Register Now ~~~~~ ss
to ~ ~

MW00780157

SPRINGER PUBLISHING
CONNECT™

Your print purchase of *An EMDR Therapy Primer: From Practicum to Practice, Third Edition* **includes online access to the contents of your book**—increasing accessibility, portability, and searchability!

Access today at:
http://connect.springerpub.com/content/book/978-0-8261-8249-4
or scan the QR code at the right with your smartphone
and enter the access code below.

M0PVE7WB

Scan here for quick access.

If you are experiencing problems accessing the digital component of this product, please contact our customer service department at cs@springerpub.com

The online access with your print purchase is available at the publisher's discretion and may be removed at any time without notice.

Publisher's Note: New and used products purchased from third-party sellers are not guaranteed for quality, authenticity, or access to any included digital components.

SPRINGER PUBLISHING
View all our products at springerpub.com

Barbara J. Hensley, EdD, is a clinical counselor in Cincinnati, Ohio, and a board-certified diplomate for the American Academy of Experts in Traumatic Stress. She served on the EMDR International Association (EMDRIA) Board of Directors as president and treasurer and has represented EMDRIA in Stockholm, Sweden, and Brussels, Belgium. She served eight years as a board member for the EMDR Research Foundation.

Dr. Hensley is an EMDRIA-certified therapist and approved consultant and regional coordinator for the Greater Cincinnati EMDR Regional Network. For the past 23 years, she has been a facilitator and logistician for the EMDR Institute trainings in Japan and throughout the United States and has served as a facilitator for Trauma Recovery (EMDR-Humanitarian Assistance Programs).

She is the creator of the Francine Shapiro Library, an online resource of EMDR research and writings. She is also the 2009 recipient of the distinguished Francine Shapiro Award for her extraordinary service and contributions to EMDR. Dr. Hensley is the co-founder of the Cincinnati Trauma Connection in Cincinnati, Ohio, an EMDR-based trauma center.

AN EMDR THERAPY PRIMER

From Practicum to Practice

Third Edition

Barbara J. Hensley, EdD

SPRINGER PUBLISHING

First Springer Publishing edition 2009; subsequent editions 2015

Springer Publishing Company, LLC
11 West 42nd Street, New York, NY 10036
www.springerpub.com
connect.springerpub.com/

Acquisitions Editor: Kate Dimock
Compositor: Transforma

ISBN: 978-0-8261-8248-7
ebook ISBN: 978-0-8261-8249-4
DOI: 10.1891/9780826182494

20 21 22 23 / 5 4 3 2 1

The author and the publisher of this Work have made every effort to use sources believed to be reliable to provide information that is accurate and compatible with the standards generally accepted at the time of publication. The author and publisher shall not be liable for any special, consequential, or exemplary damages resulting, in whole or in part, from the readers' use of, or reliance on, the information contained in this book. The publisher has no responsibility for the persistence or accuracy of URLs for external or third-party Internet websites referred to in this publication and does not guarantee that any content on such websites is, or will remain, accurate or appropriate.

Library of Congress Cataloging-in-Publication Data

Names: Hensley, Barbara J., author.
Title: An EMDR therapy primer : from practicum to practice / Barbara J. Hensley.
Identifiers: LCCN 2020032085 (print) | LCCN 2020032086 (ebook) | ISBN
   9780826182487 (hardcover) | ISBN 9780826182494 (ebook)
Subjects: MESH: Eye Movement Desensitization Reprocessing--methods | Stress
   Disorders, Post-Traumatic--therapy | Case Reports
Classification: LCC RC489.E98 (print) | LCC RC489.E98 (ebook) | NLM WM
   425.5.D4 | DDC 616.85/210651--dc23
LC record available at https://lccn.loc.gov/2020032085
LC ebook record available at https://lccn.loc.gov/2020032086

Printed in the United States of America.

Contents

Foreword

Dr. Francine Shapiro's now-famous walk in the park took place in 1987. The first EMDR study was published 2 years later in 1989. The EMDR community celebrated its 30th anniversary at the EMDR International Association (EMDRIA) Conference in Anaheim, California, in 2019. Today, 30 years later, there are trained EMDR therapists on all continents except Antarctica. The efficacy of EMDR therapy has been demonstrated repeatedly, and it is included as a treatment of choice by mental health groups in the United States (American Psychiatric Association, 2004; Department of Veterans Affairs and Department of Defense, 2004; Substance Abuse and Mental Health Services Administration [SAMHSA], 2011) and abroad (Australian Centre for Posttraumatic Mental Health, 2007; Bleich et al., 2002; Clinical Resource Efficiency Support Team, 2003; United Kingdom Department of Health, 2001; World Health Organization, 2013). We have come a long way!

BACK HISTORY

In the summer of 1989 in San Jose, California, there was a brown-bag luncheon for therapists sponsored by the Giarretto Institute. The guest speaker was an unknown psych intern who presented a case with video clips showing work with a client who was a Vietnam War veteran. As Dr. Shapiro explained her method of treatment from her recently published dissertation (Shapiro, 1989a, 1989b), there was a lot of eye-rolling and uncomfortable shifting in chairs. Then she showed the video. The audience quieted. She had our attention. The client was changing before our eyes. We were witnessing the rapid processing of trauma but did not understand why it was happening.

In the winter of 1989, the Santa Clara County Psychological Association held a special trauma response meeting for earthquake debriefing. After my presentation (Lendl & Aguilera, 1989), Dr. Shapiro approached me and invited me to her upcoming training. She was looking for trauma-trained community therapists to join her "eye movement desensitization (EMD)" team. EMD was considered at the experimental stage, but she wanted to start judiciously training as research proceeded. She did not think it was ethical to withhold treatment when it seemed to alleviate suffering so quickly and thoroughly. In the spring–summer of 1990, the first U.S. EMD training began.

At the 2002 EMDRIA Conference in Coronado, California, I met Dr. Barbara Hensley. She was in her first year on the EMDRIA board and serving as treasurer. I was immediately impressed by her dedication to EMDR and her no-nonsense work ethic. She epitomized the EMDR therapist Dr. Shapiro encouraged us all to become by utilizing all her talents to benefit EMDR and her community.

Dr. Hensley spent 30 years mostly in management for the state of Ohio. She learned to hone the ability to pinpoint needs, harvest resources, and bring solutions to fruition. With her colleague, Dr. Irene Giessl, she founded the multidisciplinary Cincinnati Trauma Connection practice with its roots in EMDR. They serve as regional coordinators for their fellow EMDR therapists and for many years sponsored top specialty trainings in their community. Dr. Hensley served a term-and-a-half as EMDRIA board president during a very difficult reorganization period. She did it quietly, gracefully, and masterfully. Despite her shyness, one of her personal goals as president was to meet as many of the EMDRIA members as possible. She wanted everyone to feel welcome and part of the EMDR community.

In 2009 when I asked her why she wanted to write this Primer, Dr. Hensley confessed that it was not her intention to write a book. She was becoming aware that many people who were trained in EMDR were hesitant to continue training or use EMDR in their practices. When questioned, they often stated that they were afraid to try such a different, "a possibly dangerous," method. She thought that a few examples might be useful. Voila! A book was born. She also said, "I wanted to make a contribution. I don't think one can do enough for EMDR .... It has changed so many lives." She continues to help EMDR therapists with her third edition. For this edition, she added sample sessions working with three special populations: military personnel and veterans, children, and the culturally diverse.

It has been my pleasure and honor to be on the editing team for this book. I believe that Dr. Hensley has written a book that is simple and basic, and that can mentor therapists who are EMDR trained and yet intimidated. It is the perfect complement to Dr. Shapiro's text (Shapiro, 2018). Learning EMDR therapy can be likened to learning a language. Having a strong foundation in grammar helps many years down the line. Ever since my Catholic grammar school education stressed diagramming sentences and studying Latin, I have appreciated the necessity for laying a strong foundation in the understanding, maintenance, and facile utilization of learned information. The importance of going back to basics cannot be overemphasized. Beyond the therapeutic relationship, a thorough understanding and meticulous use of the EMDR methodology will nurture the best EMDR treatment and therefore the greatest therapeutic effects when applied appropriately. This book brings us back to the basics.

I can see EMDR therapists rereading Dr. Shapiro's book chapter by chapter as they move through Dr. Hensley's Primer. And I can hear what Dr. Shapiro would say to us after every training: "Did you learn something? Are you having fun?" Please keep this in mind as you are reading the Primer.

Jennifer Lendl, PhD

REFERENCES

American Psychiatric Association. (2004). *Practice guidelines for the treatment of patients with acute stress disorder and posttraumatic stress disorder*. Author.
Australian Centre for Posttraumatic Mental Health. (2007). *Australian guidelines for PTSD*. University of Melbourne.
Bleich, A., Kotler, M., Kutz, E., & Shaley, A. (2002). *Guidelines for the assessment and professional intervention with terror victims in the hospital and in the community*. Israeli National Council for Mental Health.
Clinical Resource Efficiency Support Team. (2003). *The management of post-traumatic stress disorder in adults*. Northern Ireland Department of Health, Social Services and Public Safety.

Department of Veterans Affairs and Department of Defense. (2004). *VA/DoD clinical practice guideline for the management of post-traumatic stress.* Veterans Health Administration, Department of Veterans Affairs and Health Affairs, Department of Defense, Office of Quality and Performance Publication 10Q-CPG/PTSD-04.

Lendl, J., & Aguilera, D. (1989). *Multidisciplined survey of therapist-reported patient response to the October 17, 1989 earthquake.* Research assessment tool used by the UCSF Center for the study of trauma.

SAMHSA's National Registry of Evidence-Based Programs and Practices. (2011).

Shapiro, F. (1989a). Efficacy of the eye movement desensitization procedure in the treatment of traumatic memories. *Journal of Traumatic Stress, 2*(2), 199–223. https://doi.org/10.1007/BF00974159

Shapiro, F. (1989b). Eye movement desensitization: A new treatment for post-traumatic stress disorder. *Journal of Behavior Therapy and Experimental Psychiatry, 20*(3), 211–217. https://doi.org/10.1016/0005-7916(89)90025-6

Shapiro, F. (2018). *Eye movement desensitization and reprocessing (EMDR) therapy: Basic principles, protocols, and procedures* (3rd ed.). Guilford Press.

United Kingdom Department of Health. (2001). *Treatment choice in psychological therapies and counseling evidence based clinical practice guideline.* Author.

World Health Organization. (2013). *Guidelines for the management of conditions that are specifically related to stress.* Author.

Preface

We are what we repeatedly do. Excellence, then, is not an act but a habit.—Aristotle

TUNING INTO THE CREATIVE FORCE

Sit back and visualize the small but exciting moment in 1987 when Francine Shapiro became aware of her eyes shifting involuntarily and simultaneously back and forth as she focused on some disturbing events in her life. If she had not stopped to notice the relief she felt as a result of this back-and-forth movement of her eyes, the long and successful journey of EMDR therapy could have ended that fateful day. Dr. Shapiro's visionary and creative spark began a quiet revolution in the field of psychotherapy—a ripple in still water.

In his book *Creativity: Flow and the Psychology of Discovery and Invention*, Mihaly Csikszentmihalyi distinguishes between what he defines as "small-c" and "big-C" creativity as he describes how creative individuals influence their respective fields and domains of knowledge. While small-c creativity is somewhat subjective, Csikszentmihalyi states that big-C is the kind of creativity that drives culture forward and redefines the state of the art (1997).

Francine Shapiro belongs to a select group of big-C creators in our world. Small-c creativity involves personal creativity, while big-C requires the type of ingenuity that "leaves a trace in the cultural matrix" (Csikszentmihalyi, 1997), something that changes some aspect of how we view or treat something in a big way. Anyone who has conducted a successful EMDR reprocessing session or has experienced its results firsthand can attest to the expanding ripples that Dr. Shapiro began and that continue to grow as we progress further into the future.

HISTORY OF EMDR THERAPY

Many of you have repeatedly heard the story of Dr. Francine Shapiro's historic walk in Vasona County Park in Los Gatos, California, in 1987. While taking a walk, she noticed that the disturbing thoughts upon which she was focusing about a recent past traumatic event in her life were suddenly disappearing. When she tried to bring them back up, these thoughts did not seem to her to have the same negative charge or significance that they had at the beginning of her walk. She began to pay careful attention, and what she noticed when a negative thought went through her mind was that her eyes began to move spontaneously in a rapid, diagonal movement. Her thoughts had shifted; and, when she tried to bring them back up, they did not have the same charge.

It was during this famous walk that Dr. Shapiro discovered the effects of spontaneous eye movement and began to develop procedures around the effects of bilateral eye movements. In 1989, she published the first controlled outcome study of eye movement desensitization (EMD) and posttraumatic stress disorder (PTSD) in the *Journal of Traumatic Stress*. During this same year, controlled studies were also published on exposure therapy, psychodynamic therapy, and hypnosis for the treatment of PTSD. In 1990, Dr. Shapiro changed the name of EMD to EMDR to recognize and acknowledge the comprehensive reprocessing effect that was taking place. It was also during this time that other forms of bilateral stimulation (tones, taps, or music) were recognized as having the same effect and began to be utilized as an alternative to the preferred eye movement. Table 1.23 briefly describes EMD and EMDR. EMD and EMDR began with a chance observation rather than emanating from an established theory. Once the discovery was made, efforts were made to find a theory that could explain it.

From the day of her fateful walk in the park, Dr. Shapiro's destiny began to change. Excited by her chance revelation, she leapt into action, finding friends and subjects to test her new discovery. She quickly set out to develop well-structured principles, protocols, and procedures around the effects of eye movements based on the consistent treatment results she and others had observed. She trained interested and excited clinicians who in turn encouraged others to learn this new methodology. The big-C ripple mounted as the first controlled study of EMDR therapy appeared in the *Journal of Traumatic Stress* in 1989. Other studies were soon to follow, and the rest is history. Dr. Shapiro's big-C creativity changed and continues to change the way trained clinicians conceptualize and treat trauma. EMDR therapy has redefined the state of the art in terms of mental health.

The big-C ripple now encompasses the world many times over—from North to South America, Africa, Europe, India, China, Japan, and Australia. It continues to grow and multiply along with many new ripples that are created every day as clients and clinicians around the world experience for the first time the power of Dr. Shapiro's personal discovery.

WHO COULD BENEFIT FROM READING THIS PRIMER

EMDR is a powerful therapeutic approach. However, without the proper training and consultation, an untrained clinician (and this includes very experienced clinicians) could put their clients at risk. A goal of this Primer is to target those clinicians who have completed the EMDR therapy two-part basic training, 10 hours of supervised consultation, and have read Dr. Shapiro's basic text (*Eye Movement Desensitization and Reprocessing: Basic Principles, Protocols, and Procedures*, 3rd ed., 2018) and *Getting Past Your Past* (2012), but still want additional information on using it skillfully. They may have experienced fear or apprehension about trying something so new and different or they may simply want to maximize their preparation and skills as they begin using EMDR therapy.

In consultation groups, clinicians often report being skeptical before EMDR therapy training, yet amazed by their practicum experiences during the training. Although they concede that using EMDR therapy has a great potential to help their clients, many still feel a reluctance to utilize what at first appears to be a radically different treatment approach. Some live in remote areas where they are the only EMDR-trained clinician for miles or where their only access to other clinicians is by boat or airplane. I hope this Primer encourages and raises the confidence levels of those trained but wanting to increase their ability to use EMDR therapy with consistent success. I also want to provide assurance to those doing EMDR therapy that they are on the right track.

Learning to implement EMDR reprocessing in sessions with a client is a process of its own; it is not an event. Thus, it is important to understand the basic theory underlying EMDR therapy before attempting to implement it. The manner in which you as the clinician implement the eight phases with a client will vary with each and every client assessed for treatment. Every client is unique, and EMDR reprocessing is not a "cookbook" approach. Therefore, familiarity with Dr. Shapiro's Adaptive Information Processing model is crucial to enhance your understanding as to why some clients make shifts readily and others experience more difficulty. As you become more adept, comfortable, and knowledgeable in EMDR therapy with *practice, practice, practice,* your EMDR therapy approach and delivery will likely change and evolve. Each client can teach you something about the process as issues become resolved and adaptive resolution is achieved.

WHAT IS INCLUDED

Much of the information contained in the following pages has already been described by Dr. Shapiro and others in the rapidly growing body of EMDR therapy literature and research. The primary intention of this Primer is to supplement Dr. Shapiro's explanation of EMDR therapy. It is not meant to be a substitute for her training or previous writings. The reader is urged to read and study them all. It adds case histories and extensive examples of successful EMDR reprocessing sessions. The cases represent composite or conglomerate portraits of the many clients with whom I have utilized EMDR therapy over the past 20 years.

This text is a Primer and, as such, the writing, examples, and illustrations are presented in a less formal and more personal manner. The Primer has been written from a practical, learning-focused approach so that the clinicians who read it can become more familiar with the principles, protocols, and procedures of EMDR therapy. It is my desire to facilitate the flow of information so that clinicians can easily and naturally begin to use their EMDR therapy training as soon as possible. This book is also geared to help clinicians reaccess information that was lost in the weeks, months, or years since they were trained.

PURPOSE OF THE PRIMER

Throughout this Primer are transcripts embellished with relevant details to illustrate important learning points. Other sessions have been created to demonstrate how to identify the touchstone event (if any), set up the procedural steps, deal with blocked processing and blocking beliefs during the Desensitization and Installation Phases, reassess the state of previously targeted material, and identify material for new processing. An attempt is made to take the clinician through complete and incomplete EMDR therapy sessions, explaining treatment rationale at given points.

The Primer is laid out in the following manner:

- **EMDR therapy overview:** A straightforward explanation of the Adaptive Information Processing model, the three-pronged approach, the types of targets accessed during the EMDR process, and other relevant information to assist in distinguishing EMDR therapy from other theoretical orientations are provided.
- **Eight phases of EMDR therapy:** The eight phases are summarized.
- **Steppingstones to adaptive resolution:** The components of the standard EMDR protocol used during the Assessment Phase are explained, and actual cases are included to demonstrate how the procedural setup is possible with various clients.
- **Building blocks of EMDR therapy:** The foundation—past, present, and future—is assessed in terms of appropriate targeting and successful outcomes.
- **Abreactions, blocked processing, and cognitive interweaves:** Strategies and techniques for dealing with challenging clients, high levels of abreaction, and blocked processing are the focus.
- **Past, present, and future:** Actual cases demonstrate various strategies to assist the client in reaching adaptive resolution of trauma.
- **Working with special populations:** This section has been added to the Primer to highlight the importance of having a special knowledge and skills in working with military personnel and veterans, children, and clients from culturally diverse populations.

A Sacred Space exercise has been added to Chapter 8, which can be used side by side with the traditional Safe (Calm) Place exercise. Simple exercises to teach clients grounding, diaphragmatic breathing, and anchoring in the present can also be found in Chapter 8. In addition, scripts for safe (calm) place, spiral technique, future template, and breathing shift are also included.

The purpose in writing this book is to offer a Primer that can facilitate the process of mental health professionals becoming more confident and experienced clinicians in EMDR therapy. The process has been simplified as much as possible with diagrams, tables, and other illustrations. Dr. Shapiro's basic text, *Eye Movement Desensitization and Reprocessing: Basic Principles, Protocols and Procedures* (3rd ed., 2018), is a masterpiece in itself and contains a wealth of information on EMDR. One needs to read her text over and over again to savor all the kernels of significant information. These kernels have been separated out by providing explanations, as well as anecdotal and illustrative examples, throughout. EMDR therapy is a significant contribution to psychology in the 20th and 21st centuries, and this Primer is offered as a further learning tool.

What is covered in this Primer is but the tip of the iceberg when it comes to all the possibilities of using EMDR therapy with clients that present from different populations, such as children, athletes, combat veterans, and couples, and those who present with more complex issues, such as dissociation, phobias, obsessive-compulsive disorder, and substance abuse. Regardless of the client populations or the types of issues that the client brings, the basics in this Primer are essential to the overall outcome and success of EMDR therapy.

EMDR THERAPY

At the 2014 Annual EMDRIA Conference in Denver, Colorado, and as the new name of this Primer reflects, Dr. Francine Shapiro encouraged clinicians in attendance to begin referring to EMDR as EMDR therapy to reflect its status as a unique, integrative psychotherapeutic approach, and to further clarify that EMDR, based on the Adaptive Information Processing model, is a therapy and not a technique. The following letter by Dr. Shapiro (2014) was sent to the membership of EMDRIA to further explain her rationale for the name change:

EMDR THERAPY

As you may know, the World Health Organization (WHO) new practice guidelines have indicated that trauma-focused Cognitive Behavioral Therapy (CBT) and EMDR therapy are the only psychotherapies recommended for children, adolescents and adults with PTSD. In addition, the glossary description in the document alleviates multiple misconceptions:

World Health Organization (2013). Guidelines for the management of conditions that are specifically related to stress. Geneva, WHO.

EMDR: This therapy is based on the idea that negative thoughts, feelings and behaviors are the result of unprocessed memories. The treatment involves standardized procedures that include focusing simultaneously on (a) spontaneous associations of traumatic images, thoughts, emotions and bodily sensations and (b) bilateral stimulation that is most commonly in the form of repeated eye movements.

Like CBT with a trauma focus, EMDR aims to reduce subjective distress and strengthen adaptive beliefs related to the traumatic event. Unlike CBT with a trauma focus, EMDR does not involve (a) detailed descriptions of the event, (b) direct challenging of beliefs, (c) extended exposure, or (d) homework.

This description makes clear that EMDR is a "therapy," not a "technique," and is based on a specific model that distinguishes it from other forms of therapy. This has important implications for our field. Given this level of validation, I believe it is important to refer to "EMDR therapy" in publications, presentations and clinical practice to eliminate the reductive misconception that it is only a "technique."

Although EMDR therapy has been fully validated only for PTSD, there are numerous research studies underway evaluating applications to a wide range of disorders. Excellent results have already been achieved with myriad diagnoses. In addition to the reduction of symptoms and the strengthening of adaptive beliefs, the client's experience of self and other typically shifts in ways that allow the person to respond more adaptively to current and future life demands. By using the term EMDR therapy we emphasize the stature of what we are practicing and the fact that it is on the same level as the most widely recognized forms of therapy: psychodynamic therapy and cognitive behavioral therapy.

As indicated below, there are important differences among the various forms of psychotherapy:

Psychodynamic Therapy

- Foundation of pathology: Intrapsychic conflicts
- Treatment: Transference/Verbal "working through"

- Cognitive Behavioral Therapy
- Foundation of pathology: Dysfunctional beliefs and behaviors
- Treatment: Direct procedural manipulations of beliefs and behaviors

EMDR therapy

- Foundation of pathology: Unprocessed physiologically stored memories
- Treatment: Accessing and processing of memories, triggers, and future templates

While EMDR therapy is an integrative approach that is compatible with a wide range of orientations, the model and methodology are unique. Likewise, although we may customize the Preparation Phase for individual clients by incorporating a variety of techniques, the conceptualizations of pathology, processing procedures and protocols are distinctly different from those of other therapies. Therefore, I hope you will all join me in consistently referring to our modality as EMDR therapy and thus provide academics, clinicians and laypeople with a clear understanding of the psychotherapy we practice.

With best wishes for a new year of peace and harmony,

Francine Shapiro, PhD

Notes From the Author

Since the first edition of this Primer in 2009, the author has heard its title pronounced in two different ways by clinicians espousing its usefulness. It was initially titled the EMDR Pri-mər and offered as an introductory textbook much like the McGuffey Primer, which was widely used in American schools from the mid-19th century to the mid-20th century. The other is the more informal pronunciation of the EMDR Prī-mər, like "priming the pump." The original intent of the EMDR Pri-mər was to mirror and to enhance the teachings detailed in Dr. Francine Shapiro's 1995/2001/2018 texts and her EMDR Institute-sponsored trainings from their inception to the present. However the reader chooses to pronounce it (Pri-mər/Prī-mər), it was my overall intention to encourage the growth of clinicians by preparing them to be more skilled, practiced, and confident in (em)powering a client's "*train down the track*" to a healthy, adaptive destination.

A new set of tables, called Derailment Possibilities, has been peppered throughout this third edition. These tables have been included to alert the engineer (i.e., the clinician) to the possible obstacles ahead on the track that may cause the "train to slow or run off the rails."

Special Acknowledgments

Victoria Britt, LCSW, LMFT   is a Clinical Social Worker and Marriage and Family Therapist in private clinical and consulting practice in Montclair, New Jersey. She is an EMDR International Association Certified Therapist and Approved Consultant and a facilitator for the EMDR Institute. A Somatic Experiencing Practitioner, she is also Assisting Faculty for the SE Institute. Ms. Britt is a specialist in the treatment of posttraumatic stress disorder, complex trauma, and dissociation and the treatment of victims of childhood sexual abuse. She was an early practitioner of Energy Psychology and is co-author of the book, *Evolving Thought Field Therapy: The Clinician's Handbook of Diagnoses, Treatment, and Theory* (2004).

Wendy Freitag, PhD   is a psychologist with a private practice in Wauwatosa, Wisconsin. She is an EMDR Institute Senior and Regional Trainer, facilitator and logistician; EMDR International Association (EMDRIA) Approved Consultant; and past EMDRIA Secretary, President and Director from 1998 to 2007; and currently serves as the President of the EMDR Research Foundation. She has extensive clinical experience in treatment of posttraumatic stress conditions, anxiety and mood disorders, grief and anger issues, facilitating personal transitions, and performance enhancement.

Irene Giessl, EdD   is a psychologist in private practice and co-founder of the Cincinnati Trauma Connection in Cincinnati, Ohio. Dr. Giessl is an EMDR International Association (EMDRIA) Certified Therapist, Approved Consultant, Regional Co-coordinator for the Greater Cincinnati EMDRIA Regional Network, and EMDR Institute facilitator and logistician. She is also a facilitator for Trauma Recovery (EMDR-Humanitarian Assistance Programs). She served on the EMDRIA Board of Directors from 2000 to 2006, including two terms as secretary. In 2011, she received the EMDRIA Outstanding Service Award in recognition of her persistence and fortitude in educating others about the value of EMDR therapy. She is also currently a member of the EMDRIA Conference Committee.

Ana M. Gómez, MC, LPC   is the founder and director of the AGATE Institute in Phoenix, Arizona. She is an EMDR Institute trainer as well as an EMDR-Iberoamerica trainer of trainers in Colombia. She is an EMDR International Association (EMDRIA) Certified Therapist and EMDRIA Approved Consultant. Ms. Gómez is the author of *EMDR Therapy and Adjunct Approaches With Children: Complex Trauma, Attachment, and Dissociation,* and *Dark, Bad Day … Go Away*; creator of the Thoughts Kit for Kids; and developer of EMDR Sandtray Protocol and the Systemic, EMDR-Attachment Informed

Program to Heal Intergenerational Trauma & Repair the Parent-Child Attachment Bond. Ms. Gómez was the recipient of the 2011 Distinguished Service Award from the Arizona Play Therapy Association and the 2012 Sierra Tucson Hope Award.

E. C. Hurley, DMin, PhD   is a psychologist in Clarksville, Tennessee, as well as the founder and CEO of Soldier Center, a community-based treatment center specializing in treating military, veterans, first responders, and their families. A retired Army colonel, his military awards include the Meritorious Service Medal (2 Oak Leaf Clusters), Bronze Star Medal, Legion of Merit, and the U.S. Army's Air Assault Medal. In 2010, Dr. Hurley was the recipient of Trauma Recovery's (EMDR-Humanitarian Assistance Programs) Elizabeth Snyker Award and, in 2019, the EMDR International Association (EMDRIA)'s Francine Shapiro Award. He is an EMDR Institute Regional Trainer and an EMDR Basic and Advanced Approved Trainer for providers serving the military, veteran and first-responder populations. A member of EMDRIA's Council of Scholars, he is author of several publications, including his book, *Clinical Guide for Treating Military and Veterans With EMDR Therapy* (in press).

Deborah Korn, PsyD   is a psychologist with a private practice in Cambridge, Massachusetts, and is an adjunct training faculty member at the Trauma Center in Boston. Dr. Korn has authored or coauthored several prominent articles focused on EMDR, including a comprehensive review of EMDR applications with complex posttraumatic stress disorder. Dr. Korn is an EMDR Institute facilitator, EMDR International Association (EMDRIA) Approved Consultant, on the editorial board of the *Journal of EMDR Practice and Research*, former clinical director of the Women's Trauma Programs at Charter Brookside and Charles River Hospitals, and a member of EMDRIA's Council of Scholars. She presents and consults internationally on the treatment of adult survivors of childhood abuse and neglect. She has been a regular presenter at the EMDRIA Conference and was invited to present EMDRIA's first "Masters Series" class.

Deany Laliotis, LCSW   is a Licensed Clinical Social Worker in private practice in Washington, DC, specializing in the treatment of complex trauma and attachment issues with EMDR therapy. She is currently the Director of Training for the EMDR Institute and is an invited speaker for EMDR both in the United States and abroad. Ms. Laliotis has also co-authored the curriculum on the Basic Course on EMDR Therapy with Francine Shapiro, as well as a chapter in the book, *Evidence-Based Treatments for Trauma-Related Psychological Disorders* (2015). She was the recipient of the Francine Shapiro Award for outstanding service and excellence in EMDR in 2015. Ms. Laliotis is also a member of EMDR International Association's Council of Scholars.

Jennifer Lendl, PhD   is a psychologist in San Jose, California, and was one of the first EMDR trainers. She is coauthor of *EMDR Performance Enhancement for the Workplace: A Practitioner's Manual* (1997). Dr. Lendl is an EMDR International Association (EMDRIA) Certified Therapist and Approved Consultant, EMDR Institute facilitator, and currently sits on the EMDRIA Conference Committee. She is also the 2006 recipient of the Francine Shapiro Award and is a frequent presenter at the annual EMDRIA Conferences.

Katy Murray, LICSW   is a Licensed Independent Clinical Social Worker in Olympia, Washington, where she has a general clinical practice with specialties in trauma-related disorders, chemical dependency, and psycho-oncology. Ms. Murray is a Trauma Recovery/ EMDR-Humanitarian Assistance Programs (HAP) trainer, the EMDR Institute's Internet Discussion Listserv Moderator, EMDR Institute facilitator, and an EMDR International Association (EMDRIA) Certified Therapist and Approved Consultant. She is on the board of the EMDR Research Foundation and is an EMDRIA Regional Coordinator. In the past, she served on EMDRIA's Standards and Training Committee. She has presented at the annual EMDRIA Conference and other EMDR specialty workshops and is a trainer for Trauma Recovery/EMDR-HAP.

Mark Nickerson, LICSW   is a psychotherapist in Amherst, Massachusetts, an EMDR Institute trainer, a participating member of the Council of Scholars, past president of the EMDR International Association, and director of EMDR Advanced Trainings and Distance Learning, LLC. He is editor/author of *Cultural Competence and Healing Culturally Based Trauma With EMDR Therapy: Innovative Strategies and Protocols* (2016) and *The Wounds Within* (2015). He conducts advanced EMDR trainings nationally and internationally on topics including cultural competence and treatment for culturally based trauma, treatment for problem behaviors, problematic anger and violence, and the effective use of EMDR protocols. He has developed award-winning innovative programs designed to reduce and resolve interpersonal conflict and is the originator of the Cycle Model as an approach to assessing and treating problem behaviors.

Zona Scheiner, PhD   is a psychologist, partner, and co-founder of both Family Therapy Associates of Ann Arbor and the EMDR Resource Center of Michigan. She is currently a provider of basic training in EMDR and was a provider of specialty trainings. In addition, Dr. Scheiner is an EMDR International Association (EMDRIA) Certified Therapist and Approved Consultant, as well as an EMDR Institute regional trainer and facilitator. In the past, she was an EMDR-Humanitarian Assistance Programs trainer and facilitator. She served on the EMDRIA Board of Directors from 1999 to 2006 and was its president in 2006. She is a past member of the EMDR Research Foundation Board and served on the EMDRIA Conference Committee for a decade. Dr. Scheiner was the 2010 recipient of the Outstanding EMDRIA Service Award for her dedication and commitment to EMDR therapy and her service to EMDRIA.

Marilyn Schleyer, PhD   is an Advanced Registered Nurse Practitioner and Clinical Counselor with a private practice in northern Kentucky. She is a retired professor and founding Chair of the Department of Advanced Nursing Studies, College of Health Professions, at Northern Kentucky University. Dr. Schleyer is credited with enlisting Northern Kentucky University to originally house and maintain the Francine Shapiro Library. She is an EMDR International Association (EMDRIA) Certified Therapist and was a board member of EMDRIA from 2003 to 2006.

Roger Solomon, PhD   is a psychologist who specializes and teaches internationally in the areas of trauma and grief. He is a long-standing EMDR Institute trainer as well as EMDR International Association Certified Therapist and Approved Consultant. He is a consultant with the U.S. Senate and has provided services to numerous government and law enforcement agencies in the United States and abroad (e.g., Federal Bureau of Investigatio (FBI), Secret Service, Polizia di Stato in Italy). He has published numerous articles and book chapters pertaining to EMDR, grief, critical incident stress, and complex trauma.

Rosalie Thomas, RN, PhD   is a psychologist in Washington state. She currently maintains an EMDR consultation practice as an EMDR International Association (EMDRIA) Approved Consultant. Dr. Thomas has served as board member, treasurer, and president of EMDRIA, as well as receiving its Outstanding Service and Francine Shapiro awards. She currently co-chairs the EMDRIA Conference Committee and serves as a board member of the EMDR Research Foundation. She is the principal author of the EMDR Researcher's Toolkit. Dr. Thomas is a facilitator and trainer for Trauma Recovery/Humanitarian Assistance Programs and facilitator and regional trainer for the EMDR Institute. She has participated in training programs throughout the United States and Asia.

Kay Werk, LISW   is a Licensed Independent Social Worker in Columbus, Ohio. She served as an EMDR senior trainer throughout the United States and Europe and is an EMDR International Association (EMDRIA) Certified Therapist and Approved Consultant. Ms. Werk has presented at EMDRIA and other conferences on the topic of EMDR and critical incident stress management and has provided numerous EMDR-Humanitarian Assistance Programs trainings in a variety of settings related to disaster response. Before she retired, she was a manager of Community Crisis Response and Critical Incident Stress Management for NetCare.

Acknowledgments

My thanks to Dr. Francine Shapiro for providing me with an opportunity to be part of the ripple she created after taking her famous walk in the park. From that memorable walk, I was motivated to create my own small ripples in writing this Primer and in creating the Francine Shapiro Library. Dr. Shapiro has had an enormous impact on my life both personally and professionally as a result of her revolutionary work. My hope is that my efforts on behalf of EMDR therapy will feed her spirit as hers have fed mine. Francine Shapiro sadly passed on June 16, 2019. She was my mentor, friend, and hero. Her contribution to trauma-focused therapy will continue to ripple throughout the world for decades to come. I also want to thank Ms. Robbie Dunton for her continued support, encouragement, and wisdom. She is the heart and energy behind EMDR therapy.

It never was my intent to write a book, let alone a Primer on the basics of EMDR therapy. While involved in working on an EMDR presentation to local colleagues, I began to think about the significance of understanding the intricacies of the EMDR therapy model. Letting that slip from my lips, friends and colleagues started to offer ideas and give feedback. It became a personal challenge to boil down "EMDR talk" into small portions so that more clinicians might be intrigued to follow the client's train down the track and not be daunted by the process. Therefore, I started writing to the novice, imagining the questions, creating tables of explanations and diagrams. Thus, the birth of this Primer. What an adventure!

There are 15 exceptional individuals who put part of their life on hold to help me edit this Primer to ensure the fidelity of EMDR therapy. It was an editing marathon in which they volunteered to engage. These wonderful women and men—Irene Giessl, Marilyn Schleyer, Victoria Britt, Kay Werk, Jennifer Lendl, Zona Scheiner, and Deany Laliotis and, later, with this second edition, Deborah Korn, Katy Murray, and Rosalie Thomas and, with the third edition, Ana Gomez, E. C. Hurley, Mark Nickerson, Roger Solomon, and Wendy Freitag—helped to make this Primer a reality. Their names are listed in the order they became involved in the project, not by their importance or level of involvement. Thanks to all of you for reading my manuscript, sometimes more than once, for your invaluable comments, and for your encouragement. Along with myself, these wonderful clinicians were trained, mentored, and/or respected and loved by Francine Shapiro. They represent the gold standard of EMDR-trained clinicians.

Special thanks to Irene Giessl for her relentless pursuit of perfection and clarity. Her support, inspiration, faith in my ability to write this Primer, and sharp eye for the flaw, moved me when courage wavered.

Thanks to Marilyn Schleyer who urged me to "keep it simple" and to provide tables and diagrams to nurture the reader's learning process. Her mentoring and constant assurance that the Primer could be an important contribution to EMDR therapy literature spurred me on.

Thanks to Jennifer Lendl. Jennifer truly is an EMDR pioneer, "a trainer before there were trainers." I am eternally indebted to her for all the time, hard work, guidance, encouragement, and support she has given throughout the entire process of writing this Primer. Jennifer read the entire manuscript over and over again to ensure its fidelity to the EMDR therapy model.

Thanks to Victoria Britt for "holding my feet to the fire," as she promised, and for consistently and continually pointing out inadvertent deviations from EMDR therapy standard procedure. Her commitment, ideas, and suggestions were deeply appreciated and valued.

Thanks to Kay Werk and Zona Scheiner for providing invaluable input from their experience as clinicians and teachers of EMDR therapy. Kay allowed me to interrupt her complicated schedule to lend an ear any time day or night with no admonishments for my uncertainties. Her gracious demeanor and complete knowledge of the EMDR therapy model calmed me when I started second-guessing my efforts. Zona was called upon later in the writing stage. She worked with amazing speed and generosity to edit all the chapters. She added valuable effectiveness.

Thanks to Deany Laliotis for her astute editing assistance on Chapter 5, "Abreactions, Blocked Processing, and Cognitive Interweaves." She graciously took time out of her busy teaching schedule to lend assistance when asked. Having EMDR therapy trainers and facilitators oversee my writing is the only way I could dare to endorse these chapters.

The second edition of the Primer has been further guided by the astute eyes and expertise of Irene Giessl, Deany Laliotis, Jennifer Lendl, Katy Murray, Zona Scheiner, and Rosalie Thomas, all excellent EMDR therapy clinicians. They are amazing women who have dedicated their professional careers to foster and further the understanding of EMDR worldwide.

As a first-time editor of the Primer, Katy Murray combed through the revised Primer, refining the text, culling out discrepancies, and adding changes and variations taken from Dr. Shapiro's basic and advanced EMDR therapy trainings.

Without question or hesitation, Rosalie Thomas generously and graciously entered the editing phase of the Primer in its eleventh hour, offering her skilled trainer's eye in refining advanced EMDR therapy concepts and detailed client transcripts. Rosalie exemplifies the essence of the EMDR therapy community by her willingness to jump to action when called upon. I greatly appreciate her efforts on the Primer's behalf.

Additional thanks go to Deborah Korn for her generosity in working with Deany Laliotis on revising and enhancing the cognitive interweave section, a very important aspect of EMDR therapy.

The third edition of the Primer could not have been accomplished without the expertise, knowledge, and experience of Wendy Freitag, Ana Gomez, E. C. Hurley, Mark Nickerson, and Roger Solomon. Thank so much for sharing your passion for EMDR therapy.

As can be seen, these women and men, made special and unique contributions to the editing of this Primer. I know they made sacrifices and encountered personal challenges along the way. All the clinicians involved in this Primer are wonderful examples of the many individuals throughout the world who have nurtured and honored the evolution of EMDR therapy. I owe all of them a deep debt of gratitude for their time, talents, and expertise. These individuals are dear friends and colleagues. They are all ripple creators extraordinaire! They are the true mothers and fathers of EMDR therapy. From my grateful heart, I offer my sincere thanks.

Thanks also to Sheri W. Sussman, past executive editor for Springer Publishing, for her encouragement and assistance throughout the writing of the first and second editions. Sheri's interest in and support for this Primer was evident from the beginning when I first was introduced to and approached her about the Primer at the EMDR International Association Conference in Phoenix, Arizona.

I have always believed in the spirit of generosity, giving freely without strings attached. This philosophy includes making financial contributions, offering pro bono therapy services, and sharing personal and professional resources to support those who might need a step up. I am so rewarded in life for taking this stance. For me, EMDR therapy is a work of the heart, spurred on by my belief in the power of EMDR's healing properties. I chose to write and assist those beginning to study EMDR therapy as a way of continuing to "pay it forward." In offering this Primer to the EMDR therapy community, it is my hope that many clinicians and their clients will reap the benefits of my efforts.

REFERENCES

Bender, S. S., Britt, V., & Diepold, J. (2004). *Evolving thought field therapy: The clinician's handbook of diagnoses, treatment, and theory.* W. W. Norton & Company.

Csikszentmihalyi, M. (1997). *Creativity: Flow and the psychology of discovery and invention.* Harper-Collins Publishers.

Gomez, A. M. (2009). *Dark, bad day...go away!* Author.

Gomez, A. M. (2013). *EMDR therapy and adjunct approaches with children: Complex trauma, attachment, and dissociation.* Springer Publishing Company.

Hurley, E. C. (2020). *Clinical guide for treating military and veterans with EMDR Therapy.* Springer Publishing Company.

Lendl, J., & Foster, S. (2003). *EMDR performance enhancement for the workplace: A practitioners' manual* (2nd ed.). Author.

Nickerson, M. (2016). *Cultural competence and healing culturally based trauma with EMDR therapy: Innovative strategies and protocols.* Springer Publishing Company.

Nickerson, M., & Goldstein, J. S. (2015). *The wounds within: A veteran, a PTSD therapist, and a nation unprepared.* Skyhorse.

Shapiro, F. (1989). Efficacy of the eye movement desensitization procedure in the treatment of traumatic memories. *Journal of Traumatic Stress, 2*(2), 199–223. https://doi.org/10.1007/BF00974159

Shapiro, F. (1995). *Eye movement desensitization and reprocessing: Basic principles, protocols, and procedures* (1st ed.). Guilford Press.

Shapiro, F. (2001). *Eye movement desensitization and reprocessing: Basic principles, protocols, and procedures* (2nd ed.). Guilford Press.

Shapiro, F. (2012). *Getting past your past.* Rodale Books.

Shapiro, F. (2018). *Eye movement desensitization and reprocessing: Basic principles, protocols, and procedures* (3rd ed.). Guilford Press.

Shapiro, F., & Laliotis, D. (2015). EMDR for trauma-related disorders. In U. Schnyder & M. Cloitre (Eds.), *Evidence based treatments for trauma-related psychological disorders: A practical guide for clinicians* (pp. 205–228). Springer Publishing Company.

Thomas, R., & EMDR Research Foundation. (2014). *EMDR early intervention research toolkit.* EMDR Research Foundation. http://www.emdrresearchfoundation.org/toolkit/

EMDR Therapy Overview

The world is round and the place which may seem like the end may also be the beginning.—Ivy Baker Priest (*Parade*, 1958)

REINTRODUCTION TO EMDR THERAPY

The goal of EMDR is to achieve the most profound and comprehensive treatment effects possible in the shortest period of time, while maintaining client stability within a balanced system.

(SHAPIRO, 2018, P. 6)

This chapter summarizes the information covered in the most recent EMDR therapy trainings, as well as Dr. Francine Shapiro's primary text (2018), in the hope of providing additional clarity to the newly trained clinician. It looks at different ways trauma can be conceptualized and includes a reintroduction to the Adaptive Information Processing (AIP) model, the concept of the three-pronged approach, targets associated with EMDR therapy, and clinical guidelines pertinent to EMDR therapy. References to educational learning materials, research, other relevant supplementary information, and key points that are important to remember during the EMDR therapy learning process are also covered.

Although the EMDR therapy principles, protocols, and procedures have been simplified with tables and figures in this Primer, it is not a mechanistic or cookie-cutter approach. EMDR therapy is a fluid process, and the results will vary from client to client. Formal training in EMDR therapy allows clinicians to initiate understanding its model, methodology, and mechanism. This knowledge, combined with their own clinical intuition, allows them to begin practicing this therapeutic approach. No one should read this book thinking that it is a substitute for formal training. EMDR therapy seems simple on its surface; however, in reality, its competent execution is complex and complicated.

Extensive familiarity with Dr. Shapiro's primary text is a prerequisite for the reading of this Primer, which is intended to supplement, not replace, her required pre-training readings. No clinician who intends to utilize EMDR therapy with clients can afford to be without *Eye Movement Desensitization and Reprocessing: Basic Principles, Protocols, and Procedures* (Shapiro, 2018). In the early days of implementation, you may need to refer to Dr. Shapiro's book daily. Read it often and use it as your primary EMDR therapy reference guide. Every time you read it, you will probably notice something that you did not quite understand or retain the first few times around. Read it thoroughly and refer to it often. It is not necessary that you memorize the book; just remember that it is there for you as an ongoing guide to your clinical work. It is also suggested that clinicians read *Getting Past Your Past* (Shapiro, 2012b). This book provides clinicians and clients alike a greater understanding of why people act the way they do. Clinicians may also read *EMDR: The Breakthrough Therapy for Overcoming Anxiety, Stress, and Trauma* (Shapiro & Forrest, 2016) as a basic overview of the clinical applications of EMDR therapy.

EMDR therapy, a reprocessing therapy, is a robust, comprehensive psychotherapeutic treatment approach comprising eight distinct phases that begin with the clinician's initial contact with the client. These include taking a thorough client history, preparing the client for the EMDR therapy process, setting up the protocol, desensitizing and reprocessing the trauma, installing a positive cognition (PC), doing a body scan to check for residual trauma, "closing down" a session, and reevaluating the status of a trauma. All eight phases must be in place in the order described previously. Chapter 2 contains an in-depth discussion of these phases.

There have been other offshoots of EMDR therapy since its inception (e.g., Grand and Goldberg, 2011; Kip et al., 2013; Pace, 2003). These techniques have their supporters and many successes may have been reported, but these treatments, to date, have little to no validation in the research literature. The efficacy of many of these models has not been tested within a scientific, empirical setting, whereas EMDR therapy's validity has been proven repeatedly.

TRAUMA

WHAT IS TRAUMA?

The diagnostic criteria for posttraumatic stress disorder (PTSD; DSM-V, 309.81; ICD-10, F43.10) cited in the *Diagnostic and Satistical Manual of Mental Disorders* (5th ed.; *DSM-5*; American Psychiatric Association [APA], 2013) is the definition used most frequently to describe acute trauma in adults. This definition describes trauma as an event experienced or witnessed by a person that results in intrusive symptoms, avoidance, negative alterations in cognitions and mood, and alterations in arousal and reactivity (APA, 2013). Flannery describes trauma as

> the state of severe fright that we experience when we are confronted with a sudden, unexpected, potentially life-threatening event, over which we have no control, and to which we are unable to respond effectively no matter how hard we try (1995).

A child who was sexually abused by her older brother may grow up to believe "I am bad" or "The world is unsafe." When an individual experiences a traumatic event, the event can become entrenched (or fixed) in the form of irrational beliefs, negative emotions, blocked energy, and/or physical symptoms, such as anxieties, phobias, flashbacks, nightmares, and/ or fears. Regardless of the magnitude of the trauma, it may have the potential for negatively impacting an individual's self-confidence and self-efficacy. The event can become locked or "stuck" in the memory network (i.e., "an associated system of information" [Shapiro, 2018, p. 30]) in its original form, causing an array of traumatic or PTSD symptoms. Triggers activate images, physical sensations, tastes, smells, sounds, and beliefs that might echo the experience as though it were the day it originally happened or cause other distortions in perception of current events. Reminders of the event have the potential for triggering an emotional or physical response. By utilizing EMDR therapy, the client can unblock the traumatic information and can fully experience and integrate the trauma toward a healthy resolution.

TYPES OF TRAUMA

Dr. Shapiro (2018) distinguishes between big "T" traumas and other adverse life experiences or disturbing life events (formerly referred to as small "t" traumas). When a person hears the word "trauma," experiences and images of man-made events such as fires, explosions, automobile accidents, or natural disasters, which include hurricanes, floods, and tornadoes, emerge. Sexual abuse, a massive heart attack, death of a loved one, Hurricane Katrina, and the 9/11 attacks on the World Trade Center by international terrorists are graphic examples of big "T" traumas. Among other descriptors, these types of traumas can be defined as dangerous and life threatening and fit the criteria in the *DSM-5* (APA, 2013) as stated previously.

Then there are the traumas Shapiro (2018) has designated as adverse life experiences. These types of events may be subtler and tend to impact one's beliefs about self, others, and the world. Adverse life experiences are those that can affect our sense of self, self-esteem, self-definition, self-confidence, and optimal behavior. They influence how we see ourselves as a part of the bigger whole. They are often ubiquitous (i.e., constantly encountered) in nature and are stored in state-dependent mode in our memory network. Unless persistent throughout the client's childhood, adverse life experiences usually do not have much impact on overall development, yet maintain the ability to elicit negative self-attributions and have potential for other long-term negative consequences. The clinical presentations that often signal the presence of past adverse life events may be low self-esteem and anxiety as well as panic disorders and/or phobias, depression, posttraumatic symptoms, and the presence of dissociative disorders. The domains of dysfunction tend to be emotional, somatic, cognitive, and relational.

To illustrate the difference between an adverse life experience and a big "T" trauma, let us consider the case of Rebecca, who grew up as "the minister's daughter." As the offspring of a local pastor, Rebecca grew up, figuratively speaking, in a glass house. She believed that her father's job rested on her behavior inside and outside of her home. In her world, everyone was watching. She was always in the spotlight, and no one seemed to want to share his or her life with her. She went through childhood with few friends. "I remember before and after church, the groups of kids forming. I was the outsider. No one invited me in." All the kids were afraid that every move they made would be reported to her daddy. Being at home was not much better. Her father was never home. He was always out "tending to his flock" and had little time left for his own family. Her mother was not of much comfort either, because she spent much of her time trying to be perfect as well. Living in a glass house was not easy for any of them, especially Rebecca, the oldest of three. By the time Rebecca entered therapy, she was a wife and mother. She thought she had to be perfect in motherhood and in her marriage as well. She became frustrated, angry, and lonely. She felt misunderstood and neglected by her husband. He was never there. He never listened. She thought she could do nothing right, as hard as she tried.

Probing into Rebecca's earliest childhood memories, no tragic or traumatic memories (i.e., big "T" traumas) emerged. As she continued to explore her past, the hardships and rigors of living in a glass house as the preacher's daughter slowly became apparent. The original target that initiated a round of EMDR reprocessing sessions focused on Rebecca "sitting on my hands in church and being a good little girl." Her negative belief about herself as she focused on this global touchstone event was "I have to be perfect." She felt isolated, over-looked, and abandoned by her parents and the parishioners of her father's church. These were undoubtedly adverse life experiences. There was no one single event or series of traumatic events that set her current problem or issue in place. It was her way of life; and how, where, and why she was forced to live as a child caused a specific set of symptoms and interfered with her living happily and successfully in the present.

The differentiation between adverse life experiences and big "T" traumas often appears too simplistic. Another way of discussing the types of trauma is to look at it in terms of shock or developmental trauma.

Shock trauma involves a sudden threat that is perceived by the central nervous system as overwhelming and/or life threatening. It is a single-episode traumatic event. Examples include car accidents, violence, surgery, hurricanes and other natural disasters, rape, battle-field assaults, and war.

Developmental trauma refers to events that occur over time and gradually affect and alter a client's neurological system to the point that it remains in a traumatic state. This type of trauma may cause interruptions in a child's natural psychological growth. Examples of developmental trauma are abandonment or long-term separation from a parent, an unstable or unsafe environment, neglect, serious illness, physical or sexual abuse, and betrayal at the hands of a caregiver. This type of trauma can have a negative impact on a child's sense of safety and security in the world and tends to set the stage for future trauma in adulthood as the sense of fear and helplessness that accompany it goes unresolved.

Table 1.1 outlines more definitely the differences between big "T" traumas and adverse life experiences or disturbing life events (i.e., small "t" traumas).

ADAPTIVE INFORMATION PROCESSING—"THE PAST DRIVES THE PRESENT"

EMDR therapy is a distinct integrative psychotherapeutic approach and is compatible with other major orientations of psychotherapy. This eight-phase approach is led by an informa-tion processing model and guides clinical practice (i.e., case conceptualization and treat-ment planning) in general.

Dr. Francine Shapiro developed a hypothetical information processing model of learn-ing called the AIP model (changed from Accelerated Information Processing model in 1995) to provide a theoretical framework and principles for EMDR therapy. Accelerated Informa-tion Processing clarifies how EMDR therapy works, and AIP guides how it is used (Table 1.2). Dr. Shapiro recognized the need to more efficiently explain the consistent treatment effects being obtained and reported from EMDR therapy.

AIP elaborates on the observed treatment effects of EMDR therapy by describing an innate physiological system that helps to transform disturbing information into adaptive resolution by psychologically integrating the information. In this model, memory networks constitute the basis of our perceptions, attitudes, and behaviors and constitute the basis of health or dysfunction. They may contain positive and negative experiences and may be adap-tive or maladaptive based on the nature of these experiences. These memories consist of stored information, such as sensory input (i.e., captured by our five senses), thoughts, emo-tions, and beliefs (Figure 1.1). Dr. Shapiro believes that disturbing events, whether big "T"

TABLE 1.1 Similarities and Differences Between Big "T" and Small "t" Trauma

BIG "T" TRAUMA	SMALL "t" TRAUMA (DISTURBING/DISTRESSING LIFE EVENTS)
Major event normally seen as traumatic May be a single- or multiple-event trauma May be pervasive Most often there is intrusive imagery Still elicits similar negative beliefs, emotions, and physical sensations Lasting negative effect on the client's sense of safety in the world	Disturbing/distressing life event that may not always be perceived as traumatic More common and ubiquitous; usually accumulates over time from childhood More often it is pervasive and ongoing Often there is <u>no</u> intrusive imagery Still elicits similar negative beliefs, emotions, and physical sensations Lasting negative effect on the client's sense of self (self-confidence, self-esteem, self-definition)
Examples: Serious accidents (e.g., automobile or bike accidents, plane crashes, serious falls) Natural disasters (e.g., earthquakes, tornadoes, tsunamis, forest fires, volcanic eruptions, floods) Man-made disasters (e.g., 9/11, explosions, fires, wars, acts of terrorism) Major life changes (e.g., serious illnesses, loss of loved ones) Physical and sexual assaults Major surgeries, life-threatening illnesses (e.g., cancer, heart attacks, craniotomies, heart bypasses) Ongoing life events (e.g., sexual abuse, domestic violence) War- and combat-related incidents	Examples: Moving multiple times during childhood Excessive teasing or bullying Persistent physical illnesses Constant criticism Rejections Betrayals Disparaging remarks Losing jobs Divorce or witnessing parental conflict Unmet developmental needs Death of pets Public shaming, humiliation, or failure Unresolved guilt Physical or emotional neglect Getting lost Chronic harassment

TABLE 1.2 Accelerated Information Processing Versus Adaptive Information Processing

ACCELERATED INFORMATION PROCESSING (HOW IT IS USED)	AIP (HOW IT WORKS)
Working hypothesis	Working model
Explains how EMDR works	Explains why EMDR works
Developed to explain the rapid manner in which clinical results are achieved	Developed to explain the clinical phenomena observed
Simple desensitization treatment effect	Entails an information processing effect

Abbreviation: AIP, Adaptive Information Processing.

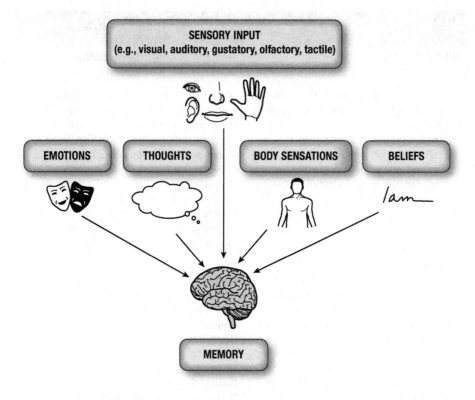

FIGURE 1.1 Diagram illustrating the components of memory.

traumas or adverse life experiences, are the primary source of our current dysfunction. When trauma happens, it causes a disruption in our information processing system, leaving any associated sights, sounds, thoughts, or feelings unprocessed and, subsequently, dysfunctionally stored as they are perceived (Shapiro, 2018). See Table 1.3 for examples of adaptive versus maladaptive resolution.

Shapiro (2018) posits that inherent in the AIP model is a psychological self-healing construct similar to the body's healing response to physical injury. For example, if you get a splinter stuck in your finger, your body's automatic response is to heal the area of injury. However, because the area is blocked by the splinter, healing cannot easily occur until the sliver is removed. In terms of mental processes, it is the inherent tendency of the information processing system to also move toward a state of health. So, even when something mildly disturbing happens, you may think about it, talk about it, and process it. You usually find that, within a day or so, you are no longer thinking so intensely about the event and, when you do, you have come to a resolution. For instance, if you are angry at your spouse, you may start to remember that your spouse has some good qualities as well as these very annoying ones. It is a case of the mind adaptively processing the disturbing material and connecting that disturbance into the larger picture of the experience. Table 1.4 demonstrates how EMDR therapy catalyzes healing and learning.

On the other hand, when a trauma occurs that is too large for your system to adequately process, it can become "stuck" (i.e., dysfunctionally stored) in the central nervous system.

TABLE 1.3 Adaptive Versus Maladaptive Resolution

ADAPTIVE	MALADAPTIVE
Big "T" (e.g., safety)	
I survived.	Driving phobia
I can learn from this.	Flashbacks
I can protect myself.	Intense driving anxiety
I am safe.	Night terrors
Small "t" (i.e., adverse or disturbing/distressing life events; e.g., responsibility)	
I am fine as I am.	Low self-esteem
I did the best I could.	Irrational guilt
I am significant/important.	Self-neglect, co-dependence

TABLE 1.4 EMDR Therapy Catalyzes Learning

TARGET	
When the target is a disturbing memory.	When the target is positive (i.e., an alternative desirable imagined future).
Negative images, beliefs, and emotions become less vivid, less enhanced, and less valid.	Positive images, beliefs, and emotions become more vivid, more enhanced, and more valid.
Before reprocessing, links to dysfunctional material.	Links with more appropriate information.
Learning is a continuum.	

Maladaptive responses, such as flashbacks or dreams, can be triggered by present stimuli, and there may be attempts of the information processing system to resolve the trauma (Shapiro, 2018). When the system becomes overloaded as just described, EMDR therapy is proving to be the treatment of choice for many to help restart this mental healing process and allow the traumas to be reprocessed. See Exhibit 1.1 for a graphical representation of the AIP model.

The AIP model also posits that earlier life experiences set the stage for later life strengths or problems. Information from earlier disturbing life events can be physiologically and dysfunctionally stored in the nervous system if not properly assimilated at the time of the event. Problematic behaviors and disorders can occur as a result. Table 1.5 describes the differences between dysfunctionally stored and adaptively stored memories.

At the time of disturbing or traumatic events, information may be stored in the central nervous system in state-specific form (i.e., the negative cognitive belief and emotional and physical sensations the client experienced at the time of the traumatic event remain stored in the central nervous system just as if the trauma is happening in the now). Over time, a client may develop repeated negative patterns of feeling, sensing, thinking, believing, and behaving as a result of the dysfunctionally stored material. These patterns are stimulated, activated, or triggered by stimuli in the present that cause a client to react in the same or similar ways

EXHIBIT 1.1 Adaptive Information Processing Model: The Information Processing System at Work

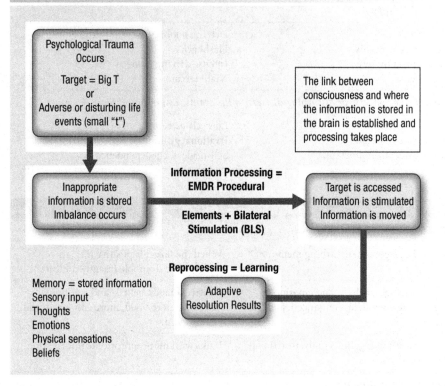

Psychological Trauma Occurs

Target = Big T
or
Adverse or disturbing life events (small "t")

The link between consciousness and where the information is stored in the brain is established and processing takes place

Inappropriate information is stored
Imbalance occurs

Information Processing = EMDR Procedural

Target is accessed
Information is stimulated
Information is moved

Elements + Bilateral Stimulation (BLS)

Reprocessing = Learning

Adaptive Resolution Results

Memory = stored information
Sensory input
Thoughts
Emotions
Physical sensations
Beliefs

Abbreviation: BLS, bilateral stimulation.

TABLE 1.5 Differences Between Dysfunctionally Stored and Adaptively Stored Memories

DYSFUNCTIONALLY STORED MEMORIES	ADAPTIVELY STORED MEMORIES
Information processing system is overwhelmed and becomes "stuck"	Information processing system is able to connect to current information and resources and adequately process information
Embraces an inappropriate, developmentally arrested lack of power in the past	Embraces an age-appropriate power in the present
Past-oriented or developmentally arrested, dysfunctional perspective	Present-oriented and age-appropriate, adaptive perspective
Stored in incorrect form of memory (i.e., implicit/motoric)	Stored in correct form of memory (i.e., explicit/narrative)
Past is present	Past is past

TABLE 1.6 Activation Components of EMDR Therapy
ACCESS
Frozen dysfunctional memory
STIMULATE
Information processing system
MOVE
Information to adaptive resolution
RESULTS
Lessening of disturbance Gained information and insights Changes in emotional and physical responses

as in the past. Shapiro (2018) states throughout her basic text that the negative beliefs and affect from past events spill into the present. By processing earlier traumatic memories, EMDR therapy enables the client to generalize positive affect and cognitions to associated memories found throughout the "neuro" networks (i.e., memory networks), thus allowing more appropriate behaviors in the present. Table 1.6 demonstrates a more simplified version of how EMDR reprocessing works (Shapiro, 2009–2017a, 2009–2017b).

Cognitive behavioral techniques, such as systematic desensitization, imaginal exposure, or flooding, require the client to focus on anxiety-provoking *behaviors* and irrational *thoughts* or to relive the trauma or other adverse life experiences. EMDR therapy accesses or develops adequate current resources, and then targets the *experiences* that caused the negative cognition, affect, and physical sensations to become "stuck" in a client's nervous system. Once the memories have been reprocessed utilizing EMDR, a physiological shift can occur that causes the disturbing picture to fade appropriately with the associated negative self-belief, feelings, and physical sensations. The "block" (i.e., dysfunctionally stored information) in the client's nervous system is shifted, and the disturbance is brought to an adaptive resolution as the natural healing process is activated. The primary byproduct of reprocessing is a decrease or elimination of the negative charge associated with the trauma or disturbing life events.

Changes in perception and attitude, experiencing moments of insight, and subtle differences in the way a person thinks, feels, behaves, and believes are byproducts as well. The changes can be immediate. Take, for instance, a session with a young woman who had been brutally raped by her ex-boyfriend. During the Assessment Phase, Andrea's terror appeared raggedly etched in her face and slumped demeanor. After many successive sets of bilateral stimulation (BLS), her pale facial features began to redden, her posture began to straighten, and her breath began to gain strength and resolve as she spontaneously stated, "He took my power that night. No more! I am taking my power back. He no longer has the

EXHIBIT 1.2 Adaptive Information Processing Model: Information Processing Mechanism

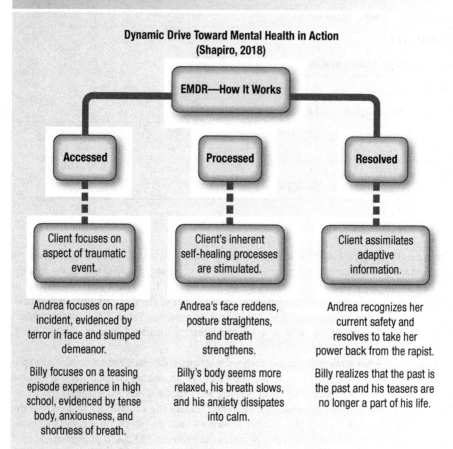

power to terrorize me!" Or consider Billy, who was teased unmercifully in high school by his football teammates. Prior to desensitization and reprocessing, he appeared tense, anxious, and short of breath. After just a few sets of BLS, his body appeared more relaxed, his breath slowed, and his anxiety dissipated into a state of calm. "That was then. This is now. They are nobody to me now."

Exhibit 1.2 demonstrates in action the inherent information processing mechanism as it highlights the changes that occurred as a result of Andrea and Billy's dynamic drive toward mental health with EMDR therapy.

Because the heart of EMDR therapy is the AIP model, it is critical that the clinician has a clear understanding of it before proceeding. An adequate conceptual understanding helps the clinician determine a client's appropriateness for EMDR therapy, as well as explain the process to the client during the Preparation Phase, so that he has some understanding of the

TABLE 1.7 Client's Experience: Adaptive Information Processing in Action

BEFORE		AFTER
Client experiences negative event, resulting in: Intrusive images; Negative thoughts or beliefs; Negative emotions and associated physical sensations	Negative experience is transmuted into an adaptive learning experience	**Client experiences adaptive learning, resulting in:** No intrusive images; No negative thoughts or beliefs; No negative emotional and/or physical sensations; An empowering new positive self-belief
What happens? Information is insufficiently (dysfunctionally) stored; Dysfunctional information gets replayed; Developmental windows may be closed		**What happens?** Information is sufficiently (adaptively) processed; Adequate learning has taken place; Development continues on a normal trajectory
Resulting in: Depression; Anxiety; Low self-esteem; Self-deprecation; Powerlessness; Inadequacy; Lack of choice; Lack of control; Dissociation		**Resulting in:** Sense of well-being; Self-efficacy; Understanding; Catalyzed learning; Appropriate changes in behavior; Emergence of adult perspective; Self-acceptance; Ability to be present

Abbreviation: AIP, Adaptive Information Processing.

potential treatment effects. Table 1.7 highlights the before and after treatment changes of EMDR in terms of the AIP model.

Using an example of a traumatic event, Table 1.8 illustrates more graphically what happens during reprocessing of a traumatic event.

For a more comprehensive explanation of AIP, read Shapiro's "Chapter 2, Adaptive Information Processing, the Model as a Working Hypothesis," in *Eye Movement Desensitization and Reprocessing: Basic Principles, Protocols, and Procedures* (3rd ed.; 2018) and "EMDR, Adaptive Information Processing, and Case Conceptualization" (Shapiro, 2007a).

As the previous tables and figures demonstrate, EMDR is an "empowerment" therapy as it provides space for a client to realize and regain personal power.

MODEL, METHODOLOGY, AND MECHANISM OF EMDR THERAPY

Why and how does EMDR therapy work? What are the fundamental procedures and elements that contribute to the EMDR therapy overall treatment effect? Unfortunately, no one really knows the neurobiological underpinnings for why EMDR therapy works. Many

TABLE 1.8 Transmutation of the Targeted Memory (e.g., What Happens During Reprocessing)

NEGATIVE EXPERIENCE	ADAPTIVE LEARNING EXPERIENCE
Example: After a heated argument, Mary is raped by her ex-boyfriend in the parking lot of a bar they just left.	

Mary experiences:		**Mary experiences:**
Intrusive images:		Cognitive restructuring of perceptions
Negative thoughts and self-beliefs (e.g., I am a bad person)		Association to positive affects
		Sense of well-being and self-efficacy
Negative emotions (e.g., shame, fear, anger, anxiety)	*Learning is catalyzed*	New insights
		Feelings of empowerment
Negative physical sensations (e.g., heart palpitations, sweaty palms, difficulty breathing)		Learning
		Greater sense of understanding
Sense of powerlessness		
Lack of choice		
Lack of control		
Inadequacy		

questions remain to be answered and, at the same time, clients experience continued positive clinical effects. The following are the three primary aspects of EMDR therapy:

1. Model—The AIP model provides the theoretical model for EMDR therapy.
2. Methodology—Eight phases of EMDR therapy plus the ethics, safeguards, and validated modifications for basic and specific clinical situations and populations.
3. Mechanism—Current hypotheses on how and why EMDR therapy works on a neurobiological level.

MODEL—HOW?

The AIP model guides its clinical practice (i.e., case conceptualization and treatment planning) and predicts the EMDR treatment effects, and it is independent from the "why" stated later. It is through the lens of the AIP model that the developmental phenomenon is understood, any clinical phenomena that arise during EMDR processing are interpreted, and successful application and positive treatment outcomes are predicted.

Guided by this information processing model, memory networks are believed to form the basis of clinical symptoms and mental health in general, and "unprocessed memories are considered to be the primary basis of pathology" (Shapiro, 2009–2017a). The important components of the model as outlined by Shapiro (1995, 2001, 2018, 2009–2017a, 2009–2017b) are summarized in Table 1.9.

There is a body of literature, including both research and case reports on a variety of clinical complaints, that illustrates the predictive value of the AIP in terms of body dysmorphic disorder (Brown et al., 1997); generalized anxiety disorder (Gauvreau & Bouchard, 2008); olfactory reference syndrome (McGoldrick et al., 2008); panic disorder with agoraphobia (Fernandez & Faretta, 2007); bonding failures (Madrid et al., 2006); depression (Uribe &

TABLE 1.9 Important Components of the Information Processing Model	

The AIP model views maladaptive/negative memory networks as the "underlying basis of both pathology and mental health."

Disturbing memories are dysfunctionally stored (i.e., perceived in the same way as when the memory was originally formed) and may disrupt the information processing system.

Emotions, physical sensations, and thoughts and beliefs associated with unprocessed memories are experienced by the client as their perceptions in the present link to the historical memory networks.

In order to be interpreted, a client's perceptions of *resent* situations link into networks of physically stored memories (negative or dysfunctional) from the *past*. In other words, *the past is present*.

As the processing begins, disruptions may be caused by high levels of emotional disturbance or dissociation, which can block adaptive processing.

When a client is processing the memory of a traumatic event, they have the opportunity to forge adaptive associations with memory networks of functional information stored in the brain. This EMDR associative process allows these connections to be made.

During processing, the unprocessed elements of a client's memory (i.e., image, thoughts, sounds, emotional and physical sensations, beliefs) have the ability to transform/transmute to an adaptive resolution. At this point, learning may take place. By discarding maladaptive information and storing adaptive information, a client has new learning that may better inform future experiences and choices.

Abbreviation: AIP, Adaptive Information Processing.

Ramirez, 2006); adolescent depression (Bae et al., 2008); PTSD (Mol et al., 2005; Raboni et al., 2006); the role of EMDR therapy in medicine (Shapiro, 2014); dental phobia (Doering et al., 2013); perpetrators with a trauma history (Ricci et al., 2006); adult attachment (Wesselman & Potter, 2009); psychosis (Heins et al., 2011; van den Berg & van den Gaag, 2012; Varese et al., 2012); peer verbal abuse (Teicher et al., 2010); obsessive-compulsive disorder (Nazari et al., 2011); borderline personality disorder (Brown & Shapiro, 2006); phantom limb pain (de Roos et al., 2010; Russell, 2008; Schneider et al., 2007; Schneider et al., 2008; Wilensky, 2006); physical punishment and mental disorders (Afifi et al., 2012); childhood trauma and children's emerging symptoms (Arseneault et al., 2012); childhood trauma and household dysfunction (Felitti et al., 1998); and biological sensitivity (Obradovic et al., 2010).

METHODOLOGY—HOW/WHAT?

EMDR therapy employs an eight-phase integrative treatment approach. Often customized to reflect a client's clinical diagnosis or individual presentation, EMDR therapy utilizes a distinct set of procedures and protocols to address a client's presenting issues. BLS is only one component of the methodology that guides this therapeutic practice of EMDR. EMDR therapy is also a three-pronged approach that includes a client's past experiences, present triggers, and a future template of how the client may want to be or respond in a situation. EMDR therapy is flexible in that it also combines aspects of a clinician's previous orientations to psychotherapy as part of the process.

For further reading on the "how" and "what" of EMDR therapy, an overview of the model and procedures is elaborated on in Table 1.10.

TABLE 1.10 Model—Adaptive Information Processing and EMDR Therapy Procedures: How/What

1997

Brown, K. W., McGoldrick, T., & Buchanan, R. (1997). Body dysmorphic disorder: Seven cases treated with eye movement desensitization and reprocessing. *Behavioural and Cognitive Psychotherapy, 25*(2), 203–207. https://doi.org/10.1017/S1352465800018403

1998

Felitti, V. J., Anda, R. F., Nordenberg, D., Williamson, D. F., Spitz, A. M., Edwards, V., Koss, M. P., & Marks, J. S. (1998). Relationship of childhood abuse and household dysfunction to many of the leading causes of death in adults: The adverse childhood experiences (ACE) study. *American Journal of Preventive Medicine, 14*, 245–258. https://doi.org/10.1016/S0749-3797(98)00017-8

2001

Ray, A. L., & Zbik, A. (2001). Cognitive behavioral therapies and beyond. In C. D. Tollison, J. R. Satterhwaite, & J. W. Tollison (Eds.). *Practical pain management* (3rd ed., pp. 189–208). Lippincott.

Shapiro, F. (2001). *Eye movement desensitization and reprocessing: Basic principles, protocols, and procedures* (2nd ed.). Guilford Press.

2002

Perkins, B., & Rouanzoin, C. (2002). A critical evaluation of current views regarding eye movement desensitization and reprocessing (EMDR): Clarifying points of confusion. *Journal of Clinical Psychology, 58*(1), 77–97. https://doi.org/10.1002/jclp.1130

Shapiro, F. (2002). *EMDR as an integrative psychotherapy approach: Experts of diverse orientations explore the paradigm prism.* American Psychological Association Press.

2004

Heim, C., Plotsky, P. M., & Nemeroff, C. B. (2004). Importance of studying the contributions of early adverse experience to neurobiological findings in depression. *Neuropsychopharmacology, 29*, 641–648. https://doi.org/10.1038/sj.npp.1300397

2005

Gold, S. D., Marx, B. P., Soler-Baillo, J. M., & Sloan, D. M. (2005). Is life stress more traumatic than traumatic stress? *Journal of Anxiety Disorders, 19*, 687–698. https://doi.org/10.1016/j.janxdis.2004.06.002

Mol, S. S. L., Arntz, A, Metsemakers, J. F. M, Dinant, G., Vilters-Van Montfort, P. A. P., & Knottnerus, A. (2005). Symptoms of post-traumatic stress disorder after non-traumatic events: Evidence from an open population study. *British Journal of Psychiatry, 186*, 494–499. https://doi.org/10.1192/bjp.186.6.494

(continued)

TABLE 1.10 Model—Adaptive Information Processing and EMDR Therapy Procedures: How/What (continued)

2006

Brown, S., & Shapiro, F. (2006). EMDR in the treatment of borderline personality disorder. *Clinical Case Studies, 5*(5), 403–420. https://doi.org/10.1177/1534650104271773

Madrid, A., Skolek, S., & Shapiro, F. (2006). Repairing failures in bonding through EMDR. *Clinical Case Studies, 5*(4), 271–286. https://doi.org/10.1177/1534650104267403

Raboni, M. R., Tufik, S., & Suchecki, D. (2006). Treatment of PTSD by eye movement desensitization reprocessing (EMDR) improves sleep quality, quality of life, and perception of stress. *Annals of the New York Academy of Sciences, 1071*(1), 508–513. https://doi.org/10.1196/annals.1364.054

Ricci, R. J., Clayton, C. A., & Shapiro, F. (2006). Some effects of EMDR on previously abused child molesters: Theoretical reviews and preliminary findings. *Journal of Forensic Psychiatry and Psychology, 17*(4), 538–562. https://doi.org/10.1080/14789940601070431

Shapiro, F. (2006). *New notes on adaptive information processing: Case formulation principles, scripts, and worksheets.* EMDR Humanitarian Assistance Programs.

Uribe, M. E. R., & Ramirez, E. O. L. (2006). The effect of EMDR therapy on the negative information processing on patients who suffer depression. *Revista Electrónica de Motivación y Emoción, 9*, 23–24.

Wilensky, M. (2006). Eye movement desensitization and reprocessing (EMDR) as a treatment for phantom limb pain. *Journal of Brief Therapy, 5*(1), 31–44.

2007

Fernandez, I., & Faretta, E. (2007). Eye movement desensitization and reprocessing in the treatment of panic disorder with agoraphobia. *Clinical Case Studies, 6*(1), 44–63. https://doi.org/10.1177/1534650105277220

Schneider, J., Hofmann, A., Rost, C., & Shapiro, F. (2007). EMDR and phantom limb pain: Theoretical implications, case study, and treatment guidelines. *Journal of EMDR Practice and Research, 1*(1), 31–45. https://doi.org/10.1891/1933- 3196.1.1.31

Shapiro, F. (2007a). EMDR, adaptive information processing, and case conceptualization. *Journal of EMDR Practice and Research, 1*(2), 68–87. https://doi.org/10.1891/1933-3196.1.2.68

Shapiro, F. (2007b). EMDR and case conceptualization from an adaptive information processing perspective. In F. Shapiro, F. Kaslow, & L. Maxfield (Eds.), *Handbook of EMDR and family therapy processes* (pp. 3–36). John Wiley & Sons.

Shapiro, F., Kaslow, F. W., & Maxfield, M. (2007). *Handbook of EMDR and family therapy processes.* John Wiley & Sons.

2008

Bae, H., Kim, D., & Park, Y. C. (2008). Eye movement desensitization and reprocessing for adolescent depression. *Psychiatry Investigation, 5*(1), 60–65. https://doi.org/10.4306/pi.2008.5.1.60

Gauvreau, P., & Bouchard, S. (2008). Preliminary evidence for the efficacy of EMDR in treating generalized anxiety disorder. *Journal of EMDR Practice and Research, 2*(1), 26–40. https://doi.org/10.1891/1933-3196.2.1.26

McGoldrick, T., Begum, M., & Brown, K. W. (2008). EMDR and olfactory reference syndrome: A case series. *Journal of EMDR Practice and Research, 2*(1), 63–68. https://doi.org/10.1891/1933-3196.2.1.63

(continued)

TABLE 1.10 Model—Adaptive Information Processing and EMDR Therapy Procedures: How/What (continued)

2008

Russell, M. C. (2008). Treating traumatic amputation-related phantom limb pain: A case study utilizing eye movement desensitization and reprocessing within the Armed Services. *Clinical Case Studies, 7*(2), 136–153. https://doi.org/10.1177/1534650107306292

Schneider, J., Hofmann, A., Rost, C., & Shapiro, F. (2008). EMDR in the treatment of chronic phantom limb pain. *Pain Medicine, 9*(1), 76–82. https://doi.org/10.1111/j.1526-4637.2007.00299.x

Solomon, R. M., & Shapiro, F. (2008). EMDR and the adaptive information processing model—Potential mechanisms of change. *Journal of EMDR Practice and Research, 2*(4), 315–325. https://doi.org/10.1891/1933-3196.2.4.315

2009

Wesselmann, D., & Potter, A. E. (2009). Change in adult attachment status following treatment with EMDR: Three case studies. *Journal of EMDR Practice and Research, 3*(3), 178–191. https://doi.org/10.1891/1933-3196.3.3.178

2010

de Roos, C., Veenstra, A., de Jongh, A., den Hollander-Gijsman, M., van der Wee, N., Zitman, F., & van Rood, Y. R. (2010). Treatment of chronic phantom limb pain using a trauma-focused psychological approach. *Pain Research & Management, 15*(2), 65–71. https://doi.org/10.1155/2010/981634

Obradovic, J., Bush, N. R., Stamperdahl, J., Adler, N. E., & Boyce, W. T. (2010). Biological sensitivity to context: The interactive effects of stress reactivity and family adversity on socioemotional behavior and school readiness. *Child Development, 1*, 270–289. https://doi.org/10.1111/j.1467-8624.2009.01394.x

Robinson, J. S., & Larson, C. (2010). Are traumatic events necessary to elicit symptoms of posttraumatic stress? *Psychological Trauma: Theory, Research, Practice, and Policy, 2*, 71–76. https://doi.org/10.1037/a0018954

Teicher, M. H., Samson, J. A., Sheu, Y.-S., Polcari, A., & McGreenery, C. E. (2010). Hurtful words: Association of exposure to peer verbal abuse with elevated psychiatric symptom scores and corpus callosum abnormalities. *American Journal of Psychiatry, 167*, 1464–1471. https://doi.org/10.1176/appi.ajp.2010.10010030

2011

Arseneault, L., Cannon, M., Fisher, H. L., Polanczyk, G., Moffitt, T. E., & Caspi, A. (2011). Childhood trauma and children's emerging psychotic symptoms: A genetically sensitive longitudinal cohort study. *American Journal of Psychiatry, 168*, 65–72. https://doi.org/10.1176/appi.ajp.2010.10040567

Heins, M., Simons, C., Lataste, T., Pfeifer, S., Versmissen, D., Lardinois, M., Marcelis, M., Delespaul, P., Krabbendam, L., van Os, J., & Myin-Germeys, I. (2011). Childhood trauma and psychosis: A case-control and case-sibling comparison across different levels of genetic liability, psychopathology, and type of trauma. *American Journal of Psychiatry, 168*, 1286–1294. https://doi.org/10.1176/appi.ajp.2011.10101531

(continued)

TABLE 1.10 Model—Adaptive Information Processing and EMDR Therapy Procedures: How/What (continued)

2011

Nazari, H., Momeni, N., Jariani, M., & Tarrahi, M. J. (2011). Comparison of eye movement desensitization and reprocessing with citalopram in treatment of obsessive-compulsive disorder. *International Journal of Psychiatry in Clinical Practice, 15*(4), 270–274. https://doi.org/10.3109/13651501.2011.590210

2012

Afifi, T. O., Mota, N. P., Dasiewicz, P., MacMillan, H. L., & Sareen, J. (2012). Physical punishment and mental disorders: Results from a nationally representative US sample. *Pediatrics, 130,* 184–192. https://doi.org/10.1542/peds.2011-2947

Shapiro, F. (2012a). EMDR therapy: An overview of current and future research. *European Review of Applied Psychology, 62*(4), 193–195. https://doi.org/10.1016/j.erap.2012.09.005

van den Berg, D. P. G., & van der Gaag, M. (2012). Treating trauma in psychosis with EMDR: A pilot study. *Journal of Behavior Therapy and Experimental Psychiatry, 43*(1), 664–671. https://doi.org/10.1016/j.jbtep.2011.09.011

Varese, F., Smeets, F., Drukker, M., Lieverse, R, Lataster, T., Viechtbauer, W., Read, J., van Os, J., & Bentall, R. P. (2012). Childhood adversities increase the risk of psychosis: A meta-analysis of patient-control, prospective- and cross-sectional cohort studies. *Schizophrenia Bulletin, 38*(4), 661–671. https://doi.org/10.1093/schbul/sbs050

2013

Doering, S., Ohlmeier, M.-C., de Jongh, A., Hofmann, A., & Bisping, V. (2013). Efficacy of a trauma-focused treatment approach for dental phobia: A randomized clinical trial. *European Journal of Oral Sciences, 121*(6), 584–593. https://doi.org/10.1111/eos.12090

Faretta, E. (2013). EMDR and cognitive behavioral therapy in the treatment of panic disorder: A comparison. *Journal of EMDR Practice and Research, 7,* 121–133. https://doi.org/10.1891/1933-3196.7.3.121

2014

Read, J., Fosse, R., Moskowitz, A., & Perry, B. (2014). The traumagenic neurodevelopmental model of psychosis revisited. *Neuropsychiatry, 4*(1), 65–79. https://doi.org/10.2217/NPY.13.89

Shapiro, F. (2014). The role of eye movement desensitization and reprocessing (EMDR) therapy in medicine: Addressing the psychological and physical symptoms stemming from adverse life experiences. *The Permanente Journal, 18,* 71–77. https://doi.org/10.7812/TPP/13-098

2015

Allon, M. (2015). EMDR group therapy with women who were sexually assaulted in the Congo. *Journal of EMDR Practice and Research, 9,* 28–34. https://doi.org/10.1891/1933-3196.9.1.28

Behnam Moghadam, M., Alamdari, A. K., Behnam Moghadam, A., & Darban, F. (2015). Effect of EMDR on depression in patients with myocardial infarction. *Global Journal of Health Science, 7,* 258–262. https://doi.org/10.5539/gjhs.v7n6p258

(continued)

TABLE 1.10 Model—Adaptive Information Processing and EMDR Therapy Procedures: How/What (continued)

2018

Shapiro, F. (2018). *Eye movement desensitization and reprocessing: Basic principles, protocols and procedure* (3rd ed.). Guilford Press.

Gauhar, M., & Wajid, Y. (2016). The efficacy of EMDR in the treatment of depression. *Journal of EMDR Practice and Research, 10*(2), 59–69. https://doi.org/10.1891/1933-3196.10.2.59

MECHANISM—WHY?

Over the past 25 years, numerous studies have indicated that eye movements have effects on a client's memory in terms of vividness, retrieval, emotional arousal, and more. Studies that evaluated EMDR therapy's mechanism of action are listed in Table 1.11.

TABLE 1.11 Mechanism of Action—Why

1996

Andrade, J., Kavanagh, D., & Baddeley, A. (1997). Eye-movements and visual imagery: A working memory approach to the treatment of post-traumatic stress disorder. *British Journal of Clinical Psychology, 36*, 209–223. https://doi.org/10.1111/j.2044-8260.1997.tb01408.x

Armstrong, M. S., & Vaughan, K. (1996). An orienting response model of eye movement desensitization. *Journal of Behavior Therapy & Experimental Psychiatry, 27*, 21–32. https://doi.org/10.1016/0005-7916(95)00056-9

MacCulloch, M. J., & Feldman, P. (1996). Eye movement desensitization treatment utilizes the positive visceral element of the investigatory reflex to inhibit the memories of post-traumatic stress disorder: A theoretical analysis. *British Journal of Psychiatry, 169*(5), 571–579. https://doi.org/10.1192/bjp.169.5.571

Wilson, D., Silver, S. M., Covi, W., & Foster, S. (1996). Eye movement desensitization and reprocessing: Effectiveness and autonomic correlates. *Journal of Behaviour Therapy and Experimental Psychiatry, 27*, 219–229. https://doi.org/10.1016/S0005-7916(96)00026-2

1999

Lipke, H. (1999). Comments on "thirty years of behavior therapy" and the promise of the application of scientific principles. *The Behavior Therapist, 22*, 11–14.

Rogers, S., Silver, S., Goss, J., Obenchain, J., Willis, A., & Whitney, R. (1999). A single session, controlled group study of flooding and eye movement desensitization and reprocessing in treating posttraumatic stress disorder among Vietnam war veterans: Preliminary data. *Journal of Anxiety Disorders, 13*, 119–130.

2000

Bergmann, U. (2000). Further thoughts on the neurobiology of EMDR: The role of the cerebellum in accelerated information processing. *Traumatology, 6*(3), 175–200. https://doi.org/10.1177/153476560000600303

(continued)

TABLE 1.11 Mechanism of Action—Why (continued)

2001

Kavanagh, D. J., Freese, S., Andrade, J., & May, J. (2001). Effects of visuospatial tasks on desensitization to emotive memories. *British Journal of Clinical Psychology, 40*, 267–280. https://doi.org/10.1348/014466501163689

2002

Rogers, S., & Silver, S. M. (2002). Is EMDR an exposure therapy? A review of trauma protocols. *Journal of Clinical Psychology, 58*, 43–59. https://doi.org/10.1002/jclp.1128

Stickgold, R. (2002). EMDR: A putative neurobiological mechanism of action. *Journal of Clinical Psychology, 58*, 61–75. https://doi.org/10.1002/jclp.1129

2004

Barrowcliff, A. L., Gray, N. S., Freeman, T. C. A., & MacCulloch, M. J. (2004). Eye movements reduce the vividness, emotional valence and electrodermal arousal associated with negative autobiographical memories. *Journal of Forensic Psychiatry and Psychology, 15*(2), 325–345. https://doi.org/10.1080/14789940410001673042

Suzuki, A., Josselyn, S. A., Frankland, P. W., Masushige, S., Silva, A. J., & Satoshi, K. (2004). Memory reconsolidation and extinction have distinct temporal and biochemical signatures. *Journal of Neuroscience, 24*(20), 4787–4795. https://doi.org/10.1523/jneurosci.5491-03.2004

2006

Lee, C. W., Taylor, G., & Drummond, P. D. (2006). The active ingredient in EMDR: Is it traditional exposure or dual focus of attention? *Clinical Psychology and Psychotherapy, 13*, 97–107. https://doi.org/10.1002/cpp.479

Servan-Schreiber, D., Schooler, J., Dew, M. A., Carter, C., & Bartone, P. (2006). EMDR for PTSD: A pilot blinded, randomized study of stimulation type. *Psychotherapy and Psychosomatics, 75*, 290–297. https://doi.org/10.1159/000093950

2007

Propper, R., Pierce, J. P., Geisler, M. W., Christman, S. D., & Bellorado, N. (2007). Effect of bilateral eye movements on frontal interhemispheric gamma EEG coherence: Implications for EMDR therapy. *Journal of Nervous and Mental Disease, 195*, 785–788. https://doi.org/10.1097/NMD.0b013e318142cf73

2008

Bergmann, U. (2008). The neurobiology of EMDR: Exploring the thalamus and neural integration. *Journal of EMDR Practice and Research, 2*(4), 300–314. https://doi.org/10.1891/1933-3196.2.4.300

Sack, M., Hofmann, A., Wizelman, L., & Lempa, W. (2008). Psychophysiological changes during EMDR and treatment outcome. *Journal of EMDR Practice and Research, 2*, 239–246. https://doi.org/10.1891/1933-3196.2.4.239

Sack, M., Lempa, W., Steinmetz, A., Lamprecht, F., & Hofmann, A. (2008). Alterations in autonomic tone during trauma exposure using eye movement desensitization and reprocessing (EMDR) – Results of a preliminary investigation. *Journal of Anxiety Disorders, 22*, 1264–1271. https://doi.org/10.1016/j.janxdis.2008.01.007

Elofsson, U. O. E., von Scheele, B., Theorell, T., & Sondergaard, H. P. (2008). Physiological correlates of eye movement desensitization and reprocessing. *Journal of Anxiety Disorders, 22*, 622–634. https://doi.org/10.1016/ j.janxdis.2007.05.012

(continued)

TABLE 1.11 Mechanism of Action—Why (continued)

2008

Stickgold, R. (2008). Sleep-dependent memory processing and EMDR action. *Journal of EMDR Practice and Research, 2,* 289–299. https://doi.org/10.1891/1933-3196.2. 4.289

2009

Friedman, D., Goldman, R., Stern, Y., & Brown, T. (2009). The brain's orienting response: An event-related functional magnetic resonance imaging investigation. *Human Brain Mapping, 30*(4), 1144–1154.

Gunter, R., & Bodnar, G. (2009). EMDR works … But how? Recent progress in the search for treatment mechanisms. *Journal of EMDR Practice and Research, 3,* 161–168.

Lilley, S. A., Andrade, J., Turpin, G., Sabin-Farrell, R., & Holmes, E. A. (2009). Visuospatial working memory interference with recollections of trauma. *British Journal of clinical psychology, 48*(3), 309–321.

2010

Bergmann, U. (2010). EMDR's neurobiological mechanisms of action: A survey of 20 years of searching. *Journal of EMDR Research and Practice, 4,* 22–42. https://doi.org/10.1891/1933-3196.4.1.22

Hornsveld, H. K., Landwehr, F., Stein, W., Stomp, M., Smeets, S., & van den Hout, M. A. (2010). Emotionality of loss-related memories is reduced after recall plus eye movements but not after recall plus music or recall only. *Journal of EMDR Practice and Research, 4,* 106–112. https://doi.org/10.1891/1933-3196.4.3.106

Kapoula, Z., Yang Q., Bonnet, A., Bourtoire, P., & Sandretto, J. (2010). EMDR effects on pursuit eye movements. *PLoS ONE, 5*(5), e10762. https://doi.org/10.1371/journal.pone.0010762

van den Hout, M. A., Engelhard, I. M., Smeets, M. A., Hornsveld, H., Hoogeveen, E., & de Heer, E. (2010). Counting during recall: Taxing of working memory and reduced vividness and emotionality of negative memories. *Applied Cognitive Psychology, 24*(3), 303–311. https://doi.org/10.1002/acp.1677

2011

El Khoury-Malhame, M., Lanteaume, L., Beetz, E. M., Roques, J., Reynaud, E., Samuelian, J. -C., Blin, O., Garcia, R., & Khalfa, S. (2011). Attentional bias in post-traumatic stress disorder diminishes after symptom amelioration. *Behavior Research and Therapy, 49*(11), 796–801. https://doi.org/10.1016/j.brat.2011.08.006

Kristjánsdóttir, K., & Lee, C. M. (2011). A comparison of visual versus auditory concurrent tasks on reducing the distress and vividness of aversive autobiographical memories. *Journal of EMDR Practice and Research, 5,* 34–41. https://doi.org/10.1891/1933-3196.5.2.34

2012

van den Hout, M., & Engelhard, I. (2012). How does EMDR work? *Journal of Experimental Psychopathology, 3,* 724–738. https://doi.org/10.5127/jep.028212

van den Hout, M. A., Rijkeboer, M. M., Engelhard, I. M., Klugkist, I., Hornsveld, H., Toffolo, M. J., & Cath, D. C. (2012). Tones inferior to eye movements in the EMDR treatment of PTSD. *Behaviour Research and Therapy, 50,* 275–279. https://doi.org/10.1016/j.brat.2012.02.001

(continued)

TABLE 1.11 Mechanism of Action—Why (continued)

2013

de Jongh, A., Ernst, R., Marques, L., & Hornsveld, H. (2013). The impact of eye movements and tones on disturbing memories involving PTSD and other mental disorders. *Journal of Behavior Therapy and Experimental Psychiatry, 44*(4), 477–483. https://doi.org/10.1016/j.jbtep.2013.07.002

Pagani, M., Hogberg, G., Fernandez, I., & Siracusano, A. (2013). Correlates of EMDR therapy in functional and structural neuroimaging: A critical summary of recent findings. *Journal of EMDR Practice and Research, 7*(1), 29–38. https://doi.org/10.1891/1933-3196.7.1.29

2014

Leer, Engelhard, and van den Hout provided corroborating evidence that recall with EM causes 24-h changes in memory vividness/emotionality.

2016

van Schie, K., Engelhard, I. M., Klugkist, I., & van den Hout, M. A. (2016). Blurring emotional memories using eye movements: Individual differences and speed of eye movements. *European Journal of Psychotraumatology, 7*, 29476. https://doi.org/10.3402/ejpt.v7.29476

van Veen, S. C., Engelhard, I. M., & van den Hout, M. A. (2016). The effects of eye movements on emotional memories: Using an objective measure of cognitive load. *European Journal of Psychotraumatology, 7*, 30122. https://doi.org/10.3402/ejpt.v7.30122

2018

Calancie, O. G., Khalid-Khan, S., Booij, L., & Munoz, D. P. (2018). Eye movement desensitization and reprocessing as a treatment for PTSD: Current neurobiological theories and a new hypothesis. *Annals of the New York Academy of Science, 1426*(1), 127–145. https://doi.org/10.1111/nyas.13882

Abbreviation: EM, eye movement.

THREE-PRONGED APPROACH

PAST, PRESENT, FUTURE

EMDR therapy is a three-pronged treatment approach that focuses on reprocessing of past events, current triggering stimuli, and adaptive rehearsal in future situations (Figure 1.2). This may seem simple, but it is often a concept that escapes many newly trained EMDR therapy clinicians.

Regardless of what you as a participant were taught in the earlier didactic trainings, what you most likely will remember is what was on the instructional sheet that sat on your lap. The first question that you asked the client was, "What old issue or old memory would you like to focus on today?" It is important to note that this question was only used in the training exercises and not in daily clinical practice. Fortunately, this teaching method has changed as the training focus now is to establish a more formalized plan that attempts to identify past events (and a touchstone event, if available), present triggers, and a future template, and to encourage the participant to process in this order. Shapiro (2006) referred to this strategy as the Treatment Planning Guide (TPG).

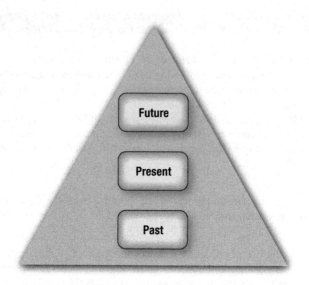

FIGURE 1.2 Self-actualization: EMDR therapy and the three-pronged hierarchy.

To completely resolve a client's issue and achieve adaptive resolution, EMDR therapy is designed to (a) address a client's past events, (b) clean out related current stimuli that might trigger distress in the client and/or reprocess difficult present experiences, and (c) prepare the client for future situations involving the same kind of circumstances (or reaction). The concept of the three-pronged approach is so important that an entire chapter in this Primer has been devoted to it (Chapter 4).

THREE-PRONGED TARGETS—EXPERIENTIAL CONTRIBUTORS TO PRESENT-DAY PROBLEMS

The order of the processing is important. First, it is necessary to strive to adaptively resolve past traumas, then process current stimuli that trigger distress, and finally do a future template on the present trigger. See Exhibit 1.3 for a breakdown of what is identified and processed under each prong of the EMDR approach.

The clinician may want to consider targeting the memories that lay the groundwork for any present problems and/or issues first. It may be a single traumatic event or what is called a *touchstone event*, a primary and self-defining event in the client's life. In AIP language, Dr. Shapiro refers to the touchstone memory as a node to which similar events *will attach* in the continuous formation of a "neuro" or memory network that is critical to the client's sense of self. It is a portal into the memory network as different associations may arise (2018; see Exhibit 1.4A and 1.4B).

Once all presently charged past events are processed (i.e., after the *touchstone event* is processed), other past events may or may not have a cognitive or affective charge remaining. The clinician may want to consider processing those that have a "charge" before continuing to recent events. Then any recent events, circumstances, situations, stressors, or other triggers that might elicit a disturbance are targeted. After the past events and present disturbances

EXHIBIT 1.3 Three-Pronged Targets: Order of Reprocessing

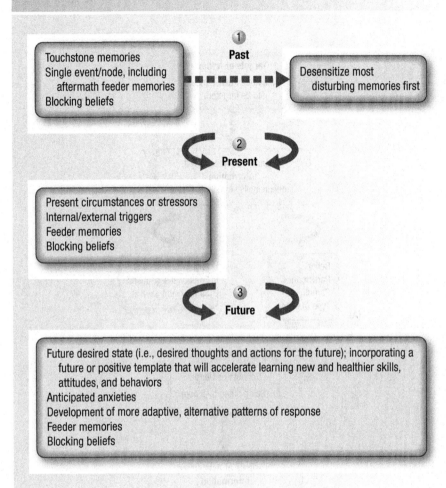

have been identified and reprocessed, focus on the future desired behavior and the client's ability to make better choices or cope more effectively. This entails education, modeling, and targeting what Dr. Shapiro calls a future or positive template (2018). It is important for the client to appropriately and properly assimilate the new information gained through the previous prongs (i.e., past, present, and future) by providing them with experiences that ensure future successes.

During recent EMDR trainings, the order of processing the three prongs (i.e., past, present, and future) and strategically identifying the touchstone event, *if any*, have been emphasized more dramatically. If trained in EMDR prior to 2008, the clinician needs to pay particular attention to Chapters 3 and 4 of this Primer.

Although the standard EMDR therapy protocol prescribes the order of processing as past, present, and future, this is not always practical or effective. Symptoms, circumstances,

EXHIBIT 1.4 (**A**) Targets or nodes and (**B**) targets or nodes with examples.

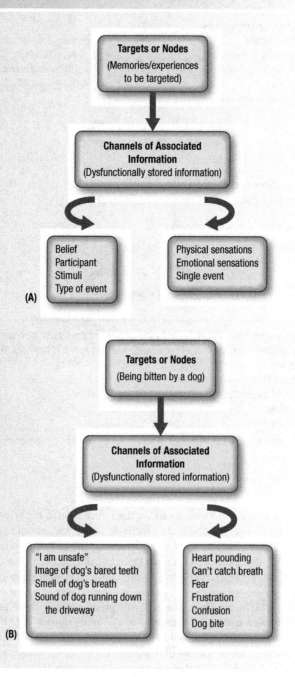

and other variables may indicate future, present, past (e.g., Inverted; Hofmann, 2005 or Reverse; Adler-Tapia, 2015 protocols) or present (e.g., recent events). The client's goals for therapy and presenting issue should determine the order of processing and the clinician should be prepared to direct the client where they need to go for a positive treatment outcome.

THE IMPORTANCE OF PAST, PRESENT, AND FUTURE IN EMDR THERAPY

The foundation of the three-pronged protocol postulates that earlier memories are processed before current events, and current events are processed before future events. Why is it so important to process these events in this order? What is the effect on the overall treatment result if it is not processed in order of past, present, and future? Earlier life experiences set the groundwork for present events and triggers. Hence, it is useful to reprocess as many of the historical associations with the triggers as possible. Once these associations have been transformed, some, if not many, present triggers will dissipate. There may, however, still be current triggers that exist outside of these channels of association that will need to be targeted and processed independently. Or there may be unprocessed material that surfaces when processing these triggers. These triggers will be the next targets to be processed.

The focus on the future template provides the client an opportunity to imaginally rehearse future circumstances and desired responses. This is yet another opening for unprocessed material to surface. The use of the future template provides the client a means of resolving any anticipatory anxiety that they may still experience in similar future situations. The three-pronged approach appears to be a bottom-up process in that the future is subsumed by the present and the present is subsumed by the past. It has been suggested that bypassing the three-pronged approach as part of the full EMDR treatment means obtaining only a fraction of the full treatment effect. If one does not complete the full protocol and believes that the material is resolved because the past has been successfully reprocessed, the client may remain unprepared for being triggered in the present and may still hold anxieties about the future.

TARGETING POSSIBILITIES

TARGETS MAY ARISE IN ANY PART OF THE EMDR THERAPY PROCESS

When a clinician instructs a client to focus on a target in EMDR reprocessing, they are asking the client to tune into a specific memory, image, person, or event or the most disturbing part of it. The target or node then becomes the pivotal point of entry into the associated psychologically stored material. If Raymond's presenting issue relates to the way he responds to his mother-in-law when she first sees him, the target he selects may be the image of her hugging and kissing him as a form of greeting. Because the target image has a constellation of associated experiences around it, Shapiro (2018) calls it a *node*.

Throughout Dr. Shapiro's clinical books (2006, 2018), she refers to several different targets that may arise in certain parts of the process. The past, present, and future targets referred to earlier are the primary focus in the EMDR therapy training. Her text also introduces the reader to other associated words, such as node, channel, cluster, and progression. Exhibit 1.5 attempts to provide a better understanding of the relationship between these types of targets from a more visual perspective.

EXHIBIT 1.5 Three-Pronged Targets: Types of Targets

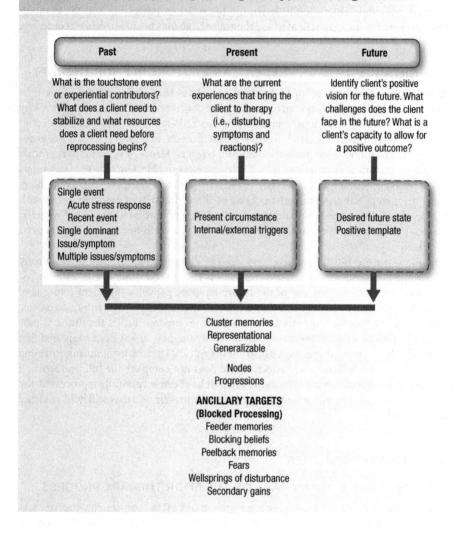

Past	Present	Future

What is the touchstone event or experiential contributors? What does a client need to stabilize and what resources does a client need before reprocessing begins?

What are the current experiences that bring the client to therapy (i.e., disturbing symptoms and reactions)?

Identify client's positive vision for the future. What challenges does the client face in the future? What is a client's capacity to allow for a positive outcome?

Single event
    Acute stress response
    Recent event
Single dominant
Issue/symptom
Multiple issues/symptoms

Present circumstance
Internal/external triggers

Desired future state
Positive template

Cluster memories
Representational
Generalizable

Nodes
Progressions

ANCILLARY TARGETS
(Blocked Processing)
Feeder memories
Blocking beliefs
Peelback memories
Fears
Wellsprings of disturbance
Secondary gains

TYPES OF EMDR TARGETS

As you think about your client sessions, do you recognize any of the types of targets, including the ancillary targets (i.e., other factors that may be contributing to a client's disturbance) listed in Exhibit 1.5? The following definitions are provided as a refresher:

TARGETS FROM THE PAST

Touchstone Memory

A memory that lays the foundation for a client's current presenting issue or problem. This is the memory that formed the core of the maladaptive network or dysfunction. It is the first time a client may have believed, "I am not good enough," or that this conclusion was formed. The touchstone event often, but not necessarily, occurs in childhood or adolescence. Reprocessing will be more spontaneous for the client if the touchstone events can be identified and reprocessed earlier in the treatment.

Example: As an adult, Mary Jane reported being uncomfortable engaging with large groups of people (i.e., 20 or more). She frequently experienced high levels of anxiety before and during office meetings, in church, and at social events. She was nervous, tentative, fearful, and unsure because she could not trust herself to be in control. During the history-taking process, it was discovered that, when she was in the second grade, Mary Jane wet her pants often. She was afraid to use the restroom because she feared its "tall, dark stalls." Students often teased her, calling her "baby" and yelling out to the other students that she had wet her pants. What she came to believe about herself was, "I cannot trust myself." This belief carried over into her later life and caused her to react tentatively in group situations.

Primary Events

These are stand-alone events that may emerge during the History-Taking and Treatment Planning, Reprocessing, and Reevaluation Phases, as well as over the course of treatment itself.

Example: Eddie entered therapy months before complaining of headaches and nightmares caused by memories of long-term sexual abuse by his paternal uncle. During treatment, Eddie reported an event involving an automobile accident that occurred 13 years ago. As a result, Eddie still had some anxiousness around driving. This was targeted once the sexual abuse issues had been resolved.

TARGETS FROM THE PRESENT

Circumstances

Situations that stimulate a disturbance.

Example: Having his principal observe one of his classes caused Pierre to flush with anxiety, even though he had been Teacher of the Year three times running and was a 25-year veteran in the public school system as a high school teacher.

Internal or External Triggers

Internal and external cues that can stimulate dysfunctionally stored information and eliciting emotional or behavioral disturbances.

Examples: Sights, sounds, smells, or sensations may be triggers. A client reports becoming triggered by driving on or near a section of roadway where they were involved in a fatal crash in which their best friend was killed. Or a client becomes anxious and ashamed when being questioned by a police officer, even though they have not done anything wrong. The client may react to their own physiological stimuli. For example, they may be triggered by a slightly elevated increase in heart rate, which they fear might lead to a panic attack. One cancer survivor was triggered by an unexplained headache and loss of appetite, leading to fears of recurrence of cancer.

TARGETS FROM THE FUTURE

Future Desired State

How would the client like to be feeling, sensing, believing, perceiving, and behaving today and in the future? What changes would be necessary? The third prong of EMDR therapy focuses on targeting a positive template that will assist in incorporating positive new learnings and anticipatory events. This stage may involve teaching the client assertiveness skills, modeling good decision making, or having the client imagine future situations, such as coaching people to help them respond more appropriately.

Example: Ryan had always been a passive guy who never could say, "No." "Peace at any cost" was his motto. The touchstone event identified with his conflict-avoidant behavior was a memory of his usually calm mother lunging at his father with a butcher knife during the heat of his father's verbal attack. Before the night was over, his father had beaten his mother so severely that she was hospitalized for three days. Once this memory had been targeted and reprocessed, Ryan felt more empowered but needed instruction on how to stand up for himself more assertively. After assertiveness training, he was able to imagine himself successfully interacting and responding appropriately in conflict-laden circumstances.

Positive Template (i.e., Imaginal Future Template Development)

A process in which the client uses the adaptive information learned in the previous two prongs to ensure future behavioral success by incorporating patterns of alternative behavioral responses. These patterns require a client to imagine responding differently and positively to real or perceived negative circumstances or situations or significant people.

Example: Joe came home from a business trip and found his wife in bed with his best friend. Joe and his wife had reconciled despite the obvious upheaval it had caused in their already shaky relationship. In the processing of this abrupt discovery, Joe had mostly worked through his reactions and feelings toward his ex-best friend, but he never wanted to interact with him again. However, both worked at the same firm, and it was inevitable that their paths would cross. What the clinician had Joe imagine was a chance meeting with this man and how Joe would like to see this encounter transpire from beginning to end.

OTHER POTENTIAL TARGETS

Node

In terms of the AIP model, a node is an associated system of information (Shapiro, 2018). It is "the biologically stored experience central to the memory network designated for therapeutic targeting" (Shapiro, 2009–2017a). It represents a memory network. A node could represent a cluster, a progression, or a feeder memory. To further clarify, a node is the *target* on which the client focuses during the reprocessing phases; and it represents the unprocessed (i.e., dysfunctional) incident. A target then is the agreed-upon incident the client focuses on and is identified in the initial treatment plan.

Example: Jeremy initially entered therapy because he had difficulty interacting professionally with his supervisor. Whenever his boss called or e-mailed asking him to come to his office, Jeremy felt like a small child being summoned to the principal's office. "What did I do now?" he thought. After a thorough investigation of his past and present, Jeremy related how he felt and reacted around his father. "I always felt as though I had done something wrong." Jeremy's father worked and traveled extensively and was not home very much. When he was, Jeremy could find his father in his office working steadily and mostly unaware of the rest of the family activities in their home. His father was gruff and matter of fact and never paid much attention to Jeremy. When he wanted something from Jeremy or would reprimand him for something he did, he would call Jeremy to his office. It was one of those memories that became the target for Jeremy's presenting issue.

Cluster Memories

These memories form a series of related or similar events and have *shared* cues, such as an action, person, or location. Each event is representational or generalizable to the other. These nodes are not targeted in the sessions in which they have been identified. The clinician usually keeps an active list of any nodes that arise during reprocessing and reevaluates them later to see if further treatment is necessary.

Example: Anna between the ages of 7 and 10 years was stung by a bee three different times. Each of these events has varying degrees of trauma attached, but each possesses a shared cue, the bees. These are cluster memories and can be grouped together as a single target.

Progression

A progression is a potential node. It generally arises during the reprocessing of an identified target during or between sets (Shapiro, 2018).

Example: Tricia was targeting incidents related to her mother publicly humiliating her when the memory of how her mother acted at her grandfather's funeral arose. The clinician knew from previous sessions that Tricia had a close, loving relationship with her grandfather and that he was her primary advocate in the family. The clinician wrote down in her notes that her grandfather's funeral may need to be targeted in and of itself. When a progression (i.e., potential target) arises, it is important not to distract the client from her processing of the current target. Rather, the clinician continues to allow the client to follow the natural processing of the present target and note any disturbance around this event that she may need to explore and target during a future session.

Feeder Memory

This type of memory has been described by Shapiro (2018) as an inaccessible or untapped earlier memory that contributes to a client's current dysfunction and that subsequently blocks its reprocessing. Unlike progressions, which typically arise spontaneously, feeder memories usually are discovered more by direct inquiry and are touchstone memories that are yet to be identified. If a client becomes stuck during reprocessing, there may be a feeder memory stalling the processing. A feeder memory also differs from a progression in that the feeder memory is an untapped memory related to the current memory being processed. When this type of memory emerges during reprocessing, it should be investigated immediately, especially if a client is blocking on an adolescent or adult memory (Shapiro, 2009–2017a, 2009–2017b). A feeder memory is usually treated before the current memory (i.e., EMDR reprocessing within EMDR reprocessing). This is unlike a progression, which is a new target (i.e., memory) that pops up during the processing of another traumatic incident (see earlier, under Progression). The progression is acknowledged and processed later. Direct questioning, floatback, and affect scan may be utilized to identify feeder memories.

Sometimes the identification and spontaneous processing of the feeder memory is sufficient to unblock the processing of the current memory. The feeder memory still needs to be checked following completion of the current memory to determine if it holds any additional disturbance. Sometimes, the current memory needs to be contained and the feeder memory reprocessed (i.e., Phases 3–6) before resuming reprocessing of the current memory.

Example: Brittany was in the midst of reprocessing a disturbing event involving malicious accusations by her mother (i.e., "You're a slut." "You must have brought it on somehow." "You deserved everything that happened."). These comments were made by her mother after Brittany at the age of 18 years was nearly raped while walking home from school two months earlier. Following several sets of reprocessing and clinical strategies to unblock or shift her processing, Brittany's level of disturbance did not change. The clinician strategically asked Brittany to focus on the words "I am dirty" (her original negative cognition) and to scan for earlier events in her life that were shameful and humiliating. The memory that finally emerged was the memory of her brothers waving her dirty underwear out a second-story window of their home for all the neighborhood boys to witness. The memory of her brothers' cruel behavior is what is called a feeder memory.

Blocking Belief

A blocking belief is a belief that stops the processing of an initial target. It is a distorted or irrational conclusion about self, others, or life circumstances (e.g., "It's not safe to get over this problem." "If I feel better, I will forget (betray, dishonor, be disloyal) _____ (fill in the blank)." "I don't deserve to get over this problem."). This type of belief may resolve spontaneously during reprocessing or may require being targeted separately. Blocking beliefs typically show themselves when the clinician is evaluating the Subjective Units of Disturbance (SUD), Validity of Cognition (VoC), or body scan. In the Desensitization Phase, the SUD level will not move below 1; in the Installation Phase, the VoC remains below 7; and in the Body Scan Phase when the body does not clear. Typically, when the clinician asks the client in the Desensitization, Installation, and Body Scan Phases to focus on where the client feels it in their body and, if needed, asks after subsequent sets, "What keeps it a _____?" or "What prevents it (i.e., SUD) from being a 0?" or, if the client is in the Installation Phase, "What keeps it a _____?" or "What prevents it (i.e., VoC) from being a 7?" the client may be able to respond with a negative belief and an appropriate, associative early memory. At this point, the processing on the initial target is stopped until the blocking belief memory has been targeted and reprocessed. This does not necessarily require a new target but may be processed with the current target. The direct questioning, floatback, and affect scan techniques are generally useful in identifying blocking beliefs. If after processing there is no change, the clinician may consider the ecological validity of the blocking belief.

Example: Heather, a sergeant in the military, returned home after sustaining injuries during a rocket attack while on a routine field mission in Afghanistan. Two of her fellow soldiers died from the blast. Heather was hit by flying shrapnel that literally left a hole in her leg. She required two subsequent surgeries, neither of which resulted in removing all the rocket shrapnel from her leg. During recuperation, Heather reported disturbing recurring dreams, flashbacks, and thoughts of the rocket attack, which were frequently accompanied by high levels of anxiety or a panic attack. While reprocessing the event, the sergeant's negative cognition was "I'm unsafe" and her PC was "I can be safe." When assessing the sergeant's PC during the Installation Phase, she reported a VoC of 6. After attempting to shift her response by asking, "Where do you feel it in your body?" with no success, Heather was asked by the clinician, "What prevents it (i.e., VoC) *from being a 7?*" Heather immediately responded with the blocking belief, "I can never be safe." Further questioning by the clinician revealed that, when Heather was 5 years old, she had been digitally penetrated by an older cousin who had said to her, "If you tell anyone what happened, you will never be safe. I will find you. And I will kill you." This is also a feeder memory in that it contributes to the current dysfunction and blocked processing. This feeder memory is represented by the blocking belief, "I can never be safe."

Peelback Memory

A peelback memory usually occurs when a touchstone has not been identified and, during reprocessing, other associations begin to "peel back" to expose prior disturbing memories. There is often confusion between a progression and a peelback memory. A peelback memory is an earlier unsuspected memory, whereas a progression is any new associated memory.

Example: After the processing of an earthquake, Taylor continued to exhibit symptoms of PTSD for which there seemed to be no reason. She continued to have many problems associated with the earthquake even though her house had remained intact, and she and others in her family did not sustain any injuries. Her initial intake showed no indications of previous trauma. On further processing of the earthquake, an early association "peeled back" a memory in her 20s when she was date raped, and then again to an even earlier time when she was molested by a neighbor in her adolescence. Her initial negative cognition, "I am not safe," may have helped to uncover these earlier memories. Unlike a feeder memory, which is an earlier disturbance that blocks the reprocessing of the event, a peelback memory emerges spontaneously during reprocessing. It is similar in terms of the emotional, physical, or cognitive content of the memory being reprocessed, but does not block the processing of the current memory being reprocessed.

Fears

Fear in the processing of targeted information can become a blocking mechanism. It stalls the process. Dr. Shapiro identified fears to include fear of the clinical outcome of EMDR therapy or the process itself, fear of going crazy, fear of losing good memories, and fear of change. Fear of the process can be readily recognized whenever a client begins to identify elements of EMDR therapy that appear to be problematic for her (2018). Also check to ensure that any expressed fears of the process are not related to secondary gain.

Example: It is not unusual for a client to express concern or fear that they are not "doing it" (i.e., the process) correctly or is afraid of extreme abreaction or that the clinician cannot handle the potential level of distress that they might express during the reprocessing.

Wellsprings of Disturbance

This phenomenon is indicative of "the presence of a large number of blocked emotions that can be resistant to full EMDR processing" (Shapiro, 2018) and is often caused by the existence of an extensive negative belief system. A wellspring is like a feeder memory in that both feed the emerging emotions. Clients who are resistant to therapy or who seek therapy involuntarily at the urging of someone else (e.g., therapy is court ordered, military command ordered, or requested by a persistent and threatening spouse or parent) are most susceptible to this phenomenon. They are in therapy because of someone else and possess no desire to report or deal with any feelings (Shapiro, 2018).

Example: A man who is forced into therapy at the urging of a disgruntled spouse may possess the belief that "real men don't cry." This belief may be associated with an earlier traumatic memory and result in the client suppressing any high level of disturbance that might otherwise naturally occur under a current circumstance (e.g., dealing with his wife's raging episodes). The true level of affective disturbance is never reached by the client, and it is this same level that contributes to the client's present dysfunction. Earlier experiences taught him that men (or boys) are not allowed to express themselves emotionally. If there is no change in the client's imagery, body sensations, or insight, but he continues to report a low level of disturbance, the wellspring phenomenon is probably in effect. When present, the clinician may need to provide additional EMDR strategies to access the blockage. See the formulas in Exhibit 1.6.

EXHIBIT 1.6 Difference Between Wellsprings of Disturbance and Blocking Belief

Blocking Belief = A negative belief about oneself that stalls reprocessing

Wellsprings of Disturbance = Negative Beliefs + Unresolved (Early Memories) + Blocked Emotions

---

The distinctions between wellsprings of disturbance and blocking beliefs are important because the presence of either determines what course of action a clinician may take to resolve the blocking issues.

Secondary Gain

A secondary gain issue has the potential of keeping a presenting issue from being resolved.

Example: Typical examples involve the following: what would be lost (e.g., a pension check); what need is being satisfied (e.g., special attention); or how current identity is preserved (e.g., "If I get over my pain, I'm abandoning those who have stood by me since the war." Or, "If I lose my disability, how will I support my family?").

Channels of Association

Within the targeted memory, events, thoughts, emotions, and physical sensations may spontaneously arise or arise when a client is instructed to go back to target (i.e., return to the original event [incident, experience]). These are called channels of association and may emerge any time during the reprocessing phases (i.e., Phases 3–6).

When cognition based, channels of association may be another level of the same plateau (responsibility/defectiveness or responsibility/action, safety/vulnerability, or power/control [or choice]) or can be another plateau entirely.

Example: Cara was in the middle of reprocessing being robbed (e.g., safety) after a movie one Friday night. After about five or six sets, she remembered that she had failed to zip up her purse while still in the theater when getting her keys out to drive home. She had a huge bank envelope largely visible for anyone to see (i.e., responsibility). When this channel cleared (i.e., continued to remain positive or remained neutral), the clinician took her back to target, and another channel of association emerged. Cara remembered seeing the robber in the movie theater and that he had been intensely staring at her. She decided it was nothing to worry about and went out to her car (e.g., choice, control).

Channels of association may emerge during reprocessing, where related memories, thoughts, images, emotions, and sensations are stored and linked to one another. The following example demonstrates a series of channels related to the client's emotions.

Example: Cara was robbed after a movie one Friday night. After one set of BLS, the fear that she reported during the Assessment Phase worsened as her hands began to tremble and chest tightened. When this channel cleared (i.e., continued to remain positive or remained neutral), the clinician took her back to target, and another emotional channel of association emerged. Cara expressed anger with the robber and with herself for being so careless with the bank envelope.

Now that you have a clearer picture of what these targets are and how they are related, can you think of examples for each? Recollect targets from some of your reprocessing sessions with clients to help you identify examples of each. Targets—*past, present, future*—especially ancillary targets, can emerge in any of the three prongs in the EMDR protocol. Refer to Exhibit 1.7 for assistance. It is important to be on the lookout for them through the entire process to ensure adaptive resolution of every aspect of the client's traumatic history.

BILATERAL STIMULATION

WHAT DOES IT DO?

BLS, along with dual attention (i.e., simultaneous awareness of the traumatic memory and the present) and the eight-phase, three-pronged protocol, are the core components of EMDR therapy. Research has validated that BLS makes a unique and effective contribution. The client simultaneously focuses on a negative aspect of an internal experience (e.g., image, thought, emotion, physical sensation) while experiencing rapid, alternating external stimuli (e.g., eye movements, taps, tones).

When Dr. Shapiro was in the early stages of developing the theory, procedures, and protocol behind EMDR therapy, she thought that it was the saccadic eye movements or eye tracking that helped to activate the information processing system, which processes the dysfunctionally stored material around a traumatic event. Alternating bilateral hand taps and auditory tones may also be utilized. The type of BLS utilized is important in terms of what the client can best tolerate while facilitating dual attention. A person with an eye disorder obviously might not be able to track a clinician's fingers well. Someone who does not like to be touched may not be able to tolerate being tapped by the clinician or the proximity of the clinician to them. The type of stimulation chosen depends on the client. Although eye movements are the preferred form of BLS, it is important to be able to offer alternative types of BLS to accommodate the client's needs.

A client's preferred means of BLS is *not* always the most effective. De Jongh et al.'s (2013) discrepant findings "suggest that patients are not the ones that should choose or decide which modality is best for them when they request EMDR therapy." Shapiro (2014) recommends eye movements as the preferred method of BLS, but also suggests that clients be offered tactile or tones when deemed necessary.

If the information during reprocessing is not moving or becomes stuck, it is important to have the client agree beforehand on two preferred directions (i.e., back and forth, up and down, or diagonal) or two types of modalities (i.e., eye movements, audio, tapping) from which the client can choose. Thus, if a need for change in direction or modality occurs, the client has agreed to their preferences in advance. Any time a change in BLS is indicated, the clinician should check with or inform the client that a change is being made before implementing the change.

EXHIBIT 1.7 Three-Pronged Targets: Types of Targets With Examples

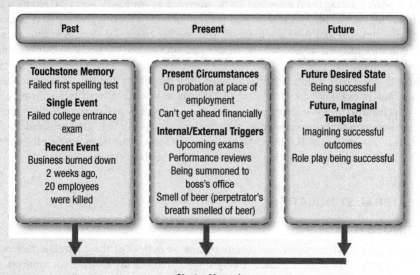

Past	Present	Future

Touchstone Memory
Failed first spelling test

Single Event
Failed college entrance exam

Recent Event
Business burned down 2 weeks ago, 20 employees were killed

Present Circumstances
On probation at place of employment
Can't get ahead financially

Internal/External Triggers
Upcoming exams
Performance reviews
Being summoned to boss's office
Smell of beer (perpetrator's breath smelled of beer)

Future Desired State
Being successful

Future, Imaginal Template
Imagining successful outcomes
Role play being successful

Cluster Memories
Failed driver's license test first time
Flunked gym in 7th grade
Was asked to quit church choir by music director

**Progression
(for later processing)**
Was kicked off the football team because he witnessed sexual misconduct between another player and coach

**ANCILLARY TARGETS
(Block Processing)
Feeder Memory**
I will fail.
Target earliest memory of having failed

Blocking Belief
In order to succeed, I need to have my father's approval.

Peelback Memory
Rape

Fear
Fear of failure

Wellsprings of Disturbance
Low level of disturbance; Inability to feel emotions
Target earliest memory of having failed and negative belief that blocks emotions

Secondary Gain
Fear of loss of identity
Who am I without this fear of failure?
Who am I if I succeed?

PREFERRED MEANS OF BILATERAL STIMULATION

Shapiro's (2018) preferred means of BLS is eye movement. All the research involved in establishing the efficacy of EMDR therapy was conducted utilizing eye movements. This type of stimulation also supports dual attention, whereby the client can attend to both internal and external stimuli. The client processes using eye movements with their eyes open so that they remain aware of their present environment.

Many studies have focused on investigating the role of eye movements in EMDR to date (Acierno et al., 1994; Andrade et al., 1997; Barrowcliff et al., 2003, 2004; Boudewyns & Hyer, 1996; Chemtob et al., 2000; Christman et al., 2003; Christman et al., 2006; Davidson & Parker, 2001; de Jongh et al., 2013; Devilly et al., 1998; Engelhard et al., 2010a; Engelhard et al., 2010b; Engelhard et al., 2011; Gunter & Bodner, 2008; Homer et al., 2016; Kavanagh et al., 2001; Kearns and Engelhard, 2015; Kuiken et al., 2002; Kuiken et al., 2010; Lee & Drummond, 2008; Lohr et al., 1995; Lohr et al., 1996; MacCulloch, 2006; Maxfield et al., 2008; Nieuwenhuis et al., 2013; Parker & Dagnall, 2007; Parker et al., 2008; Parker et al., 2009; Patel & McDowall, 2016; Pitman et al., 1996; Propper & Christman, 2008; Renfrey & Spates, 1994; Rimini et al., 2016; Sack et al., 2016; Samara et al., 2011; Sanderson & Carpenter, 1992; Schubert et al., 2011; Servan-Schreiber et al., 2006; Sharpley et al., 1996; Smeets et al., 2012; Solomon et al., 1992; van den Hout et al., 2001; van den Hout et al., 2011, 2012; van Etten & Taylor, 1998; van Veen et al., 2015; Wilson et al., 1996; Zarghi, 2015).

Two dominant theories have emerged as a result of these research studies about the effects of eye movement during EMDR: (a) eye movements have a tendency to interfere with working memory by reducing emotionality and vividness of autobiographical memories (Andrade et al., 1997; Barrowcliff et al., 2003; Barrowcliff et al., 2004; Engelhard et al., 2010a, 2010b, 2011; Gunter & Bodner, 2008; Kavanagh et al., 2001; Maxfield et al., 2008; Schubert et al., 2011; van den Hout et al., 2001) and (b) eye movements are linked into the same processes as rapid eye movement (REM) sleep (Barrowcliff et al., 2004; Christman et al., 2003; Christman et al., 2006; Elofsson et al., 2008; Kuiken et al., 2002, 2010; Parker & Dagnall, 2007; Parker et al., 2008, 2009; Sack et al., 2008; Schubert et al., 2011; Stickgold, 2002, 2008). Stickgold (2002) proposed that "the repetitive redirecting of attention in EMDR induces a neurobiological state, like that of REM sleep" (i.e., the effect of BLS is related to REM in a waking state).

Studies suggest that eye movements are superior to tones (van den Hout et al., 2012) and saccadic eye movements are superior on all parameters in all conditions to vertical eye movements (Parker et al., 2008). One study found that eye movements increased the true memory of an event (Parker et al., 2009). No research presently exists to support having the client process with his eyes closed. Lee and Cuijpers (2013) reported positive effects of eye movements in their meta-analysis.

Table 1.12 outlines the randomized studies of hypotheses regarding eye movements in EMDR reprocessing.

SHORTER OR LONGER? SLOWER OR FASTER?

During the Preparation Phase, BLS is originally introduced with the safe (calm) place and any other resource enhancement or stabilization exercises deemed appropriate by the clinician prior to using EMDR reprocessing and, then again, during reprocessing in the Desensitization, Installation, and Body Scan Phases. There is a difference in the speed and number of BLS passes used. A single pass in terms of BLS is a "round trip" from center to right, then to left, and back to center again. A series of passes make up a "set." The recommended rate of speed is slower, and the number of round-trip passes is fewer (i.e., 4–6 round

TABLE 1.12 Hypothesis Regarding Eye Movements—Randomized Studies to Date

1996

Sharpley, C. F., Montgomery, I. M., & Scalzo, L. (1996). Comparative efficacy of EMDR and alternative procedures in reducing the vividness of mental images. *Scandinavian Journal of Behaviour Therapy, 25,* 37–42. https://doi.org/10.1080/16506079609456006

EMs superior to control conditions in terms of reducing image vividness.

1997

Andrade, J., Kavanagh, D., & Baddeley, A. (1997). Eye-movements and visual imagery: A working memory approach to the treatment of posttraumatic stress disorder. *British Journal of Clinical Psychology, 36,* 209–223. https://doi.org/10.1111/j.2044-8260.1997.tb01408.x

EMs superior to control conditions in terms of reducing image vividness and emotionality.

2001

Kavanagh, D. J., Freese, S., Andrade, J., & May, J. (2001). Effects of visuospatial tasks on desensitization to emotive memories. *British Journal of Clinical Psychology, 40,* 267–280. https://doi.org/10.1348/014466501163689

EMs superior to control conditions in terms of reducing within-session image vividness and emotionality.

van den Hout, M., Muris, P., Salemink, E., & Kindt, M. (2001). Autobiographical memories become less vivid and emotional after eye movements. *British Journal of Clinical Psychology, 40*(2), 121–130. https://doi.org/10.1348/014466501163535

EMs superior to control conditions in terms of reducing image vividness and emotionality.

2002

Kuiken, D., Bears, M., Miall, D., & Smith, L. (2002). Eye movement desensitization reprocessing facilitates attentional orienting. *Imagination, Cognition and Personality, 21*(1), 3–20. https://doi.org/10.2190/L8JX-PGLC-B72R-KD7X

EMs superior to control conditions when correlated with increased attentional flexibility.

2003

Barrowcliff, A., Gray, N., MacCulloch, S., Freeman, T., & MacCulloch, M. (2003). Horizontal rhythmical eye movements consistently diminish the arousal provoked by auditory stimuli. *British Journal of Clinical Psychology, 42*(Pt 3), 289–302. https://doi.org/10.1348/01446650360703393

EMs superior to control conditions in terms of reducing arousal provoked by auditory stimuli.

Christman, S. D., Garvey, K. J., Propper, R. E., & Phaneuf, K. A. (2003). Bilateral eye movements enhance the retrieval of episodic memories. *Neuropsychology, 17,* 221–229. https://doi.org/10.3758/PBR.15.3.515

Saccadic (not tracking) EMs superior to control condition in episodic retrieval.

(continued)

TABLE 1.12 Hypothesis Regarding Eye Movements—Randomized Studies to Date (continued)

2004

Barrowcliff, A. L., Gray, N. S., Freeman, T. C. A., & MacCulloch, M. J. (2004). Eye-movements reduce the vividness, emotional valence and electrodermal arousal associated with negative autobiographical memories. *Journal of Forensic Psychiatry and Psychology, 15(2)*, 325–345. https://doi.org/10.1080/14789940410001673042

In testing the reassurance reflex model, EMs were found to be superior to control conditions in terms of reducing image vividness and emotionality.

2006

Christman, S. D., Propper, R. E., & Brown, T. J. (2006). Increased interhemispheric interaction is associated with earlier offset of childhood amnesia. *Neuropsychology, 20*, 336. https://doi.org/10.1037/0894–4105.20.3.336

EMs may induce a change in: (a) interhemispheric interaction and (b) attendant psychological change in episodic retrieval.

Servan-Schreiber, D., Schooler, J., Dew, M. A., Carter, C., & Bartone, P. (2006). EMDR for PTSD: A pilot blinded, randomized study of stimulation type. *Psychotherapy and Psychosomatics, 75*, 290–297. https://doi.org/10.1159/000093950

In this study, patients with single-event PTSD were provided three consecutive sessions, each with a different type of auditory and kinesthetic stimulation; 21 patients with single-event PTSD (average IES: 49.5) received three consecutive sessions of EMDR with three different types of auditory and kinesthetic stimulation. All three types of stimulation proved useful with the one conferring the additional benefit of alternating stimulation.

2007

Parker, A., & Dagnall, N. (2007). Effects of bilateral eye movements on gist based false recognition in the DRM paradigm. *Brain and Cognition, 63*, 221–225. https://doi.org/10.1016/j.bandc.2006.08.005

Bilateral saccadic EM groups "were more likely to recognize previously presented words and less likely to falsely recognize critical non-studied associates" (p. 223).

2008

Gunter, R. W., & Bodner, G. E. (2008). How eye movements affect unpleasant memories: Support for a working-memory account. *Behaviour Research and Therapy, 46(8)*, 913–931. https://doi.org/10.1016/j.brat.2008.04.006

Support for working-memory account of the benefits of EM.

Lee, C. W., & Drummond P. D. (2008). Effects of eye movement versus therapist instructions on the processing of distressing memories. *Journal of Anxiety Disorders, 22(5)*, 801–808. https://doi.org/10.1016/j.janxdis.2007.08.007

Significant reduction in distress for EM in post-treatment and follow-up.

Maxfield, L., Melnyk, W. T., & Hayman, C. A. G. (2008). A working memory explanation for the effects of eye movements in EMDR. *Journal of EMDR Practice and Research, 2(4)*, 247–261. https://doi.org/10.1891/1933-3196.2.4.247

Supported the working memory explanation on the effects of EM on dual-attention tasks on autobiographical memory.

Parker, A., Relph, S., & Dagnall, N. (2008). Effects of bilateral eye movement on retrieval of item, associative and contextual information. *Neuropsychology, 22*, 136–145. https://doi.org/10.1037/0894-4105.22.1.136

(continued)

TABLE 1.12 Hypothesis Regarding Eye Movements—Randomized Studies to Date (continued)

2008

Bilateral saccadic EM group superior on retrieval of the item and associative and contextual information.

2009

Parker, A., Buckley, S., & Dagnall, N. (2009). Reduced misinformation effects following saccadic bilateral eye movements. *Brain and Cognition, 69*, 89–97. https://doi.org/10.1016/j.bandc.2008.05.009

Supports hypothesis of the effects on episodic memory and interhemispheric activation.

2010

Engelhard, I. M., van den Hout, M. A., Janssen, W. C., & van der Beek, J. (2010a). Eye movements reduce vividness and emotionality of "flashforwards." *Behaviour Research and Therapy, 48*, 442–447. https://doi.org/10.1016/j.brat.2010.01.003

In non-dual task condition and while thinking of future-oriented images, EMs resulted in reduced ratings in image vividness and emotional intensity.

Engelhard, I. M., van den Hout, M. A., Janssen, W. C., & van der Beek, J. (2010b). The impact of taxing working memory on negative and positive memories. *European Journal of Psychotraumatology, 1*, 5623. https://doi.org/10.3402/ejpt.v1i0.5623

Compared Tetris to EMs.

Kuiken, D., Chudleigh, M., & Racher, D. (2010). Bilateral eye movements, attentional flexibility and metaphor comprehension: The substrate of REM dreaming? *Dreaming, 20*, 227–247. https://doi.org/10.1037/a0020841

Found differential effects between EM and non-EM conditions.

2011

Engelhard, I. M., van den Hout, M. A., Dek, E. C. P., Giele, C. L., van der Wielen, J.-W., Reijnen, M. J., & van Roij, B. (2011). Reducing vividness and emotional intensity of recurrent "flashforwards" by taxing working memory: An analogue study. *Journal of Anxiety Disorders, 25*, 599–603. https://doi.org/10.1016/j.janxdis.2011.01.009

Found with EMs on recall only; there was a trend toward reduced vividness of intrusive images and emotionality.

Samara, Z., Bernet M., Elzinga, B. M., Heleen A., Slagter, H. A., & Nieuwenhuis, S. (2011). Do horizontal saccadic eye movements increase interhemispheric coherence? Investigation of a hypothesized neural mechanism underlying EMDR. *Frontiers in Psychiatry, 2*, 4. https://doi.org/10.3389/fpsyt.2011.00004

In healthy adults, 30 seconds of bilateral saccadic EMs "enhanced the episodic retrieval of non-traumatic emotional stimuli."

Schubert, S. J., Lee, C. W., & Drummond, P. D. (2011). The efficacy and psychophysiological correlates of dual-attention tasks in eye movement desensitization and reprocessing (EMDR). *Journal of Anxiety Disorders, 25*, 1–11. https://doi.org/10.1016/j.janxdis.2010.06.024

EMs led to increased reduction in distress, decrease in heart rate at onset of EMs, decrease in skin conductance during EMs, increase in heart rate variability and respiration as EMs continued, and increased frequency of orienting responses at the start of exposure.

van den Hout, M. A., Engelhard, I. M., Rijkeboer, M. M., Koekebakker, J., Hornsveld, H., Leer, A., Toffolo, M. B. J., & Akse, N. (2011). EMDR: Eye movements superior to beeps in taxing working memory and reducing vividness of recollections. *Behaviour Research and Therapy, 49*, 92–98. https://doi.org/10.1016/j.brat.2010.11.003

(continued)

TABLE 1.12 Hypothesis Regarding Eye Movements—Randomized Studies to Date (continued)

2011

Supports a working memory account of EMDR therapy and that EMs are superior to the effects of beeps on negative memories.

2012

Smeets, M. A. M., Dijs, M. W., Pervan, I., Engelhard, I. M., & van den Hout, M. A. (2012). Time-course of eye movement-related decrease in vividness and emotionality of unpleasant autobiographical memories. *Memory, 20*(4), 346–357. https://doi.org/10.1080/0 9658211.2012.665462

Supports the theory that emotionality reduces only after vividness has dropped.

van den Hout, M. A., Rijkeboer, M. T., Engelhard, I. M., Klugkist, I., Hornsveld, H., Toffolo, M., & Cath, D. (2012). Tones inferior to eye movements in the EMDR treatment of PTSD. *Behaviour Research and Therapy, 50*, 275–279. https://doi.org/10.1016/j. brat.2012.02.001

In this study, EM were proven to be more beneficial than tones. It was unclear if tones added to recall only.

2013

de Jongh, A., Ernst, R., Marques, L, & Hornsveld, H. (2013). The impact of eye movements and tones on disturbing memories involving PTSD and other mental disorders. *Journal of Behavior Therapy and Experimental Psychiatry, 44*, 477–483. https://doi.org/10.1016/j. jbtep.2013.07.002

Evidence for the value of employing EMs in EMDR treatment, and evidence that a client's preference of BLS (EMs, tactile, or auditory) may not necessarily be the most effective form of bilateral stimulation.

Nieuwenhuis, S., Elzinga, B. M., Ras, P. H., Berends, F., Duijs, P., Samara, Z., & Slagter, H. A. (2013). Bilateral saccadic eye movements and tactile stimulation, but not auditory stimulation, enhanced memory retrieval. *Brain and Cognition, 81*, 52–56. https://doi. org/10.1016/j.bandc.2012.10.003

Functional connectivity between the two hemispheres of the brain increased by bilateral activation of the same.

2015

Kearns, M, Engelhard I. M. (2015). Psychophysiological responsivity to script-driven imagery: An exploratory study of the effects of eye movements on public speaking flashforwards. *Frontiers in Psychiatry, 6*, 115. https://doi.org/10.3389/ fpsyt.2015.00115

Using the control condition of imagery and EM while holding a mental image of a scenario in mind showed a significant decrease in heart rate, thus providing a measure of emotionality.

van Veen, S. C., van Schie, K., Wijngaards-de Meij, L. D., Littel, M., Engelhard, I. M., & van den Hout, M. A. (2015). Speed matters: Relationship between speed of eye movements and modification of aversive autobiographical memories. *Frontiers in psychiatry, 6*(45), 1–9. https://doi.org/10.3389/fpsyt.2015.00045

This study demonstrated that image vividness did not decrease emotionality over time. This is consistent with a working memory hypothesis that states that highly vivid images responded better to fast EMs while less vivid ones responded better to slower EMs.

(continued)

TABLE 1.12 Hypothesis Regarding Eye Movements—Randomized Studies to Date (continued)

2016

Homer, S. R., Deeprose, C., & Andrade, J. (2016). Negative mental imagery in public speaking anxiety: Forming cognitive resistance by taxing visuospatial working memory. *Journal of Behavior Therapy and Experimental Psychiatry, 50,* 77–82. https://doi. org/10.1016/j.jbtep.2015.05.004

It was established as hypothesized that reduction in vividness of represented imagery (i.e., public speaking was visualized less vividly; generated less anxiety when imagined) was more effected by EM than auditory task.

Sack, M., Zehl, S., Otti, A., Lahmann, C., Henningsen, P., Kruse, J., & Stingl, M. (2016). A comparison of dual attention, eye movements, and exposure only during eye movement desensitization and reprocessing for posttraumatic stress disorder: Results from a randomized clinical trial. *Psychotherapy and Psychosomatics, 85*(6), 357–365. https://doi. org/10.1159/000447671

When eye fixation and exposure control were compared to bilateral EMs, both were found to be equally effective as well as superior to exposure alone at posttest.

Abbreviations: BLS, bilateral stimulation; EM, eye movement; IES, Impact of Event Scale; PTSD, posttraumatic stress disorder.

trips) when using BLS with resource, coping, relaxation, and stress reduction exercises and strategies. Slower and shorter sets are utilized in stabilization efforts to not activate any disturbing material prior to actual reprocessing.

While using BLS when reprocessing, including installation and, when necessary, the body scan, the speed is tolerably comfortable (i.e., much faster) for the client and number of passes is increased (i.e., from 20 to 24 round trips to start, lengthen to 36 to 40 as needed during the reprocessing phases). The number of sets of BLS is determined by attention to the client's response and is customized to the needs of the client. Faster and longer sets of BLS are more likely to activate linkages to other memory networks and trigger associated channels of information. The longer and faster the eye movement, the faster the associative linkages occur. Always increase the speed of BLS with caution because, if associative linkages come too fast for a client's window of tolerance, it can lead to a loss of dual awareness. Faster BLS may impede effective processing and consequently lead to slower reprocessing. On the other hand, if a client is trying to "think" rather than just observe during reprocessing, faster eye movements can help move him into actual reprocessing.

During the Desensitization Phase, the suggested average number of BLS sets (i.e., 20–24 longer, faster sets, then lengthen to 36–40 or as needed by the client) is only a starting point for the client's processing. As the clinician wants to avoid sets that are too long or too short, it is suggested that she begin with 20 or more passes and watch the client's facial expressions and body language to determine the best length for any set. After this initial set, the clinician may customize the number of sets according to the client's need or response.

Some clients may require shorter or longer and/or slower or faster sets. For instance, clients who are anxious and/or unsure of the process may require longer sets of BLS. In addition, some clients need more time to shift from an external (outward) to an internal (inward) focus. The longer sets of BLS create adequate time for the client's processing to unfold and increase the likelihood of the client experiencing success with reprocessing. If a clinician watches eyes and other body language, clues will usually arise that indicate the appropriate pace and number of BLS sets. It is always appropriate to ask the client for feedback as well.

TABLE 1.13 Bilateral Stimulation—Fast or Slow? Short or Long?	
SLOW, SHORT SETS (4–6) **ELICIT A RELAXATION RESPONSE** **(SLOWS DOWN THE TRAIN)**	**FAST, LONG SETS (24–36)** **ELICIT AN ACTIVATION RESPONSE** **(SPEEDS UP THE TRAIN)**
Safe (calm) place	Reprocessing
Resource development	Installation
Resource development and installation	Body scan
	Future template

In terms of desensitization and speed, eye movements (or passes) that are too slow tend to stimulate a relaxation response and may not facilitate sufficient dual attention. Therefore, it is imperative for optimal processing that the clinician facilitates the passes as fast as the client can comfortably tolerate. In addition, the clinician should avoid long pauses between sets without a specific reason (e.g., the client feels the need for clinician connection). The client is discouraged from talking at any length between sets. It is suggested that the clinician minimally or nonverbally acknowledge what the client has reported and say, "Notice that" or "Go with that."

Although the purpose of the Installation Phase is to fully integrate a positive self-assessment with the targeted information, there is still the possibility that other associations could emerge that may need to be addressed. The faster, longer sets of BLS facilitate the emergence of any lingering disturbing material related to the original targeted event. Remember, a completely successful treatment of the original target memory cannot be attained until the early memories that caused the blocking belief are reprocessed. There is little research regarding this widely practiced distinction in the speed and number of sets of BLS. However, it is considered a guideline by many EMDR trainers, consultants, facilitators, and clinicians.

Except for the reprocessing phases of treatment, shorter, slower sets of BLS (approximately 4–6) are used to reinforce and strengthen the client's positive networks. The clinician wants to ensure that the client's brain is not activated in such a way as to associate the positive networks with maladaptive experiences. Especially with more complex cases, the client may not possess sufficient adaptive memory networks; and the client must have access to adaptive memory networks for reprocessing to occur. During the Installation Phase, the sets of BLS should be longer and faster (i.e., 20–24 to start, lengthen to 36–40 as needed) because the client is strengthening the connection between the newly processed memory and its connection to other existing adaptive information networks and/or continued reprocessing of associated negative networks as well. Therefore, when a clinician wants to manage a client's response, use slow, shorts sets; when a clinician wants to allow a client's associations to roam freely, use longer, faster sets. Table 1.13 demonstrates when to use long or short and slow or fast sets of BLS.

Note: If a positive association occurs during reprocessing, do not slow the speed of the BLS or decrease the number of sets. During Phases 3 to 6, the sets of BLS are faster and longer as there is always the possibility of negative associations emerging at any phase.

CONTINUOUS BILATERAL STIMULATION

Although there may be clinicians who administer one continuous sequence of BLS throughout the Desensitization, Installation, and Body Scan Phases, Shapiro (2018) clearly outlines the reasons for breaking the stimulation into sets (Table 1.14).

Note: If a clinician uses continuous BLS during the reprocessing phases 3 through 6, it should not be called EMDR therapy.

TABLE 1.14 Reasons for Breaking Bilateral Stimulation Into Sets

Provides an opportunity for the clinician to determine if processing has occurred based upon the client's feedback.

Gives the client a break from processing, especially if a set contained an intense abreactive response.

Helps a client reorient in terms of present time and consequent safety (i.e., helps to keep "one foot in the present") and thereby facilitates dual awareness.

Allows a client to share any new revelations or insights that arise during processing.

Allows a clinician to reaffirm a client's experience throughout the process.

Enables a client to better integrate any new information that emerges on a verbal or conscious level.

Allows a clinician to continually reassess or judge the need for any additional clinical interventions or strategies.

Provides multiple opportunities for a clinician to give and a client to receive encouragement and reassurance.

In terms of abreactive responses, it solidifies for a client that they are larger than the disturbing experience and in control as they demonstrate they can approach and distance from the disturbance during these breaks.

Abbreviation: BLS, bilateral stimulation.

Table 1.15 lists what can happen if BLS (i.e., in terms of speed and number of sets) is used inappropriately.

TABLE 1.15 Derailment Possibilities—Bilateral Stimulation Errors

Using long and fast sets when doing stabilization
Doing so may activate processing prematurely (i.e., speeds up the train) and cause a client to begin processing any dysfunctionally stored past memories or present triggers. Short, slow sets of BLS are indicated when facilitating stabilization.

Using short and slow sets when doing reprocessing
Slow, short BLS may stimulate a relaxation response and inhibit a client from being appropriately activated by the targeted incident/event. When doing reprocessing, the BLS should be tolerably uncomfortable for the client. Using slow, short sets may also not facilitate dual awareness. It becomes too easy for a client to become absorbed in the memory when following eye movements that are too slow or too short. Long, fast sets of BLS are indicated when reprocessing is occurring.

Note: Wilson et al. (1996) and Schubert et al. (2011) found that faster BLS may at times cause a compelled relaxation response.

(continued)

TABLE 1.15 Derailment Possibilities—Bilateral Stimulation Errors (continued)

Continuing with eye movements if a client reports pain or dryness because of the process

If this occurs, switch to a previously agreed upon, alternate form of BLS. For example, if a client was reportedly poked in the eye when they were a child, auditory or tactile stimulation may be a better alternative.

Pausing too long in between sets

There should be a specific reason for pausing too long between sets. Maybe the client is overwhelmed, "needs" to talk, or wants assurance that they are "doing it right." If the client tends to relay everything that happened between sets, gently explain the information they give is for baseline reasons only (i.e., to let the clinician know where they are in the process), that the "mind is faster than the mouth," and only minimal information is needed between sets. When a clinician or client talks excessively between sets, it inhibits the reprocessing (i.e., slows the train) of the targeted material.

During reprocessing, using sets that are too long or too short

Using sets that are too long may cause a client to lose track of the primary event and become overwhelmed with too many thoughts, images, and emotions, and may inhibit or derail processing. Sets that are too short may inhibit processing by not giving a client enough time to initiate complete processing. The rule of thumb is to start with 20-plus sets of eye movements and judge from a client's response (i.e., facial expression and body language) to determine what the appropriate number of sets is for each individual client. However subtle, a client will usually give a clue as to when a set is complete.

Using continuous BLS (i.e., taking no breaks)

Using continuous BLS throughout an entire EMDR session follows the same logic previously for long sets. The primary purpose of stopping the train is so dysfunctional information may be unloaded and more adaptive information may be loaded. Also, taking a break between sets helps a client keep "one foot in the present."

Continuing with BLS when the client has indicated that he is finished with the set

It is not uncommon for a client to look at a clinician and say, "Can we take a break right now? I need to say something." In the event this occurs, simply stop the train and allow the client to unload any material; and restart the train when the client is willing and able.

Abbreviation: BLS, bilateral stimulation.

HOW TO DO EYE MOVEMENTS

Table 1.16 outlines the specific criteria outlined by Shapiro (2018) on the proper and acceptable way to facilitate eye movements in terms of preference, duration, speed, distance, height, and more.

TABLE 1.16 How to Do Eye Movements

Before concentrating on emotionally disturbing material

Initially using horizontal or diagonal eye movements, find the best fit for a client (e.g., horizontal, vertical, diagonal).

Note: The vertical eye movements may be preferred if a client has a history of vertigo. It is also reported to be helpful in reducing extreme emotional nausea, agitation, eye tension, or dizziness. Vertical eye movements have been known to produce a calming effect.

Experiment to find a client's comfort level (i.e., distancing, speed, height).

Switch immediately to an alternate form of BLS if a client reports eye pain or dryness.

Generate a full eye movement set by moving a clinician's hand from one side of a client's range of vision to the other.

The speed of the eye movement should be as rapid as possible and without any undue physical discomfort to a client.

Use at least two fingers as a focal point (i.e., two fingers held together is usually the preferred number in American culture).

With palm up approximately 12 to 14 inches from a client's face (i.e., preferably chin to chin or contralateral eyebrow, some say shoulder to shoulder), hold two fingers upright and ask a client, "Is this comfortable?"

Note: It is important to determine distance and placement of the eye movement with which a client is the most comfortable prior to the Assessment Phase.

Demonstrate the direction of the eye movements by starting in the middle and slowly moving the fingers back and forth in a client's visual field, and then ending in the center.

Evaluate and monitor a client's ability to track the moving fingers. Start slowly and increase the rate of speed to the fastest a client can comfortably tolerate physically and still keep in their window of emotional intensity.

Ask a client during this testing phase if they have any preferences in terms of speed, distance, and height prior to concentrating on any negative emotions or dysfunctional material.

After concentrating on emotionally disturbing material

Listen to the client's feedback to determine if adequate processing is taking place at the end of a session.

If the client appears comfortable and shifts are occurring, maintain the predetermined speed.

If the client is uncomfortable and shifts are not occurring, the clinician may need to adjust the speed, direction, and number of eye movements.

If the client appears stuck (i.e., after successive sets of eye movements, the client reports no shifts), change the direction of the eye movement.

If a client experiences difficulty (i.e., manifests in irregular eye movements or "bumpiness") following a clinician's fingers, attempt to assist the client to establish a more dynamic connection and sense of movement control that results in smoother tracking by instructing the client to "push my fingers with your eyes."

Assess the client's comfort, preferred speed, and ability to sustain eye movements by listening to their feedback between sets.

(continued)

TABLE 1.16 How to Do Eye Movements (continued)

If the client reports an increase in positive shifts, continue to maintain the same direction, speed, and duration.

Note: If a clinician believes it might be beneficial, it is appropriate to experiment. However, a client's feedback should be the final determinant whether to decrease or increase the duration of a set.

Continue BLS until a shift or plateau is observed in the client, unless the client utilizes their stop signal.

If a client experiences weakness in their eye muscles, they may be unable to do more than a few eye movements at a time.

If a client is experiencing high levels of anxiety, demonstrates a tracking deficit, or finds them aversive, they may be unable to track hand movements.

Note: If this occurs, reprocess the underlying experience of discomfort and, if need be, use the two-handed approach or auditory or tactile stimulation. The two-handed approach entails having the clinician position their closed hands on opposite sides of the client's visual field at eye level and then alternating raising right and left index fingers while instructing the client to move their eyes from one raised finger to the other. This type of BLS creates an orienting or attentional response and eliminates the need for client tracking.

Abbreviation: BLS, bilateral stimulation.

IS BILATERAL STIMULATION EMDR THERAPY?

BLS is but one component of EMDR therapy. Stimuli, such as directed and accelerated eye movements, are used to activate the client's information processing system as they focus on a past trauma, present-day trigger, or future event. Over the years, many beginning students of EMDR therapy, consultees, and even seasoned veterans have referred to BLS as EMDR. BLS is used when facilitating the sacred space, safe (calm) place, and resource development exercises (Chapter 8). When coupled solely with BLS, does this mean that sacred space, safe (calm) place, resource installation, or even the reprocessing phases are EMDR therapy? EMDR therapy is clearly identified as an eight-phase, three-pronged process. If one of the phases is eliminated or substituted with something else, it can no longer be called EMDR therapy.

IMPORTANT CONCEPTS TO CONSIDER

MEMORY NETWORK ASSOCIATIONS

No one knows what a memory network looks like, but these networks represent the basis of the AIP model. Metaphorically, Dr. Shapiro pictures these networks as a series of channels "where related memories, thoughts, images, emotions, and sensations are stored and linked to one another" (Shapiro, 2018). The negative memory network associations may consist of a series of memories linked to a person (e.g., critical mother); auditory, tactile, or other sensory stimuli (e.g., the sound of a car backfiring); events (e.g., automobile accident, plane crash, tornado); physical sensations (e.g., chest or leg pain); emotions (e.g., fear, sadness); or beliefs (e.g., I am unlovable). The goal is to assist the client's progression through these memory networks and toward an adaptive resolution.

STOP SIGNAL

It is important to heed a client's wishes to ensure a sense of safety in the therapeutic environment. EMDR treatment is a choice, and the desire to stop or continue in whatever context is a choice as well. It is one a clinician should always respect. It is imperative a client always feels that the process is a choice and not an imposition or demand. So, if a client asks to stop reprocessing, the clinician should stop *immediately*.

In the Preparation Phase, the client is asked to provide the clinician with a cue that indicates they want to stop the processing. It may be a hand, finger, or body gesture. The client may simply just turn away or hold their arms up in the air. Whatever the cue is, the processing should be discontinued immediately when used. This allows the client to maintain an ongoing sense of comfort, safety, and control. When this cue to stop is utilized, the clinician assists the client in accessing whatever is needed to stabilize the client and to proceed with the processing. Discontinue all BLS until the client is willing and able to continue reprocessing. The clinician may explore what is needed in order that reprocessing may resume. The clinician should inquire of a client, "What happened? Why do you want to stop?" "Do you need to slow down or just take a break?" Perhaps a client needs to take a break because they are confused or overwhelmed, or they simply want to share concerns about the processing itself. The clinician may ask, "Why did you stop?" (i.e., "What stopped the train?") and address any concerns the client may have. And then, "What is it you need to continue processing?" (i.e., What does the client need in order to get back on the train?). The clinician also needs to ensure the client has what they need before continuing processing. If a client still insists that they do not want to continue, a clinician should respectfully use the procedures for *closing down* an incomplete session and only return to processing when a client is ready (Shapiro, 2009–2017a, 2009–2017b). The clinician may ask the client at this point to access their safe (calm) place, use a container strategy, or do some other stabilization exercise to help them to ground, to bring energy back into the body, or bring them into the present moment. The clinician should explore what the client needs to be in place in order to resume processing in the session or at the next session. If a client does not want to continue, do not implement BLS as it may reactivate the processing. Table 1.17 demonstrates some appropriate ways for a client to indicate they want to discontinue or pause the process.

It is important <u>not</u> to accept words for stop signals (e.g., "Stop," "No more," "I can't do this," "I want to throw in the towel," or "Whoa!") as it may be confused with what is going on in the processing.

The stop signal is tantamount to having a cord on a train the passenger can pull to indicate to the engineer that they want the train to stop for some reason. For instance, the client may need an added rest before the next stop or may want to get off the train. Ultimately, it is the engineer (i.e., clinician) who stops the train when signaled by the client in some way to stop.

At the beginning of each session, the clinician may remind the client of the chosen stop signal by saying, "If at any time you feel you have to stop, raise your hand (i.e., remind client of desired stop signal)."

TABLE 1.17 Stop Signals
"If at any time you feel you have to stop, (remind the client of chosen stop signal)." "Is this a comfortable distance and speed?"

Hand gestures

Hand Signal	Time-Out Signal

Body gestures

Standing up
Crossing arms or knees
Putting hands over mouth, ears, or eyes
Cyclist stop signal

EMDR THERAPY IS NOT HYPNOSIS

A frequent question asked by clients is, "Is EMDR hypnosis?" When this question is asked, the clinician may want to spend some time with the client explaining the basic differences between the two. Clients may be concerned that EMDR reprocessing will induce a deep trance state where they may lack control. Unlike hypnosis, EMDR reprocessing causes a state of heightened emotional arousal. This is an important distinction for the clinician to make when this question arises.

The differences between hypnosis and EMDR therapy are summarized in Table 1.18.

WHAT ONCE WAS ADAPTIVE BECOMES MALADAPTIVE

Some behaviors are learned. Some serve us well and others do not. Some serve us for a period in our life and eventually become a nuisance. For example, a client who was repeatedly sexually molested by a relative as a young child may have learned to dissociate during the molestation. This was their automatic coping response to the fear and pain of the trauma at the time of the abuse. Years later, as an adult, they may still find themself dissociating during stressful situations in their work and life. As a child, dissociation was the only response available and allowed them to cope; it worked well at the time. As a maturing adult, the dissociation begins to cause problems at home, at school, and/or at work.

DEVELOPING AND ENHANCING ADAPTIVE NETWORKS OF ASSOCIATION

Before processing of the negative networks may begin, clients with more complex cases may need to access, strengthen, and reinforce positive life experiences and adaptive memories (e.g., positive resources and behaviors, learning, self-esteem). It is possible to access

TABLE 1.18 Differences Between EMDR Therapy and Hypnosis

EMDR	HYPNOSIS
Integrative psychotherapy model.	Medium within which EMDR may be practiced and enhanced (Brown, 2006).
Efficacious treatment for PTSD (Bisson et al., 2007; Spates et al., 2009).	Case reports available that suggest the efficacy of hypnosis for trauma treatment outcomes (Cardena et al., 2009).
Bilateral eye movements are utilized.	Bilateral eye movements occur in hypnosis, but usually are ignored (Bramwell, 1906).
EEG readings taken during EMDR reprocessing show a brain wave pattern within normal waking parameters (Nicosia, 1995).	Theta (Sabourin et al., 1990), beta (De Pascalis & Penna, 2009), or alpha (Meares, 1960) waves are characteristic of hypnotized subjects.
During desensitization, the client may be in a state of heightened emotional arousal.	After induction, the client usually is in a deep hypnotic state.
Clinician follows a set procedure and generally does not include clinician-generated suggestions (i.e., lacks suggestibility; Hekmat et al., 1994).	There is no set procedure and includes clinician-generated suggestions (i.e., encourage suggestibility).
Each set of eye movements lasts about 30 seconds.	Client is in a trance lasting anywhere from 15 to 45 minutes or longer.
Memories may emerge, but memory retrieval is not the primary purpose.	Is often used for memory retrieval.
Images of memories generally become more distant and less vivid, and more historical.	Images of memories are generally enhanced and made more vivid and experienced in real time.
Clients tend to jump from one associative memory to another.	Clients follow a moment-by-moment ("frame by frame") sequence of events.
Eyes are usually open.	Eyes are closed throughout the induction and treatment phase.
Uses BLS (e.g., eye movements, taps, tones).	Does not use BLS.
Clients appear more alert, remain conscious, and are less susceptible to inappropriate suggestion.	Clients are less alert, not conscious, and more susceptible to suggestion.
Does not induce a trance state.	Induces a trance state.
Dual focus of attention is deliberately maintained at all times.	Dual focus of attention may occur (Harford, 2010).
For long-term trauma issues, duration of treatment is often brief.	For long-term trauma issues, duration of treatment is often lengthy.

Abbreviations: BLS, bilateral stimulation; PTSD, posttraumatic stress disorder.

these positive experiences by developing new and enhancing existing positive networks described as follows.

Developing New Positive Networks

(a) New positive experiences are created when the clinician teaches the client safe (calm) place and other stress management and relaxation techniques; (b) the initial introduction of BLS with stabilization exercises creates a positive experience with eye movements or other forms of BLS; and (c) the use of slower, shorter sets of BLS with the safe place, sacred space, or resource development and installation (RDI) imagery helps to create a positive experience for a client by inducing and fortifying agreeable or satisfying feelings (e.g., sense of safety, self-confidence, assurance) that currently exists within a client's positive neural networks. The goal is to create a positive experience in which a client begins to trust the BLS process, as well as strengthening and enhancing the therapeutic alliance. This may become its own positive network.

Enhancing Already Existing Positive Networks

Investigate and determine what positive life experiences and adaptive memories already exist. As the client holds these positive experiences in mind, the clinician implements BLS until the client feels the earlier positive emotions. If a client cannot come up with a positive memory, have them imagine one and facilitate the same steps mentioned previously. Identifying these positive memories is an important part of the Preparation Phase and facilitates later processing. This exercise works particularly well with a child who may need a stronger sense of safety or assurance before undergoing reprocessing.

Example: Adalia presents with a history of anxiety. The clinician asks the client to imagine a time in her past when she felt empowered and safe and instructs her to imagine how it might have felt to look, feel, and act that way again in a positive way. As she imagines this positive image, the clinician initiates short and slow sets of BLS until she can feel in the present what she believes it felt like in the imagined scene. This exercise works well with children.

Regardless of how and when they come about, it is important for these positive networks to be present and accessible for reprocessing to occur. With clients who have trouble in identifying positive networks of association or role models, plan on a longer preparation time before any processing of negative experiences.

STATE VERSUS TRAIT CHANGE

Shapiro (2008) differentiated between state and trait change. She defined a state change as momentary or transitory, whereas a trait change reflected a permanent change. A state change is a change of mind. It instills a sense of hope in the client. A state change also requires the use of coping mechanisms to continue the change, whereas a trait change no longer requires the same. With a trait change, the client changes how they see or view the event and, as a result, can experience it differently.

When a client changes their perspective about a previous traumatic event and has the needed skills, they can function more appropriately. An example of a state change is the client saying, "I am able to soothe myself by breathing and using my safe (calm) place when my boss asks me to come to his office. I feel much calmer." A trait change may be, "I am no longer triggered when my boss asks me to come to his office." To simplify, "states are weather" whereas

TABLE 1.19 State Versus Trait	
STATE	**TRAIT**
Momentary or transitory change.	Permanent change.
Change of mind.	Changes the way a client sees or views an event and thus can experience it differently.
Coping skills may be required.	Coping skills are not required.
"I am able to soothe myself by breathing and using my calm/safe place when my boss asks me to come to this office. I feel much calmer."	"I am no longer triggered when my boss asks me to come to his office."
Resourcing tends to cause state changes.	Processing tends to lead to trait changes.
States are weather.	Traits are climate.

All traits are states, but not all states are traits.

"traits are climate." "All traits are states" but "not all states are traits" (Shapiro, 2006). See Table 1.19 for a better understanding of the differences between the two.

DUAL AWARENESS—INTERNAL/EXTERNAL BALANCE

Dual awareness or mindfulness, or what Dr. Shapiro calls "dual focus of attention" (2018), allows the client to maintain a sense of present awareness and for the client's internal processes to function without interference during reprocessing. It allows the client to be a nonevaluative observer with respect to whatever emerges during a reprocessing session. It helps the client keep "one foot in the past and one foot in the present." The client is on the "train" watching the scenery go by.

One of the primary reasons to teach a client grounding and breathing skills and anchoring them in the present is to help them learn to keep one foot in the present while reprocessing something traumatic from their past. This provides them with a dual focus of attention and reduces the possibility or risk of a client dissociating, blanking out, becoming overwhelmed, and/or resisting. Teaching them these skills prior to the reprocessing will help facilitate a smoother therapeutic experience. It also allows the client to maintain a sense of safety in the present while accessing and stimulating negative information from the past. The clinician can solidify the client's connection to the present by utilizing verbal reassurances, such as "Good," "You're doing fine," "It's over," or "You're safe now." The clinician may also stop and change the direction or speed of the BLS. When a client is in an abreactive state, these types of clinical strategies are particularly important to help the client maintain an external focus (Shapiro, 2018).

ECOLOGICAL VALIDITY (I.E., SOUNDNESS)

In attempting to discern whether a client's target has been resolved, look at what resolution of this traumatic event would look like in the real world given the individual, the timing, and the situation. To what degree does the current situation "fit" the circumstances? Ask yourself, "If a client was processing a rape that occurred months before and the rapist was still on the loose, would it be appropriate for them to continue to feel fear and demonstrate vigilance around this event?" The answer depends on how their information processing system works. Is there a reason they may be or may think they are still in danger? Is their sense of vigilance and fear around the rapist emotionally appropriate under the circumstances?

How does one recognize ecological validity? And how do you work with it within the EMDR therapy framework? First, use Wolpe's SUD scale (Wolpe, 1990; Exhibit 1.8).

EXHIBIT 1.8 Subjective Units of Disturbance Scale

Developed by Joseph Wolpe in 1969, the modified SUD scale is an 11-point Likert scale utilized to measure the subjective units of disturbance being experienced and reported by a client at a given time.

Neutral/No Disturbance   **Highest Disturbance**

| 0 | 1 | 2 | 3 | 4 | 5 | 6 | 7 | 8 | 9 | 10 |

Abbreviation: SUD, Subjective Units of Disturbance.

The SUD scale is an 11-point Likert scale utilized to rate the anxiety level of a memory being accessed by a client in the present. When you ask the client during the Desensitization Phase to focus on the original event (incident, experience) and again ask, on a scale from 0 to 10, "How disturbing does it <u>feel *now*</u>?" and the client says a 1, the clinician needs to check out what is blocking (i.e., blocking belief) desensitization of the original target by: (a) having the client focus on where they feel it in their body; and by asking (b) "What keeps it a 1 (or .5 or 2)?"; or (c) "What keeps it from being a 0?" In the case of a rapist, the client might respond, "He's still out there." Ask the client to "go with that" and continue to process to a more complete resolution. Do not assume that the client has reached the end of the channel just yet. Continue to process and check the SUD again before proceeding to the Installation Phase.

If the client still clings to the 1 (or .5 or 2) and "he's still out there," you can consider this to be ecologically valid. Ecological validity is one of the reasons the clinician should go directly to the Installation Phase without the client's SUD level getting down to a 0. The SUD scale will be discussed in more depth in Chapters 2 and 3.

A blocking belief may also arise in the Installation Phase when evaluating the VoC, a 7-point semantic differential scale that measures the validity (i.e., felt sense of the trueness or falseness) of the client's stated PC. If the client reports a VoC of 6 or 6.5, use the same questioning mentioned earlier when the SUD does not equal 0 (i.e., focus on where the client feels it in their body, "What keeps it a 6.5?" "What prevents it from being a 7?") to discern if there is: (a) a blocking belief, (b) feeder memory, or (c) ecological validity.

Dr. Shapiro has been known to say, "Forgiveness is like rain—it may or may not happen." If a client forgives someone who has hurt them, it does not mean they use poor judgment with respect to that individual (e.g., they will never leave their children with a past abuser). However, clients often arrive at forgiveness or compassion more quickly and more completely than they might with other forms of therapy. A clinician must be alert to not use their own experiences or experiences of their other clients to determine "ecological validity" for any specific client. If processing stops at a certain place, first attempt to remove the block by changing the direction or modality of the BLS. Always get the client's permission before doing so. Then do a couple more sets of BLS before determining if it is ecologically valid for the person to move further toward forgiveness or compassion.

SIDE BENEFITS OF EMDR THERAPY

The primary goal of EMDR therapy is to reprocess any irrational, negative cognitions; emotions; sensory stimuli (e.g., images, sounds, smells, tastes); and physical sensations associated with a trauma. It does not, however, remove or eliminate any irrational, negative sensations and cognitions related to a traumatic event. In the rape example mentioned earlier, it may be ecologically appropriate that the client maintain a healthy sense of fear and an appropriate level of vigilance until the rapist has been caught and their physical safety is ensured. It does not change the client's negative thoughts and feelings about the rapist and what they did to them.

Reprocessing will not eliminate any negative thoughts, emotions, or physical sensations that are appropriate to the situation. For example, a client may experience hate toward their abusive, neglectful, and distant mother. In response to ongoing experiences, the client may have developed low levels of self-esteem and confidence. Reprocessing may be successful in improving the client's self-esteem and other issues, but the client may or may not still feel hatred toward their mother.

EMDR therapy does not have the potential for making one fall back in love with their significant other if one does not love them, secure a raise at their job if one does not deserve one, believe that their abusiveness to another was acceptable, or make one the next race car champion of the Indy 500 if one does not have the ability to drive a race car. It cannot make the true untrue or the untrue true. It only can decompress the negative thoughts, feelings, and physical sensations from the client's internal system so that natural healing can take place. In the process of EMDR therapy, new insights may occur; behavior, perceptions, and attitudes can shift; and physical and emotional responses can change.

HOLISTIC NATURE OF THE APPROACH

Even though it has been around for more than 30 years, EMDR is very much a "cutting edge" therapy. One of the reasons that it continues to be cutting edge is that it appears to be a permanent means of flushing traumatic memories with the accompanying negative cognitions, emotions, and physical sensations from the client's system in a way that seems unique. It is a whole-system approach. It can reach down into the depths of a client's despair, attach itself to every negative element connected to a traumatic event, and then flush it out.

COOKIE-CUTTER APPROACH

EMDR therapy is not a one-size-fits-all approach. It is neither mechanistic nor cookie-cutter. Clients are as different as night and day and sessions can vary from simple to complex depending on a client's trauma history. Each client is approached individually in terms of history-taking, treatment planning, preparation, and target focus. Some clients will benefit from eye movements while others may do better with other forms of BLS. The speed and the length of the set will vary from client to client. Some will need more and different forms of preparation. Not only do clinicians approach each client differently, each client responds differently to EMDR treatment as well. EMDR therapy is not simply a matter of a clinician waving their fingers in front of a client's eyes as they focus on a trauma. From beginning to end, each client is treated as unique and special as the clinician helps them to navigate his way through his trauma to adaptive resolution.

USEFUL METAPHORS

TRAIN METAPHOR

While no longer a major form of transportation in America and the experience of riding a train is unfamiliar to many, the use of the train metaphor continues to be Shapiro's primary means of explaining the intricate principles, protocols, and procedures inherent in EMDR therapy.

Dr. Shapiro prescribes the use of a train metaphor to help clients move along their processing "tracks." Reference to and use of this metaphor will be utilized frequently throughout this Primer. During the Desensitization Phase, this metaphor can be applied as a means of noticing yet distancing the client from fear of the trauma. Dr. Shapiro favors this metaphor because it conveys a sense of movement and safety (Shapiro, 2006). The train metaphor may be used throughout the reprocessing as needed. It goes like this: "In order to help you just notice the experience, imagine riding on a train and the feelings, thoughts, etc., are just scenery going by" (Shapiro, 2018).

During the reprocessing, the image of the train going down the track is also used to encourage the client to continue. The passenger is the client, and the scenery represents the dysfunctional information that they are reprocessing. The clinician might say, "It's just old scenery. Just watch it go by." This metaphor is a reminder to the client that the train passes the scenery as quickly as it appears.

Dr. Shapiro describes the processing as "metaphorically like moving down a train track" (Shapiro, 2006). From the point of origination to the destination, there are freight depot stops where useless cargo (i.e., dysfunctional information) is unloaded and new, useful cargo (i.e., adaptive information) is loaded (i.e., adaptive resolution). In between stops, resources may need to be loaded for the client to continue the trip down the track, debris may need to be cleared from the track, and/or linkages to adaptive networks can occur. See Exhibit 1.9 for a pictorial rendition of this metaphor. Again, the damaged material is unloaded and discarded at the freight depots found along the track during the stopping and starting of the BLS. It is also at this freight depot where adaptive information is loaded. When the train reaches its final destination, the client has reached adaptive resolution. Metaphorically, the processing stimulated by the assessment questions and BLS move the train down the track toward adaptive resolution.

Whether suggesting the train or another example, the metaphor is an option being offered to a client if the trauma becomes too much to bear and distancing from it will allow reprocessing to continue. Installation of the metaphor is unnecessary.

During an abreaction, the train metaphor is a useful strategy for supportively assisting a client to allow movement down the tracks. The clinician can assist by saying, "It's just old information. Watch it like scenery going by."

Dr. Shapiro also uses the train metaphor to describe information that moves adaptively from dysfunctional to functional. It is a common experience for a client's once-vivid negative images, affect, and cognitions to become less vivid and less valid while the opposite happens

EXHIBIT 1.9 Adaptive Information Processing Model—Metaphoric Train Moving Down the Track Toward a More Adaptive, Functional Resolution

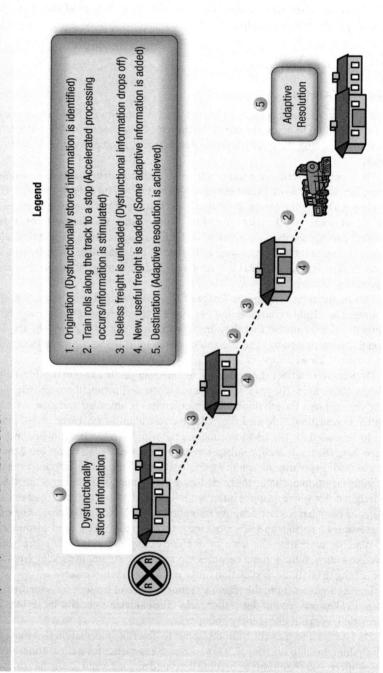

Legend

1. Origination (Dysfunctionally stored information is identified)
2. Train rolls along the track to a stop (Accelerated processing occurs/information is stimulated)
3. Useless freight is unloaded (Dysfunctional information drops off)
4. New, useful freight is loaded (Some adaptive information is added)
5. Destination (Adaptive resolution is achieved)

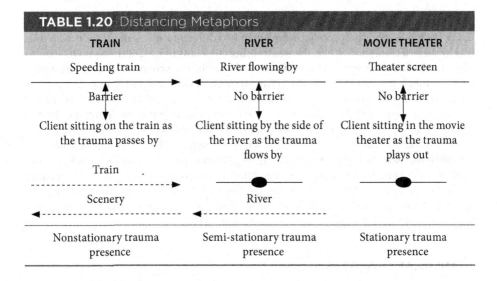

TABLE 1.20	Distancing Metaphors	
TRAIN	**RIVER**	**MOVIE THEATER**
Speeding train	River flowing by	Theater screen
Barrier	No barrier	No barrier
Client sitting on the train as the trauma passes by	Client sitting by the side of the river as the trauma flows by	Client sitting in the movie theater as the trauma plays out
Train		
Scenery	River	
Nonstationary trauma presence	Semi-stationary trauma presence	Stationary trauma presence

to the positive images, affect, and cognitions. Can you visualize a train traveling down its track? Each time the dysfunctional information is stimulated or when accelerated processing takes place, the train moves down the track and stops. At each stop, the client unloads dysfunctional information and loads more functional or adaptive information. The train continues on this route until it reaches its final destination (i.e., adaptive resolution). One of the important elements of this journey that should not escape the client is that the choice to make a return trip down the same track and revisit the scenery that emerged is optional.

Although seemingly archaic, the use of the train metaphor versus others (i.e., movie theater, river) makes more sense for several reasons. It conveys the sense of movement and safety that Shapiro emphasizes (2018). It is a distancing metaphor. First, the train moves forward at a rapid rate of speed as it distances the client from the trauma while the scenery recedes in the distance at the same rate of speed. In addition, there is a visual barrier between the client who sits on the train and the scenery passing by outside the train. The protective barrier between the client and trauma helps to create a greater sense of safety. See a representation of this idea by the comparison with the other distancing metaphors in Table 1.20.

TUNNEL METAPHOR

Another metaphor used by Shapiro (2018) is driving a car through a tunnel. To get through the tunnel as quickly as possible, the driver will need to increase their pressure on the accelerator (i.e., "You are in a tunnel. Just keep your foot on the pedal and keep moving."). In EMDR reprocessing, the eye movements or other BLS act as the accelerator (i.e., the processing of the dysfunctional information is accelerated by the speed and length of the BLS). This metaphor is utilized to encourage the client to pass through the tunnel as fast as possible (i.e., keep moving his eyes quickly). If they ease up on the accelerator or choose to stop during transit, the car moves slower; and it takes much longer to get through the tunnel. Or they are left in the midst of unprocessed material.

HAND METAPHORS

Using the hand as her prop, Shapiro explained two different aspects of the treatment process by using a metaphor. When she was training clinicians in EMDR therapy, Dr. Shapiro often used a hand metaphor to emphasize and explain the progression of the treatment effects through the memory network. With the back of her hand facing outward and her fingers pointing downward, she would explain the processing of an identified traumatic memory. The top part of the hand represented the target or node (i.e., the traumatic event or some aspect of it, such as thought, belief, body sensation) and her fingers the different channels of association that the client had to progress through to achieve adaptive resolution.

With the palm facing outward and fingers pointing downward, Dr. Shapiro would use another hand metaphor to demonstrate the different components of a memory. The top part of the hand represented the memory and the fingers the different aspects of the memory network—sensory (e.g., visual, auditory, olfactory, tactile, gustatory), thoughts, emotions, body sensations, and thoughts and beliefs (see Figure 1.1).

ANCILLARY TARGETS

A yellow or red board in train lingo is a fixed signal to slow and eventually stop a train. When an engineer encounters one of these, they know they need to stop and then, if possible, proceed with caution, depending on what is farther down the line. In some cases, there may be workers and equipment ahead indicating that the track is being repaired, or there may be an obstacle or debris blocking the tracks that needs to be cleared. Blocking beliefs (e.g., "I do not deserve good things" or "If I get over this, I will betray (be disloyal) to my buddies") and feeder memories (e.g., an unconscious memory that is emotionally feeding the targeted memory network) can activate yellow or red boards. When one of these emerges, it could be an indicator to a clinician that they may need to slow the "train" with successive sets of BLS or switch tracks to clear the track of this additional debris. Once this track has been cleared, the track is switched once again to allow the original "train" to continue down the line.

SECONDARY GAINS

Secondary-gain issues tend to obstruct or stall processing. Therefore, it is advisable for a clinician to attempt to ferret these out prior to any actual processing taking place. In the History-Taking Phase and Treatment Planning Phase, the clinician may investigate the presence of these gains by asking the client if they are aware of any reasons why processing might be unsuccessful. Is there something a client may be uncomfortable giving up to help resolve the issues they bring to therapy? What other issues are served by the presenting complaint, such as positive consequences (e.g., pension checks); needs (e.g., fear of dishonoring the dead by getting better and moving on; fear of bears may keep a wife from going on camping trips with her husband); or identity issues (e.g., fear of loss of professional or social identity)? Identify what feeds these secondary gains (e.g., low self-esteem, irrational fears, boundary issues, lack of assertiveness). Whatever the issues are, these fears need to be resolved before a successful therapeutic outcome can be expected or maintained. A clinician also needs to ensure that a client has the stability and resources available, which assists them in giving up the gains. Noncompliance may also be related to other fears (e.g., fear of success, fear of terminating therapy, fear of failure). When this occurs, the clinician may ask the client, "What is the worst that could happen?" or "What would change if you were successful?" The secondary-gain issues and fears may need to be addressed before any successful processing can occur.

BLOCKING BELIEFS

Blocking beliefs generally arise during EMDR processing toward the end of the Desensitization, Installation, and Body Scan phases. They become evident when a client's SUD level does not lower to a 0, VoC does not rise to a 7, or a clear body scan is not achieved.

SUBJECTIVE UNITS OF DISTURBANCE AND THE EMERGENCE OF BLOCKING BELIEFS

If, after repeated applications of different directions and types of BLS, the client cannot attain a 0 for a SUD level, the clinician may ask the client to: (a) focus on where they feel it in their body. If it still does not lower, the clinician is directed to look for the presence of a dysfunctional blocking belief by asking (b) "What keeps it a 1 (or .5 or 2)?" or (c) "What prevents it from being a 0?" If a benign or nonproblematic blocking belief (e.g., "I don't believe in absolutes") arises, the clinician should ask the client to "Just notice that," and add another set of BLS. Sometimes this allows the SUD to drop to 0. If not, then proceed to the Installation Phase.

To probe further for a blocking belief, the clinician may ask the client, "Is there a part of you that might have concerns about getting over this problem?" or "What would happen if you were to completely get over this problem?" and initiate one of more sets of BLS in order to bring forth the concern or an association to the client's consciousness. Examples of responses that may emerge are, "It's not safe to get over this problem," I don't deserve to get over this problem," or "If I feel better, I will forget about what happened."

If a dysfunctional blocking belief surfaces and, after successive sets of BLS, it does not remit, the clinician should target it with full reprocessing (i.e., Phases 3–6). This means that processing of the original target should be stopped until the blocking belief has been identified, targeted, and reprocessed. After a blocking belief has been successfully processed, the clinician should reevaluate the original targeted event and then complete the Desensitization Phase and proceed to the Installation Phase.

VALIDITY OF COGNITION AND THE EMERGENCE OF BLOCKING BELIEFS

Except for the wording, the same procedures cited earlier for blocking beliefs and the SUD level apply to blocking beliefs and the VoC. For assessing a blocking belief at the Installation Phase, the clinician asks the client: (a) to focus on where they feel it in their body; (b) "What keeps it a 6.5?"; or (c) "What prevents it from being a 7?" When assessing a client's level of validity, ecological validity should be taken into consideration by the clinician. What current life circumstances may keep a client's VoC from rising to a 7? If a client is processing a rape and their PC is, "I am safe," her 7 level may not be realistic or possible for them if their rapist is still at large. If blocking beliefs are revealed during the Installation Phase, they need to be fully processed using phases 3 through 6. Once it has been reprocessed, the clinician should reevaluate the original targeted event and then complete the Desensitization Phase and proceed to the Body Scan Phase.

BODY SCAN AND THE EMERGENCE OF BLOCKING BELIEFS

Blocking beliefs can emerge anywhere during EMDR treatment, including the body scan. If a blocking belief emerges during this phase and it appears more dysfunctional than innocuous, it should be targeted and processed with full reprocessing (i.e., Phases 3–6). Once resolved, the original target should be accessed, processed, and completed at the Body Scan Phase.

FEEDER MEMORIES

When Shapiro (2018) first began developing and implementing eye movement desensitization (EMD) in 1989, she started by targeting a client's current dysfunction. The result was that, when a client focused on their negative reaction to present stimuli, they would become more anxious and processing remained blocked. What she readily discovered was after several sets of BLS and often earlier, related memories would spontaneously emerge; and the client would get better once the processing of them was complete. It was then that Dr. Shapiro developed and introduced the three-pronged protocol—past, present, and future—whereby her first area of focus changed from a client's presenting issue to the precipitating event that fueled their current dysfunction.

At this stage of development, Dr. Shapiro also began asking a client to focus on a presently held negative belief and scan back in the past for an earlier time they may have had this negative belief about themself. Because of these changes, Shapiro (2018) wrote, "The theoretical assumption of EMDR treatment is that any current dysfunctional reaction (with the exception of organically or chemically based pathologies) is always the result of a previous experience, although, of course, not necessarily one from childhood" (p. 181).

The earlier untapped memories that may emerge and appear to continue to feed a client's current dysfunction and block successful processing are called *feeder memories* and may arise in any of the three stages of the EMDR approach. Clinicians are now encouraged to initially treat the earlier memories with the standard protocol, followed by the present triggers and desired future outcome.

There are several ways to elicit the existence of feeder memories from a client: (a) direct questioning, (b) floatback, and (c) affect scan. If a feeder memory surfaces during the processing of another related event, these strategies may be utilized to ascertain the existence of a feeder memory within the reprocessing session or may be targeted later.

In addition to ancillary targets, there are other client obstacles that may obstruct reprocessing. In these cases, the clinician will need to determine the cause and rectify to initiate or continue processing. The obstacles highlighted in Table 1.21 were adapted from Dr. Shapiro's work (2009–2017a, 2009–2017b).

TO INTERVENE OR NOT TO INTERVENE

As a rule of thumb or when in doubt, *do not intervene* during reprocessing. Simply say, "Go with that." There are many indicators of successful processing, such as shifts: (a) in the memory itself; (b) from one memory to another; (c) in the reported changes or the emergence of new images, sounds, cognitive content, levels of affect, or physical sensations; (d) in a client's self-worth, self-efficacy, affect, and self-assessment; and (e) from dysfunctional to adaptive. It is important for a clinician to remember anything that emerges between sets is related to a client's experience, and only memories associated in some way with this

TABLE 1.21 Obstacles to Processing

OBSTACLES	REASONS
Headaches, nausea, and dizziness	Secondary-gain issues May be artifact of eye movements Client resistance State of hypervigilance May be part of the memory itself May be the result of dissociation or dissociative disorder
Client cannot feel	Memory may be processed fully Client cannot tolerate affect Presently held beliefs exist that inhibit feelings (e.g., Big boys don't cry/If I start to cry, I will never stop. It is dangerous, unsafe, or shameful to express feelings) Cultural or gender restraints or constraints with parents
Ototverbalizing	May serve as a buffer Client believes he is supposed to talk
Client blaming	Client was mandated to therapy (i.e., client uncooperative or unresponsive) Client shuts down experience

experience will emerge. To ensure the success of the reprocessing, it is imperative that a client be allowed on his own to discern the importance of the connections of all associations that may arise. As these associations arise and connections are made, the sets are continued, and the need to engage in any complex EMDR interventions is curtailed.

Table 1.22 provides some examples of changes that may occur in multimemory and single-event channels of association. When any of these shifts occur, stay out of the way and say, "Go with that."

EYE MOVEMENT DESENSITIZATION VERSUS EMDR THERAPY

In 1987, Dr. Shapiro inadvertently discovered the effects of spontaneous eye movements while focusing on disturbing thoughts of her own. She developed standardized procedures and a protocol that she called *EMD*. Two years after Dr. Shapiro's famous walk in the park, her seminal article, "Efficacy of the Eye Movement Desensitization Procedure in the Treatment of Traumatic Memories" (1989a), was published in the *Journal of Traumatic Stress*. In 1991, Dr. Shapiro renamed her psychotherapeutic method EMDR to recognize its shift from a desensitization paradigm to one of information processing.

While EMDR protocols are used within EMDR therapy to accomplish reprocessing of traumatic memories and comprehensive treatment, EMD is a brief strategy that can be used to reduce symptomatic reactions to a specific target or cluster of targets. EMD intentionally limits the linkages to associated memories. Associations that are reported outside of the target memory require that the client be returned to the target, the SUD reassessed, and BLS be initiated.

TABLE 1.22 Patterns of Response	
CHANGES IN MULTIMEMORY ASSOCIATIVE CHANNELS	**EXAMPLES**
Dominant belief inherent in trauma	The memory of a boat accident brings up an associated memory of being bullied and physically assaulted by classmates in the second grade (both shared the same negative belief, "I am powerless").
Major participant or perpetrator	A client associates being beaten by his mother with his mother driving drunk while he was in the car.
Pronounced stimuli	While processing waking up to a bedroom fire set by a lit cigarette, a firefighter remembers an associative memory of being overcome by smoke in a raging prairie fire.
Specific type of event	During the processing of a memory when a teller was robbed at gunpoint, an associated memory of being pistol-whipped in a previous robbery years earlier emerges.
Dominant physical sensations	As a client processes their childhood memories of being tied to a bedpost by a babysitter while their parents were away, an associated memory of being assaulted and tied up so the perpetrator can flee spontaneously surfaces.
Dominant emotions	Disappointment over being passed over for a much-deserved promotion is shared with an associated memory of failing a CPA exam for the third time.
CHANGES IN SINGLE-EVENT ASPECTS OF MEMORY	**EXAMPLES**
Images	Change in content or appearance: A father's outraged face becomes a smiling one. Change to an image of a different but associated event: The image of a father's outraged face changes to remembering his anger when he failed a class. Change to a different aspect of the same event: The image of a father's outraged face changes to one of a grief-stricken man. Shift in perspective: A son begins to see the image of his father's outraged face as more pathetic or laughable. Expansion of a scene to include more details: Original image picture is one where a son sees the outrage on his father's face upon hearing that his son was expelled from school. As processing continued, the scene opened up; and he suddenly remembered he was expelled because of a physical fight that ensued on school property between his father and himself. The father started the fight.

(continued)

TABLE 1.22 Patterns of Response (continued)

CHANGES IN MULTIMEMORY ASSOCIATIVE CHANNELS	EXAMPLES
	Shifts in the appearance of an image: The image of an outraged father may become larger (or smaller), blurs or fades, becomes closer (or more distant), turns gray or black or white, transforms into a still image, or disappears altogether.
Sounds	Shifts in the sound of a voice: The voice of an outraged father's voice may become softer, louder, quieter, distorted, or simply becomes mute. Shifts in dialogue: The son suddenly commences to voice words of assertiveness toward his outraged father. Shifts in language: The son is from Germany and reverted to his first language to express his assertiveness toward his outraged father.
Cognitions	Emergence of insight: As processing continues, the son suddenly realizes that the outrage his father demonstrates toward him is really about his father's sense of failure. A polar shift occurs: In the earlier part of processing, the son's negative cognition (e.g., "I am not good enough") is replaced by a positive one (e.g., "I am okay as I am").
Emotions	Increases/decreases in intensity: After the first set of BLS, the son's fear of his outraged father becomes overwhelming (or becomes less fearful). Shifts from one emotion to another: The son's fear of his outraged father changes to disgust, or crying changes to laughter. Shifts toward more appropriate or ecologically valid emotions: The son's emotion shifts from fear to sadness to disgust during the course of processing.
Physical sensations	Reexperiences physical sensations tied to the emotions: The son experiences chest pains and shortness of breath as he processes fear of his father. Experiences physical sensations felt at the time of the original event: The son feels a punch in his stomach as he processed a memory where his outraged father hit him in the gut. Increases/decreases in intensity: The son's physical sensations of being hit in the stomach become less/more intense during subsequent sets of BLS. Shifts in the location: The physical sensation of being hit in the gut moves from the heart to the throat.

(continued)

TABLE 1.22 Patterns of Response (continued)	
CHANGES IN MULTIMEMORY ASSOCIATIVE CHANNELS	**EXAMPLES**
	Shifts in the type of sensations felt in a certain location: The son's stomach awareness changes from nauseous to tight to feeling empty.

Abbreviations: BLS, bilateral stimulation; CPA, Certified Public Accountant.

If during BLS, the client reports a free association that appears unrelated to the precipitating event, gently say "Ok, now I would like you to go back to the bombing incident (name the event), what do you notice now?" Obtain a SUDS rating each time the client returns to the target memory. After obtaining the SUDS instruct, "Just think of that ..." (and then initiate the next set of BLS).

(RUSSELL & FIGLEY, 2013, P. 99)

The clinician may find the use of EMD helpful when the goal is to desensitize a current or recent disturbing incident without accessing an associative memory network of experiences. This helps the client to decrease reactivity, obtain emotional regulation, and maintain dual awareness. This intervention can be used on its own or as a bridge to reprocessing. In these instances, EMD works much like other stabilization techniques, in that it helps a client establish or regain a sense of resiliency and mastery.

EMD is being used in the treatment of recent traumatic events or episodes and in several specific situations. One is when the target is an intrusive element, such as a disturbing image, sensation, thought, or feeling. Another is when processing overwhelms the AIP system. Switching briefly to EMD often helps to reduce the distress enough to start the processing again (Shapiro & Laub, 2014).

The EMD procedure possesses the capacity to: (a) desensitize a highly disturbing or traumatic event, often within one session without an intense emotional reaction; (b) result in cognitive restructuring of the negative self-assessment along with a diminished visual representation of the original image; and (c) shift thoughts, feelings, and behaviors (Shapiro, 1989a).

Table 1.23 outlines the differences between EMD and EMDR.

The procedure initially developed by Shapiro (1989a) has evolved to more closely resemble the standard protocol, with deviations as follows (follow the standard Assessment Phase as completely as possible):

ASSESSMENT PHASE

1. Select a single memory and an image (or picture) that represents the worst part of the memory/incident.
   What image (or picture) represents the worst part of the experience?
   If no image/picture, When you think of the experience, what do you get?
2. Identify a negative belief (e.g., "I'm not safe," "I should have done something," "I have no control," or "I am helpless") which goes *best* with the target memory or image.
   What words go best with the image (or picture) that express your negative belief about yourself now?
3. Identify a desired PC, such as "I'm safe now," "I did the best I could," or "It's over."

TABLE 1.23 Eye Movement Desensitization Versus EMDR

EMD	EMDR
Informed by desensitization model. Procedure for desensitization. Used for decreasing reactions, reducing arousal, and increasing stability to individual memories; symptom reduction while minimizing spontaneous associations to other experiences; and with clients who appear prone to emotional overwhelm, dysregulation, or outside of window of tolerance.	Informed by the AIP model. Psychotherapeutic orientation. Used for comprehensive cognitive and emotional restructuring.
Brief sets of alternating eye movements or tapping facilitate effective desensitization.	Longer sets of eye movements, alternating taps and tones, facilitate information reprocessing.
Average number of passes is 12–24.	Average recommended number of passes of BLS is 20–24 to start, lengthen to 36–40 as needed (the number of passes is generally customized to the client's response).
Sets are continued only as long as necessary to desensitize reactions to the target.	There is no limit to the number of sets.
Treatment effect Reduction of the fear and anxiety related to the disturbing memory.	**Comprehensive treatment effect** Reduction in fear and anxiety. Replacement of negative emotions with positive ones. Emergence of insight. Change in body sensations. Surfacing of new behaviors. Negative events transformed to adaptive learning experiences.

Abbreviations: AIP, Adaptive Information Processing; BLS, bilateral stimulation; EMD, eye movement desensitization.

When you bring up that image (or picture), what would you like (or prefer) to believe about yourself now?
4. Determine the validity of the client's PC (i.e., rate the VoC on a scale of 1–7).
When you focus on that image (or picture), how true do those words, (repeat positive cognition), feel to you now on a scale from 1 to 7, where 1 feels completely false and 7 feels completely true?
5. Identify the associated emotions.
When you bring up that image (or picture) and those words, (repeat negative cognition), what emotion(s) do you feel now?
6. Determine the level of disturbance (i.e., rate the SUD on a scale of 0–10) based on the memory or image and the negative belief.

From 0, which is neutral or no disturbance, to 10, which is the worst disturbance you can imagine, how disturbing does it feel to you <u>now</u>?

7. Identify the physical location of the body sensations.
   Where do you <u>feel</u> it in your body?

DESENSITIZATION PHASE

8. Instruct the client to focus on the image, the negative belief, and where they feel it in their body, and initiate a set of BLS (i.e., faster, but with only 12–15 passes; set of BLS). Shorter sets of BLS are utilized with EMD to limit access to associations.
   I would like you to bring up that image (or picture), those negative words (repeat negative cognition), and notice where you feel it in your body. Just let whatever happens, happen (set of BLS).

9. After each set of BLS, instruct the client to
   Take a breath. (Pause.) Let it go. Then ask, *What are you noticing?*
      The clinician should note the response, and then gently return the client to the target, NC, and reassess the SUD. After obtaining the SUD, instruct the client to "Just think of that," and initiate the next set of BLS (i.e., 12–15).
   When you bring up that image (or picture) and those negative words, using a scale from 0, which is neutral or no disturbance, to 10, which is the worst disturbance you can imagine, how disturbing does it feel to you <u>now</u>?

10. Repeat this process until the client reports little or no disturbance (i.e., SUD = 0 or ecologically sound) and no new intrusive symptoms emerge.

11. Once the SUD has stopped decreasing, the clinician moves to the Installation Phase.
    When you focus on that image (or picture), do the words, (repeat positive cognition), still fit, or is there another positive statement you feel would be more suitable?
    When you focus on that image (or picture), how true do those words, (repeat positive cognition), feel to you now on a scale from 1 to 7, where 1 feels completely false and 7 feels completely true?
    Hold the two together. The clinician initiates BLS.
    On a scale from 1 to 7, how true do those words, (repeat positive cognition), feel to you <u>now</u> when you focus on the original experience?

The clinician continues to install the PC as long as the reprocessing keeps becoming more and more adaptive. If the reported VoC does not increase to 7, the clinician will check for ecological appropriateness. The existence of blocking beliefs should be considered.

Continue to the Closure phase. See Chapter 6 for a complete transcript using EMD with a client. Please note that a Body Scan is not initiated using EMD as the clinician does not want to run the risk of opening up associative links.

PRACTICAL TIPS TO REMEMBER

PRACTICE, PRACTICE, PRACTICE

Practice, practice, practice is this Primer's mantra. In the EMDR Weekend 1 and 2 Trainings you were introduced to EMDR therapy—but, because of time limitations, you may not have fully integrated its substance and protocol into your own therapeutic paradigm. Learning EMDR therapy comes from the *actual doing of it*. Even skilled clinicians who have conducted hundreds of sessions have the potential for learning something new every time they execute the process with a client. It is only from practicing EMDR that excellence and expertise can be derived; so, the mantra *practice, practice, practice* cannot be overly emphasized.

FOLLOW THE SCRIPT VERBATIM

Newly trained EMDR therapy clinicians are strongly encouraged to follow Dr. Francine Shapiro's script verbatim in the Assessment Phase. Dr. Shapiro has chosen every word for a specific reason, and these words have been tested and validated repeatedly in one context or another in session after session with clients presenting various mental health issues. It is important for the clinician to understand the intent and implications of the wording of the well-researched protocol before implementing individual styles of eliciting the same information. In addition, it is highly beneficial for clinicians to follow the scripts provided for Phases 4 through 6. Clinicians who learned the script in the early days of EMDR therapy may notice how it has been refined throughout the past 30 years.

If you have been recently trained or have decided to finally put your EMDR training to use, sit with a copy of the standard protocol in your lap as you implement the Assessment Phase with clients (see Chapter 3). Reading the script verbatim may feel unnatural at first, but you can expect to feel more at ease as you learn the procedural steps. Sitting with the pages in your lap and reading the script as it is written can also serve as good modeling for your client as they watch you work with something new on their behalf. As they become more familiar with the protocol and what words are required in each part, the clinician will most likely develop their own style for setting up the EMDR protocol. The words in the Assessment Phase necessary to optimize receiving the desired processing outcome have been underlined in this chapter and in subsequent ones for your recognition and convenience.

The EMDR Fidelity Rating Scale (EFRS) was developed by van der Kolk et al. (2007) to evaluate adherence to EMDR therapy's eight phases of treatment (i.e., Phases 1–8) and three-pronged protocol (i.e., past, present, future). The EFRS can help a clinician evaluate use of the standard EMDR therapy protocol with memories associated with adverse life events or current triggers. A modified version of this scale (Korn et al., 2018) can be found on the EMDR Research Foundation website (see https://emdrfoundation.org/research-grants/emdr-fidelity-rating-scale/). Clinicians are strongly encouraged to become familiar with this helpful scale. The more fidelity a clinician demonstrates, the better treatment outcome for the client.

Consider logging onto the Trauma Recovery/EMDR Humanitarian Assistance Programs (TR/EMDR-HAP) website to contribute to a worthy cause. You may want to consider purchasing the laminated SUD/VoC Scale Chart or the EMDR Progress Notepad. These items may be purchased online at the TR/EMDR-HAP website (https://www.emdrhap.org/content/). The worksheets can assist you in being more consistent and successful from client to client. The laminated chart may save time and help the client to distinguish a belief from a feeling and to select a negative belief appropriate to their situation. It is not an uncommon reaction for a client to look like a deer caught in the headlights when asked, "What words go best with the picture that express your *negative belief* about yourself *now*?" Having said this, use this placard sparingly. In all cases, it is imperative that the client be given ample opportunity to provide the clinician with a negative and positive cognitions on their own. When a client seemingly does not understand what is being asked for, the clinician should be knowledgeable and skilled in ways to tease these cognitions out before handing them the placard.

KNOW YOUR CLIENT

Before you begin using the reprocessing phases, it is important that you know your client well. Know their strengths and weaknesses. Know their abilities and their limitations. Know their ego deficits. Know their coping mechanisms and strategies. Know their support system—or lack of it. Some clients may not be appropriate or ready for EMDR trauma processing. There could be situations, however, in which you will not have the luxury of waiting weeks to know your client before beginning reprocessing. Then it becomes imperative that you gain as much information as you can about your client in a brief period, particularly when situations or circumstances indicate a necessity of serious caution.

STAY OFF THE TRACKS

The hallmark of EMDR reprocessing is facilitating a client's flow of association and allowing the client to get to the end of the "track" on their own. After completion of the Assessment Phase, the clinician is encouraged to be very limited in what they say, such as "Take a breath. (Pause.) Let it go." "What are you noticing *now*?" "Good." "Go with that." "Notice that." The clinician does not say much of anything else unless the client appears stuck in the process.

The most appropriate and easiest method to stay out of the way is by consistently maintaining a position of quiet neutrality. During the process, the clinician encourages the client by saying "Good" or "You're doing fine." Beyond this, the clinician must be careful not to physically or verbally express what they believe or think about a client's responses between sets of BLS. It is imperative that the clinician allow the client to own the reprocessing of their traumatic event and not be encumbered by the clinician's interventions, comments, or questions. Remember, the clinician is not the agent of change: the client is.

TRACKING THE CLIENT

It is important for the clinician to write down as much as possible of what the client says during the Assessment Phase, especially the exact wording of the client's negative and positive cognitions and key words from their descriptions of traumatic events. Why? Because it is important to use exact wording when activating what the client says. If a client provides a negative cognition, such as "It's my fault," and a clinician reframes it as "I'm responsible," the clinician may have inadvertently distorted what the client originally meant. In doing so, the clinician has also placed themselves in the client's process. Because the clinician reframed it that way, the client may begin to interpret it as "I'm responsible," simply because the clinician said it. "It's my fault" and "I am responsible" may or may not mean the same to the client. To the degree that it does not, it can alter the direction of processing. During the remaining reprocessing Phases 4 through 6, clinicians often find it helpful to write down what the client says. However, if writing down what the client says during reprocessing slows, interrupts, or hinders in any way the client's flow, stop writing and opt to listen and observe more closely what the client is experiencing in the moment.

KEEP IT SIMPLE

In the early days of your EMDR experience as a clinician, try to keep it simple. Do not go straight from the training to your office and select the most challenging client to conduct your first reprocessing session. Select someone with a less complex trauma, such as a client who presents with a single-event trauma. Maybe someone has recently been involved in an automobile accident that relates to no other traumatic event in their life. As will be described in Chapter 4, when the three-pronged approach is discussed, multiple-event traumas are more comprehensive, will take a longer time frame to deal with, and require more skill than a client who presents with a single event. As a new EMDR clinician, you may not yet have the skill level required to deal with multiple-event traumas.

POWER OF NOW

One of the most emphasized words in the EMDR protocols is "now." Why? Because we are asking the client what they believe negatively about themself, what they want to believe positively about themself, and what are the negative emotions and physical sensations that go with the event they are focusing on "now." How are they being affected in the present by something that happened to them 2 months, 2 years, or 20 years ago? How are they being affected now?

The clinician may need to repeat the "now" over and over to a client. The client may get confused between how they felt "then" about an incident and how they feel "now" and ask questions that indicate their confusion. "Do you mean then or *now*?" And they could say, "Then it felt awful, but *now* it does not feel so bad." If this happens during the Assessment Phase, the clinician may need to reevaluate whether the client has chosen an appropriate target. Remember, the clinician is looking to relieve the client of a memory that is charged with negativity. Use Exhibit 1.10 to help remember this important point.

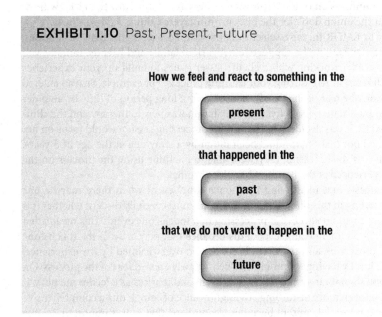

EXHIBIT 1.10 Past, Present, Future

How we feel and react to something in the

present

that happened in the

past

that we do not want to happen in the

future

ONE MORE TIME

A good rule to remember during EMDR reprocessing with a client is that any time something is positively reinforced with BLS, it strengthens the focus of reinforcement. So, when a client reports a positive direction in the reprocessing, say "Go with that" just one more time before returning to target. After the client reaches the SUD of 0, VoC of 7, and a clear Body Scan, say "Go with that" one or more times to reinforce the positive treatment effect and/or to allow deepening of the PC (Shapiro, 2018, 2009–2017a, 2009–2017b). If the clinician is consistent with this rule, the success of the EMDR will be enhanced. In any case, it is important to continue BLS if positive material continues to emerge or strengthen in any part of the client's reprocessing experience.

When reinforcing a positive effect during the Desensitization, Installation, and Body Scan Phases, the BLS will be faster and the length of the sets longer (i.e., 20–24 round-trip passes to start, lengthen to 30–40 as needed) than during the Preparation Phase, when using the safe (calm) place and other resource-building exercises (i.e., slower 4–6 round-trip passes). As indicated earlier, slower and shorter sets are utilized in stabilization efforts to not activate any disturbing material prior to actual reprocessing with EMDR. The primary reason for utilizing faster, longer sets during Phases 3 through 6 is that negative associations may emerge at any phase. Faster, longer sets facilitate the resolution of the negative material, adaptive resolution, and generalization.

SOLO RUN

Client selection is always an important part of the EMDR therapy process, but more so when a clinician is choosing clients for a first solo run. Clinicians may want to select clients with whom they have a strong client–clinician relationship. Pick the less complicated cases. Think of a client's trauma as an onion. How many layers are there? How thick? How thin? So, when looking at the onion, look for the one- or thin-layered skins. And go slowly.

If you are new to EMDR therapy, select a client with more strengths than weaknesses, adequate coping mechanisms, and a supportive network of family and friends. Initially, you may also want to consider working with a client's lesser issues to build up your experience and the client's confidence in AIP during your learning process. For example, Sharon entered therapy 3 weeks prior. She had been sexually abused over a long period of time by an older brother who had an intellectual disability. Because Sharon was new to therapy and the clinician was new to EMDR, it was decided that her first reprocessing session would focus on her fear of dogs. It turned out that Sharon had been bitten by a stray dog at the age of 5 years. Because the session was so successful, they were able to continue using the process on the sexual abuse she experienced at the hands of her older brother.

Dr. Shapiro suggests first identifying the "touchstone" event when there may be one (2008). Before proceeding in this direction, however, one must carefully discern whether it is possible for the client to attain successful processing of a touchstone event. This means that the client must be able to tolerate any level of disturbance that may arise. If the touchstone event is chosen for processing and the client becomes too overwhelmed by the experience, much time could be lost by having to "undo" the client's newly created fear of the process. On the other hand, if you do not target the touchstone event and it arises as a feeder memory, it has the potential to be even more disturbing. The significance of completing a comprehensive history and obtaining informed consent becomes clearer here; that is, it is important for the client to be informed of the potential for accessing feeder memories during the reprocessing of any chosen target.

In this chapter, an attempt has been made to help refamiliarize the reader with basic concepts inherent in EMDR and/or to provide valuable updates to EMDR therapy. Throughout subsequent chapters, case examples will be provided along with teaching points that attempt to explain the clinician's strategies or to point out techniques prescribed by Dr. Shapiro during reprocessing.

SUMMARY STATEMENTS

1. EMDR therapy is an integrative psychotherapeutic approach and is guided by the AIP model. The AIP model "provides the theoretical framework and principles for treatment and an explanation of the basis of pathology and personality development" (Shapiro, 2018). As an integrative psychotherapeutic approach, EMDR therapy is distinct from cognitive behavioral therapy, experiential, and psychodynamic approaches, although it is not exclusive and may be informed by or used together with these approaches.
2. EMDR therapy has eight distinct phases.
3. EMDR therapy is a three-pronged approach addressing the past, the present, and the future.
4. BLS is not EMDR therapy. It is only one component.
5. During the active reprocessing phases of EMDR therapy, dual awareness should be maintained always: one foot in the present, and one foot in the past.
6. EMDR therapy is a fluid, dynamic approach that entails the clinician using all their clinical skills. It is neither mechanistic nor a cookbook approach.
7. The heart of EMDR therapy is the AIP model. As such, it is critical that the clinician have a clear understanding of it to proceed with EMDR practice.
8. Practice, practice, practice. This is how we learn the model.
9. Know your client thoroughly.
10. Stay out of the client's way. The reprocessing is about the client, not the clinician.

REFERENCES

Acierno, R., Tremont, G., Last, C., & Montgomery, D. (1994). Tripartite assessment of the efficacy of eye-movement desensitization in a multiphobic patient. *Journal of Anxiety Disorders, 8*, 259–276. https://doi.org/10.1016/0887-6185(94)90007-8

Adler-Tapia, R. (2015). *EMDR psychotherapy case conceptualization with a reverse protocol* [Conference presentation]. Twentieth EMDR International Association Conference, Philadelphia, PA.

Afifi, T. O., Mota, N. P., Dasiewicz, P., MacMillan, H. L., & Sareen, J. (2012). Physical punishment and mental disorders: Results from a nationally representative US sample. *Pediatrics, 130*(2), 184–192. https://doi.org/10.1542/peds.2011-2947

Allon, M. (2015). EMDR group therapy with women who were sexually assaulted in the Congo. *Journal of EMDR Practice and Research, 9*, 28–34. https://doi.org/10.1891/1933-3196.9.1.28

American Psychiatric Association. (2013). *Diagnostic and statistical manual of mental disorders* (5th ed.). Author.

Andrade, J., Kavanagh, D., & Baddeley, A. (1997). Eye-movements and visual imagery: A working memory approach to the treatment of posttraumatic stress disorder. *British Journal of Clinical Psychology, 36*, 209–223. https://doi.org/10.1111/j.2044-8260.1997.tb01408.x

Armstrong, M. S., & Vaughan, K. (1996). An orienting response model of eye movement desensitization. *Journal of Behavior Therapy & Experimental Psychiatry, 27*, 21–32. https://doi.org/10.1016/0005-7916(95)00056-9

Arseneault, L., Cannon, M., Fisher, H. L., Polanczyk, G., Moffitt, T. E., & Caspi, A. (2011). Childhood trauma and children's emerging psychotic symptoms: A genetically sensitive longitudinal cohort study. *American Journal of Psychiatry, 168*, 65–72. https://doi.org/10.1176/appi.ajp.2010.10040567

Bae, H., Kim, D., & Park, Y. C. (2008). Eye movement desensitization and reprocessing for adolescent depression. *Psychiatry Investigation, 5*(1), 60–65. https://doi.org/10.4306/pi.2008.5.1.60

Barrowcliff, A. L., Gray, N. S., Freeman, T. C. A., & MacCulloch, M. J. (2004). Eye-movements reduce the vividness, emotional valence and electrodermal arousal associated with negative autobiographical memories. *Journal of Forensic Psychiatry and Psychology, 15*(2), 325–345. https://doi.org/10.1080/14789940410001673042

Barrowcliff, A. L., Gray, N. S., MacCulloch, S., Freeman, T. C., & MacCulloch, M. J. (2003). Horizontal rhythmical eye movements consistently diminish the arousal provoked by auditory stimuli. *British Journal of Clinical Psychology, 42*(Pt 3), 289–302. https://doi.org/10.1348/014466503603360703393

Behnam Moghadam, M., Alamdari, A. K., Behnam Moghadam, A., & Darban, F. (2015). Effect of EMDR on depression in patients with myocardial infarction. *Global Journal of Health Science, 7*, 258–262. https://doi.org/10.5539/gjhs.v7n6p258

Bergmann, U. (2000). Further thoughts on the neurobiology of EMDR: The role of the cerebellum in accelerated information processing. *Traumatology, 6*(3), 175–200. https://doi.org/10.1177/153476560000600303

Bergmann, U. (2008). The neurobiology of EMDR: Exploring the thalamus and neural integration. *Journal of EMDR Practice and Research, 2*(4), 300–314. https://doi.org/10.1891/1933-3196.2.4.300

Bergmann, U. (2010). EMDR's neurobiological mechanisms of action: A survey of 20 years of searching. *Journal of EMDR Research and Practice, 4*, 22–42. https://doi.org/10.1891/1933-3196.4.1.22

Bisson, J. I., Ehlers, A., Matthews, R., Pilling, S., Richards, D., & Turner, S. (2007). Psychological treatments for chronic posttraumatic stress disorder. Systematic review and meta-analysis. *British Journal, 190*, 97–104. https://doi.org/10.1192/bjp.bp.106.021402

Boudewyns, P. A., & Hyer, L. A. (1996). Eye movement desensitization and reprocessing (EMDR) as treatment for posttraumatic stress disorder (PTSD). *Clinical Psychology and Psychotherapy, 3*, 185–195. https://doi.org/10.1002/(SICI)1099-0879(199609)3:3<185::AID-CPP101>3.0.CO;2-0

Bramwell, J. M. (1906). *Hypnotism*. Alexander Moring, Ltd.

Brown, D. (2006). *Treatment of attachment pathology in patients with trauma-related diagnoses.* Workshop presented at the Annual Trauma Conference, Harvard Medical School, Boston, MA.

Brown, K. W., McGoldrick, T., & Buchanan, R. (1997). Body dysmorphic disorder: Seven cases treated with eye movement desensitization and reprocessing. *Behavioural and Cognitive Psychotherapy, 25*(2), 203–207. https://doi.org/10.1017/S1352465800018403

Brown, S., & Shapiro, F. (2006). EMDR in the treatment of borderline personality disorder. *Clinical Case Studies, 5*(5), 403–420. https://doi.org/10.1177/1534650104271773

Calancie, O. G., Khalid-Khan, S., Booij, L., & Munoz, D. P. (2018). Eye movement desensitization and reprocessing as a treatment for PTSD: Current neurobiological theories and a new hypothesis. *Annals of the New York Academy of Science, 1426*(1), 127–145. https://doi.org/10.1111/nyas.13882

Cardena, E., Maldonado, J., van der Hart, O., & Spiegel, D. (2009). Hypnosis. In E. B. Foa, T. M. Keane, & M. J. Friedman (Eds.), *Effective treatments for PTSD: Practice guidelines from the International Society for Traumatic Stress Studies* (2nd ed., pp. 427–457). Guilford Press.

Chemtob, C. M., Tolin, D. F., van der Kolk, B. A., & Pitman, R. K. (2000). Eye movement desensitization and reprocessing. In E. B. Foa, T. M. Keane, & M. J. Friedman (Eds.), *Effective treatments for PTSD: Practice guidelines from the International Society for Traumatic Stress Studies* (pp. 139–155, 333–335). Guilford Press.

Christman, S. D., Garvey, K. J., Propper, R. E., & Phaneuf, K. A. (2003). Bilateral eye movements enhance the retrieval of episodic memories. *Neuropsychology, 17*, 221–229. https://doi.org/10.3758/PBR.15.3.515

Christman, S. D., Propper, R. E., & Brown, T. J. (2006). Increased interhemispheric interaction is associated with earlier offset of childhood amnesia. *Neuropsychology, 20*, 336. https://doi.org/10.1037/0894-4105.20.3.336

Davidson, P. R., & Parker, K. C. H. (2001). Eye movement desensitization and reprocessing (EMDR): A meta-analysis. *Journal of Consulting and Clinical Psychology, 69*, 305–316. https://doi.org/101037//0022–006x.69.2.305

De Jongh, A., Ernst, R., Marques, L., & Hornsveld, H. (2013). The impact of eye movements and tones on disturbing memories involving PTSD and other mental disorders. *Journal of Behavior Therapy and Experimental Psychiatry, 44*(4), 477–483. https://doi.org/10.1016/j.jbtep.2013.07.002

De Pascalis, V., & Penna, P. M. (2009). 40-Hz EEG activity during hypnotic induction and hypnotic testing. *International Journal of Clinical and Experimental Hypnosis, 38*(2), 125–138. https://doi.org/10.1080/00207149008414507

de Roos, C., Veenstra, A., de Jongh, A., den Hollander-Gijsman, M., van der Wee, N., Zitman, F., & van Rood, Y. R. (2010). Treatment of chronic phantom limb pain using a trauma-focused psychological approach. *Pain Research & Management, 15*(2), 65–71. https://doi.org/10.1155/2010/981634

Devilly, G. J., Spence, S. H., & Rapee, R. M. (1998). Statistical and reliable change with eye movement desensitization and reprocessing: Treating trauma with a veteran population. *Behavior Therapy, 29*, 435–455. https://doi.org/10.1016/S0005-7894(98)80042-7

Doering, S., Ohlmeier, M.-C., de Jongh, A., Hofmann, A., & Bisping, V. (2013). Efficacy of a trauma-focused treatment approach for dental phobia: A randomized clinical trial. *European Journal of Oral Sciences, 121*(6), 584–593. https://doi.org/10.1111/eos.12090

El Khoury-Malhame, M., Lanteaume, L., Beetz, E. M., Roques, J., Reynaud, E., Samuelian, J. C., Blin, O, Garcia, R., & Khalfa, S. (2011). Attentional bias in post-traumatic stress disorder diminishes after symptom amelioration. *Behavior Research and Therapy, 49*(11), 796–801. https://doi.org/10.1016/j.brat.2011.08.006

Elofsson, U. O., von Scheele, B., Theorell, T., & Sondergard, H. P. (2008). Physiological correlates of eye movement desensitization and reprocessing. *Journal of Anxiety Disorders, 22*(4), 622–634. https://doi.org/10.1016/j.janxdis.2007.05.012

Engelhard, I. M., van den Hout, M. A., Dek, E. C. P., Giele, C. L., van der Wielen, J.-W., Reijnen, M. J., & van Roij, B. (2011). Reducing vividness and emotional intensity of recurrent "flashforwards" by taxing working memory: An analogue study. *Journal of Anxiety Disorders, 25*, 599–603. https://doi.org/10.1016/j.janxdis.2011.01.009

Engelhard, I. M., van den Hout, M. A., Janssen, W. C., & van der Beek, J. (2010a). Eye movements reduce vividness and emotionality of "flashforwards". *Behaviour Research and Therapy, 48*, 442–447. https://doi.org/10.1016/j.brat.2010.01.003

Engelhard, I. M., van den Hout, M. A., Janssen, W. C., & van der Beek, J. (2010b). The impact of taxing working memory on negative and positive memories. *European Journal of Psychotraumatology, 1*, 5623. https://doi.org/10.3402/ejpt.v1i0.5623

Faretta, E. (2013). EMDR and cognitive behavioral therapy in the treatment of panic disorder: A comparison. *Journal of EMDR Practice and Research, 7*, 121–133. https://doi.org/10.1891/1933-3196.7.3.121

Felitti, V. J., Anda, R. F., Nordenberg, D., Williamson, D. F., Spitz, A. M., Edwards, V., Koss, M. P., & Marks, J. S. (1998). Relationship of childhood abuse and household dysfunction to many of the leading causes of death in adults: The adverse childhood experiences (ACE) study. *American Journal of Preventive Medicine, 14*, 245–258. https://doi.org/10.1016/S0749-3797(98)00017-8

Fernandez, I., & Faretta, E. (2007). Eye movement desensitization and reprocessing in the treatment of panic disorder with agoraphobia. *Clinical Case Studies, 6*(1), 44–63. https://doi.org/10.1177/1534650105277220

Flannery, R., Jr. (1995). *Posttraumatic stress disorder: The victim's guide to healing & recovery.* Crossroad.

Friedman, D., Goldman, R., Stern, Y., & Brown, T. (2009). The brain's orienting response: An event-related functional magnetic resonance imaging investigation. *Human Brain Mapping, 30*(4), 1144–1154. https://doi.org/10.1002/hbm.20587

Gauhar, M., & Wajid, Y. (2016). The efficacy of EMDR in the treatment of depression. *Journal of EMDR Practice and Research, 10*(2), 59–69. https://doi.org/10.1891/1933-3196.10.2.59

Gauvreau, P., & Bouchard, S. (2008). Preliminary evidence for the efficacy of EMDR in treating generalized anxiety disorder. *Journal of EMDR Practice and Research, 2*(1), 26–40. https://doi.org/10.1891/1933-3196.2.1.26

Gold, S. D., Marx, B. P., Soler-Baillo, J. M., & Sloan, D. M. (2005). Is life stress more traumatic than traumatic stress? *Journal of Anxiety Disorders, 19,* 687–698. https://doi.org/10.1016/j.janxdis.2004.06.002.

Grand, D., & Goldberg, A. (2011). *This is your brain on sports: Beating blocks, slumps and performance anxiety for good!* Dog Ear Publishing.

Gunter, R. W., & Bodner, G. E. (2008). How eye movements affect unpleasant memories: Support for a working-memory account. *Behaviour Research and Therapy, 46*(8), 913–931. https://doi.org/10.1016/j.brat.2008.04.006

Harford, P. M. (2010). The integrative use of EMDR and clinical hypnosis in the treatment of adults abused as children. *Journal of EMDR Practice and Research, 4*(2), 60–75. https://doi.org/10.1891/1933-3196.4.2.60

Heim, C., Plotsky, P. M., & Nemeroff, C. B. (2004). Importance of studying the contributions of early adverse experience to neurobiological findings in depression. *Neuropsychopharmacology, 29,* 641–648. https://doi.org/10.1038/sj.npp.1300397

Heins, M., Simons, C., Lataste, T., Pfeifer, S., Versmissen, D., Lardinois, M., Marcelis, M., Delespaul, P., Krabbendam, L., van Os, J., Myin-Germeys, I. (2011). Childhood trauma and psychosis: A case-control and case-sibling comparison across different levels of genetic liability, psychopathology, and type of trauma. *American Journal of Psychiatry, 168,* 1286–1294. https://doi.org/10.1176/appi.ajp.2011.10101531.

Hekmat, H., Groth, S., & Rogers, D. (1994). Pain ameliorating effect of eye movement desensitization. *Journal of Behavior Therapy and Experimental Psychiatry, 25*(2), 121–129. https://doi.org/10.1016/0005-7916(94)90004-3

Hofmann, A. (2009). The inverted EMDR standard protocol for unstable complex post-traumatic stress disorder. In M. Luber (Ed.), *Eye movement desensitization (EMDR) scripted protocols: Special populations* (pp. 313–328). Springer Publishing Company.

Homer, S. R., Deeprose, C., & Andrade, J. (2016). Negative mental imagery in public speaking anxiety: Forming cognitive resistance by taxing visuospatial working memory. *Journal of behavior therapy and experimental psychiatry, 50,* 77–82. https://doi.org/10.1016/j.jbtep.2015.05.004

Hornsveld, H. K., Landwehr, F., Stein, W., Stomp, M. P. H., Smeets, M. A. M., & van den Hout, M. A. (2010). Emotionality of loss-related memories is reduced after recall plus eye movements but not after recall plus music or recall only. *Journal of EMDR Practice and Research, 3*(4), 106–112. https://doi.org/10.1891/1933-3196.4.3.106

Kapoula, Z., Yang, Q., Bonnet, A., Bourtoire, P., & Sandretto, J. (2010). EMDR effects on pursuit eye movements. *PLoS ONE, 5*(5), e10762. https://doi.org/10.1371/journal.pone.0010762

Kavanagh, D. J., Freese, S., Andrade, J., & May, J. (2001). Effects of visuospatial tasks on desensitization to emotive memories. *British Journal of Clinical Psychology, 40,* 267–280. https://doi.org/10.1348/014466501163689

Kearns, M., & Engelhard I. M. (2015). Psychophysiological responsivity to script-driven imagery: An exploratory study of the effects of eye movements on public speaking flashforwards. *Frontiers in Psychiatry, 6,* 115. https://doi.org/10.3389/fpsyt.2015.00115

Kip, K. E., Sullivan, K. L., Lengacher, C. A., Rosenzweig, L., Hernandez, D. F., Kadel, R., Kozel, F. A., Shuman, A., Girling, S. A., Hardwick, M. J., & Diamond, D. M. (2013). Brief treatment of co-occurring post-traumatic stress and depressive symptoms by use of accelerated resolution therapy. *Frontiers in Psychiatry, 4*(11). https://doi.org/10.3389/fpsyt.2013.00011

Korn, D. L., Maxfield, L., Stickgold, R., & Smyth, N. J. (2018). *EMDR Fidelity Rating Scale (EFRS), version 2.* https://emdrresearchfoundation.org/research-grants/emdr-fidelity-rating-scale/

Kristjánsdóttir, K., & Lee, C. W. (2011). A comparison of visual versus auditory concurrent tasks on reducing the distress and vividness of aversive auto-biographical memories. *Journal of EMDR Practice and Research, 5*(2), 34–41. https://doi.org/10.1891/1933-3196.5.2.34

Kuiken, D., Bears, M., Miall, D., & Smith, L. (2002). Eye movement desensitization reprocessing facilitates attentional orienting. *Imagination, Cognition and Personality, 21*(1), 3–20. https://doi.org/10.2190/L8JX-PGLC-B72R-KD7X

Kuiken, D., Chudleigh, M., & Racher, D. (2010). Bilateral eye movements, attentional flexibility and metaphor comprehension: The substrate of REM dreaming? *Dreaming, 20*, 227–247. https://doi.org/10.1037/a0020841

Lee, C. W., & Cuijpers, P. (2013). A meta-analysis of the contribution of eye movements in processing emotional memories. *Journal of Behavior Therapy and Experimental Psychiatry, 44*(2), 231–239. https://doi.org/10.1016/j.jbtep.2012.11.001

Lee, C. W., & Drummond, P. D. (2008). Effects of eye movement versus therapist instructions on the processing of distressing memories. *Journal of Anxiety Disorders, 22*(5), 801–808. https://doi.org/10.1016/j.janxdis.2007.08.007

Lee, C. W., Taylor, G., & Drummond, P. D. (2006). The active ingredient in EMDR: Is it traditional exposure or dual focus of attention? *Clinical Psychology and Psychotherapy, 13*(2), 97–107. https://doi.org/10.1002/cpp.479

Leer, A., Engelhard, I. M., & van den Hout, M. A. (2014). How eye movements in EMDR work: Changes in memory vividness and emotionality. *Journal of Behavior Therapy and Experimental Psychiatry, 45*(3), 396–401. https://doi.org/10.1016/j.jbtep.2014.04.004

Lilley, S. A., Andrade, J., Turpin, G., Sabin-Farrell, R., & Holmes, E. A. (2009). Visuospatial working memory interference with recollections of trauma. *British Journal of Clinical Psychology, 48*, 309–321. https://doi.org/10.1348/014466508X398943

Lipke, H. (1999). Comments on "thirty years of behavior therapy" and the promise of the application of scientific principles. *The Behavior Therapist, 22*, 11–14.

Lohr, J. M., Tolin, D. F., & Kleinknecht, R. A. (1995). An intensive investigation of eye movement desensitization of medical phobias. *Journal of Behavior Therapy and Experimental Psychiatry, 26*, 141–151. https://doi.org/10.1016/0887-6185(95)00036-4

Lohr, J. M., Tolin, D. F., & Kleinknecht, R. A. (1996). An intensive investigation of eye movement desensitization of claustrophobia. *Journal of Anxiety Disorders, 10*, 73–88. https://doi.org/10.1016/0887-6185(95)00036-4

MacCulloch, M. (2006). Effects of EMDR on previously abused child molesters: Theoretical reviews and preliminary findings from Ricci, Clayton, and Shapiro. *Journal of Forensic Psychiatry and Psychology, 17*(4), 531–537. https://doi.org/10.1080/14789940601075760

MacCulloch, M. J., & Feldman, P. (1996). Eye movement desensitisation treatment utilises the positive visceral element of the investigatory reflex to inhibit the memories of post-traumatic stress disorder: A theoretical analysis. *British Journal of Psychiatry, 169*(5), 571–579. https://doi.org/10.1192/bjp.169.5.571

Madrid, A., Skolek, S., & Shapiro, F. (2006). Repairing failures in bonding through EMDR. *Clinical Case Studies, 5*(4), 271–286. https://doi.org/10.1177/1534650104267403

Maxfield, L., Melnyk, W. T., & Hayman, C. A. G. (2008). A working memory explanation for the effects of eye movements in EMDR. *Journal of EMDR Practice and Research, 2*(4), 247–261. https://doi.org/10.1891/1933-3196.2.4.247

McGoldrick, T., Begum, M., & Brown, K. W. (2008). EMDR and olfactory reference syndrome: A case series. *Journal of EMDR Practice and Research, 2*(1), 63–68. https://doi.org/10.1891/19333196.2.1.63

Meares, A. (1960). *A system of medical hypnosis.* The Julian Press.

Miller, E., & Halpern, S. (1994). *Letting go of stress.* Inner Peace Music.

Mol, S. S. L., Arntz, A., Metsemakers, J. F. M., Dinant, G., Vilters-Van Montfort, P. A. P., & Knottnerus, A. (2005). Symptoms of post-traumatic stress disorder after non-traumatic events: Evidence from an open population study. *British Journal of Psychiatry, 186*, 494–499. https://doi.org/10.1192/bjp.186.6.494

Nazari, H., Momeni, N., Jariani, M., & Tarrahi, M. J. (2011). Comparison of eye movement desensitization and reprocessing with citalopram in treatment of obsessive-compulsive disorder. *International Journal of Psychiatry in Clinical Practice, 15*(4), 270–274. https://doi.org/10.3109/13651501.2011.590210

Nicosia, G. J. (1995). A brief note: Eye movement desensitization and reprocessing is not hypnosis. *Dissociation, 8*(1), 69.

Nieuwenhuis, S., Elzinga, B. M., Ras, P. H., Berends, F., Duijs, P., Samara, Z., & Slagter, H. A. (2013). Bilateral saccadic eye movements and tactile stimulation, but not auditory stimulation, enhance memory retrieval. *Brain and Cognition, 81*, 52–56. https://doi.org/10.1016/j.bandc.2012.10.003

Obradovic, J., Bush, N. R., Stamperdahl, J., Adler, N. E., & Boyce, W. T. (2010). Biological sensitivity to context: The interactive effects of stress reactivity and family adversity on socioemotional behavior and school readiness. *Child Development, 1*, 270–289. https://doi.org/10.1111/j.1467-8624.2009.01394.x

Pace, P. (2003). *Connecting ego states through time with EMDR and lifespan integration* [Conference presentation]. Eighth EMDR International Association Conference, Denver, CO.

Pagani, M., Di Lorenzo, G., Monaco, L., Niolu, C., Siracusano, A., Verardo, A. R., Lauretti, G., Fernandez, I., Nicolais, G., Cogolo, P., & Ammaniti, M. (2011). Pretreatment, intratreatment, and posttreatment EEG imaging of EMDR: Methodology and preliminary results from a single case. *Journal of EMDR Practice and Research, 5*(2), 42–56. https://doi.org/10.1891/19333196.5.2.42

Pagani, M., DiLorenzo, G., Verardo, A. R., Nicolais, G., Monaco, L., Lauretti, G., Russo, R., Niolu, C., Ammaniti, M. Fernandex, I., & Siracusano, A. (2012). Neurobiological correlates of EMDR monitoring—an EEG study. *PLoS ONE, 7*(9), 1–12. https://doi.org/10.1371/journal.pone.0045753

Parker, A., Buckley, S., & Dagnall, N. (2009). Reduced misinformation effects following saccadic bilateral eye movements. *Brain and Cognition, 69*, 89–97. https://doi.org/10.1016/j.bandc.2008.05.009

Parker, A., & Dagnall, N. (2007). Effects of bilateral eye movements on gist based false recognition in the DRM paradigm. *Brain and Cognition, 63*, 221–225. https://doi.org/10.1016/j.bandc.2006.08.005

Parker, A., Relph, S., & Dagnall, N. (2008). Effects of bilateral eye movement on retrieval of item, associative and contextual information. *Neuropsychology, 22*, 136–145. https://doi.org/10.1037/0894-4105.22.1.136

Patel, G. J., & McDowall, J. (2016). The role of eye movements in EMDR: Conducting eye movements while concentrating on negative autobiographical memories results in fewer intrusions. *Journal of EMDR Practice and Research, 10*(1), 13–22. https://doi.org/10.1891/1933-3196.10.1.13

Perkins, B., & Rouanzoin, C. (2002). A critical evaluation of current views regarding eye movement desensitization and reprocessing (EMDR): Clarifying points of confusion. *Journal of Clinical Psychology, 58*(1), 77–97. https://doi.org/10.1002/jclp.1130

Pitman, R. K., Orr, S. P., Altman, B., Longpre, R. E., Poire, R. E., & Macklin, M. L. (1996). Emotional processing during eye movement desensitization and reprocessing therapy of Vietnam veterans with chronic posttraumatic stress disorder. *Comprehensive Psychiatry, 37*, 419–429. https://doi.org/10.1016/S0010-440X(96)90025-5

Propper, R. E., & Christman, S. D. (2008). Interhemispheric interaction and saccadic horizontal eye movements: Implications for episodic memory, EMDR, and PTSD. *Journal of EMDR Practice and Research, 2*(4), 269–281. https://doi.org/10.1891/1933-3196.2.4.269.

Propper, R. E., Pierce, J., Geisler, M. W., Christman, S. D., & Bellorado, N. (2007). Effect of bilateral eye movements on frontal interhemispheric gamma EEG coherence: Implications for EMDR therapy. *Journal of Nervous Mental Disorders, 195*(9), 785–788. https://doi.org/10.1097/NMD.0b013e318142cf73

Raboni, M. R., Tufik, S., & Suchecki, D. (2006). Treatment of PTSD by eye movement desensitization reprocessing (EMDR) improves sleep quality, quality of life, and perception of stress. *Annals of the New York Academy of Sciences, 1071*(1), 508–513. https://doi.org/10.1196/annals.1364.054

Ray, A. L., & Zbik, A. (2001). Cognitive behavioral therapies and beyond. In C. D. Tollison, J. R. Satterhwaite, & J. W. Tollison (Eds.), *Practical pain management* (3rd ed., pp. 189–208). Lippincott.

Read, J., Fosse, R., Moskowitz, A., & Perry, B. (2014). The traumagenic neurodevelopmental model of psychosis revisited. *Neuropsychiatry, 4*(1), 65–79. https://doi.org/10.2217/NPY.13.89

Renfrey, G., & Spates, C. R. (1994). Eye movement desensitization: A partial dismantling study. *Journal of Behavior Therapy and Experimental Psychiatry, 25*, 231–239. https://doi.org/10.1016/0005-7916(94)90023-X

Ricci, R. J., Clayton, C. A., & Shapiro, F. (2006). Some effects of EMDR on previously abused child molesters: Theoretical reviews and preliminary findings. *Journal of Forensic Psychiatry and Psychology, 17*(4), 538–562. https://doi.org/10.1080/14789940601070431

Rimini, D., Molinari, F., Liboni, W., Balbo, M. Daro, R., Viotti, E., & Fernandez, I. (2016). Effect of ocular movements during eye movement desensitization and reprocessing (EMDR) therapy: A near-infrared spectroscopy study. *PlusOne, 11*(10), e0164379. https://doi.org/10.1371/journal.pone.0164379

Robinson, J. S., & Larson, C. (2010). Are traumatic events necessary to elicit symptoms of posttraumatic stress? *Psychological Trauma: Theory, Research, Practice, and Policy, 2*, 71–76. https://doi.org/10.1037/a0018954

Rogers, S., & Silver, S. M. (2002). Is EMDR an exposure therapy? A review of trauma protocols. *Journal of Clinical Psychology, 58*(1), 43–59. https://doi.org/10.1002/jclp.1128

Rogers, S., Silver, S. M., Goss, J., Obenchain, J., Willis, A., & Whitney, R. L. (1999). A single session, group study of exposure and eye movement desensitization and reprocessing in treating posttraumatic stress disorder among Vietnam War veterans: Preliminary data. *Journal of Anxiety Disorders, 13*(1–2), 119–130. https://doi.org/10.1016/S0887-6185(98)00043-7

Russell, M. C. (2008). Treating traumatic amputation-related phantom limb pain: A case study utilizing eye movement desensitization and reprocessing within the Armed Services. *Clinical Case Studies, 7*(2), 136–153. https://doi.org/10.1177/1534650107306292

Russell, M. C., & Figley, C. R. (2013). *Treating traumatic stress injuries in military personnel: An EMDR practitioner's guide.* Routledge Publishing.

Sabourin, M. E., Cutcomb, S. E., Crawford, H. J., & Pribram, K. (1990). EEG correlates of hypnotic susceptibility and hypnotic trance: Spectral analysis and coherence. *International Journal of Psychophysiology, 10*, 125–142. https://doi.org/10.1016/0167-8760(90)90027-b

Sack, M., Hofmann, A., Wizelman, L., & Lempa, W. (2008). Psychophysiological changes during EMDR and treatment outcome. *Journal of EMDR Practice and Research, 2*(4), 239–246. https://doi.org/10.1891/1933-3196.2.4.239

Sack, M., Lempa, W., Steinmetz, A., Lamprecht, F., & Hofmann, A. (2008). Alterations in autonomic tone during trauma exposure using eye movement desensitization and reprocessing (EMDR)—Results of a preliminary investigation. *Journal of Anxiety Disorders, 22*(7), 1264–1271. https://doi.org/10.1016/j.janxdis.2008.01.007

Sack, M., Zehl, S., Otti, A., Lahmann, C., Henningsen, P., Kruse, J., & Stingl, M. (2016). A comparison of dual attention, eye movements, and exposure only during eye movement desensitization and reprocessing for posttraumatic stress disorder: Results from a randomized clinical trial. *Psychotherapy and Psychosomatics, 85*(6), 357–365. https://doi.org/10.1159/000447671

Samara, Z., Bernet, M., Elzinga, B. M., Heleen, A., Slagter, H. A., & Nieuwenhuis, S. (2011). Do horizontal saccadic eye movements increase interhemispheric coherence? Investigation of a hypothesized neural mechanism underlying EMDR. *Frontiers in Psychiatry, 2*, 4. https://doi.org/10.3389/fpsyt.2011.00004

Sanderson, A., & Carpenter, R. (1992). Eye movement desensitization versus image confrontation: A single-session crossover study of 58 phobic subjects. *Journal of Behavior Therapy and Experimental Psychiatry, 23*, 269–275. https://doi.org/10.1016/0005-7916(92)90049-o

Schneider, J., Hofmann, A., Rost, C., & Shapiro, F. (2007). EMDR and phantom limb pain: Theoretical implications, case study, and treatment guidelines. *Journal of EMDR Practice and Research, 1*(1), 31–45. https://doi.org/10.1891/1933-3196.1.1.31

Schneider, J., Hofmann, A., Rost, C., & Shapiro, F. (2008). EMDR in the treatment of chronic phantom limb pain. *Pain Medicine, 9*(1), 76–82. https://doi.org/10.1111/j.15264637.2007.00299.x

Schubert, S. J., Lee, C. W., & Drummond, P. D. (2011). The efficacy and psychophysiological correlates of dual-attention tasks in eye movement desensitization and reprocessing (EMDR). *Journal of Anxiety Disorders, 25*, 1–11. https://doi.org/10.1016/j.janxdis.2010.06.024

Servan-Schreiber, D., Schooler, J., Dew, M. A., Carter, C., & Bartone, P. (2006). Eye movement desensitization and reprocessing for posttraumatic stress disorder: A pilot blinded, randomized study of stimulation type. *Psychotherapy and Psychosomatics, 75*(5), 290–297. https://doi.org/10.1159/000093950

Shapiro, E., & Laub, B. (2014). The recent traumatic episode protocol (R-TEP): An integrative protocol for early EMDR intervention (EEI). In M. Luber (Ed.), *Implementing EMDR early mental health interventions for man-made and natural disasters: Models, scripted protocols, and summary sheets* (pp. 193–207). Springer Publishing Company.

Shapiro, F. (1989a). Efficacy of the eye movement desensitization procedure in the treatment of traumatic memories. *Journal of Traumatic Stress, 2*(2), 199–223. https://doi.org/10.1007/BF00974159

Shapiro, F. (1989b). Eye movement desensitization: A new treatment for post-traumatic stress disorder. *Journal of Behavior Therapy and Experimental Psychiatry, 20*(3), 211–217. https://doi.org/10.1016/0005-7916(89)90025-6

Shapiro, F. (1995). *Eye movement desensitization and reprocessing: Basic principles, protocols and procedures* (1st ed.). Guilford Press.

Shapiro, F. (2001). *Eye movement desensitization and reprocessing: Basic principles, protocols and procedures* (2nd ed.). Guilford Press.

Shapiro, F. (2002). *EMDR as an integrative psychotherapy approach: Experts of diverse orientations explore the paradigm prism.* American Psychological Association Press.

Shapiro, F. (2006). *EMDR: New notes on adaptive information processing with case formulations principles, forms, scripts and worksheets, version 1.1.* EMDR Institute.

Shapiro, F. (2007a). EMDR, adaptive information processing, and case conceptualization. *Journal of EMDR Practice and Research, 1*(2), 68–87. https://doi.org/10.1891/1933-3196.1.2.68

Shapiro, F. (2007b). EMDR and case conceptualization from an adaptive information processing perspective. In F. Shapiro, F. Kaslow, & L. Maxfield (Eds.), *Handbook of EMDR and family therapy processes* (pp. 3–36). John Wiley.

Shapiro, F. (2009–2017a). *The EMDR approach to psychotherapy—EMDR Institute basic training course: Weekend 1 of the two part basic training.* EMDR Institute.

Shapiro, F. (2009–2017b). *The EMDR approach to psychotherapy—EMDR Institute basic training course: Weekend 2 of the two part basic training.* EMDR Institute.

Shapiro, F. (2012a). EMDR therapy: An overview of current and future research. *European Review of Applied Psychology, 62*(4), 193–195. https://doi.org/10.1016/j.erap.2012.09.005

Shapiro, F. (2012b). *Getting past your past: Take control of your life with self-help techniques from EMDR therapy.* Rodale Books.

Shapiro, F. (2014). The role of eye movement desensitization and reprocessing (EMDR) therapy in medicine: Addressing the psychological and physical symptoms stemming from adverse life experience. *Permanente Journal, 18*(1), 71–77. https://doi.org/10.7812/TPP/13-098

Shapiro, F. (2018). *Eye movement desensitization and reprocessing: Basic principles, protocols and procedures* (3rd ed.). Guilford Press.

Shapiro, F., & Forrest, M. S. (2016). *EMDR: The breakthrough therapy for overcoming anxiety, stress, and trauma* (2nd ed.). Basic Books.

Shapiro, F., Kaslow, F. W., & Maxfield, M. (2007). *Handbook of EMDR and family therapy processes.* John Wiley.

Sharpley, C. F., Montgomery, I. M., & Scalzo, L. (1996). Comparative efficacy of EMDR and alternative procedures in reducing the vividness of mental images. *Scandinavian Journal of Behaviour Therapy, 25*, 37–42. https://doi.org/10.1080/16506079609456006

Smeets, M. A. M., Dijs, M. W., Pervan, I., Engelhard, I. M., & van den Hout, M. (2012). Time-course of eye movement-related decrease in vividness and emotionality of unpleasant autobiographical memories. *Memory, 20*(4), 346–357. https://doi.org/10.1080/09658211.2012.665462

Solomon, R. M., & Shapiro, F. (2008). EMDR and the adaptive information processing model: Potential mechanisms of change. *Journal of EMDR Practice and Research, 2*(4), 315–325. https://doi.org/10.1891/1933-3196.2.4.315

Solomon, S. D., Gerrity, E. T., & Muff, A. M. (1992). Efficacy of treatments for posttraumatic stress disorder: An empirical review. *Journal of the American Medical Association, 268*, 633–638. https://doi.org/10.1001/jama.1992.03490050081031

Spates, C. R., Koch, E., Cusack, K., Pagoto, S., & Waller, S. (2009). Eye movement desensitization and reprocessing. In E. B. Foa, T. M. Keane, M. J. Friedman, & J. A. Cohen (Eds.), *Effective treatments for PTSD: Practice guidelines from the International Society for Traumatic Stress Studies* (2nd ed., pp. 279–305). Guilford Press.

Stickgold, R. (2002). EMDR: A putative neurobiological mechanism of action. *Journal of Clinical Psychology, 58*(1), 61–75. https://doi.org/10.1002/jclp.1129

Stickgold, R. (2008). Sleep-dependent memory processing and EMDR action. *Journal of EMDR Practice and Research, 2*(4), 289–299. https://doi.org/10.1891/1933-3196.2.4.289

Suzuki, A., Josselyn, S. A., Frankland, P. W., Masushige, S., Silva, A. J., & Satoshi, K. (2004). Memory reconsolidation and extinction have distinct temporal and biochemical signatures. *Journal of Neuroscience, 24*(20), 4787–4795. https://doi.org/10.1523/jneurosci.5491-03.2004

Teicher, M. H., Samson, J. A., Sheu, Y.-S., Polcari, A., & McGreenery, C. E. (2010). Hurtful words: Association of exposure to peer verbal abuse with elevated psychiatric symptom scores and corpus callosum abnormalities. *American Journal of Psychiatry, 167*, 1464–1471. https://doi.org/10.1176/appi.ajp.2010.10010030

Uribe, M. E. R., & Ramirez, E. O. L. (2006). The effect of EMDR therapy on the negative information processing on patients who suffer depression. *Revista Electrónica de Motivación y Emoción, 9*, 23–24.

van den Berg, D. P. G., & van der Gaag, M. (2012). Treating trauma in psychosis with EMDR: A pilot study. *Journal of Behavior Therapy and Experimental Psychiatry, 43*(1), 664–671. https://doi.org/10.1016/j.jbtep.2011.09.011

van den Hout, M. A., Engelhard, I. M., Rijkeboer, M. M., Koekebakker, J., Hornsveld, H., Leer, A., Toffolo, M. B. J., Akse, N. (2011). EMDR: Eye movements superior to beeps in taxing working memory and reducing vividness of recollections. *Behaviour Research and Therapy, 49*, 92–98. https://doi.org/10.1016/j.brat.2010.11.003

van den Hout, M. A., & Engelhard, I. (2012). How does EMDR work? *Journal of Experimental Psychopathology, 3*, 724–738. https://doi.org/10.5127/jep.028212

van den Hout, M. A., Engelhard, I. M., Smeets, M. A., Hornsveld, H., Hoogeveen, E., and de Heer, E. (2010). Counting during recall: Taxing of working memory and reduced vividness and emotionality of negative memories. *Applied Cognitive Psychology, 24*(3), 303–311. https://doi.org/10.1002/acp.1677

van den Hout, M. A., Muris, P., Salemink, E., & Kindt, M. (2001). Autobiographical memories become less vivid and emotional after eye movements. *British Journal of Clinical Psychology, 40*(2), 121–130. https://doi.org/10.1348/014466501163535

van den Hout, M. A., Rijkeboer, M. M., Engelhard, I. M., Klugkist, I., Hornsveld, H., Toffolo, M. J., & Cath, D. C. (2012). Tones inferior to eye movements in the EMDR treatment of PTSD. *Behaviour Research and Therapy, 50*(5), 275–279. https://doi.org/10.1016/j.brat.2012.02.001

van der Kolk, B. A., Spinazzola, J., Blaustein, M. E., Hopper, J. W., Hopper, E. K., Korn, D. L., & Simpson, W. B. (2007). Randomized clinical trial of eye movement desensitization and reprocessing (EMDR), fluoxetine, and pill placebo in the treatment of posttraumatic stress disorder: Treatment effects and long-term maintenance. *Journal of Clinical Psychiatry, 68*(1), 37–46. https://doi.org/10.4088/JCP.v68n0105

van Etten, M. L., & Taylor, S. (1998). Comparative efficacy of treatments for posttraumatic stress disorder: A meta-analysis. *Clinical Psychology & Psychotherapy, 5*, 126–144. https://doi.org/10.1002/(SICI)1099-0879(199809)

van Schie, K., Engelhard, I. M., Klugkist, I., & van den Hout, M. A. (2016). Blurring emotional memories using eye movements: Individual differences and speed of eye movements. *European Journal of Psychotraumatology, 7*, 29476. https://doi.org/10.3402/ejpt.v7.29476

van Veen, S. C., Engelhard, I. M., & van den Hout, M. A. (2016). The effects of eye movements on emotional memories: using an objective measure of cognitive load. *European Journal of Psychotraumatology, 7*, 1–11. https://doi.org/10.3402/ejpt.v7.30122

van Veen, S. C., van Schie, K., Wijngaards-de Meij, L. D., Littel, M., Engelhard, I. M., & van den Hout, M. A. (2015). Speed matters: Relationship between speed of eye movements and modification of aversive autobiographical memories. *Frontiers in Psychiatry, 6*(45), 1–9. https://doi.org/10.3389/fpsyt.2015.00045

Varese, F., Smeets, F., Drukker, M., Lieverse, R., Lataster, T., Viechtbauer, W., Read, J., van Os, J., Bentall, R. P. (2012). Childhood adversities increase the risk of psychosis: A meta-analysis of patient-control, prospective- and cross-sectional cohort studies. *Schizophrenia Bulletin, 38*(4), 661–671. https://doi.org/10.1093/schbul/sbs050

Wesselmann, D., & Potter, A. E. (2009). Change in adult attachment status following treatment with EMDR: Three case studies. *Journal of EMDR Practice and Research, 3*(3), 178–191. https://doi.org/10.1891/1933-3196.3.3.178

Wilensky, M. (2006). Eye movement desensitization and reprocessing (EMDR) as a treatment for phantom limb pain. *Journal of Brief Therapy, 5*(1), 31–44. https://doi.org/10.1186/1471-2474-14-256

Wilson, D., Silver, S. M., Covi, W., & Foster, S. (1996). Eye movement desensitization and reprocessing: Effectiveness and autonomic correlates. *Journal of Behavior Therapy and Experimental Psychiatry, 27*, 219–229. https://doi.org/10.1016/S0005-7916(96)00026-2

Wolpe, J. (1990). *The practice of behavior therapy* (4th ed.). Pergamon Press.

Zarghi, A. (2015). Memory editing with emphasizing the role of EM in EMDR. *International Clinical Neuroscience Journal, 2*(2), 66–70. https://doi.org/10.22037/icnj.v2i2.9473

2

Eight Phases of EMDR Therapy

It's all knowing what to start with. If you start in the right place and follow all the steps, you will get to the right end.—Elizabeth Moon (*The Speed of Dark*, 2003)

INTRODUCTION

EMDR therapy is an eight-phase protocol. Dr. Shapiro and the EMDR International Association (EMDRIA) are precise about what EMDR therapy is and what it is not; and, if you eliminate one of the eight phases, it cannot be called EMDR therapy. The intention of this chapter is to briefly touch on some of the eight phases and more extensively on others. An effort is made to enhance and expand on key areas that can assist the clinician in client selection, target selection, and adaptive resolution. Table 2.1 offers a description of the goals and objectives of each phase as described by Shapiro (2009–2017, 2018).

TABLE 2.1 Eight Phases of EMDR Therapy

1. History-Taking and Treatment Planning—Take a general history from the client and develop an appropriate treatment plan.	Has all the relevant client information been gathered (e.g., life experiences, childhood development, family of origin, cultural and gender issues, ethnic and religious influences, familial and peer relationships)?
	Has risk or crisis assessment on the client been performed?
	Has the client been evaluated for affect tolerance, integrative capacity, trust, and self-regulation?

(continued)

TABLE 2.1 Eight Phases of EMDR Therapy (continued)

Has the client's history of attachment been assessed?

Have the client's strengths and internal/external supports and resources been assessed?

Have the client's selection and readiness been determined?

Have all the standard history-taking questionnaires and diagnostic psychometrics been administered?

Has the client been screened for dissociative disorders?

Have the client's developmental deficits been identified?

Has the client's level of complexity and resources to set the pace of treatment been determined?

Have needed skills and behaviors been identified?

What experiences have set the pathology for the client's present symptoms?

Have potential targets and sequencing of targets (i.e., past, present, future) been identified and secondary gains addressed?

If appropriate, has the client's touchstone event(s) been identified?

Have the client's current psychosocial factors been evaluated?

Has all relevant background information been obtained?

Is the client suitable for the EMDR reprocessing phases of treatment?

Is the client able to access identified experiences and maintain dual awareness so that reprocessing is able to occur?

Have safety and trust been established between the clinician and client?

Is the client able and has the client agreed to provide the clinician accurate feedback in terms of internal experiences during the reprocessing of a memory?

Have medical considerations been assessed and addressed?

Has the treatment plan been developed collaboratively with the client, and is it consistent with the treatment goals?

Are there any events a client is not ready to discuss?

(*continued*)

TABLE 2.1 Eight Phases of EMDR Therapy (continued)

2. Preparation—Introduce and prepare client for EMDR therapy	Has an appropriate relationship been established with the client?
	Has the client been formally introduced to EMDR therapy?
	Has the client been educated about the EMDR process?
	Have the client's fears been assessed and addressed?
	Has informed consent been established via the client's verbal understanding and agreement to continue with EMDR therapy?
	Has the client's stability been assured?
	Can the client self-soothe?
	Have coping strategies (i.e., stabilization/affect tolerance, train metaphor, stop signal, safe/calm place) been introduced?
	Has BLS been introduced (i.e., type, speed, distance, seating arrangement)?
	Have timing considerations been taken into account (e.g., client has an important meeting or clinician is going on vacation)?
	Are there current life stressors in the client's life that may be exacerbated as a result of EMDR therapy?
	Again, is the client able to maintain dual awareness?
3. Assessment—Access, activate, and assess target using three-pronged approach for EMDR processing and primary aspects of memory (image, NC, PC, VoC, emotions, SUD, and body location)	Has a target image been obtained? If no image is identified, has the client answered the question, "When you think of the memory, what do you get?"
	Have the NC and PC been identified?
	Has the validity of PC been rated using the VoC scale?
	Have the relevant emotions been identified?
	Has the level of disturbance been rated using Wolpe's SUD scale?
	Have discomfort or physical sensations experienced by the client been identified?
4. Desensitization—Reprocess selected targets (and all related channels of association) toward an adaptive resolution (SUD = 0)	Be sure to:
	Begin the reprocessing by bringing up the image, NC, and location of negative physical sensations.
	Use a speed of BLS that is tolerable for the client, starting with about 20 passes and customizing the number of passes to the client's response. Generally, 20–24 round trips to start, lengthen to 36–40 as needed.

(continued)

TABLE 2.1 Eight Phases of EMDR Therapy (continued)

	Avoid talking, analyzing, summarizing, or clarifying. Return to target only after the end of a channel has been reached. Do not interrupt a client's abreactive experience, but do provide periodic supportive statements to maintain dual focus. Use strategies for blocked processing and cognitive interweaves sparingly and effectively. Ask for a SUD rating only when all channels of association have been completely cleared or when you are unsure if the client is moving. Determine if the desensitization is complete before moving on to installation. Does SUD = 0? Check to see if ecological validity applies if SUD >0 (i.e., greater than 0). Have all channels of association been fully processed?
5. Installation—Recheck appropriateness and validity of PC Utilizing BLS, integrate positive effects when linked to original target (VoC = 7)	Does PC still fit? Can the client easily pair the target memory and PC? Add BLS (speed and frequency consistent with what is used in Phases 4 and 5). Customize to the client's response as needed. Does VoC = 7? Are there emerging blocking beliefs or feeder memories? Is ecological validity appropriate?
6. Body Scan—Complete processing of residual elements associated with traumatic memories by linking original event and PC and check for bodily discomfort. Use BLS to clear any remaining physical disturbance. (Completed treatment = clear body scan)	Is body scan clear? Has all residual disturbance associated with the target been fully processed? Are there unresolved negative physical sensations that need to be reprocessed? If needed, use sets of BLS (speed and frequency consistent with what is used in Phases 4 and 5) until the client reports a clear body scan.
7. Closure—Appropriately close a complete or incomplete session	Has the client been briefed as to what to expect after a complete or incomplete session? Has the client's stability been ensured after EMDR processing (e.g., shifting states from a focus on the memory to full, present, grounded awareness to minimize difficulties between sessions)?

(continued)

TABLE 2.1 Eight Phases of EMDR Therapy (continued)

	Has the client been requested to keep a log? Does the client need stabilizing using the Safe (Calm) Place or other regulatory exercise?
8. Reevaluation and use of the EMDR standard three-pronged protocol	Has the successful completion of relevant material been determined? Has the client's log been checked? Has the client's SUD level been rechecked and memory fully reprocessed, if necessary? Has anything new emerged since the last session? Does the client need to complete the reprocessing of the memory targeted the last session to SUD = 0, VoC = 7, and is body scan clear, or move to a new target? Have all three prongs (i.e., past trauma, present triggers, future desired directions) been identified, processed (or installed)?

Abbreviations: BLS, bilateral stimulation; NC, negative cognition; PC, positive cognition; SUD, Subjective Units of Disturbance; VoC, Validity of Cognition.

PHASE 1: CLIENT HISTORY AND TREATMENT PLANNING

The History-Taking and Treatment Planning Phase has a threefold purpose. The data collection that occurs in this phase provides all the information customarily acquired by most clinicians, as well as providing the client with the information needed for informed consent. This phase drives the client selection process and helps the clinician identify potential treatment targets that emerge from examining the positive and negative events in a client's past, present, and future. This is the phase in which the clinician determines whether a client is able to tolerate reprocessing. These factors include client stability, integrative capacity, affect and distress tolerance, attachment history, readiness to change, and current psychosocial factors. The client's clinical presentation aids the clinician in determining the need for titration of history-taking, as well as the need for additional resources. This phase of EMDR supplements the clinician's normal history-taking procedures.

INFORMED CONSENT AND SUITABILITY FOR TREATMENT

In Phase 1, the client gives consent to the use of EMDR therapy based on their appreciation and understanding of the facts and implications of possible treatment outcomes. In this first phase, the clinician begins to gather information pertinent to the client's readiness, willingness, stability, and ability to engage in the EMDR process. The clinician will take a complete and thorough client history using whatever methodology they are comfortable with, identify the presenting problems, and establish treatment goals in the same way they might for clients with whom they will not be using EMDR therapy. The next step is to utilize this information plus valuable data collected from risk or crisis assessments, depression

TABLE 2.2 History-Taking and Treatment Planning

PURPOSE

- The data collection that occurs in this phase provides the client with all the information needed for informed consent and drives the process by which the client's appropriateness and readiness for EMDR reprocessing (i.e., Phases 3–6) is evaluated.
- A biopsychosocial and diagnostic interview, which evaluates a client's treatment goals, affect and self-regulation skills and other resources, and readiness for EMDR treatment, is conducted.
- It helps the clinician identify potential treatment targets that emerge from examining the positive and negative events in a client's past, present, and future.
- This is the phase in which the clinician begins to know the client and develops an AIP-informed case conceptualization and treatment plan that guides Phases 2 to 8. This plan represents the overall treatment contract between the clinician and the client.
- Potential targets, including touchstone events if available, are identified.

Abbreviation: AIP, adaptive information processing.

inventories, diagnostic and dissociative evaluations, and the presence of internal and external supports, along with the client's strengths and limitations, to assess a client's suitability for treatment. During the biopsychosocial and diagnostic interview, the clinician attempts to identify a client's early childhood resources and strengths, negative experiences, and nodal events (e.g., abuse, neglect, loss of betrayal, medical issues, development deficits, memory lapses). See Chapter 8, Informed Consent and EMDR Therapy, for more information on EMDR therapy and informed consent.

To begin an initial assessment of the client's appropriateness for EMDR therapy, the following questions need to be answered: Is the client ready for EMDR therapy? Will the client benefit from EMDR therapy? Is the client able to self-regulate? Finally, does the client consent to the use of EMDR therapy? See Table 2.2 for the purpose.

CLIENT SELECTION CRITERIA

The client selection criteria are diverse and obtained from various sources. First, examine safety factors relevant to the client to assist in determining appropriate candidates for EMDR therapy. For instance, does the client possess a sufficient level of trust? Before initiating EMDR reprocessing, it is essential to ensure that there is an *adequate level of trust* between client and clinician. For many clients, trust reserves are often depleted by the time they get to EMDR treatment. In addition, the clinician may be asking the client to share intimate details of their life. Facts that they have never shared with anyone may emerge during EMDR therapy. Although clients are not required to share all details with the clinician, this may occur or could be helpful from the client's perspective. That is why it is important to build and establish adequate rapport with the client, sometimes in very short periods of time, to maximize the success of the EMDR processing. A client who has a history of severe abuse is screened more intensely than others to identify their appropriateness and readiness for this treatment, as trust is likely to be more difficult to develop.

The goal for the client is to trust enough to proceed safely with EMDR processing. The necessary levels of trust will vary with the complexity and the trauma experiences of the client.

CLIENT'S SUITABILITY AND READINESS FOR EMDR THERAPY

Shapiro (2009–2017a, 2009–2017b) recommends checking the client's stability, integrative capacity, affect tolerance and regulation, attachment history, and readiness to change before any reprocessing takes place. The goal here is to discern whether or not the client is able to board and ride the train down the track and arrive safety at the final destination.

1. **Stability:** Has the clinician assessed the client's current level of psychosocial functioning? Has the clinician evaluated the client's ability to control behavior and/or manage emotional responses? Has the clinician determined the availability of the client's internal and external resources?
2. **Integrative capacity:** Does the client have the ability to stay present or to maintain dual awareness, present a coherent narrative, or to take in and utilize new information? Does the client have access to positive (integrated) memory networks?
3. **Affect tolerance/regulation:** Does the client have the ability to access and tolerate a positive and/or negative state? Does the client have the ability to manage their experience for a period of time? Can the client sustain high or varying levels of emotion throughout the EMDR process? Does the client have the ability to shift from one emotional state to another?
4. **Attachment history:** What is the consistency and duration of the client's early relationships? What is the level of disruption, if any, of the client's early relationships? What is the client's ability to establish and maintain relationships of any kind?
5. **Readiness to change:** Are there any external factors (e.g., child, spousal, employment, or legal demands) that may impede or interfere with or preclude a client's successful treatment outcome? Have all complicating factors (e.g., limits, secondary/tertiary gains/losses) been identified? Does the client have a current and active issue with substance abuse or other compulsive disorders? Does the client have the capacity and motivation to change?
6. **Behaviors that interfere with EMDR therapy:** In order to maintain a client's safety and the continuing integrity of the therapeutic relationship, it is recommended that any behaviors (e.g., addictions, obsessions, and compulsions; avoidance or withdrawal; compliance issues, such as coming late, cancellations, payment) that may potentially interfere with processing be identified and addressed prior to reprocessing (Shapiro, 2009–2017a, 2009–2017b).

As the client's needs and reactions to the treatment change after each session, the clinician needs to constantly reevaluate suitability and readiness, as well as benefits. This evaluation is a process, not a one-time event.

In addition, the clinician also needs to take into consideration the client's responses to the following questions:

■ Does the client have a medical condition that might preclude them as a candidate for the EMDR reprocessing phases (e.g., a stress-related illness, epilepsy or pseudoseizures, heart condition, high-risk pregnancy, withdrawal from substances)?
■ Are there any contraindications for the use of eye movements (e.g., eye pain, detached retina, corneal scratches)?

- What is the age of the client?
- What medications does the client take that may impact the speed and generalization of the EMDR reprocessing phases (i.e., benzodiazepines)?
- Is the client inpatient or outpatient?
- Is the client a danger to others?
- Does the client have a history of violent or assaultive behavior?
- Is there a history of neurological impairment that may prevent the client from succeeding with the EMDR process?
- Is the client physically able to sustain intense emotion?
- Has the client been in counseling before? With whom? Why? How long? Does the client have a history of treatment failure?
- Does the client have a history of alcohol or drug abuse? If so, would an increase in use or relapse be life-threatening? Is the client actively using alcohol or drugs or recently entered recovery?
- Has the client had any serious suicide attempts? Is there current suicide risk?
- Has the client engaged in self-mutilation (e.g., cutting, burning, or picking)?
- Have indicators of poor psychological development been identified and addressed (e.g., years of unsuccessful psychotherapy, present memory lapses, depersonalization, derealization, somatic symptoms, flashbacks, intrusive thoughts, chronic life instability)?
- Does the client have impending legal proceedings that need coordination with an attorney?

In addition, the clinician may want to assess previous therapy that the client has had (i.e., reason, focus, length, quality), previous losses, and present relationships with significant others and children (Shapiro, 2006a). See Shapiro's (2006a) *EMDR: New Notes on Adaptive Information Processing With Case Formulation Principles, Forms, Scripts, and Worksheets* for further assistance in taking a more thorough history of the client. Included in part of the booklet is an Intake Case Conceptualization Form. Dr. Shapiro suggests that the questions therein be incorporated into the History-Taking and Treatment Planning Phase to aid case conceptualization and management. This booklet can be purchased from the Trauma Recovery website (EMDR-HAP; https://www.emdrhap.org/content/). See Chapter 8, D: EMDR Therapy-Related Resources, for more information on trauma recovery. *New Notes on Adaptive Information Processing With Case Formulation Principles, Forms, Scripts, and Worksheets* was drawn from a preconference presentation called *Know the Why and How to Choose Your What: Some Essentials of EMDR Model and Methodology"* that Shapiro gave in 2006.

SCREENING FOR DISSOCIATIVE DISORDERS

While preparing a client for EMDR therapy, it is important to screen them for a dissociative disorder. Familiarize yourself with the clinical signs of dissociative disorders and use of the Dissociative Experiences Scale (DES). See Chapter 8, D: EMDR Therapy-Related Resources, for signs and symptoms of dissociative disorders and information on the DES. Screen every potential EMDR client for dissociative disorders as special preparation is needed to stabilize dissociative clients. This screening will take into consideration the number of years the client was involved with unsuccessful psychotherapy, past episodes of depersonalization and/or derealization, history of memory lapses, occurrence of flashbacks and intrusive thoughts, existence of Schneiderian symptoms (i.e., audible thoughts, hallucinated voices, thought

TABLE 2.3 Cautionary Note
If your areas of expertise do not match the diagnoses or age of the clients who present as possible candidates for EMDR therapy, it is your ethical responsibility to refer them on to someone who specializes in EMDR therapy and those particular diagnoses (i.e., dissociative disorders, substance use disorders) or age groups (i.e., children, adults, seniors). EMDR therapy is meant to be a treatment for the types of clients you normally see and does not make you an expert in areas beyond your specialization. If a clinician does not possess training in specialized populations, such as dissociation, eating disorders, children, sports or performance enhancement, or addictions, these clients should be referred to someone who has that specialized training.

broadcasting, thought insertion, thought withdrawal, delusion perception, and somatic passivity), and presence of somatic symptoms. Furthermore, if these symptoms are present, it will be necessary to lay special groundwork to aid in safely accessing the dysfunctionally stored material while maintaining client stability. For further information, the reader is also encouraged to refer to the International Society for the Study of Trauma and Dissociation's *Guidelines for Treating Dissociative Identity Disorder in Adults, Third Revision* (2011).

See the cautionary note in Table 2.3 about dealing with special-population clients with whom you have no expertise.

CLIENT WILLINGNESS TO DO EMDR THERAPY

Once the answers to these questions have been fully investigated by the clinician, assess the client's willingness to continue treatment utilizing all phases of EMDR therapy. Ask: "Is EMDR therapy something that you might like to consider as a course of treatment?" In cases where an adequate level of mutual trust and safety has been established between the client and the clinician, EMDR reprocessing may be initiated early in the therapeutic relationship. It is optimal that the client also possesses a high level of comfort with the clinician. Therefore, ask, "Are you comfortable with our starting the reprocessing at this time?" If the answer is affirmative, the clinician may move forward with embarking on the remaining phases of EMDR therapy. It is also important for the clinician to be available for support and follow-up immediately after beginning reprocessing.

As the clinician, be careful about initiating EMDR reprocessing phases with a client and then leaving town, let alone the country, for an extended length of time. It may also be best that the client is not engaged in an extended trip shortly after beginning trauma processing. The clinician can also suggest that the client select a time for processing in which there is nothing particularly demanding on their schedule following the session.

ASSESSMENT

In the treatment planning stage of Phase 1, a closer look at the client's presenting problems is undertaken. Once the client's suitability for EMDR therapy has been established, the clinician can better identify the negative events in the client's past, present, and future that need targeting. The questions that follow are typical of what a clinician may want to consider before implementing reprocessing with a client.

- What targets appear to have set the groundwork for the client's presenting issue?
- What negative reactions does the client possess in the present that can be traced to experiences in their past?
- Which of these targets appear to have potential to fill in deficits in the client's life and optimize a healthier level of functioning?
- Is the client able to access these identified experiences and process them to successful resolution?

In Phase 1, the clinician attempts to complete the client's clinical picture by investigating and including all pertinent details before initiating processing of their traumas. Once a solid outline of these pictures begins to emerge, the clinician can begin to set targets for the Treatment Planning stage to determine possible interventions.

TREATMENT PLANNING IN EMDR THERAPY

EMDR treatment planning may be simple in the case of a single-event trauma, or it may be more complicated. A single-event trauma can be the easiest to process and often the most successful. It could represent a one-layered onion. A multiple-event trauma is more comprehensive. This entails identifying the earliest dysfunctional memories associated with the client's presenting problems or issues or what are called *touchstone memories*. In either case, the clinician also needs to identify present situations and experiences that trigger the dysfunction and the alternative future behaviors that ensure the success of therapy.

In the manuals for Weekend 1 (2009–2017a) and Weekend 2 (2009–2017b) trainings, Dr. Shapiro presented a worksheet for the clinician to use as a checklist to ensure that necessary criteria have been evaluated before pursuing EMDR therapy with a client. A modification of this worksheet appears in Table 2.4. In addition, treatment planning includes identification of needed resources or skills necessary for successful reprocessing with dual awareness and stability between sessions.

These questions will not be answered as briefly as the table might suggest, but be aware that all of them need to be considered in some fashion. It is up to the clinician to decide whether to simply check off each criterion met by the client. Alternatively, the clinician can rate each item on a scale of 1 to 3 to record the client's level of appropriateness for EMDR therapy in each criterion. In either case, this can be a valuable tool.

ELEMENTS PERTINENT TO EMDR THERAPY

There are other factors the clinician may also want to consider during the History-Taking and Treatment Planning Phase of EMDR therapy. The clinician may want to consider previous therapy the client has experienced. What was the client's reason for seeking therapy? How long did the therapy last, and what was the outcome? There could be a need to seek more information concerning the past and current state of the client's relationships with the significant individuals in their life—parent, lover, spouse, boss, coworkers, children, and friends. How does the client self-soothe (e.g., relaxation, exercise, meditation, substances or other compulsive behaviors)? Table 2.5 provides a list of pertinent questions specific to EMDR.

TABLE 2.4 EMDR Therapy Selection Criteria			
CRITERIA	**OK**	**PROBLEM**	**CONSULTATION NEEDED**

Client Stability/Developmental Deficits/Ability to Manage Stress

Client has been screened for dissociative
  disorders (use DES, SCID-D, or MID).
Indicators of poor psychic development have
  been identified:
    1. years of unsuccessful psychotherapy
    2. depersonalization and/or derealization
    3. memory lapses
    4. flashbacks and intrusive thoughts
    5. somatic symptoms
Chronic instability at home and/or work
Client's capacity to maintain dual awareness has
  been established.
Secondary-gain issues have been identified and
  appropriately addressed.
Severity of possible newly activated issues have
  been considered.
Client's capacity to understand and
  communicate has been established.

Acute Presentations
Caution and case consultations have been used
  for the following situations:
    1. life-threatening substance abuse
    2. recent suicide attempts
    3. self-mutilation
    4. major loss, illness, or injury
    5. serious assaultive/impulsive behavior
    6. psychotic episode(s)
    7. active alcohol/drug use
    8. dissociative disorders

Stabilization
Adequate stabilization/self-control strategies are
  in place.
Client has a workable means of managing
  distress during and between sessions.
Client has adequate life supports (e.g., friend,
  relatives).
If necessary, client has the viable means to
  dissipate disturbance during and/or after
  sessions.

(continued)

TABLE 2.4 EMDR Therapy Selection Criteria (continued)			
CRITERIA	OK	PROBLEM	CONSULTATION NEEDED
System issues that might endanger the client have been identified and addressed.			
Client wherewithal to call for help if indicated has been established.			
Client is safe at home.			
Medical marijuana use has been determined.			
Medical Considerations			
General physical health, medical condition, and age have been considered.			
Current medications have been identified.			
Inpatient care has been considered or arranged.			
If needed, use of eye movements has been cleared by physician.			
Any other neurological impairments or physical complications have been identified and addressed.			
Any first-trimester cautions or other complications have been assessed in case of pregnancy.			
Time Considerations/Readiness			
Treatment has been timed around client's projects, demands, and/or work schedules.			
Availability of both clinician and client for support and follow-up has been ensured.			
Willingness and ability of the client to continue treatment has been assessed.			
Ninety-minute sessions, if possible, have been arranged.			
Legal obligations have been considered.			

Abbreviations: DES, Dissociative Experiences Scale; MID, Multidimensional Inventory of Dissociation; SCID-D, Structured Clinical Interview of Dissociative Disorders.

CANDIDATES FOR EMDR THERAPY

Not everyone who walks into your office is a potential candidate for EMDR therapy. In looking at both clients discussed subsequently, Isabella and Marie, as candidates for EMDR therapy, the clinician might want to consider the criteria specified by Dr. Shapiro before proceeding to the processing stage.

Keep in mind that, as a clinician seeks answers to these questions, they are looking for patterns—clusters of similar events, responses, and symptoms (e.g., irrational negative beliefs, behaviors, emotions, body sensations, people, places, or things) and other parallels between the client's past and present.

TABLE 2.5 History-Taking
ELEMENTS PERTINENT TO EMDR THERAPY
Criteria
What are the specific symptoms (i.e., negative emotions, cognitions, behaviors, and somatic complaints) reported by the client? Have the symptoms changed?
What set the disturbance in motion? What was the initial cause or incident associated with the symptoms?
Does the client report or describe a specific internal picture, cognition, or feeling?
Are there current triggers? If so, what are their frequency, timing, and settings?
How long has the client been aware of the presenting problem/issue?
Does the client report past occurrences of a similar event?
Is this a part of a bigger trauma/complex/multiple trauma?
Does the client remember the first time they felt this way?
Are there other similar events that might be clustered in this same group of events?
Does the client allude to or report alternative complaints, such as substance abuse, eating disorders, relationship problems, or somatic problems?
How is the client being affected at present?
What is the client's desired state? How does the client want to feel?
Does the client have secondary-gain issues?
Does the client have a good support system in place?

Case Example: Isabella

Isabella came into the clinician's office and stated that she was extremely disillusioned with her marriage and wanted to decide what to do about it. She stated that she "loved" her husband a great deal and that he was a wonderful man, but she was no longer "in love" with him. In her most recent past, she had become enamored and eventually became sexually involved with one of her male coworkers. She alleged no abuse in her childhood or her marriage. The rest of her history appeared unremarkable in terms of other traumatic events. She simply no longer loved her husband and longed for something more with another man.

Is Isabella a candidate for EMDR reprocessing phases? Consider the following:

1. **Symptoms:** When Isabella arrived, she was rushed and breathless. She was extremely apologetic for being late for her first appointment and talked hurriedly as she explained the situation with her husband and current lover. She stated that she was confused and frustrated and no longer loved her husband and was in a quandary as to what to do about it. She did not want to hurt or leave him but was opposed to living with a man with whom she could no longer experience emotional and sexual intimacy in the ways she did when they were younger.
2. **Initial causes:** It was not until she initiated a friendship with a coworker that she realized how isolated and lost she was in her marriage. She felt more like she was living with her brother than her husband.

3. **Past occurrences:** After starting up the friendship, Isabella realized that she had been unhappy in her marriage for a long time.
4. **Other complaints:** Isabella's infidelity was a one-time occurrence for which she felt remorse.
5. **Constraints:** Isabella continues to be unhappy in her marriage, confused as to what to do, and remorseful for her infidelity.
6. **Desired state:** Isabella wants to be happily married.

Isabella did not appear to be an immediate candidate for EMDR reprocessing phases. After exploring her many options, the clinician and Isabella entered into the problem-solving process to find out what had occurred in her marriage over the years that made her "fall out of love" with her husband and what could be done to light a new fire under it. After a few weeks of therapy, Isabella was asked to bring her husband, Antonio, to therapy with her. He had no idea she was in therapy, nor did he know that she was unhappy in their marriage. After a few months of counseling, their relationship was renewed and moved to a more intimate level. As you can see, EMDR reprocessing phases did not appear to be an appropriate intervention with this client or her husband.

Note: EMDR reprocessing might have been used with either of the two to focus on issues that caused them to feel "separate and isolated" from one another later on in their therapeutic process or to resolve the trauma of the affair that may have an impact on Isabella's or Antonio's ability to deepen their relationship.

Case Example: Marie

Marie had been involved in a car accident 2 months earlier. Since then, she had not been able to get behind the wheel without experiencing feelings that she associated with loss of control.

1. **Symptoms:** Marie reported feeling depressed and anxious. She had been medicated for anxiety and depression for as long as she could remember. A history of both was evident from her other comments, but they had become "more exaggerated after the accident." She stated that she was often nauseous and light-headed even at the thought of driving a car. As a passenger, she reported being agitated and hypervigilant. She could not ride in a car for long periods of time or tolerate busy intersections without experiencing a near panic. Whoever drives her must take long and complicated detours to avoid major intersections along their route. Currently, the client only gets into the passenger side of the car if she needs go to the doctor. She will not enter a car for any other reason. As a result, she has not been able to work.
2. **Initial cause:** When she was 10 years old, Marie was involved in an accident in which her mother and younger sister were killed. This is the touchstone memory.
3. **Past experiences:** When she was in college, a fire broke out in one of the lower floors in her dorm. Marie was trapped on the seventh floor of the dorm for 4 hours before it was safe for her to take the elevator to the dorm's lobby.
4. **Other complaints:** Since the accident, Marie becomes anxious and agitated if she does not feel in complete control, especially while riding in a car.
5. **Constraints:** Low affect tolerance and inability to adequately self-soothe.
6. **Desired state:** She sought self-empowerment and peace behind the wheel.

Marie's trauma was appropriate for EMDR therapy. She had a history of previous events during which she felt out of control. The clinician taught Marie the Safe (Calm) Place exercise and other skills for managing acute episodes of anxiety before initiating reprocessing (i.e., Phases 3–6) for the automobile accident in which her mother and younger sister were killed and then the subsequent occurrences where she similarly felt out of control. Many of her present symptoms and dysfunctions disappeared after these events were fully processed. Marie had been experiencing residue from these events every time she entered a busy intersection. After several months of success-fully processing the car accident, dorm incident, and other disturbances where she previously felt out of control, Marie terminated and began living a more secure, stable existence. And she was able to get behind the wheel of a car once again.

Note: With clients having more complex presentations, it may be necessary to titrate the history-taking over a longer period of time.

WHAT DOES AN ADAPTIVE INFORMATION PROCESSING-INFORMED TREATMENT PLAN LOOK LIKE?

In the development of an adaptive information processing (AIP)-informed treatment plan, the clinician identifies a client's history of past trauma, present triggers, and future responses: (a) In terms of past trauma, the clinician maps out and brings to a client's conscious aware-ness the memory network of past experiences that inform their presenting issue(s). Once these negative experiences have been identified, they are segregated into symptoms clusters (i.e., clustered by negative self-beliefs, intense emotional responses, maladaptive behaviors, body sensations, senses, people, places, things, specific negative events). In each cluster, the first and worst experiences as well as any other contributing past experiences are identified and processed. During this process, the clinician observes any emotional responses to past associations that the client may have that connect to their present difficulties. (b) Once all the past trauma in the cluster have been successfully processed, the clinician assists the client in identifying current people, places, and situations that continue to trigger negative reactions, responses, and behaviors. Any triggers that are still active due to second-order conditioning (i.e., as a result of residing in a separate memory network) are processed using Phases 3 through 6. Other traumatic events that occurred in the recent past may also be identified and reprocessed. These events may not possess a historical component but may generate symptoms that indicate a need for further treatment. (c) A present trigger has been identified and processed, and the clinician helps the client identify any response(s) to possible future situations and prepare for potential challenges related to the present trigger. A future template is created and processed for each trigger identified by the client. In this prong of the protocol, the clinician also assists the client in identifying any anticipatory anxiety or patterns of avoidance and developing alternative patterns of response that will prove to be more adaptive to the client (Shapiro, 2009–2017a, 2009–2017b).

PHASE 2: PREPARATION

While history-taking and treatment planning lay the groundwork, the Preparation Phase sets the therapeutic framework and appropriate levels of expectation for the client (Shapiro, 2018). In this phase, the primary goal is to prepare the client to process a disturbing target utilizing EMDR Phases 3 to 6. Over the past few years, client preparation has been emphasized more heavily in trainings. It is often a "make or break" aspect of successful EMDR therapy. The Preparation Phase may be brief or lengthy depending on the complexity of a client's clinical landscape. It is about: (a) educating and communicating to the client what to expect before, after, and during the EMDR process (e.g., mechanics, procedures, outcome); (b) building confidence in the client in terms of safety, assurance, and the therapeutic alliance; (c) continuing the informed consent process; (d) setting expectations for the process; and (e) teaching coping skills (e.g., safe [calm] place, containment, resource development, life management skills, relaxation) as needed to assure that the client can maintain dual awareness during reprocessing and stability during and between sessions. It is in this phase that the clinician determines if the client is able, willing, and ready to board the train.

SETTING THE STAGE FOR EFFECTIVE REPROCESSING

It is during the Preparation Phase that the clinician begins to set the stage for effective reprocessing. There are specific tasks identified by Shapiro (2018) that the clinician does before initiating the reprocessing of disturbing material with the client: (a) safety within the therapeutic relationship is ensured, (b) EMDR theory is explained and the model is described, and (c) potential concerns, issues, and emotional needs are addressed. These tasks are identified in Table 2.6.

TABLE 2.6 Client Preparation	
SETTING THE STAGE FOR EFFECTIVE PROCESSING	
A safe therapeutic relationship is established.	A clinical stance is adopted. A bond is formed with the client. Rapport, trust, and safety have been established.
The process and its effects are explained in detail.	Preparing the client in terms of education and informed consent is assured (see Chapter 8, C: Informed Consent and EMDR Therapy). The theory behind EMDR therapy is explained. The AIP model is briefly described. Eye movements (or other form of BLS) are introduced, demonstrated, and tested. Medical considerations are considered. The client's stability has been assessed, and coping strategies have been introduced. The client is able to create a safe (calm) place or other skills for shifting emotional states. Timing is appropriately planned.
The client's concerns and potential emotional needs are evaluated.	Expectations are set. Client fears are addressed. Current stressors are identified.

Abbreviations: AIP, adaptive information processing; BLS, bilateral stimulation.

Maintaining a Safe Therapeutic Environment

Establishing sufficient rapport, trust, and safety is essential in the therapeutic relationship. The same is true of EMDR therapy, but often the clinician may have a very short time to form this kind of bond with the client. As a result, a clinician's demonstration of flexibility, respect, and accommodating attitudes toward the client's sense of safety and need for reassurance becomes more pronounced. Because clinicians may implement reprocessing after a few weeks of first meeting a client, a sufficient level of trust and adequate bonding must take place before it is attempted.

Explanation of the EMDR Process and Its Effects

The importance of providing the client with a descriptive and informative explanation of reprocessing during these phases (i.e., Phases 3–6) cannot be stressed enough. Unfortunately, many EMDR-trained clinicians do not say more than, "I just learned this new technique. Let's try it." And, without hesitation, the clinician leads the client into setting up the procedural steps outlined in the Assessment Phase without telling the client what the acronym EMDR stands for or providing an adequate explanation of what is involved.

The client needs to be provided with a simple, general understanding of the theory behind EMDR therapy and how their brain originally stores information. The amount of information supplied varies with the age of the client (i.e., children need far less information) and the expressed desire of the client for more or less information. EMDRIA sells pamphlets for adults, children, and adolescents, called *EMDR Brochure for Clients* (2019), which can be used as an option for this process. These pamphlets are also printed in Spanish and French (see Chapter 8, D: EMDR Therapy-Related Resources, for more information on EMDRIA). In 2012, Dr. Shapiro wrote the book *Getting Past Your Past: Take Control of Your Life with Self-Help Techniques from EMDR Therapy*. This is an excellent resource about EMDR therapy for clients and other laypeople.

Because clients frequently report feeling "stuck" in terms of emotions or body sensations, Shapiro's (2018) explanation of how trauma gets locked into the central nervous system, gets triggered by internal and external stimuli, and results in a flood of intense emotional and physical sensations can support clients' understanding. In addition, it can be helpful to elaborate on how bilateral stimulation (BLS) helps to free the "stuck" information and allows the locked information to emerge to the surface, integrate, resolve, and flush out. However, this may be too much information for some clients. Use clinical judgment as to how much psychoeducation to provide.

Shapiro (2018) also suggests describing the model in terms of connecting the target with adaptive networks. Exhibit 2.1 presents a graphic understanding of the theory about how the brain stores a disturbing event: (a) when a traumatic event occurs, the brain stores it in an isolated memory network and prevents it from linking up with more adaptive information. As a result, no learning can take place; (b) once the EMDR reprocessing has been initiated, appropriate links between the maladaptive and adaptive information occur, and shifts begin to emerge that allow learning to take place; and (c) if reprocessing has been successfully completed, all necessary links between memory networks have been addressed, learning has taken place, and the event is no longer disturbing.

It is important for the clinician to spend an adequate amount of time explaining to the client the possibilities and options regarding BLS. Several methods of BLS have been developed over the years, such as alternating taps and sounds, or even the butterfly hug (i.e., crossing arms in front of the chest with the tips of the fingers of each hand resting just below the clavicle on each side while gently tapping from side to side; Artigas et al., 2000; Artigas &

EXHIBIT 2.1 How the Brain Stores a Disturbing Event

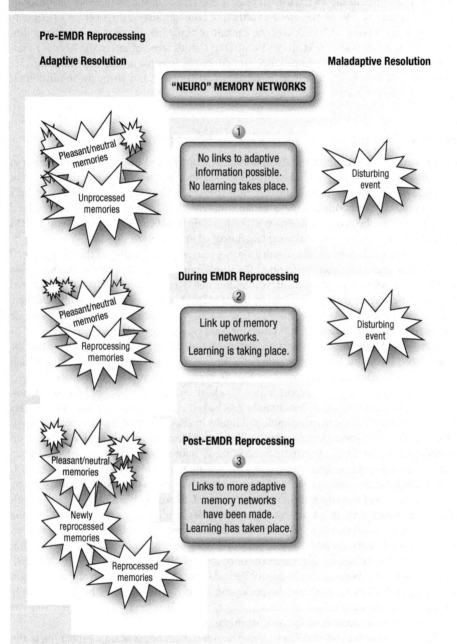

Pre-EMDR Reprocessing

Adaptive Resolution   Maladaptive Resolution

"NEURO" MEMORY NETWORKS

Pleasant/neutral memories

Unprocessed memories

1

No links to adaptive information possible.
No learning takes place.

Disturbing event

Pleasant/neutral memories

Reprocessing memories

During EMDR Reprocessing

2

Link up of memory networks.
Learning is taking place.

Disturbing event

Pleasant/neutral memories

Newly reprocessed memories

Reprocessed memories

Post-EMDR Reprocessing

3

Links to more adaptive memory networks have been made.
Learning has taken place.

Jarero, 2005; Boël, 1999, 2000; Jarero, 2002) or Tarzan tap (i.e., crossing arms in front of the chest with the fists of each hand resting just below the clavicle on each side while gently tapping from side to side [Bill Brislin, personal communication, November 16, 2019]). Because *most* research to date has been done using eye movements, it has become the preferred means of BLS for most clinicians. Thus, it is important to inform the client of this as other options may be explored. De Jongh et al. (2013) address the use of other forms of BLS.

When assessing for the appropriate type of BLS to utilize with a client, it is optimal to assess and monitor their physical limitations. Do they suffer from a hearing deficit? Do they wear glasses? Do they have problems moving their eyes back and forth (i.e., side to side) in a brisk movement? Do they have mobility in their body to tap their own knees or shoulders? Because different types of BLS are used, check to see if the client can tolerate eye, audio, or tactile movement. Remember to take these options into consideration when assessing the proper stimulation for each client.

What effect does the BLS have? Although the mechanism of action is unknown at this time, there is a great deal of informed speculation as to how it works. What happens when we intentionally shift our focus back and forth at an increased rate of speed? Does it cause us to process information, experiences, or trauma more efficiently? With more advanced computer technology becoming available, such as information from single-photon emission computed tomography and computed axial tomography scans, we are able to gain clearer understanding of how the brain works and how it may respond to BLS during EMDR reprocessing.

Safe (Calm) Place and Other Coping Strategies

Although these techniques will not be covered in depth in this Primer, there are various calming, soothing, relaxing, containing exercises with which the clinician may want to become more familiar. Several are described in the EMDR therapy literature, and there are myriad options available to the clinician, including different breathing techniques, imagery, hypnosis, biofeedback, and somatic and muscle relaxation exercises. These maximize the likelihood that the client will be able to handle the level of disturbance that could arise before, during, or between reprocessing sessions. Some of these techniques may also be useful when closing down incomplete sessions. It is optimal for clients to be trained in some of these self-control techniques prior to implementing processing. It is also recommended that EMDR therapy not be pursued if a client does not respond to or is unable to use any of these coping strategies. At the very least, it is strongly recommended that the clinician teach the Safe (Calm) Place exercise (see Chapter 8, A: EMDR Phase 2 Exercises), a mechanism for self-regulation. Once created by the client (with assistance or guidance from the clinician), the clinician can encourage the client to return to it before, during, or after a reprocessing session, especially if they are experiencing a high level of emotional disturbance. With more complex clients who display affect dysregulation, resource development and installation (RDI; Leeds, 1998; Leeds & Shapiro, 2000) is suggested.

Clinicians can experiment with various techniques listed subsequently until it is determined that a client can tolerate or reduce levels of disturbance caused by the dysfunctionally stored material in their central nervous system. Although all clients need to be familiar with and use self-regulation techniques, some clients may be able to do it more easily on their own; so, for them only a limited number of these techniques may be necessary for stabilization.

There is a broad range of possibilities that aid in the goal of successful processing and can also be used by clients in a session or between sessions for symptom reduction and relaxation:

To help prepare a client for processing:

1. Safe (Calm) Place (see Chapter 8, A: EMDR Phase 2 Exercises)
2. Sacred Space (see Chapter 8, A: EMDR Phase 2 Exercises)
3. Resource Development Steps (see Chapter 8, B: EMDR Therapy Scripts)
4. Mindfulness/meditation techniques
5. Other coping skills if more appropriate

For incomplete sessions or additional stabilization:

6. Lightstream Technique (Shapiro, 1991–1995; see Chapter 8, B: EMDR Therapy Scripts)
7. Miller and Halpern's *Letting Go of Stress* (1994)
8. Container (see Chapter 8, B: EMDR Therapy Scripts) and conference room technique
9. Grounding, diaphragmatic breathing, and anchoring in the present exercises (see Chapter 8, A: EMDR Phase 2 Exercises)
10. Breathing shift (see Chapter 8, B: EMDR Therapy Scripts)
11. Spiral technique (see Chapter 8, B: EMDR Therapy Scripts)
12. Autogenic training
13. Hatha yoga
14. Tai chi
15. Visualization
16. Guided imagery
17. Self-control and relaxation exercises
18. Basic self-care
19. Four elements (i.e., air, fire, water, and earth) stabilization technique formulated by Elan Shapiro for use with terrorist victims in Israel (Shapiro, 2006a).

The utilization of the techniques during the Preparation Phase is often the client's first introduction to BLS and provides them with a realistic peek into how a session may proceed during actual processing.

WHAT FACTORS INDICATE A GREATER NEED FOR STABILIZATION?

There are factors that may indicate a greater need for client stabilization (i.e., resourcing) in the Preparation Phase (Shapiro, 2018). These include, but are not limited to, a client's pervasive difficulty with affect and/or affect regulation (i.e., client's ability to maintain or increase positive feelings and minimize defense states) and with socializing and communicating individually and relationally; trouble with routine changes that can trigger into high arousal states; difficulty managing negative behavioral responses (e.g., impulsivity, bullying, teasing, tantrums); presence of disruptive dissociative symptoms (e.g., memory loss/amnesia, detachment or out of body experiences, blurred sense of reality/distorted reality); self-injurious (e.g., cutting, biting, hitting, burning) or addictive behaviors (e.g., substance abuse, sex, gambling); evidence of suicidality (e.g., ideation, plans, attempt); limited access to appropriate external resources (e.g., familial, filial, or professional, or significant figures); or violent urges and/or behaviors (e.g., physical and verbal aggression).

In preparing clients with the difficulties and issues above, it is important to stabilize them so that processing can be facilitated (Shapiro, 2018). In doing so, the clinician will employ strategies that will help the client increase the window of tolerance and, therefore, increase the client's capacity to experience positive and negative affective experiences and to be able to develop more positive neural networks. The clinician may also utilize strategies that help the client increase the ability to self-regulate and, as a result, help the client manage any current triggers through the development of these adaptive coping strategies, increase the client's ability to shift states and track emotional and somatic responses, and increase the capacity for mindfulness (i.e., to observe rather than react). The goals of these interventions are to strengthen the client's sense of safety and confidence in self, the therapeutic dyad, and the EMDR therapy process. These interventions may consist of psychoeducation through the AIP lens; sessions on affect regulation and resource strategies for self-use; learning to identify and strengthen positive experiences that may occur before, during, or after a session, and to be able to desensitize triggers that occur daily that are normally disruptive and dysregulating.

SAFE (CALM) PLACE—STABILIZATION AND ASSESSMENT

Shapiro (2018) prescribes the use of the Safe (Calm) Place exercise throughout the EMDR process. It assists in preparing a client to process traumatic events, to close incomplete sessions, and to help equalize or stabilize a client's distress in session if the information that emerges is too emotionally disruptive. It has been redesignated safe (calm) place over the years because it was found that some clients have been traumatized to a high degree, making it ecologically impossible for them to imagine that a "safe" place can exist. The clinician can have the client create a calm place instead.

Note: When utilizing this exercise with veterans or military personnel, the use of a "secure" place may be more appropriate. Table 2.7 provides a simple description of uses of this exercise.

The Safe (Calm) Place exercise also assists in preparing the client for processing in two important ways: (a) It serves to introduce the client to BLS in a comfortable way before it is used with disturbing material. If necessary and, according to the strengths and needs of the client, the clinician may suggest or name the type of place the client could create, such as a place of courage, a peaceful place, or a place for time out, and (b) It can be utilized to evaluate the client's ability to shift from one positive state to another without the intrusion of any negative associations. Both are helpful in evaluating a client's readiness and appropriateness for EMDR.

As with any technique utilized with a client, it is important to use caution. Listed in the following are cautionary elements with which the clinician needs to be aware when using the safe (calm) place for self-regulation, symptom reduction, or relaxation (Shapiro, 2018).

1. The initial development of a safe (calm) place may be disturbing to the client and increase their levels of distress. If this does occur, reassure the client that it is not unusual for this to happen. Then assist the client in developing another safe (calm) place or initiate another self-regulating exercise. At other times, developing another safe (calm) place is unnecessary. Sometimes disturbance occurs because the clinician has used too fast or too many sets of BLS and the client has associated with the disturbing material. At other times, the client is trying to hold the image of the place rather than focusing solely on the "pleasant sensations in your body," as the script suggests. Because BLS will reduce the vividness of images, this is not surprising. In either case, the clinician should refresh the sensory aspects of the place through guided imagery until the client is able, once again, to experience pleasant sensations in the body. Then

TABLE 2.7 Use of Safe (Calm) Place—The Why and the How

WHY

Prepares client for processing.

Introduces and provides client with a positive experience with BLS.

Temporary rest (i.e., relief, break) between sets.

Technique to deal with dysfunctional material and high levels of disturbance that may emerge before, during, or after sessions.

Functions as a temporary state change strategy; when needed/desired by client, it is used to shift the client out of the processing mode and into a temporary state change to manage high levels of distress.

Aids in closing *down* a session (i.e., *when time is running out or an in-between session self-regulation strategy*).

Ensures that the client can ride the train by maintaining dual awareness.

HOW

See Chapter 8, A: Exercise for the Safe (Calm) Place Script.

NOTE

This exercise was originally adapted from a variation of a guided visualization included on Emmett Miller's (1994) "Letting Go of Stress" tape. In more complex presentations, Shapiro (2018) suggests substituting situations of "courage" or "strength" or other resourcing adjectives in this exercise for clients who may need to access positive affects between sessions. The result of this suggested change was the Resource Development Steps exercise found in Chapter 8, B: EMDR Therapy Scripts.

Abbreviation: BLS, bilateral stimulation.

reinitiate BLS with the instructions, "Just focus on the pleasant sensations in your body and allow yourself to enjoy them. Just focus on these pleasant sensations and follow my fingers (or taps or tones)." Be sure to use only a few (i.e., 4–6) slow sets of BLS and then recheck the client's experience.

2. Pairing the BLS with the development of the safe (calm) place has the ability to bring some clients to high levels of negative affect very quickly. For example, the client may be in the process of developing a safe (calm) place in a meadow and suddenly the image of the rapist appears as a dark figure overshadowing it. In a case like this, try again to develop a place that continues to be safe (calm) to them, probably a different place, as the current image has been "intruded" on by distressing material.

3. Negative associations may be activated if negative memories spontaneously link with the client's safe (calm) place during its development. For example, a client who happens to be a police officer is preparing to reprocess a memory of seeing their partner shot in a confrontation with a gang member. On introducing BLS to their newly developed safe (calm) place of a favorite location on the college campus they attended, a memory of exchanging gunfire with a group of marauding student protesters on a local college

campus several years ago emerges. When this happens, the clinician should assist the client in developing another safe (calm) place.

4. Some clients may be unable to develop a safe (calm) place. In this case, the clinician may need to utilize other strategies, many of which are described in the Appendices, to shift out of states of disturbance. If unable to use any coping strategies, the clinician should reevaluate the client's appropriateness for EMDR processing or they may need to develop a more complex focus on treatment along with more advanced stabilization.

5. Slow, short sets of BLS are utilized to reduce the risk that a client may be activated by any negative associations.

Table 2.8, "Derailment Possibilities—Safe (Calm) Place," provides some cautions that if not heeded could keep "the train from leaving the depot."

TABLE 2.8 Derailment Possibilities—Safe (Calm) Place

Remember, this safe (calm) place is always available to you. Just let me know if you need to return to it at any time.

Selecting a safe (calm) place or other resource that may be linked to a distressing or disturbing event
A client may select a place that is generally represented as safe (calm), for example, a meadow, but find that it is too closely associated with a traumatic event (e.g., being raped in a meadow as a teenager). If this becomes the case, the client needs to create another safe (calm) place.

Providing *only* one relaxation exercise or self-control technique to use between sessions
The clinician should attempt to provide the client with a safe (calm) place and a variety of other relaxation exercises to relieve any negative disturbance that may arise between sessions.

Selecting a safe (calm) place
Again, it is important to "stay out of the way" and allow the client to identify and/or create their own refuge.

Forgetting to ask for and/or install the cue word
Strictly follow the safe (calm) place script word for word until you are familiar with the order, content, and intent of each step. The "cue" word is a crucial part of the Safe (Calm) Place exercise.

Selecting a safe (calm) place that is more appropriate for a child (e.g., under the bed, deep into a closet, under the porch) than an adult
A safe (calm) place that is associated only with childhood can lead the client to a past focused/dissociated state and may fail to ensure present orientation and grounding.

Selecting a safe (calm) place that is associated with an individual who may be part of the necessary reprocessing material (e.g., a church where the clergyman who molested the client still preaches)

(continued)

TABLE 2.8 Derailment Possibilities—Safe (Calm) Place (continued)

In this case, it would be appropriate for the client to visualize an entirely different safe (calm) place.

Doing sets of BLS that are too long or too fast
In order to avoid stimulating channels of association linked to disturbing material, it is important to do short, slow sets when utilizing BLS to stabilize the client.

Reinstalling safe (calm) place or doing resourcing when it is unnecessary
It is not necessary to reinstall the safe (calm) place before every EMDR session. Simply remind the client of their cue word and their ability to elicit it at any point during the process (i.e., before, during, and after EMDR).

Continuing reprocessing with a client who obviously is unable to use self-control techniques to shift out of a state of distress
These clients may need to be evaluated for sufficient ego strength and self-soothing skills and may possibly need more frontloading in terms of stabilization before reprocessing can begin.

Abbreviation: BLS, bilateral stimulation.

During the Preparation Phase, the clinician routinely reassesses the client's stability and provides coping strategies to enhance and strengthen the client's sense of calm, grounding, or safety before, during, and between reprocessing sessions. The clinician may want to be equipped with a repertoire of stabilization and resource development interventions prior to starting processing. Safe (calm) place, relaxation exercises, metaphors, anxiety-control skills, stress-reduction strategies, and other resources can provide safe and calm means to assist a client in processing their most traumatic experiences. For more complex trauma presentations, the use of RDI is recommended (see the following section).

RESOURCE DEVELOPMENT AND INSTALLATION, DISSOCIATION, AND EGO STATE THERAPY

Although not covered at length in this Primer, a discussion of the Preparation Phase also needs to include RDI, dissociation, and Ego State Therapy. A brief description of each follows. Additional resources on these topics can be found in the Resources section (see Chapter 8, D: EMDR Therapy-Related Resources).

Resource Development and Installation

Clinicians use RDI as a prerequisite to prepare clients with more complex affect dysregulation (i.e., limited capacities to emotionally self-regulate) for EMDR. RDI (Korn & Leeds, 2002; Leeds, 1998; Leeds & Shapiro, 2000) was developed as a means of enhancing a client's ability to alter their affective and behavioral states adaptively by heightening their access to functional memory networks. RDI provides a debilitated client who exhibits unstable behaviors (e.g., dissociation, mutilation or other self-injurious behaviors, addictions, eating disorders) a means of accessing, developing, and strengthening positive introjects and increasing affect regulation. Guidelines and protocol for EMDR RDI can be located in

Chapter 8, A: EMDR Phase 2 Exercises, in Shapiro's (2018) basic text. Before proceeding to the Assessment Phase, consider what is needed to stabilize the client and whether the client has adequate affect regulation skills and adequate internal and external resources to safely and effectively reprocess the disturbing memories.

Note: See Resource Development Steps in Chapter 8, B: EMDR Therapy Scripts. This is a resource development intervention similar to the Safe (Calm) Place exercise suggested by Shapiro (2018) to work with affect management and behavior change.

What Is Dissociation?

Realizing that you do not know how to recognize dissociation or deal with it adequately when it occurs in a session with a client is as important as knowing what dissociation is. Simply stated, dissociation is disconnection of things usually associated with each other. This can be a disconnection from the memories of an event and the attached emotion, knowledge, behavior, and/or sensation that happened as a result of a past or presently occurring event. It can also be a "disconnect" of various aspects of the self. Dissociation is often driven by overwhelming of the information processing and affect regulation systems. That is why it is important to keep a client within the therapeutic "window of tolerance" during treatment. Clients can and often do dissociate during traumatic events. Dissociation is a valid, automatic, and often critical defense mechanism during a traumatic event but can be problematic if it occurs during an EMDR session, particularly if the clinician does not recognize that it is transpiring or does not know how to ameliorate its occurrence. Along with a thorough clinical assessment, it is highly suggested that before initiating EMDR with a client, the clinician administers the DES (Bernstein & Putnam, 1986). For some highly dissociative clients, more robust clinical instruments may be necessary for thorough diagnosis (e.g., Structured Clinical Interview of Dissociative Disorders [SCID-D], Steinberg, 1994, or Multiscale Inventory of Dissociation [MID], Dell, 2006).

Ego State Therapy

In the late 1970s, Watkins and Watkins developed Ego State Therapy. It employs family and group therapy techniques "to resolve conflicts between various 'ego states' that constitute a 'family of self' within a single individual" (Watkins & Watkins, 1997). Ego State Therapy techniques can be utilized in EMDR therapy with clients who have complex posttraumatic stress disorders, dissociative disorders, performance enhancement difficulties, and problems associated with serious illness. Some clients enter therapy with dissociated parts that are unable to cope with the symptoms that have emerged as a result of their traumas. Hence, it becomes imperative in the history-taking to identify a client's fragmentation and alienation, then define the appropriate ego state, and select the somatosensory and affect management strategies to help these challenging clients. Integrating ego-state techniques with EMDR therapy can be highly useful and successful with clients possessing dissociative disorders (see Table 2.9).

CONTAINER

Usually introduced in the Preparation Phase, a container is an imaginary receptacle created through visualization, where a client places any residual images, feelings, beliefs, perceptions, urges or cravings, worries, thoughts, and other sensations left over from an EMDR

TABLE 2.9 Cautionary Note

Dissociation is not a simple state, and clinicians who have not been formally and adequately trained to treat dissociative disorders or dissociative symptoms when they arise in sessions should immediately seek supervision or refer the client to someone who does have this training. EMDRIA-approved basic trainings do provide an overview of dissociation, but time constraints do not permit in-depth discussion. Note that many of the advanced EMDRIA-approved trainings do concern themselves with the subject of EMDR therapy and dissociative disorders. (The *ISST-D Guidelines for the Treatment of Dissociative Identity Disorder* [2011] may be downloaded from www.isst-d.org).

Abbreviations: EMDRIA, EMDR International Association; ISST-D, International Society for the Study of Trauma and Dissociation.

reprocessing session for safekeeping. This empowers the client to keep intrusive traumatic material at bay until she is able and willing to open it up again and continue to address issues that arise in therapy. The container helps keep the past in the past and the client fully functional in the present.

A container usually has the ability to be locked, sealed, tied, glued, nailed, or otherwise secured; so the client makes a choice to open or not before the next session. The container is an important tool in EMDR therapy. According to Murray (2011), its purposes are numerous: (a) it has the ability to enhance a client's stability and affect tolerance, (b) it provides information as to the client's ability to continue through to the Assessment Phase and reprocessing, and (c) it can be used to close down incomplete sessions or between sessions to manage any disturbances that may arise. Scripts for the Container exercise can be found in Chapter 8, B: EMDR Therapy Scripts and Murray (2011).

The clinician can also use other containment strategies to shift the client's focus of attention and to help regulate affect: (a) Instruct the client to set aside the memory(ies)/associations for a later time by saying, "If you can, visualize putting these memories in a container for another time. Would/could you do that?" and (b) Instruct the client to focus their attention toward or away from the memory(ies)/associations by saying, "Allow yourself to set aside any thoughts, worries, or anxieties and focus on being in the present moment. You can always come back to them later; and" (c) Instruct the client to pause/rest by saying, "Allow yourself to set aside any thoughts and/or association for a few seconds. Notice that you are here and not there. Notice that you can put it way and leave it there, and when you're ready, you can come back to it. Notice that you're the one in control now" (Shapiro, 2009–2017a, 2009–2017b).

ADDRESSING THE CLIENT'S FEARS AND EXPECTATIONS

Client Expectations

The client can expect to be able to maintain a sense of safety and of being in control. These are critical for safe processing. If, during the reprocessing effort, the client indicates that they want to stop, the clinician needs to honor their request. To do otherwise might seriously undermine treatment effects and the integrity of the therapeutic relationship. The clinician assists in helping the client maintain that dual awareness, reassuring them that the surfacing emotions and memories are transient and that they are in no real danger in the present.

Client Fears

It is in the Preparation Phase where the clinician addresses any fears the client may have about the process and instills hope, however thin and tattered they may have perceived it to be. And it is this shred of hope that sets up the client's potential for success in the EMDR process.

After an explanation of the EMDR theory, the clinician is encouraged to introduce metaphors (e.g., train or video) or analogies that may be used during the actual reprocessing of the client's disturbing material. The client can then have familiarity with those metaphors if the clinician references them during the ensuing session. Other concerns or fears may be addressed at this time.

In summary, the clinician informs the client about the nature of EMDR and what they might expect as a result of EMDR reprocessing; establishes an adequate therapeutic relationship through bonding, rapport, and honesty; and ensures client safety, stability, and their ability to maintain their control over the process.

Caution: If the client cannot self-soothe, do not proceed to a trauma focus. Do more frontloading of stabilization and affect management skills to ensure the client is adequately stabilized and can tolerate any affect that may emerge before proceeding to the Assessment Phase.

MECHANICS OF EMDR THERAPY

As previously mentioned, the clinician determines what type of BLS (e.g., eye movements, tactile, auditory) is to be used with the client and establishes a stop signal in the event that the client needs or wants to discontinue processing. In addition, the clinician needs to establish a comfortable seating position with the client, as well as the range, speed, and direction of the BLS.

Seating Arrangement

One of the elements emphasized during basic EMDR therapy training is the seating arrangement between the clinician and the client. The suggested arrangement for clients with whom the clinician is utilizing hand movements to facilitate eye movements is what is called *two ships passing in the night*. In keeping with another concept, *staying out of the way*, the clinician positions themself in front of and off to the side of the client so that they are out of the client's peripheral vision. If the clinician is utilizing one of the electronic forms of BLS, such as the EyeScan models (i.e., lightbar), AudioScan, or Tac AudioScan (neurotekcorp. com), the clinician wants to be sure they are out of the client's range of vision during the sets of BLS, while still visible to the client (if they choose to turn their head) between sets.

Range, Distance, Speed, Direction, and Number of Bilateral Stimulation Sets

Some clients cannot comfortably tolerate certain directions and speeds of eye movement. This is why it is important to find the best fit when proceeding with processing. In these cases, the range, distance, direction, speed, and number of sets of eye movements may be varied until a comfortable formula is found for the client. Hence, as the client holds their head stationary, the clinician demonstrates the centerline-to-centerline movement of fingers while also testing for distance, range, direction, and speed variance. These elements should be tolerably comfortable for the client.

The distance refers to the proximity of the clinician's fingers from the centerline of the client's face. The range should be tested prior to any reprocessing efforts with the client. The clinician facilitates this by holding two fingers approximately 12 to 14 inches from the client's face and saying, "Is this comfortable?" If not, the clinician continues to move their fingers out and asks the same question until the client reports a comfortable placement and distance.

Using two fingers as the focal point, the clinician moves them from one side of the client's range of vision to another. In place of fingers, the clinician could also use a pen, ruler, wand, finger puppet, or pointer to facilitate eye movements.

The clinician should also pretest the rate of speed of the eye movements by establishing a speed that is tolerably comfortable for the client. The clinician commences the eye movements, increasing in speed to determine the client's ability to track. Allow the client to express any preferences in terms of distance, height, or speed before focusing on any disturbing material. When establishing an appropriate distance and speed, the clinician says, "Is this a comfortable distance and speed?"

The direction of the eye movements may vary from vertical to horizontal. Eye movements may also be diagonal, circular, or in a figure-eight pattern. The ease and speed of the eye movements should be evaluated frequently to ensure successful and complete reprocessing of the dysfunctional material.

The duration or the number of sets utilized should be determined by the client's verbal and nonverbal feedback. The suggested number of initial passes (i.e., one round trip, centerline to centerline, shoulder to shoulder) ranges from 20 to 40. When actual processing has begun, the clinician should listen closely for any feedback from the client about the number of passes, speed, and distance. If the client reports discomfort or if the material does not seem to readily shift, adjustments in speed, distance, direction, and number of passes (i.e., eye movements, tones, and taps) may be necessary.

There is more than one type of eye movement available to the client as well as other forms of BLS if a client is unable to tolerate the eye movements. Although it has limitations in terms of speed, the two-handed approach entails a clinician holding a closed hand at each end of the client's visual field and alternating raised fingers from end to end. The clinician may also use tapping and/or sounds as alternate forms of BLS.

Special caution and consideration should be given to clients who wear glasses, contacts, bifocals, or trifocals. In case of dryness or eye irritation, it can be suggested that the client has their contact lens case available in the event their contacts need to be removed in order to more comfortably continue reprocessing. It may be preferable for clients with contacts to utilize other forms of BLS. In the case of a client who wears glasses, give them the choice of tracking the eye movements with or without glasses or using other forms of BLS. In all cases, the clinician and the client should agree on at least two forms of BLS prior to reprocessing in case the mode of stimulation needs to be changed in the middle of the process (see Shapiro, 2011, for more information on the mechanics of eye movements).

PHASE 3: ASSESSMENT

As target selection has been accomplished in previous phases, assessment is simply the measurement and amplification of the targets already selected. This is the phase in which the components of the target are identified, and baseline measures are taken. The order of the EMDR components (i.e., image, negative cognition [NC], positive cognition [PC], Validity of Cognition [VoC] scale, emotions, Subjective Units of Disturbance [SUD] scale, and body location) is specifically designed to access and stimulate the dysfunctional target material. Assessment should always be done in the order of the script because it moves from "seeing and thinking about it" to "feeling it." This is why a client's level of distress may become increasingly more agitated during the Assessment Phase, and the clinician needs to be prepared to activate processing soon after completion of the assessment to ease their disturbance.

IDENTIFY, ASSESS, AND MEASURE

The three words that Shapiro uses to represent this phase are *identify, assess,* and *measure* (2018). By consulting the treatment plan, the target memory for reprocessing is chosen; and the clinician assists and supports the client in *identifying* a specific pivotal picture and *assessing* its toxicity. This is accomplished by determining the NC and PC, and specific negative emotion(s) and body sensation(s) associated with the event. Then baseline *measurements* of the client's responses to and progress within the phase are established and monitored (see Table 2.10; Shapiro, 2012a).

Identifying the Target

The memory selected for reprocessing is identified in the first two phases of EMDR (see Chapters 3 and 4 for more information about target possibilities).

Identifying the Image

In order to assist the client in establishing a link between consciousness and the location where the memory is stored in the brain, the clinician assists the client in identifying an

TABLE 2.10 Assessment		
IDENTIFY	**ASSESS**	**MEASURE**
Target	**Image** **NC** **PC/Desired State** **Specific Emotion(s)** **Location of Body Sensation:** "Where do you feel it (i.e., the disturbance) in your body?"	VoC (1–7) of desired cognition. "When focusing on the image (or picture; or if no picture, the event), how true do the words (repeat the positive cognition) feel to you *now*?" **SUD** (0–10) "When focusing on the event (incident, experience)*, how disturbing does it feel to you *now*?"

* The SUD measures the level of disturbance of the entire memory.
Abbreviations: NC, negative cognition; PC, positive cognition; SUD, Subjective Units of Disturbance; VoC, Validity of Cognition.

image (or picture) that best represents the entire incident or the "worst" (i.e., most upsetting) part of it. It does not matter whether the image (or picture) is clear or distinct. In fact, it is not unusual for the image to present as blurred or fragmented. If there is no image (or picture), the clinician instructs the client to focus on the *event* (incident or experience).

Assessing the Negative and Positive Cognitions, Emotions, and Location of the Physical Sensations

Along with the memory to be identified and treated (i.e., the target) and the image (or picture) that represents it, the clinician assists the client in identifying the negative self-belief or statement (i.e., NC), the desired direction of change (i.e., PC) verbalized by the client, and the emotions and location of the physical sensations associated with it.

1. When the client voluntarily or involuntarily stimulates stored information associated with the identified image (or picture) of the specific traumatic event, perceptions may come to the surface that could distort what a client perceives in the present. These perceptions are explicitly expressed in an NC identified by the client (e.g., negative, self-referencing, generalizable, irrational, dysfunctional, and possessing emotional resonance). For example, shame and self-hatred can be explicitly expressed in the NC, "I am not good enough."
2. The PC is a positive reflection of what the client would like to believe about themself (i.e., desired direction of change) as they focus on the image (or picture) of the targeted event and on the opposite side of a personal issue or theme indicated by the NC. For example, "I am a failure" versus "I am able to succeed."
3. As the client focuses on the image (or picture), they are asked to name the specific *emotional sensations* that also emerge (i.e., the shame and self-hatred described earlier).
4. The clinician asks the client to initiate a body scan to determine the location of the *physical sensations* associated with the disturbance. For example, "Where do you feel it in your body?"

Measuring the *Validity of Cognition* and the *Subjective Units of Disturbance*

The VoC scale is used to measure the PC for current validity as the client thinks of the incident and to ensure that it is attainable and not a result of wishful thinking on the part of the client. It is rated to provide a baseline measurement as to how true (i.e., "How true do those words *feel*?") and how believable the cognition feels to the client (i.e., Does it constitute wishful thinking on the part of the client?). The VoC scale is shown in Exhibit 2.2.

EXHIBIT 2.2 Validity of Cognition Scale

Completely False   Completely True

| 1 | 2 | 3 | 4 | 5 | 6 | 7 |

Table 2.11 briefly explains the why, how, and cautions of the VoC scale.

The SUD scale is a measurement of the gut-level of *emotional disturbance* being experienced by the client. The SUD scale is shown in Exhibit 2.3.

Table 2.12 briefly explains the why, how, and cautions of the SUD scale.

These scales benefit both clinician and client in that they provide an indicator of the client's progress during the EMDR process. The components of the Assessment Phase

---

TABLE 2.11 Validity of Cognition—The Why and the How

WHY?

When measured during the Assessment Phase, assesses on a gut-level the validity of a client's PC now as they think about the image (or picture) or event (incident, experience, i.e., how strongly a client believes their selected PC). The measurement of the VoC scale at this point during the process helps a client to see "light at the end of the tunnel."

When measured in the Installation Phase, determines what further work may need to be done before the installation of the PC is considered completed (e.g., continuing sets of BLS until VoC = 7, identifying and processing blocking beliefs, feeder memories, ecological validity)

When measured in the Installation Phase, assesses the appropriateness of the PC (e.g., if the VoC does not increase after a few successive sets, the clinician may need to reevaluate the appropriateness of a chosen PC and if another positive belief would be a better fit)

When measured in the Installation Phase, increases the self-efficacy of the client as validity of a PC continues to increase

---

HOW?

"When you focus on the image (or picture; or if no picture, "event"), how true do those words _____ (e.g., "I am safe.") feel to you now on a scale from 1 to 7, where 1 feels completely false and 7 feels completely true?"

"On a scale from 1 to 7, how true do those words _____ (e.g., "I am competent.") feel to you now?"

NOTE

It is important to ensure that a client's PC is appropriate and possible. A red flag for this risk is when the client reports an initial VoC rating of 1. If this occurs, the client may be engaging in wishful or magical thinking, which is indicative of a PC that will be almost impossible to achieve. Consider the case of a client who physically abused his 5-year-old son within the past 3 months. His PC is, "I am a good father." This statement is clearly untrue. No matter how one thinks about it, a good father does not beat up a young son. No matter his remorse, there is no way for this father to achieve this desired belief within the near future. In this instance, "I can learn from my mistakes and be a good father" may be a far more appropriate PC.

Abbreviations: BLC, bilateral stimulation; NC, negative cognition; PC, positive cognition; VoC, Validity of Cognition.

EXHIBIT 2.3 Subjective Units of Disturbance Scale

Neutral/No Disturbance   Highest Disturbance

◄ –

0   1   2   3   4   5   6   7   8   9   10

are considered to be the steppingstones to adaptive resolution, and Chapter 3 has been entirely dedicated to stressing its importance. In this phase, the assessment questions activate the trauma memory network. The assessment questions are asked at the beginning of the train ride. They are what stokes the fire that finally forces the train down the track to its final destination.

DISPARATE SCALING BETWEEN SUBJECTIVE UNITS OF DISTURBANCE AND VALIDITY OF COGNITION

Many clinicians find the disparate and reverse scaling on the SUD (i.e., 0–10) and VoC (i.e., 1–7) scales confusing and annoying. Why not scale them the same? Either 0 to 10 or 1 to 7?

TABLE 2.12 Subjective Units of Disturbance—The Why and the How

WHY?

Helps the clinician and client determine which memories need to be targeted.
Rates the intensity of a client's disturbance.
When used in the Desensitization Phase, assesses the degree of change in a client's level of disturbance and determines when desensitization is complete (SUD = 0 or ecologically valid).

HOW?

"From 0, which is neutral or no disturbance, to 10, which is the worst disturbance you can imagine, how disturbing does it feel to you <u>now</u>?"

NOTE

The clinician should be cognizant of which emotion(s) a client is rating and ensure the client is rating negative not positive emotions. It is also important for a client to name the emotion(s). If more than one emotion is named, however, the level of disturbance is always on the entire incident, not the emotions alone.
The SUD does not specifically measure the intensity of an emotion but, rather, the level of disturbance of the event (incident, picture). A person may feel some sadness but not be disturbed by it (SUD = 0). The client may experience no residual emotion but still feel disturbance related to a body sensation (e.g., arousal when they think of the sexual abuse).

Abbreviation: SUD, Subjective Units of Disturbance.

One of the reasons Shapiro presented these scales this way is to indicate the direction of desired change (i.e., increase vs. decrease). In the reprocessing phase, the desired direction of change for the client's level of distress is to *decrease* it (i.e., 0) and in the Installation Phase, the clinician looks for the validity of the client's PC need to *increase* it (i.e., 7) to ensure success in both phases (see Exhibit 2.4).

Moreover, the SUD scale is a Likert scale modeled after Wolpe (1990), who used a scale from 0 to 100. A Likert scale measures agreement/disagreement on a particular statement (e.g., "How disturbing is it to you now?") and in the Assessment Phase it measures the level of disturbance from neutral or no disturbance (i.e., 0) to the highest disturbance (i.e., 10) the client can imagine. The VoC scale is a semantic scale which is more subjective. It measures how much of a trait or quality the item has (i.e., "On a gut level, how true do those words, 'I am _____ (PC)' feel to you now?"). The VoC measures the validity of the cognition from totally false (i.e., 1) to totally true (i.e., 7).

EXHIBIT 2.4 Desired Direction of Change: Decrease in Subjective Units of Disturbance and Increase in Validity of Cognition

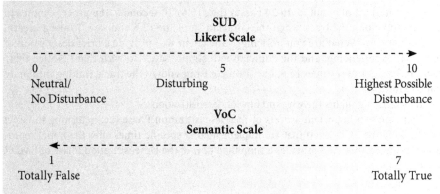

SUD
Likert Scale

0	5	10
Neutral/	Disturbing	Highest Possible
No Disturbance		Disturbance

VoC
Semantic Scale

1		7
Totally False		Totally True

Abbreviations: SUD, Subjective Units of Disturbance; VoC, Validity of Cognition.

PHASE 4: DESENSITIZATION

WHEN DOES IT BEGIN?

By the end of the Assessment Phase, the train is now loaded and ready to start down the first level of reprocessing associations. The goal of the Desensitization Phase is to reprocess every level of association identified along the track until the level of disturbance is down to a 0. The "active" reprocessing phases of EMDR therapy (i.e., *reprocessing* and *desensitization*) begin when the clinician instructs the client, "Focus (or Concentrate) on that image (or picture) (do not describe the image/picture) and those words _____ (repeat the client's negative cognition, 'I am _____'). Notice where you feel it in your body and follow my fingers (or alternative form of bilateral stimulation)." (*Note:* The

TABLE 2.13 Desensitization—The Why and the How
WHY?
Addresses a client's disturbing imagery and other sensory details, cognitions and thoughts, emotions, and body sensations Elicits insights and appropriate associations, including linkage of the memory to adaptive information
HOW?
Repeated sets of BLS are used with appropriate variations and changes of focus as needed until a client's initial reported SUD lowers to a 1 or 0.

Abbreviations: BLS, bilateral stimulation; SUD, Subjective Units of Disturbance.

clinician does not refer back to all aspects identified in the Assessment Phase—only the image or incident, the NC, and where it is felt in the body.) Once these instructions are given, the reprocessing is initiated and continues with subsequent sets of BLS until the SUD is 0, VoC is 7, and body scan is clear. The clinician begins the agreed-on form of BLS. After an initial set of about 20 to 24 passes (i.e., 15 to 20 seconds), the process comes to the first stop along the track when the clinician stops the BLS and says, "Take a breath. (Pause.) Let it go. What are you noticing?" The client will provide a brief description of what he is experiencing, and the clinician will simply say, "Go with that ('Notice that,' 'Be with that.')" and resumes BLS. The train continues down the track, linking into more adaptive information.

Table 2.13 highlights the why and how of desensitization.

There are two important aspects of the Desensitization Phase (i.e., returning to target and checking the SUD level) that are implemented at specific times after the initial reprocessing begins. Exhibit 2.5 provides a simplified flow of the Desensitization Phase of EMDR therapy.

WHAT ABOUT REPROCESSING?

The title of the Desensitization Phase may prove inadequate as it does not describe all that it entails. It may be more appropriate to consider this the Desensitization Phase of the Reprocessing Phases. Desensitization or removal of the disturbance associated with the initial target is actually only a side benefit of this phase. The PC restructuring (e.g., "I am bad" to "I am good"); integration of perception (i.e., from that of the 3-year-old who experienced the original trauma to that of the 30-year-old who is processing the trauma); new insights or "Aha" experiences; and positive changes in previously reported emotional and physical sensations are significant as well. The typical outcome of the desensitization represents the removal of the disturbing material, whereas reprocessing is the actual reprocessing of the material and includes the association or linkage with adaptive information. Resultant restructuring of the cognition, spontaneous emergence of insights, and other positive shifts usually do not occur without this important component.

EXHIBIT 2.5 Desensitization Flow Chart

Desensitization and reprocessing begins: "Focus on that image (or picture) and those words, (repeat the client's NC). Notice where you feel it in your body and follow my fingers." Clinician reprocessing begins with a set of BLS. The clinician ends each set with, "Take a breath. Let it go. What are you noticing *now?*" The client reports what they are noticing. Go to **A.**

A. **Continue with additional sets of BLS and the client report:** If something new or distressing surfaces, repeat **A.** If nothing new or distressing surfaces or client's reports are neutral or positive for two or more consecutive sets of BLS, go to **B.**

B. **Go back to target:** Ask the client, "When you go back to the original experience, what are you noticing now?" The client reports what they are noticing. Say, "Go with that," and implement another set of BLS. Go to **A** and continue with sets of BLS until nothing new or distressing surfaces or client's reports are neutral or positive for two or more consecutive sets of BLS. It may be necessary for the client to return to target **(B)** several more times before all the negatively associated material has been accessed and reprocessed. If, after going back to target and doing another set of BLS, the client reports nothing new or distressing, go to **C.**

C. **Check the SUDs:** Ask the client, "When you bring up the experience, on a scale of 0 to 10, where 0 is no disturbance and 10 is the highest disturbance you can imagine, how disturbing does it feel to you now?" If the client's SUD = 1 or greater, check for a feeder memory or blocking belief, and go to **A.** If the client's SUD = 0, go to **E.** If the client's SUD >0 or 1 and nothing is shifting, go to **D.**

D. **Implement another set of BLS:** If still no change, ask the client, "Where do you feel it in your body?" and implement an additional set of BLS. If still no change, ask the client, "What keeps it a _?" or "What prevents it from being a 0?" If still no change, the clinician should be alerted to check for ecological soundness or validity. If the client's SUD = 0 or ecological soundness has been established, go to **E.**

Note: The clinician is cautioned against considering ecological soundness when the VoC is moderate or high.

E. **Implement another set of BLS:** If the SUD continues to equal 0 (or ecologically valid), proceed to the Installation Phase.

Abbreviations: BLS, bilateral stimulation; NC, negative cognition; SUD, Subjective Units of Disturbance; VoC, Validity of Cognition.

PURPOSE OF THE DESENSITIZATION PHASE

The primary purpose of this phase of the EMDR treatment protocol is to (a) identify, reprocess, and flush out the dysfunctionally stored material associated with the original target and all channels of association (i.e., images, cognitive, emotional, or physiological nodes that link with other past experiences), and (b) desensitize the emotional impact of the memory. As the processing of the information unfolds, the clinician can observe shifts in client awareness, progression of insights, and noticeable changes in the original target information in terms of image, affect, thoughts, sounds, sensations, or beliefs.

ASSOCIATIVE PROCESSING

Clients may report different aspects of the memory. They may mention changes in imagery (e.g., an angry face changes to a happy or neutral face). A new memory could emerge. A change in the presenting image can occur; details in the presenting image may unfold (e.g., the most terrifying moment of the traumatic event being targeted emerges); or a single image that represents a disturbing aspect of an event may change (e.g., intrusive thoughts, flashbacks, recurring nightmare images). Clients sometimes notice auditory and cognitive changes. They may also experience a diminishing negative emotion, indicative of the memory becoming less toxic and thus desensitized. Each of these shifts is processed completely as it emerges. Once fully processed, the client can be instructed to reaccess the original target.

The general tendency during reprocessing, whether the client is reporting new or shifting information, is for the disturbance to be less disturbing with each successive set. Even if this is not the case and the disturbance increases, reprocessing may still occur. The client may have accessed or experienced another aspect of the memory, and it is being metabolized at a different level. It is a safe assumption thatas the disturbance lessens progressively from set to set, the targeted channel is being cleared of dysfunctional debris.

In between sets of BLS, it is imperative that the clinician listens carefully to what the client reports so that the next focus of reprocessing can be adequately identified, and the clinician's next intervention can be strategically orchestrated. When one channel of association has been addressed and exhausted, as indicated by two neutral or positive reports in a row, the client is instructed to return to the original target to discern the presence of new channels needing processing. Each of these channels is linked psychologically to the other. Although the client focuses on the target, the information can be shifted in different ways. It may be linked by shifting images, thoughts, sounds, tastes or smells, insights, sensations, or beliefs. New memories, emotions, and changes in body sensations may also shift the information in various ways. This is what Shapiro (2018) calls *associative processing*. Depending on which of these manifests, the clinician will decide what action may be taken. Remember, desensitization of these channels cannot be completed until the dysfunctional material associated with the targeted event has been eliminated. Table 2.14 provides an outline of the possible changes in focus between sets identified by Shapiro (2018), examples (where applicable), and the clinician's response under the circumstances.

EVALUATING CHANNELS OF ASSOCIATION

In the Desensitization Phase, each line of association that emerges during the reprocessing of the client's disturbing material may be evaluated at several levels. Is the progression

TABLE 2.14 Associative Processing

Clients tend to report their experiences in terms of changes in imagery, tastes or smells, sounds, sensations, thoughts, and emotions

CHANGE IN	EXAMPLE	IF THEY EMERGE ... BECOMES THE FOCUS OF THE NEXT SET (I.E., "GO WITH THAT." ADD BLS)
TASTES OR SMELLS	The smell of aftershave or the taste of tobacco left behind after father's molestation of daughter	Taste or smell If it fades and no new associations, return to original target
IMAGERY		
New Memory		
One memory	The memory of her father opening the door	Memory
Several memories	The memories of the molestation and breakfast with the family the next morning	Most disturbing memory
All memories are equally disturbing	Both memories above are highly disturbing.	Last memory to appear
Endless stream of associated memories (i.e., 10–15)	Bits and pieces of multiple molestations stream through client's consciousness	Return to original target after each shift.
Transient memory	Memory of their first sexual encounter with a boyfriend	If needed, retarget after presenting memory has been completely reprocessed.

(continued)

TABLE 2.14 Associative Processing (continued)

Clients tend to report their experiences in terms of changes in imagery, tastes or smells, sounds, sensations, thoughts, and emotions

CHANGE IN	EXAMPLE	IF THEY EMERGE … BECOMES THE FOCUS OF THE NEXT SET (I.E., "GO WITH THAT." ADD BLS)
Image Changes		
Negative image emerges	Father yelling	Negative image
Neutral or positive image emerges	Father singing softly to himself while gardening or sitting silently on his rocking chair in the evenings	Early in session: Target a set or two to see if it strengthens; readdress the original issue as soon as possible. Later in session: Continue until strengthening ceases.
Two images emerge, one positive, one negative	Father singing and yelling	Negative one
Incident Unfolds	Frame-by-frame scenes of the molestation emerge chronologically	Client focuses on each scene in separate sets until resolution is achieved.
Appearance Changes		
Image itself changes in appearance	Father appears to be getting bigger and bigger	Changes in appearance. If client states the image is "blurry," ask the client to concentrate on it.
Image disappears, disturbance remains		Tell the client to "Just think of the incident" and concentrate on physical sensations. Continue the sets until the disturbance is resolved.
SOUNDS AND THOUGHTS		
Negative **Statement or Idea**	"I am a total failure."	Ask the client, "Where do you feel it in your body?" If thought persists, implement proactive version of EMDR (e.g., cognitive interweave).

(continued)

TABLE 2.14 Associative Processing (continued)

Clients tend to report their experiences in terms of changes in imagery, tastes or smells, sounds, sensations, thoughts, and emotions

CHANGE IN	EXAMPLE	IF THEY EMERGE … BECOMES THE FOCUS OF THE NEXT SET (I.E., "GO WITH THAT" ADD BLS)
Mismatch Client deliberately brings something to consciousness	Client reports thinking of something funny	Determine whether client has deliberately attempted to bring something to consciousness that is inconsistent with the elements associated with the original target. If the determination is positive, ask the client, "Are you doing or saying anything deliberately?" If so, instruct the client to stop and to "Just let it happen, without judging or trying to force anything to happen."
Positive Thought If positive thought emerges If no change in positive thought If positive thought strengthens If both a positive and negative thought emerge at once	"I am a success." "I am a failure. I can be successful at some things."	Initiate additional sets. Return to original target. Initiate additional sets. Initiate additional sets.
Insights Become progressively more adaptive		The clinician instructs the client to "Go with that."
SENSATION AND AFFECT		
New Emotion **Shifting Body Sensations**	"I am feeling unusually sad." "My stomach is beginning to cramp."	The clinician will ask the client, "Where do you feel it in your body." Physical sensations. Initiate additional sets.

Abbreviation: BLS, bilateral stimulation.

or sequential processing that is occurring therapeutically relevant? When can a clinician assume that a channel has been cleared out? What does the clinician need to do when it is determined that an end of a channel has been reached? What happens after retargeting the original incident and no new associations, emotions, sensations, thoughts, or images emerge? Table 2.15 is designed to answer these questions and more.

TABLE 2.15 Evaluation of Association

IDENTIFY, EVALUATE, MEASURE

Evaluate associations for …
Progression (i.e., disturbance is more or less disturbing).
Other aspects of the memory being experienced.
Any change in image, sounds, smells, beliefs, emotions, sensations.

A channel of association has been cleared when …
The client experiences no disturbance.
The associations have reached a reasonable stopping point; or
Nothing new emerges after two consecutive sets of BLS.

When enhanced associations cease …
Instruct client to retarget the original incident by saying, "When you focus on the original event (incident, experience), what are you noticing now?" Wait for client's response and then initiate another set.
Process emerging channels.
After each channel has been cleared, instruct the client to return to the original target.

When the original incident has been retargeted and no new associations, emotions, sensations, or images emerge after two consecutive sets of BLS …
Recheck the client's SUD level.
If the client reports a SUD equal to 0, it is considered to be desensitized; and the installation of the PC may begin.
If SUD becomes stuck at 1 or 2, focus on the body sensation and add BLS.
If there is still no change, ask, "What makes it a ___ ?" or "What prevents it from becoming a 0?" Once identified, add BLS. If still no change, probe for additional blocking beliefs or feeder memories.
If there is a *feeder memory*, first say, "Just notice that," and add BLS. If it does not resolve, then target it directly beginning with Phase 3. When resolved, return to the current target and complete reprocessing.
If a response indicates the presence of a *blocking belief* (e.g., "If I get my hopes up too high, the other shoe will drop"), first say, "Go with that," and add BLS to see if the blocking belief clears on its own. If the SUD continues to be over 0 (or not yet ecologically valid), implement the full EMDR reprocessing (i.e., Phases 3–6) on the memory where the client came to believe the blocking belief.
If the client's response seems appropriate given the circumstance (e.g., "It's difficult to feel totally safe knowing the rapist is out on bond"), first say, "Go with that," and add BLS to see if there is any change. If the SUD continues to be over 0, the level of disturbance may be considered ecologically valid. Initiate the Installation Phase.

TABLE 2.15 Evaluation of Association (continued)

If the client has arrived at the end of a channel and time is running out ...

Go directly to the Closure Phase. Do not return to target, as this may open up a new channel of association with a yet untapped disturbance.

If the client makes a statement that reflects a blocking belief limiting further progress ...

Acknowledge the statement and do at least two sets of BLS to see if it will clear on its own. The clinician can also ask, "Do you remember where (or when) you learned that?"

If necessary, using floatback identify the memory associated with the origination of the limiting/blocking belief and add repeated sets of BLS before returning to target. If the limiting statement/blocking belief continues to impede full desensitization, it may require reprocessing of the associated memory (using Phases 3–6) before returning to the Desensitization Phase of the original memory. Before advancing to the Installation Phase, examine all SUD levels higher than 0 for ecological validity. Accept the limitation only if it appears reasonable and has ecological validity.

Abbreviations: BLS, bilateral stimulation; SUD, Subjective Units of Disturbance.

END OF CHANNEL?

When associations appear to have reached the end of a channel or when nothing new or disturbing appears after two or more successive sets of BLS, the clinician redirects the client back to the original target. "When you focus on the original event (incident, experience), what are you getting *now*?" (Or "What are you noticing *now*?") A new set of BLS is initiated regardless of whether the client reports negative or positive associations. Even if the client reports positive images or reports "nothing," which is quite often the case, continue the BLS for at least two sets. It is not unusual for unexpected channels of association to open up at this point in time. If this happens, simply reprocess the material in the usual manner and redirect the client once again to the original target after the channel appears to have been completely cleared of dysfunctional material. (*Note:* When the clinician says, "What do you notice now?" and the client says, "Nothing," it is important for the clinician to question the client by asking, "What does 'nothing' mean?" or "Where did your mind go as you were noticing nothing?" Or, "Do you notice 'nothing' or 'numbness' in your body?" Sometimes, "nothing" may mean that the client is experiencing a condition of numbness, has dissociated, or simply can no longer access the memory. At other times, "nothing" may reflect clients' misperception that whatever is in their awareness is not relevant. The answer the client gives will depend on what the clinician does (i.e., continue processing, return to target, or utilize a strategy to unblock the processing).

Only when the client reaches a point at which no new associations, images, sensations, thoughts, or emotions come to the forefront will the clinician ask the client, "Focus on the original event (incident, experience). On a scale of 0 to 10, how disturbing does it *feel* to you *now*?" If the client answers, 0, the original target is said to be desensitized. Transcripts of client sessions, which include the Desensitization Phase, are provided in Chapter 6.

What happens if the SUD reported by the client is more than 0? Consider the following:

Clinician: From 0, which is neutral or no disturbance, to 10, which is the worst disturbance you can imagine, how disturbing does it feel to you now?
Client: It feels like a 2.

The clinician implements another set of BLS.

Clinician: How disturbing does it feel to you now?
Client: It is the same.
Clinician: Where do you feel the 2 in your body?
Client: In my head.

When a client initially reports a SUD >0, the clinician's first line of action is to have the client focus on where the client feels it in their body.

Clinician: Where in your head?
Client: My forehead.

It does happen that a client will report a sensation in their head that is not necessarily of a physical nature. Instead of questioning whether it is cognitive or physical, just ask the client the same question as mentioned previously. You do not risk leading the client away from an important component of their processing in asking this question. Do not try to lead a client during reprocessing. Remember that what is being processed is about them, not you.

Clinician: Go with that. Take a breath. (Pause.) Let it go. What comes up for you now?

The phrase, "Let it go," is intentionally stated this way as it vaguely refers to "letting go" of the breath and the memory.

Client: It's the same.
Clinician: What emotions are you feeling?
Client: I'm feeling a little wary.

The client has reported a low-grade negative emotion. If the client had reported a more positive emotion at this time, the clinician could redirect the client to assess negative emotions if they remain.

Clinician: What keeps it from being a 0?
Client: I don't deserve to be happy.

The client's response reveals what is called a *blocking belief.* The clinician could ask, "Do you remember when you first learned this, or first had that thought?" If there is time, the experience(s) creating the belief should be processed. If not, this information will need to be carried over to another session and be targeted with an associated memory for the full EMDR reprocessing (i.e., Phases 3–6). Once resolved, return to the current target and complete Phases 4 through 8.

Clinician: (Change direction of eye movement.) Go with that. Take a breath. (Pause.) Let it go. What are you getting now?

If the client still reports no change, the clinician will need to check for ecological sound-ness. The clinician does not proceed beyond the Desensitization Phase of EMDR unless the client's SUD is 0 or ecological soundness has been validated (see Chapter 1 for explanation of ecological soundness).

WHEN TO RETURN TO TARGET?

Table 2.16 provides a more comprehensive understanding of the why and how of returning to target. Table 2.17 provides guidelines for returning to target (i.e., the original incident or event) and taking the client's SUD level. Returning to target has the potential of activating another channel of association. Therefore, if there is insufficient time to reprocess new material, the clinician is advised to close down a session as incomplete rather than returning to target.

TABLE 2.16 Going Back to Target—The How and the Why

WHY?

To discern whether or not there are additional channels of dysfunctional material that need to be reprocessed when there is no change after two consecutive sets of BLS.

To reorient the client to the target if the client or the clinician is confused about where the processing has gone in relationship to the target.

To commence the Installation Phase.

To complete the body scan.

HOW?

After a client has come to the end of a channel of association:

"When you go back to the original memory (incident, experience), what are you noticing now? [Pause as the client provides a response.] Go with that."

Abbreviation: BLS, bilateral stimulation.

TABLE 2.17 Desensitization Phase—When to …

Return to original target if …	Take a SUD (0–10) if …
An end of channel is identified by repeated neutral, positive, or vague responses by the client.	After returning to target and doing two more sets of BLS, the client still reports neutral or positive material.
After at least two consecutive sets of BLS, the client reports no change.	Client's progress is being checked.
After a set of BLS, client does not have a response to, "What are you noticing now?"	The end of the desensitization is identified (SUD = 0).
The associations reported by the client are too vague or unrelated to the original target.	The client reports a SUD >0, then do the following in order: Focus on client-reported location of body sensation and add BLS.

(continued)

TABLE 2.17 Desensitization Phase—When to ... (continued)

	Ask what prevents it from being a 0. If identified, do BLS. Search for feeder memories or blocking beliefs using direct questioning, floatback, or affect scan. Consider ecological soundness. Explore further for additional feeder memories or blocking beliefs.
Change characteristics of BLS if	
Client reports a headache, dizziness, or nausea. No shift in information is reported or observed.	Differences need to be accommodated.
... then change direction or change type of BLS	**... then change length and speed or change type of BLS**

Abbreviations: BLS, bilateral stimulation; SUD, Subjective Units of Disturbance.

WHAT TO DO IF THE SUBJECTIVE UNITS OF DISTURBANCE BECOME STUCK

What happens when the SUD level becomes stuck at a 1 or 2?

1. Ask the client, "Where do you feel it in your body *now*?" and add BLS.
2. If the SUD is still not equal to 0, the clinician may check for blocking beliefs by asking the client, "What keeps it a _____?" or "What prevents it from becoming a 0?" If a blocking belief is identified, the clinician adds BLS until the blocking belief has been completely reprocessed.
3. If the SUD is still not equal to 0, the clinician may probe for additional blocking beliefs or feeder memories. Note that blocking beliefs may be spontaneously processed (i.e., an EMDR reprocessing session within an EMDR reprocessing session) or may be the target in a subsequent reprocessing session (i.e., "Where did you learn that belief?"). As mentioned previously, additional blocking beliefs may be uncovered using direct questioning, floatback, or affect scan techniques.
4. If SUD is still not equal to 0, the clinician may check for ecological soundness (Shapiro, 2009–2017a).

HOW LONG DOES IT LAST?

The Desensitization Phase in some instances may last no longer than 5 to 10 minutes or may span over numerous sessions. Some sessions can move smoothly from start to finish without the clinician saying anything more than, "Take a breath. (Pause.) Let it go. What are you noticing now?" followed by, "Go with that" or words of encouragement, such as

"Good. You're doing fine." This is what is called *spontaneously reprocessing*. At times, you may experience other sessions that are full of verbal and nonverbal cognitive interweaves (see Chapter 5) every step of the way. Just like every client, each session is unique. Anything can and will happen. Go with the flow, keep out of the way, and let whatever happens, happen. This is a good EMDR mantra for both the clinician and the client.

WHEN TO PROCEED TO THE INSTALLATION PHASE?

Remember, the rule of thumb for this stage is that the SUD level is reduced to a 0 before proceeding to the Installation Phase. Does this always happen? Not necessarily. We need to allow for ecological validity in some instances. What keeps it from being a 0? In other words, is this response most appropriate for this client under their unique circumstances?

Table 2.18, "Derailment Possibilities—Desensitization," has been compiled to demonstrate to the clinician the potential obstacles to unobstructed processing.

TABLE 2.18 Derailment Possibilities—Desensitization

"Bring up that picture, those negative words _____ (repeat the client's NC), notice where you are feeling it in your body."

The clinician may instruct the client to "follow my fingers" if using eye movements or initiate other modes of BLS (e.g., taps, tones).

Initiating BLS without instructing the client to bring up the image, NC, and body sensations

When initiating desensitization, use the words above in the order presented to initiate reprocessing for a client.

Instructing the client to "stay" focused on the image/target

As the image/target is a starting point, the clinician instructs the client to "Just let it go wherever it goes," thus allowing associations to spontaneously emerge. The client may get confused and try to hold on to the target and have difficulty getting started as a result. Prior to initiating desensitization and reprocessing, the clinician may say to the client, "The image is a starting point, not a staying point. Focus on the image for a few moments and then release to allow other associations to spontaneously emerge."

Providing or repeating the description of the image or any details of the memory being processed

This is contraindicated in the protocol. Repeating back details of a client's memory is an intrusion into their processing. When referring to the event, refer to the "original incident or experience." If the client cannot remember where they started in the beginning, give as little detail as possible.

Failing to closely observe the client's non-verbal cues during the BLS

The clinician should closely observe any changes in expression, breathing, skin tone, posture, etc., during the BLS to help determine the length of the set.

(continued)

TABLE 2.18 Derailment Possibilities—Desensitization (continued)

Failing to listen to what a client says between sets
The clinician should listen attentively in order to identify the client's next focus for processing (e.g., a client's last statements, another aspect of a client's experience, or possibly a new target).

Asking the client to focus on: 1) the emotions identified during the Assessment Phase; 2) the physical sensations described by the client (e.g., a deep pain in the pit of my stomach); 3) a sensation in place of an image; or 4) "All that"
Always instruct the client to bring up the picture, the NC, and where (*not what*) they feel it in their body. Do not repeat the details.

Encouraging or allowing a client to control the processing
The clinician may hear from the client that they are "trying to" do something between sets (e.g., "I am trying to slow my breathing and trying to accept what happened"). When this occurs, reinforce the client's process by saying, "Just notice what comes up. Don't control it in any way. Just let what happens, happen." The clinician may need to explore ways to deal with the client's resistance to affect associated with the memory (e.g., additional resourcing).

Abbreviations: BLS, bilateral stimulation; NC, negative cognition.

TAKING A BREAK

At the end of a set of BLS, when the clinician says, "Take a breath. Let it go," the clinician stops the eye movements (or other form of BLS) and asks the client, "What are you getting now?" or "What comes up for you now?" This is essential to maintain dual attention and is done for several reasons: (a) During BLS, information pertinent to the targeted traumatic event is stimulated. Stopping the processing allows time for the dysfunctional information to drop off and adaptive information to be consolidated. (b) This brief interruption allows the clinician to reevaluate the client's progress and to judge if reprocessing has taken place. (c) During this break, the client's concentration and intensity of focus is interrupted, and the client is given permission to rest, reorient, and verbalize what happened during the set. It also provides the client with a sense of empowerment. (d) Finally, it provides the client with an opportunity to verbalize their internal process and understand whatever changes have taken place more readily (Shapiro, 2018).

PHASE 5: INSTALLATION

WHAT OCCURS?

When all channels of association revealed throughout the reprocessing are completely cleared (i.e., SUD = 0 or ecologically valid), the clinician can embark on the Installation Phase. It is during this phase that the PC is linked to the original event (incident or experience). Installation occurs when the positive self-assessment established by the client is fully integrated with the targeted information. To allow this, the clinician rechecks the current *appropriateness*, *applicability*, and *validity* of the PC reported in the Assessment Phase. Table 2.19 provides a clearer view of the why and how of the Installation Phase.

TABLE 2.19 Installation—The How and the Why

WHY?

Sets the desired direction of change

Stimulates the appropriate alternative and adaptive neuro networks

Offers clinician/client a baseline from which to assess a client's progress

If a better PC fails to materialize before or during desensitization, provides an opportunity for the client to give a positive statement that can be used for rapid installation

Improves a client's self-esteem and installs generalized self-enhancement as their train moves further down the track

May increase generalization to other associated memories or present triggers that will be targeted as part of the treatment plan

Ensures "enhanced integration of the cognitive reorganization" (Shapiro, 2018)

HOW?

"Focus on the original event (incident, experience). Do those words, _____ (e.g., 'I am competent'), still fit, or is there another positive statement you feel would be more suitable?"

"Focus on the original event (incident, experience) and those words, _____ (e.g., 'I am competent'). From 1, which is completely false, to 7, which is completely true, how true do they feel now?"

"Hold them together." Initiate BLS utilizing standard long/fast sets that are typical of all reprocessing phases

Abbreviations: BLS, bilateral stimulation; PC, positive cognition.

PROCEDURAL CHANGE TO THE PROCESSING OF THE VALIDITY OF COGNITION

In the VoC Phase, the clinician checks the appropriateness of the PC obtained in the Assessment Phase (i.e., "Is 'I am _____ (positive cognition)' still what you would like to believe about yourself as your focus on the original event or is there another one that is more appropriate?"). Regardless what the client wants to believe, the VoC is evaluated on a scale of 1 (i.e., totally false) to 7 (i.e., totally true). BLS is then initiated for 20–40 sets. After each subsequent set, the clinician rechecks the VoC on a scale of 1 to 7 (i.e., "As you focus on the original event, how true do those words, 'I am _____,' feel to you now on a scale of 1 to 7?"; Shapiro, 1995, 2001, 2018).

Rather than check the VoC after each successive set (i.e., "How true does it feel now?"), it is recommended the clinician simply say, "Go with that" after each successive set of BLS until two or more neutral or positive passes have occurred (Deany Laliotis, personal communication, December 1, 2019). When this occurs, the clinician goes back to the original event and those words, "I am _____ (positive cognition)," to determine what direction of change, if any, has occurred. This allows for the possibility of other negative associations to emerge. This is similar to the steps for checking the SUD when a client gets to the end of a channel of association in the Desensitization Phase.

After each set, the clinician asks the client, "What are you noticing now?" and once the client responds, the clinician says, "Go with that." Once the clinician feels the client has reached a VOC = 7 or ecological validity has been obtained, the client it taken back to target and the desired PC and asked, *Bring up the event and those words,* 'I am _____ (positive cognition)'. How true do those words feel to you now on a scale of 1 to 7?" If the client responds with a comment and reports the VoC as <7, processing continues with additional sets of BLS until 7 (or 6, if ecologically valid) is achieved. If the client responds "7," it is suggested the VoC be reinforced with an additional set of BLS. If it continues to be 7, the clinician can move the client on to the Body Scan Phase.

Whatever way the clinician decides to help the client process the VoC is fine. Either strategy is efficient and amenable to successful processing.

Table 2.20, "Derailment Possibilities—Installation," has been compiled to demonstrate to the clinician the potential obstacles to the installation process.

TABLE 2.20 Derailment Possibilities—Installation

"Do the words (repeat PC) still fit or is there another positive statement you feel would be more suitable?"
"Focus on that event and those words.' _____ (repeat selected PC)'. On a scale from 1 (completely false) to 7 (completely true), how true do they feel to you now?"
"Hold them together." Initiate BLS.
"On a scale from 1 to 7, how true do those words, '_____ (repeat selected PC),' feel to you now?"

Failing to check if the PC is still appropriate before completing installation
The clinician should always check the appropriateness of the PC identified by the client in the Assessment Phase. Be open for the possibility that a more appropriate or powerful PC may have emerged spontaneously during successive sets of desensitization. The client should use the PC that is most meaningful and acceptable to him.

Failing to ask the client to pair the selected PC with the original memory
Linking the original memory (or its current manifestation) with the PC strengthens the associative bond between the two. In the event the memory (e.g., being snubbed at a birthday party by her peers) is triggered in the future, it may be accompanied by a stronger, more adaptive response (e.g., "I am worthy").

Instructing the client to focus on the original image (or picture)
The installation of the PC requires that a client focuses on the entire memory or event rather than the original starting image (or picture). This question is asked in a more general form because the original image may have disappeared or has been replaced by another that is more appropriate.

Instructing the client to focus on the body by saying, "Where do you feel it in your body?" or "What keeps it a (SUD level)?" or "What prevents it from being a 0?"
Asking these questions indicates the clinician is confused by the order of the phases. The order is: (a) desensitization (SUD = 0; check for blocking beliefs or feeder memories if SUD still >0), (b) installation (check for appropriateness and install PC), and (c) body scan (i.e., "What is happening in the body now?").

(continued)

TABLE 2.20 Derailment Possibilities—Installation (continued)

Asking for the SUD after the completion of the Installation Phase (i.e., installing PC with a VoC of 7)
This is a common occurrence. Again, it is important to remember the order of the phases of treatment. Installation only occurs after the completion of the Desensitization Phase. There is no need to recheck the SUD level once it has already been established at the end of Phase 4.

Installing a PC without a SUD of 0. Installation should occur after the original target has been desensitized
A SUD level of 0 is indicative of this. Exceptions: Presence of ecological validity (i.e., client's response seems appropriate to the situation)

Continuing to accept the original cognition when the VoC does not improve
If a client selects the original cognition as appropriate and the VoC rating does not increase after several successive sets of BLS, it should be reexamined. The client's self-efficacy should have increased with the processing of the previously dysfunctional material, and this increase should be reflected in the strengthening of the PC selected. If this does not occur, a substitute PC should be found and installed.

Failing to check for blocking beliefs or feeder memories when the VoC <7
If the VoC does not rise after repeated changes in direction of eye movement or the VoC does not rise beyond a 5 or 6, the clinician will need to check for the emergence of other associations. If a blocking belief or feeder memory arises, reprocess using Phases 3 to 6. If the association proves innocuous, nonproblematic, and does not resolve after a few sets of BLS, proceed to the Body Scan.

Abbreviations: BLS, bilateral stimulation; PC, positive cognition; SUD, Subjective Units of Disturbance; VoC, Validity of Cognition.

EVALUATE APPROPRIATENESS OF ORIGINAL COGNITION

Because so much baggage is shifted or lost and new insights are being boarded at the various stops during the "train ride," what the client originally wanted to believe about herself may now be different. She may need a stronger PC to complete the process. It may have gone from, "It's over. I am safe" to "I am a powerful person." The fact that a more powerful and appropriate PC surfaced after desensitization was complete is indicative that the client has moved further along the information-processing track.

To provide the client with an opportunity to evaluate the appropriateness of the original PC, the clinician asks, "When you bring up that *original* incident, do the *words,* '_____ (e.g., 'I am competent)' *still fit,* or is there another positive statement you feel would be more suitable (or appropriate)?" It is imperative that the client chooses the cognition that resonates the most with them as they focus on the original target. If you help the client to identify a PC at this stage, do so cautiously. Remember, the process belongs to the client; and the clinician needs to keep their distance from the "moving train." The clinician does not want to impede or derail the "train" with any attempts to be helpful.

VALIDITY OF THE POSITIVE COGNITION

During this phase, the positive effects of the chosen cognition identified are being linked and can be fully integrated with the target memory. Imagine that the client chooses the original PC. The baseline measurement has already been established. Has the VoC changed? To assess, the clinician asks, "As you focus on the incident, how true do the words '_____ (e.g., 'I am competent')' feel now on a scale of 1 to 7, where 1 is completely false, and 7 is completely true?" If the VoC does not increase after repeated sets, the PC will need to be rechecked and, possibly, a substitute may be considered.

LINK TO ORIGINAL TARGET

Once an appropriate PC is chosen, it is linked with the original target. At this stage of the process, the original target is likely to be quite different than it was when reprocessing began. Clients often describe it as cloudy, in the distance, untouchable, foggy, unclear, or far way. The client is asked to hold the event in mind while repeating the PC silently to themselves in this way: "Focus on the event, and hold it together with the words '_____ (e.g., 'I am competent')'." Successive sets of BLS follow. Because the Installation Phase is still part of reprocessing, the length and speed of the set are similar to those determined in the Desensitization Phase.

WHEN IS INSTALLATION COMPLETE?

Like desensitization, installation continues until there are no longer changes and the VoC continues to be a 7. Continue to do BLS as long as the VoC of 7 is strengthening and becomes more adaptive. When it is a 7 and further BLS no longer causes it to shift in a functional way, the clinician then implements the body scan.

HOW TO DISCERN THE PRESENCE OF A BLOCKING BELIEF

If the VoC does not rise to a 7, it is a signal for the clinician to look for blocking beliefs or emerging associations that need to be addressed, such as "If I don't have this problem, I won't know who I am." The clinician checks for a blocking belief by asking the client, "What keeps this from going to a 7?" Or "What is the worst thing that would happen if this went to a 7?" If a blocking belief arises, implement another set of BLS and say, "Go with that."

If the client insists on sticking with their blocking belief and it seems without much content and the VoC is nearly a 7, the clinician can proceed to the body scan. If the blocking belief has some punch and does not improve with successive sets of BLS, the clinician will need to assess for ecological soundness (see Chapter 1 for definition of ecological soundness). There are occasions when the blocking belief becomes a target for a full EMDR reprocessing (i.e., Phases 3–6). It is not until the earlier memories behind the blocking belief are successfully reprocessed at the next session(s) that the reprocessing of the original target can be completed. Once the earlier memory has been successfully processed, the clinician needs to reevaluate the original target and complete the installation.

PHASE 6: BODY SCAN

Dysfunctionally stored material often manifests itself somatically. After having successfully installed the client's PC, the clinician asks them to reassess their body from head to toe for residual body tension, tightness, unusual or unfamiliar sensations, or even positive changes that might still be present. Table 2.21 presents the why and how of the body scan.

In implementing a body scan at this juncture, the clinician is looking for residual blocking beliefs or other material (e.g., major areas of resistance, associated networks containing dysfunctional information that might not be fully integrated). The amelioration of the cognitive, emotional, and physical sensations will increase the probability of a positive treatment effect.

The client is asked to focus on the original targeted event, the PC, and any identified physical discomfort. The clinician continues with successive sets of BLS until the tension has been lifted. This is what the clinician says to initiate a body scan: "Close your eyes and keep in mind the original event (incident, experience) and the words (e.g., 'I am competent.'). Then bring your attention to the different parts of your body, starting with your head and working downward. Any place you find tension, tightness, or unusual sensation, let me know." If positive sensations arise, use BLS to strengthen. If negative sensations arise, use BLS to decrease them and continue to reprocess until they subside or disappear. With standard sets (speed and length) of BLS used in the other reprocessing phases, the client is able to decrease or eliminate negative sensations or increase positive sensations that are identified.

If the physical sensations do not dissipate, first switch to diagonal eye movements and add another set or two of BLS. This often helps to move somatic material. If the physical sensations still do not shift, another channel or other associated networks of information may be present and will need to be processed before the current session will be considered complete. Positive sensations that emerge are reinforced with shorter sets (i.e., 4–6) of BLS. It is not unusual for a client to report an obvious injury when scanning their body (e.g., pain in the back from a ruptured disk or upset stomach from something they had for lunch). When these types of bodily discomforts are reported, continue the body scan in the prescribed manner. There may

---

TABLE 2.21 Body Scan—The Why and the How

WHY?

Evaluates and addresses any residual body tension, tightness, or unusual sensations

Opens or reveals other channels of association that may be appropriate for reprocessing

Highlights major areas of resistance

HOW?

"Close your eyes and keep in mind the original event (incident, experience) and the words, '_____ (i.e., positive cognition; e.g., "I am competent.')" Then bring your attention to the different parts of your body, starting with your head and working downward. Any place you find any tension, tightness or unusual sensation, tell me."

be chronic or acute problems showing up physiologically that are affecting their psychologically as well. In these instances, three things can happen: (a) the discomfort may dissipate or remit completely; (b) the client may remember another incident that had not been anticipated by either the clinician or the client, which will need to be reprocessed at the next session (e.g., a pain in the lower back may cause a memory of being molested at age 5 years to emerge); or (c) there is no change, because the bodily discomfort is unrelated to the current processing.

The key point to remember during the body scan is that the reprocessing of the dysfunctional material is not considered complete until the body scan is clear (i.e., free of residual negative associated sensations). Do not proceed to the next target until it is clear. If there is not enough time in the session to ensure the completion of this phase, either extend the session or close it down and address anything that is not completed at the next session.

Table 2.22, "Derailment Possibilities—Body Scan," has been compiled to demonstrate to the clinician the potential obstacles to the Body Scan Phase.

TABLE 2.22 Derailment Possibilities—Body Scan

"Close your eyes and keep in mind the original event (incident, experience) and the words _____ (repeat selected PC). Bring your attention to the different parts of your body, starting with the top of your head and working downward. Any place you find any tension, tightness, or unusual sensation, please tell me."

Failing to do a body scan
No reprocessing is considered complete or successful without the inclusion of the body scan.

Failing to pair the negative body sensations with the original event (incident, experience) and/or the installed PC
Follow the script as prescribed.

Instructing the client to focus on the original picture/image
A body scan is facilitated by having the client focus on the original event (incident, experience) rather than the image (or picture) targeted in the Assessment Phase.

Concluding a body scan when the client still reports residual physical sensations
The body scan is not complete until the client reveals no tension or associated negative sensations.

Failing to initiate successive sets when the client continues to report negative physical sensations
Successive sets of BLS should be continued until all negative physical residue has been desensitized.

Performing a body scan when there are only a few minutes left in a session
The clinician should ensure that the client does not end a session with high levels of disturbance or in the middle of an abreaction. A body scan always has the potential for setting off new channels of dysfunctional information (e.g., fears, resistance) that may take more than a few minutes to reprocess. Ensure that the client leaves the office in a stable condition.

(continued)

TABLE 2.22 Derailment Possibilities—Body Scan (continued)

Asking the client, "Is everything okay?"
A body scan evaluates and addresses residual body tension. The clinician facilitates processing by refraining from asking questions or making comments.

Asking the client questions about what is revealed during a body scan (e.g., "Did you find any tightness in your chest?")
The clinician should refrain from asking or asking as few questions as possible.

Asking the client the status of a previously reported body sensation (e.g., "Do you still feel it in your chest?")
Trust the process. Unless a blocking belief or a feeder memory arises, the body scan usually eliminates any negative physical sensations by the end of a session without any further assistance from a clinician.

Requesting a descriptive appraisal of any body sensations the client may report (e.g., "How much does it hurt?")
As it does not provide any useful information, the clinician should refrain from asking these kinds of questions.

Asking for body sensations only
At this point, channels of association, blocking beliefs, feeder memories, or negative emotions may still emerge. As the client scans their body, just let whatever happens, happen.

Initiating a body scan before the completion of desensitization and installation
The body scan should only be performed after all other parts of the process have been fully completed.

Naming the body parts as the client scans down his body
The client should be encouraged to scan down their body by their own design and at their own pace.

Encouraging the client to do the body scan with their eyes open
Eyes should remain closed during the scanning of the body and then open for the BLS during the body scan.

Failing to strengthen any positive physical sensations that arise
Successive sets should always be done to strengthen these positive physical sensations.

Abbreviations: BLS, bilateral stimulation; PC, positive cognition.

PHASE 7: CLOSURE

LEVELS OF CLOSURE

The Closure Phase of EMDR therapy refers to either properly shutting down an incomplete session or ending a completed session. This phase also includes debriefing the client after each session, instructing the client to maintain a log between sessions, and giving guidelines for in-between sessions. Regardless of whether the session is complete or incomplete, the primary goal of this phase is to ensure that the client is returned to "a state of emotional equilibrium" (Shapiro, 2018) by the end of the session (i.e., to ensure the client's stability at the end of a session and between sessions). At this point, all processing has stopped, and the client is directed to focus on or access neutral or other positive networks that are not associated to the targeted network.

STRATEGIES FOR CLOSING SESSIONS

Strategies for closing down completed and incomplete sessions are different.

Completed Session

A session is complete when SUD = 0, VoC = 7, and the body scan is clear (Exhibit 2.5). When a session has been successfully completed, the clinician indicates to the client that it is time to stop and provides encouragement and assurance by saying, "You have done very good work today. How are you feeling?" In addition, the clinician debriefs the client by further asking, "As you review your experience in our session today, what positive statement can you make to express what you have learned or gained?"

Incomplete Session

As Exhibit 2.5 depicts, a session is considered incomplete if one of the standard procedural steps has not been completed (i.e., SUD >0, VoC <7, or no clear body scan).

EXHIBIT 2.5 Formulas for Completed and Incomplete Target Sessions

Completed Target Session =

(SUD = 0) + (VoC = 7) + (Clear body scan)

Incomplete Target Session =

SUD >0
(SUD = 0) + (VoC <7)
(SUD = 0) + (VoC = 7) + (No clear body scan)

When it is necessary to close down an incomplete session, do not: (a) recheck the SUD or VoC levels, (b) refer back to the PC, or (c) do a body scan, as these acts may reactivate processing. If the clinician feels that they are at a good stopping point, they notify the client, asks the client's permission to stop, and tells the client why. For instance, "We are near the end of our time together, so we need to stop. Are you okay with that?" It is at this juncture that the clinician may suggest containment, stress reduction, progressive breathing, relaxation exercises, or the Lightstream Technique to help return the client to their normal functioning. Remind the client of their safe (calm) place. As additional processing may take place between sessions, it is important that the client be stabilized before leaving the clinician's office. As the processing can continue, instruct the client to use self-soothing strategies in between sessions. Assure the client that they can call between sessions, if needed. Once the client is stabilized, encourage and debrief the client in the same manner described earlier for completed sessions. "You have done some good work today. How are you doing?" "As you consider your experience today, what positive statement can you make that expresses how you feel?" Or, "What have you learned or gained today?" Do not use BLS after asking these statements.

INSTRUCTIONS FOR CLOSING ALL SESSIONS (COMPLETE AND INCOMPLETE)

"The processing we have done today may continue after the session. You may or may not notice new insights, thoughts, memories, or dreams. If you do, just notice what you are experiencing. Take a snapshot of it (what you are seeing, feeling, thinking, and the trigger), and keep a log. We can work on this new material next time. If you feel it is necessary, call me"; or something similar.

Table 2.23 presents the why and how of complete and incomplete closure.

TABLE 2.23 Closure: Complete or Incomplete—The Why and the How

WHY?

Returns a client to a state of emotional equilibrium to ensure stabilization between sessions
Assures that the client no longer has "one foot in the past" but instead is fully oriented to "here and now"

HOW?

Do this by providing the client with detailed instructions at the end of each session:
Instruct the client to use a variety of relaxation techniques (e.g., safe (calm) place, sacred space, Lightstream Technique) to assist them in maintaining a relative state of calm:

"I suggest we do a relaxation (or a container) exercise before we stop." Or, "I suggest we _____ (fill in the blank)."

Remind the client that disturbing images, thoughts, or feelings may continue between sessions and that these disturbances are indicative of further processing. Instruct the client to keep a log of any disturbing memories, dreams, thoughts, or situations that arise between sessions, as these disturbances may be the target of future sessions. Provide the client with realistic expectations as to what may surface in terms of negative or positive responses between sessions:

"Processing may continue after our session. You may or may not notice new insights, thoughts, memories, physical sensations, or dreams. Please make a note of whatever you notice. We will talk about that at our next session. Remember to use the self-control techniques as needed."

The clinician may need to use their own clinical judgment in determining whether special attention needs to be focused on a client to minimize the opening of new negative channels of association or whether the client has the ability to manage any negative emotions that arise as a result of continued reprocessing between sessions. In this case, the clinician may suggest to the client the use of the Safe (Calm) Place exercise, Container, and/ or relaxation exercises to utilize between sessions. The clinician may also want to assign the client homework to help manage whatever comes up in the interim, such as practicing self-control techniques and using the trigger, image, cognition, emotion, and sensation (TICES) grid.

These are the instructions that Shapiro (2009–2017a, 2009–2017b) provides for closing down all reprocessing sessions: "Processing may continue after our session. You may or may not notice new insights, thoughts, memories, physical sensations, or dreams. Please make a note of whatever you notice. We will talk about that at our next session. Remember to use self-control techniques as needed." Table 2.24, "Derailment Possibilities—Closure," outlines some common oversights when it comes to the Closure Phase of treatment.

TABLE 2.24 Derailment Possibilities—Closure

INCOMPLETE SESSIONS

Initiating a complete session closure when the session is incomplete
When a session is incomplete, it is the clinician's responsibility to debrief the client and to return them to an adequate level of equilibrium before they leave the office. Adequate closure techniques (e.g., Lightstream, Safe (Calm) Place exercise, visualizations) need to be agreed upon before reprocessing commences in the event that the client continues to demonstrate high levels of disturbance.

Failing to use relaxation, visualization, Container, Safe (Calm) Place, etc.
Maintaining client stability between sessions is extremely important and easily facilitated by these techniques. Therefore, it is the clinician's charge to attempt to bring the client back to a state of relative calm and mastery before completely closing down a session. Clients should be encouraged to use these self-control techniques to dissipate any disturbance that may emerge between sessions. Here is a list of potential client consequences as a result of insufficient closure:

1. Client is destabilized between sessions, experiencing emotional lability
2. Client does not feel "present" and grounded, indicative of dissociation
3. Client experiences flashbacks or other intrusions from the memory network between sessions
4. Client may notice an increased urge or inclination to use maladaptive coping strategies that may be related to the memory or memory network being reprocessed (e.g., a client in recovery who is reprocessing childhood trauma that is also associated with beginning to use substances may find themself having increased cravings for alcohol)
5. Client may become more reactive to present triggers associated with the memory being reprocessed
6. Client may experience increased dissociation between sessions

---

(continued)

TABLE 2.24 Derailment Possibilities—Closure (continued)

Continuing with EMDR reprocessing if the client is unable to completely eliminate moderate levels of disturbance with the previous self-control techniques
If the client is unable to eliminate moderate levels of disturbance using self-control techniques, EMDR reprocessing should be postponed until the client is able to tolerate high levels of disturbing material. More frontloading is indicated.

Going back to target, NC, body, or checking for a SUD level prior to ending a session
It is important to find a neutral place for the client to stop. Having a client refocus on any of these components will risk bringing up additional disturbing or distressing material or activating another negative channel of association. Again, shifting states for a client is necessary for closing a session; and some type of relaxation exercise or self-control technique is preferable.

Encouraging the client to focus on distress and then using BLS to bring the client to their safe (calm) place
The purpose of closing down a session is to bring the client back to complete equilibrium at the end of every session.

Doing additional BLS after the client has been brought back to their safe (calm) place
Doing so may stimulate more negative material or activate another channel of association

Instructing the client to focus on her distress (e.g., incompetency, fear of snakes, belief that they are unlovable)
One of the purposes of closing down an incomplete session by invoking a relaxation response or "container" is to provide an opportunity to shift states and terminate reprocessing. Having a client focus on their distress may activate more disturbing material or open another negative channel of association.

FOR ALL SESSIONS

"The processing we have done today may continue after the session. You may or may not notice new insights, thoughts, memories, or dreams. If you do, just notice what you are experiencing. Take a snapshot of it (what you are seeing, feeling, thinking, and the trigger), and keep a log. We can work on this new material next time. If you feel it is necessary, call me."

Neglecting to perform any closure at all
It is important for a client to know what to expect after each session and what is normal and what is not. That is, a client should know that additional processing occurs regularly between sessions and is evidenced by any disturbing images, thoughts, or emotions that may emerge and that these are healthy signs of continued processing. Even if a client experiences little or no obvious processing, the clinician should not fail to perform debriefing and closure at the end of each session. Ending a session in this way can provide the client with a sense of accomplishment and self-efficacy. So regardless if little or no processing has been completed within a session, debriefing and closure should *always* be conducted.

(continued)

TABLE 2.24 Derailment Possibilities—Closure (continued)

Failing to debrief the client at the end of every EMDR session
Decompensation may occur with any client, especially one who may be suicidal. Failing to debrief a client of the possibilities increases this danger. It is important that the clinician provide the client with realistic expectations (negative and positive) about between-session processing. This information helps the client to better maintain a sense of equilibrium.

Failing to provide adequate time at the end of a session to conduct the required closure
Conduct a 45-, 50- to 90-minute session allowing for adequate processing and time at the end of the session to facilitate appropriate closure.

Allowing the client to leave the office with an unresolved abreaction
If a client's trauma is insufficiently processed at the end of a session, the clinician should inform the client that may continue to experience high levels of distress after a session. The clinician should make concerted attempts to bring the client back to a balanced state of equilibrium and also assess whether it is safe for them to drive home.

Forgetting to inform the client that they can call in between sessions as needed
The clinician should inform a client of their availability during the preparation phase of EMDR and at the end of an incomplete session.

Debriefing with the client about the specifics of their EMDR session
Processing continues regardless of what the status of the sessions is at the end (i.e., complete or incomplete), and resolution is still possible in the interim (i.e., between the current and subsequent sessions) even if the session is incomplete.

Failing to ask the client to maintain a TICES log
By having the client keep a log or journal of any negative thoughts, situations, dreams, and memories helps them to cognitively distance themself from the same by the simple act of writing it down on a piece of paper. The client is asked to take a snapshot of anything negative that emerges in the interim. This may or may not be used as a target in a subsequent session. This is often a difficult task to get a client to do. Ask instead that the client to jot something down on his phone and bring it up at the next session.

Using a relaxation or self-control technique that has not previously been introduced to the client
It is more efficient to use a technique during closure with which the client has been previously successful than to experiment with something new.

Abbreviations: BLS, bilateral stimulation; NC, negative cognition; SUD, Subjective Units of Disturbance; TICES, trigger, image, cognition, emotion, and sensation.

ASSESSMENT OF CLIENT'S SAFETY

Regardless of whether the session is complete or incomplete, Shapiro (2018) suggests that the clinician remind and instruct the client in these key points as they leave an EMDR reprocessing session:

1. End the reprocessing using the Safe (Calm) Place exercise, the Lightstream Technique, or other containment strategies to return the client to a more present-focused, functional state of mind.
2. Additional processing may occur between sessions; additional disturbing material in the form of images, thoughts, or emotions may arise.
3. It is important to instruct the client to keep a log or journal of negative material (i.e., situations, thoughts, emotions, dreams) that may arise between sessions. The act of writing provides the client with an emotional distancing technique. The negative material collected in the log may serve as targets for future sessions (see Chapter 8, B: EMDR Therapy Scripts under TICES Log). Although having the client keep a log between sessions is an ideal practice, some clients may be resistant. Just remember, it is neither necessary nor critical to the rest of the process.
4. To ensure client stability, encourage the client to utilize visualization and relaxation techniques between sessions. If they need to write down something disturbing in the TICES log in between sessions, instruct them to use one of the self-control techniques that they were taught following entry into the log. Once they have written something in their log, it helps them to externalize the initial disturbance (or "container" it).
5. It is important for the clinician to provide the client with reasonable and realistic expectations of what might be the negative and positive reactions that a client could encounter before, during, and after a session.

WHAT CAN HAPPEN AFTER A SESSION?

Shapiro (2009–2017a, 2009–2017b) sums it up in this statement to the client:"Processing may continue after our session. You may or may not notice new insights, thoughts, memories, physical sensations, or dreams. Please make a note of whatever you notice. We will talk about that at our next session. Remember to use one of the self-control techniques once a day and after each time you write something in your log."

PHASE 8: REEVALUATION

Reevaluation is an ongoing process of assessing the reprocessing of relevant material before, during, and after EMDR processing sessions. Reevaluation is conducted at the beginning of the next session following an EMDR therapy session to determine if: (a) the treatment effect has held, (b) any other relevant channels of association have emerged, (c) any new experiences stimulated dormant networks, and (d) any new changes need to be implemented to be successfully integrated into a client's life.

Reevaluation is also conducted before terminating treatment to ensure: (a) the client is able to integrate into their larger social systems and (b) all relevant material has been completely processed. Has each individual target been resolved? Has ecological validity been determined? Has all associated material been reprocessed in terms of past, present, and future? Has the client experienced adequate assimilation with a healthy social system?

WHAT HAS CHANGED AND WHAT IS LEFT TO DO?

In the next scheduled session, the clinician elicits information as a follow-up to the client's previous EMDR reprocessing. What has changed? What have you noticed since your last session? What images, emotions, thoughts, insights, memories, or sensations have emerged, if any? Have you noticed changes in symptoms or behaviors? What were your responses to these changes? Have new dreams or other material surfaced as a result? What are your reactions and responses to triggers?

In addition to reevaluating what has changed in the client's life since the previous EMDR session, the clinician will also reassess the specific target work that was done. Has the individual target been resolved? Instruct the client to bring up the memory or trigger targeted in the previous session and say, "Bring up the memory we have been working on. What image represents the worst part of it as you think about it now? What emotions are you experiencing now? On a scale from 0 to 10, how disturbing is it? Where do you feel it in your body?" If the memory was completely reprocessed at the end of the last session (i.e., SUD = 0, VoC = 7, and body scan is clear) and the memory continues to hold no disturbance, the next memory or trigger in the treatment plan can be targeted using Phases 3 to 6. If the reprocessing was incomplete in the prior session, resume at the appropriate phase of reprocessing. Once all phases are completed (i.e., SUD = 0, VoC = 7, and body scan is clear), the client is ready to tackle the next traumatic memory or trigger.

The clinician is encouraged to ask the client these questions regardless of whether the previous session was complete or incomplete. The questions are solicited to ensure the resolution of the targeted issue, the presence of ecological validity, the determination of whether associated material has been activated that must be addressed in the current or subsequent sessions, and the existence of resistance on the part of the client.

RESUMING REPROCESSING IN AN INCOMPLETE SESSION

If an event from the previous session was not fully processed (i.e., SUD >0, VoC <7, and lack of a clear body scan), the clinician will resume the processing of the unfinished target (see Table 2.25).

The aforementioned script is prescribed by Dr. Shapiro for resuming an incomplete session. Notice that the script focuses on the worst part of the memory *now*, the emotions, SUD level, and body sensations. No mention is made of the negative or PC or VoC. The clinician begins the session in this manner because the original image/picture may or may not have been resolved in the past session. By focusing on what is the worst part "now," the clinician allows the client's next channel of association to emerge spontaneously. It is possible that the NC may have changed since the process began. In the Assessment Phase, the clinician determined how the memory was stored initially when implementing the Assessment Phase (i.e., the clinician determined what the worst part was in terms of image [or picture], NC, PC, VoC, SUD, and location of the body sensations). In subsequent sessions, the goal is to access memories as they are currently stored, which most likely have changed since the previous session. To begin the reprocessing again, the clinician says, "Focus on that the image (or picture) and where you feel the sensations in your body," and initiates a set of BLS.

REEVALUATION OF TREATMENT EFFECTS

Have new aspects of the memory or other earlier associated memories emerged during the interim between this session and the last that need to be addressed? This is also the time to

TABLE 2.25 Resuming Reprocessing an Incomplete Session

Use a target memory if SUD >0, VoC <7, or body scan is not clear as reported from a previous session

Reaccess the memory

Clinician: Bring up the *memory we have been working on*. What is the image that represents the worst part of it as you think about it now? Or ask, what is the worst part of the memory as you think of it now?

When resuming the processing of an unfinished target from a previous session, the clinician is not required to identify the NC and PC or the VoC.

Client: Okay. It is not as intense as before, but I do still see my brother shaking the axe at me threateningly.

Identify the client's current emotions around the event

Clinician: What emotions are you experiencing now?

Client: Now that I focus on it, I can feel the fear intensify.

Identify the current level of disturbance (i.e., SUD)

Clinician: On a scale of 0 to 10, how disturbing does this incident *feel* to you *now*?

Client: It's about a 4.

Identify location of physical sensations associated with the incident

Clinician: Where do you *feel* it in your *body*?

Client: In my chest.

Resume Desensitization and Reprocessing

Clinician: Focus on that memory, where you feel the sensations in your body, and follow my fingers (or implement BLS of choice).

Use if the target memory is SUD = 0, VoC <7, and the body scan is not clear

Complete Installation Phase and Body Scan

Use if target memory is SUD = 0, VoC = 7, and body scan is not clear

Complete the body scan

In all cases, follow procedural steps through the Closure Phase

Note: Do not reference the NC.
Abbreviations: BLS, bilateral stimulation; NC, negative cognition; PC, positive cognition; SUD, Subjective Units of Disturbance; VoC, Validity of Cognition.

refer to the client's log or journal to assess changes in behavior or the way they are responding to the world.

Reevaluation of treatment effects takes place at the beginning of each session following an EMDR reprocessing session. After a brief evaluation of changes in how the client acts, feels, senses, or believes, instruct the client to focus on the finished target from the previous session to see if treatment has held and ask, "On a scale of 0 to 10, how disturbing is it to you now?" If the treatment effect appears to have held (i.e., SUD = 0), proceed with processing other appropriate targets. If the client reports something other than a 0, reprocessing of the disturbing material is in order, unless it is determined that there is ecological validity.

REEVALUATION AND TREATMENT PLANNING

Reevaluation focuses on integrating each session into the client's full treatment plan. The clinician assesses how the prior reprocessing session has impacted the client's internal responses and behaviors and how it may have affected individuals with whom the client interacts. This determination allows the clinician to assess what attention needs to be directed toward the client's interpersonal system issues.

The Reevaluation Phase is much more than just a reassessment of previously targeted material to see if treatment has held or additional processing is required. Reevaluation also requires the clinician to actively integrate each targeting session within the client's overall treatment plan and calls for the clinician to assess appropriate targets and outcome in terms of the three-pronged approach (i.e., the client's past, present, and future). The client's stability and functioning between sessions is evaluated to determine if additional Phase 2 stabilization and resourcing may be needed prior to the resumption of reprocessing. In this regard, Shapiro (2018) states that attention must be paid to four factors: (a) resolution of individual target, (b) addressing associated material that may have been activated within a target, (c) reprocessing of all necessary targets in all three prongs, and (d) adequate assimilation accomplished within a healthy social system.

Not only do individual EMDR sessions need to be reevaluated, the clinician also needs to reassess whether the appropriate targets and subsequent outcomes have been attained in relation to the three-pronged protocol (i.e., past, present, and future). A treatment plan structured within EMDR therapy is not complete until all childhood trauma has been processed utilizing all three stages of the protocol. Whether working on past, present, or future targets, or single- or multiple-event targets, the clinician is constantly reevaluating the successful processing of targeted material to ensure that all dysfunction has been reprocessed and that treatment effects continue to be maintained.

FINAL REEVALUATION STAGE

The final reevaluation stage of EMDR therapy will conclude with whatever follow-ups are necessary to determine when it is appropriate for a client to terminate therapy. It is important to remember that the treatment effect may not be generalized to every possible disturbance experienced by the client. It is possible that other issues may arise in the future and that clients may come back to therapy at a later date in an attempt to resolve these issues. Then there is what Shapiro (2018) calls a *natural unfolding process*, which may indicate that the process continues even after therapy has concluded. When this happens, it is not an indication that the EMDR treatment process was a failure. The unfolding of new disturbing material is an opportunity for learning at a different level. Life is a dynamic process, and learning takes place on a minute-by-minute basis even after therapy has concluded.

So, another reevaluation is made prior to the client terminating therapy. In this instance, the clinician will evaluate to discern if the client's symptoms have been reduced or eliminated in a manner that is ecological to the client. In terms of a comprehensive treatment approach, the clinician may make a systematic evaluation of the overall progress of the client in resolution of main themes and detect whether the client has successfully integrated treatment gains into their current life context.

Before termination is considered complete, the clinician may:

Past

1. Ensure that any primary events identified during the course of treatment have been resolved.
2. Scan for other unresolved memories by having the client focus on each of their previously identified NCs or scan chronologically through their life for the same.
3. Reevaluate any events that may have emerged during the processing of a primary target.
4. Identify any cluster memories that have not been resolved through the generalization effect.

Present

1. Reprocess (i.e., Phases 3–6) any current stressors—conditions, situations, people—that continue to evoke any maladaptive behaviors.
2. Identify and address residual sources of maladaptive patterns of response (e.g., physical sensations, urges) that may be a byproduct of second-order conditioning.

Future

1. Ensure all triggers have been reprocessed with desired outcomes or potential changes in the future.
2. Discern whether a client has been successfully able to integrate positive changes from the reprocessing and apply these changes in a positive way in their daily life (Shapiro, 2011).

PIVOTAL POINTS IN THE REEVALUATION PHASE

Table 2.26 presents a summary of pivotal points that Shapiro (2018) has identified for reevaluation to take place. Reevaluation is a dynamic and continuous process. Table 2.27, "Derailment Possibilities—Reevaluation," provides some common mistakes made during the Reevaluation Phase of treatment.

TABLE 2.26 Summary of Reevaluation Phase

Global Inquiry Reevaluate the state of the client's life since the last session.	What has the client noticed since the last session? What has changed? Say, "Tell me what you have noticed different in your life since our last session?" and ask these questions: "Have you noticed any changes in how you respond to the issue we have been working on?" "Have you noticed any insights? Dreams? Changes in behavior or symptoms?"

(continued)

TABLE 2.26 Summary of Reevaluation Phase (continued)

Target Specific:	Reevaluation of previously targeted material:
Reevaluate targeted material processed during the previous session.	Has the memory targeted in the prior session been resolved? Does it require further processing?
	Has the new information been appropriately and adequately integrated by the client?
	Have additional targets emerged as a result of previous processing?
	Have other memories or NCs arisen that were not identified in the History-Taking and Treatment Planning Phase?
	Say, "As you think about the incident we focused on during our last session, what are you noticing now?" and ask these questions:
	"What has changed or what is different about the incident now?"
	"Any new insights or thoughts?"
	"Any new connections?"
	And then say, "When you think of the incident, on a scale from 0 to 10, how disturbing is it now?"
Reevaluation occurs during critical or pivotal points in treatment.	Have all appropriate targets and subsequent outcomes been attained in terms of past, present, and future?
	Have feeder memories that emerged been processed?
A final reevaluation will end with an extensive follow-up period.	Is the client ready to conclude BLS?

Abbreviation: BLS, bilateral stimulation.

TABLE 2.27 Derailment Possibilities—Reevaluation

"Tell me what you have noticed different in your life since our last session."
"Any changes in how you respond to the issue we have been working on?"
"Any new insights?"
"Any dreams?"
"Any changes in behavior?"
"Any change in your symptoms?"

Only performing a final reevaluation
Reevaluations are important to complete at the start of every session which has been preceded by EMDR reprocessing. Revaluation continues to inform the treatment planning process.

Failing to reevaluate at the beginning of each session
At the beginning of each session (after the first reprocessing session), the clinician checks with the client to see if the treatment effects from the previous session have been maintained by having the client reaccess the target from the previous session.

(continued)

TABLE 2.27 Derailment Possibilities—Reevaluation (continued)

The clinician reviews the client's responses to determine if further reprocessing is needed. Revaluation is performed for two reasons: (a) unforeseen ramifications of the treatment effects may have emerged that need attention, and (b) new targets may have arisen. The treatment can be determined to be successful only after sufficient reevaluation of previous reprocessing and any resulting behavioral effects. Every EMDR reprocessing session (i.e., Phases 3–6) should be integrated into a complete treatment plan.

Targeting new material before previous targets have been fully reprocessed
Previous targets need to be fully integrated before initiating reprocessing with a new target. Exceptions may be in the event of feeder memories or blocking beliefs which impede processing. In these cases, "EMDR reprocessing within EMDR reprocessing" may need to be done.

Failing to complete any form of reevaluation
Reevaluation is the eighth phase of EMDR therapy, and the process is not considered complete without it. Even in the event of single-event traumas, re-evaluation needs to be performed. One to three follow-up appointments may be necessary to evaluate treatment effects. In terms of a multiple-event trauma, there may be many reevaluation sessions.

Failing to integrate the targeting sessions with the overall treatment plan
During the Reevaluation Phase, Shapiro (2018) suggests that the following questions be asked and answered to ensure complete integration of the targeted material with the overall treatment plan: (a) Has the individual target been resolved? (b) Has associated material been activated that must be addressed? (c) Have all the necessary targets been reprocessed to allow the client to feel at peace with the past, empowered in the present, and able to make choices for the future? and (d) Has an adequate assimilation been made within a healthy social system?

Reread Chapters 4, 5, and 6 in *Eye Movement Desensitization and Reprocessing: Basic Principles, Protocols, and Procedures* (2018) by Dr. Francine Shapiro.

SUMMARY STATEMENTS

1. EMDR therapy is an eight-phase integrative treatment approach. It is not one or two phases—it is eight.
2. Know your client. Know your client well.
3. There must be an adequate level of trust between the clinician and client for EMDR processing to be successful.
4. If your areas of expertise or specialization do not include the client's diagnosis, it is the your ethical responsibility as a clinician to refer the client to a professional who is appropriately trained. This applies if the client is new. If not, get the appropriate supervision.
5. It is not necessary for the clinician to know all the details about a client's trauma. What is important is that the clinician allows the client to process the trauma without interference. Stay out of the client's way. Stay out of their process.

6. If a sufficient level of trust or bonding has not been established, do not undertake EMDR processing.
7. The explanation of the model that supports EMDR therapy is presented in a way that fosters instilling hope and understanding in terms of how a client begins to comprehend their coping and defense mechanisms.
8. Do not implement EMDR reprocessing (i.e., Phases 3–6) unless the client is ready.

REFERENCES

Artigas, L., & Jarero, I. (2005). [The butterfly's embrace]. *Revista de Psicotrauma para Iberoamérica, 4*(1), 30–31 [Spanish].

Artigas, L. A., Jarero, I., Mauer, M., Lopez Cano, T., & Alcala, N. (2000). *EMDR and traumatic stress after natural disasters: Integrative treatment protocol and the butterfly hug* [Poster presented]. EMDR International Association Conference, Toronto, ON.

Bernstein, C., & Putnam, F. (1986). Development, reliability, and validity of a dissociation scale. *Journal of Nervous and Mental Diseases, 1*, 727–735. https://doi.org/10.1097/00005053-198612000-00004

Boël, J. (1999). Child & adolescent issue: A closer look—The butterfly hug: Some history and updates in its use with children. *EMDRIA Newsletter, Special Edition, 4*(4), 11–13.

Boël, J. (2000). *The butterfly hug plus drawings: Clinical and self-care applications* [Paper presentation]. EMDR International Association Conference, Toronto, Ontario.

de Jongh, A., Ernst, R., Marques, L., & Hornsveld, H. (2013). The impact of eye movements and tones on disturbing memories involving PTSD and other mental disorders. *Journal of Behavior Therapy and Experimental Psychiatry, 44*(4), 477–483. https://doi.org/10.1016/j.jbtep.2013.07.002

Dell, P. F. (2006). The multidimensional inventory of dissociation (MID): A comprehensive measure of pathological dissociation. *Journal of Trauma & Dissociation, 7*(2), 77–106. https://doi.org/10.1300/J229v07n02_06

EMDR International Association. (2019). *Brochure for clients.* Author.

International Society for the Study of Trauma and Dissociation. (2011). Guidelines for treating dissociative identity disorder in adults, third revision. *Journal of Trauma & Dissociation, 12*(2), 115–187. https://doi.org/10.1080/15299732.2011.537247

Jarero, I. (2002). The butterfly hug: An update. *EMDRIA Newsletter, 7*(3), 6.

Korn, D., & Leeds, A. (2002). Preliminary evidence of efficacy for EMDR resource development and installation in the stabilization phase of treatment of complex posttraumatic stress disorder. *Journal of Clinical Psychology, 58*(12), 1465–1487. https://doi.org/10.1002/jclp.10099

Leeds, A. M. (1998). Lifting the burden of shame: Using EMDR resource installation to resolve a therapeutic impasse. In P. Manfield (Ed.), *Extending EMDR: A casebook of innovative applications* (1st ed., pp. 256–281). W. W. Norton.

Leeds, A. M., & Shapiro, F. (2000). EMDR and resource installation: Principles and procedures for enhancing current functioning and resolving traumatic experiences. In J. Carlson & L. Sperry (Eds.), *Brief therapy with individuals and couples* (pp. 469–534). Zeig, Tucker & Theisen.

Miller, E., & Halpern, S. (1994). *Letting go of stress.* Inner Peace Music.

Murray, K. (2011). Container. *Journal of EMDR Practice and Research, 5*(1), 29–32. https://doi.org/10.1891/1933-3196.5.1.29

Shapiro, E. (2011). Suggestions for teaching the application of eye movements in EMDR. *Journal of EMDR Practice and Research, 5*(2), 73–77. https://doi.org/10.1891/1933-3196.5.2.73

Shapiro, F. (1991–1995). *EMDR: The lightstream technique.* EMDRHAP.

Shapiro, F. (1995). *Eye movement desensitization and reprocessing: Basic principles, protocols and procedures* (1st ed.). Guilford Press.

Shapiro, F. (2001). *Eye movement desensitization and reprocessing: Basic principles, protocols and procedures* (2nd ed.). Guilford Press.

Shapiro, F. (2006a). *EMDR: New notes on adaptive information processing with case formulations principles, forms, scripts and worksheets, version 1.1.* EMDR Institute.

Shapiro, F. (2006b). *Know the why and how to choose your what: Some essentials of EMDR model and methodology* [Paper presentation]. Preconference presentation at the 11th EMDR International Association Conference, Philadelphia, PA.

Shapiro, F. (2012a). EMDR therapy: An overview of current and future research. *European Review of Applied Psychology, 62*(4), 193–195. https://doi.org/10.1016/ j.erap.2012.09.005

Shapiro, F. (2012b). *Getting past your past: Take control of your life with self-help techniques from EMDR therapy.* Rodale Books.

Shapiro, F. (2018). *Eye movement desensitization and reprocessing: Basic principles, protocols and procedures* (3rd ed.). Guilford Press.

Shapiro, F. (2009–2017a). *The EMDR approach to psychotherapy—EMDR Institute basic training Course: Weekend 1 of the two part basic training.* EMDR Institute.

Shapiro, F. (2009–2017b). *The EMDR approach to psychotherapy—EMDR Institute basic training Course: Weekend 2 of the two part basic training.* EMDR Institute.

Steinberg, M. (1994). *Structured clinical interview for DSM-IV® dissociative disorders (SCID-D-R).* American Psychiatric Publishing.

Watkins, J. G., & Watkins, H. H. (1997). *Ego states: Theory and therapy.* W. W. Norton.

Wolpe, J. (1990). *The practice of behavior therapy* (4th ed.). Pergamon Press.

3

Steppingstones to Adaptive Resolution

All great truth passes through three phases.
First it is ridiculed, then violently attacked, and finally accepted as self-evident.
—Arthur Schopenhauer (*Chemurgic Digest,* 1951)

ASSESSMENT PHASE

BACK TO BASICS

It is only after the clinician has obtained an adequate history, has determined that the client is an appropriate candidate, and has prepared the client for EMDR therapy that the Assessment Phase can begin. This phase entails two elements. First, the clinician and client confirm the previously selected target memory (i.e., identified target as part of the overall treatment plan), identifying the image (or picture) and its cognitive, emotional, and physical components. Second, baseline measurements are established in terms of total disturbance and the credibility of the positive cognition (PC; i.e., how possible is it given the circumstances?).

The components of the standard EMDR procedure remain consistent whether the clinician is targeting single- or multiple-event traumas, past traumas, present triggers, or future events. In all cases, the clinician will be trying to identify targets that encompass the past, present, and future.

Variations of the EMDR procedural steps are used in specific and special situations (e.g., phobias, obsessive compulsive disorder, and chronic pain). These variations, however, still incorporate the main ingredients of the EMDR procedural steps. Many of these protocols can be found in Shapiro's (2018) book *Eye Movement Desensitization and Reprocessing: Basic Principles, Protocols and Procedures*. These variations will not be covered at this time. Instead, this Primer will be focusing on the standard EMDR protocol to ensure that the clinician has a grasp of all that it entails. Scripted protocols for basic and special situations (Luber, 2009a), special populations (Luber, 2009b), man-made and natural disasters (Luber, 2015), anxiety and mood-related conditions, and trauma- and stress-related conditions (Luber, 2016a) are available as well.

HOW MUCH DO YOU NEED TO KNOW?

After completion of the first two phases (i.e., History-Taking and Treatment Planning, and Preparation), the clinician then proceeds to the Assessment and Desensitization (and Reprocessing) phases. A common question that clinicians may ask is, "How much do I need to know about the memory itself?" The answer is that the clinician needs to know only what the client wants to reveal, or even less. This is the beauty of EMDR therapy. The clinician is not required to know all the painful details of a traumatic event in order for the process to be successful. The clinician can encourage the client to provide only a brief description of the disturbing event (e.g., "My uncle chased me with a dead bird"), explaining that it is not because you do not want to listen, but that it is unnecessary for you to know it all for them to process successfully.

Many clients who come to our doors have told their stories several times to previous clinicians. If there is sufficient information for the Assessment Phase, the clinician probably has enough detail for the client to bring their traumatic memory to a successful resolution without unnecessary retraumatization. Reprocessing is the client's internal process. What they want and need us to know can only be revealed by them when they are willing, able, and ready.

TARGET ASSESSMENT

In order to facilitate appropriate information processing and achieve psychological change through healthier associations, it is imperative that a client make connections to the appropriate targets to gain access to the dysfunctional material that drives a client's current pathology.

EFFECTIVE EMDR THERAPY EQUALS EFFECTIVE TARGETING

The Assessment Phase begins by confirming the specific target that the clinician and client previously agreed upon as part of an extensive treatment plan. In selecting the target, the clinician considered whether it was the most effective for resolving the client's issue. An effective target leads the way to the dysfunctionally stored *material* and, thus, the dysfunctional memory *networks*. Targets generally emerge during a thorough evaluation of the client's presenting problems. From the client's responses to the questions in the History-Taking and Treatment Planning Phase, the clinician is able to help identify salient targets for the client. As stated earlier, in your initial interviews with the client, watch and listen for behavioral, emotional, cognitive, and physical cues; the duration of the presenting issue; how the problem manifests in the present; and what the client needs to be more adaptive in the future. In addition, determine whether the client possesses adequate affect tolerance and stability to process the negative states and access anything positive that may arise during the EMDR process.

If a client presents with a single disturbing or traumatic event, target selection is simply a matter of identifying the worst part of the event. The clinician, however, will also identify any present triggers and future template whenever appropriate. With multiple disturbances and traumatic incidents, target identification and selection become more complicated.

TABLE 3.1 Indicators of Obstructed Memory Networks

MEMORY LAPSES

Able to retrieve only negative memories when there is evidence of positive memories as well	A client witnessed their father having a fatal heart attack. The only memories they can currently access are the last moments of their father's life as he struggled to breathe.	Once the target is processed, the positive events will emerge.

DISSOCIATION

A client presents as highly symptomatic but claims no memory of any traumatic events.	A client presents with a sense of danger, but no traumatic events in the client's life support the presence of this symptom.	Target a specific occurrence of the symptom, preferably either earliest or worst.

ACCESS RESTRICTED TO NEGATIVE MATERIAL

Despite the fact that positive memories have been experienced, a client is only able to access negative ones.	A client's best friend struggled for years with recurring and debilitating colon cancer and eventually died. When they think of their friend, they are overwhelmed with a sense of powerlessness. Their only images of their friend are when they were in hospice.	Target all the memories that contain the disturbing images.

CHARACTERISTICS OF EFFECTIVE TARGETS

The target should be as specific as possible and can be an image (or picture), complete or partial memory of an event, sight, sound, taste, touch, dream, metaphor, fantasy, or recurring thought or fear that something is going to happen. A target should be concrete rather than abstract. Simply targeting "fear of flying" is too diffuse or vague. However, the specific target of experiencing extreme turbulence in an airplane 33,000 feet above the ground during a violent storm is more concrete and a more appropriate target for EMDR reprocessing. There may also be a number of obstructions to the memory network that could be targeted. Table 3.1 describes these obstructions and how to deal with them.

Table 3.2 represents possible obstacles when selecting appropriate targets for processing.

HOW IS THE MEMORY ENCODED?

In assessing how a memory is presently encoded in the client's memory network, Shapiro (2018) suggests asking questions such as, "What **image (or picture)** represents the incident (i.e., representative)?" or "What **image (or picture)** represents the worst part of the **incident** (i.e., most disturbing)?" or "When you focus on the **incident**, what do you get (i.e., if no picture)?" In essence, the clinician is asking the client, "How is it stored now?" This does not include inquiries at this point about what the client feels and believes about themself. Emerging information may be in the form of tastes, sounds, or smells.

TABLE 3.2 Derailment Possibilities—Target Selection

What image (or picture) represents the event (i.e., representative)? or what image (or picture) represents the worst part of the event (i.e., most disturbing)? or when you focus on the event, what do you get (i.e., if no picture)?

Considering the image (or picture) of the incident as the target rather than the memory
The target includes an *image* (or *picture*) that represents the worst part of the event. It is a "freeze frame" picture that encapsulates what happened at the time of the event. It is the image (or picture) that immediately overwhelms a client with fear, dread, anger, sadness, etc., when they focus on the event. If no picture, the target may be accessed through another sensory aspect of the memory (e.g., sound, smell, taste) that is the most disturbing.

Selecting a target that is too vague or diffuse
The target should be more specific than general (i.e., an event where the client experienced extreme disturbance while flying as a passenger in an airplane vs. fear of flying).

Selecting a target unrelated to the presenting symptom(s)
A target should be related to the presenting symptoms as they are indicative of dysfunctionally stored material.

Unless a more recent experience(s) is causing the client's intrusive symptomology, selecting a target memory that is not a relevant, earlier experiential contributor
As most pathology is forged by relevant, earlier life experiences, these events should be processed first. If not, processing may become derailed by feeder memories.

For multiple-event traumas, not clustering the events together
In this case, multiple events should be clustered together; and a representative incident should be selected for each cluster.

Not targeting each present trigger separately
Due to second-order conditioning and previously paired association, it is possible that each may have become independently disturbing.

Case Example: Jennifer

Take the example of Jennifer, who reported being molested by her English teacher when she was a sophomore in high school. The teacher in question had requested that she stay after school one afternoon to help him prepare some special handouts for his class the next day. While helping him, this teacher came up behind her, nudged his head into her hair, kissed her on the neck, and fondled her. Jennifer let out a faint cry and ran from the room. She ran down the hall and out the side door of the school, where she found her brother waiting to give her a ride home. Jennifer never told anyone of her experience outside of therapy. She is a junior now and is encountering difficulties relating to boys her own age and men in authority positions.

Jennifer had never experienced anything like this before. She indicated that her childhood was uneventful. She felt that she had lived a relatively normal life until this point. So, when she asked the client what part of this particular trauma she wanted to work on, the clinician stated it in this way, "What image (or picture) represents the entire incident?" Her answer was, "The car ride home. I felt so ashamed." The clinician asked the question in this manner because it was: (a) a one-time event; (b) she had a clear memory associated with the event; and (c) there appeared to be no other parts to the memory that might have been as disturbing. Alternately, the clinician could have asked, "What is the worst part of this memory?" The client might have replied, "When he came up behind me." In this case, the clinician would have targeted both the worst part and, if they did not emerge spontaneously during the processing, any remaining disturbing fragments (e.g., the ride home).

APPROPRIATENESS OF THE TARGET

In assessing the appropriateness of the selected target, it may be helpful to ask the following question: Does the image or event identified by the client represent a single incident that will potentially gain access to the dysfunctionally stored information? Refer to Figures 3.1–3.6 to see how the individual blocks of the procedural steps build a powerful tool to assist the client in activating their natural healing process.

As many clinicians can attest, single-incident trauma is generally not the type of case that they deal with on a day-to-day basis with their clients. Target selection with clients having complex posttraumatic stress disorder (PTSD) or other complex psychological profiles requires a different approach from that described earlier for single traumatic or disturbing events. In these cases, several clinical aspects may require treatment, and each target needs to be identified and fully processed to obtain positive treatment effects.

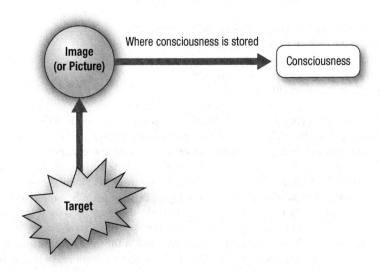

FIGURE 3.1 Steppingstones to adaptive resolution: Image, picture.

A multiple-trauma victim may be asked to cluster their traumatic incidents into groups of like events. They are then asked to choose an incident that is representative of the group to serve as the target. Some clinicians may use historical timelines or genograms to elicit the same type of information from the client. Others may arrange and treat them in chronological order. Some will arrange them in chronological order, but treat the most disturbing event first and then proceed chronologically to treat what remains. Shapiro (2006) developed a Treatment Planning Guide (TPG), which attempts to identify and address past, present, and future events, incidents, issues, and desired outcomes associated with the presenting problem.

ASSESSMENT OF COGNITIONS

ELEMENTS OF NEGATIVE AND POSITIVE COGNITIONS

In terms of the train metaphor, the negative cognition (NC) represents the obstacle on the track that keeps a client from resolving or learning from a past experience; and the PC helps a client take a glimpse down the tracks to see what may be possible. As the train traverses down the track, negative images, thoughts, emotions, physical sensations, and other psychic debris are unloaded, and more positive aspects of the same are loaded until the train reaches its final destination.

The negative belief often pops up spontaneously as the client focuses on the memory. The NC is another indication of how the memory is stored. If not, it is optimal or suggested to take time assisting clients in the selection of the most appropriate cognitions, particularly the negative. The selection of appropriate cognitions predicts greater success in accessing the dysfunctionally stored material surrounding the event. When the proper cognitions are identified, "all roads should lead to Rome." That is, all memory networks lead to resolution of the trauma. Accurate cognitions also assist the generalization and resolution of other traumatic memories existing in the same domain in the client's system.

The NC and PC share common components, such as

- self-referencing (i.e., typically using an "I" statement),
- stated in the present because they still exist in the present,
- focusing on the presenting issue,
- generalizable to other related events, and
- concrete, rather than abstract.

The NC is a self-denigrating or self-limiting irrational belief, whereas the PC represents a shift in self-perception that opens up new possibilities for the client. NCs aid in eliciting associated affect. When the client focuses on the disturbing event and the words, "I am unsafe," the client can still feel fear, confusion, and shame in the present. PCs provide marked evidence of the client's desired direction for change, for instance, "I am safe now" or "I am free of fear, confusion, and shame." As a desired goal, PCs are initially somewhat believable and acceptable. If the cognitions are totally unbelievable, they may need some modifications (e.g., "I am safe" vs. "I am beginning to believe I am safe").

Both the NC and PC are self-referencing and stated in the present tense and, therefore are usually, with some exceptions, preceded by an "I" statement. Both are generalizable, that is, they can be related to clusters of similar events or areas of concern. The NC focuses on the client's presenting issue, whereas the PC focuses on the client's desired direction of change.

TABLE 3.3 Purpose of Cognitions	
NC	**PC**
Highlight irrationality (or dysfunctionality) of the belief for client.	Set a direction for treatment.
Stimulate dysfunctional material.	Stimulate appropriate alternative memory networks.
Establish a baseline from which to measure progress.	Establish a baseline from which to measure progress.

Abbreviations: NC, negative cognition; PC, positive cognition.

For example, "I am a bad person" could be a presenting issue, and "I am a good person" might be the desired direction of change. Table 3.3 provides a simple view of the purpose of cognitions in the standard procedural steps.

WHAT IS A COGNITION?

It is important to know what cognitions are *not* as well as what they are. Cognition involves conscious intellectual activity, such as thinking, reasoning, and remembering. For the purposes of EMDR therapy, cognitions are beliefs. NCs are not feelings, such as "I am scared." They are *not* true statements. In the case of a driver who ran a red light and crashed into another car, the statement, "I was not in control" would be true and an inappropriate negative self-referencing belief if targeting the actual event. Table 3.4 provides a more extensive view of how to and how not to structure NC and PC.

TEASING OUT NEGATIVE AND POSITIVE COGNITIONS

How do you elicit effective NC and PC without putting words into the client's mouth? When assisting the client in forming her NC and PC, the clinician might say, "What words go best with that image (or picture) that express your *negative belief* about yourself *now*? I am." This reminds the client to frame the belief in the present. The clinician is silently saying, "I am what? Please fill in the blank." The client may still attempt to frame their beliefs in different ways, such as "I cannot succeed" for the negative belief or "I can succeed," or "I will succeed" for the positive belief. All are correct.

What if the client says, "I am not successful at my job?" Is this an acceptable NC? This particular cognition only pertains to the client's job. Should the NC (as well as the PC) be generalizable to other areas in the client's life where they might feel they do not succeed? What would be a better cognition, and how would you tease it out? How about, "What does this make you believe about yourself in general?" The statement, "I cannot succeed" has a stronger potential for generalizing to all areas of the client's experience and becoming a more appropriate NC. The corresponding PC may become, "I am a success" or "I can learn to be successful" or even "I can be successful in some ways."

What if a client's response to the clinician's elicitation of a NC is, "I have failed"? In some instances, depending on the client's target, this may be a true statement. The clinician can respond with, "When you focus on (repeat description), what negative belief do you have about yourself? What does that say about you as a person?"

TABLE 3.4 Characteristics of Negative Cognition and Positive Cognition

NC		PC	
WHAT ARE THEY	**WHAT THEY ARE NOT**	**WHAT THEY ARE**	**WHAT THEY ARE NOT**
Self-referential (i.e., usually preceded by an "I")	Statements of simple emotion (e.g., "I am afraid or angry.")	Self-referential (i.e., usually preceded by an "I")	Absolute statements—words like "never" and "always"—are inappropriate (e.g., "I will always be in control.").
Stated in the present	Accurate descriptions of disturbing circumstances, social references, attributes of others or client (e.g., "My father molested me.")	Stated in the present	Magical thinking (e.g., "I am a good father") when the father has recently been caught molesting his child
Focuses on the presenting issue	Blatant overgeneralizations (e.g., "I am the worst person in the world" or "I am alone")	Focuses on the presenting issue	EMDR processing cannot make a silk purse out of a sow's ear. However, one can say, "I can atone for my behavior" or "I can learn to be a good father"
Reflects a belief (i.e., cannot be a simple statement of emotion or a description of circumstances)	Description of fact (e.g., "My mother was scary" or "My mother despised me")	Ecologically sound (i.e., it is possible under client's circumstances)	Negations of negative thinking (e.g., "I am not guilty")
Often irrational and/or dysfunctional	True and rational (e.g., "I was overwhelmed.")	Generalizable to related events	
Generalizable to related events		The word "not" is not used in the statement	

(continued)

TABLE 3.4 Characteristics of Negative Cognition and Positive Cognition (continued)

NC		PC	
WHAT ARE THEY	**WHAT THEY ARE NOT**	**WHAT THEY ARE**	**WHAT THEY ARE NOT**
Cannot be removed if true or installed if false		Reflects a positive and desired direction of change	
Concrete rather than abstract		Not clinician imposed	
Interpretive rather than descriptive		Does not contain words like "always" or "never"	
Elicits associated affect		Concrete rather than abstract	
		Possesses emotional resonance	
		Often elicits positive emotion	

Abbreviations: NC, negative cognition; PC, positive cognition.

If a client responds to the NC question with an emotion (e.g., "I am scared"), the clinician can respond by saying, "What *negative belief* about you goes with that fear?" Or the clinician can reframe the client's response by saying, "In your worst moment, what *negative belief* do you have about yourself *now* when you focus on the event?" In either case, the clinician may be able to elicit an appropriate NC.

Watch for wishful thinking. For instance, a client frames the NC as "I am not perfect" and the PC as "I am perfect." In ordinary life, no one is perfect. In this instance, the clinician might say, "Does that mean you believe _____ (fill in the blank) about yourself?" to help the client reframe the cognitions in a more realistic way.

Sometimes a client may generalize their response when the clinician elicits the NC and PC to their entire life or to another memory. In this event, the clinician may want to remind the client that they are framing their response around the image (or memory, if no picture) being focused on at the moment.

When a client focuses on the image (or picture) representative of the worst part of the memory being processed and cannot easily provide a negative or positive self-referencing belief, the clinician can offer several general NCs as a demonstration of what is being asked, such as "So, for example, I'm wondering if it is more like 'I'm not safe,' or 'I can't trust,' or 'I'm not good enough,' or 'It's my fault.' Do any of those seem to fit?" The clinician should always offer at least three or four suggestions and draw from the informational plateaus most likely to fit the situation being presented. This is to give examples, not to put words into the client's mouth. In these cases, it is important for them to verbally and/or nonverbally indicate to the client that they have permission to choose or reject anything offered as an alternative by the clinician (Shapiro, 2018). If the client still is unable to provide a negative belief, the clinician could hand them the list of cognitions available in the training manual or the laminated Subjective Units of Disturbance (SUD) or Validity of Cognition (VoC) scale placard sold online by Trauma Recovery/EMDR-Humanitarian Assistance Programs. The front side of the placard illustrates the SUD scale and the VoC scale in more graphic detail as a visual aid for children and adults. The other side provides a sample list of NC and PC. Use this strategy sparingly, as it is important for the client to self-generate a NC or PC if possible.

Sometimes clients will provide an emotional response rather than a belief-oriented one. If the client reports an emotional statement, the clinician may respond, "What negative belief about you goes with the (repeat the emotion)?" (Shapiro, 2018).

In working with a client setting up the protocol, they may express more than one NC at a time, such as, "I am unlovable and unworthy." When this happens, ask them to "Focus on the image (or picture). Which negative belief resonates *the most* with the image (or picture)— worthiness or lovability?" Every negative belief opens up another maladaptive memory network, so the clinician intentionally will limit the NC to one per target during the Assessment Phase. Others may emerge during the reprocessing, and that is okay.

At other times, the client may provide NC and PC which are not parallel, such as "I am unworthy" (NC) and "I am lovable" (PC). How would you tease out which negative semantic theme the client associates with the image (or picture)? You could say one of the two things. First, you might say, "If you would like to *believe*, 'I am lovable' as you focus on the image (or picture), what does that make you *believe negatively* about yourself *now*? What is the *flip* side of 'I am lovable'?" Or you might say, "What is the *flip* side of 'I am unworthy' for you?"

Some clinicians believe the NC and PC need to be perfectly parallel to be effective. If the client says his NC is "I am bad," his PC needs to be, "I am good." Some conclude the cognitions only need to be similar. So, what does that mean? Here are some examples:

IMAGE (OR PICTURE) INCIDENT	NC	PC
Rape	I am dirty.	I am okay.
Assault	I am in danger.	I am fine.

Abbreviations: NC, negative cognition; PC, positive cognition.

Dr. Shapiro (2018) states that the PC is *generally* a 180-degree shift from the NC. In any case, the clinician assures that the PC expresses a positive self-assessment that verbalizes the same thematic schema or issue conveyed in the NC.

There are also clinicians who advocate that NC and PC do not necessarily have to be parallel or compatible. For example, Ralph was involved in an automobile accident where his hand was severed. His NC is "I am unsafe," while his PC is, "I can be whole again." There continues to be diversity of belief as to whether the compatibility of the NC and PC is necessary for more complete processing of the target. Some clinicians believe the process works better when the cognitions are parallel. Others say it does not matter. Use of clinical judgment is required in all cases where the cognitions do not match. In this Primer, it is urged that the clinician only accept a PC that is on the same informational plateau (i.e., responsibility/defectiveness, safety/ vulnerability, or power/control [or choice]) as the NC.

Especially under the pressure of processing past trauma, many of our clients are unable to come up with these beliefs. Some cannot distinguish a belief from a feeling. Some just cannot think that quickly on their feet. And some simply go blank. Rather than retraumatize them further by thinking they cannot process correctly, simply offer a range of examples as described above, or say, "Here's my 'cheat sheet.' Focus on the trauma and see if any of the beliefs on the left side of the placard resonate." If the client selects more than one negative belief, ask them to pick the one that resonates the most as they focus on the image (or picture). Even with the use of the laminated SUD/VoC scale, allow the client to come up with a corresponding PC. If they cannot, ask them to look at the NC they selected off this placard and ask if the PC horizontal to it fits. If it does, they can go with that. *Note*: Again, use the placard only as a method of last resort or as a teaching tool. If time allows, the clinician may probe further, if necessary, to assist the client to come up with a NC of their own. "What makes this image (or picture) the worst part?" Have a therapeutic discussion about what the image (or picture) means to the client. Help the client put their feelings into words. Take as much time as needed to tease out an appropriate NC.

Can the protocol be continued without assessing for a NC? Shapiro (2018) states "when the thoughts, emotions, or situation appear to be too confusing or complex, it is appropriate to continue without the negative cognition." In all cases, the clinician attempts to elicit a NC. Information gathered in the Assessment Phase can assist the clinician in drawing out an appropriate NC from the client that resonates with the targeted memory. The existence of a NC allows for more complete accessing and processing of the dysfunctional information attached to the targeted event.

See Table 3.5 for a more complete listing of NCs and PCs. The NCs usually cluster around themes of responsibility/defectiveness (i.e., self-worth/shame or action/guilt), safety/vulnerability, or power/control (or choice). Some of these NC and PC combinations were cited by Dr. Shapiro (1995, 2001, 2018, 2009–2017a, 2009–2017b).

It is not unusual for a client to have difficulty selecting a PC. If this happens, do not spend an excessive amount of time on the process. What is most important is the client having a positive EMDR experience. Remember, they will have another chance to provide a PC in the Installation Phase, so complete the protocol without a PC, if necessary. It may or may not slow down the processing, but the processing probably will not be halted because of it.

TABLE 3.5 Examples of Negative Cognition and Positive Cognition

NC	PC
Responsibility/Defectiveness	
I am not good enough	I am good enough/fine as I am
I don't deserve love	I deserve love; I can have love
I am a bad person	I am a good (loving) person
I am incompetent	I am competent
I am worthless/inadequate	I am worthy; I am worthwhile
I am shameful	I am honorable; I am okay
I am not lovable	I am lovable
I am a failure	I can succeed
I deserve only bad things	I am deserving good things
I am permanently damaged	I am/can be healthy
I am ugly (my body is hateful)	I am fine/attractive/lovable
I do not deserve …	I can have/deserve …
I am stupid/not smart enough	I am intelligent/able to learn
I am insignificant/unimportant	I am significant/important
I am a disappointment	I am okay just the way I am
I deserve to die	I deserve to live
I deserve to be miserable	I deserve to be happy
I am different (don't belong)	I am okay as I am
I have to be perfect (out of inadequacy)	I am fine the way I am
Responsibility/Action	
I should have done something*	I did the best I could
I did something wrong*	I learned/can learn from it
I should have known better*	I do the best I can/can learn
I am shameful/stupid/bad person	I am fine as I am
I am inadequate/weak	I am adequate/strong
Safety/Vulnerability	
I cannot trust anyone	I can choose whom to trust
I cannot protect myself	I can learn to protect myself
I am in danger	It's over; I am safe now
I am not safe	I am safe now
I am going to die	I am safe now
It is not okay (safe) to feel/show my emotions	I can safely feel/show my emotions
Control/Power (or Choice)	
I am not in control	I am now in control
I am powerless/helpless	I now have choices
I cannot get what I want	I can get what I want
I cannot stand up for myself	I can make my needs known
I cannot let it out	I can choose to let it out
I cannot be trusted	I can be trusted
I cannot trust myself	I can/learn to trust myself
I cannot trust my judgment	I can trust my judgment
I cannot succeed	I can succeed
I have to be perfect/please everyone	I can be myself/make mistakes
I can't handle it	I can handle it

*What does this say about you (e.g., I am shameful/I am stupid/I am a bad person)?

Abbreviations: NC, negative cognition; PC, positive cognition.

INFORMATIONAL (CLINICAL, COGNITIVE, OR EMOTIONAL) PLATEAUS

Inadequately processed memories often do not have access to much-needed information needed for a client to experience adaptive resolution. When this occurs, distortions begin to surface that manifest in negative emotions and beliefs about the client as a person, the pervasiveness of which helps to identify a client's clinical theme. The NCs and PCs rendered by clients are often organized into the following themes (i.e., self vs. other, past vs. present, internal vs. external locus of control; Shapiro, 2009–2017a, 2009–2017b):

Responsibility (i.e., client attributes the problem to self rather than to other; possible overidentification with perpetrator)

- Defectiveness (i.e., self-worth/shame; "I am something wrong" or "I am the problem")
- Action (i.e., guilt; "I did something wrong" or "I am the cause of the problem.")

Clients who report NCs and PCs which belong to the responsibility (defectiveness/action) informational plateau often represent with distorted conclusions and confusion about self, between self and others, and between standards of adults versus that of a child (e.g., "I am not good enough," "I am bad.").

Challenge: To separate self from other; to separate self from "something bad was done to me" versus "I am bad"; to designate appropriate responsibility.

Safety/Vulnerability (i.e., distinguish between present and past conditions of safety)
Cognitions (e.g., "I am unsafe" or "I am in danger") on this informational plateau often deal with continued confusion between current conditions of safety even after a threat has passed and experiences of high levels of fear and/or numbness due to thwarted fight/flight.

Challenge: To separate past conditions of safety from present circumstances surrounding safety.

Power/Control (or Choice; i.e., distinguish between past and present locus of control)
Clients who report cognitions (e.g., "I am powerless" or "I am not in control") in this informational plateau often are confused about present-day locus of protocol (i.e., client continues to feel powerless/helpless in the present as a result of something that happened in the past).

Challenge: To shift locus of control (i.e., from external to internal) by helping the client realize as an adult they have choices that as a child they were powerless to make in the past, they can make better or have more choices now, and going forward or can enlist the competent adult to reparent the child.

For examples of the NCs and PCs under each of these information plateaus, please see Table 3.6. These informational plateaus are generally processed in this order.

In the earlier case of Jennifer, the NCs and PCs might be elicited as follows:

Clinician: Jennifer, what words go best with that image (or picture) that express your *negative* belief about yourself now?

"How do you define yourself?" or "What adjectives do you give yourself?" might be more preferable questions in this phase for other cultures (Shapiro, 2018).

Jennifer: I did something bad.
Clinician: What does that make you believe about yourself now?
Jennifer: That I am bad.

TABLE 3.6 Criteria for Negative Cognition and Positive Cognition

NC

Self-referential (i.e., usually preceded by an "I")
Stated in the present
Focuses on the presenting issue
Reflects a belief (i.e., cannot be a simple statement of emotion or a description of circumstances)
Often irrational and/or dysfunctional
Generalizable to related events
Cannot be removed if true or installed if false
Concrete rather than abstract
Interpretive rather than descriptive
Elicits associated affect

PC

Self-referential (i.e., usually preceded by an "I")
Stated in the present
Focuses on the presenting issue
Ecologically sound (i.e., it is possible under client's circumstances)
Generalizable to related events
The word "not" is not used in the statement
Reflects a positive and desired direction of change
Not clinician imposed
Does not contain words like "always" or "never"
Concrete rather than abstract
Possesses emotional resonance
Often elicits positive emotion

Abbreviations: NC, negative cognition; PC, positive cognition.

If a client has difficulty coming up with a negative belief, the clinician may explain how the self-limiting assessments the client has are irrational and what they know to be true may be incongruent with the emotional responses that emerge along with it. Or the clinician might ask the client to "State what you think of yourself in your worst moments, even if you know it isn't true?" (Shapiro, 2018).

Clinician: When you bring up that image (or picture) what would you like (or prefer) to believe about yourself now?
Jennifer: Well, I guess, that I am good.

If a client is unable to come up with an appropriate NC, the clinician might ask, "What thoughts do you have about yourself?"

In assisting clients to formulate cognitions that will optimally aid resolution of their trauma, the clinician can use the checklist below to ensure that all components of each cognitive level have been considered (Table 3.6).

See Figure 3.2 to identify the completion of the cognitive part of the Assessment Phase.

Table 3.7 outlines the common mistakes made by the clinician that may derail successful reprocessing.

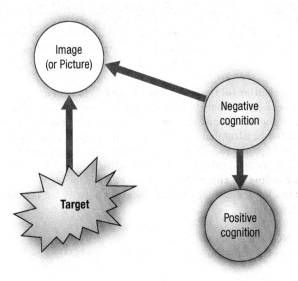

FIGURE 3.2 Steppingstones to adaptive resolution: Cognitions.

TABLE 3.7 Derailment Possibilities—Negative Cognition and Positive Cognition

NCS (NEGATIVE SELF-STATEMENT ASSOCIATED WITH AN EVENT)

What words go best with that image (or picture) that express your negative belief about yourself now?

If no picture, what words go best with that event (incident, experience) that express your negative belief about yourself now?

Accepting a statement that does not meet all the requisite criteria
The NC should be negative, irrational, self-referential, presently held, reflect a client's presenting issue, resonate with his associated affect, and generalize to other like events.

Investigating the NC (or PC) using the Socratic method or in any other complex manner
Always follow the script above, which directly links the negative belief to the image (or picture).

Asking for the NC without a clear reference to the targeted image (or picture)
It is important that the client focus on the original targeted image (or picture) as they develop an appropriate NC. Otherwise, the "train" may not get out of the station.

Accepting more than one NC at a time (e.g., "I am unsafe and helpless") during the Assessment Phase
Each cognition may open a different associated memory network. It is important to find the NC that resonates best with the image (or picture) at hand.

(continued)

TABLE 3.7 Derailment Possibilities—Negative Cognition and Positive Cognition (continued)

Accepting a statement that is a description of what the client is feeling (e.g., "I am sad")
A NC is a belief—not a thought, emotion, or physical sensation.

Automatically suggesting (or imposing) the NC (or PC) to a client
Suggesting a NC to a client should be performed judiciously and only after a client's failed attempts to come up with one on their own. And it should be performed in such a way to openly indicate to the client that it is fine to reject or accept the clinician's suggestions. Do so cautiously, as imposing NCs or PCs on a client may have a detrimental effect despite a clinician's attempt to do so delicately and unobtrusively.

Automatically handing the client a list of NCs (or PCs)
It is important to allow the client to discover their own negative self-talk. Offer the list only as a possible last resort.

Asking for the NC in reference to the past
Elicit the negative belief that resonates best with the image "in the now."

Accepting a statement that is factually true (e.g., "I was powerless")
In the case where an adult presents with issues of childhood sexual abuse, this is a truthful description of a past condition and which EMDR processing cannot change.

Accepting a statement that relates the specifics of an event or a description of circumstances (e.g., "I failed my licensure exam three times")
NCs represent a statement or belief *only* about oneself (e.g., "I am a failure"), *not* other people, places, or things.

Accepting a statement that references the misfortunes of a client's earlier life experiences
Often clients verbalize statements such as "Life was unfair" or "My coach did not like me." When this occurs, simply say, "What does that say about you as a person?" or "What does that make you believe about yourself now?" EMDR processing does not have the ability to change traumatic or distressing life events. However, it may alter what a client negatively believes about themself as a result of these events.

Accepting a statement that is too diffuse or disruptive
It may be appropriate to omit the NC if an issue appears to be too diffuse or disruptive (i.e., too confusing, too distressing, too difficult) to a client's process. Particularly in the earlier stages, ineffective and inefficient processing effects may occur when any of the components of the standard protocol are utilized, so omitting the NC for any reason should be the exception.

Pressing a client for the NC when their thoughts, emotions, or situation seem to be too confusing or complex
In this instance, it is appropriate to continue without the NC.

PC

When you bring up that image (or picture), what would you prefer to believe about your-self now?

(continued)

TABLE 3.7 Derailment Possibilities—Negative Cognition and Positive Cognition (continued)

Accepting a statement that does not meet all the requisite criteria of a PC
A PC should be self-referential, focus on desired state or direction of change, believable, generalizable to like events, and compatible but not necessarily identical with the NC.

Investigating the PC using the Socratic method or in any other complex manner
Always follow the script above, which directly links the preferred positive belief to the image (or picture).

Automatically suggesting (or imposing) a PC in lieu of using the question as stated above
Ask the question, "What words best describe what you would like to believe about yourself now?"

Accepting a statement that is not compatible or is not on the same informational plateau (i.e., responsibility/defectiveness, responsibility/action, safety/vulnerability, or power/control [or choice]) as the NC
The PC represents a client's desired state and is generally a 180-degree shift from the NC. Developing compatible NC and PC most often help facilitate a smoother process in terms of realigning other like incidents for processing within the cluster, using fewer cognitive interweaves, and ensuring the integration of a completed VoC and clear body scan as the train approaches its final stop. For more complex presentations, the clinician may need to accept the cognitions that a client provides (i.e., the best they can do in the moment) despite their incompatibility. The important point is not causing a client undue distress by trying to make the cognitions fit. If a client cannot come up with a compatible PC, accept the one they give or abandon the development of the PC altogether. The client is provided another opportunity for its development in the Installation Phase.

Accepting a statement that is a negation of the NC (e.g., "I am not a failure" or "I am not to blame")
Statements such as these do not stimulate or directly link to the positive information that is stored in the client's neuro networks as strongly and efficiently as more positive statements, such as "I can succeed" or "I did the best I could." Whenever possible, a PC should represent a self-assessment with implications for a brighter future.

Accepting a statement that is absolute or one that uses "always" or "never"
A PC must be reasonable and realizable.

Asking for the PC in reference to the past
Elicit the positive belief that resonates best with the image (or picture) and what a client would like to believe about themself "in the now."

Accepting a statement without a reference to the self and/or a magical connotation (e.g., "They did the best they could" or "My mother is good")
EMDR processing does not have the ability to change actual events of the past or the personality attributes of a client or others.

Abbreviations: NC, negative cognition; PC, positive cognition, VoC, Validity of Cognition.

During the initial learning stages of EMDR therapy, the development of NC and PC can be challenging. To help understand the difference between a belief and a thought, a belief and an emotion, a belief and a truth, and the improbable and the possible, see Table 3.8.

ASSESSMENT OF THE VALIDITY OF COGNITION

VALIDITY OF COGNITION SCALE

The SUD and the VoC are emotional and cognitive rating scales designed and utilized by the clinician to provide a baseline measure for client and clinician alike. The VoC is a 7-point Likert scale which provides a baseline (or pretreatment) measure of strength (i.e., truth) of a client's PC while focusing on the target memory. It is assessed at the beginning of the process after the PC is defined and reassessed in the Installation Phase to see if the original cognition is still appropriate.

Prior to initiating reprocessing, the VoC usually needs to be at least a 2 to be considered a workable cognition. It is very difficult for a client to go from "total disbelief" to "total belief." If a client reports an initial VoC rating of 1 (i.e., completely false), the clinician assesses whether it is unrealistic, improbable, or impossible to achieve (i.e., red flag). The clinician must evaluate the ecological soundness of the cognition in terms of the client and the event. Therefore, the clinician assesses the suitability and degree of success the client may experience in assimilating a PC with a low VoC level. In some cases, the client's PC may simply be titrated to raise the VoC level. For instance, a 1 rating for "I am in control" could be changed to "I can learn to have better control," thereby rendering the VoC at least a 2 (Figure 3.3). If a client reports a VoC of 1, the clinician may ask, "Is this possible for you to get to?" If the client says, "Yes," leave it alone. If the client says, "No," the clinician may say, "Let's see if we can change this just a little to come up with a belief that is attainable."

If a client reports a VoC of 5, 6, or 7, the clinician may begin to wonder if the client is measuring the level of validity in their head. In this case, direct the client to focus on their gut and say, "Is this in your head or gut?" If the client says, "head," instruct the client to "close your eyes and bring up the event. How true does (repeat client's positive cognition) feel now?"

ASSESSMENT OF EMOTIONS

EMOTION

The next step in the Assessment Phase is the identification of the negative emotion(s) associated with the event or issue. This is simply where the client identifies the emotion(s) they are currently feeling when thinking about the original event (incident, experience) and the NC. Let us go back to Jennifer and see what emotions she was able to recognize: "Jennifer, when you bring up the incident and those words, 'I am bad,' what emotion(s) do you <u>feel now</u>?" "Fear, anger, confusion."

In this case, we want to know what Jennifer feels *now* as she focuses on the incident and her NC, *not when it happened*. She may not be feeling the same emotions that she felt at the time the incident happened; and, in her case, she was able to identify more than one emotion. She was afraid her teacher might approach her again. She was angry at what he did and confused about what to do and how to feel about it (Figure 3.4). If the client identifies only one emotion, the clinician does not need to probe for more. The clinician should accept the client's answer and move on.

TABLE 3.8 Negative Cognition and Positive Cognition

NC	PC	CORRECT YES/NO	IF "NO," WHY NOT?	APPROPRIATE COGNITION	INFORMATIONAL PLATEAU(S)
I am **unworthy**	I am **safe.**	No	NC/PC are incompatible. **Response:** Does this mean you believe "I am unsafe?" or "I am unworthy?" Which one fits best as you focus on the image/picture (if no picture, event)?	I am unworthy *and* I am worthy. or I am unsafe (or I am in danger) *and* I am safe.	Responsibility/defectiveness Safety/vulnerability
I am unsuccessful **at my job.**	I am a success. I can succeed.	No	NC lacks generalizability. NC is possible description of fact. *See response below	I am a failure. I cannot succeed.	Responsibility/defectiveness
I am unsafe. I am in danger.	I will **always** be safe.	No	The word *always* makes the PC an absolute statement. **Response:** How could you say what you would prefer to say about yourself without being so absolute, "I am _____?"	I will be safe. I can be safe. I am safe.	Safety/vulnerability
I **have failed.**	I can be successful.	No	NC is possible description of fact; true and rational *See response below	I am a failure.	Responsibility/defectiveness
I am **scared.**	I am safe.	No	Fear is a statement of a simple emotion, not a belief. *See response below	I am in danger. I am unsafe.	Safety/vulnerability
I am incapable of **working with my father.**	I am capable.	No	NC lacks generalizability. NC is possible description of fact *See response below	I am incapable.	Responsibility/defectiveness

(*continued*)

TABLE 3.8 Negative Cognition and Positive Cognition (continued)

NC	PC	CORRECT YES/NO	IF "NO," WHY NOT?	APPROPRIATE COGNITION	INFORMATIONAL PLATEAU(S)
I was doubtful I could escape.	I am safe.	No	NC lacks generalizability. Doubt is a mental state, not a belief. NC is stated in the past tense. *See response below	I am unsafe.	Safety/vulnerability
My boss hated my work.	I am good enough.	No	NC is an accurate description of disturbing circumstances. NC may be a description of fact. *See response below	I am not good enough.	Responsibility/ defectiveness
I am imperfect.	**I am perfect.**	No	In ordinary life, no one is perfect. "I am perfect" is a magical statement (i.e., wishful thinking) and not very realistic. *See response below	I have to be perfect. I am fine as I am.	Responsibility/ defectiveness
I will get hurt if I exercise.	I am safe.	No	NC lacks generalizability. NC is possible description of fact. *See response below	I am unsafe.	Safety/vulnerability
I am different.	I am special.	Yes	Note: NC/PC speaks to the client belief about self-value.		Responsibility/ defectiveness
I don't belong.	I do belong.	Yes			Responsibility/ defectiveness Belongingness/ connection

(continued)

TABLE 3.8 Negative Cognition and Positive Cognition (continued)

NC	PC	CORRECT YES/NO	IF "NO," WHY NOT?	APPROPRIATE COGNITION	INFORMATIONAL PLATEAU(S)
I am **a bad** singer.	I am adequate.	No	NC lacks generalizability. NC is possible description of fact. **Response:** In general, what does that make you believe about yourself as a person?	I am inadequate.	Responsibility/ defectiveness
I am **full of** shame.	I am fine as I am.	No	NC is a description of client's self perception NC is possible description of fact *See response below	I am shameful.	Responsibility/ defectiveness
I am **unloved.**	I am **loved.**	No	Statements in this context that end in "ed" are usually about someone else other than the client. *See response below	I am unlovable. I am lovable.	Responsibility/ defectiveness
I cannot be trusted.	I can be trusted.	Yes			Power/control/choice
I **was** **overwhelmed.**	I am powerful. I have some power	No	NC is true and rational statement *See response below	I am powerless	Power/control/choice
I am an oddball/ weirdo.	I am unique.	Yes			Responsibility/ defectiveness

(continued)

TABLE 3.8 Negative Cognition and Positive Cognition (continued)

NC	PC	CORRECT YES/NO	IF "NO," WHY NOT?	APPROPRIATE COGNITION	INFORMATIONAL PLATEAU(S)
(If the client has abused his child in the past) I am a bad father.	**I am a good father.**	No	Because the father abused his child, it is unrealistic to assume just because he successfully reprocessed his abuse that he automatically becomes a "good" father. **Response:** Tease out further by saying, "Because you were a bad father, what does this say about you as a person?" or "What does that say about you now?"	I can learn to be a good father.	Responsibility/ defectiveness
I cannot safely show my emotions.	**I can safely show my emotions.**	No	Lacks generalizability. *See response below	I am unsafe. I am safe.	Safety/vulnerability
I cannot trust anyone.	I can choose who to trust.	Yes			Power/control/choice
My mother hated me immensely.	**My mother loved me immensely.**	No	Not self-referential NC/PC stated in the past tense Does not reflect a belief—description of fact Lacks generalizability *See response below	I am unlovable. I am lovable.	Responsibility/ defectiveness
I did something wrong.	**I was just a child.**	No	NC/PC are incompatible. PC is stated in the past tense. PC is a statement of fact. *See response below	I did the best I could.	Responsibility/action

(continued)

TABLE 3.8 Negative Cognition and Positive Cognition (continued)

NC	PC	CORRECT YES/NO	IF "NO," WHY NOT?	APPROPRIATE COGNITION	INFORMATIONAL PLATEAU(S)
I am an incompetent **employee.**	I am competent.	No	Lacks generalization **Response:** In general, what does that make you believe *negatively* about yourself as a person?	I am incompetent.	Responsibility/ defectiveness
I am to blame.	I am okay.	Yes			Responsibility/action
I am guilty.	I am **not guilty.**	No	Word *not* in PC is a negation of NC **Response:** How could you rephrase this statement to make it more positive: "I am _____?"	I did the best I could, or I can be forgiven.	Responsibility/action
I do not deserve love.	I deserve to love.	Yes			Responsibility/ defectiveness
I am going to die.	I can live.	Yes		I am going to be okay (This is a good cognition, especially if a client is focusing on a specific phobia, such as flying).	Responsibility/action
I am **unwanted.**	I am **wanted.**	No	Statements in this context that end in "ed" are usually about someone else other than the client. *See response below	I am unacceptable. I am acceptable.	Responsibility/ defectiveness

(continued)

TABLE 3.8 Negative Cognition and Positive Cognition (continued)

NC	PC	CORRECT YES/NO	IF "NO," WHY NOT?	APPROPRIATE COGNITION	INFORMATIONAL PLATEAU(S)
I am unlovable and unworthy.	I am lovable.	No	NC/PC should only use one belief at a time. **Response:** As you focus on the image/picture (if no picture, event), which of these statements resonates the highest; "I am unlovable," or "I am unworthy"?	I am unlovable. I am lovable. or I am unworthy. I am worthy. One or the other—not both	Responsibility/defectiveness
I am weak.	I can be strong.	Yes			Responsibility/defectiveness
I am valueless and sad.	I have value.	No	Combining a belief with statement of simple emotion **Response:** Valueless is what you believe; sadness is how you feel. Focus again on the image/picture (if no picture, event). What words best express your *negative* belief about yourself now?	I am valueless.	Responsibility/defectiveness
I am **the worst person in the world.**	I am good. I am fine as I am.	No	Blatant overgeneralization *See response below	I am bad.	Responsibility/defectiveness
I am **always** bad.	I am good.	No	Word *always* makes this an absolute statement **Response:** In general, what does that make you believe *negatively* about yourself as a person?	I am bad.	Responsibility/defectiveness

(continued)

TABLE 3.8 Negative Cognition and Positive Cognition (continued)

NC	PC	CORRECT YES/NO	IF "NO," WHY NOT?	APPROPRIATE COGNITION	INFORMATIONAL PLATEAU(S)
I am powerless.	I can (will) be powerful.	Yes			Power/Control/Choice
I am a failure.	I am **not** a failure.	No	Word *not* in PC is a negation of negative thinking **Response:** How could you rephrase this statement to make it more positive: "I am _____"?	I am successful. I can be successful.	Responsibility/ defectiveness
I am defective.	I am whole.	Yes			Responsibility/ defectiveness
Life was unfair.	**Life is fair.**	No	NC/PC are not self-referential. NC/PC lack generalizability. NC stated in past tense 'See response below	I cannot get what I want. I can get what I want.	Responsibility/action
I failed my licensure exam three times.	**I passed my licensure exam.**	No	NC/PC lack generalizability. NC/PC are stated in the past tense. NC/PC are possible description of fact 'See response below	I am a failure. I am a success. I can be successful.	Responsibility/ defectiveness
I am to blame.	I am **not** to blame.	No	Word *not* in PC is a negation of negative thinking **Response:** How could you rephrase this statement to make it more positive: "I am _____"?	I did the best I could.	Responsibility/action

(continued)

TABLE 3.8 Negative Cognition and Positive Cognition (continued)

NC	PC	CORRECT YES/NO	IF "NO," WHY NOT?	APPROPRIATE COGNITION	INFORMATIONAL PLATEAU(S)
I am bad.	I am **always** good.	No	Word *always* makes NC an absolute statement **Response:** In general, what does that make you believe *positively* about yourself as a person?	I am good.	Responsibility/ defectiveness
I am not "normal."	I am "normal."	Yes			Responsibility/ defectiveness Belongingness/ connection
I **was** powerless.	I have some power.	No	NC is stated in the past tense. NC is possible description of fact *See response below	I am powerless.	Power/control/choice
I am **never** worthwhile.	I am worthwhile.	No	Word *never* makes NC an absolute statement *See response below	I am worthless.	Responsibility/ defectiveness
I am incompetent.	I am competent **and happy**.	No	NC/PC should only use one belief at a time. Happiness is a state of being versus a belief. **Response:** Competent is what you would like to believe; happy is what you would like to feel. Focus again on the image/picture (if no picture, event). What would you prefer to believe about yourself now?	I am competent.	Responsibility/ defectiveness

*Response: What does this say about you as a person?

Abbreviations: NC, negative cognition; PC, positive cognition.

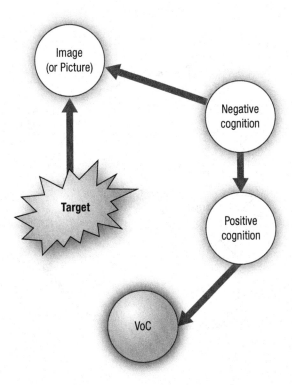

FIGURE 3.3 Steppingstones to adaptive resolution: Validity of Cognition.

Abbreviation: VoC, Validity of Cognition.

ASSESSMENT OF CURRENT LEVEL OF DISTURBANCE

SUBJECTIVE UNITS OF DISTURBANCE SCALE

The SUD scale was originally developed by Wolpe (1990) and is an 11-point Likert scale (i.e., a unidimensional scaling method developed by Likert [1932]) utilized in EMDR therapy to measure a client's subjective experience of how distressing an event feels for them at the present moment. It is meant to measure the level of disturbance of the entire memory. The SUD is taken after the client has identified what emotions they are feeling during the Assessment Phase and again as the Desensitization Phase appears to be nearing completion to indicate whether processing is complete and resolution of the disturbance has been achieved. It can also be used at the end of a channel of association to determine the client's level of progress. The SUD level should also be assessed as a gut-level feeling by the client.

To determine a client's initial SUD level, the clinician simply asks, "From 0, which is neutral or no disturbance, to 10, which is the worst disturbance you can imagine, how disturbing does it feel to you <u>now</u>?" Note that the client has not been redirected to the original incident or to their NC. The SUD follows the elicitation of emotion but refers to the entire incident. As such, the clinician is asking how the client feels now with regard to the old incident or

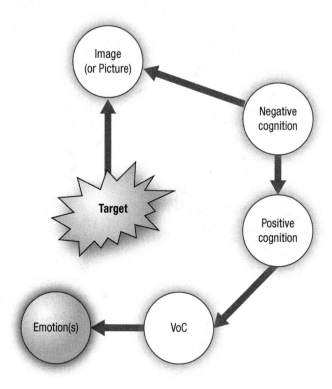

FIGURE 3.4 Steppingstones to adaptive resolution: Emotions.

Abbreviation: VoC, Validity of Cognition.

"How are you <u>feeling now</u>?" (e.g., fear over initiating the process) or "How disturbed are you now?" The SUD is a baseline measurement that helps the clinician to know the client's level of disturbance. It also provides information to the client as to how the process is progressing.

It is not unusual for clients to experience a range of different emotions during a reprocessing session. The SUD does not reflect the level of disturbance with each emotion. It is a measure of the total disturbance.

During the Desensitization Phase when a client reports a SUD level of 0, the clinician may assume that the client's memory has been totally desensitized. Often, the SUD level at the end of a session does not reach zero. The client's original target may not be fully processed (leading to SUD = 0) at the end of the session, but the SUD will most likely have decreased to some degree.

These scales can be confusing to a client, especially since one measures their progress by decreasing in value and the other by increasing in value. If a client questions this, the clinician may provide them with a plausible and simple explanation: "Well, if you think of it in this way, it makes it easier to understand. The EMDR standard protocol is set up in a way so as to decrease the negative emotional charge of your trauma and to increase the charge to your desired direction of change" (Figure 3.5).

Table 3.9 lists common mistakes made by clinicians with regard to the VoC and SUD.

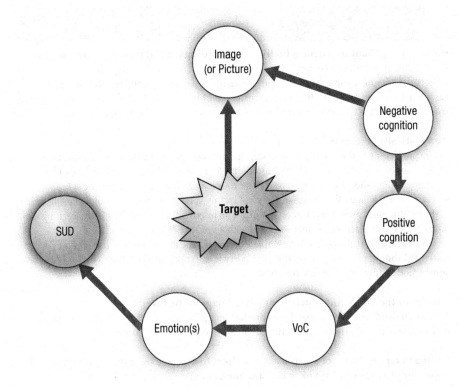

FIGURE 3.5 Steppingstones to adaptive resolution: Subjective Units of Disturbance.

Abbreviations: SUD, Subjective Units of Disturbance; VoC, Validity of Cognition.

TABLE 3.9 Derailment Possibilities—Validity of Cognition and Subjective Units of Disturbance

VOC

Provides a baseline and ensures that the PC is possible

> *When you think of that image (or picture), how true (or believable) do the words (PC) feel to you now on a scale of 1–7, where 1 feels completely false and 7 feels completely true?*

Asking for the VoC on a 0–7 scale
The correct scale is 1–7.

Eliciting a VoC that is in reference to a general event
VoC should be in reference to the image (or picture) previously identified.

Obtaining the VoC by asking a question other than the one stated above
Do not ask, "How true is it today?"

(continued)

TABLE 3.9 Derailment Possibilities—Validity of Cognition and Subjective Units of Disturbance (continued)

Proceeding without the client actually understanding the significance of the VoC
If the client appears confused by what they are asked, the clinician may say, "Remember, sometimes we know something with our head; but it feels differently in our gut. In this case, what is the gut-level feeling of the truth now of [clinician states the positive cognition], from 1 (completely false) to 7 (completely true), as you think of the image?"

Automatically accepting a VoC of 1
Before proceeding to the next assessment step, it is appropriate for the clinician to assess the PC in terms of potential flaws in ecological validity, logic, and applicability. The PC should be appropriate and valid with a client's present environment. Although a client may be able to successfully assimilate a PC with such a low VoC rating, it is often an indicator of the unsuitability of the PC. In some cases, it may be best to suggest an intermediate PC, such as "I am learning that I have choices" to replace the PC that was rated with a VoC of 1 "I have choices."

While it might change, an attainable PC is desirable at the onset of processing. This initial PC should possess a modicum of validity (i.e., truth) for the NC/PC dialectic to have some traction toward cognitive resolution.

Asking for the VoC without pairing it to the image (or picture)
The initial words are "When you focus on that image (or picture) (i.e., original image or picture), how true do those words (repeat positive cognition) feel to you now?"

Failing to repeat the exact words used by a client to describe their PC in reference to the image (or picture; e.g., I am okay vs. I am fine as I am)
It is imperative that the clinician repeat the PC exactly as the client has given it to them. The clinician should write down the cognitions so they may be easily accessed when needed.

Failing to check with the client regarding the trueness of the PC on a "gut" level for an initial VoC of 5 or above
If a VoC appears to be too high, it may be because (a) they *know* it is true, (b) but do not *feel* it is true, and (c) they are not pairing it to the disturbing image (or picture). Depending upon the outcome, the clinician may need to assist the client in further teasing out the appropriate NC and PC.

During the Installation Phase, failing to regularly check for the VoC after each set
Unlike Desensitization Phase measurement of the SUD scale, the clinician checks the VoC regularly if changes continue to occur in the Installation Phase.

SUD

On a scale from 0 to 10, where 0 is neutral or no disturbance and 10 is the highest disturbance you can imagine, how disturbing does the incident feel to you now?

Asking for the SUD on a scale of 1–10
Correct scale is 0–10.

Asking for the SUD before obtaining the PC, VoC, and emotion(s)
Again, follow the exact order of the Assessment Phase.

(continued)

TABLE 3.9 Derailment Possibilities—Validity of Cognition and Subjective Units of Disturbance (continued)

Assigning the SUD to the emotion(s)—e.g., sadness, fear, or anger—identified in the Assessment Phase

The SUD is evaluated on the total disturbance level.

Abbreviations: NC, negative cognition; PC, positive cognition; SUD, Subjective Units of Disturbance; VoC, Validity of Cognition.

ASSESSMENT OF PHYSICAL SENSATIONS

BODY SENSATIONS

The final question that you will ask Jennifer is, "And where do you feel it in your body now?" She might respond, "In my stomach." The somatic component is an important piece of the client's traumatic jigsaw puzzle. The clinician is asking the client where she is feeling the disturbance in her body when she evokes a disturbing image (or picture) with the NC. Jennifer most likely had a physical reaction while the event was occurring. She might have felt it in her stomach then, or maybe not. She might have felt it in her stomach whenever she brought the incident up, or maybe not. What is important is where she feels it in her body while she is currently focusing on the event. We do not need or want to know what she was feeling before, during, or after the event in her body. We need to know where she feels it in her body *now* when setting up the last of the Phase 3 procedural steps.

The significance of body sensations in the Assessment Phase cannot be overemphasized. When a client is focusing on a traumatic memory, the emergence of physical sensations may be associated with emotional tension (e.g., tight muscles or rapid breathing), physical sensations stored at the time of a traumatic event (e.g., physically feeling the pain where a perpetrator hit the victim in the jaw), or NCs.

Notice that the clinician says, "Where do you feel it in your body now?" In doing so, the clinician is assuming that the client is feeling it somewhere in his body, even if they say, "Nowhere." It is inappropriate to say, "What do you feel in your body?" or "How do you feel it in your body?"

As you can see, the body's physical responses to a trauma are an important aspect of the treatment. When the clinician asks the client, "Where do you feel it (the disturbance) in your body now?" there is a clear assumption that there is physical resonance to dysfunctional material (Shapiro, 2018). Later, when we cover the reprocessing phases, the clinician will see that as long as physical sensations linger, the reprocessing is considered incomplete. Residual tension and atypical physical sensations must be absent for reprocessing to be complete (Figure 3.6).

As stated earlier, it is important to mimic Dr. Shapiro's words as closely as possible when assessing the components of the client's targeted memory in preparation for EMDR processing. Her script for the Assessment Phase procedure is followed precisely in this Primer as well.

CASE EXAMPLES

The following cases are composites of clients and events. Where appropriate, notes have been inserted to serve as teaching points.

Note: If this is the first time a client has experienced EMDR reprocessing, it is a good practice to introduce the client to it by saying, "When a disturbing event occurs, it can get

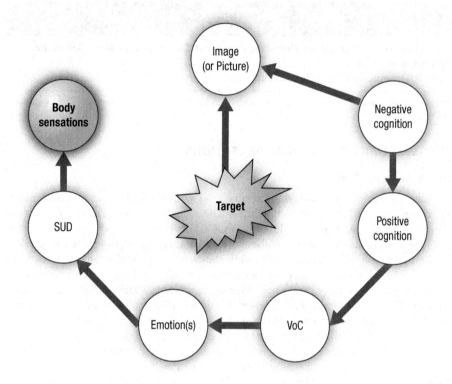

FIGURE 3.6 Steppingstones to adaptive resolution: Body sensations.

Abbreviations: SUD, Subjective Units of Disturbance; VoC, Validity of Cognition.

locked in the brain with the original picture, sounds, thoughts, feelings, and body sensations. EMDR reprocessing seems to stimulate the information and allows the brain to reprocess the experience. That may be what is happening in rapid eye movement (REM) or dream sleep—the eye movements (tones, tactile) may help to process the unconscious material. It is your own brain that will be doing the healing, and you are the one in control" (Shapiro, 2018). If the client ends up having multiple reprocessing sessions, the clinician can say, "Just let whatever happens, happen" and remind the client to distance themself from the trauma by saying, "To help you 'just notice' the experience, imagine riding on a train or watching a video; and the images, feelings, and thoughts are just going by."

Case Example: Terry

Terry, a 40-year-old male, suffered from severe anxiety and depression and a phobia of dead animals, especially birds of any kind. When Terry first arrived, he was sluggish and disoriented. His wife joined him in sessions for the first couple of times because she acted as his historian. He had lost track of the last few years in terms of doctors, medications, and episodes. He was scared but knew he needed something more than talk therapy for him to get better. As part of his history, the clinician discovered that his mother had married many times during his childhood and usually to very abusive men. Because of this, Terry had experienced what seemed to him lifetimes of trauma before he graduated from high school.

When Terry arrived to begin EMDR reprocessing, he was visibly shaken. "I'm scared," he said. "I'm afraid it is not going to work." Because of his discomfort with reprocessing, it was decided to start with a less disturbing memory, that of being chased with a dead bird by his Uncle Roger.

It is important for the clinician to provide the following instructions to the client prior to the initiation of the Assessment Phase. If provided prior to the Desensitization Phase: (a) the client has to pull themself out of the memory in order to listen and understand the clinician's instructions and (b) the clinician has interrupted any access the client has just established with the targeted memory.

Often, we will be doing a simple check on what you are experiencing. I need to know from you exactly what is going on with as clear feedback as possible. Sometimes things will change and sometimes they won't. There are no "supposed to's" in this process. So just give as accurate feedback as you can as to what is happening without judging whether it should be happening or not. Just let whatever happens, happen. [Remember to tell the client about the STOP hand signal.]

Here is how the protocol of Terry's fear of dead birds was set up.

Clinician: Last week, Terry, you stated that you wanted to start with the memory of your uncle chasing you with a dead bird. Can you elaborate *briefly*?

The briefer, the better. The clinician does not necessarily need to know the details. It is about the client being able to resolve his trauma as completely as possible. The focus is on the client spending time processing the event rather than describing all the details of it. If the clinician already knows enough about the memory, the client will not be asked to elaborate at all.

Terry: I must have been around 3 years old. I was playing in the yard when I spotted a strange looking "*thing*" in the yard. It turned out to be a dead bird. I always was a curious kid. Because I wanted to know what it was and what it did, I ran to Uncle Roger and showed him the dead bird. Uncle Roger immediately took the dead bird away from me, thrust it into my face, and began to chase me with it.

Clinician: What image (or picture) represents the worst part of the incident?

Once a client has revealed a traumatic memory, the clinician asks him for a single image (or picture) as the initial focus, an image (or picture) that represents a link to neurological and dysfunctional material. If no picture, focus on the entire event.

Terry: It was his evil laugh. He chased me and laughed hysterically.

The sound that the client has selected is very concrete (e.g., "his evil laugh" rather than "always being treated cruelly by my uncle"). This is an important element of an effective target. Terry's sensory access to the memory is a sound, his uncle's evil laugh, rather than an image or picture. The clinician should adapt the standard script appropriately.

Clinician: Terry, what words go best with that sound that express your *negative* belief about yourself now?
Terry: I am in danger.

This is an excellent NC. It is irrational (or dysfunctional), negative, and self-referencing. It is stated in the present and focuses on the client's presenting issue. And it can be generalized to other traumatic events in which the client may feel unsafe. It also reflects the associated effect of fear identified later by the client.

Clinician: When you bring up the sound, what would you like to believe about yourself now?
Terry: I am not in danger.

This PC is not acceptable or effective. The way it is stated, it is simply a negation of the NC as it appears above. A negative (i.e., "no," "not") within a positive statement does not bring the client to their desired direction of change. This is when it becomes necessary for the clinician to tease it out without putting words into the client's mouth, if at all possible.

Clinician: How can you phrase that in a more positive direction?
Terry: Oh, I don't know. How about, "I am safe?"

Does this cognition fit the criteria for a PC? Yes, it does. It is a positive, self-referencing belief. It reflects the client's desired direction of change. It is generalizable to other areas of the client's life. And it provides clear indication of a positive associated affect. In addition, the PC in this instance matches the theme in the NC. Both deal with the theme of safety.

Note that the cognitions are not perfectly parallel in this example (i.e., "I am in danger" and "I am safe"). They are comfortably similar, and this is okay. It is important to use the client's words, not what we think the client's words ought to be.

Clinician: Good. Terry, when you focus on the sound, how true do those words, "I am safe," feel to you now on a scale from 1 to 7, where 1 *feels* completely false and 7 *feels* completely true?
Terry: Two. It does not feel very true.
Clinician: When you bring up that sound and those words, "I am in danger," what *emotion(s)* do you feel now?
Terry: Fear! Total fear!
Clinician: From 0, which is neutral or no disturbance, to 10, which is the worst disturbance you can imagine, how disturbing does it feel to you <u>now</u>?

Notice that the clinician ends most questions with the word *now*. The clinician is not interested in what the client believed negatively at the time of the event or what physical and emotional sensations they experienced then. They want to know what is happening in the present—in the *now*. This is an important point because some clients will report what they believed, felt, and experienced then. Clients will even base the SUD on how disturbing the event was at the time it occurred if the clinician is not clear that they are asking about the client's disturbance *now*. Make sure that the client knows the difference, because it could adversely affect the processing.

Terry: It's an 8.
Clinician: Where do you feel it in your *body* <u>now</u>?
Terry: In my gut.

A client's bodily response to trauma is an important aspect of treatment and provides a valuable addition of information apart from the verbalizations provided by the client (Shapiro, 2018). When a client is asked where the body sensation is located in their body, what that clinician is really asking is, "Where does the dysfunctional material physically resonate in your body?"

Sometimes it may be difficult for a client to identify where they feel the disturbance in their body. When this is the case, the clinician can assist the client in assessing body sensations by referring them back to their original SUD level. For example, if the client reported a SUD level of 9, the clinician might say, "You reported a 9 as the level of disturbance. Where do you feel the 9 in your body?" If the client is still having difficulty, say "Close your eyes and notice how your body feels. Now I will ask you to think of something; and, when I do, just notice what

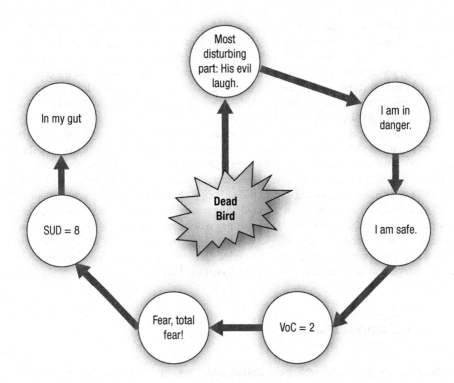

FIGURE 3.7 Steppingstones to adaptive resolution: Body sensations.

Abbreviations: SUD, Subjective Units of Disturbance; VoC, Validity of Cognition.

TABLE 3.10 Protocol Setup: Terry	
Target:	When he was around 3 years old, Terry found a dead bird in the yard. Piqued by his curiosity and his thirst to know more, he brought the dead bird to show his Uncle Roger. Uncle Roger took the dead bird, immediately thrust it in Terry's face, and chased him with it.
Image/worst part:	It was his evil laugh. He was chasing me and laughing hysterically.
NC:	I am in danger
PC:	I am safe
VoC:	2
Emotion:	Fear
SUD:	8
Body:	Gut

Abbreviations: NC, negative cognition; PC, positive cognition; SUD, Subjective Units of Disturbance; VoC, Validity of Cognition.

changes in your body. Okay, notice your body. Now, focus on the sound (or bring up the image/picture). Tell me what changes. Now add the words, 'I am in danger.' Tell me what changes." See Figure 3.7 for a graphical picture of the EMDR components in the Assessment Phase for Terry.

When you are going through the Assessment Phase procedural steps with the client, it is important to write down everything as it is done in Tables 3.9–3.12. Write down exactly what the client says, not what the clinician thinks the client says, and reflect the words back to them in their exact language when the need arises. If a clinician were to say to Terry, for example, "When you focus on the event and those words, 'I am unsafe' (what Terry did not say) instead of 'I am in danger' (what Terry did say), what emotions come up for you now?" the clinician has not allowed the client's process to work for them. The clinician is using their words, not the client's. This format also gives a broader perspective of the client's responses to the questions in the protocol.

This was a straightforward setup. Even though this client had not reprocessed with EMDR before, they were able to understand and provide what was needed without too much effort. This is not always the case. It sometimes will become necessary for the clinician to tease out what is needed to smooth the way for adequate processing of the dysfunctionally stored material around the targeted event. Table 3.10 is a reminder for the clinician to write down everything the client says during the Assessment Phase.

Case Example: Mariko

Mariko suffered severe neck, back, and shoulder injuries during a car accident with a drunk driver 2 years ago while proceeding north on a divided four-lane highway. Mariko told the police officer that she saw a vehicle heading toward her. While she tried to avoid the car, Mariko became hemmed in by other moving traffic and was struck by the vehicle, driven by a young woman. Mariko's car was hit on the passenger side and spun around before it came to rest backwards, partially in the highway median. Mariko had collided with a 27-year-old woman who was driving in the wrong direction. At the time, the woman stated that she did not know she was driving the wrong way and was unsure how that happened.

Immediately following the accident, Mariko was rushed to a local hospital with significant injuries. She later had to have back surgery as a result. When Mariko came to therapy, she stated that she had not been able to drive since the accident. As a single parent, she was the sole provider of income for herself and her two children. Mariko realized the importance of getting back behind the wheel of her car as soon as possible. She was mending physically and nearing the time when her long-term disability would expire.

Clinician: Mariko, what image (or picture) represents the worst part of the incident?

Because there was more than one possible image (or picture) the client could select that was linked to the event, the clinician asked the client to select the image (or picture) that held the most disturbance. It would be inappropriate and counterproductive for the clinician to target the entire narrative rather than the most disturbing aspect of the client's experience.

If the client cannot name an image (or picture) that represents the worst part, the clinician may ask, "When you think of the accident, what do you get?"

Mariko: Seeing the car heading toward me and not being able to do anything to get out of the way. There were cars on both sides and behind me. There was just nowhere for me to turn. I had no choice but to get hit by this oncoming car.

Clinician: What words go best with that image (or picture) that express your negative belief about yourself now? I am (the client fills in the blank).

Mariko: I was afraid.

This is not an appropriate NC. Why? While it is self-referencing, is it a belief? No, it expresses the emotion of fear. The task then is to tease out the negative belief that is associated with this negative emotion.

Clinician: I understand that you were afraid. What is the belief about yourself now that goes with the fear? Or "What does the fear make you believe about yourself now?"

Mariko: That I am out of control. I feel so helpless.

Here the client has stated one belief, "I am out of control," and is feeling a sense of helplessness that might be translated into, "I am helpless."

The clinician teases this out further so that they can obtain the belief that goes with the negative emotion the client has already expressed.

Clinician: As you focus on the image (or picture), which *belief*, lack of control or helplessness, resonates the most now?

Mariko: Lack of control.

Clinician: So "I am out of control" is what you believe about themself as they focus on the event now?

The NC is restated to be certain that this is what the client believes about themself as they focus on the past event. This cognition meets all the criteria for an appropriate NC. It is self-referencing. It is stated in the present. It is generalizable, and it reflects the negative emotion that the client associates with their current difficulties.

Mariko: Yes.

Clinician: When you bring up that image (or picture), what would you like to believe about yourself now?

Mariko: I can take care of myself.

Clinician: What could be the flip side of "I can take care of myself" for you?

Mariko: I can't take care of myself.

Clinician: Does this resonate with you as you focus on the incident, or does, "I am out of control"?

Mariko: I am out of control.

Clinician: What is the reverse of "I am out of control" for you?

Mariko: I always have control.

The PC cannot be an absolute statement. Therefore, avoid the use of words such as "always," and "never." When this happens, assist the client in reframing their cognition to something more reasonable or realistic.

Clinician: Is it possible to always have control?

Mariko: Probably not.

Clinician: What would be a more reasonable version of "I always have control"?

Mariko: I have control, I guess.

Clinician: When you bring up that image (or picture), is this what you would like to believe about yourself now?

Mariko: Yes.

Clinician: Mariko, when you focus on that image (or picture), how true do those words, "I have control," feel to you now on a scale from 1 to 7, where 1 *feels* completely false and 7 *feels* completely true?

Mariko: It's a 1. It's not true at all.

When the client states that the positive belief feels like a 1, it is indicative that this might not actually be a realistic goal for the client. It may just be part of the client's magical thinking that they can have control over all people, places, and things. So, we need to fine-tune it so that the PC is more realistic and attainable.

Clinician: Is it realistic to state in this situation that you have control?

Mariko: No. Probably not.

Clinician: What might a more realistic preferred belief look like for you as you focus on the event?

Mariko: I have some control.

Clinician: And how true does, "I have some control" feel on a scale of 1 to 7 now?

Mariko: It's not much higher. Let's say a 2.

TABLE 3.11 Protocol Setup: Mariko	
Target:	Car accident 2 years ago
Image/worst part:	Seeing the car heading toward her and not being able to do anything to get out of the way
NC:	I am out of control
PC:	I have some control
VoC:	2
Emotion:	Fear
SUD:	10
Body:	Stomach and chest

Abbreviations: NC, negative cognition; PC, positive cognition; SUD, Subjective Units of Disturbance; VoC, Validity of Cognition.

Clinician: When you bring up that image (or picture) and those words, "I am out of control," what emotion(s) do you feel now?
Mariko: Fear. I still feel so afraid.

Notice that the NC resonates with the associated affect stated by the client.

Clinician: From 0, which is neutral or no disturbance, to 10, which is the worst disturbance you can imagine, how disturbing does it feel to you now?
Mariko: I'm terrified.
Clinician: Where do you feel it in your *body* now?
Mariko: In my stomach and in my chest.

The clinician is cautioned to refrain from offering cognitive restructuring or psychoeducation during this phase.

Table 3.11 is a reminder for the clinician to write down everything the client says, especially during the Assessment Phase.

Case Example: Geraldo

Originally presenting with generalized anxiety, Geraldo had successfully reprocessed the death of his younger brother. Previously, he had worked through guilt over his brother's death and his wish that he could have done something more to help his brother through his lingering illness. He worried incessantly about the stress of his brother's death on his fragile mother's health, but obsessed more about the day when she would pass and the pain he anticipated that he would feel.

Geraldo came from a family of one brother and three sisters. Now that his brother was dead, there was no one to carry out the family lineage. Tragically, he discovered at a very young age that he was sterile as a result of an earlier bout with meningitis. He did have three sons whom he and his wife adopted at birth. But he still felt that he had failed in his familial responsibility to carry on the family name. These were the issues that Geraldo had previously successfully reprocessed with EMDR. Yet, there was one final lingering splinter that still seemed to stick out as he focused on his brother's death.

His younger brother's new wife was still in the picture. Prior to his death, his brother apparently was unable to manage his financial matters on his own. He had set up a will in which he named his wife the chief beneficiary but did not name his wife as the executor of the will. He named Geraldo instead, which created two problems. Geraldo became overwhelmed by the intricacies of the legal matters with which he had to deal. His brother's wife was not happy about the arrangement and caused difficulties within the family.

Most of Geraldo's apprehension centered on his feelings of inadequacy involving legal matters of any kind. He was a teacher, not a lawyer. It was his insecurity regarding the meetings with the lawyer handling his brother's will that bothered him the most.

Clinician: When you focus on the situation, what do you get?
Geraldo: The last meeting with my brother's lawyer. I felt so inept at legal matters. I don't want to disappoint my brother even in death.
Clinician: What image (or picture) represents the worst part as you think of it now?
Geraldo: I remember stuttering when the lawyer started asking me questions about what was in the will. I never stutter.
Clinician: What words go best with that image (or picture) that express your *negative* belief about yourself now?
Geraldo: I am incompetent.
Clinician: When you bring up that picture, what would you *like* to *believe* about yourself *now*?
Geraldo: I am competent.
Clinician: Geraldo, when you focus on that image (or picture), how true do those words, "I am competent" feel to you now on a scale from 1 to 7, where 1 *feels* completely false and 7 *feels* completely true?

If the client has difficulty coming up with a number value for the VoC, the clinician explains further by saying, "Remember, sometimes we know something with our head, but it feels differently in our gut. In this case, what is the gut-level feeling of the truth of (repeat PC) from 1 being completely false and 7 being completely true?"

Geraldo: It feels, well maybe, about a 3.
Clinician: As you bring up the image (or picture) and those words, "I am incompetent," what *emotion(s)* come up for you now?
Geraldo: I am feeling really apprehensive about these meetings. I possess a lot of self-doubt, too.
Clinician: From 0, which is neutral or no disturbance, to 10, which is the worst disturbance you can imagine, how disturbing does it feel to you now?
Geraldo: It's only about a 5. I thought it would be higher.

TABLE 3.12 Protocol Setup: Geraldo	
Target:	Last meeting with his brother's lawyer
Image/Worst part:	Stuttering in the meeting
NC:	I am incompetent
PC:	I am competent
VoC:	3
Emotion:	Apprehension and self-doubt
SUD:	5
Body:	Stomach

Abbreviations: NC, negative cognition; PC, positive cognition; SUD, subjective units of disturbance; VoC, validity of cognition.

Geraldo reported feeling apprehension and doubt. The SUD level measures total disturbance, rather than the level of disturbance on each separate emotion identified.

Clinician: Where do you feel it in your *body*?
Geraldo: I don't know.

Some clients are unable to report body sensations, no matter how hard a clinician tries to coach them. When this is the case, the clinician only needs to have the client focus on the identified components of the target and concentrate on assisting in locating the emotions in their body as reprocessing progresses through the immediate or successive sessions. Another approach is to utilize the client's calm (or safe) place to elicit body consciousness and then refocus the client on the target memory to assist them in noticing the change in their body.

Clinician: Do you remember your safe (calm) place represented by the word "mountain?"
Client: Yes.
Clinician: Please bring it up. (Pause.) Notice how that feels to be there *now*. Head to toe … how safe, how relaxing? Let me know when you have it by nodding your head. (Pause.) Good. Now, bring up the disturbing incident. What changes in your body?
Client: I feel jittery in my stomach.

Table 3.12 is a reminder for the clinician to write down everything the client says during the Assessment Phase.

Case Example: Henri

Henri and his clinician had been working for weeks identifying and clearing out old memories that were fueling his current symptoms. He was feeling better and better about how he was handling his relationship with his wife, 15 years his junior.

Despite his successes in therapy, Henri continued to be self-loathing. It was this negative deep-seated feeling about himself that he simply could not lose. "I hate myself," he would say. "I simply do not like myself, and I do not know why." When asked about historic events and memories that may have elicited this feeling, he could identify none. Consequently, the clinician first works with Henri to identify a specific memory before proceeding to the Assessment Phase.

Clinician: Focus on the words, "I hate myself." Where do you feel that self-hatred in your *body*?
Henri: In my gut.
Clinician: What *emotion* is associated with that *physical sensation* in your gut?
Henri: Anxiousness.
Clinician: As you focus on those words, "I hate myself," the *physical sensation* in your gut, and the anxiousness that you feel, what words go best that describe your *negative* belief about yourself right now?
Henri: I am worthless.

Having identified his negative self-belief, "I am worthless" and the negative emotion associated with this self-belief, the clinician led Henri into the floatback technique (see Chapter 4).

Note: The steps for setting up Phase 3 Assessment and the floatback technique are similar. The clinician asks the client to focus on the issue (e.g., Henri's experience of thinking, "I hate myself") and identify the emotion(s) and NC associated with the issue.

Clinician: Henri, bring up that (negative) belief, "I am worthless" and the emotions you are feeling now and let your mind float back to the earliest time when you may have felt this way before and just notice what comes to mind (Shapiro, 2009–2017a,b).

Henri floated back to when he was 5 years old. He was in the basement playing while his dad was busy cutting on a piece of plywood. The plywood had been placed between two saw-horses. He did not remember what his dad was working on. He just wanted to play and was busy doing so when his dad jerked him up and placed him firmly on the piece of plywood. And then his father continued cutting with his circular saw.

Henri was terrified. All he remembers seeing and hearing from that point on was the buzzing of the saw as it made its way toward him. His father used Henri as an anchor to keep the board from shifting out of place while he made his cuts. Henri said, "I shook. I cried. I was so scared." Aggravated, his father jerked him off the board, threw him angrily on the floor, picked up his 3.5-year-old sister, Martha, made her take Henri's place on the plywood, and continued his project.

It was at this point that the clinician set up the EMDR protocol around this event, and Henri was able to process to a successful resolution.

Clinician: What image (or picture) represents the incident?
Henri: I can still see myself standing on the board.
Clinician: What words go best with that image (or picture) that express your *negative* belief about yourself now?
Henri: I am weak. Afraid. I can't do it. I am incompetent.

Except for one, the client rattled off several statements which could possibly serve as the NC around this event. "I am afraid" is not an appropriate NC. It is a feeling. Because there were appropriate NCs available, the clinician did not say, "Fear is what you feel. What does that make you believe about yourself as you focus on the event?" The clinician believed that it was more important to weed out the best cognition from the three that the client provided. Had the clinician not done this, it is possible that the results would have turned out differently. This was a judgment call on his part. As you will see later, the client did bring this trauma to a successful resolution.

Clinician: Other than feeling afraid, which one of those statements resonate the most when you focus on the event?

Henri: I am incompetent.

If Henri was unable to recall his previous statements (i.e., "I am weak. Afraid. I can't do it. I am incompetent"), the clinician may repeat them and ask the same question as earlier.

Clinician: When you bring up that image (or picture), what would you like to believe about yourself <u>now</u>?

Henri: I am competent.

Clinician: When you focus on that image (or picture), how *true* do those words, "I am competent," feel to you now on a scale from 1 to 7, where 1 *feels* completely false and 7 *feels* completely true?

Henri: About halfway. Maybe a 3.

Clinician: When you bring up that image (or picture) and those words, "I am incompetent," what emotion(s) do you feel <u>now</u>?

Henri: Anger and fear mostly.

Clinician: When you bring up the image (or picture) on a scale from 0 to 10, where 0 is no disturbance and 10 is the worst disturbance you can imagine, how disturbing does it feel to you <u>now</u>?

Henri: It's pretty high. Let's say an 8.

Clinician: Where do you feel it in your body?

Henri: In my chest.

Table 3.13 is a reminder for the clinician to write everything down that the client says, especially during the Assessment Phase.

RECENT TRAUMATIC EVENTS AND SINGLE-INCIDENT TRAUMAS

Most clinical problems are treated with the 11-step standard EMDR procedure (i.e., image, NC, PC, VoC, emotion, SUD, location of body sensation, desensitization, installation, body scan, and closure) and the standard three-pronged approach (i.e., targeting the past, present, and future). However, protocols are available for special populations (e.g., children, couples, sexual abuse victims, combat veterans, or clients with dissociative disorders) or special conditions or disorders (e.g., phobias, performance anxieties, substance abuse, and pain control). It is important not to overlook the importance and differences in processing these types of events utilizing EMDR. These cases may require special protocols or customized treatment regimens (Shapiro, 2018) and are beyond the scope of this Primer. Explanations and examples of many of these are available (Luber, 2009a, 2009b, 2015, 2016a, 2016b) from other sources.

In Chapter 1, incidents described as recent and single-incident traumas were identified and discussed. Because references to each type of trauma are interspersed throughout the Primer, the specific protocols outlined by Dr. Shapiro (2018) are presented here as well.

TABLE 3.13 Protocol Setup: Henri	
Target:	When he was 5 years old, his experience of his father using him as an anchor to hold a board while cutting it with a saw
Image/worst part:	I can still feel myself standing on the board
NC:	I am incompetent
PC:	I am competent
VoC:	3
Emotion:	Anger and fear
SUD:	8
Body:	Chest

Reminder: Reprocessing includes the Desensitization, Installation, and Body Scan phases. Reprocessing is complete when SUD = 0, VoC = 7, and the body scan is clear.
Abbreviations: NC, negative cognition; PC, positive cognition; SUD, subjective units of disturbance; VoC, validity of cognition.

RECENT TRAUMATIC EVENTS PROTOCOL

Dr. Shapiro developed the Recent Traumatic Events Protocol for incidents that still contain separate disturbing aspects or fragments of an event and have not had adequate time in which to fully consolidate into one primary memory. As a result, it becomes necessary to target each separate aspect of the traumatic event by separately targeting and assessing for each the image, NC, PC, VoC, emotions, SUD, and body sensations using the standard protocol. Case Example—Patrick is an example of the Recent Traumatic Events Protocol (Luber, 2015; Shapiro, 2018). Further information on the Recent Traumatic Events Protocol can be found in Chapter 8, B: EMDR Therapy Scripts.

Case Example: Patrick

Approximately 3 months before coming to therapy, Patrick was directly involved in a chemical explosion and fire at the plant where he worked as a maintenance technician. Although many others were taken to the hospital as a result of this explosion, Patrick was the only seriously injured employee and the only one who was in the room where hazardous materials had spilled and caught fire. He had just checked a valve in the vicinity of the explosion and was walking away when the explosion occurred. His shocking comment about himself was, "Thirty more seconds, and I would have been toast." After determining appropriateness for EMDR therapy and orientation to present safety through safe (calm) place and grounding techniques, the Recent Traumatic Events Protocol would proceed as follows.

1. *Obtain a narrative history*

Clinician: Patrick, tell me what you remember from beginning to end. That might be when you knew it was over, or even until now.

   Utilizing the recent events protocol, the clinician asks the client to relate the details of the event in narrative form.

Patrick: I had just finished checking a valve on my regular safety rounds and was walking away and, "BOOM!" I didn't know what was happening. I just knew I had to get out of there quickly. I don't even know where I was when the explosion occurred. I just know that I had to get out. I was disoriented. It was dark and smoky. I didn't know which way to go. I was panicking because I couldn't breathe. I kept thinking, "What happened? What happened?" And, I don't know how, but I quickly reached the door to the outside. The second the light and air hit my eyes, they started burning. I threw myself down in the snow and started rolling around. It was so cold. I threw snow on my face and rubbed my eyes with it. I hadn't been out long when Bill and Pete grabbed me and led me back into another entrance of the building. Bill said, "You know the drill," and threw me into a cold shower, clothes and all. I still couldn't see. I was freezing. It was so cold. Whenever I tried to get out of the shower, one of them would push me back in. Then they made me take all my clothes off and shoved me back in. (This was a documented safety procedure. It was important that Patrick got all the chemicals off his body to ensure that no further complications might arise.) God, it was cold! I was freezing. Next thing I remember is being loaded into the ambulance. I kept thinking, "What happened? Why me? Where's my wife? I can't see. I can't see! Why can't I see?" My wife arrived at the hospital about the same time that I did. The doctor told us both that the burns were pretty bad, and I'd have to stay in the hospital. I still couldn't see. "Oh God. Why me?" When I was in the hospital, I kept retracing my steps. "Was it me? Did I do something wrong?"

Clinician: Anything else?

Patrick: I was in the hospital for a while. They kept treating my eyes and checking pressure and stuff like that. That was really hard on my wife and my kids. Then, my vision started to clear a little bit. It was really blurry, and the light hurt. Then it started getting better.

Clinician: And where do things stand now?

Patrick: Well, my vision is okay right now. I still have to go in and get the pressure checked regularly and will probably need a corneal transplant in the future. I went back to work last week, but I sure get anxious when I have to go in and check those valves. I'm not sure I can do it.

2. *Target the most disturbing aspect of the memory*

   There are several experiences in Patrick's narration that could be treated as separate events (e.g., the explosion, not being able to see or breathe inside the building after the explosion, the air and light hitting his face and eyes and the burning sensation that occurred, the shower experience, the ride to the hospital, and being told by the doctor that it looked pretty bad). As the client is providing a narrative, the clinician records these separate events.

Clinician: Patrick, is there a particular part of your story that is more distressing than another?
Patrick: Not being able to see.

Patrick was able to identify the most disturbing part of his memory. Although not shown here, the clinician would set up the EMDR standard procedure specified in the Assessment Phase by identifying the image, NC, PC, VoC, emotions, SUD, and physical sensations associated with what Patrick has identified as the worst aspect of his memory of the explosion. This memory fragment would then be reprocessed with the standard Desensitization and Installation phases. The body scan would be skipped at this point. It is assumed that, given the other unprocessed parts of the entire sequence of events, it would be impossible to get a clear body scan. It would not be surprising if the PC did not reach a 7. There are other targets relating to this same event that may need to be reprocessed first before this can occur, such as his hospitalization and/or aspects of his medical treatment, impact on his family and work.

Note: Because Patrick's trauma involved potential injury to his eyes, the type of bilateral stimulation chosen by the clinician was tapping rather than eye movements.

3. *Target the remainder of the narrative in chronological order*
After the worst part of the memory has been reprocessed, the clinician needs to target the remaining events in the client's narrative in chronological order. If they were to have identified one of the events to be more disturbing than the rest, the clinician would target this one first and then the remainder as they occurred during the telling of their story. Each target is treated separately in terms of the standard EMDR protocol (i.e., Phases 3–5) up through the Installation Phase, being mindful to exclude the body scan for each. The body scan is initiated only after the last target of this traumatic event has been identified and addressed so that all the associated negative physical sensations can be eliminated.

4. *Visualize entire sequence of the event with eyes closed*
Once all the separate events in Patrick's narrative have been identified and reprocessed, the client is asked to visualize the entire sequence of the event from start to finish.

Clinician: Patrick, close your eyes and visualize the entire sequence of events of the explosion.
Patrick: Okay.
Clinician: Any time a disturbance arises in any form (i.e., visual or auditory, emotional, cognitive, or somatic), stop and open your eyes. (Pause.)
Patrick: Why? Why did it happen to me? The company had just replaced the valve. Didn't anyone check it to see if it was connected correctly?

Something disturbing has arisen. Because it is still disturbing, the clinician would implement Assessment, Desensitization, and Installation phases again with this newly identified disturbance. Once this has been processed, they would then ask the client to visualize the entire sequence of the event once again from the beginning to see if further disturbances arise. If so, they would reprocess each disturbance that surfaces using the standard protocol (i.e., Phases 3–5).

5. *Visualize entire sequence of events with eyes open*
   When the client is able to run the experience through and no distressing material comes up, the clinician moves to the Installation Phase. An overall PC is identified: "As you think of the entire experience, from beginning to end, what would you like to believe about yourself now?" The PC might be something like "It's over. I survived." Once the overall PC is identified, have them hold the PC and visualize the entire event one more time from beginning to end with their eyes open. Add long set of bilateral stimulation. The client is asked to give the "stop" signal when their processing has been completed. This is continued until the VoC is 7. As an additional check, the client closes their eyes and reviews the entire event along with the PC. This is to ensure that the VoC equals 7 for the entire event. If not, target that part of the memory until the VoC feels completely true (7) or to a degree that is ecologically valid.

6. *Conclude with body scan*
   Once this open-eyed visualization has been completed, a normal body scan is done.

7. *Process present stimuli, if necessary*
   Any current situations (triggers) that lead to distress are also processed using the standard protocol (i.e., Phases 3–6). With present triggers, you need not use the modifications outlined above. In Patrick's case, this included having to check the valves and his concerns about a corneal transplant in the future. His PC in both situations was "I'm strong. I can do it."

8. *Develop a future template*
   After reprocessing each present trigger, the client is instructed to run a movie of the desired response for coping with a similar situation or challenge in the future. The process for the future template is described in detail in the next chapter.

CAVEATS WHEN USING THE RECENT TRAUMATIC EVENTS PROTOCOL

There are several caveats (Shapiro, 2018) the clinician needs to keep in mind when administering the Recent Traumatic Events Protocol (Table 3.14).

HOW DO YOU KNOW WHEN ITS USE IS APPROPRIATE?

A common question regarding recent events is: "How recent is recent?" Or "How does a clinician know when a memory has consolidated or is consolidated enough to use the standard three-pronged approach?" There are two possibilities in answering this question. First, if a client is processing the worst part of a traumatic incident and other channels of association open up, the event may have been consolidated. Second, if the first memory reprocessed using the Recent Traumatic Events Protocol processes down to a 0 SUD and 7 VoC, it is likely that the memory has been consolidated. In either case, the past, present, and future prongs need to be processed. Refer to Exhibit 3.1 for the illustrative example related to Case Example—Patrick.

TABLE 3.14 Caveats Associated With Recent Events Protocol

The clinician must ensure that the timing for this intervention is adequate (i.e., within 2–3 months of recent event).

The client should be able to give a narrative account of the event and be oriented to the present before initiating this protocol.

The clinician may need to reprocess present distressing stimuli (e.g., startle response, reminders of the event, nightmares) that may emerge for a client after reprocessing the entire event.

Reprocessing of a recent event may take more than a few sessions. Be patient with the process if it does.

Distressing material from unresolved earlier events with the same thematic issues (e.g., safety) as the recent event may surface during or after the reprocessing.

SINGLE-INCIDENT TRAUMAS

A client may present with a single traumatic event. When this occurs, the clinician will want to consider using the standard EMDR procedure and apply it to the following targets identified by Dr. Shapiro (2018) if they are available: (a) the memory (or image) associated with a traumatic event, (b) a flashback scene the client has experienced, (c) a recurring dream or nightmare or the most disturbing or traumatic scene in the dream, (d) stimuli that trigger the client in the present, and (e) the incorporation of a future template.

With single-event traumas, there are some targeting possibilities the clinician may want to consider. For instance, are there historical linkages that need to be elicited? Or, are there additional related events associated to the traumatic event (Shapiro, 2009–2017a, 2009–2017b)? If possible, thorough questioning during the intake interview may help to elicit this information.

SINGLE TRAUMATIC EVENT PROTOCOL

Case Example: Rayshawn

Rayshawn was involved in a bank robbery when he was working as a teller at a local bank. The bank robber stormed into the bank, brandishing a gun. The gunman jumped over the counter and held the gun to Rayshawn's head, demanding he put money in a canvas bag that he shoved into Rayshawn's hand. The robber fled the scene within a matter of minutes and was not seen again until 6 months later. The same unmasked bank robber entered the same bank, held a knife to a teller's throat, demanded money, and fled. The gunman was apprehended 10 minutes after the robbery and was sent to jail. As Rayshawn was one of two who could identify the gunman, he eventually ended up testifying at the robber's trial. As the gunman had been involved in other robberies where bank employees had been injured or killed, he was easily convicted and sentenced to death row.

EXHIBIT 3.1 Recent Traumatic Events Protocol

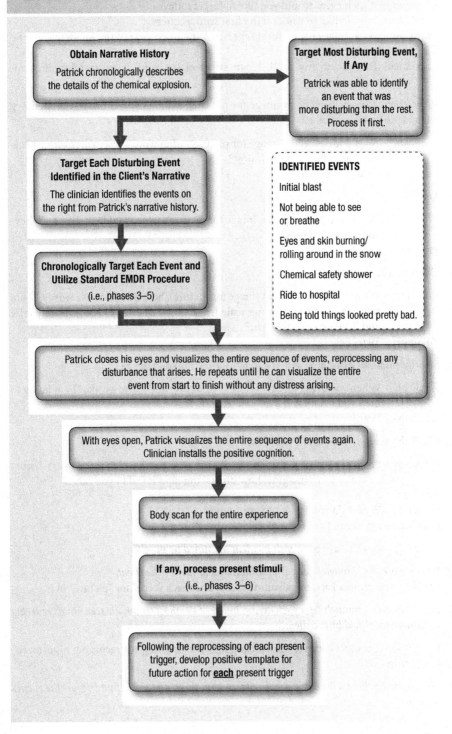

Obtain Narrative History

Patrick chronologically describes the details of the chemical explosion.

Target Most Disturbing Event, If Any

Patrick was able to identify an event that was more disturbing than the rest. Process it first.

Target Each Disturbing Event Identified in the Client's Narrative

The clinician identifies the events on the right from Patrick's narrative history.

IDENTIFIED EVENTS

Initial blast

Not being able to see or breathe

Eyes and skin burning/ rolling around in the snow

Chemical safety shower

Ride to hospital

Being told things looked pretty bad.

Chronologically Target Each Event and Utilize Standard EMDR Procedure

(i.e., phases 3–5)

Patrick closes his eyes and visualizes the entire sequence of events, reprocessing any disturbance that arises. He repeats until he can visualize the entire event from start to finish without any distress arising.

With eyes open, Patrick visualizes the entire sequence of events again. Clinician installs the positive cognition.

Body scan for the entire experience

If any, process present stimuli

(i.e., phases 3–6)

Following the reprocessing of each present trigger, develop positive template for future action for **each** present trigger

1. *Identify the image (or picture) that represents the entire incident.*

   Clinician: Which event would you like to target today?
   Rayshawn: I would like to work on the first bank robbery.
   Clinician: What image (or picture) represents the worst part of the incident (or trau-
   matic event)?
   Rayshawn: The gun to my head. I can still feel the cold, hard barrel against my
   forehead.

   If the client cannot identify an image (or picture), ask, "As you think of the memory,
   what is the worst part of it?"

   Clinician: As you focus on the image (or picture), what words best express your negative belief about yourself now?
   Rayshawn: I am going to die.

2. *Identify the client's PC.*

   Clinician: When you bring up that image (or picture), what would you like to believe
   about yourself now?
   Rayshawn: I am safe.

3. *Check for the Validity of Cognition.*

   Clinician: When you focus on that image (or picture), how *true* do those words, "I am
   safe," feel to you now on a scale from 1 to 7, where 1 *feels* completely false
   and 7 *feels* completely true?
   Rayshawn: Two.

4. *Identify emotions associated with the image (or picture) and the NC.*

   Clinician: When you bring up that image (or picture) and those words, "I am going to
   die," what emotion(s) do you feel now?
   Rayshawn: Fear.

5. *Check the Subjective Units of Disturbance*

   Clinician: From 0, which is neutral or no disturbance, to 10, which is the worst distur-
   bance you can imagine, how disturbing does it feel to you now?
   Rayshawn: Eight.
   Clinician: Where do you feel it in your body?
   Rayshawn: My chest. I am having difficulty breathing.

6. *Process Phases 4 through 6 for each incident identified by the client*

7. *Process Phases 4 through 6 for each flashback identified by the client.*
   Use the same protocol above, substituting the "flashback scene" for "picture" in it.

8. *Process Phases 4 through 6 for each dream image of the most traumatic scene in a recurring
   nightmare identified by the client.*

   Use the same protocol above, substituting the "dream image or recurring nightmare"
   for "picture" in it.

9. *Elicit from the client a list of the people, places, situations, and so on, that triggers the client's
   trauma.*

> *Clinician:* Rayshawn, can you identify any situations, events, or any other stimuli that trigger your memory of the gun being held to your head?
> *Rayshawn:* The biggest one is when I see a flash—like the sun off someone's ring or car keys. I get startled and then become extremely anxious.
> *Clinician:* Anything else?
> *Rayshawn:* I get edgy and irritated whenever someone comes at me fast or stands too close to me.

10. *Process Phases 4 through 6 for each trigger identified by the client.*
    Use the same protocol mentioned earlier.

    > *Clinician:* What trigger would you like to work on today?
    > *Rayshawn:* The flash of metal.

11. *Immediately following the reprocessing of a present trigger, install a future template for that trigger (see Luber, 2009b, pp. 129–132, on the steps to incorporating a future template for each trigger identified in a single event trauma).*

12. *Closure.*
    Whether the reprocessing is unfinished or complete, end EVERY reprocessing session with Phase 7—Closure to ensure that the client is well grounded.

TREATMENT PLANNING GUIDE

Treatment planning and target selection are usually structured using Shapiro's (2006) TPG. The guide may also be structured around recent trauma, single-incident trauma, and presenting problems defined by NC and PC, problem behavior, disturbing affect or body sensation, and external stimuli, such as odor, touch, experience, situation, perpetrator, or anniversary date. A more comprehensive plan may revolve around a complex presentation (e.g., complex PTSD or client with an Axis II diagnosis). A treatment plan may also be generated using chronological timelines and genograms during the History-Taking and Treatment Planning Phase. In any case, the incident/event selected for targeting in the Assessment Phase comes from some version or variety of the TPG suggested by Dr. Shapiro.

It is during the initial intake interview that the clinician begins noting and recording the past, present, and future (i.e., anticipated) negative and positive incidents/events reported by the client. It is from this collection of recorded events that the clinician may develop a TPG utilizing the three-pronged format. It is here that the clinician can uncover past experiences that resonate with the presenting problem, beginning with the touchstone event (if any), past events, present triggers, and future desired outcomes. See Chapter 8, B: EMDR Therapy Scripts for more information on Dr. Shapiro's TPG.

SUMMARY STATEMENTS

1. Try to not confuse the Assessment Phase with the assessment taken during the History-Taking and Treatment Planning Phase. History-taking and treatment planning are used to evaluate a client's total "rail" system (light or complex), where the Assessment Phase loads the "train" in readiness to head down one specific "track."
2. An assessment for past, present, and future is made with all types of client presentations. This assessment is completed for a target immediately preceding the Desensitization Phase.

3. Targets are more concrete versus abstract, more specific than general.
4. NC and PC do not need to be perfectly parallel. However, they generally focus on the presenting issue and address the same thematic schema.
5. Write down as much as possible during the Assessment Phase. It is important to be able to accurately reflect what the client has said.

REFERENCES

Likert, R. (1932). A technique for the measurement of attitudes. *Archives of Psychology, 22* 140, 55.

Luber, M. (2009a). *Eye movement desensitization and reprocessing (EMDR) scripted protocols: Basics and special situations.* Springer Publishing Company.

Luber, M. (2009b). *Eye movement desensitization and reprocessing (EMDR) scripted protocols: Special populations.* Springer Publishing Company.

Luber, M. (2015). *Implementing EMDR early mental health interventions for man-made and natural disasters: Models, scripted protocols, and summary sheets.* Springer Publishing Company.

Luber, M. (2016a). *Eye movement desensitization and reprocessing (EMDR) therapy scripted protocols and summary sheets: Treating trauma- and stressor-related conditions.* Springer Publishing Company.

Luber, M. (Ed.). (2016b). *Eye movement desensitization and reprocessing (EMDR) therapy scripted protocols and summary sheets: Treating anxiety, obsessive-compulsive, and mood-related conditions.* Springer Publishing Company.

Shapiro, F. (1995). *Eye movement desensitization and reprocessing: Basic principles, protocols and procedures* (1st ed.). Guilford Press.

Shapiro, F. (2001). *Eye movement desensitization and reprocessing: Basic principles, protocols and procedures* (2nd ed.). Guilford Press.

Shapiro, F. (2006). *EMDR: New notes on adaptive information processing with case formulations principles, forms, scripts and worksheets, version 1.1.* EMDR Institute.

Shapiro, F. (2009–2017a). *The EMDR approach to psychotherapy—EMDR Institute basic training Course: Weekend 1 of the two part basic training.* EMDR Institute.

Shapiro, F. (2009–2017b). *The EMDR approach to psychotherapy—EMDR Institute basic training Course: Weekend 2 of the two part basic training.* EMDR Institute.

Shapiro, F. (2018). *Eye movement desensitization and reprocessing: Basic principles, protocols and procedures* (3rd ed.). Guilford Press.

Wolpe, J. (1990). *The practice of behavior therapy* (4th ed.). Pergamon Press.

4

Building Blocks of EMDR Therapy

Although the world is full of suffering, it is full also of the overcoming of it.
—Helen Keller (*Optimism*, 1900)

EMDR THERAPY IS A THREE-PRONGED APPROACH

In the client History-Taking and Treatment Planning Phase of EMDR therapy, the clinician begins the process of identifying past disturbances or traumatic experiences, present triggers or difficult recent experiences, and anticipated future occurrences or situations related to the presenting issue chosen as the focus of treatment. These are the true building blocks of EMDR therapy. A client's success with EMDR therapy relies on a balanced focus on all three prongs of the EMDR protocol and the order of processing in which they are accessed and reprocessed. It is on these blocks—past, present, and future—that the momentum and treatment effects can build and the healing process can be completed.

When new to EMDR therapy, it is easy to overlook the remaining prongs, especially the third. Clinicians may become accustomed to focusing on a client's past for answers to what is happening in the present and possibly the present situations that continue to create difficulty, but do not always get an opportunity to process the final prong. Some EMDR clients feel so good after having resolved some of their past issues and present triggers that they terminate therapy prematurely.

As the three prongs of EMDR therapy are reviewed, return the focus to assessing appropriate targets and outcomes in relationship to past, present, and future. An understanding of this relationship is important to the construction of an EMDR Treatment Planning Guide suggested by Shapiro (2006) to ensure the successful accomplishment of overall treatment goals.

BUILDING BLOCKS OF EMDR THERAPY: PAST, PRESENT, AND FUTURE

A client who has experienced a single traumatic event can usually be treated by targeting the original traumatic memory and additional past incidents related to the primary event (e.g., car accident and related traumas: the car catching on fire while trapped in the car; being told she would never walk again; the long, difficult recovery) and any presenting situations that continue to trigger anxiety (e.g., driving on the same mountain road). Clients who present with multiple issues and/or symptom presentations, or with complex presentations of traumatic life events or extreme stress over a prolonged period, will require a more comprehensive treatment approach. When a client's history is traumatically complex, it is important to identify and treat these three areas of concern: touchstone memories and other contributor memories, present triggers, and future alternative behaviors. Whether targeting single or multiple traumatic events, it may be necessary to sequentially target the traumatic event(s) and present triggers/recent experiences that have manifested as a result, and work on skills a client needs to be more successful or comfortable in the future (Figure 4.1).

In the first prong of EMDR treatment, the clinician and client work together to reprocess any past incidents associated with the presenting issue and, if present, the early and critical touchstone memories (i.e., crucial memories that set the foundation for a client's current disturbance). The second prong is much like the first in that the clinician and client focus on reprocessing (i.e., Phases 3–6), present triggers (e.g., people, circumstances, places, or other forms of stimuli that activate disturbing reactions or responses), or difficult present experiences. The third prong focuses on alternative behaviors to aid the client in meeting their future therapeutic goals.

Although past incidents, present triggers and experiences, and future outcomes associated with the presenting issue are initially identified in the History-Taking and Treatment Planning Phase, they may also emerge anywhere throughout the eight phases (e.g., emergence of blocking beliefs or feeder memories, during reprocessing, between sessions). Figure 4.2 identifies the treatment planning guidelines suggested by Shapiro (2009–2017a, 2009–2017b) and will serve as the targeting model for this Primer.

Note: In earlier EMDR trainings, clinicians were taught to identify and reprocess targets *in order of* past, present, and future. Although this remains largely true, the clinician is encouraged, when needed, to modify the three-pronged protocol to meet the clinical demands with which a client presents (Shapiro, 2009–2017a, 2009–2017b). For learning purposes, the standard three-pronged protocol will be discussed. The conditions that

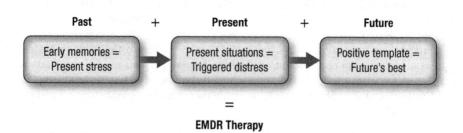

FIGURE 4.1 Three-stage protocol: Building blocks of EMDR therapy.

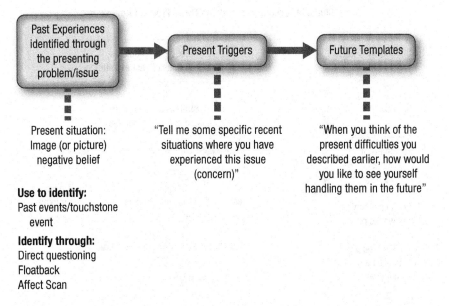

FIGURE 4.2 Three-stage protocol.

may be present to fit the demands of altering the protocol will be covered later in the chapter.

CLINICAL PRESENTATION POSSIBILITIES

Clients initially present to therapy specific issues, problems, and disturbing events that are accompanied by a constellation of symptoms (i.e., cognitive, affective, somatic, and behavioral; Shapiro, 2009–2017a, 2009–2017b). The presenting issue can be driven by associated negative cognitions (NCs) such as "I am unsafe" or "I am different (i.e., don't belong)." It may be defined by a problem behavior or a self-destructive pattern, inappropriate or negative affect (e.g., overwhelming sadness), or physical sensation (e.g., unexplained chronic headaches). Or it may be activated by external stimuli such as touch (e.g., brushing up against something or someone), odors (e.g., the smell of aftershave or alcohol), an experience (e.g., driving past an intersection where a bad accident occurred), or an anniversary date (e.g., the death of a loved one). Clinical presentations may be simple (e.g., acute stress, recent event, single incident, specific presenting problem, circumscribed problems or set of experiences) or complex (e.g., multiple issues or problems, pervasive experiences of unresolved childhood abuse and/or neglect, unresolved childhood or adult onset traumatic experiences, comorbidity of disorders, diffuse presentations, pervasive history of early trauma).

A pictorial conceptualization of the types of presenting issues for EMDR therapy identified by Shapiro (2018) and how they fit the three-pronged targeting and reprocessing plan can be found in Figure 4.3. As the figure demonstrates, there are several types of traumas with which a client can present, but clients do not always present with a trauma. They more often come in with symptomatology, such as depression, anxiety, or panic attacks.

Here are some types of traumas and other issues with which clients may initially present.

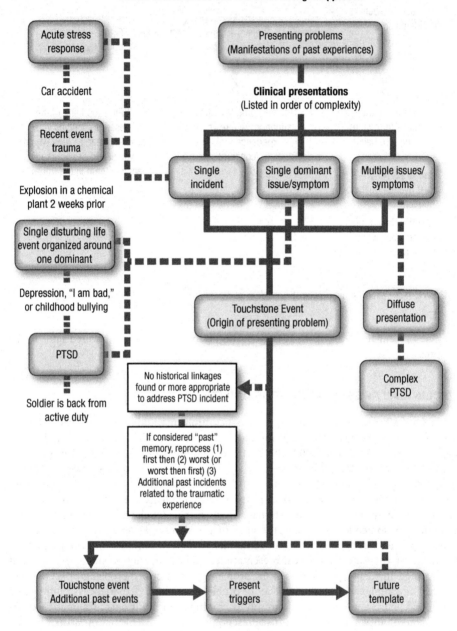

FIGURE 4.3 Clinical presentations and three-pronged approach.

Abbreviation: PTSD, posttraumatic stress disorder.

SIMPLE SYMPTOM PRESENTATIONS

Acute Stress Response (i.e., Fight or Flight)

This is a response to an acute traumatic event that has happened within the past 48 hours and has caused a set of symptoms directly attributed to the event. After 48 hours, it becomes acute stress disorder.

Example: Kelly was working as a cashier at a fast-food restaurant when a man wearing a ski mask walked up to the counter, pulled out a revolver, pointed it at her, and shouted angrily, "Give me all the money in the drawer or I will shoot you." Three days after the event, Kelly came to therapy complaining of fatigue, irritability, and sleeplessness. She had frequent nightmares of the event and found it increasingly difficult to concentrate.

Recent Event Trauma

A recent traumatic event is when "the memory has not had sufficient time to consolidate into an integrated whole" in terms of information processing (Shapiro, 2001). For recent events, the clinician will use the EMDR protocol for recent traumatic events. A recent event is one that has occurred within a 2- to 3-month period.

Example: Within 3 months of his accident, Patrick came to therapy after being seriously injured in an explosion at the chemical plant storage facility where he worked. He continues to experience flashbacks, intrusive thoughts and nightmares, anxiety, sleeplessness, and fatigue. He remains in a constant state of hypervigilance and experiences frequent bouts of anxiety. A complete transcript of Patrick's EMDR recent traumatic event session can be found in Chapter 3 under the heading Recent Traumatic Events Protocol.

Single Incident

A single traumatic incident is a one-time occurrence of a traumatic experience. It may entail an accident, vehicular or otherwise (e.g., plane, automobile, bicycle, rollerblade fall, skiing accident), a natural disaster (e.g., hurricane, tornado, flood, forest fire), crime (e.g., mugging, rape, robbery, home invasion), and other types of trauma. It may have a profound effect on a client's ability to negotiate their world or may affect their ability to sleep, relate to others, and/or function in ways that they were able to before the event occurred. Psychological symptoms of depression, anxiety, isolation, and increased use of alcohol and drugs may occur following a single traumatic event. A single traumatic event has the potential for the client to develop posttraumatic stress disorder (PTSD).

Example: A passenger train traveling between Cincinnati and Washington, DC, collided into a parked, unmanned freight train. Dimitri, a freight rail operator, had mistakenly diverted the passenger train and, as a result, it slammed into a stationary freighter. The lead engine and some of the passenger cars derailed. There were 10 crew members and 134 people aboard the train when the collision occurred. The engineer and conductor were killed. The railroad worker cited for the accident had been experiencing symptoms of anxiety and increased arousal, including sleeping difficulties, irritability, concentration issues, exaggerated startle response, increased motor activity, tenseness, and hypervigilance.

Note: Acute stress, recent event, and single incident may all apply to the same incident.

Specific Presenting Problem Characterized by the Following (in a Limited Context)

An event or series of events may be categorized as a single issue or symptom if there is a dominant theme or issue organized around a single symptom (e.g., client has a single negative irrational core belief about self, patterns of behavior, affect, body sensations, and other sensory input, people, places, and situations, dreams, and specific time periods). These types of presentations may be exacerbated by an adverse life experience (i.e., small "t") that occurred in early childhood.

Example: Jesse was on the swim team at his high school. He had a strong sense of competitiveness and had won major swim competitions in prior years. This year he was beginning to fall way below the mark in competitions. The clinician learned that Jesse's swim coach was aggressive and often hurled verbal insults (e.g., "You're stupid." "You're fat." "You will never measure up."). Jesse began to exhibit pervasive anxiety and issues of self-doubt. Other possible single presenting symptoms in this case could be a belief of "I am no good," having frequent leg cramps, or perfectionist behavior in all areas of his life.

Any Circumscribed Problem (or Set of Experiences) Whether Acute or Long-Standing and Within a Specific Context

This is context-specific (i.e., learning that happens in a specific situation/setting and only happens again in a similar situation/setting). It is important to understand the context (i.e., the circumstances present at the time) in which a client's behavior continues to happen.

Example: In social situation with colleagues, Irena is often belligerent and rude. The circumstances that occur which manifest this behavior is when a colleague teases her about something she did while at work (e.g., presenting the wrong report at an important meeting) in front of other colleagues. She often leaves these events feeling confused, embarrassed, and shameful. In high school she was on the debate team where she often prepared for the wrong debate. Her fellow debaters would likely tease her about this when in debate-related social gatherings.

Diagnoses: Posttraumatic Stress Disorder, Adjustment Disorder, and Acute Stress Disorder

Posttraumatic Stress Disorder

The client has experienced a life-threatening event or series of events that meet diagnostic criteria for PTSD outlined in the *Diagnostic and Statistical Manual of Mental Disorders* (5th ed.; American Psychiatric Association, 2013) and has experienced hyperarousal, intrusions, and/or avoidance of stimuli that trigger negative symptoms with possible origins in early childhood incidents of neglect and/or abuse. Cases of simple PTSD involve single-event traumas (e.g., war and violence, natural or man-made disasters, accidents, and sudden losses or serious illnesses) or a cluster (i.e., repeated or similar) of similar events (e.g., physical or sexual abuse). The symptoms of simple PTSD stem from the occurrence of a critical event. The clinician needs to identify the incident, including earlier contributing events, if any, the triggers, including current manifestations (e.g., nightmares, flashbacks, recurring dreams), and future templates.

Example: A young woman witnessed a fatal car–pedestrian accident while driving on the interstate on her way to work. The victim was a pedestrian who was killed instantly, and the speeding car that hit her did not stop. Nine months later, the woman is still finding it more and more difficult to drive on the interstate. She becomes extremely tense and anxious while driving on more than two-lane highways, has experienced several full-blown panic attacks while driving in high-speed interstate traffic, and has had difficulty getting up on the mornings she has to go to work. Regarding a prior history, the client's past is unremarkable. In the case of this tragic incident, the accident itself is the touchstone event and hence was the first to be targeted and reprocessed in the sessions that followed.

COMPLEX CLINICAL PRESENTATIONS

Multiple Problems/Issues

It is not uncommon for a client to seek therapy to overcome more than one presenting problem and/or symptom (e.g., overreactions to current stressors, trouble at work, drinking too much). These types of clinical presentations are characterized by multiple issues, problems, or symptoms caused by a client's prolonged/sustained exposure to abuse/neglect with a negative cumulative effect on a client over a lifetime.

Example: A client presented with both work-related difficulties and grief issues, citing ongoing symptoms of depression, anxiety, and frequent panic reactions. His wife had died 3 years earlier having suffered a brain aneurysm. Because of the stressful nature of his high-profile job and his immediate need to care for his three small children, his focus went straight from the funeral to full speed ahead in getting his life together. As his children got older and the demands of his job became greater, the client began to regularly experience symptoms of anxiety and depression. His boss put him on notice for his absenteeism, being late for work and leaving early, and missing deadlines and meetings. In this case, numerous incidents have caused his pathology, but he does not meet the full diagnostic criteria for PTSD.

Pervasive Experiences Regarding Severe Childhood Abuse/Neglect

Maltreatment in childhood can come in many and any form and can have a lifelong and intergenerational impact on a child. The long-term consequences of childhood abuse and neglect include physical (e.g., traumatic brain injuries from head trauma, malnutrition, diabetes, lung and heart disease, cancer, migraines, arthritis, high blood pressure), psychological (e.g., isolation tendencies, pervasive fear and mistrust, academic difficulties, low self-esteem, depression, attachment and relationship difficulties), cognitive (e.g., delayed intellectual ability, poor school performance, attention deficits), and behavioral (e.g., sexual risk-taking, alcohol and substance abuse, juvenile delinquency and criminality, perpetration of maltreatment), ramifications which can be further exacerbated by other adverse experiences (e.g., parental divorce or substance abuse, domestic violence, poverty, war). The extent of these consequences is often determined by the age and developmental status of the child at the onset of the child abuse and neglect.

Example: Aalia was born to a single mother who suffered from an intellectual disability. Her mother's primary coping mechanism for dealing with her limitations resulted in ongoing drug abuse and prostitution. Aalia was born into poverty, witnessed perpetrator violence against her mother and herself, experienced frequent bullying at school, was teased for often appearing disheveled and dirty, suffered from malnutrition, and was frequently sexually molested by her mother's customers. As a toddler, Aalia had to feed and dress herself the best she could because her mother was often not present and, if she was, she was engaged in illicit behavior with other adults. Over the intervening years, Aalia experienced severe bouts of depression, low self-esteem, and anger. She isolated and distrusted everyone around her, especially men. As an adolescent, she sexually molested other children.

Adult-Onset Traumatic Experiences

When one thinks of adult-onset trauma, images of Holocaust survivors and Vietnam War veterans may come to mind. Despite a client's developmental history, life-threatening assaults, acts of terrorism, war, torture, genocide, and extreme danger may have a profound and devastating impact even on a client with a healthy sense of self. This type of trauma may also encompass major catastrophes, such as 9/11, natural disasters, serious accidents—anything that disrupts the fundamental aspects of a client's self-experience in terms of sense of agency, affectivity, time, safety, and bodily integrity is called into question (Boulanger, 2005).

Example: Kamara was drinking excessively, frequently breaking down, fighting, and generally feeling like he wanted to strangle someone most of the time. He felt like a shell of his former self. He had gone from being a hardworking, compassionate, independent man to someone who had hand tremors so badly that he could not tie his shoes and night terrors and flashbacks so vivid that he felt like he was in a war zone at night. In his early 20s, he had spent one deployment in Iraq while serving in the military. In high school, Kamara was a star quarterback, homecoming king, popular, and academically successful and hopeful. He was from an intact family. He went to college and excelled at the same level and achieved high levels of success. Because of his love of his country and a sense of duty and gratitude for his blessings, he enlisted in the Army right out of college. He wanted to serve in whatever capacity to show his gratitude for a life well lived. After 9 months, he was mustered out of the military.

Comorbidity of Disorders

Clients who present with comorbidity (i.e., coexistence of two or more disorders, such as depressive disorders, substance abuse disorders, bipolar disorder, obsessive-compulsive disorder, personality and dissociative disorders) often have increased levels of distress, symptomatology, social impairment, and other disabilities than those diagnosed with a single disorder, such as PTSD.

Example: Six years ago, Niro was involved in a six-car collision when a whiteout occurred on a mountain passage he was driving. Although he did not know at the time, the accident resulted in several fatalities. Over the intervening years, he began to experience frequent bouts of sadness, anxiety, and depression. He began to drink more often and to drink larger quantities than he ever had before. The depression deepened, and his alcohol use accelerated to the point that he could no longer hold a job.

Pervasive History of Early Trauma

A client with this type of trauma often presents with a history of low self-esteem and relationship issues, difficulties with affect regulation, and symptom clusters across various contexts. When dealing with a client possessing a pervasive history of early trauma, a clinician is encouraged to explore the client's history of abuse and neglect, any past or current medical issues, the impact of trauma and neglect on a client's psychosocial development, familial relationships, academic performance, and social skills. Attachment history and losses should also be explored along with primary attachment figures and relationships with anyone outside the immediate family (e.g., extended family, friends, co-workers, present and past clinicians). In addition, the clinician should explore any negative impact pervasive early trauma has had on the client's self-esteem which may have resulted in dysfunctional behaviors, negative beliefs about self and others, home and work difficulties, and compromised self-care. The clinician should examine any difficulties the client has with affect regulation and compromised regulatory capacity (i.e., ability to tolerate positive and negative emotional states outside the window of tolerance) as well as the client's reported maladaptive behaviors and compulsions that are utilized to manage dysregulated emotional states.

Example: Tyrone was kidnapped by a drifter when he was 3 years old. Throughout his 5-year captivity, he was severely sexually, physically, emotionally, and verbally abused. As Tyrone became older, his captor feared he would try to run away so he chained and padlocked him to his bed at night and when he was left alone in the country cabin that they shared. He was often denied bathroom and shower privileges and spent weeks and months without a clean change of clothes. His meals consisted of discarded, half-eaten scraps of food left in trash bins by local restaurants in a nearby town. When Tyrone was finally rescued, he was severely emaciated, suffered developmental delays, was selectively mute, and exhibited waves of intense anger and hostility, as well as anxiety and depression, and engaged in self-injurious behavior.

Vague or Diffuse Presentations

A client may present as one who appears to have a "perfect" life history but feels joyless and unfulfilled and does not know why. The client may complain of many vague symptoms with unknown origins. When asked about past traumas or disturbing life events, they may answer, "I can't think of anything." This is what is called a vague or diffuse presentation. In this case, the clinician needs to strategically tease out potential targets. The clinician may want to consider a more extensive look into the client's symptom origin and developmental history, including a history of disrupted attachment, neglect, and ubiquitous disturbing experiences that may not occur to the client as significant or worthy of mention. It should be noted that the apparent lack of significant history may be a red flag for a dissociative disorder, and a careful screening using the Dissociative Experiences Scale (DES) and diagnostic tools may be required. In these cases, history taking may need to be titrated—with an emphasis on stabilization using Phase 2 interventions and integrating other stabilization or skills-building techniques.

If past contributory experiences continue to be elusive, it may be productive to identify recent experiences of the issue and use the floatback technique or affect scan to link to earlier, more defined experiences. The usual chronological ordering of targets may need to be altered. A current experience of the issue may be reprocessed first, and, if the processing becomes blocked or loops, the clinician can trace back through floatback or affect scan for the source of any blocking beliefs or emotions. Once identified, the earlier memories can be reprocessed using Phases 3–6. With vague or diffuse presentations, a thorough accounting of her medical history and a depression screen in addition to dissociation screening would also be in order.

With this type of presentation, the client may report numerous experiences over their lifetime that could have produced their current pathology (i.e., severe depression; history of panic attacks; interpersonal, familial, and professional problems; or some dissociation). However, the client does not remember much of their childhood and/or may not meet the full diagnostic criteria for 309.81 (PTSD).

Example: Bennie originally presented to therapy at the request of the couples counselor that he and his wife had been seeing for several months. The couple experienced issues between them when he found the existence of mold in their home. The mold was successfully remediated and needed repairs were made with a few weeks. It was at this point that he developed a strong sense of guilt (i.e., for not protecting his children) and betrayal (i.e., by the house) and began to not trust anyone. His need to be in control also heightened. He could not cite any past contributory memories and claimed to have had an exemplary childhood, and the clinician could not trace his symptom presentation back to anything in his past beyond a girlfriend cheating on him in high school and his perfectionistic tendencies as an athlete.

Diagnoses: Complex Posttraumatic Stress Disorder, Addictions and Compulsive Disorders, Mood Disorders, Phobias, Dissociative Disorders, Personality Disorders

Complex Posttraumatic Stress Disorder

Complex Posttraumatic Stress Disorder (C-PTSD) is characterized by: (a) a complex presentation of traumatic life events over an extended period; (b) often including early abuse, neglect, or attachment disruptions; and (c) presenting with symptoms of a personality disorder and/or dissociation. Additionally, individuals with complex PTSD may experience difficulties with emotional regulation, self-perception, relationships with others, and one's sense of meaning.

Example: Sandra's mother died when she was 5 years old. Her abusive father was left to care for their four young children. He sexually abused and beat Sandra if she was not totally submissive and obedient from the time her mother died until she ran away from home at the age of 17 years. She was used as a replacement for his deceased wife and told it was her job because she was the oldest female. She became highly dissociative. If the client is too unstable, additional interventions and options for the order of reprocessing have been discussed in literature addressing EMDR therapy with clients having symptoms of complex PTSD and/or dissociation. In these cases, the inverted (Hofmann, 2009) or the reverse (Adler-Tapia, 2015) protocols may be used. These protocols reorganize the order of processing from past, present, and future to future, present, and past (i.e., future rehearsal, present triggers, and past events) so that the client may focus on developing hope, integrative capacity, and skills for the future. Use these protocols to address present challenges and triggers before processing any foundational trauma. Eye movement desensitization (EMD) may also be an option when reprocessing a highly disturbing target as it can help reduce the Subjective Units of Disturbances (SUDs) quickly and limit associations. See the section EMD Versus EMDR in Chapter 1. For more information on these protocols and other options for dealing with clients possessing symptoms of C-PTSD, reference the Francine Shapiro Library (emdria.omeka.net).

The presenting problems in each type of case (simple symptom, vague or diffuse, and the comprehensive presentations—single and multiple) need to be processed in the order of past events (touchstone event and all additional past events), present triggers, and future templates.

The types of a client's possible presenting issues have been limited in this Primer to those covered in the EMDR therapy Weekend 1 and 2 trainings. Other possibilities for presentation types may be of a relational nature (e.g., divorce or sibling rivalry), ongoing stressful events, someone who is in imminent danger (e.g., being stalked), or other complex presentations.

FIRST PRONG: EARLIER MEMORIES/TOUCHSTONE EVENTS

TOUCHSTONE EVENT

A touchstone event is synonymous with the earliest memory the client can remember that created the foundation for the client's present dysfunction or pathology. It is usually identified during the History-Taking and Treatment Planning Phase. In some cases, touchstone events may not be apparent in Phase 1. They may emerge spontaneously during processing or may be revealed through the clinician's use of strategies for blocked processing or other interventions, such as direct questioning, floatback technique, and affect scan. And, with some cases, the event that brings the client to treatment is the touchstone event.

The touchstone event brings home the fact that our presenting problems are often linked to traumatic or other disturbing events in the past (i.e., "the past is present"; Shapiro, 2009–2017a,b). Except for clients who present with an intense recent trauma or those who may not be initially able to tolerate going back to a painful touchstone event (e.g., a police officer losing their partner in the line of duty), the client's touchstone event is generally identified and reprocessed first.

Past events may be recent events, other adult events, or childhood experiences. Note that the symptoms presented by the client are not always precipitated by events in the past. There are cases where the presenting issue is the issue and the target, that is, there is no earlier touchstone event. This may be true in relational issues, ongoing stressful events, or recent traumatic events.

A simplified example of uncovering the touchstone event in an EMDR-directed session begins with the client presenting a problem (i.e., complaint, issue, or concern) on which they would like to work. Maybe the client is having a difficult time saying "no" or handling stress in the workplace. Perhaps they are experiencing relationship issues or have anxiety attacks in elevators. To uncover more information about the presenting issue, the clinician either asks the client explicitly if they can relate some specific and recent situations or events where they experienced their concern, or remembers the first time they encountered the problem. If not forthcoming, the clinician may need to obtain the information implicitly through intensive history taking.

In the case of a client who has difficulty saying "no," the clinician might ask, "Tell me about some recent situations where you have experienced that issue." A summary of the client's possible answers can be found as follows:

- Volunteering to take on extra work at the office even when they know they already have more work than they can handle.
- Agreeing to take care of their sister's three dogs for a week when they cannot find time to adequately care for their own two dogs.
- Being the only one of five siblings who visits their mother twice a week and does their grocery shopping before they do their own.

The client may have an entire laundry list of events that fits the criteria of the presenting issue. In this case, the clinician needs to sort out which incident is most disturbing and representative of the issue (i.e., "Which is the most disturbing recent incident that represents your issue?"). "My boss knew I would never say 'no' to his personal requests. He never once stopped to think about my feelings and what I thought about what he was asking." This experience exemplified their presenting issue and was used as the starting point for identifying past, present, and future targets.

STRATEGIES FOR ACCESSING THE TOUCHSTONE MEMORY

Direct questioning, the floatback technique, and the affect scan can be utilized to access the touchstone event. As an organizing technique, it is probably most useful for the beginning

EMDR clinician to utilize these tools in the order presented here. During the history-taking process, the clinician attempts to identify a recent time the client remembers experiencing the current difficulty that represents the presenting issue (e.g., their boss asked them to pick up their laundry yesterday, and they were unable to say "no"). Once a recent incident is identified, the clinician attempts to elicit an image (or picture) and an associated NC (e.g., "I am insignificant.") as well as the emotions and body sensations associated with the recent incident.

DIRECT QUESTIONING (I.E., GO BACK)

Through direct questioning, the clinician assists the client in identifying past events where the client felt or believed something similar. The earlier the event, the better (e.g., somewhere in the formative years of the client's life—from birth to 10 years). Remember, the clinician is probing for the touchstone memory, if there is one. The following are some questions clinicians might ask to elicit this information:

- When was the first time you remember feeling, thinking, or reacting that way?
- When was the first time you heard (or learned) "I am insignificant?"
- What incidents come to mind from childhood or adolescence?

In addition to the earliest event, other related past memories are identified.

FLOATBACK TECHNIQUE (I.E., THINK BACK)

If the client is unable to identify the touchstone through direct questioning, the clinician's next option is to use the floatback technique (Browning, 1999; Young et al., 2002) to elicit the past event that is foundational to the development of the current dysfunction. The floatback is an imagery exercise that acts as a bridge to earlier dysfunctional memories. Use the floatback technique:

- If the NC is clear (e.g., "I am insignificant") and is identified as a relevant and important part of the client's presenting issue (i.e., inability to say "no").
- When the present event is not fully accessible.
- If the NC is unclear or difficult to access. The floatback technique can still be implemented to access the touchstone event responsible for the client's current dysfunction by using the client's current emotions or physical sensations as a bridge to the past.

If the NC is clear, the clinician instructs the client to focus on the earliest identified memory up to this point, the NC, and emotions associated with the event by saying, "Float back to the earliest time when you experienced these." Or, if the client cannot easily focus, consider saying, "Now, bring up that negative belief (i.e., 'I am insignificant') and the emotions you are feeling now, and let your mind float back to the earliest time when you may have felt this way; and just notice what comes to mind."

AFFECT SCAN (I.E., FEEL BACK)

A hypnotherapeutic technique called an affect bridge was developed by Watkins (1971). This is like what we use in EMDR therapy when we ask a client, "When was the first time you experienced this emotion?" In either case, the client is asked to focus on the most recent memory of an event as a starting point for scanning back into time through similar memories to find the original memory or the cause of the client's presenting problem or issue. The affect scan (Shapiro, 1995; independently developed and without the hypnotic/reliving component contained in Watkins, 1971) is probably the easiest and quickest way to get to the touchstone event and can be the most powerful. However, it may elicit higher levels of emotion and body sensation that the client may not be prepared to experience. Thus, the floatback technique may be preferred with clients who have a higher level of negative affect. Note that the affect scan can be extremely effective when: (a) the NC is not clearly stated; (b) the earliest memory has not been able to be identified; and (c) the client becomes stuck during reprocessing, and the clinician checks for a feeder memory.

To initiate the affect scan, the clinician instructs the client to "Bring up that experience (i.e., the last memory identified in the floatback), the emotions, and the sensations that you are having now; and allow yourself to scan back for the earliest time you experienced something similar."

If nothing emerges, the clinician may want to explore family of origin issues with the client by inquiring, "Do you remember feeling like this in your family when you were young?" Or, "As you were growing up in school or in the neighborhood, do you remember similar things happening?" It is important *not* to limit exploration of the touchstone event to their family of origin. The disturbing event may have happened outside the familial circle (e.g., molestation by a neighbor, bullying on the playground).

An affect scan may also be used during processing if a client becomes mired in an emotional state and the bilateral stimulation (BLS) will not shift it. It may also be used to find blocking beliefs and feeder memories when SUD >0, Validity of Cognition (VoC) <7, and body scan will not clear completely.

Note: The memory device "Go back, think back, and feel back" was developed to help the clinician to conceptualize the focus of direct questioning, floatback, and affect scan (B. Korzun, personal communication, April 15, 2015).

It is not unusual for a client to come to therapy to work specifically on an early pivotal experience that happens to be the touchstone event. There are cases in which a client cannot identify an earlier memory and weeks later it may (i.e., most likely, but not always) spontaneously emerge. Touchstone events are usually traumatic or other disturbing events that occur in a client's formative years from birth to age 10. It is best to find the earliest possible memory for reprocessing because it is identified as the event that laid the foundation for the client's current problem. Exceptions to this may be: (a) clients who present with intense recent trauma (e.g., the client may not be able to tolerate going back to the touchstone event [i.e., firefighter losing a friend in a fire]); (b) returning military personnel involved in combat; or (c) survivors of an acute recent trauma, such as first responders and medical emergency personnel (Shapiro, 2009–2017a, 2009–2017b).

These techniques are used when appropriate, but not without caution as they may increase clients' current levels of distress. In all instances, it is important to ensure that clients have sufficient affect tolerance to handle whatever comes up and feel safe within the therapeutic relationship. In the case that follows, the client's presenting issue will be used to elicit the touchstone event with the direct questioning, floatback, and affect scan techniques.

Finding a touchstone event is a strategic process in terms of when, how (as seen earlier), and if ever (i.e., there is no touchstone event). See Table 4.1 for a more extensive view of the differences and sequencing of these strategies.

TABLE 4.1 Strategies for Accessing Touchstone Memory

Before preceding to direct questioning, floatback, and affect scan (in this order), ensure that:

1. a recent incident which represents the current difficulty is identified.
2. an image and NC are identified.

DIRECT QUESTIONING

"When was the first time you remember feeling (thinking, reacting) that way?"
"When was the first time you heard (or learned) _____?"
"What incidents come to mind from childhood or adolescence?"

FLOATBACK TECHNIQUE (NEGATIVE COGNITION + EMOTIONS)

Use floatback if:
Client is unable to identify the touchstone memory through direct questioning.
The NC is clear and identified as a relevant and important part of the client's presenting issue.
The present event is not fully accessible.
Client demonstrates a higher level of negative affect.

If the NC is clear, the client focuses on the earliest memory identified in direct questioning, the NC, and emotions associated with the event
"Float back to the earliest time when you experienced these."

If the client has difficulty focusing, say:
"Bring up that <u>negative belief</u> and the emotions you are feeling now and let your mind float back to the <u>earliest</u> time when you may have felt this way and notice what comes to mind."

AFFECT SCAN (MOST RECENT MEMORY + EMOTIONS + PHYSICAL SENSATIONS)

Use affect scan, if:
Client is unable to identify the touchstone memory through the use of the floatback technique.
NC is unclear and difficult to access. In this case, use the client's current emotions and physical sensations as a bridge to the past; or

If a touchstone is not identified using floatback, say:
"Bring up that experience (i.e., the most recent memory identified in the floatback), the <u>emotions</u>, and the <u>physical sensations</u> that you are having now, and allow yourself to scan back for the earliest time you experienced something similar."

Abbreviation: NC, negative cognition.

Case Example: Betty

Betty, a 55-year-old retiree, had been suffering with depression and low self-esteem after a long-drawn-out divorce from her husband of 36 years. She had great success with EMDR in the past, and she was determined to use it again to help with current relationship issues.

Betty wanted to be in a loving relationship. She thought it was a possibility after she had undergone the empowering effects of EMDR. Six months before coming back to therapy, Betty had met Richard, a wonderful man who was warm, compassionate, smart, and independent. She was comfortable with herself in this relationship.

Betty came into the session upset over an incident involving Richard. Both maintained separate residences and spent time away from each other with their own children and other family members. So, Betty had looked forward to spending time with him over the entire Labor Day weekend. When her companion left on Sunday morning instead of that night, she was devastated and could not understand why. She cried the entire day and was upset with herself.

This case will be utilized to demonstrate the use of direct questioning, floatback, and affect scan in identifying Betty's touchstone event.

Target:	Richard left rather than spend the day with me.
Image/worst part:	Being in my empty house after he drove away.
NC:	I am unimportant.
Positive cognition (PC):	I am important.
Emotions:	Loneliness, sadness
Body:	Throat, stomach

Identifying the Touchstone Through Direct Questioning

Because of Betty's previous history in therapy, the clinician knew that this was not an isolated event and that there was an inherent relationship pattern that had been with Betty for most of her life. The clinician wanted to identify the earliest event that established the foundation for her current symptoms.

Here is how the *direct questioning* went:

Clinician: Are there earlier times in your life when you thought that you were unimportant?

Betty: Yes, I remember in college my dorm mates often excluded me from social events.

Clinician: Can you think of any other times when you thought that you were unimportant?

Betty: Yes, my father was rather distant. He never had much to say or do with me. Once he just looked at me and grunted.

Clinician: As you focus on that experience and the negative thoughts, are there any childhood memories that come up?

Betty: I remember waking up from an afternoon nap. I had had a nightmare. I was terribly afraid, so I ran to find my mom. I said, "Mommy, mommy, hold me. I'm scared." My mother just looked at me and said, "Not now. I don't have time for you right now, little missy."

If the touchstone had not been identified using direct questioning, the clinician may consider using the floatback technique.

Identifying the Touchstone Event Using Floatback

When implementing the floatback technique, the client is asked to repeat the <u>last</u> identified memory that was accessed from the direct questioning technique. For the purposes of demonstration, the clinician assumes that the earliest memory identified up to this point was the memory of her distant father just looking at her and grunting.

Clinician: As you focus on that event (incident, experience) and the negative thoughts, are there any <u>earlier</u> childhood memories that come up?
Betty: No, I can't think of anything.
Clinician: Okay, now bring up that <u>negative belief</u> (i.e., 'I am unimportant') and the <u>emotions</u> you are feeling now and let your mind <u>float back</u> to the <u>earliest</u> time when you may have felt this way and just notice what comes to mind.
Betty: I remember waking up from an afternoon nap. I had had a nightmare. I was terribly afraid, so I ran to find my mom. I said, "Mommy, mommy, hold me. I'm scared." My mother just looked at me and said, "Not now. I don't have time for you right now, little missy."

If, again, Betty had been unable to access an earlier or touchstone memory, the clinician could also explore family of origin issues at this point by asking, "Any incidents from your family of origin where the negative thought 'I am unimportant' come to mind?"

If the touchstone had not been identified using the floatback technique, the clinician may consider utilizing the affect scan.

Identifying the Touchstone Event Using Affect Scan

If the client is still unable to identify an earlier memory, utilize the affect scan by incorporating the earliest memory already identified from the floatback technique. The affect scan can be used to access the touchstone event based on her emotional and physical sensations. Be sure to start by using the client's earliest memory identified in the floatback. Again, the clinician assumes that the earliest memory identified up to this point was the memory of her distant father just looking at them and grunting.

Clinician: Bring up that event (incident, experience; i.e., the <u>earliest</u> memory identified in the floatback), the <u>emotions</u>, and the <u>sensations</u> that you are having now, and allow yourself to <u>scan back</u> for the earliest time you experienced something similar.
Betty: I remember waking up from an afternoon nap. I had had a nightmare. I was terribly afraid, so I ran to find my mom. I said, "Mommy, mommy, hold me. I'm scared." My mother just looked at me and said, "Not now. I don't have time for you right now, little missy."

Note that direct questioning was employed first to see if Betty could recall an earlier time in her life when she experienced similar thoughts of "I am unimportant." It was only after it was determined that she could not that the floatback technique was utilized. Remember, floatback and affect scan may occasionally cause the client to experience high levels of

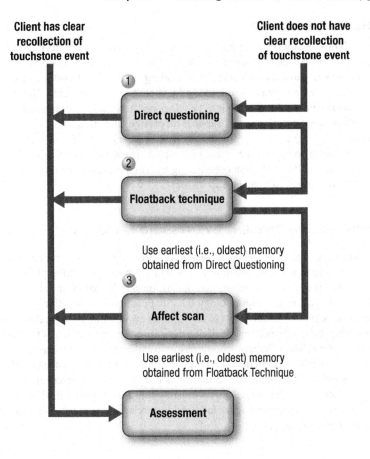

FIGURE 4.4. Past event: Strategies for identifying touchstone event.

emotions and body sensations that they might not be able to tolerate at the time. Use these two techniques cautiously.

It is not always necessary to have a NC to identify a touchstone memory. If it cannot be accessed, you can use the affect scan "to use the sensations as a bridge to the past" (Shapiro, 2006).

If appropriate, identify and reprocess the touchstone memory before continuing with the processing of later past memories, present triggers, and future situations when using either direct questioning, floatback, or the affect scan. (Note: There is not always a touchstone memory to reprocess.) Once the memory has been accessed and it is determined that the client is ready to begin the reprocessing phases of treatment, use the procedural steps to complete the assessment using this identified earliest memory for processing (Figure 4.4).

When the touchstone event and all the past events have been identified using the methods described earlier, they need to be targeted and reprocessed before continuing to the next prong. Once completed, the clinician then progresses to targeting and reprocessing the client's present triggers and future templates.

TOUCHSTONE REVISITED

Current EMDR therapy training places a greater emphasis on identifying and targeting a touchstone event before reprocessing other memories that arise. However, the training focus in no way negates the importance of dealing with present issues as they arise. Be cautious about being overzealous in looking for these touchstone events. There may not be one, or it may not be significant enough (i.e., does not have sufficient emotional resonance) to utilize effectively. Sometimes, an orange is an orange. The clinician needs to be aware of the clinical choices (or trauma presentations listed earlier) to determine whether a client's current focus needs to be on the present or the past. The appropriateness of the clinician's recommendations will be apparent considering the client's presenting issues, current functioning (including affect tolerance), and history.

SECOND PRONG: PRESENT EVENTS AND TRIGGERS

The second step of the three-pronged protocol is identifying and reprocessing the present events and situations that continue to resonate with the presenting problem. In other words, identify all current situations, conditions, or people that (a) may be continuing to trigger the client's current symptomology (i.e., inappropriate or negative emotions, physical sensations, beliefs, or behaviors), (b) continue to evoke avoidant or maladaptive behaviors or emotional disturbance, or (c) elicit physical sensations and urges that are residual sources of the same. These current situations are initially obtained during the early clinical intake interviews with the client; they may be added to after the past memories are successfully processed. The client should reprocess conditional responses, events, and other stimuli associated with the presenting problem using the standard EMDR protocol (i.e., Phases 3–6) with each present trigger followed by a related future template before moving on to the next present trigger.

WHAT TO LOOK OUT FOR

When processing present disturbances, the clinician also attends to the following:

1. **Ecological validity:** Is the level of disturbance appropriate for the client's circumstances? For example, the client states that they cannot reach a 0 or 1 on the SUD scale by saying, "I don't ever want to forget that this happened." This refers to a client, for example, who had a serious motor vehicle accident where someone in the other car died. They were no longer traumatized by the event. Their driving and ability to be a passenger had returned. Even though the accident was not their fault, the fact that someone had died because of the accident made them say that a 1 was enough. For them, there could not be a 0 level of disturbance for something that had such an impact on a family. Consider another example where a client is recovering from colon cancer. Currently, they are in remission with a good chance of long-term survival. However, in processing the diagnosis and the treatment, they were unable to reach a 0 SUD level. The cancer had totally changed their life, and it was impossible for them to say that the impact was totally over.
2. **Blocking beliefs:** Is there an inappropriate belief actively involved in the current disturbance? In an example of a domestic violence case, the client might be unable to reach a 0 on the SUD scale because of the emerging belief "I can't let this go since I am not worthy enough to feel safe."

3. **Peelback memories:** Did an earlier associated memory emerge? Even when targeting an obvious critical incident in the present, such as a rape, associations to earlier experiences may surface.

4. **Feeder memories:** Is an earlier memory feeding the underlying disturbance identified in a non-childhood target? For instance, a client is processing their most recent disturbing incident of being stuck in an elevator when a memory of being trapped in a closet that was being held shut by their older brother emerges. This is a memory that was not accessed during the History-Taking and Treatment Planning Phase or the reprocessing of past memories.

Comprehensive history taking prior to EMDR processing is helpful in identifying these types of beliefs and memories and curtailing stalled processing later. If they do arise, use of the floatback technique or the affect scan can help identify the earlier memories.

Many of the triggers present at the beginning of EMDR therapy will no longer exist once the touchstone and other past events have been identified and reprocessed. Current events or situations that previously induced a high level of disturbance may no longer cause the symptoms reported by the client in the past. The negative behaviors, emotions, sensations, and thoughts associated with the earlier events may have been flushed out and no longer accessible. The client's present distress may have been resolved and the trauma can now be considered a learning experience, rather than something to be looked on with dread.

In this case, these triggers do not continue to cause any symptoms because the negative emotions, sensations, thoughts, and behaviors associated with the traumatic event are no longer stored in the memory network. The current stress caused by the trauma has been transformed into a learning experience.

Some triggers may still be active due to *second-order conditioning* (see below). Two things may be happening: (a) the previously targeted distress may have sensitized numerous existing stimuli in the present that have become independently disturbing and (b) another previously unaccessed memory network may be activated by the distress. The generalization effect did not resolve everything and, hence, these triggers will need to be accessed and targeted separately to reach resolution (Shapiro, 2009–2017a, 2009–2017b).

In this part of the process, the clinician has the client access a recent event so that the level of disturbance, if any, can be evaluated: "Bring up the last time you remember feeling/ behaving (fill in the blank)." If there is still disturbance, implement Phases 3 to 6.

HOW CAN TRIGGERS REMAIN ACTIVE AFTER SO MUCH PROCESSING?

There are at least three reasons why some present triggers may be active after all past events have been reprocessed:

1. **Second-order conditioning:** Second-order conditioning refers to a conditioned stress response created because of past distress being repeated in the presence of certain situations. In the case of a process phobia called cyberphobia (i.e., fear of computers or working on a computer), for example, there could be additional stimuli that need to be processed separately because of unrelated circumstances or events that may trigger the fear. In this case, the client may become frightened on hearing that their young child is learning to use the computer in school, their wife has signed up for a computer class to learn word processing, or their older daughter is begging for a laptop of her own.

2. **Fed by information left over from earlier events:** This information was not processed because every channel of association has not been cleared.
3. **Recent situations may have occurred where the emotions and perceptions are different than the earlier event:** These triggers are freshly charged by recent events and have been stored in memory along with other emotions and perceptions that are different from those in previously processed events.

Each trigger will need to be assessed and reprocessed, and then a future template can be performed on a related future challenge prior to reprocessing the next present trigger. The clinician will need to direct the client in assessing recent events that were originally distressing and then determine whether the events are still disturbing. An instruction may be, "Bring up the last time you remember feeling/behaving (fill in the blank). (Pause.) What do you get?" If a disturbance is still present, the clinician will reprocess each event identified. The recent event or trigger will be reprocessed until SUD = 0, VoC = 7, and the body scan is clear. A future template is then installed for each trigger by imagining an encounter with the situation sometime in the future or reprocessing anticipatory anxieties about such an encounter.

Case Example: Peter

Peter, a proud military person who served his country voluntarily and honorably, was back from his second tour of duty in South Asia. His wife and he presented initially for couples counseling, but it quickly became clear that Peter needed individual work. All efforts at marital counseling were suspended and Peter came to therapy for his individual issues. Peter worked for weeks on both early childhood and war experiences so that he could successfully navigate his civilian world. He was eating and sleeping better, his irritability had almost completely abated, and his marriage was beginning to flourish.

Certain things still triggered him, however, such as loud noises, gunshots, flashes of light of any kind, and construction zones. With these in mind, the clinician and Peter set out to process his startle responses to these external triggers. The following is Peter's session.

ASSESSMENT

Target: Peter lives in hunting country and had been bird hunting many times before the war without much attention to the sound of gunshots around him. "Birdshot," he said, "is so heavy that it does not travel far, nor can it do much damage at large distances." *While he was in therapy, he happened to go hunting with his friends.* During the hunt, someone fired in his general direction—not an uncommon event—and the shot exploded yards before him. "I hit the ground," he said. "I thought I was going to die."

Image/worst part: The worst part was the sound of the birdshot coming toward him.
NC: I'm in danger.
PC: It's over. I'm safe now.

VoC:	2
Emotions:	Anger, fear, irritation
SUD:	8
Body:	Chest

DESENSITIZATION

Clinician: Bring up the sound, those words, "I'm in danger," and where you feel it in your body. Just let it go wherever it goes. Just let whatever happens, happen (set of BLS). Take a breath. (Pause). Let it go. (Pause.) What comes up for you now?

Notice the change in the language in the discussion. The client reported a sound rather than an image (or picture) as the worst part.

Peter: Am I doing this right?

It is not unusual for clients to question before, during, and after EMDR processing whether they are "doing it right." These are common questions: What if I don't do it right? Am I doing it right?

Clinician: There is no right or wrong way to do EMDR processing. Everyone does it differently. Just trust the process and let happen whatever happens. Go with that (set of BLS). Good. You're doing fine. Take a breath. (Pause.) Let it go. (Pause.) What are you noticing <u>now</u>?
Peter: Okay. I feel my chest tightening up.

It is important for the clinician to maintain neutrality throughout the client's reprocessing.

Clinician: Go with that (set of BLS). Good. Good. Take a breath. (Pause.) Let it go. (Pause.) What's happening <u>now</u>?

Take a breath with the client to model how it is done. Otherwise, many clients may not fully inhale and exhale. Modeling complete inhalations and exhalations for the client facilitates their reprocessing of the trauma. Breathing is an important component of the reprocessing of traumatic memories as it inherently enables the client to let go of the negative sludge that has been laying stagnant in the client's system. However, the clinician should not take this too far. Guiding the client in breathing exercises during reprocessing may interfere with sufficient access to the memory for successful reprocessing.

Peter: No change. I feel it in my chest.
Clinician: Go with that (set of BLS). Take a breath. (Pause.) Let it go. (Pause.). What are you noticing <u>now</u>?
Peter: It has moved to my stomach.
Clinician: Go with that (set of BLS). Good. You're doing fine. Take a breath. (Pause.) Let it go. Pause.) What are you noticing <u>now</u>?
Peter: It feels like it is moving just above my legs.
Clinician: Go with that (set of BLS). Good. Take a breath. (Pause.) Let it go. (Pause.) What's happening <u>now</u>?

Peter: I'm feeling pretty good.

Clinician: Go with that (set of BLS). Let it go. Take a breath. (Pause.) Let it go. (Pause.) What do you get <u>now</u>?

Peter: It's about the same.

Clinician: Go with that (set of BLS). Good. Take a breath. (Pause.) Let it go. (Pause.) What are you getting <u>now</u>?

Notice that the clinician encourages the client throughout the process.

Peter: I'm safe now. It's over.

Clinician: Go with that (set of BLS). Take a breath. (Pause.) Let it go. (Pause.) What are you noticing <u>now</u>?

Peter: It's the same.

Clinician: When you go back to the <u>original</u> event (incident, experience), what are you getting now?
      (Reminder: Original event [incident, experience]—the recent experience of hunting where someone fired in his general direction.)

Peter: I'm feeling really relaxed.

Clinician: Go with that (set of BLS). Good. Good. Take a breath. (Pause.) Let it go. (Pause.) What comes up for you <u>now</u>?

Peter: I'm not feeling anything.

Clinician: What does "I'm not feeling anything" mean?

The clinician is asking this question because they are unclear about what is happening. This could be a sign of dissociation, or it could represent completed reprocessing of this channel of association (i.e., nothing simply means nothing).

Peter: I feel kind of numb.

Clinician: What does numb mean?

Client: I don't feel anything.

Again, the clinician attempts to discern whether the client is stuck, dissociating, or if processing of this channel of association is complete.

Clinician: Go with that (set of BLS). Take a breath. (Pause.) Let it go. (Pause.) What are you noticing <u>now</u>?

Peter: I am getting tingly all over.

Clinician: Notice that (set of BLS). Good. Take a breath. (Pause.) Let it go. (Pause.) What are you noticing <u>now</u>?

Peter: There's something in my head. I don't know what it is. It's not a headache. It's numbness. I can't describe it. I don't hurt. I can just feel something going on.

Clinician: Go with that (set of BLS). You're doing fine. Take a breath. (Pause.). Let it go. (Pause.) What are you getting <u>now</u>?

Peter: Nothing.

Clinician: What does "nothing" mean?

Peter: I feel good. Relaxed. Calm.

Clinician: Go with that (set of BLS). Good. Good. Take a breath. (Pause.) Let it go.(Pause.) What are you getting *now*?

Peter: It's the same. I feel good. Still relaxed. Still good.
Clinician: When you go back to the <u>original</u> event (incident, experience), what are you getting now?
Peter: It's over. I am safe.
Clinician: Go with that (set of BLS). Good. Good. Take a breath. (Pause.) Let it go. (Pause.) What are you noticing <u>now</u>?
Peter: I feel safe.
Clinician: When you focus on the <u>original</u> event (incident, experience), on a scale from 0 to 10 where 0 is neutral or no disturbance and 10 is the worst disturbance you can imagine, how disturbing is the event (incident, experience) to you <u>now</u>?
Peter: 1.
Clinician: What prevents (keeps) it from being a 0?

If a blocking belief emerges, and depending at which phase it appears, it is reprocessed with BLS until SUD = 0, VoC = 7, or body scan is clear. The clinician also needs to consider any new skills needed by the client and ecological validity when dealing with blocking beliefs.

With clients who have issues with numbers and/or perfection, a clinician may say instead, "What makes it (1 or 2)?" or "Is it better or worse?" It is important to be flexible.

Peter: My knowing that I'm going to get mad if it happens again. My believing that my body will react.
Clinician: Go with that (set of BLS). Take a breath. (Pause.) Let it go. (Pause.) What's happening <u>now</u>?
Peter: I'm really relaxed.
Clinician: Go with that (set of BLS). Good. Take a breath. (Pause.) Let it go. (Pause.) What are you noticing <u>now</u>?
Peter: I am still relaxed.

Remember that one criterion for returning to target is for the client to provide at least two neutral or positive responses.

Clinician: Focus on the <u>original</u> event (incident, experience) and tell me what comes up. What comes up for you now?
              (Reminder: Original event [incident, experience]—the recent hunting experience when someone fired in his general direction.)
Peter: Nothing.
Clinician: Go with that (set of BLS). Take a breath. (Pause.) Let it go. (Pause.)What's happening <u>now</u>?
Peter: I am as relaxed as I have ever been.
Clinician: When you focus on the <u>original</u> event (incident, experience), on a scale from 0 to 10 where 0 is neutral or no disturbance and 10 is the worst disturbance you can imagine, how disturbing is the event (incident, experience) to you <u>now</u>?
Peter: Zero.
Clinician: Go with that (set of BLS). Good. Take a breath. (Pause.) Let it go. (Pause.).How disturbing does it feel <u>now</u>?
Peter: Zero still.

INSTALLATION

Clinician: Focus on the <u>original</u> event (incident, experience). Do those words, "It's over. I'm safe now" still fit, or is there another positive statement you feel would be more suitable?

Peter: Yeah. It's over. I am safe now.

Clinician: When you focus on the <u>original</u> event (incident, experience), how true do those words, "It's over. I'm safe now," feel to you now on a scale from 1 to 7 where 1 feels completely false and 7 feels completely true?

Peter: 7.

Clinician: Focus on the <u>original</u> event (incident, experience) and hold it together with the words, "It's over. I'm safe now" (set of BLS). Take a breath. (Pause.) Let it go. (Pause.) On a scale of 1 to 7, how true do those words, "It's over. I'm safe now," feel to you when you focus on the original event (or experience)?

Peter: It's still a 7. I feel relieved.

BODY SCAN

Clinician: Close your eyes and focus on the original event (incident, experience) and those words, "It's over. I'm safe now." Scan your body from head to toe for physical discomfort. If you feel anything, let me know.
(Reminder: Original event [incident, experience]—the recent experience of hunting where someone fired in his general direction.)

Peter: It's a void. Relief. It's like I kicked something out. There is space for something else now.

Clinician: Go with that (set of BLS). You're doing fine. Take a breath. (Pause.) Let it go. (Pause.) What are you getting <u>now</u>?

Peter: Nothing.

Clinician: Peter, what does "nothing" mean?

Peter: I'm good. I feel great.

Clinician: Go with that (set of BLS). You're doing fine. Take a breath. (Pause.) Let it go. (Pause.) What are you noticing now?

Peter: I'm good.

CLOSURE

Clinician: The processing we have done today may continue after the session. You may or may not notice new insights, thoughts, memories, or dreams. If so, just notice what you are experiencing. Take a snapshot of what you are seeing, feeling, thinking, and any triggers, and keep a trigger, image, cognition, emotion, and sensation (TICES) log. Then do a Safe (Calm) Place exercise to rid yourself of the disturbance. We can work on this new material next time. If you feel it is necessary, you may call me.

Peter came back the next week impressed with his progress. He stated that his startle response was "back to normal." He said, "I don't seem to be as jumpy as I was before. I'm home. I am happy, and I just want to get on with my life." The clinician would then suggest using the Future Template to help Peter to do just that. They would likely use the next time he is going hunting or hears "birdshot" as the similar future situation.

PRESENT TRIGGERS SUBSUMED BY THE REPROCESSING OF THE TOUCHSTONE EVENT

As a client reprocesses triggers, other reported triggers may dissipate. There are times when a client's present triggers are cleared by simply reprocessing earlier or touchstone memories. So, when the clinician revisits the presenting problem, the triggers often no longer exist.

An example of this is Yolanda, a client who experienced extreme fear whenever her boss asked to see her. "Whenever I stood before him, I felt like a 7-year-old who was in trouble. I never could shake the fear of it. The minute I would get an e-mail or a telephone call requesting my presence, I could immediately feel myself shrinking. By the time I got to his office, I was a mess. I just knew I had done something wrong. I had screwed up."

During the initial history-taking interview, the client shared with the clinician that whenever she misbehaved at home, her mother always said, "Wait until your father gets home." Her dad never really talked to or played with her, so when he called for her, she knew she was in trouble. This was a ubiquitous (i.e., constantly encountered) touchstone event. She could not recall one incident, because there were so many. They were similar in that she would shrink inside the second her dad called for her. She knew the reason he was summoning her could not be good and that consequences for her ill behavior would be worse.

After the original event (incident, experience) had been fully processed, the clinician went back to the event that brought her to counseling in the first place so that she could process the present triggers. It turned out to be no longer relevant, as it had been fully resolved by processing the touchstone events. The processing of the earlier events had turned the current difficulty into an important learning experience.

THIRD PRONG: FUTURE EVENTS AND FUTURE TEMPLATES

A future (or positive) template is utilized as a means of addressing avoidance, adaptation, and actualization within the EMDR process (Shapiro, 2018). The third prong of the approach focuses on a client's ability to identify and make choices and utilizes a protocol for developing a future, positive template that will help the client to incorporate appropriate future behaviors. The clinician will apply a future template for each trigger identified by the client. Some clinicians may reprocess all the present triggers before working with future templates, while others create a future/positive template following the reprocessing of a present trigger, and then process the next present trigger.

GOALS OF THE FUTURE TEMPLATE

The goals of creating a future template are diverse: (a) to provide the client time to practice or rehearse a behavior (i.e., imaginal/behavioral rehearsal) or to develop a desired action plan or skill building for an actual event in the future before going out into the world (i.e., in vivo) or that is adaptive to the client's current life context; (b) to identify and reprocess residual or anticipatory anxiety; (c) to provide another opportunity to reveal the client's hidden negative beliefs, fears, and/or inappropriate responses; and (d) to strengthen any adaptive skills, behaviors, and/or emotional or sensory responses that have emerged or developed in the client's memory system.

There are three types of future templates with distinct goals. The first type is the third prong of reprocessing when the past trauma and present triggers have all been cleared, and the goal is to take the new learning into future situations. It is uncomplicated and straightforward, following the future template procedure and using long and faster sets of BLS. The second, future rehearsal, is a skills-building and imaginal rehearsal future template that helps a client develop a repertoire of skills and strengthen their confidence. This is often done before all targets have been reprocessed and follows the resource development protocols more closely, using short and slower BLS. The third addresses anticipatory anxiety and the exploration of new and more adaptive patterns of behavior. Future anxieties are "flash forwards" and are addressed using the standard protocol for present triggers. The ultimate outcome of the third prong is to assure that the client has assimilated new information, including real or imaginal experiences of adaptive functioning, which may translate to future successes.

SKILLS BUILDING AND IMAGINAL REHEARSAL

For this type of future template, the clinician does not need to implement a full assessment of the target. They can start with simply having the client imagine the anticipated event in their mind. For example, if a client processed memories involving a significant person or a significant situation in the past, they would be asked to imagine a future meeting with the person or future situation to see if further disturbances arise. If a disturbance does arise, it could be dealt with by several interventions (e.g., education, modeling of appropriate behaviors, assertiveness training, exploration of boundaries, and reprocessing of the disturbing material). If a client's disturbance is inappropriate, clusters of events are evaluated for unresolved issues. See Table B.1 in Chapter 8 for the steps to these important processes.

STEPS NEEDED PRIOR TO CREATING A POSITIVE TEMPLATE

Before a future template can be installed, it is necessary that the earlier memories that set the groundwork for the client's presenting problem/issue and present stimuli that elicit dysfunctional material be successfully reprocessed and education and/or skills training (e.g., assertiveness training or social customs and norms awareness) be initiated. In addition, a full exploration is undertaken to examine how a client wishes to perceive, feel, act, or believe in the present and in the future.

Here are the steps that are completed prior to creating a positive template:

1. Resolve earlier memories and present triggers, internal and external.
2. Explore how the client sees themself in the future in terms of thinking, feeling, perceiving, acting, and believing.
3. Identify and teach appropriate skills, such as assertiveness training, social skills, and mindful behavior.
4. Refer for nonpsychological skills (i.e., computer classes, public speaking).
5. Identify anticipated future stressors that emerge during the reprocessing of past and present events.
6. Use future template following the successful reprocessing of each present trigger.

PROCEDURAL STEPS FOR INSTALLING A FUTURE TEMPLATE (SHAPIRO, 2017A, PP. 99–100)

The installation of a future template is a two-phase process: (1) the client identifies a future situation in which they would like to develop an adaptive response, and (2) the client focuses on a challenging scenario(s) to the future situation where unanticipated or undesirable outcomes could arise where adaptive responses could be generated.

Phase 1: Future Template—Desired Outcomes

Once the steps outlined in Exhibit B.1 of Chapter 8 have been completed, the clinician may say to the client, "We have worked on past experiences in relation to your presenting problems, as well as present situations that have triggered your distress. Today, I would like to suggest that we work on how you would like to respond in the future to similar situations."

This introduction may be worded more carefully to reflect the situation (Shapiro, 2009–2017a, 2009–2017b). For example, if the client is in treatment for grief following the death of a child, the clinician might alter the wording to say, "Now let's work on how you'd be able to respond in the future when you might experience a loss."

Until now there was no script for identifying the future situation and PC. This step entails a dialogue between the clinician and client to discern, such as, "How do you want to see yourself responding to this situation? What would you like to believe about yourself as you do?" A script for the phases 1 and 2 of the future template are provided below for each step so the clinician can follow the flow and the intent of the third prong of the standard EMDR therapy protocol.

Step 1: The clinician instructs the client to identify a future situation where they would like a more adaptive response. The clinician also ensures that the client has the necessary skills to implement an adaptive response and helps the client identify a desired PC connected with it. This cognition may or may not be the same one the client used previously when resolving the present trigger. *Phase 1 dialogue:* "Identify a future situation related to _____ where you want a more adaptive response. What would you like to believe about yourself as you accomplish this?"

Step 2: While holding in mind the desired PC and associated emotions, the clinician instructs the client to imagine a situation responding appropriately to a similar situation in the future. *Phase 1 dialogue:* "I'd like you to imagine yourself responding effectively with a similar situation in the future. With the positive belief, 'I am _____,' and a feeling of _____ (e.g., calm, confidence), imagine stepping into this situation. Notice how you are handling the situation and what you are thinking, feeling, and experiencing in your body."

There is no BLS implemented at this point. After a short pause, ask the client, "What are you noticing now?" Then proceed accordingly:

1. If their response is *positive*, instruct the client to target the situation as the clinician reinforces with BLS and then install the PC until the VoC = 7 (or if ecologically appropriate). *Phase 1 dialogue:* "Focus on the situation and the words, 'I am _____' (i.e., positive cognition). How true do those words feel to you now on a scale from 1 to 7, where 1 feels completely false and 7 feels completely true?"
   The clinician asks the client to "Bring up the image and the words, 'I am _____' (i.e., positive cognition), and follow my fingers."
   The clinician initiates sets of BLS (i.e., 20 or more) until the VoC = 7 (or if ecologically appropriate).
2. If the client's response is *neutral* (or uncertain), the clinician asks for clarification (such as lack of familiarity or need for a plan) in order to generate a desired response from the client and the situation is retargeted as described at the beginning of Step 2.
3. If the response is *negative*, identify any difficulties, problem solve, and generate a desired response (e.g., blocks, anxieties, fears) and retarget the scene described at the beginning

of Step 2. If the client cannot generate a desired response due to a negative association (i.e., another past event), the clinician instructs the client to *contain* the negative association and retarget the scene described at the beginning of Step 2. However, if the client remains blocked, further processing of the past event(s) may be indicated.

Note: The "desired response" describes how the client would like to respond in an anticipated future situation. What would they like to be doing, thinking, feeling, and so on? For example, if their boss asked them to come to their office, their desired response may be, "I could do so calmly without anxiety and agitation."

Step 3: While holding in mind the PC, the clinician asks the client to run a movie of the situation from start to finish of responding adaptively to the situation. *Phase 1 dialogue:* "Now I would like you to run a movie of dealing effectively with this situation, holding in mind those words, 'I am _____.'"

The clinician adds BLS as the client runs the movie in order to enhance the positive feelings and process any disturbance that may arise. If the client runs into any difficulties or blocks, ensure that they can run the movie from beginning to end with a sense of confidence and satisfaction.

Note: If the client remains blocked and unable to run the movie from start to finish, further processing of past events may be indicated.

Phase 2: Future Template—Generate Challenging Situations

Once the adaptive response to a future situation and the PC have been identified and installed, the clinician has the client visualize challenging situations that might occur in the future and how they may respond.

Step 1: The clinician instructs the client to create multiple scenarios where an unanticipated or undesirable outcome could occur and where the client can generate favorable or adaptive responses to the future situation and desired outcome described in first phase of the future template. *Phase 2 dialogue:* "I'd like you to think of a challenging situation that could occur. What are you noticing?"

Step 2: While holding in mind the desired PC and associated emotions, the clinician instructs the client to imagine responding appropriately to a similar situation in the future. *Phase 2 dialogue:* "I'd like you to imagine yourself coping effectively with this challenging situation. With the new positive belief, 'I am _____,' and the feeling of _____ (e.g., joy, happiness, contentment), imagine stepping into this situation. Notice how you are handling the challenging situation and what you are thinking, feeling, and experiencing in your body."

If the client's response is positive, reinforce with BLS and then proceed with the installation of the PC. *Phase 2 dialogue:* "Focus on the situation and the words, 'I am _____' (i.e., positive cognition), how true do those words feel to you now on a scale from 1 to 7, where 1 feels completely false and 7 feels completely true?"

When the client provides the VoC, the clinician asks the client to "Bring up the image and the words, 'I am _____' (i.e., positive cognition), and follow my fingers." The clinician implements BLS until the VoC = 7 (or if ecologically appropriate).

If the client's response is negative, the clinician identifies any difficulties, debriefs, and processes as needed. The clinician may also help the client problem solve and help the client to generate a desired response. Then the clinician targets the scene above and installs the PC.

TABLE 4.2 Anticipatory Anxiety

Like traumatic and other adverse life events, anticipatory anxiety may be addressed according the standard EMDR protocol (i.e., Phases 3–6).

To proceed with the reprocessing, the SUD level is likely to be no higher than 3 to 4. If the SUD is higher than 3 to 4, the clinician will need to retarget feeder memories or present triggers.

In dealing with anticipatory anxiety, the Desensitization Phase should be brief. If it is not and the SUD level is above 4, then the three-pronged reprocessing approach (past, present, and future) will need to be re-implemented.

Abbreviation: SUD, Subjective Units of Disturbance.

Step 3: The clinician instructs the client to run a movie of one of the challenging situations using BLS to enhance and reinforce. This process is repeated until VoC = 7 (or ecological validity is established) and an adaptive response occurs throughout.

THIRD PRONG: MISUNDERSTOOD, DISREGARDED, AND FORGOTTEN

The third prong of the EMDR approach is probably the most misunderstood and, often, most disregarded for clinicians who are new to EMDR therapy. One of the reasons may be that the client is often surprised to see what progress can be made so quickly in the first and second prongs of the approach that the response to future events gets lost. As a clinician, it is important to stay focused and to ensure that all three prongs of the approach are adequately and successfully processed before termination.

If there is hesitancy by the client in approaching the future template, it may be an indicator of incomplete processing of past issues, present triggers, or secondary gain issues. If a feeder or earlier memory arises, they may find it necessary to process the contributing event and stimuli before continuing. In either case, provide needed education and assist in reprocessing these memories before the installation of a future template. The future (or positive) template may be thought of as a continuation of the Installation Phase of the EMDR procedural steps. See Table 4.2 with some instructions and cautions when dealing with issues of anticipatory anxiety.

If a client's presenting issues encompass memories of significant people, places, or situations, the client could be asked to imagine themselves with that person, that place, or that situation. Unresolved materials may need to be accessed and resolved, clusters of events reevaluated, residual dysfunctional memories targeted and reprocessed, assertiveness or boundary setting explored and retargeted, or use of a positive template employed to assimilate the newly uncovered information and to help the client identify appropriate adaptive behaviors. The focus on the third prong assures the incorporation of new and appropriate future actions or behaviors and is vital to the client's continued movement toward adaptive resolution.

Again, each trigger identified in the present prong needs a future template. This process may be part of one session, or it may span many sessions depending on time and number of present triggers. Even though some triggers are neutral after a client processes past events (i.e., VoC = 7) and the trigger does not have to be processed utilizing Phases 3 to 6, the use of a future template for those triggers may still be helpful.

To reiterate, there are three basic types of future templates. One simply takes the PC or new learning into a future situation and strengthens it using the future template procedure. Another addresses anticipatory anxiety, which is reprocessed using the 11-step standard EMDR procedure (i.e., image or picture, NC, PC, VoC, emotion, SUD level, location of body sensation, desensitization, installation, body scan, and closure). The third uses skills building and imaginal rehearsal, which does not require a full Phase 3 Assessment.

With skills building and imaginal rehearsal, the client imagines an adaptive response in the future to a previously disturbing person, place, or thing, uncomfortable situation or circumstance, and/or doing a particularly upsetting future action. It is like "running a movie" of a potentially disturbing or upsetting action or event and the optimal behavioral responses to it. Positive beliefs and sensations are identified, and an enhancing PC is incorporated. The clinician leads the client in successive sets of BLS as a means of assimilating information and incorporating it into a positive template for future action. During this imaginal rehearsal, residual negative beliefs or sensations are identified and reprocessed as needed.

The clinician may also want to consider doing a brief future rehearsal each time the client has a reprocessing session, regardless of whether it is complete or not, especially if a client's focus is on performance issues or anticipated events. For example, if a client hesitates during a reprocessing session on a different issue because they fear they are "doing it wrong," a short future rehearsal at the end of the session may focus on the client "doing it right." Or, with someone having immediate performance issues at school but is working on a past event that precipitated the anxiety, they may need a few moments at the end of the session to focus on further developing their repertoire of skills of enhancing their confidence by rehearsing future situations.

FUTURE TEMPLATE—EXAMPLES

Case Example: Michael

When leaving work, Michael remembered that he needed to buy a gallon of milk before going home. As he turned a corner to make his way to the grocery store, a young boy ran in front of his car. Michael stomped on his brakes and swerved dramatically to the right, but he could not stop his car before grazing the child. The little boy suffered a broken leg and was taken by ambulance to the hospital. This was a single-event trauma. Nothing in Michael's life compared to the look on the little boy's face just before he was hit. It took several sessions of reprocessing to alleviate his suffering from the memory.

During previous therapy sessions, the clinician and Michael had successfully processed several current triggers, including his driving anxiety and driving around dusk, the time of day when the accident occurred. Michael also had a dread of encountering the little boy's parents, such as at church or at the mall. The future template script developed by Shapiro (2009–2017a, 2009–2017b) will be utilized to create a future template for Michael regarding his anxiety around driving at dusk and his dread of unexpectedly encountering the parents.

Michael needed to be self-empowered, so the clinician elected to help him develop a positive template around the potential events. Driving at dusk (i.e., desired outcome) and potentially encountering the boy's parents (i.e., problem-solving situation) were challenging future templates. These sessions proceeded as follows:

DESIRED OUTCOME

Trigger:	Fear of driving at dusk.
PC:	I am safe.
Future template:	Driving at dusk.
Clinician:	We have worked on the accident as well as present situations that have triggered your distress. Now let's work on how you would like to be able to respond to similar situations in the future.
Michael:	Okay.
Clinician:	Identify a future situation related to fear of driving at dusk where you would want a more adaptive response. What would you like to believe about yourself as you accomplish this?
Michael:	*Driving at dusk, especially in heavy traffic or driving toward the sun,* still scares me. I guess I would have to say I want to believe, *I am safely in control.*

The client has identified a situation and a positive belief he would like to have a positive response to in the future.

Clinician:	I'd like you to imagine yourself responding more effectively in a similar situation in the future. With the new positive belief, "I am safely in control," and feeling the fear, imagine stepping into this situation. Notice how you are handling the situation and what you are thinking, feeling, and experiencing in your body. (Pause.) What are you noticing now?

There is no BLS initiated at this point.

Michael:	I can feel myself getting anxious, and my chest feels tight as I imagine driving at dusk.

Michael's response is *negative*, so the clinician asks him to focus on his body sensations. Sets of BLS are added until Michael reports a neutral response. (Note that, if the client's response is neutral or positive, other strategies are available [see Chapter 8, B: EMDR Therapy Scripts]).

Clinician:	Focus on your body sensations (set of BLS). Take a breath. (Pause.) Let it go. (Pause.) What are you noticing <u>now</u>?

If the client continues to report negative responses, the clinician may elicit a desired response from the client utilizing BLS, introduction of new information, new skills or resources, and the use of direct questioning, floatback, or affect scan.

Michael:	I can feel my chest tighten up, and I am having difficulty breathing.
Clinician:	Go with that (set of BLS). Take a breath. (Pause.) Let it go. (Pause.) What's happening <u>now</u>?
Michael:	It's the same. I just can't seem to breathe.

Even at this stage, a new level of association may emerge; and the client may need to return to reprocessing.

Clinician: Are there other times in your life when you remember feeling this way?

The clinician uses direct questioning as a means of eliciting a desired response from the client.

Michael: Now that I think about it, I have always had a difficult time driving at dusk, especially in heavy traffic or driving toward the sun. It's like my eyes cannot adjust. It's anxiety-provoking for me much of the time.

Clinician: Go with that (set of BLS). Take a breath. (Pause.) Let it go. (Pause.)What's happening <u>now</u>?

Michael: I feel calm, relaxed, and confident. Up to the point of the accident, nothing bad ever happened. I always managed to negotiate the traffic despite the adverse elements.

Clinician: Go with that (set of BLS). Take a breath. (Pause.) Let it go. (Pause.) What are you noticing <u>now</u>?

Michael: I am picturing myself driving down the road and dusk is just beginning to set in. I am feeling even more relaxed.

The clinician will add additional sets of BLS if the client continues to report additional positives.

Clinician: Go with that (set of BLS). Take a breath. (Pause.) Let it go. (Pause.) What are you noticing <u>now</u>?

Michael: Nothing new. Still feeling more empowered, calm, confident, relaxed.

Clinician: Go with that (set of BLS). Take a breath. (Pause.) Let it go. (Pause.) What are you noticing <u>now</u>?

Michael: It's the same. I feel good. I am picturing driving at dusk in heavy traffic and feeling relaxed, calm, and confident. My chest continues to feel relaxed.

Now that the client's response continues to be positive, the clinician will pair the future template with the PC the client formulated in assessing the trigger of driving at dusk. Install using BLS until VoC = 7.

Clinician: Hold your positive belief (i.e., "I am safely in control") along with that situation. On a scale from 1 to 7, how true does it feel <u>now</u>?

Michael: It's 6 and three quarters.

Clinician: Go with that (set of BLS). Take a breath. (Pause.) Let it go. (Pause.) How true does it feel <u>now</u>?

Michael: It's really high. I would say it's a 7. I always have some control.

Clinician: Go with that (set of BLS). Good. Take a breath. (Pause.) Let it go. (Pause.) How true does it feel <u>now</u>?

Michael: It is a 7.

The clinician initiates BLS until the VoC = 7 (or if ecologically appropriate).

Clinician: Now I would like you to run a movie of dealing effectively with this situation while holding in mind the positive belief, "I am safely in control." (The client runs the movie.) What are you noticing now?

As the clinician adds BLS, the client runs the movie to strengthen positive feelings and process any disturbance that may arise. If the client encounters any blocks, the clinician will address them in the same way as above until the client is able to play the movie from beginning to end with a sense of confidence and satisfaction.

Client: Nothing comes up.
Clinician: Go with that (set of BLS). Take a breath. (Pause.) Let it go. (Pause.) What are you noticing now?
Client: The same.

PROBLEM-SOLVING SITUATION

Trigger: Dread of encountering the little boy's parents.
PC: I have some control.
Future Template: Encountering the little boy's parents.

It is here that the clinician instructs the client to create multiple scenarios where there might be an unanticipated or undesirable outcome. The client is asked to generate an adaptive response to the situation.

Clinician: We have worked on the accident as well as present situations that have triggered your distress. Now let's work on how you would like to be able to respond to possible situations connected to the incident in the future.
Michael: Okay.
Clinician: I'd like you to think of some challenge you may experience around this situation and what you would like to believe about yourself as a result.
Michael: I have a fear of running into his parents and I would like to believe, "I have some control."
Clinician: What are you noticing?
Michael: This has been a fear of mine since the accident. I just think it's inevitable that I will run into them some day. It makes me sick to think about it.

The client's response is *negative*, so the next step is for the clinician to ask the client to focus on any body sensations he may be having and to add BLS until the sensations dissipate.

Clinician: What are you noticing in your body?
Michael: My stomach feels so queasy, and my chest aches.
Clinician: Go with that (set of BLS). Take a breath. (Pause.) Let it go. (Pause.) What are you noticing <u>now</u>?
Michael: The sensations in my stomach and chest have eased somewhat, but I feel more anxious.
Clinician: Go with that (set of BLS). Take a breath. (Pause.) Let it go. (Pause.) What are you noticing <u>now</u>?

Michael: I am starting to get some relief.

Clinician: Go with that (set of BLS). Take a breath. (ause.) Let it go. (Pause.) What are you noticing <u>now</u>?

Michael: It has eased. I imagined passing them while driving in my car. They just looked at me. There was no expression good or bad in their faces.

Clinician: Go with that (set of BLS). Take a breath. (Pause.) Let it go. (Pause.) What are you noticing <u>now</u>?

Michael: It's good. My chest stopped aching, and my stomach feels normal. I can imagine meeting them without feeling the anxiety I felt before.

The clinician may throw in a challenge.

Clinician: What if it doesn't go as you imagined? Do you have a plan?

Michael: Oh my. That makes me a bit nervous.

Clinician: Go with that (set of BLS). Take a breath. (Pause.) Let it go. (Pause.) What are you noticing <u>now</u>?

Michael: If I see them I will put all my nervous thoughts in a container, or I will take breaths and, maybe, turn up the volume on my radio.

Clinician: Go with that (set of BLS). Take a breath. (Pause.) Let it go. (Pause.) What are you noticing <u>now</u>?

Michael: That makes it better. If they don't respond in a nice way, I can just turn away. I don't want to make them uncomfortable either. And, besides, it turned out all right. Their son is okay. His leg did heal. I heard he was playing soccer again on his team.

Clinician: Go with that (set of BLS). Take a breath. (Pause.) Let it go. (Pause.) What are you noticing <u>now</u>?

Michael: I feel at ease. It will be okay if I run into them. I can handle it.

Clinician: What are you noticing in your body?

The clinician will add additional sets of BLS if the client continues to report additional positives.

Clinician: Go with that (set of BLS). Take a breath. (Pause.) Let it go. (Pause.) What are you noticing <u>now</u>?

Michael: Since it's all over, I could even contact them to see how he's doing. That would feel much better than avoiding them!

Clinician: Go with that (set of BLS). Take a breath. (Pause.) Let it go. (Pause.) What are you noticing <u>now</u>?

Michael: I feel really good about it.

Now that the client's response continues to be *positive*, the clinician will pair the future template with the PC the client formulated in assessing the trigger of driving at dusk. Install using BLS until VoC = 7.

Clinician: "Focus on the situation and the words, 'I am _____' (i.e., positive cognition). How true do those words feel to you now on a scale from 1 to 7, where 1 feels completely false and 7 feels completely true?"

The clinician asks the client to "Bring up the image and the words, 'I am _____' (i.e., positive cognition), and follow my fingers."

The clinician initiates sets of BLS until the VoC = 7 (or if ecologically appropriate).

Michael:	It's totally true. 7.
Clinician:	Go with that (set of BLS). Take a breath. (Pause.) Let it go. (Pause.) How <u>true</u> does it feel <u>now</u>?
Michael:	Seven.
Clinician:	Are there important things from today that you want to remember?
Michael:	That for me the war is over. I am safe now and free to enjoy my life with my family.

Regardless of whether a session is complete or incomplete, the clinician may use intermediate gains, what the client has learned during the session, and strengthen it with a future resource.

Clinician:	The processing we have done today may continue after the session. You may or may not notice new insights, thoughts, memories, or dreams. If so, just notice what you are experiencing. Take a snapshot of what you are seeing, feeling, thinking, and any triggers, and keep a TICES log. Then perform a Safe (Calm) Place exercise to rid yourself of the disturbance. We can work on this new material next time. If you feel it is necessary, you may call me.

MODIFICATIONS OF THE THREE-PRONGED APPROACH

In most clinical presentations, the three-pronged approach will be applied (Shapiro, 2009–2017a, 2009–2017b). However, in some cases, the clinician may begin EMDR treatment by processing a recent past memory (i.e., secondary trauma) rather than a more pervasive early childhood experience that was uncovered in the history-taking process. This situation occurs when a client presents with intrusive symptoms that have arisen because of an event in a client's recent past (e.g., military combat, accident, injury, and illness) and appears to be unrelated to the early childhood experiences identified in the History-Taking and Treatment Planning Phase. For instance, despite a client's violent history of early childhood sexual and physical abuse, the intrusive symptoms occurring in the present may need to be resolved before reprocessing the abuse memories if possible. In this case, the clinician may target the more recent experiences to stabilize the client for future processing of earlier events.

If the client lacks confidence in themself or EMDR therapy, presents with a diffuse clinical picture (i.e., earlier experiences are global, difficult to identify, or ubiquitous), or appears unstable in terms of their current psychosocial functioning or affect tolerance, the clinician may also consider modifying the three-pronged approach to meet the client's current clinical demands. The client may present with a desire for symptom reduction or changes that may require a more comprehensive treatment plan. The client may enter therapy with the intention of working on a specific issue or memory (e.g., fear of flying). The clinician should explain to the client that other memories may emerge during processing. The clinician and the client should determine in advance a strategy to be used if this occurs, including continuing or putting disturbing material in a container.

Another example of when to sidestep the typical three-pronged processing sequence is when a client is constantly triggered by external events. In this case, the client may need to focus on present triggers to achieve some level of stabilization before past events may be targeted.

SUMMARY STATEMENTS

1. There are three prongs to the EMDR therapy approach—past, present, and future.
2. Three primary strategies can be used to access the touchstone event—direct questioning, floatback technique, and affect scan.
3. A touchstone event from childhood does not always exist.
4. A future template should be installed for each trigger identified in the treatment planning process or during treatment.
5. The three-pronged protocol may be modified to meet a client's current clinical demands.

REFERENCES

Adler-Tapia, R. (2015). *EMDR psychotherapy case conceptualization with a reverse protocol.* Presentation at the 20th EMDR International Association Conference, Philadelphia, PA.

Adler-Tapia, R., & Settle, C. (2008). *EMDR and the art of psychotherapy with children.* Springer Publishing Company.

American Psychiatric Association. (2013). *Diagnostic and statistical manual of mental disorders* (5th ed.). Author.

Boulanger, G. (2005). *Wounded by reality: Understanding and treating adult onset trauma.* Routledge.

Browning, C. (1999). Floatback and float forward: Techniques for linking past, present, and future. *EMDRIA Newsletter, 4*(3), 12, 34.

Hofmann, A. (2009). The inverted EMDR standard protocol for unstable complex post-traumatic stress disorder. In Luber M. (Ed.), *Eye movement desensitization (EMDR) scripted protocols: Special populations* (pp. 313–328). Springer Publishing Company.

Shapiro, F. (1995). *Eye movement desensitization and reprocessing: Basic principles, protocols and procedures* (1st ed.). Guilford Press.

Shapiro, F. (2001). *Eye movement desensitization and reprocessing: Basic principles, protocols and procedures* (1st ed.). Guilford Press.

Shapiro, F. (2006). *EMDR: New notes on adaptive information processing with case formulations principles, forms, scripts and worksheets, version 1.1.* EMDR Institute.

Shapiro, F. (2009–2017a). *The EMDR approach to psychotherapy—EMDR Institute basic training Course: Weekend 1 of the two part basic training.* EMDR Institute.

Shapiro, F. (2009–2017b). *The EMDR approach to psychotherapy—EMDR Institute basic training Course: Weekend 2 of the two part basic training.* EMDR Institute.

Shapiro, F. (2018). *Eye movement desensitization and reprocessing: Basic principles, protocols and procedures* (3rd ed.). Guilford Press.

Watkins, J. G. (1971). The affect bridge: A hypnotherapeutic technique. *International Journal of Clinical and Experimental Hypnosis, 19,* 21–27. https://doi.org/10.1080/00207147108407148

Young, J. E., Zangwill, W. M., & Behary, W. E. (2002). Combining EMDR and schema-focused therapy: The whole may be greater than the sum of the parts. In Shapiro F.(Ed.), *EMDR as an integrative psychotherapy approach: Experts of diverse orientations explore the paradigm prism* (1st ed., pp. 181–208). American Psychological Association.

5

Abreactions, Blocked Processing, and Cognitive Interweaves

Healing is a matter of time, but it is sometimes also a matter of opportunity.
—Hippocrates

WHEN THE ENGINE HAS STALLED

STALLED PROCESSING

Many EMDR clients process in a straightforward manner with few, if any, direct therapeutic interventions on the part of the clinician. For others, however, processing to completion without any additional interventions is unlikely. The reasons for blocked processing are varied and multifaceted. The question then becomes: How can the clinician facilitate the client's spontaneous movement toward an adaptive resolution?

This chapter explores guidelines for facilitating abreactions, strategies for blocked processing, and applying more proactive interventions for achieving full treatment effect. To the degree possible, these interventions are intended to mimic a natural progression toward resolution. Clinicians who are trained in EMDR therapy are already familiar with many of the strategies included in this chapter, particularly the strategies for clients who present with affect regulation difficulties or with complex trauma. Clinical supervision and/or consultation in these cases are always recommended.

In this chapter, three types of client responses—normal, overaccessing, and underaccessing—and strategies the clinician can apply when the client displays either low or high levels of emotions and/or blocked processing are explored. The client may appear to be confused or overwhelmed, struggling to maintain dual awareness, unable to access body sensations and/or emotions, to shift the experience on their own, or simply reports that "nothing" is happening. In other words, the train has stalled and it becomes the clinician's responsibility to identify and clear the debris and keep the client moving down the tracks.

Later in the chapter, a new and improved categorization of cognitive interweaves is presented (Laliotis, 2000; Laliotis & Korn, 2015) which outlines for the clinician a more systematic approach on how and when to intervene during the processing. These categories identify specific actions the clinician may take using the eight types of interweaves to help facilitate effective processing, particularly for more traumatized clients.

ABREACTION

WHAT IS IT?

For ancient Greek dramatists, the term *abreaction* was used to describe the purging effect that the release of emotion provides. It is a flow of intense emotions with the overall effect of releasing high levels of affect (Jackson, 1999). The meaning of abreaction has not changed much in the ensuing millennia. In today's world of clinical psychology, it continues to represent a verbal and often emotional and physical expression or discharge of affect. From a psychoanalytic perspective, abreaction involves releasing emotional tension achieved through recalling a repressed traumatic experience.

In EMDR therapy, conscious and unconscious material is stimulated in the memory network, and the client reexperiences the emotions in the same or reminiscent fashion of how they experienced the original incident or experience (i.e., at a high level of disturbance). At other times, a client may experience their reactions to a event in a way they were unable to at the time it actually occurred. For example, a client who had been physically restrained, frozen in their response, can experience for the first time their reaction to the event by experiencing emotions such as anger and hurt as well as the fear and anxiety they felt at the time. Conversely, during traditional talk therapy, a clinician will offer a holding environment where they witness, reassure, and express empathy for the client as they experience emotions in the present related to past events. In EMDR therapy, while the clinician is also providing that holding environment, it is the client's own brain that is reprocessing the past experience with all the current information that was unavailable at the time of the event, thereby transmuting the way the memory is actually stored in the brain. The client never has to reexperience the event in the same way because the arousal has been released, and the memory is now stored with all the information that is currently available.

Although abreaction is an integral part of the healing process for many clients, it can also be challenging as it requires the client to allow difficult emotions in the context of a disturbing experience or set of experiences. The clinician's role is to help the client tolerate the emotional distress while maintaining dual awareness of the present moment in order to facilitate a full reprocessing effect and effective resolution of experience.

PREPARING THE CLIENT FOR ABREACTIONS

During the Preparation Phase, it is very important that the client be made aware that abreactions or high levels of emotional distress may occur during the session and that: (a) it is a normal phenomenon in EMDR processing, (b) the clinician will be there to help them through it, and (c) once the client is on the other side of an abreaction, and, assuming there are no undiscovered pockets of dissociation, the symptoms will abate or disappear altogether. Before any reprocessing is initiated, the client will be reminded that they are in control of their experience in the present (unlike the past). There are ways in which they can maintain some distance from the experience, including: (a) imagining being on a train and allowing the vivid images to be scenery that passes by, (b) imagining watching a DVD and using their mental remote control, or (c) placing a thick protective glass between themself and the perpetrator. At the beginning of a session, the client is reminded that they have a stop signal that they can use, should they need it.

WHAT HAPPENS WHEN A CLIENT ABREACTS?

There are many ways in which a client can abreact. If a client's original trauma consisted of a near drowning, they may find it difficult to breathe or catch their breath in the present. If they were being chased in the woods by a perpetrator, their breath may rise and fall rapidly and inconsistently. If a client had been grabbed roughly and slapped sharply during the targeted abuse, the actual marks made by the hands of the abuser may appear on their face or arm. If the client is a war veteran, they can mimic the self-protective maneuvers that they used to protect themself when they were attacked. Clients may gasp, scream, shake, sob, choke, or cringe. When this occurs, the clinician gently encourages the client to allow for the completion of the experience, supporting the client through their reaction while simultaneously helping them maintain dual awareness until it is over and completely in the past.

From an information processing perspective, when a client experiences a strong emotional response during reprocessing, it is information being released. So, if a client is crying during reprocessing, let them cry. Remember that emotional responses have a beginning, middle, and end, and that information is being released and reprocessed as it is occurring. Strong emotions are part of reprocessing for many clients, particularly clients with a pervasive history of early trauma over a prolonged period of time. Successive sets of bilateral stimulation (BLS) are maintained until the intense reaction dissipates. If a client tends to close or cover their eyes when crying, the clinician may change the modality of stimulation in order to allow the processing to continue uninterrupted (i.e., changing from eye movements to auditory and/or tactile). Or the clinician could say, "It's okay to cry. Just follow my fingers." Or the clinician can simultaneously be verbally supportive by saying, "It's in the past," "It's old stuff," "Just notice it," or "It's over, you're safe now," and/or "That's it. Stay with it. You're doing fine." This encouragement and reassurance help the client maintain dual awareness so the brain can reprocess the experience while moving toward a more adaptive resolution. The clinician can also use the tunnel or train metaphors suggested by Shapiro (2018): "You are in the tunnel, just keep your foot on the pedal and keep moving" and "It's just old information. Watch it like scenery going by" are alternatives to help the client continue processing during an abreaction. All these strategies may help a client move through their emotional responses. If a client asks to stop, it is imperative that the clinician honor the request.

The client, by stopping, has an opportunity to reorient to the present. Often, the clinician will then initiate contact with the client to help them reorient, offering reassurance and support. Sometimes the clinician will initiate a state change intervention, such as the calm (safe) place, sacred space, or other self-control strategies, until the client is ready to resume reprocessing. It is important for the clinician to negotiate a plan of action based on the client's needs, as well as the client's capacity to continue. Incorporating the client's feedback into a plan of action is an important contrast to earlier experiences where they have no control or choice. Once the clinician understands what the client is experiencing or is concerned about, the clinician can offer the necessary support in order to help the client resume processing at the earliest opportunity.

ABREACTION GUIDELINES

Table 5.1 lists guidelines provided by Shapiro (2018) to aid in dealing effectively with client abreaction during EMDR.

STRATEGIES FOR MAINTAINING PROCESSING

If changes are not occurring while a client is reprocessing, the first line of approach is to change the way the BLS is being administered. The clinician may change speed (e.g., faster, slower); direction (e.g., up, down, diagonal, elliptical); and/or modality (e.g., taps, tones). In the Preparation Phase, the clinician has already introduced the client to the different modes and has identified the best fit. Before changing the modality during the processing, the clinician informs the client of the proposed change. If a change in BLS does not effectively facilitate movement, the clinician may ask the client to shift their focus to their body or return to target. It is suggested that the clinician attempt these strategies outlined earlier at the first signs of blocked processing as these strategies are mechanical and do not address the emotional, psychological, or content of the client's experience.

OVERRESPONDERS AND UNDERRESPONDERS: GUIDELINES FOR CLIENTS WHO DISPLAY TOO LITTLE OR TOO MUCH EMOTION

There are three types of client responses possible during reprocessing—normal, underaccessing, and overaccessing. Normal processing is when the client's experience is shifting on its own with relative ease and with minimal assistance on the part of the clinician, and spontaneous processing is occurring. When the client has difficulty managing their experience, this is known as overaccessing; they may be upset at a level that is higher than they can maintain. A client who is overaccessing may or may not possess the needed resources or affect tolerance to comfortably deal with accessing the information as it is currently stored in the memory network. It is also possible that the client is accessing a particularly difficult aspect of their experience and needs additional support and encouragement to stay with it and get through it. The overall goal is to continue with the set(s) until the intensity subsides. When underaccessing occurs, the client has minimal access to one or more aspects of their experience and appears to be blocked. In order to allow the client to access the traumatic event more fully, the clinician may use strategies that access, deepen, and accelerate the processing (Shapiro, 2009–2017a, 2009–2017b).

It is not unusual for the same client to overrespond or underrespond at times, just as it is typical that some clients will generally overrespond or underrespond to the demands of EMDR processing. It is important for the clinician to be aware of the client's inclinations under stress so that the appropriate strategy will be applied to help the client meet the processing demands (Figure 5.1).

Remember, the goal is to facilitate processing when it is not occurring spontaneously. These strategies are designed to slow down or speed up the processing in order to help the client access and tolerate the material that is coming up. This allows the client to be able to continue processing with greater safety and containment.

Tables 5.2A and 5.2B outline Shapiro's (2018) strategies to intervene in the processing for both underresponders and overresponders. As described earlier, TICES is an acronym for trigger = image, cognition, emotion, and sensation.

TABLE 5.1 Abreaction Guidelines	
GUIDELINES	**WHAT DOES IT MEAN?**
EMDR assists in allowing a client to release distress.	EMDR reprocessing is a catalyst for change. It does not cause high levels of emotional disturbance for the client; it allows the client to access it, reexperience it (if necessary), and eliminate it.
Abreactions have three parts—a beginning, middle, and end.	The abreactions that occur are generally short-lived in nature and can be considered to be nothing more than a "flash in the pan" when compared to the emotional upset that occurred in the original experience.
Information is usually being processed during EMDR treatment.	Although the client can become disturbed during the processing, the disturbing material is transformed and the client is moved to a state of resolution.
A clinical position of detached compassion is called for during an abreactive demonstration by a client.	The clinician must demonstrate balanced detachment during the client's reprocessing of a traumatic event (i.e., the clinician should be very empathic without rushing in to "fix" the client).
What a clinician or others might need during an abreactive response is usually what the client needs as well.	The clinician provides a calm and stable presence that will ensure the client's sense of safety, calm, and support.
A sense of safety in the present when processing events in the past is crucial to effective processing.	The clinician reassures the client that it is "old stuff" they are experiencing by providing a metaphor that helps them maintain a sense of control and informs them to keep their eyes open so that the processing can continue. Sometimes the client just needs to hear they are safe at that moment.
Monitor the client's nonverbal responses for indications that a new level of processing has occurred or that the set can be terminated.	Observe minimal cues that often accompany abreaction, such as changes in eye movement, breathing, posture, skin color, or bodily tension.
Continue the BLS until the abreaction has ended.	Continue the BLS while the changes are occurring and for several passes after the client relaxes to help solidify conscious or cognitive connections.

Abbreviation: BLS, bilateral stimulation.

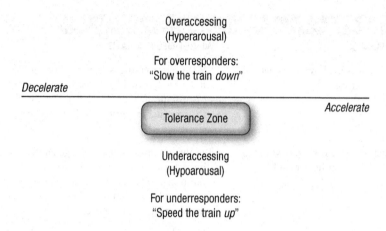

FIGURE 5.1 Overaccessing versus underaccessing.

TABLE 5.2A Strategies for Maintaining Reprocessing (Overaccessing)

DECELERATION (FOR OVERREPONDERS)

Dual awareness (i.e., can maintain a present awareness while revisiting the disturbing material)
Ask the client, "How are you doing?"
Remind the client about the stop signal.
Remind client of clinician's continued presence.
Offer compassion and support.
Say to client, "It's over. It's in the past. You're here now, looking back on the experience." or "You're here in my office. I am with you."

Narrowing the focus of attention
Increase or decrease speed or length of eye movements (or other forms of BLS).
Concentrate only on body sensations: "Where do you feel it in your body?" or "Where do you feel it (i.e., emotion) in your body?"
Concentrate on thoughts about the event rather than emotions.

Mechanics strategies
Continue BLS, but:
Consider changing to tapping or auditory processing.
Change the length of the sets (i.e., shorter or longer).
Change the direction or slow speed of the bilateral movements.
If closed, ask client to open eyes.

TICES strategies (in order):
Change color of image to black and white.
Visualize a perpetrator without action (i.e., freeze-frame).

(continued)

TABLE 5.2A Strategies for Maintaining Reprocessing (Overaccessing) (continued)

DECELERATION (FOR OVERREPONDERS)

Instruct client to visualize the disturbing event further away, eventually seeing it coming closer.

Visualize barrier to obscure part of the memory, then remove.

Provide client with the reality check, "It's in the past."

Instruct client to focus on one thought, emotion, or sensation at a time.

Reduce the number of passes and then gradually increase if a client does not seem to be responding.

Increase the number of passes if a client seems to be blocked.

Abbreviations: BLS, bilateral stimulation; TICES, trigger, image, cognition, emotion, and sensation.

TABLE 5.2B Strategies for Maintaining Reprocessing (Underaccessing)

ACCELERATION (FOR UNDERRESPONDERS)

Initial strategies

Increase speed, length, direction, and intensity of BLS, depending on stimulus used (i.e., eye movements, auditory, tactile).

Concentrate only on body sensations. Where do you feel it in your body?

Where do you feel it (i.e., emotion) in your body?

Change the mode of BLS, or try a combination of two.

Increase the number of BLS sets.

Check for feeder memories (i.e., any memory that may be emotionally feeding or impeding the reprocessing of the current target).

TICES strategies (in order)

For blocked processing to increase access:

Instruct the client to return to target and scan for new visual data.

If there is tension in the jaw or throat, check to see if there are words that need expression.

Check to see if the client's muscle tension indicates a need to move/act; instruct the client to move/act during BLS.

Instruct the client to scan the original target for any sounds or smells.

Instruct the client to scan the original target for any disturbing conversations.

To increase feeling and responsiveness:

Redirect to NC to access more disturbance.

Add color to black-and-white picture.

Visualize an "actionless" perpetrator into action.

Instruct the client to imagine getting closer to the event.

Offer the client some other behavioral stimulus (e.g., change the client's seating) so the original event can be experienced more actively.

Instruct the client to focus on several sensations at once.

Instruct the client to focus on several emotions at once.

Abbreviations: BLS, bilateral stimulation; NC, negative cognition.

The TICES alternative procedural strategies listed in Tables 5.2A and 5.2B enable a client to relate to the memory in a way that provides them with a sense of empowerment (i.e., "I am larger than the disturbance") and feeling of being in control. These strategies can also mimic spontaneous processing (i.e., the clinician asks the client to deliberately do what has not occurred spontaneously on its own).

Table 5.2A provides concrete examples a clinician can use for a client who displays a high level of uncomfortable emotions that have remained unchanged after two successive sets of eye movements.

These strategies utilize mechanics and TICES interventions to restart processing of a client who is blocked or to amplify processing of a client who reports feeling too little or maintains too much distance from the target memory. The TICES strategies also assist the client by mimicking spontaneous processing (Shapiro, 2009–2017a, 2009–2017b).

CAUTIONARY NOTE

When intervening during a client's abreaction by using any of the suggestions available in Tables 5.2A and 5.2B, the clinician is encouraged to maintain a position of detached compassion with the client. This posture allows the clinician to be present with the client, offering containment of the client's experience, as well as being an empathic witness. Newly trained EMDR practitioners who are not experienced at handling abreactive processes are encouraged to consult with a more experienced EMDR practitioner.

RETURNING TO TARGET TOO SOON?

A common error of novice EMDR practitioners is to have the client return to target too soon or too often. This can circumvent the client's processing and possibly even prevent the client from completely clearing out the dysfunctional material stored in the channels of association that would otherwise be accessed and processed. However, there are also times when a clinician may determine that more frequent returning to target is helpful.

When is it appropriate to return to target? When associations (i.e., changing imagery, sounds, sensations, emotions, tastes, smells) appear to level off in a channel, the client is instructed to return back to the target memory. For example, if during the processing of a rape, the client is focusing on the smell of the rapist and they can no longer smell them, it may be time to return to target. A return to target may also be warranted when associations are not changing. Another reason that a return to target is appropriate is if the clinician is confused about whether the client is processing the material (e.g., random thoughts that are seemingly unrelated).

There are several reasons the clinician might redirect a client back to the original target: (a) when a client's feedback between each set of BLS is consistently positive or neutral, (b) to identify and activate another channel of association, (c) to check in on the client's progress, (d) to determine whether or not the end of desensitization has been reached, (e) to refocus on the original target, (f) if you cannot identify changes at the end of processing after two sets of BLS, (g) if the client is lost or confused after questioning the client, and (h) if the ecological soundness is present. Another reason for taking a client back to target is when a client appears to be distracted. If it feels like a client is running around in circles or losing focus, take them back to target so that they have a starting point from which to begin processing again (Shapiro, 2009–2017a, 2009–2017b, 2018).

STRATEGIES FOR BLOCKED PROCESSING

BLOCKED PROCESSING

Have you ever had a client who seemed to stop responding favorably to EMDR processing? What do you think happened? What was your response? Did you stop the BLS? Did you do anything to help restimulate the processing? What are the indications of blocked processing in an EMDR session?

Clinical intervention is needed when the spontaneous linkage between dysfunctional and adaptive becomes blocked during the processing of a client's traumatic event. Strategies for blocked processing (i.e., a strategy utilized in EMDR to restimulate processing that appears to be "stuck") may include: (a) changing the mechanics (i.e., speed, intensity, direction, or modality) of the BLS; (b) changing from eye movements to tactile or auditory stimulation; (c) changing the client's focus (i.e., thought, feeling, physical sensation, sensory—taste or smell) by saying, "Where do you feel it in your body?" or "Is there an emotion that goes with that body sensation?" to (d) utilizing a strategy for blocked processing or cognitive interweave to help move the client's traumatic memory to adaptive resolution (Shapiro, 2018). It is recommended that the clinician use the order specified earlier to assist the client with minimal interference.

IDENTIFYING BLOCKED PROCESSING

Processing can be considered to be blocked during a reprocessing session if: (a) the client reports no change in two or more successive sets of reprocessing; (b) the same thoughts, emotions, and bodily sensations occur in successive sets of BLS; or (c) the Subjective Units of Disturbance (SUD) scale continues to be the same for two subsequent sets of BLS. If one of these three situations occurs, the clinician can attempt to remove the block by using one of the mechanical strategies listed in the previous section. When these strategies are unsuccessful, offering a cognitive interweave would be the next step to stimulate movement.

The strategies for blocked processing of the primary (i.e., original target) and ancillary targets (i.e., contributing factors) have been condensed in Tables 5.3 and 5.4. These strategies may be used to restimulate processing in the event it becomes "stuck." If ancillary targets arise, the clinician should be open to the possibility that they may need to be reprocessed before returning to the primary event.

TABLE 5.3 Strategies for Blocked Processing

PRIMARY TARGET

Processing has stopped when a client's response remains unchanged after two consecutive sets of BLS.

The clinician can restimulate processing of an immediate target in the following order by:

Returning to the original target and changing the direction, length, speed, and height of horizontal movements (if using eye movements) or a combination of these changes or change to alternate stimulus (e.g., tapping and tones).

(continued)

TABLE 5.3 Strategies for Blocked Processing (continued)

The clinician should only change direction or alternate stimulus with the next set—not within a set.

Focusing on physical sensation

Focusing only on physical sensations of a client while altering the BLS.

Focusing only on the most pronounced sensation (if more than one is reported).

Verbalizing or giving voice to certain types of body tension (e.g., throat, jaw) and the associated affect (e.g., anger, rage).

Acting out movement (e.g., punching, kicking) associated with a particular emotion (e.g., anger).

Pressing or focusing attention on a body sensation that will not shift and has no associated images or thoughts.

Scanning for

Something that is more disturbing than the original event being targeted.

A sound effect that remains disturbing.

A dialogue that occurred during the traumatic event.

Alterations (i.e., in focus of attention or actual target)

Ask the client to alter the appearance of the image (e.g., smaller, dimmer, more faded, in black or white, rather than color).

Have the client visualize the perpetrator *only*—not what they are doing or what they did do.

Alter the target event in terms of time and distance (e.g., have the client imagine the perpetrator in the hallway rather than on top of the bed).

When different events emerge during processing in a particular channel, one event may appear to have a higher disturbance level. If, in subsequent sets, the client concentrates on the thoughts and feelings of this specific event, allow the client to process this event until the thoughts and feelings begin to possess a milder level of disturbance. Then redirect the client back to the image of the last event with a significant level of disturbance.

Reintroduce the original NC, along with the last disturbing image.

If processing becomes stuck at a low level of disturbance, processing can be restimulated by asking the client to add the statement, "I'm safe now. It's over."

If processing is stuck at a 1 or 2 SUD, ask "What keeps it from becoming a 0?"

Scan for feeder memories or blocking beliefs.

If, during the Installation Phase, the client is not processing appropriately, the clinician reassesses the client's PC for appropriateness.

If the PC is not going up to a 7, ask "What keeps it from becoming a 7?"

Scan for feeder memories or blocking beliefs.

If processing is blocked or not progressing during the body scan

Focus on the sensation and add BLS.

Scan for feeder memories with similar sensations.

Abbreviations: BLS, bilateral stimulation; NC, negative cognition; PC, positive cognition; SUD, Subjective Units of Disturbance.

PRIMARY TARGETS FOR BLOCKED PROCESSING

If processing has remained unchanged after two successive sets of BLS, the clinician may assume that processing has stalled on the tracks. The strategies in Exhibit 5.2 offer variations in procedure to jump-start processing by asking the client to deliberately do something. It is recommended that altering the direction, speed, or length of eye movements and focusing on body sensation(s) be tried first. If these strategies do not work to unblock the processing, the reprocessing session should be terminated and other avenues of treatment explored.

See Table 5.3 for strategies developed by Shapiro (2018) to be used in clearing debris from a client's "track."

ANCILLARY TARGETS FOR BLOCKED PROCESSING

When processing does not resume after one or more of these strategies have been employed, the clinician should look for ancillary targets or other factors that may be causing the block. These factors include feeder memories, blocking beliefs, and fears (i.e., fear of going crazy, fear of the worst-case scenario, fear of losing good memories, fear of change, fear of losing respect or losing contact with the clinician, and wellsprings of disturbance). Review Chapter 1 for definitions and examples of these variables. Shapiro (2018) stresses that the earliest memories that contribute to present dysfunction are generally targeted first in order to minimize the possibility of later memories that are out of the client's awareness from blocking the processing. See Table 5.4 for more sophisticated strategies to address this issue.

TABLE 5.4 Strategies for Blocked Processing

ANCILLARY TARGETS

Strategies for working with blocks caused by undiscovered channels of association

Feeder memories
Floatback: The client is asked to float back to an earlier time that incorporates the NC or any emotions or sensations. This strategy is indicative of looking for an earlier disturbing memory related to a current experience.
Affect Scan: The client is asked to think about the target experience with the emotions and sensations and scan the memory for something similar in the past.

Blocking beliefs
What prevents it (i.e., client's SUD score) from being a 0?
What prevents it (i.e., client's VoC score) from being a 7?
What prevents it (i.e., the body scan) from being clear?
If a blocking belief does not emerge, ask the client to close their eyes, focus on the situation, and verbalize anything that comes to mind. The clinician would then scan the client's dialogue for negative blocking beliefs.
Examples: "I don't believe in extremes."
              "Nothing is perfect."

(continued)

TABLE 5.4 Strategies for Blocked Processing (continued)

Fears

The client's fears and secondary gain issues must be addressed before targets can be reengaged and processing continued.

Examples

Going crazy: "What if I lose my mind during this process?" *Response:* "There have been no reports of anyone losing her mind before." This is usually because the information during reprocessing comes quickly and, seemingly, out of nowhere. The clinician should reassure the client that their brain is just gathering similar experiences along the way.

Losing good memories: "If I lose this memory, I will lose my loved one." Or "If I don't have the memory, did it really happen?" *Response:* "Is there another way to hold this in memory that is not so _____ (fill in the bank, e.g., painful, hurtful, negative)?" The clinician may let the client know that good memories may also strengthen with reprocessing. It is important to pay attention to the client's pace so that they can adapt and incorporate changes along the way.

Not being able to handle the treatment process: "What if I don't do it right?" *Response:* "There is no right or wrong way to do EMDR reprocessing." It is important to pay attention to the client's pace so that they can adapt and incorporate changes along the way.

Change: "With change there is a loss." *Response:* Deal with the loss change can bring beforehand. The clinician should help the client address the potential change and/or loss before any changes take place.

Worst case scenario: "I will start crying, and I will not be able to stop." *Response:* "Has that ever happened to you before?"

Losing respect of the clinician: "If I tell you my deepest secrets, will you lose respect for me?" *Response:* "Your memories will process whether you tell me or not." The same holds true for clients with issues of guilt and shame.

Losing contact with the clinician: If a client has been with a clinician for years, there may be a fear of losing their support system. *Response:* "I will still be your therapist, but we can work on expanding your support system."

Wellsprings of disturbance

The clinician targets the early memories associated with blocking beliefs that hinder a client's ability to feel emotions.

Note: Precise definitions and examples of these ancillary targets can be found in Chapter 1.
Abbreviations: NC, negative cognition; SUD, Subjective Units of Disturbance; VoC, Validity of Cognition.

THE ART OF THE COGNITIVE INTERWEAVE

Cognitive interweaves introduce information or offer another perspective into the processing track when it gets stuck and the mechanical strategies of jump-starting the process have been unsuccessful. The cognitive interweave can be one of the most challenging EMDR strategies for newly trained as well as seasoned clinicians to understand and apply effectively. Although EMDR is a client-centered psychotherapy approach, the clinician is expected to guide the process to facilitate a successful resolution. Thus, the cognitive

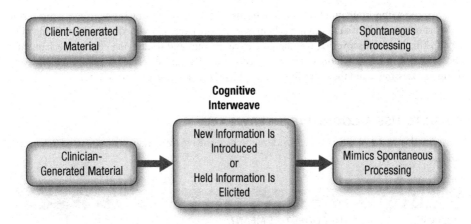

FIGURE 5.2 Understanding the cognitive interweave.

interweave is subject to underuse, overuse, misuse, and misunderstanding. However, if used sparingly and deliberately, it is an elegant and artful means of facilitating EMDR processing. As with any intervention, timing, accuracy, and appropriateness are paramount to positive treatment outcomes.

WHAT IS A COGNITIVE INTERWEAVE?

The cognitive interweave is a statement or a question that is being offered to the client by the clinician in response to a blockage in the processing or to facilitate relevant connections, optimize generalization effects, help the client with affect regulation, address defensive responses, and to maintain dual awareness. When the client is working on attachment-related trauma, it is also used to help the client feel supported and understood and to bring attention to the fact that they are not alone in their experience.

> **Client-Generated Material + Clinician = Derived/Elicited Statements (Cognitive Interweave) = Access to Adaptive Information (hence, reprocessing continues)**

Or, see Figure 5.2 for a more graphic example.

USING A COGNITIVE INTERWEAVE EFFECTIVELY

In order to utilize cognitive interweaves most effectively, it is necessary to begin collecting information from the earliest contact with the client. It is "a sensuous flowing together of presenting problems, client behavior, and clinician skills" (Zangwill, 1997) and emphasizes the importance of recognizing, collecting, and utilizing a client's vulnerabilities and schemas (i.e., broad organizing principles that help the client make sense of their life experience, such as a sense of "defectiveness)" (Young et al., 2003). Shapiro (2018) states, "clinicians will be able to use the cognitive interweave most beneficially if they are aware of the relevant clinical issues" and "can introduce new adaptive perspectives in a progressive manner that parallels the typical client's natural healing process."

The most important question to ask in terms of effectively utilizing the cognitive interweave is: What are your client's underlying schemas, and how have they coped with them (Zangwill, 1997)? This entails discovering the client's clinical themes and underlying coping mechanisms and collecting the information to use later to construct strategically placed cognitive interweaves during processing to aid the client in reaching adaptive resolution of their trauma.

WHEN TO USE A COGNITIVE INTERWEAVE

Table 5.5 shows the circumstances under which cognitive interweaves can be used (Shapiro, 2018).

TABLE 5.5 When to Use a Cognitive Interweave	
REASON	**WHAT DOES THIS MEAN?**
Looping	The clinician has used EMDR reprocessing variations to unblock processing and, even after successive sets of eye movements, the client continues to remain at a high level of disturbance with the same negative thoughts, affect, and imagery reoccurring.
Insufficient information	The client is unable to progress cognitively or behaviorally because they did not have the appropriate data, or the client has the information and, for whatever reason, is not connecting with it.
Lack of generalization	Processing does not generalize to ancillary targets, despite the client's achieved success in reaching a positive emotional plateau with respect to a targeted event.
Time dilemma	Time is running out, and the client erupts into an abreaction or fails to process an abreaction sufficiently. The target may be multifaceted (i.e., more than one NC is associated with it). More time may be needed to reprocess.
Extreme emotional stress	If the client is abreacting to the point of exhaustion, the clinician needs to intercede.

Abbreviation: NC, negative cognition.

Case Example: Renee

Renee, now 25, was 10 years old when she was involved in a car accident in which her 34-year-old mother was seriously injured. Renee was strapped in the front seat opposite her mother, who was driving, when a semi-truck hit them head on. Her vivid memories include her mother being unconscious and slumped over the steering wheel while Renee crawled out of the window of the car and rushed to the other side to help her mother. The impact of the semi-truck rendered it impossible to budge the bent and crumbled door. No matter how hard she tried, she could not open the door to rescue her mother. The smell of gasoline helped Renee to choke back her tears as she tried to tug the door open. She was near hysteria when the firemen pushed her aside and pulled her mother out of the car just before it exploded into a fiery inferno. She stood and watched as her unconscious and helpless mother was removed from the car with a crowd of strangers looking on in horror. In a matter of minutes, Renee's world became empty and unsafe, and she went on to live a life of anxiousness and uncertainty.

Renee had experienced fear, terror, disbelief, and helplessness as she viewed her trapped mother, and she continued to experience deep sadness and guilt for her mother's injuries. When Renee presented for therapy 15 years later, she was overweight, struggling with insomnia, and having frequent nightmares and flashbacks of the accident. She also suffered from depression and anxiety.

According to the Adaptive Information Processing (AIP) model (Shapiro, 2018), Renee's information processing system (i.e., her natural healing mechanism) "stalled on the tracks" the day of the accident. The elevated levels of stress that she experienced that tragic day persisted long after the accident had taken place until EMDR therapy helped her to clear the emotional and sensory debris from the "track" so that processing could occur. The most disturbing parts of the event were left on the "track" (i.e., the image of her mother slumped helplessly over the steering wheel, the firemen pulling her away from the devastating scene, the fiery explosion, the range of emotions she felt throughout the event, the rise of her adrenaline as she climbed out of the car to rush to her mother's aid) and instead were generating symptoms because they were stuck in her memory in the same state-specific form in which she had originally experienced it. This dysfunctional material stored in Renee's nervous system subsequently was responsible for the symptoms described previously, and she was eventually diagnosed with posttraumatic stress disorder (PTSD).

As with many people who suffer from PTSD, years later, when she passed by an automobile accident or heard about an explosion on the news, Renee would experience the same fear, terror, disbelief, and helplessness, as if the accident were occurring all over again. The information (i.e., thoughts, images, cognitions, emotions, sensations) from the original accident had been isolated in its own memory network and frozen in time. Neither new learning, nor the passage of time, was able to impact the way she reacted to these triggers. It was only when the memory networks were connected through EMDR processing that insight and integration could naturally occur. With the aid of EMDR therapy, Renee was able to bring up the accident and assimilate the related negative information into its proper perspective (i.e., that it belonged to the past) and then was able to release the negative and the distorted cognitive content.

CHOICES OF COGNITIVE INTERWEAVES

Case Example: Renee (continued)

Shapiro (2018) identifies and explains several choices of cognitive interweaves.

It was during a session where Renee ran into a huge timber lying on her "train track." No matter what strategy was used to unblock processing, nothing seemed to work. When she accessed this particular part of the memory, Renee expressed inappropriate feelings of guilt for failing to be the one who got her mother out of the car.

Nothing in Renee's previous learning or education seemed to provide salvation from her guilt. What was needed was a piece of dynamite to obliterate the debris from the blocked "track." During this session, a cognitive interweave was utilized to remove the timber from her "track." It was used to strategically introduce new, but pertinent, information to Renee's system to quick-start her stalled healing process.

Renee: If I only could have jerked the car door open. I could have helped her. I should have done something differently.

The issue of responsibility comes to the foreground.

Clinician: Renee, I'm confused. Are you saying that a 10-year-old should have been strong enough to open a jammed car door and drag an adult to safety?
Renee: Well, I suppose not.
Clinician: Go with that.

From the examples in Table 5.6, a number of different interweaves could have been utilized if continued processing did not cause a spontaneous change in her feelings.

In introducing the information in that manner, Renee was able to get in touch with her more adaptive adult perspective and assist in linking the information that was deliberately inserted to the appropriate memory networks. Renee's perspective, somatic responses, and personal referents of the accident came from that of a 10-year-old, the age she was at the time of the accident. The cognitive interweave served to link dysfunctional information stored in an isolated memory network to Renee's present-day adult and to activate the adaptive material stored in a healthier network. This provided her with a more realistic adult perspective of the accident.

After successfully processing the guilt she had felt for her mother's car accident, Renee realized that she was just a child at the time of the accident. Since the accident she had difficulty riding in a car for sustained periods of time, and it was a struggle for her to drive. During a subsequent session, she began seeing images of the semi-truck hitting them head on and her mother's injured body slumped over the steering wheel. Renee's reprocessing had stalled for the last few sets of BLS. The following excerpt illustrates how the clinician attempted to unblock her processing and address her confusion around the issue of safety:

Renee: I just keep seeing the semi coming at us. It is as if it were yesterday. It came so fast and "bang," it was over. The next thing I noticed was my mother's limp body slumped over the steering wheel. I don't know if she was breathing or not. I didn't take time to think about myself. When I think of it now, I am fearful.
Clinician: Where do you feel the fear in your body?

The clinician used a TICES strategy for blocked processing to bring attention to Renee's somatic experience so that she can "move the train further down the track."

Renee: In my chest.
Clinician: Go with that.
Renee: I am so vigilant when I drive now. I can never take my eyes off the road. I never feel safe in the car. I'm always too tense in the car.

TABLE 5.6 Choice of Cognitive Interweaves		
CHOICE	**PURPOSE**	**EXAMPLES**
New information or perspective	Used when the client lacks the information needed to correct a maladaptive cognition.	*Renee:* I should have been able to get the car door open. I did not try hard enough. *Clinician:* Most 10-year-old children do not have the strength to do what you are suggesting, even in the best of circumstances. Were you stronger than most children your age? *Renee:* No. *Clinician:* Go with that.
"I'm confused …"	The clinician uses this when it is believed the client already knows the answer to the question.	*Clinician:* I'm confused. Who was bigger, you or the fireman? *Renee:* The fireman. *Clinician:* Just think of that.
"What if it were your child?"	As a variation of the above, this interweave uses the client's children (if any) as a convenient intervention.	*Clinician:* Do you mean that, if it was your daughter who was trying to get you out of the car, you would want her to stay and save you regardless of the outcome? *Renee:* No! I would want my daughter safe and out of harm's way. *Clinician:* Go with that.
Metaphor/ analogy	The clinician uses stories (i.e., fables, fantasies, personal stories) to introduce therapeutic lessons to the client.	*Clinician:* Recently, I watched a segment on the news about a 10-year-old boy. His father was up in a tree cutting limbs with a chain saw when he cut the limb he was sitting on. He fell 10 feet out of the tree and then the limb dropped on him. Someone videotaped the little boy trying to lift that big limb off his father. He tried really hard, but he was not strong enough. He had to stand back and let his relatives take charge. *Renee:* Oh, there wasn't anything I could have done either. I was so small. *Clinician:* Go with that.
"Let's pretend"	To help the client move through issues of inappropriately placed responsibility, the client is asked to visualize a more positive outcome to the issue at hand.	*Clinician:* Pretend that your mother would say something to you if she were here now. What would she say? *Renee:* I'm glad you're safe. There was nothing you could have done to get me. You did the right thing. I love you. *Clinician:* Go with that.

(continued)

TABLE 5.6 Choice of Cognitive Interweaves (continued)		
CHOICE	**PURPOSE**	**EXAMPLES**
Socratic method	The clinician leads the client to a logical conclusion by asking questions that are easily answered.	*Renee:* I feel like I am to blame. *Clinician:* What could you have done differently? *Renee:* I could have smashed the window in. *Clinician:* Did you have anything that you could have used to smash the window in? *Renee:* No. *Clinician:* Did the firemen break the window in and save your mother? *Renee:* Yes. *Clinician:* Go with that.

The issue of safety emerges. The clinician probed further by eliciting information with a pertinent question.

Clinician: Is that what your mother did? She took her eyes off the road.
Renee: Yes. No. For some odd reason, I am seeing my mother slumped over the steering wheel before the semi hit us.
Clinician: Just think of that.
Renee: She was …. Oh, my God! My mother had a seizure!!! That's why the semi hit us. I never made that connection before. My mother was an epileptic, and she had a seizure. She hit the truck and not the other way around. She couldn't help it. That's why the truck driver was not charged. I never could figure that one out. It was no one's fault. My mother would have kept us safe if she could!

Renee never made this connection before this moment in the processing, even though her mother had told her at the time of the accident that she had a seizure.

Clinician: Go with that.
Renee: No wonder I am so tense when driving. I thought that if I ever took my eyes off the road, I would crash just like my mom. She couldn't help it. It wasn't her fault. She didn't mean to ….
Clinician: Go with that.

After this session, Renee was able to drive with a higher comfort level. She started to relax more and, in her eyes, actually became a better driver. The resolution of her issue of safety also opened the door to a variety of choices in her life. Previously, Renee had never traveled too far from home. It was beyond her comfort level. Being more comfortable behind the wheel empowered her to drive to different places and try new activities. She actually accepted a teaching position one summer that required her to drive 50 miles round trip to another city.

After the issues of responsibility/defectiveness, safety/vulnerability, and power/control (or choice) were resolved, Renee was able to complete the session by reaccessing and fully processing the original target. Once the block dissipates, the client continues to process associated channels of dysfunctional material that may still exist.

Regardless of how a client moves through these important plateaus, the successful negotiation of one plateau facilitates the possibility of resolution in the next. The client may successfully negotiate these plateaus on their own, or they may be assisted by the use of questioning or educating by the clinician.

COMPARISON BETWEEN STRATEGIES FOR BLOCKED PROCESSING AND COGNITIVE INTERWEAVES

Strategies for blocked processing can be described as cognitive (e.g., "What negative thoughts go with that event?"), somatic (e.g., "Where do you feel that in your body?"), affective (e.g., "What are you feeling right now?"), or general (e.g., "What do you need right now?"). Changing the direction, speed, intensity, or location when using or changing alternatives for BLS can be effective strategies for blocked processing. These strategies tend to question, inform, and challenge the client's obstacles (i.e., blocked beliefs, secondary gains or losses, feeder memories, ancillary targets, negative abreactions, performance anxiety, or lack of safety) during episodes of blocked processing until they are removed from the "track." They are designed to help the client's processing to move further down the existing "track" by removing the obstacle impeding progress.

See Table 5.7 for an encapsulated view of the differences between the two.

RESPONSIBILITY/DEFECTIVENESS, SAFETY/VULNERABILITY, AND POWER/CONTROL (OR CHOICE)

The optimal outcome of reprocessing entails the client coming to an adaptive resolution. This occurs as appropriate memory networks spontaneously link to each other and move

TABLE 5.7 Comparison Between Strategies for Blocked Processing and Cognitive Interweaves

STRATEGIES FOR BLOCKED PROCESSING	COGNITIVE INTERWEAVES
Reactive	Proactive
Uses client's spontaneous processing system.	Mimics client's spontaneous processing.
Concentrates directly on client's emerging material.	Introduces new information or a new perspective.
Helps remove obstacles from the client's "track".	Helps the client lay new "track".
Useful when the "train" has stopped on the "tracks".	Useful when the "train" is still moving, however slowing down. Accurate timing and sequencing is needed.
Questions, challenges, and informs.	Confronts three major issues: Responsibility/defectiveness, safety/vulnerability, power/control (or choice). Fitted to the client.
Used usually before a cognitive interweave.	Usually used only as a last resort.

TABLE 5.8 Issues of Responsibility/Defectiveness, Responsibility/ Action, Safety/Vulnerability, and Power/Control (or Choice)			
ELEMENTS OF POSITIVE TREATMENT EFFECTS FOR TRAUMA SURVIVORS			
PLATEAU	**OBJECTIVE**	**DESIRED COGNITIVE SHIFT**	**DESIRED EMOTIONAL SHIFT**
Responsibility/ defectiveness Responsibility/ action	Recognition and attribution of appropriate responsibility.	"It was my fault" to "I did the best I could". "I should have done something" to "I did the best I could".	Guilt, shame, or self-blame to self-acceptance.
Safety/ vulnerability	Awareness of present sense of safety.	"I'm in danger" to "It's over. I am safe now".	Feelings of fear or lack of safety to relative sense of present safety.
Power/control (or choice)	Confidence in ability to choose alternative actions when necessary.	"I am not in control" to "I am now in control".	Helplessness to empowerment.

the targeted issue to adaptive resolution. In cases of early trauma, Shapiro (2018) believes a client's perspective becomes distorted in terms of responsibility/defectiveness, safety/vulnerability, and power/control (or choice; Table 5.8).

Examples of effective cognitive interweaves addressing responsibility/defectiveness, safety/vulnerability, and power/control (or choice) follow.

Responsibility/Defectiveness and Responsibility/Action Interweaves

- "Whose responsibility is it?"
- "Is that about you or them?"
- "Whose fault is it?"
- "I'm confused. Who was bigger, you or he?"
- "Let's pretend. If you could say something to him, what would it be?"
- "Would you expect any 10-year-old to know what to do in that type of situation?"

Safety/Vulnerability Interweaves

- "Are you safe now?"
- "Can he (i.e., the perpetrator) hurt you now?"
- "If he (i.e., the perpetrator) tried something now, what would you do?"

Power/Control (or Choice) Interweaves

- "What happens when you think of the words 'As an adult, I know I have choices' or 'I can now choose' or 'I am now in control?'"

These issues are often processed in this order for processing to be the most effective (Figure 5.3).

Generally processed in this order

Responsibility/ Defectiveness and Action	Safety/ Vulnerability	Power/Control (or Choice)
Guilt, blame, shame	Perceived lack of safety Danger	Helplessness Powerlessness No choice

FIGURE 5.3 Cognitive and emotional plateaus.

Case Example: Susie

When Susie was 10 years old, her uncle took her back behind his house to see the new shed he had built. This was her favorite uncle, so Susie was excited to share this with him. Once in the shed, her uncle grabbed her and pushed her down. Before she could do anything, he was on top of her, his hand clasped over her mouth so that she could not scream.

The following transcript demonstrates an example of a client moving through these plateaus spontaneously and naturally.

Target:	Being sexually abused by her uncle at age 10.
Image:	The worst part of the experience for Susie was when her uncle turned around, grabbed her, and roughly pushed her down on the floor of the shed.
Negative cognition (NC):	I am powerless.
Positive cognition (PC):	I have power now in my life.
Validity of Cognition:	2
Emotions:	Fear, shame, disgust, guilt
SUD:	8
Body:	Down there (the client points to her genital area).
Clinician:	Susie, bring up that image those words, "I am powerless," and where you feel it in your body. Just let it go wherever it goes (set of BLS). Take a breath. (Pause.) What's coming up *now?*
Susie:	I see him on top of me, tearing at my clothes. I can hear children in the background playing and giggling. I can feel his weight on me. I tried to fight with him, but I was too weak.
Clinician:	Notice that (set of BLS). Good. You're doing fine. Take a breath. (Pause.). Let it go. (Pause.) What are you getting *now?*
Susie:	He kept pushing against me.
Clinician:	Notice that (set of BLS). Good. Take a breath. (Pause.) Let it go. (Pause.) What are you noticing *now?*
Susie:	I am feeling a sharp pang in my chest.
Clinician:	Go with that (set of BLS). Good. Take a breath. (Pause.) Let it go. (Pause.) What are you noticing *now?*

Susie: He touched me. I let him …. I allowed it …. He told me he loved me. It was my fault. He asked me to come with him … and I did. I am such a bad person.

The client is expressing inappropriate feelings of guilt and is accepting the blame for going with her uncle to his shed.

Clinician: Go with that (set of BLS). Good. Take a breath. (Pause.) Let it go. (Pause.) What are you noticing *now?*

Susie: He said what we were doing together was special and our own little secret. He told me that, if I told anyone, he would go to jail. He said if he went to jail it would be my fault. But it wouldn't be. He was bad, not me. It was not my fault. I was so small. I did nothing wrong. I am not a bad person. He is.

The attribution of responsibility belongs solely to the perpetrator. The client making this emotional connection is tantamount to her resolving the first of three informational plateaus in her reprocessing.

Clinician: How does that make you feel toward yourself?

Susie: Better … that I am a good person.

The client has spontaneously shifted from "I am a bad person" to "I am a good person." She no longer feels that she is to blame for what happened with her uncle in the shed.

Clinician: Go with that (set of BLS). Good. Good. Take a breath. (Pause.) Let it go. (Pause.) What's happening *now?*

Susie: It's not my fault. No child asks to be treated in this way.

The cognitive and emotional shift continues to materialize in terms of the guilt and blame that she so readily attributed to herself only moments before.

Clinician: Just go with that (set of BLS). You're doing fine. Take a breath. (Pause.)Let it go. (Pause.) What are you noticing *now?*

Susie: I feel dirty. I feel so ashamed. I feel so vulnerable and helpless. I am so scared. I need to get away from him.

Client spontaneously opens another associated channel of her experience. This one involves the issue of *safety.* This cognitive and emotional plateau will need to be resolved as well before proceeding on to the next plateau.

Clinician: Where do you feel it in your body?

Susie: My stomach, chest, and legs.

Clinician: Go with that (set of BLS). Good. Good. Take a breath. (Pause.) Let it go. (Pause.) What's happening *now?*

Susie: Every time I saw my uncle after the incident, like at family functions, he would just smirk and wink at me. I was afraid he would try to do it again. I can still feel the fear.

Clinician: Where do you feel it in your body?

Susie: My heart is beating more rapidly, and I feel like there's a weight on my chest.

Clinician: Just notice that (set of BLS). Good. Take a breath. (Pause.) Let it go. (Pause.) What are you noticing *now?*

Susie: My uncle died several years ago. He had a heart attack while driving to work. He plowed into a tree. He died instantly. He can never hurt me again. I never have to see him at family events. I never have to feel the revulsion and hatred I felt for him every time I saw him.

The client continues to realize that she is safe from her perpetrator. As an adult, she does not need to fear for her safety.

Clinician: Just notice that (set of BLS). Good. Take a breath. (Pause.) Let it go. (Pause.) What comes up for you *now?*

Susie: I am feeling calmer ... and safer. I never have to see him again. It's over. I have other family members who care for me and love me.

The client spontaneously separated the past from the present. She is safe now. He is dead, and he cannot hurt her anymore.

Clinician: Go with that (set of BLS). Good. Take a breath. (Pause.) Let it go. (Pause.) What's coming up *now?*

Susie: I don't know if I can ever be free of him ... the tainted feeling still lingers. What he did to me defined me for so many years. How do I get rid of that? How do I move on still knowing what he did to me and the years that he took from me?

Clinician: Just go with that (set of BLS). You're doing fine. Take a breath. (Pause.) Let it go. (Pause.) What are you noticing *now?*

Susie: Maybe I can be free of him. I no longer feel responsible. And I feel safe knowing he is dead. Maybe I can be free of him.

Clinician: Go with that (set of BLS). Good. Good. Take a breath. (Pause.) Let it go. (Pause.) What are getting *now?*

Susie: It's up to me. He's dead and cannot hurt me now. I can choose to live free of him. He can't hurt me anymore. I won't let him. I can take my power back.

The third plateau begins to emerge. The client realizes her ability to *choose* to live free of the effect her uncle has had on her.

Clinician: Just go with that (set of BLS). Good. Take a breath. (Pause.) Let it go. (Pause.) What are you noticing *now?*

Susie: I am feeling strong. I feel like he is gone, and there's nothing he can do now. That's just the way it is.

Dr. Shapiro (2018) contends that these themes should be processed in order of responsibility/defectiveness, responsibility/action, safety/vulnerability, and power/control (or choice). Susie was able to spontaneously move through these cognitive and emotional plateaus successfully on her own. However, this does not happen with all trauma survivors. In some instances, the clinician may need to introduce or stimulate the issues of responsibility/ defectiveness, responsibility/action, safety/vulnerability, and power/control (or choice) for the client by strategically utilizing the cognitive interweave.

In an effort to demonstrate how this is done, Susie's transcript will be altered, allowing the clinician to utilize cognitive interweaves to elicit the same information around these three important issues.

Responsibility/Defectiveness (i.e., "I am Something Wrong")

Susie: Whenever he would touch me, he would tell me what a bad girl I was. I felt so bad. I must have deserved it.

Clinician: If that were your daughter and that had happened to her, would you think she was bad?

Susie: Of course not.

The clinician did for the client what she could not do for herself by weaving together the appropriate memory networks and associations. As a result, the client is able to transmute her belief, "I am a bad person," into "I am a good person."

Clinician: Go with that (set of BLS). Good. Good. Take a breath. (Pause.) Let it go. (Pause.) What's happening *now?*

Responsibility/Action (i.e., "I Did Something Wrong")

Susie: He told me what we were doing together was special and our own little secret. He told me that if I told anyone, he would go to jail. He said if he went to jail it would be my fault.

Clinician: Whose fault was it? Yours or his?

Client: It's his, not mine. I did not do anything wrong. He did. It's not my fault. I was so small. I did nothing wrong. He is guilty of doing something wrong, not me.

Clinician: He was the adult in the room.

Susie: Yes, and I was just a child. I did not do anything wrong. Something wrong was done to me. I can learn from this and move on.

With the use of an appropriate interweave, the client was able to discern that the responsibility for the abuse happening belonged to her uncle, and she was able to transmute "I did something wrong" into "It was not my fault. I did not do anything wrong, and I can learn from it."

Clinician: Go with that (set of BLS). Good. Good. Take a breath. (Pause.) Let it go. (Pause.) What's happening *now?*

Safety/Vulnerability

Susie: Every time I saw my uncle after the incident, like at family functions, he would just smirk and wink at me. I was afraid he would try to do it again. I can still feel the fear.

Clinician: Where do you feel it in your body?

Susie: My throat. I could just scream. What if he tries to do it again?

Clinician: Where is your uncle now?

Susie: Oh my. My uncle died several years ago. I had forgotten. He had a heart attack while driving to work. He plowed into a tree. He died instantly. He can never hurt me again. I never have to see him at family events. I never have to feel the revulsion and hatred I felt for him every time I saw him.

Using a cognitive interweave to bring the client back into the present where her adult self lives, the clinician is able to demonstrate to the client that her uncle is no longer a danger to her.

Clinician: Just notice that (set of BLS). Good. Take a breath. (Pause.) Let it go. (Pause.) What are you getting *now?*

Power/Control (or Choice)

Susie: I don't know if I can ever be free of him. What he did to me defined me for so many years. How do I get rid of that? How do I move on still knowing what he did to me and the years that he took from me?
Clinician: What choices do you have today as an adult that you didn't have then as a child?
Susie: I never thought of that. As a child I really didn't have much choice, did I?
Clinician: Go with that (set of BLS). Good. Let it go and take a breath. (Pause.) What is happening *now?*
Susie: Right! Right! I do have choices now that I did not have then … I am feeling calmer … and safer. I never have to see him again. I always felt tainted by what he did to me. I choose not to feel that way anymore.

With the assistance of the clinician, the client is able to proceed to the plateau of choice.

SOCIAL CONNECTION AND BELONGING INFORMATIONAL PLATEAU

Based upon the quest and emergence of cultural competence in EMDR therapy, another informational plateau has been recommended to recognize aspects of social connection and belonging. Use of these cognitions is appropriate when a client experiences socially based trauma and adversity, such as social exclusion, ostracism, oppression, discrimination, or stigmatization (e.g., racism, ethnic discrimination, elitism, adultism, anti-religious fervor, classism, sexism, gender bias, ageism, heterosexism), microaggressions, and acculturation challenges which tend to foster an atmosphere of isolation, empowerment, and social insecurity (Nickerson, 2019). Table 5.9 reflects socially based NCs and PCs appropriate for inclusion in this informational plateau.

TABLE 5.9 Social Connection and Belonging Informational Plateau: Examples of Negative Cognition and Positive Cognition

NC	PC
I do not belong.	I do belong (deserve to belong).
I am alone.	I have others with me (deserve).
I am disconnected.	I can connect with others.
I am an oddball/misfit.	I am unique.
I am not "normal."	I am "normal."
I am an outsider.	I have my "groups."
I am different.	I am who I am.
I am invisible.	I deserve to be seen/included.

Abbreviations: NC, negative cognition; PC, positive cognition.

TABLE 5.10 Types and Examples of Cognitive Interweaves		
TYPE	**PURPOSE**	**EXAMPLES**
Validating	Validates the client's experience, functioning as a witness. Helps maintain dual awareness. Helps the client feel supported.	That's right. That's good. You're doing fine. That makes sense to me. I can really appreciate how you feel.
Clarifying/ mirroring	Helps the client feel understood. Mirroring back to the client what you hear them saying; invoking observing ego function. Could also be in the form of a question when you want to check the client's progress.	Do you mean you're feeling like … You mean that … Let me make sure I'm understanding what you're saying … So, part of you feels _____, and another part of you feels ____, is that right? So, you're thinking about _____, is that right? So, you're feeling _____, is that right? So, you're noticing the _____ in your body?
Focusing	Keeping the client focused on their process. Keeping the client in the moment; expanding their present level of awareness. Deliberately focusing the client's attention away from aspects of their experience or toward an aspect of their experience. In more complex cases, helping the client deconstruct aspects of their experience in order for them to be able to be reprocessed.	Just notice … what's it like for you to notice that you're _____ now. What are you experiencing now? What are you feeling right now? Where do you feel it in your body? What are you thinking about? Tell me what you see. What aspect of the memory stands out for you/ is bothering you right now? Who is your emotion directed at? What's it like for you to recall this right now? What's it like to notice that you're feeling _____ now? What's it like to know that you did the best you could? What's it like to name this _____ right now? If a client says, "I'm stuck," the clinician may say, "What part are you stuck on?" As you're saying _____, notice what it feels like at this moment … in your body. Just take a few moments to let it sink in. Focus on the part of you that _____, and the other part of you that _____, and notice what happens.

(continued)

TABLE 5.10 Types and Examples of Cognitive Interweaves (continued)

TYPE	PURPOSE	EXAMPLES
Accessing/ questioning	Series of questions designed to move the client from the general to the specific, from the present to the past, from the past to the present, from the present to the future. Build affect, somatic, and cognitive bridges.	Go back to the incident … what comes up for you now? Thoughts? Feelings? Body sensations? As you think about this memory/experience, what is the belief you're having about yourself now? What does that say about you that you could do that? Where does that (feeling, thought, sensation) take you? When have you felt this way before? Where did you get that message from? Whose voice is that? What would you like to say to that person/voice now? Where/when did you first learn …? What are you saying to yourself about this right now? What would you like to hear instead? What do you need right now? What resource do you need in order to _____ (in the context of reprocessing)? If you could do anything to make it better at this moment, what would it be? Is there a part of you that knows exactly what to do? Is there a part of you that is unsure about _____? Focus on the part of you that _____, and the other part of you that ___, and notice what happens?
Informing/ education	Offering the client information that they already have but is not available in the moment. Offering information the client may not already have but would be useful in facilitating their process. Normalizes the client's experience. Corrects misinformation. Gives the client permission when they need it. Uncouples components of the experience that do not belong together.	As a child you were _____. As an adult you are _____. What did the doctor tell you? Other women/men would have the same reaction in your shoes. I would like you to consider that it does not always have to be this way. I would like you to consider that it will not always be this way. It is okay to _____. Using a metaphor or a story to get a point across

(continued)

TABLE 5.10 Types and Examples of Cognitive Interweaves (continued)		
TYPE	**PURPOSE**	**EXAMPLES**
Challenging	Inviting the client to consider another perspective. Challenging the immature logic of the child. Challenging the client when they apply the standards of an adult to a child. Challenging resistance to letting go of the problem or to move toward health. Challenging blocking beliefs that are informed by erroneous connections.	So, let me make sure I understand what you are saying …. She/he was an adult and you were a child. Who was responsible? Which of you was bigger? So, you are saying that it was your job to keep yourself safe as a child. If you were to get over this problem, what would it be like? Imagine it …. What would it take to move forward? What do you need to hold on to before you can let the rest of it go? Is there a part of you that wants to hold on to this problem? Is afraid to let go of the problem? If there were a good reason to hold on to the (emotion, problem, issue), what would it be? What other ways could this need be satisfied? What is keeping it from feeling even better than it does at this moment?
Integrating	Rehearse. Redo. Replace. Future template. Meaning. Past/present. Present/future.	What positive belief do you have about yourself right now that you were able to _____ (positive thing)? Imagine how it can be different now and in the future. Let yourself imagine how you wished it could have been. If you could do it differently right now, how would you do it? If you could replace it with _____, what would that be? What would you like to say to the kid right now that you wished someone had said back then? What would you like to do right now that you wished someone had done for you back then? What does the little boy/girl need/want right now? Imagine it. As you look back on this experience now, how do you make sense of it?
Resourcing	Eliciting resources in a specific context during reprocessing. Helping the client develop resources in a specific context.	What you do need right now to continue? What would it take to make it feel more tolerable right now? Just notice that you are an adult looking back on this experience.

(continued)

TABLE 5.10	Types and Examples of Cognitive Interweaves (continued)	
TYPE	**PURPOSE**	**EXAMPLES**
	Resourcing as a preparation for trauma work. Resourcing as a container to maintain dual awareness, to resume reprocessing, or to close down an incomplete session. Bring in a religious figure or archetype as a source of guidance and wisdom or as someone who can help them feel at peace.	I would like to remind you that while you are afraid of what you might feel (or what you might come up with), the worst is already over, and you have all the resources of an adult. What would feel safe right now? What do you need in order to feel safer? What resource do you need in order to _____ (before installing resource)? If you could put this away until our next session, where would you put it or what would you put it in?

TABLE 5.11A	Clinical Interweave Categories (EMDDRRIIA)
CATEGORY	**GOALS**
Experiential	Help client access and bring attention to all components of memory and present experience. Assist client in up-regulating arousal, tracking and deepening affective/somatic experience, noticing cognitive shifts and expanding field of consciousness. Support the client in approaching dissociated aspects of memory/experience, bringing them more fully into awareness.
Modulation	Help client down-regulate arousal to stay within the window of tolerance. Maintain dual attention. Includes the use of soothing, containing, distancing, titrating, grounding, orienting, and unblending strategies.
Defense	Decrease blocks to processing by acknowledging and appreciating defenses from a place of compassion and empathy. Recognize efforts of "protective parts" and address internal conflicts to increase access to relevant memories and affective/somatic/cognitive material. Ultimately, help client approach inner experience as defenses are minimized or relinquished.
Developmental repair	Create an opportunity for an intrapsychic "corrective emotional experience" to help with shame/guilt, profound despair, and aloneness. Facilitate developmental repair by connecting the adult self with the child selves/parts to address unmet and unrecognized longings and needs.

(continued)

TABLE 5.11A Clinical Interweave Categories (EMDDRRIIA) (continued)	
CATEGORY	**GOALS**
Relational	Provide an interpersonal "corrective emotional experience" and undo sense of aloneness through recognition and support from the clinician. Activate the client's social engagement system, increase sense of safety and security, and facilitate co-regulation, increasing capacity for exploration and processing.
Informational	Provide information, education, and adaptive adult perspectives in an attempt to facilitate processing. Information offered is in response to what is missing and, therefore, what is needed for adaptive resolution.
Integration	Facilitate generalization of learning, address present and future scenarios, assist with integration of new experiences and perspectives into self-identity and personal narrative. Help client find meaning in experiences of the past and reevaluate sense of purpose for the present and future. Optimize treatment effects by ensuring that plateaus of responsibility, safety and power have been resolved.
Action	Encourage the completion of thwarted fight/flight responses, helping the client move from a stance of immobilization/submission and powerlessness to mobilization/action and control. Facilitate restoration and expression of a full range of adaptive actions. Encourage verbalization of unspoken words or enactment of desired actions to achieve a sense of completion, triumph, and justice.

Abbreviation: EMDDRRIIA, experiential, modulation, defense, developmental repair, relational, informational, integration, and action interweaves.

USE THE COGNITIVE INTERWEAVE WITH COMPLEX TRAUMA

While encouraging both clinician and client to "let whatever happens, happen" in EMDR reprocessing, it is often more complicated with complex trauma. A client who has been multitraumatized, especially in early childhood, often has difficulties with affect regulation and maintaining dual awareness and has dissociative processes that make it challenging for them to allow the processing to unfold naturally and with minimal assistance on the part of the clinician. In addition, their developmental deficits often result in a lack of important skills that are required to tolerate the demands of the processing.

Laliotis (2000) and then Laliotis and Korn (2015) categorized types of cognitive interweaves that bring attention to the purpose or action that is being taken on the part of the clinician as well as offering a more elaborate set of choices to more effectively navigate the moment-to-moment clinical demands of working with all clients, but most especially with complex trauma. A client with complex trauma has greater fragmentation in their memory networks, making it more difficult to access adaptive information and memory networks spontaneously. In addition to offering a client information they do not have, the use of cognitive interweave allows them to stay in their process, keeping them emotionally resourced in tracking the duality between present and past so they are less likely to get overwhelmed or shut down. Additionally, developmental repair is often required to fill in what was needed at the time in the client's childhood but was not available. For example, the child of a chronically ill parent who learned not to speak up for themself may need permission to assert their needs. Furthermore, for clients with these attachment issues, it is important for the clinician to use the relational dimension of EMDR processing, bringing attention to the empathic attunement of the clinician as well as the recognition that they are not alone in the experience.

The above examples of cognitive interweaves in Table 5.10 were adapted from Laliotis (2000):

Tables 5.11A and 5.11B show the categories of interweaves that describe their purpose and the action being taken on the part of the clinician, along with examples of each. Tables 5.11A and 5.11B "Clinical Interweave Categories (EMDDRRIIA)," was adapted from Laliotis and Korn (2015). (EMDDRRIIA is an acronym for Experiential, Modulation, Defense, Developmental Repair, Relational, Informational, Integration, and Action interweaves).

Cognitive interweaves allow a clinician to help a client remove obstacles to stalled processing. Please consider reasons that may cause a train to leave its tracks in terms of a clinician's use of the cognitive interweave as outlined in Table 5.12, "Derailment Possibilities—Cognitive Interweaves."

Other references for the applications of cognitive interweave can be found in Shapiro's Chapter 7, "Working with Abreaction and Blocks," and Chapter 10, "The Cognitive Interweave: A Proactive Strategy for Working with Challenging Clients," in *Eye Movement Desensitization and Reprocessing: Basic Principles, Protocols, and Procedures* (2018). Other books and articles are also available. See Gilson and Kaplan (2000) and Dworkin (2003).

If the strategies outlined previously (i.e., strategies for blocked processing, cognitive interweave) do not work to unblock the processing, the reprocessing session should be terminated, and other avenues of treatment explored.

SUMMARY STATEMENTS

1. Blocked processing is first addressed by changing eye movements (i.e., speed, length, direction) or changing the client's focus of attention.
2. A client should be informed beforehand of any changes in BLS, including a brief explanation of the clinician's rationale, and used only with the client's expressed consent.
3. When using a strategy to reactivate stalled processing and a shift occurs, allow the reprocessing to resume on its own to the extent possible. It is important to go back to the original target in order to ensure that the client is reprocessing the memory unaided by the clinician's interventions.
4. The cognitive interweaves described in this chapter are designed to mimic spontaneous processing and to facilitate change. It is important to remember that it is the client's brain doing the work.
5. The cognitive interweave is a powerful intervention.
6. Spontaneous processing is the most desirable processing as it is determined totally by the client's own brain and AIP mechanism.
7. "All targets must be reaccessed and processed in undistorted form" (Shapiro, 2009–2017a).

TABLE 5.11B Clinical Interweave Categories (EMDDRRIIA)

CATEGORY	ACTIONS	EXAMPLES
Experiential	Bring attention to the client's moment-to-moment experience. Facilitate mindfulness to all components of experience.	What emotions are connected to that? Where do you feel that in your body? What are you seeing or sensing or hearing? What words or thoughts go with that? What impulses or urges are you aware of? What's it like for you in this moment? What's it like to feel _____?
	Help the client clarify, reflect on, and express what they are experiencing.	Notice what it's like for you to be able to handle these feelings right now. Do you mean you're feeling _____? So, a part of you feels _____ and another parts of you feels _____. Is that right? So, you're thinking/feeling/noticing that …. Is that right? Can you put some words on that experience?
	Broaden or narrow the focus of attention.	Can you stay with that (image, feeling, sensation) just a little longer? Can you come back to the (image, feeling, sensation)? Is there more there? Can we put the other feelings/ issues to the side now and just try to stay with …? Notice that you can zoom out and look at the memory as a whole.
	Help the client track the unfolding of the experience through mirroring and shared observations.	I see … I can sense that …. Something shifted in your body when you said that …. You look like you are about to cry. Yes, these seems to be so much pain there … such big feelings.

(continued)

TABLE 5.11B Clinical Interweave Categories (EMDDRRIIA) (continued)

CATEGORY	ACTIONS	EXAMPLES
	Facilitate access to and experience of different aspects of self or "parts."	Maybe you could look inside and see if there is a part of you that feels differently or has a different idea about this. Can you sense that (younger, scared, angry) part of you? Would you be willing to hold both parts of you and be curious about what happens next? Notice the part of you that is moving your leg right now and be curious about what that part of you might be experiencing.
Modulation	Enlist observing ego as a witness.	Be a passenger on a train. Just watch the scenery go by. It's old stuff. Just notice that you are an adult now, looking back on this experience. Can you observe your response rather than be completely absorbed in it?
	Separate arousal from trauma-related emotions, thoughts, images, and sensations by facilitating dual awareness.	Drop the content/story for the moment. Stay only with what you are experiencing in your body right now. As you notice what's happening in your body, remember: It's not happening now. Your body is just processing old stuff.
	Unblend adult self from traumatized child parts (to maintain dual attention and self-regulation).	See if you can separate your adult self from your child self. Ask that (younger, traumatized, frightened) part to step back and not overwhelm you. If the client has difficulty unblending: Feel yourself here with me as an adult. Notice what it's like as you look at me and hear my voice here in the present. You'll be most helpful to this child if you're able to remain separate (but connected) from him/her. If client is able to unblend: What do you notice now as you look through your adult eyes, thinking about that experience and about yourself as a child?

(continued)

TABLE 5.11B Clinical Interweave Categories (EMDDRRIIA) (continued)

CATEGORY	ACTIONS	EXAMPLES
	Limit associations and work to contain affect, material, and/or memories.	Would you be okay to set that (memory, association) aside for another time and finish with the memory we started with? If you could put this away until next session, where/what would you put it/in? Imagine putting it into a container.
	Titrate the intensity of affective experience. Slow down the processing. Establish boundaries.	What would it take to make it feel just a little more tolerable right now? Imagine letting in only one drop or 1 percent of the feeling …. Imagine a (protective bubble, emotion dial, TV with picture within a picture, faucet with a slow leak).
	Help client recognize that they are in control of what is happening in the moment; help the client approach their inner experience.	I'm wondering if you can give yourself permission to feel into your experience just a little at a time …. Notice that you can actually control your experience now. What [resource] do you need in order to continue? Imagine having/feeling that resource. Notice that you can choose what you want to do right now.
	Match the resource with the client's process in the moment: Somatic resource with body sensations that are uncomfortable or disturbing. Visual resource with a disturbing image of other aspects of self or "parts." Affective resource with a disturbing affect. Cognitive resources with a disturbing thought.	As you notice the lightness in your chest, notice also where in your body you're feeling ok … perhaps in your feet or legs or … Notice that you can see yourself now in the present at the same time that you're seeing yourself as a child. Notice that you can feel into the experience of safety in this moment while you touch into the fear. Notice that you, as an adult, have a different idea about what is going on than the child.

(continued)

TABLE 5.11B Clinical Interweave Categories (EMDDRRIIA) (continued)

CATEGORY	ACTIONS	EXAMPLES
	Ground and orient.	Feel your feet on the floor/your back against the chair. Look around the room and notice the familiarity of THIS space. Notice the sound of my voice. Stand up. Lengthen your spine. Push against the wall. Stretch your arms out. Catch this ball.
	When in a state of hyperarousal, help the client gain access to components of experience. (See also Experiential Interweaves)	Notice the numbness; notice where you feel it in your body. Let yourself be curious about what you might be feeling beneath the numbness. See if you can sense into what is going on through your body. Let your body speak to you in its own language and be captive to what comes up.
Defense	Name the defense.	Notice the shutdown that occurs every time I ask you what is happening.
	Work with the resistance/block in the body.	Where do you feel that (hesitation/fear/shutdown/protective wall) in the body? Stay with that.
	Validate the defense; encourage access of disavowed emotions. Guide client back to affect/body.	I know that this is how you protected yourself for a long time; maybe it's finally safe enough to let yourself feel now what you couldn't feel back then (grief, anger, longing, etc.). Even though it's never been okay to feel (grief, anger, longing, etc.), can you let yourself experience those feelings now? If yes, just allow yourself to feel into the emotion now.
	Unblend the "protective part" from the "traumatized part." Validate the emotional need and renegotiate the strategy (defense).	I understand that this part of you is concerned and wants to protect you. Would this protective part be willing to relax back just a bit to allow us to work with the traumatized part for a few moments? If the protective part is unable/unwilling to relax back: Ask this protective part what they are afraid will happen if they were to relax back. Would that protective part be willing to explore other ways of (keeping them safe, managing the feelings/pain, making sure they can handle it)?

(continued)

TABLE 5.11B Clinical Interweave Categories (EMDDRRIIA) (continued)

CATEGORY	ACTIONS	EXAMPLES
	Explore for relevant earlier memories connected to blocked processing, fears, and/or beliefs.	When have you experienced this before? Where did you learn to respond that way? Whose voice is that?
	Float back to explore for relevant associations.	Notice the feelings, thoughts, and sensations coming up here. Let your mind float back to an earlier time when you responded this way. What do you get?
	Remove the pressure.	No rush. It's important to be kind to yourself …. Just take your time with what's coming up.
	Coach.	You can stay with this. You can do this! I'm totally with you. You're not alone this time. I'm right here. Let's stretch a little.
	Make the conflict/resistance explicit.	So, notice that one part of you really wants to let go of the anger, while another part isn't so sure. Notice both at the same time and be curious about what happens next.
Developmental repair	Acknowledge and validate unmet developmental needs.	What does that child need now (that you wished someone would have done for you back then and didn't)?
	Connect the adult with the child part to repair unmet needs.	Imagine offering this to them Notice that you can go to this child now and they don't have to be alone in this experience. Let this child know that you see/hear them. Perhaps you can tell them that you understand how awful it was and that you are sorry. Go ahead and take this child out of that situation. Take them somewhere safe. Somehow, you'll know exactly what to say or do for this child. They may need you to simply hang out or be present with them. Or, they may simply need some form of touch from you. If the client is still unable to take a step toward connection with the child: Perhaps, you could … (offer a suggestion to the client).

(continued)

TABLE 5.11B Clinical Interweave Categories (EMDDRRIIA) (continued)

CATEGORY	ACTIONS	EXAMPLES
		Perhaps we could approach him/her together and ….
		If you were to step into that scene, you would tell them that ….
		If (e.g., resource person) were to step into that scene, image what they would say to that child.
	Check receptivity of child.	How is this child responding to you?
		Is this child feeling accepted and understood by you right now?
		What's it like for this child to know that you're there with them?
		If the child is not receptive:
		Can you understand why they might be hesitant to let you in?
		Can you let them know that you understand why they are (scared/mistrustful, angry, and unable to respond)?
		Take it slow and allow for their experience.
	Give back the responsibilities/burdens.	Can you "give back" to your parents the responsibility of keeping the family safe?
		Can you consider it was wrong for them to ask you to take care of them when you were so little?
	Fully acknowledge the emotional impact of having unmet needs/longings from childhood.	What's it like to contemplate the impact of these experiences?
		Would it be okay to let yourself know now what you couldn't let yourself know then?
		Would you be willing to consider that your parent will never be the parent you needed as a child?
		Can you allow yourself to feel the grief connected to this realization?
		What's it like to acknowledge that you will never be parented in the way you needed as a child?

(continued)

TABLE 5.11B Clinical Interweave Categories (EMDDRRIIA) (continued)

CATEGORY	ACTIONS	EXAMPLES
Relational	Use relationship with the clinician as a counterpoint to past aloneness.	Notice that you're not by yourself right now … not at this time. Stay with it and stay with me. Just notice that you're not alone in this. Do you feel me with you? I'm not going to let you drown. I'm right here. Whatever comes up, we'll deal with it together.
	Reassure and address unspoken fear (being too much, not enough, overwhelming to the clinician, etc.).	What do you see when you look at my face? Notice that (unlike your parent) I'm not scared or overwhelmed or sitting in judgment.
	Use agreed-upon touch.	Would it be helpful if I put a hand on your back so you can feel my support? If you'd like, you can rest your hand in my hand.
	Ask client to stretch with you.	Are you willing to work this edge with me for a minute or two? I'll help you.
	Recognize, support, reassure, validate.	Uh huh. Hmmm. Yes. Of course. That's right. So much pain. Such big feelings.
	Undo shame with compassion and empathy.	My heart is breaking for you right now. Notice what it's like to feel my compassion for you right now. I'm so sorry that this happened to you.
	Provide permission and encouragement to take in support.	Go ahead and express what you're feeling. Notice that it's okay with me … that your feelings, your needs are not too much. In fact, I welcome them.
	Meta-process. Make the experience dyadic. Check client's receptivity.	What's it like for you to tell me this? Notice what it's like for you to be seen/understood by me in this moment. I'm wondering what it's like for you to see me so incredibly touched by your experience. What is it like for you to share this experience with me … to have us share this experience together? I am feeling _____ right now. Does that make sense to you? Is it okay with you that I'm feeling _____?

(continued)

TABLE 5.11B Clinical Interweave Categories (EMDDRRIIA) (continued)

CATEGORY	ACTIONS	EXAMPLES
Informational	Provide psychoeducation Examples: • Function of emotions • Appropriate responsibility • Nature of attachment • Role of "parts" • Fight/flight/freeze	Tears are welcome and healthy. They allow you to transform grief and move on. Children are never responsible for abuse. Attachment is biologically driven. Of course you were looking for attention. This part may seem like the enemy, but s/he is actually trying to help and protect you. You probably wanted to fight back or flee but you couldn't. The terror was too great, and your body froze. That's just what happens when you are facing an overwhelming threat. You can help your body know that it's safe now and it can begin to relax.
	Normalize reactions, needs, and experiences where appropriate.	This is a normal, understandable reaction. Other people probably would have done the same thing in that kind of situation. Just like when you touch a hot stove and react, arousal is an involuntary reflex. It's just what your body does. Of course, you were lonely and needed attention. You were a little girl, and no one was taking care of you.
	Question/challenge distorted perceptions and rigidly held beliefs. Invite the client to consider other points of view.	What if this happened to your daughter/best friend? What would you say to them? Who would you hold responsible? What do you imagine a good parent might say/do in this situation? If you could invite _____ into the scene, what would they say? I'm confused … you mean a child can cause a parent to drink?
	Offer metaphors, analogies, and stories to offer perspective.	Just like running a marathon, it takes time and practice; and you're in it for the long run. While there's no way to undo what happened, perhaps there is a way to balance the scales going forward.

(continued)

TABLE 5.11B Clinical Interweave Categories (EMDDRRIIA) (continued)

CATEGORY	ACTIONS	EXAMPLES
	Reference common fairy tales, Bible stories, popular culture, images from nature, etc.	It's like a jigsaw puzzle, where you can't see the whole picture until you have all the pieces. You're like the child in "The Emperor's New Clothes." You knew the truth, tried to get others to see it, but couldn't.
	Orient to current context; age and height, time and place, current sense of safety.	Notice that you're here and you are safe now. Look at your hands. How old do they appear to you? Where do you live now? How old are you? How tall are you? Send this information out to all parts of you.
Integration	Facilitate generalization of learning, linking new beliefs and sense of self to present and future goals. Float forward to explore anticipatory anxiety. Utilize future templates.	What would you like to be able to do now and in the future that you couldn't do before? Imagine it. When you think of speaking to your (mother/father/boss), what comes up What happens inside? Imagine speaking up to ____. Notice what it's like to use your voice now. So, from this place of (mastery, triumph, readiness), imagine yourself taking center stage.
	Integrate new experiences, perspectives, and learning into sense of self and evolving life narrative.	What is it like to finally have an adult understanding of the child's experience? What positive belief do you have about yourself now, after successfully (expressing your true feelings, recognizing that it wasn't your fault, etc.)? Yes, and imagine how it can be different now and in the future. How does this [set of] experience(s) inform how you see yourself? What feels like the most important thing you learned about yourself or for yourself today?

(continued)

TABLE 5.11B Clinical Interweave Categories (EMDDRRIIA) (continued)

CATEGORY	ACTIONS	EXAMPLES
	Help the client make meaning out of their life experiences.	As you look back on this experience now, how do you make sense of it? What has changed in how you think about your life's purpose?
	Highlight appropriate responsibility.	What's it like for you to realize that you were holding yourself responsible for your parents' failures? What's it like to have helped your child self unload that burden of responsibility?
	Highlight present safety.	What's it like to know that it is truly over and that you are truly safe now? What's it like for your younger self to know that you are able to keep themself safe?
	Highlight power and choices in the present. Check work to ensure plateaus of responsibility, safety, and power have resolved in relation to the target memory; look for confusion or blocks about past versus present.	What's it like for you to recognize that you have a choice today? What's it like to realize that you are not being held back by anything or anyone at this point in your life? Notice what it's like to be able to give your child self exactly what they need [rather than having them waiting or looking for someone else to give it]. Is there any part of you that has any confusion about your responsibility in this experience? Is there any part of you that is confused about the current conditions of safety as you look back on the memory? Is there any part of you that is confused about the power/control/choices you didn't have in the past that you have now in your life?
Action	Facilitate the completion of a thwarted fight/flight response in imagination.	How do you experience that (anger, hurt, resentment) inside of you? What does it want to do? Is there any impulse or urge that wants to come out? What does your (hand, foot, jaw, etc.) want to do? Imagine doing it now.

(continued)

TABLE 5.11B Clinical Interweave Categories (EMDDRRIIA) (continued)

CATEGORY	ACTIONS	EXAMPLES
	Facilitate the completion of a thwarted fight/flight response by helping the client track and feel into the body's action impulse.	Just feel into that impulse in your body to do now what it was unable to do at the time … just sense into it … notice it … trusting your body to do [finish] now what it was unable to do [finish] back in time.
	Facilitate discharge of excessive arousal by allowing for somatic release of thwarted fight/flight response.	Notice the (shaking, trembling, temperature, changes, vocal sounds, etc.) and allow it to move through you. It's how your body is releasing all that stored up energy.
	Facilitate the expression of specific attachment-related actions/gestures in imagination.	Tell the child that it's okay/safe to reach out now.. Imagine reaching out to that little child and holding them close. Imagine asking your spouse (in present day life) for help and letting them comfort you. Imagine yourself feeling relaxed, secure, and able to enjoy your partner's safe touch.
	Facilitate the action of "giving back" responsibility for others and "letting go" of emotional burdens. (in the past or present; out loud or in imagination; right here, right now or in imagination)	It was your parents' responsibility to keep your sister safe, not yours. Are you ready to "give back" to your parents what is theirs? Okay, imagine doing that right now. Imagine handing that responsibility back to them. Imagine giving that shame back to them. It's theirs, not yours. Or, do it right now. Take this (object) and notice what it feels like to let go.
	Give permission to verbalize unspoken words and/or engage in desired actions in order to achieve a sense of completion, triumph, and/ or justice.	What would you like to say to them (the perpetrator) now that you couldn't say back then? Imagine it. What would you like to do now that you couldn't do back then? Imagine it … Go ahead and say/do it now …. As you think of all the people who have hurt you, what actions would represent true justice in your mind (e.g., send them to jail, share their misdeeds with their families, humiliate them in public)?

(continued)

TABLE 5.11B Clinical Interweave Categories (EMDDRRIIA) (continued)

CATEGORY	ACTIONS	EXAMPLES
	(in the past or present; out loud or in imagination; right here, right now or in imagination)	Is there anything that you need to say or do to reclaim your voice, your dignity, and/or your power? What would you want to see happen to them? Go ahead and imagine/say that.
	Encourage client to move from a passive (powerless) to an active (choices) stance.	Follow up. Is there more? Is there anything else that needs to happen? Continue with this until it feels completely satisfying. Imagine fighting back. What would you say or do right now if they were here? Imagine that there are no limits. Stay with it until it feels satisfying enough or complete.
	Help the client with permission, words, or actions when they are frozen, scared, or stuck.	I'm wondering if you want to say or do something. Does that feel possible? How would it be for you to give yourself permission …? Can you say, "I'm mad at you for betraying me"? Can you imagine slamming the door in their face?
	Encourage a mini exercise to explore somatic resources and possible adaptive action when the client is unable to move from immobilization to action (temporarily let go of traumatic content).	Push against the wall with your hands. Feel our strength. Feel the energy in your body. Throw this pillow with me. Notice what it's like to throw it lightly/to throw it hard. Hold your hands up and say "Stop" as I approach you. Pay attention to your own personal boundary. Notice what it's like to take action on your own behalf. Walk around the room and feel the freedom of movement. Find your stride. Have fun with it.

Abbreviation: EMDDRRIIA, experiential, modulation, defense, developmental repair, relational, informational, integration, and action interweaves.

TABLE 5.12 Derailment Possibilities—Cognitive Interweaves

Using a cognitive interweave before a clinician has been properly trained and supervised in its use

The cognitive interweave is a powerful strategy to help a client jump-start processing. A newly trained clinician should use it only after they have adequate practice and supervision. A clinician should be proficient with the basic EMDR protocol and methodology prior to facilitating a cognitive interweave.

Using a cognitive interweave when spontaneous processing appears to be occurring

The cognitive interweave was designed to be used only when spontaneous processing appears to be insufficient to achieve a client's therapeutic goals. Cognitive interweaves are to be used when a client is looping, lacks sufficient information, processing does not generalize to ancillary targets, or if a client is abreacting and there is not enough time in a session to appropriately process information. If these reasons are not present, refrain from using this strategy.

Failing to determine if blocked processing is due to other reasons

The clinician should first determine whether blocked processing is due to other aspects of the treatment process (e.g., adequate preparation, existence of secondary gains or blocking beliefs, safety issues).

Using a cognitive interweave(s) as a means of analyzing, summarizing, reflecting, etc. (i.e., an excuse for talking)

Cognitive interweaves should be used sparingly by the clinician so that a client possesses and retains the ability to process the material internally. This will greatly enhance a client's self-esteem, self-efficacy, and self-empowerment.

After a cognitive interweave has been used, not allowing a client to return to spontaneous processing with successive sets of BLS

Once a blockage has been removed, the clinician should allow the client to return to spontaneous processing. Any time the clinician has intervened to facilitate processing, it is important to return to the target and reprocess without intervention by the clinician to ensure that a client has successfully integrated new information.

Failing to use the cognitive interweave selectively

If at all possible, allow a client to utilize their own processing system to full integrate any information that may arise during the reprocessing phase.

Abbreviation: BLS, bilateral stimulation.

REFERENCES

Dworkin, M. (2003). Integrative approaches to EMDR: Empathy, the inter-subjective, and the cognitive interweave. *Journal of Psychotherapy Integration, 13*(2), 171–187. https://doi.org/10.1037/1053-0479.13.2.171

Gilson, G., & Kaplan, S. (2000). *The therapeutic interweave in EMDR: Before and beyond: A manual for EMDR trained clinicians.* EMDR Humanitarian Assistance Programs.

Jackson, S. (1999). *Care of the psyche: A history of psychological healing.* Yale University Press.

Laliotis, D. (2000). *Advanced applications of cognitive interweave and resource development in EMDR* [Paper presentation]. EMDR International Association Conference, Austin, TX.

Laliotis, D., & Korn, D. (2015). *Clinical interweave categories (EMDDRIIA)*. Authors.

Nickerson, M. (2019). Advancing cultural competence in EMDR therapy and EMDR Training. In D. Laliotis, M. Masciandaro, & M. Nickerson (Eds.), *Trainer Facilitator Day 2019*. EMDR Institute Inc.

Shapiro, F. (2009–2017a). *The EMDR approach to psychotherapy—EMDR Institute basic training course: Weekend 1 of the two part basic training*. EMDR Institute.

Shapiro, F. (2009–2017b). *The EMDR approach to psychotherapy—EMDR Institute basic training course: Weekend 2 of the two part basic training*. EMDR Institute.

Shapiro, F. (2018). *Eye movement desensitization and reprocessing: Basic principles, protocols and procedures* (3rd ed.). Guilford Press.

Young, J. E., Klosko, J. S., & Weishaar, M. E. (2003). *Schema therapy: A practitioner's guide*. Guilford Press.

Zangwill, W. M. (1997). *The dance of the cognitive interweave* [Paper presentation]. EMDR International Association Conference, San Francisco, CA.

6

Past, Present, and Future

Since we cannot change reality, let us change the eyes which see reality.
—Nikos Kazantzakis (*The Son,* 1965)

EMDR THERAPY CASE EXAMPLES

In this chapter, the clinician will be reintroduced to the basic components of EMDR therapy through transcripts of therapy sessions. The EMDR reprocessing sessions are introduced in order of past (Airi, Karen), present (Delores, Breanna), and future (Jimmy), as well as with the use of the cognitive interweave and informational plateaus (Kevin) and eye movement desensitization (EMD; Harlan). These are simple, uncomplicated sessions. These cases are presented in this way to demonstrate to the reader what a successful session looks like when the client reprocesses disturbing material without any interventions by the clinician. As a newly trained EMDR therapy clinician, it is inadvisable to implement EMDR therapy starting with your most difficult client. Begin using this approach with clients with whom you believe success is possible for them and you. And *practice, practice, practice.* It is wise for any novice EMDR therapy-trained clinician to seek consultation as a strategic course of action with an EMDRIA Approved Consultant.

The following questions cover some of the basic information needed to complete a successful EMDR reprocessing session.

QUESTIONS

After a set of bilateral stimulation (BLS), what does the clinician say?

Can EMDR reprocessing change something that is real or factual?

Has adaptive resolution been achieved when the clinician returns the client back to the original target?

How does the clinician know that the client is at the end of a channel of association?

How does the clinician close down the EMDR therapy process? How fast should the BLS be?

How is setting up a future template different from setting up the standard EMDR protocol for a past event or present trigger?

How many times should the clinician reinforce positive treatment effects identified by the client?

How often should the clinician reinforce and encourage the client throughout the EMDR process?

Is a positive cognition (PC) reflective of what the client believes or would like to believe about themself as they focus on a trauma?

Is EMDR therapy focusing on then or now?

Is it ever okay to initiate reprocessing without first establishing a negative cognition (NC) associated with the traumatic event being processed by the client?

Is the issue with which the client presents necessarily the same as the image they eventually reprocess?

Is there any way for the clinician to utilize a negative physical sensation expressed by the client to further their process?

What are the characteristics of NCs and PCs?

What does the clinician do if the client begins to cry or visibly emote in any way?

What does the clinician do if the client only reports physical sensations between sets?

What does the clinician do if the client reports newly emerging memories or changes in what the client originally reported at the beginning of the EMDR reprocessing?

What does the clinician do if the client states more than one NC or PC related to a specific traumatic memory or event?

What does the clinician do when the client cannot come up with an appropriate NC?

What does the clinician say to the client between sets? What is appropriate? What is not appropriate?

What does the clinician say after each set of BLS? What does the Validity of Cognition (VoC) measure?

What is an option if the client reports an emotion during the feedback process?

What words does the clinician use to initiate processing with the client? When is it appropriate for the clinician to return the client back to the original target?

When is it appropriate to ask the client what their Subjective Units of Disturbance (SUD) level is?

When is it appropriate to initiate the actual reprocessing of the client's traumatic event?

When should the client proceed with the Installation Phase?

Why does the clinician redirect the client back to an original target?

Why is it imperative that the clinician does not intrude upon the client's process?

Why is it important for the clinician *to stay out of the client's way*?

Why is it important for the clinician to reinforce any positive shifts by the client?

Why is it important for the clinician to provide encouragement to the client during and between sets of BLS?

Should SUD = 0 be reinforced with a set of BLS? VoC = 7? Body scan = clear?

Why does the clinician check in with the client between sets of BLS? How does the clinician initiate it?

At the beginning of the Installation Phase, why does the clinician ask the client whether the original PC is appropriate or not?

Can EMDR reprocessing work successfully with a general target?
What can the clinician do if the client continues to give a narrative report of what happened the day of the trauma?
What does the clinician do if they keep witnessing movement in the client's process?
What does the clinician do if there is no movement of any kind in the client's reprocessing efforts for two or more sets of BLS?
When is it appropriate for the clinician to check the client's current SUD level?
When is it appropriate for the clinician to redirect the client back to the original target?
Why does the clinician check in so frequently with the client?
What is the hallmark of EMDR therapy?

In the following transcripts, it is assumed that the clinician has completed Phases 1 and 2 (i.e., History-Taking and Treatment Planning, and Preparation). The client's history has been outlined to provide the reader with a clearer understanding of the client's chosen targets. Read the following cases and, when finished, come back and answer the questions again. Be prepared to write down the components of the target (i.e., NCs and PCs, emotions, and body sensations) and baseline responses (i.e., VoC and SUD) identified by the client.

In each case, when the clinician asks the client to focus on the original event (incident, experience), the client's original target has been placed in brackets with a reminder (e.g., Reminder: Original incident—when Tom was bitten by a snake when he was in the second grade) to help the user remember the original target's wording. If the reprocessing takes the client far afield, the clinician may need to remind the client of the target memory. However, do not repeat the target image back to the client. The words are placed there only as a reminder to the clinician of the client's original target. *In order to reinforce learning, some of the salient elements of EMDR therapy have been repeated more than once.*

Because of the simplistic nature of a Primer, the following cases mirror more what happens in EMDR therapy much of the time—with no or very few interventions. It is important for the clinician to be able to master the basics of EMDR therapy before utilizing it with more complicated cases. The reader is directed to the many EMDR therapy books and articles (see the Francine Shapiro Library at emdria.omeka.net for more sophisticated examples of EMDR processing sessions).

PAST

Case Example: Airi

Situation:	At age 20, the client was jammed up against a blackboard by several students' desks during a tornado that occurred during one of her college classes.
Type of presentation:	Single incident.
Symptoms:	Depression, lethargy, poor appetite, joylessness.
Issues	Unable to attend classes (eventually flunked out), reacts to extreme weather conditions, unable to hold a job, and has had multiple failed relationships.

Airi was looking out of a window daydreaming in one of her classes at a small college in the Midwest. With little warning, the previously clear sky became immersed with large, rapidly growing clouds until it resembled a grayish black wall. She remembers the clamor of constant thunder in the background and then the torrents of rain that began to descend almost instantly. The day had become night, and the tornado sirens began to roar and signal everyone to head for cover. But it was too late for her to seek cover. Her classmates scrambled for safety in the darkened corridors. The force of the wind popped the windows out of their panes. Desks, papers, and other debris whipped around erratically and dangerously. Within minutes, hail as big as golf balls began to pummel the ground, some flying through the now glassless windows. Airi found herself jammed up against the blackboard by two or three of the students' desks. She was quite shaken but appeared to be okay.

This was Airi's first and only encounter with disaster. Having been brought up in a loving home in what she called a "normal" childhood, she had not experienced any kind of trauma, certainly not one of this magnitude. In her case, this was a one-time event. Even so, she did not fare so well. She found herself isolating in her room and unable to attend classes, especially if the weather was not sunny and clear. She became more and more lethargic and depressed. She had lost her appetite and her joy for living.

By the time Airi reached the clinician's office, she was 25 years old. She appeared haggard and pale. A year after the tornado, she had flunked out of school, had been involved in multiple failed relationships, and could not hold down a job.

Target:	The tornado.
Image:	Sitting quietly in my chair and being flattened against the blackboard.
NC:	I cannot protect myself.
PC:	I can protect myself.
VoC:	2.
Emotion(s):	Terror, helplessness.
SUD:	10.
Body:	Below belly button.

Although not repeated for each transcript that follows, before the Assessment Phase begins the clinician says to the client, "Often we will be doing a simple check on what you are experiencing. I need to know from you exactly what is going on with as clear feedback as possible. Sometimes things will change, and sometimes they won't. There are no 'supposed to's' in this process. So just give as accurate feedback as you can as to what is happening without judging whether it should be happening or not. Just let whatever happens, happen." Remember to tell the client about the "stop" hand signal.

The clinician usually needs to repeat the complete instructions once to a client, unless the client has difficulty remembering what is expected of them from session to session. The clinician instructs just before desensitization and reprocessing begins, "Focus on the event (incident, experience), those words (NC), and where you feel it in your body. Just let whatever happens, happen. Let it go wherever it goes."

Alternatively, the clinician may also say: "Remember, it is your own brain that is doing the healing, and you are the one in control. I will ask you to mentally focus on the target and to follow my fingers with your eyes. Just let whatever happens, happen; and we will talk at the end of the set. Just tell me what comes up, and don't discard anything as unimportant. New information that comes to mind is connected in some way. If you want to stop, just raise your hand" (Shapiro, 2018).

The following is a transcript of Airi's first reprocessing session.

ASSESSMENT

Clinician: Last time we met, you indicated to me that you wanted to work on the memory of being in a tornado. What image (or picture) represents the most disturbing (or most traumatic) part of the incident?

As a part of an overall treatment plan, this memory was agreed upon by the client and the clinician in the History-Taking and Treatment Planning Phase as the touchstone memory related to the presenting issue. The target memory had been identified, but the image that represents it had not. The clinician invited her to select a single image with which to begin. She has many potential images, so the clinician asked her for the most disturbing part of the memory. By asking this question, the information about the incident becomes stimulated and accessible.

Airi: It all happened so fast. Within seconds, everything changed. One minute I am daydreaming out the window. The next minute, I find myself flattened like a pancake up against a blackboard with desks piled on top of me. I don't remember anything in between. That's the most disturbing part for me, the time in between sitting quietly in my chair and being flattened against the blackboard, not knowing exactly how I got there.

Clinician: What words go best with the image (or picture) that express your *negative belief* about yourself <u>now</u>?

This question can be difficult for some. Airi could have become confused between a feeling and a belief and blurted out something like "I was scared." Or, perhaps, she might have provided a description of circumstances, such as "I was not in control." In Airi's case, this is a true statement. She was not in control. EMDR does not have the power to change something that is true or factual. And it does not have the power to change a past thought. If the client does not come up with a belief, try to elicit an appropriate one by asking, "What does that make you believe about yourself now?"

Airi: I cannot protect myself.

Airi's NC is appropriately stated in the present and is a belief about herself. It is not an emotion or a statement of circumstance. It is also self-limiting. In this case, Airi had quickly decided on an appropriate negative belief. What if she had initially responded with two or more NCs, such as "I am helpless," "I am powerless," or "I cannot protect myself"? These are three separate beliefs. The clinician may help the client elicit the NC that best fits as she thinks about herself with respect to this event. In this case, the clinician might say, "As you focus on the incident, which belief resonates the best?" Remember, the clinician is looking for a belief the client has that continues *now* as a result of this experience.

The clinician should be cautious about feeding cognitions to the client despite the temptation to do so. Make every effort to solicit these cognitions from the client. And then, only if the client continues to have difficulty, pull out a list of NCs and matching PCs (Table 3.4) or the placard developed by Trauma Recovery/EMDR Humanitarian Assistance Program (HAP). If the client continues to have difficulty, it becomes appropriate for the clinician to offer potential cognitions. When cognitions are offered, two or more should be suggested to avoid the client only agreeing to a NC to please the clinician.

Clinician: When you bring up that image (or picture), what would you *like* to *believe* about yourself <u>now</u>?

Airi: I can protect myself.

Does Airi's belief as stated meet all the criteria for an appropriate PC? The "I" in the statement is indicative that it is self-referential, and it is stated in the present. *Safety* is her desired direction of change; it is future oriented. It is a positive assessment that is generalizable in that it could influence her perception of past events, current assessment, and future expectations.

Clinician: When you focus on that image (or picture), how true do those words, "I can protect myself," feel to you now on a scale from 1 to 7, where 1 feels *completely false* and 7 feels *completely true*?

Airi: I am not sure what you mean.

Clinician: Remember, sometimes we know something with our head, but it feels differently in our gut. In this case, what is the *gut-level feeling* of the truth of "I can protect myself," on a scale of 1 to 7, where 1 is completely false and 7 is completely true?

Does this belief reflect wishful thinking, or is it an actual possibility for Airi? The VoC measures the possibility of the PC. If the PC is not possible, the VoC is not valid either.

Airi: It's about a 2. Maybe a little less than that.

Often 1 or *totally false* indicates that the client may have difficulty believing the PC though it is what she would like to believe. The clinician could assist her to come up with wording that would make the statement more believable (e.g., "I can protect myself" might become "I can learn to protect myself."). Even with her answer of 2, there is a need to assess Airi's ability to assimilate this PC successfully. The clinician believed she could.

Clinician: When you bring up that image (or picture) and those words, "I cannot protect myself," what emotions do you <u>feel now</u>?

Airi: Terror. And I feel helpless.

Clinician: From 0, which is neutral or no disturbance, to 10, which is *the worst disturbance you can imagine*, how disturbing does it feel to you <u>now</u>?

Airi: Oh, that's easy. It's a 10!

Clinician: Where do you <u>feel</u> it in your body?

Airi: I feel it below my belly button.

DESENSITIZATION

Clinician: I would like you to bring up that image (or picture), those negative words "I cannot protect myself," and notice where you feel it in your body. Just let whatever happens, happen (set of BLS).

Remember to maintain an air of neutrality and encourage the client throughout the process. The clinician is still watching, guiding, nurturing, and accepting, while remaining compassionate but detached from the client's responses to the processing.

If the clinician is using something other than fingers to facilitate eye movements or some other form of BLS, activate it to start and stop the stimulation.

After this initial set of BLS, the image and the NC are not referred to again.

Airi: (Takes a breath)

Sometimes, the client will spontaneously take a breath. It is up to the clinician whether to ask the client to take another one. In either case, the clinician asks the client, "What are you getting now?" or "What's coming up now?"

Clinician: That's it. Take a breath. (Pause.) Let it go. (Pause.) What are you getting <u>now</u>?
Airi: I am resistant to going there.

"What are you getting now?" refers to the thoughts, emotional and physical sensations, and images that may have emerged during reprocessing.

During EMDR reprocessing, the clinician checks in frequently to ascertain the client's current condition and to see if new information has emerged. The client reports dominant image, emotional, and/or physical sensations. Based on what the client reports, the clinician will direct the client to "Go with that," "Notice that," or return to the original target if the clinician feels a new plateau of processing has been reached.

If using eye movements, the clinician initially uses horizontal movements to ensure effectiveness.

One of the basic strategies for encouraging a client to maintain a dual focus of awareness is for the clinician to utilize periodic supportive statements. Dr. Shapiro (2018) suggests the following statements: "That's it. Stay with it. You're doing fine." "It's old stuff." "That was then. This is now." "Just notice it." "It's in the past." "It's over. You're safe now."

The clinician is encouraged to maintain a receptive response.

Clinician: Use your stop signal if you need it.

It is important for the clinician to continually monitor the client's verbal and non-verbal signals (i.e., breathing, posture, facial expression, energy level) and to check in with the client as needed. In this instance, the client may or may not have wanted to stop processing as indicated by her words, "I am resistant to going there."

Airi: No, I'm fine. I need to do this.
Clinician: Okay. Just notice that (set of BLS). Go with it. You're doing fine. Take a breath. (Pause.) Let it go. (Pause.) What's coming up for you <u>now</u>?

Remember to be undemanding when asking the client to report on new information, images, emotions, or when dominant sensations have arisen between sets. The clinician needs only to determine if the actual reprocessing has taken place. Allow the client to report what is most salient to them at the time of the processing. Do not elicit this information by asking the client specifically "What are you feeling?" or "What is it that you see?"

When pausing between sets of eye movements, it is inappropriate to say "relax" or "close your eyes."

Airi: I remember how excited I was when I first saw the clouds forming and saying to myself, "I wonder if this is a tornado." I was so excited. I can feel the excitement now. I had never seen one up close before.

Clinician: Go with that (set of BLS). You're doing fine. Take a breath. (Pause.) Let it go. (Pause.) What are you noticing <u>now</u>?

Airi: The excitement turned to panic when I saw my classmates running toward the door. Before I could react, I could feel myself being lifted from my chair. I was terrified.

It is evident that information is being processed when the client describes a shift in one of the distinct aspects of the memory (i.e., image, sound, cognition, emotion, physical sensation). Another indicator is when a new event arises that is linked associatively (i.e., by an inherent belief, major participant or perpetrator, pronounced stimuli, specific event, dominant emotions, or physical sensations) with the original event (incident, experience).

Clinician: Notice that (set of BLS). You're doing fine. Take a breath. That's it. (Pause.).Let it go. (Pause.) What comes up for you <u>now</u>?

The clinician is encouraged to make comments like "Good" or "You're doing fine" to reinforce the client's efforts and to reassure them that they are reprocessing correctly. The clinician may want to be mindful to listen supportively and compassionately. This is a team-driven approach (i.e., clinician and client). As such, the clinician is encouraged to inhale and exhale along with the client. It helps to establish and solidify the bonding that is important to the process (Shapiro, 2018). Some clients may be uncomfortable with the word "good." In these cases, use the phrase "That's it."

Airi: I can still feel the terror.
Clinician: Where do you feel it in your body?
Airi: All over. I feel electrified.

When a client identifies an emotion during the processing, ask them where (not what) they feel in their body.

Clinician: Notice that (set of BLS). You're doing fine. Take a breath. (Pause.) Let it go. (Pause.) What are you noticing <u>now</u>?
Airi: It's the same. It doesn't seem to be going away.
Clinician: How are you doing? Do you want to continue? Do you want to take a minute?
Airi: No. I think I can continue.

At this point, the clinician may offer a distancing strategy (e.g., change direction or speed of BLS) to further facilitate reprocessing.

Clinician: Good. Start where you left off and notice that (set of BLS). That's it. Good. Good. Just notice it. You're in the tunnel. Just keep your foot on the pedal and keep on moving. It's over. You're safe now. Take a breath. (Pause.) Let it go. (Pause) Take another breath. Take another. Good. That's good. (Pause.) What are you getting <u>now</u>?

After each set of BLS, the clinician asks for feedback. And the clinician may ask for it in several different ways, such as "What's coming up now?" "What are you getting now?" "What's happening now?" "What are you noticing now?" It is important to include the word *now* so that the client is reminded to respond with whatever they are dealing with at that moment only what they end up with.

Airi: I'm remembering the tornado siren and how frightening that feels right now.

The new image the client described now becomes the focus of concentration for the next set of BLS.

It is also suggested that, if Airi's shifts in information were primarily cognitive, the clinician may want to increase the number of movements back and forth to 36 or 48 (or, for some clients, a set of less than 24) to see if the client responds better. It is unnecessary to count the exact number of movements. The clinician's attention remains on the client's facial expressions and other body cues, rather than on counting the exact number of movements.

Clinician: Where do you feel it in your body?
Airi: In my chest.
Clinician: Notice that (set of BLS). You're doing fine. Good. Good. Let the memory peel off. Take a breath. (Pause.) Let it go. (Pause.) What are you noticing <u>now</u>?
Airi: I feel calmer.
Clinician: Go with that (set of BLS). Take a breath. (Pause.) Let it go. (Pause.) What comes up for you <u>now</u>?
Airi: It's the same. I just feel calm and relaxed.
Clinician: When you focus on the <u>original</u> event (incident, experience), what do you get <u>now</u>? *(Reminder: Original incident—At age 20, the client was jammed up against a blackboard by several students' desks during a tornado that occurred during one of her college classes.)*

Notice that the clinician asks the client to focus on the original incident, not specifying "the time in between sitting quietly in my chair and being flattened against the wall." When the clinician asks the client to focus on the original incident, they may also use words like "memory" or "experience" where appropriate.

Airi: I see that the glass has been blown from the windows. My classmates are frantic. There is chaos everywhere.

Just notice as successive channels of association are revealed.

Clinician: Go with that (set of BLS). That's it. Take a breath. (Pause.) Let it go. (Pause.) What are you noticing <u>now</u>?
Airi: I am looking around, and now I'm seeing that the other students appear disheveled. They are dazed and bruised, but they are okay. I am okay. It feels good.
Clinician: Go with that.
Airi: Everything happened so fast. One moment there's a classroom and everything is normal. A few minutes later, everything is chaotic, and debris is everywhere. I am vulnerable. I was then and I feel so now.
Clinician: Notice that (set of BLS). It's just old information. Watch it like it is scenery going by. Take a breath. (Pause.) Let it go. (Pause.) What are you noticing <u>now</u>?

Again, continue to reinforce the client by saying "You're doing fine" or some other words of encouragement during or at the end of a set. It helps keep the client grounded and in the present to hear the clinician's voice. The clinician also needs to remain grounded in the present with their client.

Dr. Shapiro (2018) strongly suggests reassuring the client during processing by gently or unobtrusively saying "Good." It is a neutral response and is preferred over "excellent" or "great." Those words imply judgment on the client's process and could impede or cloud the client's progress.

Airi:	There's a commercial where the punch line is, "When life comes at you fast." I think it is about insurance or something. I don't remember. That's how I felt that my life was coming at me fast and that it might be ending fast. In the blink of an eye, everything had changed.
Clinician:	Go with that (set of BLS). Good. Take a breath. (Pause.) Let it go. (Pause.) What are you getting <u>now</u>?

Do not try to interpret all the details the client provides between sets of BLS. By asking questions like, "What are you getting now?" the clinician tries to determine how the information surrounding the original event (incident, experience) is stored now while the client is reprocessing.

Airi:	I am feeling calmer. I survived with only a few scratches. I am going to be okay. I am okay.
Clinician:	Go with that (set of BLS). Good. It's over. It's in the past. Take a breath (Pause.) Let it go. (Pause.) What are you noticing <u>now</u>?
Airi:	I am feeling great!
Clinician:	When you focus on the <u>original</u> event (incident, experience), what do you get <u>now</u>?
Airi:	I can't seem to retrieve it. It feels far away. It's distant somehow.
Clinician:	Go with that (set of BLS). Just notice it. Take a breath. (Pause.). Let it go. (Pause.) What comes up for you <u>now</u>?
Airi:	It's time to move on with my life.
Clinician:	When you focus on the <u>original</u> event (incident, experience), on a scale from 0 to 10, where 0 is neutral or no disturbance and 10 is the worst disturbance you can imagine, how disturbing is the event (incident, experience) to you <u>now</u>?
Airi:	It is a 0. I just can't connect with it.

She has reported a 0 level of emotional disturbance. The clinician reinforces it by doing another set of BLS.

Clinician:	Go with that (set of BLS). Good. Take a breath. (Pause.) Let it go. (Pause.) What are you getting <u>now</u>?
Airi:	It's still a 0.

Once the SUD level is a 0, we can consider the original target to be desensitized. Then, and only then, the clinician proceeds to the Installation Phase. At this point, all channels of revealed dysfunctional information appear to have been processed.

INSTALLATION

Clinician: Do the words, "I can protect myself," *still fit*, or is there another positive statement you feel would be more suitable?

Airi: I can learn to protect myself fits better.

Clinician: Focus on the <u>original</u> event (incident, experience) and those words, "I can learn
to protect myself." From 1, which is *completely false*, to 7, which is *completely*
<u>true</u>, how *true* do they <u>feel now</u>?

Airi: 6.5.

If the VoC keeps getting stronger or becomes more adaptive, the clinician continues
reprocessing the PC. If the client reports a 6, 7, or, in this case, a 6.5, the clinician will continue with additional sets of BLS to strengthen and continue until it can be strengthened no
further. Then the clinician can implement the body scan.

If the client reports a VoC of 6 or less, the clinician will need to check the appropriateness and decide whether to address with additional reprocessing of existing blocking
beliefs.

Clinician: Focus on the event (incident, experience) and hold it together with the words "I
can learn to protect myself" (set of BLS). On a scale of 1 to 7, how <u>true</u> do those
words, "I can learn to protect myself" feel to you <u>now</u> when you focus on the
<u>original</u> event (incident, experience)?

Airi: It's a 7.

Reinforce the PC as well.

Clinician: Go with that (set of BLS). Take a breath. (Pause.) Let it go. (Pause.) How <u>true</u> do
they <u>feel now</u>?

Airi: It still feels totally true.

BODY SCAN

Clinician: Close your eyes and keep in mind the <u>original</u> event (incident, experience)
and those words, "I can learn to protect myself." Then bring your attention to
different parts of your body, starting with your head and working downward.
Any place you feel tension, tightness, or unfamiliar or unusual sensations, tell
me.

Airi: I feel some tightness in my throat.

The body scan is the last phase of the procedural reprocessing steps, and processing is
not considered complete until all residual dysfunctional material associated with the original
experience has dissipated.

If there is insufficient time in a session to complete a body scan, a clinician may resume
this phase at the next session.

If the client reports either a negative/uncomfortable or positive/comfortable sensation
during the body scan, it will be followed by BLS. For a positive or comfortable sensation, it
will serve to strengthen it. If a negative or uncomfortable sensation is reported, the reprocessing will continue until it has dissipated.

It is possible that new associations may emerge during the Body Scan Phase and, if they do, they should be completely reprocessed.

With a body scan, the BLS remains at the same length and speed as before. Negative physical sensations will be processed, and positive physical sensations may be reinforced.

Remember that reprocessing is considered incomplete until the body scan is clear of any residual, inappropriately associated body sensations and that the associated body responses are congruent with the neutralized memory and the PC.

Clinician: Notice that (set of BLS). Good. Take a breath. (Pause.) Let it go. (Pause.) What are you getting <u>now</u>?

Airi: The tightness has dissipated, and I'm feeling really calm.

The clinician at this point initiates another set of BLS to reinforce the positive or comfortable physical sensations the client is experiencing.

Clinician: Notice that (set of BLS). Good. Take a breath. (Pause.) Let it go. (Pause.)What is happening <u>now</u>?

Airi: I am relaxed and calm.

Clinician: Hold the event (incident, experience) in mind again and rescan your body. (Pause.) What do you get?

Airi: The same. I am very calm and very relaxed.

Before ending, the clinician instructs the client to hold the memory in mind along with the PC and scan the body again. Before moving on from the body scan, the clinician ensures there is no residual tension, tightness, or physical discomfort of any kind. When clear, the clinician moves onto the next phase of the process.

FUTURE RESOURCING

Clinician: As you review your experience in our session today, what positive statement can you make to express what you have learned or gained?

Airi: That not only can I protect myself, but that I did protect myself.

As an additional enhancement of the positive, the clinician may ask the client what they have learned or gained during the session regardless if it is a completed or unfinished session.

Clinician: Anything else?

Airi: That life can happen fast and that I need to appreciate and savor what I have day by day.

As will be seen later, some clinicians advocate using future resourcing as a part of closure to solidify any intermediary gains or a positive treatment outcome. The full procedure for *future resourcing* uses the Resource Development Protocol. When used as a part of closure, the procedure is abbreviated and focuses on any identified intermediary gains. Essentially, the clinician asks the client to identify and hold the new learning, pair it with an upcoming situation or challenge, then add BLS. Since all targets have not yet been completely repro-cessed, future resourcing uses short, slow BLS.

Clinician:	Is there a situation coming up in the next few days in which you would like to have a sense that "I can protect myself?"
Airi:	It's tornado season again. I am anticipating the high winds and possible hail.
Clinician:	I'd like you to imagine yourself effectively being in that situation with a sense of knowing you can protect yourself and savoring what you have day to day. (Pause.) What are you noticing?"
Airi:	I feel a rush of energy. And then I see myself looking for cover. I can take care of myself. I need to enjoy and appreciate each day as it occurs. I need not sit in anticipation of another tornado. If it occurs, it occurs. I can and will handle it at the time if it happens.
Clinician:	Just notice it (set of <u>slow</u> BLS). Good. Take a breath. (Pause.) Let it go.(Pause.) What are you noticing <u>now</u>?
Airi:	I just feel confident in my ability to keep myself safe.
Clinician:	Go with that (set of <u>slow</u> BLS). Good. Take a breath. (Pause.) Let it go. (Pause.) What are you noticing <u>now</u>?
Airi:	Just energized, but calm.
Clinician:	On a scale of 1 to 7, how <u>true</u> do those words, "I can learn to protect myself." feel to you <u>now</u> when you focus on the <u>original</u> event (incident, experience)?
Airi:	7.
Clinician:	Go with that (set of <u>slow</u> BLS). Good. Take a breath. (Pause.) Let it go. (Pause.) How <u>true</u> do they <u>feel now</u>?
Airi:	It's still 7.

CLOSURE

Clinician:	The processing we have done today may continue after the session. You may or may not notice new insights, thoughts, memories, or dreams. If so, just notice what you are experiencing. Take a snapshot of what you are seeing, feeling, thinking, and any triggers and keep a log or trigger, image, cognition, emotion, and sensation (TICES) grid. Then do the Safe (Calm) Place exercise to rid your-self of the disturbance. We can work on this new material next time. If you feel it is necessary, you may call me.

At the end of a completed session, a client is asked to practice established self-control tech-niques and to use a TICES grid to keep track of any associations that emerged between sessions.

Note: Airi only had one issue that she wanted to focus on in therapy and only one past memory associated with her presenting issue. No other memories emerged during history-taking or reprocessing. Before termination can occur, the clinician will target any remaining present triggers having a SUD = 0 using the reprocessing phase (i.e., Phases 3–6) and install appropriate future templates of the present issue for each present trigger. If she did present with other issues, the clinician will complete the processing of the triggers and installation of future templates of this first issue before addressing other presenting issues. In other words, each presenting issue will have its own treatment plan.

Case Example: Karen

Situation:	When Karen was 13 years old, she dropped her pet cat off a second-story balcony.
Type of presentation:	Single-event trauma.
Symptoms:	Guilt, shame.
Issues:	Dealing with injustice in her life.

Karen was 35 years old and had been seeing the clinician for 3 months. One day she came in and said "EMDR is good. I can see the effect in all areas of my life." What she had discovered as one of the many insights since beginning EMDR therapy was that a theme of injustice appeared to permeate her life—injustices done to her and others and injustices she had perpetrated onto others. She wanted to start with what she had done to others.

Target:	She dropped her pet cat off a second-story balcony.
Image:	Sound of cat shrieking before it hit the grass.
NC:	I am bad.
PC:	I am good.
VoC:	3.
Emotion(s):	Guilt, shame.
SUD:	10.
Body:	Chest.

ASSESSMENT

Clinician: Last time we met, you indicated to me that you wanted to work on the memory of dropping your pet cat off a second-story balcony. *What image represents the most traumatic (or most disturbing) part of the incident?*

Karen: I can still hear my cat shrieking before hitting the grass.

Sometimes memory is stored as a sound or a smell, rather than as an image. The clinician should adjust the language appropriately.

Clinician: What words go best with the sound that express your *negative belief* about yourself <u>now</u>?

Karen: I am bad.

Clinician: When you bring up that sound, what would you *like* to *believe* about yourself <u>now</u>?

Karen: I am good.

If the client were to state the NC as "I am not good," or her PC as "I am not bad," the clinician may help the client to reframe the cognitions more appropriately by asking the client "Can you state your positive belief more positively?" For instance, "Do you mean, 'I am good'?" The reframing question is preferable because it allows the client a *choice* of what she would like to believe.

Clinician: When you focus on that sound, how true do those words, "I am good," feel to you now on a scale from 1 to 7, where 1 feels *completely false* and 7 feels *completely true*?

Karen: 3.

Clinician: When you bring up that sound and those words, "I am bad," what emotions do you <u>feel now</u>?

Karen: Guilt. Shame.

Clinician: From 0, which is neutral or no disturbance, to 10, which is *the worst disturbance you can imagine,* how disturbing does it feel to you <u>now</u>?

Karen: Definitely a 10!

Clinician: Where do you <u>feel</u> it in your body?

Karen: In my chest.

DESENSITIZATION

Clinician: Karen, I would like you to bring up that sound, those words, "I am bad," and where you feel it in your body. Just let whatever happens, happen (set of BLS). Take a breath. (Pause.) Let it go. (Pause.) What's coming up *now*?

Notice that, when setting up the client to perform the actual processing, the clinician does not recount how the client described her initial target or draw the client's attention back to her reported negative emotions.

Incorrect: "Focus on the image of something 'bad' you did to your cat, those words, 'I am bad,' those feelings of guilt and shame, and where you feel it in your chest." The focus begins to change as the protocol setup emerges. Image (or sound), emotions, and physical sensations may begin to shift, even as they are being reported. The clinician does not repeat back to the client her description of the event, her emotions, or the exact place she feels it in her body because the image (or sound) and where she felt it may already be changing. The clinician does not want to hinder the client's process by asking her to start all over again. Without repeating it, simply have the client focus on the image (or sound), the exact words she has chosen as her NC, and where she feels it in her body. After this initial set of BLS, the image and the NC (or, in this case, the sound) are usually not referred to again.

Correct: "Focus on the image (or picture) (or, if no picture, the event [incident, experience]), those words, 'I am bad' and where you feel it in your body." The clinician, however, repeats the NC just as the client said it. It is a belief that has shaped a lifetime and is deeply engrained in the client's psyche.

Metaphorically, instructing a client to focus on the image/event (incident, experience), NC, and where they feel it in their body is the equivalent of directing three laser beams at the dysfunctionally stored material.

Karen: It makes me want to cry. I feel prickly and sweaty all over.

Clinician: Go with that (set of BLS). Good. Take a breath. (Pause.) Let it go. (Pause.)What comes up for you <u>now</u>?

After each set of BLS, the clinician asks for feedback. And the clinician may ask for it in several different ways, such as "What's coming up now?" "What are you getting now?" "What's happening now?" "What are you noticing now?" It is important to include the word <u>now</u> so that the client is reminded to respond with whatever she is dealing with at that moment. It is not necessary for her to recount everything that happened to her between sets.

Karen: I am feeling less sweaty and less anxious.
Clinician: Go with that (set of BLS). Good. Take a breath. (Pause.) Let it go. (Pause.) What are you getting <u>now</u>?

Consistently say words like "Notice that" or "Go with that." Thoughts, emotions, and physical sensations are meant to flow.

One of the aims of EMDR reprocessing is to get whatever is stuck into a flowing mode. Thoughts, emotions, or physical sensations are not static for very long without changing even slightly from one level to another (e.g., feeling extreme pain in your stomach to feeling less pain) or changing one kind to another (e.g., sadness turning into anger).

Karen: I'm feeling better.
Clinician: Notice that (set of BLS). Good. Take a breath. (Pause.) Let it go. (Pause.) What are you getting now?
Karen: I feel much better than when we started.
Clinician: Notice that (set of BLS). Good. Take a breath. (Pause.) Let it go. (Pause.) What are you getting now?
Karen: I'm still feeling better.
Clinician: Karen, when you focus on the original event (incident, experience), what do you get <u>now</u>?
               (Reminder: Original target—She dropped her pet cat off a second-story balcony.)

Note again that, when the clinician took Karen back to the target, she asked her to go back to the original event (incident, experience)—she did not ask her to focus on dropping her pet cat off a second-story balcony or the shrieking sound the cat made before it hit the grass. This is an important point. As the clinician, you do not describe the event to the client for several reasons. From the time a client describes their target, the entire memory may begin to change or transform. It begins to lose some of its power over the client. We do not want to interfere with the client getting their power back. And, we may run the risk of tampering with the memory by not describing it fully or accurately.

Karen: I feel some remorse, but I do not feel as guilty as I did.
Clinician: Where do you feel it in your body?
Karen: My heart area.
Clinician: Notice that (set of BLS). Good. Good. Take a breath (Pause.) Let it go. (Pause.) What's coming up <u>now</u>?

Try to take a breath with the client. It serves to keep you grounded in the present with the client. During sets, it is easy for the clinician to drift off and think about other things. It also helps you to sidestep the negativity being dispelled by the client. This is not directly addressed in Dr. Shapiro's works but is something that some clinicians are finding as they experience the process with their clients.

Karen: I was with her when she was put to sleep years later.
Clinician: Notice that (set of BLS). Good. Take a breath. (Pause.) Let it go. (Pause.)What are you noticing <u>now</u>?
Karen: (Spontaneously blurted out ...) I just had the strangest thought. I remember where I found her. Pause.) It's gone ... the guilt and remorse are gone.

Clinician: Notice that (set of BLS). You're doing fine. Take a breath. (Pause.) Let it go. (Pause.) What are you getting now?

It is important to give the client lots of encouragement throughout the EMDR process, especially during a client's first EMDR reprocessing session. It is not uncommon for the client to think that they are not doing it correctly.

Karen: Nothing.

When processing gets stuck: When a client says, "Not much," "I'm just not getting (feeling) anything right now," or "Nothing," the clinician says, "What does that mean?" What are you noticing in your body right now?" or "What is the last image/thought you remember?" "Where did your mind go as you noticed nothing?"

Clinician: What does "nothing" mean?
Karen: The guilt and remorse are gone.
Clinician: Notice that (set of BLS). Good. Take a breath. (Pause.) Let it go. (Pause.) What comes up for you <u>now</u>?
Karen: I just feel light. It feels so good.
Clinician: Karen, when you focus on the <u>original</u> event (incident, experience), what do you get <u>now</u>?

The client appears to have reached the end of a channel, so the clinician redirected her back to the target to see if Karen had other accessible channels in need of processing. She did. Since there was enough time in the session to deal with new material that might have emerged, the clinician asked the client to go back to the original memory (i.e., memory that was addressed during the initial setup—dropping her pet cat off a second-story balcony). If there is not enough time to clean out another channel of association, close down and follow the procedure for an incomplete session.

When directing a client back to the target, it is unnecessary for the clinician to describe the experience. It may be stored differently now.

Karen: I still have a little sadness but not the guilt.
Clinician: Where do you feel it in your body?
Karen: In my chest as well.
Clinician: Notice that (set of BLS). Take a breath. (Pause.) Let it go. (Pause.) What are you noticing <u>now</u>?
Karen: It's weird. I went to my safe place, and somebody was there. It was weird but nice.

Typically, it is important for the client to tell the clinician when she wants to go to her safe (calm) place rather than going there spontaneously on her own. However, since this is what occurred naturally during the reprocessing, the clinician just says, "Go with that" or "Notice that."

Clinician: Notice that (set of BLS). Take a breath. (Pause.) Let it go. (Pause.) What's happening <u>now</u>?
Karen: I feel all right. I don't feel the sadness anymore.

Clinician: Go with that (set of BLS). Good. Take a breath. (Pause.) Let it go. (Pause.) What comes up for you <u>now</u>?

Karen: Great. I feel wonderful.

Clinician: When you focus on the original event (incident, experience), what do you get <u>now</u>?

Again, the client appeared to be at the end of another channel, so the clinician redirected her back to the original target.

Karen: I can't seem to retrieve the image … it's blurred or something.

At this point, the client appears to have exhausted all open channels, so the clinician asked her to again rate her disturbance on a scale of 0 to 10. It is only when you determine or find evidence that a client has cleared out all negative cognitive, emotional, and physical residue from the targeted material that you ask for a new SUD level.

Clinician: When you focus on the original event (incident, experience), on a scale from 0 to 10, where 0 is neutral or no disturbance and 10 is the worst disturbance you can imagine, how disturbing is the event (incident, experience) to you <u>now</u>?

Karen: It's a 0.

Remember that the goal is to process the client's negative experiences toward an adaptive resolution. What this means in terms of the SUD level is that a 0 must be achieved for the process to be completed. There are exceptions, such as the ecological soundness.

INSTALLATION

Clinician: Focus on the original incident. Do those words, "I am good" still *fit*, or is there another positive statement you feel would be more suitable?

Karen: Yes. I learned from it.

Clinician: Focus on the <u>original</u> event (incident, experience) and those words, "I learned from it." From 1, which is *completely false*, to 7, which is *completely true*, how <u>true</u> do they <u>feel now</u>?

Karen: I feel totally relaxed. It's a 7.

Clinician: Focus on the event (incident, experience), and hold it together with the words, "I learned from it" (set of BLS). Take a breath. (Pause.) Let it go. (Pause.) How true do the words, "I learned from it," <u>feel</u> to you <u>now</u> on a scale of 1 to 7?

Karen: Still a 7.

Clinician: Notice that (set of BLS). Take a breath. (Pause.) Let it go. (Pause.) How <u>true</u> do they <u>feel now</u>?

The clinician adds reinforcement to the validity of the cognition to ensure that it remains a 7.

Karen: 7. I never thought I could feel this way about the incident.

BODY SCAN

Clinician: Close your eyes and focus on the <u>original</u> event (incident, experience) and those words, "I learned from it." Now bring your attention to the different parts of your body, starting with your head and working downward. Any place you find tension, tightness, or unfamiliar or unusual sensations, let me know.

Karen: I feel totally relaxed.

The body scan is implemented at this stage of the process to ensure that there are no residual aspects of the target that need reprocessing. If the body sensations change in either direction, the clinician will continue to do additional sets until the change is complete. If discomfort is reported, BLS is implemented until it subsides. Then repeat the body scan procedure. After a neutral body scan, the clinician implements an additional set of BLS to help set in the neutral or positive change.

Clinician: Just notice that (set of BLS). Take a breath. (Pause.) Let it go. (Pause.) What are you getting <u>now</u>?

Karen: Still relaxed.

Clinician: Hold the event (incident, experience) in mind again and rescan your body (Pause.) What do you get?

Karen: I continue to feel relaxed.

Even though this is a completed session, present triggers have not been addressed. As with Airi, the clinician may choose to help Karen strengthen positive intermediate gains by including a future resource.

CLOSURE

Clinician: The processing we have done today may continue after the session. You may or may not notice new insights, thoughts, memories, or dreams. If so, just notice what you are experiencing. Take a snapshot of what you are seeing, feeling, thinking, and any triggers and keep a log or TICES grid. Then do a Safe (Calm) Place Exercise to rid yourself of the disturbance. We can work on this new material next time. If you feel it is necessary, you may call me.

Direct the client to keep a log of newly emerging after-session insights, dreams, memories, and thoughts. At the next session, ask the client "What has changed since you did the EMDR reprocessing? What is different?" Many may say "Not much" or "Nothing significant." However, as the conversation progresses, the clinician can often point out something the client said to them that indicates something has changed.

How about the ambiguity of the target? Was it a problem? What did the client do "bad" to her pet? Originally, the client started to launch into a long dialogue about the pet without telling the clinician what she had done. She became emotionally agitated, and the clinician stopped her. The clinician told the client that she did not need to talk about it but could process it instead. It was not revealed what happened to the cat until after the session was completed. Reportedly, Karen was pressured by her friends and dropped her cat off a second-story balcony and into her yard. The cat was not injured.

When Karen said, "I know where I found her," why did the clinician not ask, "Where did you find her?" Did the cat run away and die somewhere, and she found it later? What happened to the cat? The clinician resisted satisfying her curiosity to ensure the integrity of Karen's process. She did learn later that Karen originally had rescued her cat—Cassie—from the side of the road where someone had dumped her. Cassie, a beautiful yellow tabby, lived to be 17.

The clinician may have completely derailed or upset her "train" from going down the "track" had she gone along with her assumption that Karen did something to make the cat die.

When Karen stated that someone was in her safe (calm) place, one might also be tempted to interrupt her process by asking "Who was in your safe (calm) place?" The clinician did ask after the reprocessing was complete and discovered that the person who showed up was Tim, her brother-in-law. Tim had died 2 years previously. He had a massive heart attack while he was cutting his grass. He came to tell her "Everything is okay."

Once a target has been fully processed, the clinician needs to reevaluate the treatment plan (or treatment planning guide) to determine the next memory that may need to be targeted and revisit the reprocessing phases to resolve it as well.

PRESENT

Case Example: Delores

Situation:	The client had been working in therapy on past issues and was slowly regaining a personal sense of power. She was triggered by an incident involving her husband.
Type of presentation:	Present trigger.
Symptoms:	Sense of lacking control of her life.
Issues:	Husband's job was in jeopardy; his exhibited alcoholic behavior; marital difficulties.

The clinician had been working with Delores on issues of self-esteem and self-control over a few months. Delores was gradually reclaiming her power as she discovered that she could express herself more confidently with the people around her. She had identified and reprocessed the childhood events that had surfaced, which initially ignited the present dysfunction in her life. However, there was a situation in her current life that triggered her.

Delores did not feel like an equal in her marriage. "Don is a good father," she would say. "He comes home every night and does anything we need him to do. He brings dinner home sometimes or occasionally he may even cook. He goes to all the girls' games and is very active in their activities." But, once the girls were put to bed, Don would drive down to the local pub and sit for hours with some old high school buddies and drink beer while they related stories about the "old days." He would come home around 11 or 11:30 p.m.

Don worked as an executive for a retail sales company. Because he did a lot of traveling, he drove a company car. Around the first of the year, Don hit another patron with his company car while trying to leave the parking lot of a bar. He got out of the car to see if the person was okay and then promptly left before the police arrived. Don was eventually apprehended and charged with a hit-and-skip accident, which he did not report to his employer. In June of the same year, the company informed Don that they were in the process of changing insurance companies. As part of the transition, they would be checking current driving records of all employees with company cars. Don feared that his job was now in jeopardy, and Delores's emotional charge surrounding the event escalated. Delores felt that she was now ready to process the event in therapy.

ASSESSMENT

Target: Hearing from Don that his job was in jeopardy because the company would learn about his hit-and-skip accident charges.

Image: The blank look on her husband's face when he told her about his company checking employee driving records. "It didn't seem to bother him."

NC: I am not in control.

Check your training manuals. You will find a list of examples of NCs and PCs. If a client is unable to come up with an appropriate cognition, either negative or positive, there is nothing wrong with handing them this list saying, "Here is a list of possible beliefs. Focus on the event (incident, experience) and tell me if one of them resonates or if it helps you to come up with one of your own."

A laminated version of the cognitions list may be purchased from Trauma Recovery/EMDR HAP.

Remember that present triggers can be identified during history taking, reprocessing, reevaluation, and/or ongoing feedback from a client's TICES log.

PC: I have some control.

The PC is also a self-referencing belief aimed at the client's *desired direction of change* (i.e., from someone who has no control to someone who has control).

VoC: 3.

The VoC scale is measuring on a *gut* level how true or false the PC feels.

Emotions: Desperation, anger, and fear.

Again, these are emotions the client *feels* in the present about something that happened in her past.

SUD: 8.

The VoC and SUD scales provide a quantitative basis and act as a reprocessing report card. The SUD is a report of the level of disturbance for the entire incident, not just the emotions felt by the client in the now.

Body: A little in my shoulder. Nothing else.

No matter how slight, the physical sensations reported by the client are targeted. A client's hands or feet may tingle. Respiration or heartbeat may accelerate. Anything identified by the client is not to be discounted.

DESENSITIZATION

Clinician: Bring up the image (or picture), those words, "I am not in control" and where you feel it in your body. Just let whatever happens, happen (set of BLS). That's it. Good. That's it. Take a breath. (Pause.) Let it go. (Pause.) What are you getting now?

After each complete set of BLS (eye movement or otherwise), the clinician instructs the client to "Take a breath. Let it go. What are you getting (or noticing) now?" The original meaning intended was for the client to "draw a curtain over the material" (Shapiro, 1995). This gave the client permission to take a break from the intensity of the material being repro- cessed, thereby creating space for the client to reorient and to verbalize any new information that has arisen. The generally accepted usage now is to say "Take a breath. (Pause.) Let it go." Regardless of which way the instructions lean, the client will tell the clinician what they are noticing. Once they are finished, the clinician will say "Go with that."

When first facilitating the BLS, begin slowly and increase the speed as fast or tolerably comfortable for the client. The speed of the BLS is adjusted to the client's need.

Delores: I feel like it has extended. It has not left my shoulders. I can feel the tension at the top of my head. It has just extended. It has not moved off me.

Clinician: Go with that (set of BLS). You're doing fine. Good. Take a breath. (Pause.) Let it go. (Pause.) What's happening now?

The clinician checks in with the client between sets to determine where the client is in the process and what has changed, if anything. The clinician then assesses the information received to determine if the client is moving toward adaptive resolution. Has new information emerged? Sometimes the information will change; sometimes it will not. Sometimes new information will emerge, and sometimes it will not. Regardless, it is important for the clinician to elicit clear feedback from the client. Neither the client nor the clinician is encouraged to judge the efficacy of the newly emerging and changing information. Just let whatever happens, happen and trust the process (Shapiro, 2018, 2009–2017a, 2009–2017b). Whether the client reports something entirely related or unrelated to the original target, the clinician will say *"Go with that"* and con- tinue the BLS. Reprocessing is in process and, as a result, associated channels may open.

A client with NCs in the area of power/control (or choice) may not like the BLS activated by the clinician. In these cases, consider allowing the client to do it for themself. The clini- cian-activated stimulation may cause the client to link into their abuse history, so empower them further by giving them control of it.

Delores: I don't know if it moved down. I am feeling it in my arms, and there is less ten- sion in my head.

Clinician: Go with that (set of BLS). Good. That's it. Take a breath. (Pause.) Let it go. (Pause.) What's coming up now?

Other than "Good," "Uh-huh," or "You're doing fine," the clinician says little more than "Let it go."

The clinician's best strategy is asking the client to focus only on the new material that emerged during the last set by saying "Go with that" or "Just notice that."

Delores: There's still tension. Maybe … It's still just tense.

Clinician: Go with that (set of BLS). Good. Take a breath. (Pause.) Let it go. (Pause.) What are you noticing now?

Delores: I feel it in my face … frustration, concern, worry.

The client reports the most dominant thought, emotion, sensation, or image. Based on what the clinician learns, she will direct the client to the new information or to the original target. In this case, the client reports some new emotions, and the clinician directs the client to focus on the new information.

Clinician: Go with that (set of BLS). Good. Take a breath. (Pause.) Let it go. (Pause.)What's happening now?

Delores: There is not much change. I feel it may be less in my face, but I feel more tension or the same here (she points to her forehead).

Clinician: Dolores, I am going to switch to the faster speed that we talked about last week. Is that okay?

Delores: Sure.

Clinician: Notice that (speed of the BLS is increased; set of BLS). That's it. Good. Take a breath. (Pause.) Let it go. (Pause.) What comes up for you now?

When asking a client what they are experiencing, the clinician uses general statements that allow them to report whatever is dominant in the moment (i.e., a change in thought, feeling, image, physical sensation, new event). The rule of thumb is that, as a significant change occurs with the set, use the same BLS (i.e., speed, length, intensity, and direction) as in the previous set. If no change occurs, vary the speed, length, intensity, or direction of the BLS. If a change fails to occur after subsequent sets, a more proactive approach may be needed (see Chapter 5).

Delores: As I focus on the event then, I feel less stressed. When I focus on the event as it affects me now, it gets worse. I feel it less in my forehead but feeling it more in my neck. I am having a difficult time splitting the two.

Clinician: Go with that (set of BLS). That's it. You're doing fine. Take a breath. (Pause.) Let it go. (Pause.) What's happening now?

Encouraging the client is important. During sets of BLS when a shift is obvious, comment positively to the client by saying at least once, "That's it. Good. That's it."

Delores: I am not sure where I should be. I keep things to myself. How can I take control?

Clinician: Notice that (set of BLS). Good. Take a breath. (Pause.) Let it go. (Pause.)What are you noticing now?

Delores: I believe that I can take control. I can choose to sit back and let the circumstance take control over me, but I can make the decision if I need and want to. I just don't want the circumstance to rule me. When I think about it this way, I don't feel so worried or feel the tension in my head and neck and face.

Movement continues to occur in the client's reprocessing of the event, so the clinician keeps tracking the client's process and progress as it occurs. The biggest responsibility the EMDR clinician has during processing is to track the client's process but stay out of the client's way. If movement of any kind is evident, the clinician needs only to say, "Go with that."

Clinician: Go with that (set of BLS). Good. That's it. Take a breath. (Pause.) Let it go. (Pause.) What comes up for you now?

If the client reports newly emerging memories or changes in the client's original image, thoughts, feelings, or sensations, the clinician supports the movement by saying "Go with that" or "Notice that." What if no movement is reported by the client? Unless it is the end of a channel, the clinician is instructed to change the direction or speed of the BLS and add another set. Or the clinician could increase the length of the set.

Delores: I am feeling a bit more relaxed. Still less tension.
Clinician: Notice that (set of BLS). Good. Take a breath. (Pause.) Let it go. (Pause.) What comes up for you now?
Delores: I am still feeling relaxed.

Delores has not reported anything new or distressing for two consecutive sets of BLS. She appears to be at the end of a channel and is unable to make more linkages at this point to the original event (incident, experience). When a client reaches the end of a channel, the clinician needs to bring the client back to target in order that they may access additional channels, if they exist.

Clinician: When you focus on the original event (incident, experience), what do you get now?
(*Reminder: Original incident—hearing from Don that his job was in jeopardy because the company would learn about his hit-and-skip accident charges.*)
Delores: I am not so much focusing on the event. I find that I am calmer and less stressed in focusing on finding strength within myself. In this situation, where I was stressed because of the jeopardy he put his family in, I feel I can make the decision to stay or go to support my family rather than him supporting the family. It is more calming and more empowering. And, again, there is less tension.
Clinician: Go with that (set of BLS). Good. Take a breath. (Pause.) Let it go. (Pause.) What's happening now?
Delores: It is an event that had nothing to do with me and, as it impacts our family, I can decide as to whether I will let this impact our family or not.
Clinician: Go with that (set of BLS). Good. Take a breath. (Pause.) Let it go. (Pause.) What comes up for you now?
Delores: My body feels relaxed. I feel more confident. I can handle this.
Clinician: When you focus on the original event (incident, experience), on a scale from 0 to 10, where 0 is neutral or no disturbance and 10 is the worst disturbance you can imagine, how disturbing is the event (incident, experience) to you now?
Delores: It's a 4. Maybe a 3. It makes me less angry. I still feel some disappointment but less angry.

Did you catch the clinician's omission? She needed to take Delores back to the original event (incident, experience) by saying "Focus on the original event (incident, experience) and tell me what comes up? What are you getting now?" before asking about the SUD level. The clinician assumed that the client was down to a 0 and jumped on it. She inadvertently forgot to have her focus on the original event (incident, experience) to check for other levels of disturbance that may have existed around this event. Fortunately, the next channel of association, the disappointment, became apparent.

Furthermore, the process would have probably been more effective if the clinician had just let her process to see if other insights would emerge.

Clinician: Go with that (set of BLS). That's it. Good.

Delores: (The client begins to talk out loud.) I'm not sure if I'm skirting it. If I focus on the disappointment, the tension comes back. If I focus on the strength in me, I feel more relaxed and confident. I don't know if it's right or wrong. It just causes tension.

Clinician: The mind moves faster than spoken word. If you process silently to yourself, it will help speed the train faster down the track. Just go with that silently to yourself (set of BLS). Good. Take a breath. (Pause.) Let it go. (Pause.) What comes up <u>now</u>?

When a positive track and a negative track come up simultaneously, focus on the negative track. After the negative is cleared, only the positive will remain.

The client may repeatedly begin speaking before being instructed to do so. When she has finished talking, the clinician may gently remind her to process silently to herself and say, "It will speed the 'train' faster down the 'track.'" And then "Go with that." Instruct the same way at the next set by saying "Just go with that silently to yourself" to make sure that she understands.

Delores: I am a little less tense. I still feel it in the same spots, but it is less prevalent … which tells me the disappointment is still there.

Clinician: Go with that (set of BLS). Good. Take a breath. (Pause.) Let it go. (Pause.) What are you noticing <u>now</u>?

Delores: It's a lot less, but it's still there.

Clinician: Go with that (set of BLS). That's it. Good. Take a breath. (Pause.) Let it go.(Pause.) What are you getting <u>now</u>?

Delores: I tell myself that it happened, but it does not have to affect me. I am my own person, and I control what I do and how I react.

Clinician: Go with that (set of BLS). That's it. Good. Take a breath. (Pause.) Let it go. (Pause.) What is happening <u>now</u>?

Delores: My body is relaxed again. The confidence is back. It feels permanent. I can handle this in my own way.

Clinician: When you focus on the original event (incident, experience) what do you get <u>now</u>?

The material the client reports has a neutral feeling, which flags that the client has reached the end of a channel. When this happens, the correct response for the clinician is to bring the client back to target.

Delores: I feel pretty calm. It's difficult to feel much as I focus on it.

No matter what the client reports, the clinician will add a set of BLS.

Clinician: Go with that (set of BLS). Good. That's it. Take a breath. (Pause.) Let it go. (Pause.) What is happening <u>now</u>?

It is only after retargeting the original event (incident, experience) and completing a set of BLS without the emergence of new associations or new images, emotions, or physical sensations that the clinician goes back and checks the client's current SUD level.

Delores: I feel relaxed and calm.

Clinician: When you focus on the original event (incident, experience) on a scale from 0 to 10, where 0 is neutral or no disturbance and 10 is the worst disturbance you can imagine, how disturbing is the event (incident, experience) to you <u>now</u>?

No change occurred, so the clinician checked the SUD level.

Delores: It's a 2.

CLOSURE

Clinician: We have run out of time, and we need to stop. We can take a further look at this next time. Are you okay with stopping right <u>now</u>?
Delores: Sure.

The goal at the end of a session is to direct the client's attention away from the disturbing information and into the present. The clinician should not take a SUD measurement at the end of a session unless the client has reached the end of what appears to be the final channel of association and the clinician is ready to proceed to the Installation and Body Scan phases. In this case, the clinician was nearing the end of the therapeutic session and did not have time to implement these two phases.

Even though they came so far in this session and the client is at a 2 in terms of SUD level, it is still considered an incomplete session. Since there is obviously more material to be processed, the installation of the client's PC and the body scan are shelved for the next session.

Clinician: You have done some very good work, and I appreciate the effort you have made. How are you feeling?

Even though the session is incomplete, it is important that the clinician provide sincere encouragement and support for the effort the client did make.

Delores: I feel better.
Clinician: You did a good job. As you review your experience in our session today, what positive statement can you make to express what you have learned or gained today?

While debriefing a client, it is optimal to leave them with a positive statement so that they will not leave dwelling on the negative with the possibility of opening other negative channels of association.

Delores: I am too dependent on others, especially my husband; and I let them lead my life. I don't like it. I don't need it. I can and will be independent is what I learned today.
Clinician: Good. What I would like to suggest we do *now* is a relaxation exercise. How would you feel about doing the Lightstream Technique?

This is an exercise the clinician had previously done with the client. She could have suggested other forms of relaxation, such as imagery or safe (calm) place. The clinician might ask "What would you like to do?" Clients often like some forms of relaxation better than others. Other possible alternatives are breathing, safe (calm) place, or container exercises.

Delores: Sure. That would be good.

Clinician leads the client in the Lightstream Technique.

When a session ends in incomplete reprocessing, the clinician needs to use judgment in terms of the client's ability to manage any emotions that may arise after they leave the session. The clinician may request that they practice some form of self-control technique between sessions and to keep a log of what emerges during the intervening week.

Clinician: The processing we have done today may continue after the session. You may or may not notice new insights, thoughts, memories, or dreams. If so, just notice what you are experiencing. Take a snapshot of what you are seeing, feeling, thinking, and any triggers and keep a log or TICES grid. Then do the Safe (Calm) Place exercise to rid yourself of the disturbance. We can work on this new material next time. If you feel it is necessary, you may call me.

In closing down an incomplete session, the clinician (a) informs the client it is time to stop, (b) gives encouragement for what they did today, (c) debriefs by asking the client specifically what they have learned or gained, (d) assures them of your availability throughout the interim week, and (e) encourages the use of safe (calm) place, relaxation, and/or container exercises.

Delores arrived at her session a week later feeling more prepared to handle whatever comes in terms of her husband's work and driving record. She and her husband had talked about how it could affect them financially. She had lost trust in her husband and believed that she needed to begin taking steps toward making herself and her children more independent of him. "I find myself distancing from him," she stated, "but also see how dependent I actually am on him. It's scary." Because Delores's SUD level ended up at a 2 at the last session, the clinician takes her back to the original event (incident, experience) to see what other layers have emerged during the intervening week.

ASSESSMENT

Target: Hearing from Don that his job was in jeopardy because the company would learn about his hit-and-skip accident charges.
Image: Husband without a job.
Emotion(s): Frustration, disappointment.
SUD: 1.
Body: Stomach, chest.

Notice that the emotions, location of body sensations, and the SUD have changed from last session. These changes provide a clear indication that processing continued after the session ended in the previous session. To ensure nothing has changed in the interim, it is important that the clinician reevaluate the prior target even if the SUD = 0, VoC = 7, and a clear body scan was reported by the client at the end of the previous session.

DESENSITIZATION

Clinician: Bring up the image (or picture) and where you feel it in your body. Just let whatever happens, happen (set of BLS). Take a breath. (Pause.) Let it go. (Pause.) What is happening <u>now</u>?

When reprocessing an event from an incomplete session, the focus is on the worst part of the event (incident, experience) <u>now</u>—not the original event (incident, experience)—and the location of body sensations. The client may have also identified current emotions associated with the event prior to when reprocessing begins.

Delores: I really feel it in my shoulders, eyes, and chest.

Clinician: Go with that (set of BLS). That's it. Good. Take a breath. (Pause.) Let it go. (Pause.) What are you noticing <u>now</u>?

Delores: I'm trying to think what being in control looks like. If I had not been so dependent, would I have reacted earlier to what had been happening all along in our marriage?

Clinician: Go with that (set of BLS). Good. Take a breath. (Pause.) Let it go. (Pause.) What's coming up <u>now</u>?

Delores: I'm feeling a lot less tension in my shoulders and neck, but I still feel it in my eyes. There's the feeling there that I can be in control.

Clinician: Go with that (set of BLS). You're doing fine. Take a breath. (Pause.) Let it go. (Pause.) What are you noticing <u>now</u>?

Delores: Again, I'm a lot less tense.

Clinician: Go with that (set of BLS). You're doing fine. Take a breath. (Pause.) Let it go. (Pause.) What are you getting <u>now</u>?

Delores: I can be in control. I have been—long before I met him. I can be again.

Clinician: Go with that (set of BLS). You're doing fine. Take a breath. (Pause.) Let it go. (Pause.) What is coming up <u>now</u>?

Delores: I will be in control again.

Clinician: Delores, when you focus on the original event (incident, experience), what do you get <u>now</u>?
(*Reminder: Original incident—hearing from Don that his job was in jeopardy because the company would learn about his hit-and-skip accident charges.*)

Delores: It's his problem, not mine.

Clinician: Go with that (set of BLS). You're doing fine. Take a breath. (Pause.) Let it go. (Pause.) What are you noticing *now*?

Delores: I can feel my body letting it go.

Clinician: Go with that (set of BLS). That's it. Good. Take a breath. (Pause.) Let it go. (Pause.) What are you noticing <u>now</u>?

Delores: Good. It's gone.

Clinician: When you focus on the original event (incident, experience), what do you get <u>now</u>?

Delores: He's the one who is losing, and I can feel more separated from that event.

Clinician: Go with that (set of BLS). That's it. Good. Take a breath. (Pause.) Let it go. (Pause.) What is coming up <u>now</u>?

Delores: Before, I was saying, "I can handle this." Now I believe, "I will handle this."

Clinician: Go with that (set of BLS). Good. Take a breath. (Pause.) Let it go. (Pause.) What are you noticing <u>now</u>?

Delores: Yes, I will handle this.

Clinician: When you bring up the original event (incident, experience) on a scale from 0 to 10, where 0 is no disturbance and 10 is the worst disturbance you can imagine, how disturbing does it feel to you <u>now</u>?

Delores: It's between a 2 and a 3. There's the reality that I must make sure I remember that it is his problem. I do not want to be pulled back into it. I want to remain separate from him. I want to decide what to do for me despite the situation. I will have to remind myself of it. I'm afraid prior concerns will come back.

The clinician erroneously believed that the client had opened and challenged all channels of association related to the current trigger. Obviously, she had not. Because EMDR reprocessing is such a fluid, dynamic process, no harm is done to the client. Simply continue with the reprocessing.

Clinician: Go with that (set of BLS). Good. Take a breath. (Pause.) Let it go. (Pause.) What's happening <u>now</u>?
Delores: I am just thinking to myself that I don't want it to come back and interrupt what I believe I need to do. I don't want it to bother me anymore. When I continue to do that, it does not have the same impact. I can call it a two. I feel like I must keep reminding myself to let it out. Let it go. It's not about me. It's not my problem.
Clinician: Go with that (set of BLS). That's it. Take a breath. (Pause.) Let it go. (Pause.) What's happening <u>now</u>?
Delores: If we continue to have to deal with it and it even involves him, I am connected in some way. It can never be a 0. I can continue to tell myself that it's not my problem. It's not my fault. Anything ahead will affect the family. Today, that's where we are.
Clinician: Go with that (set of BLS). You're doing fine. Take a breath. (Pause.) Let it go. (Pause.) What are you noticing <u>now</u>?
Delores: The same. I just must go day by day and regain my control a day at a time. But, I can and will handle it.
Clinician: Go with that (set of BLS). Good. Take a breath. (Pause.) Let it go. (Pause.) What are you getting <u>now</u>?
Delores: I can have some control, and I can have it now.
Clinician: Delores, when you bring up the original event (incident, experience) on a scale from 0 to 10, where 0 is no disturbance and 10 is the worst disturbance you can imagine, how disturbing does it <u>feel</u> to you <u>now</u>?
Delores: It's a 0!
Clinician: Go with that (set of BLS). You're doing fine. Take a breath. (Pause.) Let it go. (Pause.) What are you getting <u>now</u>?
Delores: I know I can regain control. I know I will.

INSTALLATION

Clinician: Focus on the original event (incident, experience). Do those words, "I have some control" still fit or is there another positive statement you feel would be more suitable?
Delores: No. I think "I am now in control" fits even better.
Clinician: Focus on the original event (incident, experience) and those words, "I am now in control." From 1, which is completely false, to 7, which is completely true, how <u>true</u> do they <u>feel now</u>?

In the Installation Phase, the clinician first checks to see if a better/ stronger PC has emerged. The selected PC is strengthened by linking it to the original incident.

Delores: 6.5.

Clinician: Focus on the event (incident, experience) and hold it together with the words, "I am now in control" (set of BLS). Take a breath. (Pause.) Let it go. (Pause.) On a scale of 1 to 7, how <u>true</u> do those words, "I am now in control," <u>feel</u> to you <u>now</u> when you focus on the original incident?

BLS in the Installation Phase is performed at the same speed and approximate duration as in the Desensitization Phase.

Note: The clinician has been instructed to check the VoC after each set. Some clinicians believe the VoC should be checked <u>frequently</u> until the PC is totally true (VoC = 7). They feel checking after each set puts too much performance demand on the client, so they suggest checking it every second or third set. Clinicians are still being taught to check the VoC after each set.

Delores: I am really beginning to believe it.

Clinician: Go with that (set of BLS). That's it. Take a breath. (Pause.) Let it go. (Pause.) How true do those words, "I am now in control," <u>feel</u> to you <u>now</u> when you focus on the <u>original</u> incident?

Delores: Still totally true. 7.

Clinician: (Set of BLS.) Take a breath. (Pause.) Let it go. (Pause.) How <u>true</u> do they <u>feel</u> <u>now</u>?

Delores: It's still a 7.

BODY SCAN

Clinician: Close your eyes and focus on the <u>original</u> event (incident, experience) and those words, "I am now in control," and scan your body from head to toe for physical discomfort. Any place you feel tension, tightness, or unfamiliar or unusual sensations, please tell me.

Delores: The pain in my neck is gone.

Clinician: Just notice that (set of BLS; pause). What comes up for you *now*? Scan your body again for discomfort (pause). What are you getting <u>now</u>?

Delores: I feel good.

Clinician: Hold the event (incident, experience) in mind again and rescan your body. (Pause.) What do you get?

Delores: The same.

Clinician: What's the difference between how you feel now versus when we started the session?

Delores: I feel more empowered, like I can make it without him if I choose to. He is no longer steering my ship. I am.

Ideally, there would be time in the session to move directly from the resolution of this present trigger to the future template. Since this not the case, the clinician may choose to help Delores strengthen this positive belief by using future resourcing. The clinician would then move to reevaluation and future template in the following session.

CLOSURE

Clinician: We need to stop for today. The processing we have done today may continue after the session. You may or may not notice new insights, thoughts, memories, or dreams. If so, just notice what you are experiencing. Take a snapshot of what you are seeing, feeling, thinking, and any triggers and keep a log or TICES grid. Then do the Safe (Calm) Place exercise to rid yourself of any disturbance. We can work on this new material next time. If you feel it is necessary, you may call me.

Whether the session is complete or incomplete, Dr. Shapiro recommends that the above closure/debriefing statement be made to the client. A review of stress control skills and strategies can also be considered (see Chapter 2).

Case Example: Breanna

Situation:	Client is triggered by an act of love and tenderness of a mother toward her infant daughter.
Type of presentation:	Present trigger.
Symptoms:	Depression, anxiety, anger, rage.
Issues:	Realization of what she missed as a child.

Breanna grew up in abject poverty in a small coal-mining town in West Virginia. Her developmental growth was further hindered by a ruthless, critical father and a mother who had been diagnosed with bipolar disorder years before. She had four older brothers, but they were too busy fending for themselves and offered little support. Because her mother was more absent than present, either laying in her bed most of the days or recovering from her mental illness at the nearest psychiatric unit, Breanna became her mother's replacement in most phases of her family's life. At an early age, she learned to cook and clean and do whatever else was expected of her.

Because she grew up poor and in the country, Breanna felt awkward around most people. And she felt alone. She never had many friends as a child, and those she did remember were short-lived. Her home was never a safe or appropriate place to bring other children home to play. Playing was not much of an option most days. Breanna suffered cruelly under the harsh words and frightening looks of her father's obvious disapproval: "He just plain didn't like women." So, Breanna grew up "motherless" and rudderless throughout her childhood and adolescence.

Breanna and the clinician worked for months trying to ease the painful fragments of her neglected and lonely past. She would make leaps of progress only to slide downhill into the sadness that kept blocking her way. She had plowed through and dissipated the rage and anger from her past and elevated her self-esteem and self-confidence. She was finally becoming comfortable around others and taking risks to be with people.

One day Breanna walked into the clinician's office and told her how deeply affected she was by watching a mother and a child while she was shopping at a local market. "I just welled up with sadness as I watched how gentle and playful this woman was with her child. I finally knew what was triggering me. It is what I missed as a child." She never really had a mother to hold her, comfort her, or protect her, or a father who would do the same. She had no one.

Breanna was realizing that this trigger plagued her often in many types of ways. So, it was decided to process the pain associated with this trigger.

ASSESSMENT

Target: Watching a mother and child in the grocery store.

Image: The image of how gentle and playful a woman was with her child at the grocery store. (*Note:* A positive experience for one person can be a negative one for another.)

NC: I am unlovable.

PC: I am lovable.

VoC: 2 to 3.

Emotion: Sadness.

SUD: 6.

Body: Stomach.

DESENSITIZATION

Clinician: Bring up that image (or picture), those negative words "I am unlovable," and notice where you feel it in your body. Just let whatever happens, happen (set of BLS). Good. Take a breath. (Pause.) Let it go. (Pause.) What comes up <u>now</u>?

Breanna: I feel sad and lonely.

During reprocessing, it is unnecessary for the client to report all the details of what comes up between sets. The clinician only needs to know what the client reports, even if it does not make sense. If there is a change, say "Go with that" and stay out of the client's way. What the client reports about an event does not need to be chronological, either. In fact, the clinician may want to discourage the client from trying to remember the exact details of the event because it can slow the processing.

Clinician: Where do you feel it in your body?

Breanna: In my heart.

Clinician: Notice that (set of BLS). Good. Take a breath. (Pause.) Let it go. (Pause.) What is coming up <u>now</u>?

Breanna: I wish someone cared about me. I wish my parents cared about me.

Clinician: Notice that (set of BLS). Just push my fingers with your eyes. Good. Take a breath. (Pause.) Let it go. (Pause.) What are you noticing <u>now</u>?

In the middle of the BLS, the client's eyes stopped moving. That is when the clinician said "Just push my fingers with your eyes" to ensure continued eye movement.

It is important to nurture the client through whatever is happening. If using eye movements, the clinician could have also wiggled her fingers up and down while continuing the bilateral movement. This draws the client's attention back to the clinician's fingers and restimulates processing.

Breanna: I was just a kid. I wish this was not my life or life story. I wish I had parents or someone to help me. I wish I had a happy childhood.

Clinician: Go with that. You're doing fine (set of BLS). Good. Take a breath. (Pause.) Let it go. (Pause.) What's coming up <u>now</u>?

Breanna: I had an image of that day in the grocery store.

Clinician: Go with that. You're doing fine (set of BLS; she begins to cry uncontrollably).

If a client starts to cry during reprocessing, it is not beneficial to halt the process. When you think they are at a stopping point, ask them to take a breath. If tears or other physical signs of emotion (e.g., reddening of the face, rapid breathing) are present, encourage and support the client to continue processing.

Have Kleenex available and visible to the client, but do not hand a tissue to a client who is crying as it might interrupt or stop the abreaction.

Clinician:	(The clinician continues with BLS and waits until Breanna has stopped crying.) Take a breath. (Pause.) Let it go. (Pause.) What's coming up <u>now</u>?
Breanna:	It's really hard not to have anyone to help or lean on. I tried to put on a good face.
Clinician:	Go with that (set of BLS). Good. Take a breath. (Pause.) Let it go. (Pause.) What's coming up <u>now</u>?
Breanna:	When I was a kid, I tried to be so tough and so strong. I don't feel tough or strong.
Clinician:	Go with that (set of BLS). Good. Take a breath. (Pause.) Let it go. (Pause.) What comes up for you now?
Breanna:	I just seem to be bouncing around with childhood memories. I remember Dad when I was in first grade. He scared me. Everyone did. I was 6, and I was afraid of people. I remember in the second grade my teacher took care of me because my mom didn't. When I was in the fourth grade, I won the Spelling Bee. I was so proud of myself, but I did not have anyone to tell. I never had any friends. I was such a weird kid. I was so alone.
Clinician:	Go with that (set of BLS). Good. Take a breath. (Pause.) Let it go. (Pause.) What comes up for you <u>now</u>?
Breanna:	I don't think I am a good person.
Clinician:	Notice that (set of BLS). Good. Take a breath. (Pause.) Let it go. (Pause.) What's coming up <u>now</u>?
Breanna:	I see myself lashing out a lot. I don't feel like people treat me very well, and I feel like I must defend myself.
Clinician:	Notice that (set of BLS). Good. Take a breath. (Pause.) Let it go. (Pause.) What's happening <u>now</u>?
Breanna:	I feel the same. I didn't know what else to do as a kid. I feel sad. I feel like I have lost so much possibility in life … being the weird kid that no one liked. It feels like I am spinning around in a circle, bouncing back from one to the other.
Clinician:	Where do you feel it in your body?
Breanna:	My lungs and arms.
Clinician:	Go with that (set of BLS). You're doing fine. Just ride the wave. Take a breath. (Pause.) Let it go. (Pause.) What's coming up <u>now</u>?
Breanna:	I can feel it mostly in my arms now. There's a lot of activity.
Clinician:	Notice that (set of BLS). Good. Good. Take a breath. (Pause.) Let it go. (Pause.) What's happening <u>now</u>?
Breanna:	I am feeling hot and tingly. I think I am not a good person.
Clinician:	Go with that (set of BLS). Good. Take a breath. (Pause.) Let it go. (Pause.) What comes up for you <u>now</u>?
Breanna:	I'm grinding my teeth. It's the same kind of sensation. My chest is tightening up. My throat really hurts.

The clinician continues to stay out of the way and just follows the client through the waves of emotion and physical tension associated with the related memories.

Clinician: Go with that (set of BLS). Good. Take a breath. (Pause.) Let it go. (Pause.) What are you noticing <u>now</u>?

Breanna: There's a raw feeling in my throat ... kind of sweet. I'm really a good person even if I am the only person who knows it. I did a really good job of finding my way in this world. I can let it go, and it's okay. I'm okay.

As the processing begins to shift, resolution (learning) becomes less maladaptive and more and more adaptive.

Clinician: Go with that (set of BLS). Good. Take a breath. (Pause.) Let it go. (Pause.) What comes up for you <u>now</u>?

Breanna: I am so happy that I tried and tried and tried until I found the help I needed. I am so proud I gave myself a chance. I have nothing but opportunities and possibilities ahead of me by letting this go. It is not who I am. It is what I survived.

Clinician: When you focus on the original event (incident, experience), what do you get <u>now</u>? (Reminder: *Original incident—Client is triggered by an act of love and tenderness of a mother toward her infant daughter.*)

Breanna: I don't get anything. The memory is a blank.

Clinician: Go with that (set of BLS). Good. Take a breath. (Pause.) Let it go. (Pause.) What are you noticing <u>now</u>?

Breanna: I can be loving and gentle with myself. I never allowed myself to be. I think I want to try to be now.

Clinician: Go with that (set of BLS). Good. Take a breath. (Pause.) Let it go. (Pause.) What is happening <u>now</u>?

Breanna: This will be a new experience. I've never done this before.

Clinician: When you focus on the original event (incident, experience), what do you get <u>now</u>?

Breanna: I feel like I have just met myself for the first time, and it feels good.

Clinician: Go with that (set of BLS). Good. Take a breath. (Pause.) Let it go. (Pause.) What comes up for you <u>now</u>?

Breanna: I like myself. No, I can love myself. I am a good person.

Clinician: When you focus on the <u>original</u> event (incident, experience), on a scale from 0 to 10, where 0 is no disturbance and 10 is the worst disturbance you can imagine, how disturbing does it <u>feel</u> to you <u>now</u>?

Breanna: It is definitely a 0.

Clinician: Just go with that (set of BLS). Good. You're doing fine. (Pause.) And again, when you focus on the <u>original</u> event (incident, experience), on a scale from 0 to 10, where 0 is no disturbance and 10 is the worst disturbance you can imagine, how disturbing does it <u>feel</u> to you <u>now</u>?

Breanna: Oh, yes. 0. Oh, finally, 0.

The clinician facilitates another set of BLS to see what emerges, if anything.

Clinician: Just notice that (set of BLS). Take a breath. (Pause.) Let it go. (Pause.) What are you getting <u>now</u>?

Breanna: 0! 0! 0!

INSTALLATION

Clinician: Do the words, "I am lovable" still fit, or is there another positive statement you feel would be more suitable?

Breanna: "I am lovable" feels right.

Clinician: Focus on the *original* event (incident, experience) and those words, "I am lovable." From 1, which is completely false, to 7, which is completely true, how <u>true</u> do they <u>feel now</u>?

Breanna: 7.

A client may report a VoC of 6 and not be able to move beyond it because they do not believe in absolutes. This can be considered an appropriate response under the circumstances, and the clinician may advance to the body scan. Alternatively, the clinician may just ask the client to notice that belief (i.e., "I do not believe in absolutes") and add another set of BLS. This may allow the VoC to become completely true. Sometimes what appears to be ecological is simply a blocking belief.

Regardless of what VoC the client reports during this phase, the client continues to process. It is possible that other channels of association, blocking beliefs, or feeder memories could still emerge at this level as well as during the body scan.

If a client has difficulty getting to a 7, the clinician may need to determine the ecological soundness of the client's response, whether the client requires new skills, or explore for the existence of a feeder memory or a blocking belief. In terms of the latter, the clinician may tag the belief and process it as a separate target in another session.

Clinician: Focus on the event (incident, experience) and hold it together with the words, "I am lovable" (set of BLS). Good. Take a breath. (Pause.) Let it go. (Pause.) On a scale of 1 to 7, how <u>true</u> do those words, "I am lovable," <u>feel</u> to you <u>now</u> when you focus on the *original* incident?

Breanna: It feels totally true. I am lovable.

Clinician: Just notice that (set of BLS; pause). What are you getting <u>now</u>?

The clinician facilitates another set of BLS to see what emerges, if anything.

Breanna: Wow! Totally true!

BODY SCAN

Clinician: Now focus on the <u>original</u> event (incident, experience) and those words, "I am lovable" and scan your body from head to toe and let me know if you notice anything. Any place you feel tension, tightness, or unfamiliar or unusual sensations, tell me.

Breanna: I feel good.

Clinician: Just notice that (set of BLS; pause). What are you getting <u>now</u>?

A client may report being exhausted, neutral, or energized after a session. If the exhaustion does not dissipate after several sets of BLS, the clinician may ask, "Do you think this is new information or are you exhausted after the session?" If the client responds "Yes," to being tired from the session, then the client should be reassured that they have done a lot of hard work, and the closure should include self-care, such as rest or relaxation. If the client is link-ing into new information and there is not enough time to continue processing, the clinician may do a container to ensure the stabilization of the client before leaving the session.

Breanna: I feel great!

Clinician: Hold the event (incident, experience) in mind again and rescan your body. (Pause.) What do you get?

Breanna: I have never felt this good.

Clinician: You did a great job.

Breanna: I had to say good-bye to the "little me." (She smiled.) That was weird. The images I got were of me as a kid, but I felt so mature. I said, "Good-bye. You can go." "Little me" was smiling and waving and telling me, "Everything is going to be okay." And she faded off into the distance. I felt like I was merging. The last time was weird. I realized that my whole life all I wanted to do was save kittens and people and fix things. I was really here to save myself and to think the only person I need to save is me.

As with Airi and the others mentioned earlier, the clinician may choose to help Breanna strengthen this new learning by using future resourcing. The clinician may ask Breanna if she anticipates a time in the next week when she will want to remember this. If the client's answer is "yes," then reinforce with a short, slow set of BLS.

CLOSURE

Clinician: The processing we have done today may continue after the session. You may or may not notice new insights, thoughts, memories, or dreams. If so, just no-tice what you are experiencing. Take a snapshot of what you are seeing, feel-ing, thinking, and any triggers and keep a log or TICES grid. Then do the Safe (Calm) Place exercise to rid yourself of the disturbance. We can work on any new material next time. If you feel it is necessary, you may call me.

FUTURE

FUTURE TEMPLATE—DESIRED OUTCOME/PROBLEM SOLVING

See Case Example: Michael in Chapter 4 for detailed transcripts of future template.

FUTURE TEMPLATE—ANTICIPATORY ANXIETY

Case Example: Jimmy

Situation:	The client saw himself as an ordinary guy married to a beau-tiful woman.
	He never felt worthy of her or that he quite measured up.
Type of presentation:	Anticipatory anxiety.

Symptoms:	Insecurity, chronic worry, lack of confidence in the relationship with his spouse.
Issues:	Fear of his wife leaving him.

Jimmy and his wife had been in and out of couples counseling for years. His wife, Megan, was a beautiful woman, and Jimmy had always thought he played second fiddle to her. He never felt that he measured up to the romantic notion of the tall and handsome knight in shining armor who could physically and sexually sweep her off her feet.

Jimmy was far from ugly, but he was not exactly stunning either. He was short and stocky, had wavy hair, and thin lips. He thought these characteristics made him unattractive, and this is how he labeled himself. Nonetheless, he wooed and won the woman of his dreams in college. They eventually married and had two beautiful children. Despite his obvious conquest, Jimmy was never confident in his ability to keep his wife. He always thought that, despite her obvious love and devotion to him, she would leave him one day.

After years of assuring Jimmy that she loved him and would not leave him, his wife did walk out on him. She left him with the kids and went to her older sister's for 3 days. She had grown weary of his chronic worrying and questioning over something that she had no intention of doing. She left in anger and frustration but came back tired and remorseful 3 days later.

Fear of his wife walking away was Jimmy's original presenting issue, and he and the clinician worked for weeks cleaning out all the touchstone events (e.g., earlier experiences of failure and not feeling worthy) that set his dysfunction into place and the present triggers that kept it in place. After these successful reprocessing sessions, his relationship with his wife became closer and his confidence in their marriage renewed.

ASSESSMENT

Target:	Possibility of his wife leaving him again.
Image:	Seeing his wife walking out on him.
NC:	I don't matter.
PC:	I do matter.
VoC:	3.
Emotions(s):	Fear.
SUD:	7 to 8.
Body:	Chest.

Here is the transcript of this session:

DESENSITIZATION

Clinician: Bring up the image (or picture), those words, "I don't matter" and where you <u>feel</u> it in your body. Just let whatever happens, happen (set of BLS). Take a breath. (Pause.) Let it go. (Pause.) What's happening <u>now</u>?

With every set of BLS, it is the intention to bring the client to a new plateau of processing. The clinician needs to stay alert to the emergence of this new information during every set. Watch the client's face, especially his breathing, eyes, and/or skin color. This is where it may show up first, even before the client realizes that a shift has occurred, such as a lessening of disturbance.

Jimmy:	I am feeling very alone. I am thinking about how hurt I would feel on my own. It's like this has all been a big farce.
Clinician:	Where do you feel it in your body?
Jimmy:	In my heart. It feels empty.
Clinician:	Go with that (set of BLS). Take a breath. (Pause.) Let it go. (Pause.) What are you noticing <u>now</u>?
Jimmy:	I would feel embarrassed if she left. What do I tell people, and what a fool I would look like.
Clinician:	Notice that (set of BLS). Take a breath. (Pause.) Let it go. (Pause.) What is coming up for you <u>now</u>?
Jimmy:	Having to tell everyone. Telling my kids and my mom would be the hardest part (Jimmy begins to cry).
Clinician:	Go with that (set of BLS). Take a breath. (Pause.) Let it go. (Pause.) What's happening <u>now</u>?
Jimmy:	And then the kids would be devastated, especially my 5-year old son, Jason.
Clinician:	Go with that (set of BLS). Take a breath. (Pause.) Let it go. (Pause.) What are you noticing <u>now</u>?
Jimmy:	I am thinking about telling my friends, other siblings, and family. It would just be so hard, so hard to do. And where would I be after that? It just didn't work out, and she doesn't love me. I feel like a failure.
Clinician:	Notice that (set of BLS). Take a breath. (Pause.) Let it go. (Pause.) What's coming up <u>now</u>?
Jimmy:	How do I recover from that? Would I feel like I could recover from that?
Clinician:	Go with that (set of BLS). Take a breath. (Pause.) Let it go. (Pause.) What are you getting <u>now</u>?
Jimmy:	I am feeling like I would make it, and I would be alright. I don't feel it in my chest as much. I feel like I would be okay. It's more about the mechanics of splitting assets and all the other complications.
Clinician:	Go with that (set of BLS). Take a breath. (Pause.) Let it go. (Pause.) What are you noticing <u>now</u>?
Jimmy:	My chest does not hurt nearly as bad.
Clinician:	Go with that (set of BLS). Take a breath. (Pause.) Let it go. (Pause.) What is coming up for you <u>now</u>?
Jimmy:	I feel okay. I feel like I would be alright. I can get through it. No mental pictures.
Clinician:	Go with that (set of BLS). Take a breath. (Pause.) Let it go. (Pause.) What are you noticing <u>now</u>?
Jimmy:	I'm having a difficult time concentrating on it. I can see my wife's face, and she is walking away from me. That would be rough. Moving out (at this point, the client placed his hand over his heart).
Clinician:	Go with that (set of BLS). Take a breath. (Pause.) Let it go. (Pause.) What are you getting <u>now</u>?
Jimmy:	It just feels manageable … that's kind of weird. It comes and goes. I guess I would feel embarrassed. I'm tired. I can't see anything happening. I'm not having the emotion I had before. I keep seeing that I am going to be okay. That's

alright. That's what keeps coming up. I'm going to be alright. I am worthy of being loved. I see that. My chest feels weird. It's a little tight, and I am a little sick to my stomach but not much.

Clinician: Go with that (set of BLS). Take a breath. (Pause.) Let it go. (Pause.). What are you getting <u>now</u>?

Jimmy: I can see myself with my wife.

Clinician: Go with that (set of BLS). Take a breath. (Pause.) Let it go. (Pause.) What's happening <u>now</u>?

Jimmy: Not a lot. My chest does not hurt.

Clinician: Go with that (set of BLS). Take a breath. (Pause.) Let it go. (Pause.) What is coming up for you <u>now</u>?

Jimmy: I can see her face to the side. She is just standing there. She looks like she feels disappointed. My chest feels a little weird.

Clinician: Go with that (set of BLS). Take a breath. (Pause.) Let it go. (Pause.) What's coming up for you <u>now</u>?

Jimmy: I think she is trying to deal with something. That's what I get. That's what it is. I'm at my mom's house for Christmas. I can see my wife. I see all the presents.

Clinician: Notice that (set of BLS). Take a breath. (Pause.) Let it go. (Pause.) What's happening <u>now</u>?

Jimmy: I'm sitting in my living room now. Everyone is excited about the presents. Everyone is there.

Clinician: Notice that (set of BLS). Take a breath. (Pause.) Let it go. (Pause.) What are you noticing <u>now</u>?

Jimmy: I guess I feel like she is not going to leave me. That's what I feel.

Clinician: Go with that (set of BLS). Take a breath. (Pause.) Let it go. (Pause.) What are you getting <u>now</u>?

Jimmy: She's not going to leave. She never was going to leave.

Clinician: When you focus on the original event (incident, experience, etc.), what do you get now?

When referring to the original event, do not say "image or picture." The focus at this point in the reprocessing is on the entire incident or experience.

When referring to the original event, the clinician should ensure that the client understands they mean the one they are currently targeting.

(Reminder: Original incident—possibility of his wife leaving him again.)

Jimmy: I can't see. I'm having a hard time concentrating on it. I can see her face. She has a smile on her face. She's not saying anything.

When a client appears to be distracted, the clinician may ask the client to refocus on the original event (incident, experience). Any time it appears that a client is running around in circles or losing focus, the clinician has the option of taking the client back to the original target so that they have a starting point from which to begin processing again.

It is not always "cut and dried" when deciding to go back to target or to instead check on the SUD scale. The rule of thumb is that a return to target occurs in the final stages of reprocessing if a client's associations seem to have stopped in a certain channel. A return to target is necessitated to discern additional channels of disturbing information or to ascertain the progression to the Installation and Body Scan phases. When we return to target, we are essentially checking to see how the incident or event is currently stored. However, going back does not necessarily mean that adaptive resolution has occurred. Prematurely going back to the target may interrupt the client's processing but will not harm them in the process.

Note that, when the clinician takes the client back to the target, she is asking him to go back to the original event (incident, experience)—she does not ask him to focus on the possibility of his wife leaving him. The clinician does not describe the event for the client for several reasons. From the time a client describes his target in any way, the entire memory may begin to change or transform. It begins to lose some of its power over the client. The clinician does not want to interfere with the client getting his power back or run the risk of tampering with the memory by not describing it fully or accurately.

Clinician:	Go with that (set of BLS). Take a breath. (Pause.) Let it go. (Pause.) What are you noticing <u>now</u>?
Jimmy:	She really does love me. I know that now.
Clinician:	When you bring up the original event (incident, experience), on a scale from 0 to 10, where 0 is no disturbance and 10 is the worst disturbance you can imagine, how disturbing does it <u>feel</u> to you <u>now</u>?
Jimmy:	Let's say a 3. There is some doubt that she will stay in the marriage. Anything is possible.
Clinician:	Go with that (set of BLS). Take a breath. (Pause.) Let it go. (Pause.) What's coming up <u>now</u>?
Jimmy:	I keep saying, "I'm okay" in my mind. I'm not sure my chest believes it, but it keeps coming up. I see that I'm a good person. I'm worthy. I'm lovable. I see that. I'm liked.
Clinician:	Go with that (set of BLS). Take a breath. (ause) Let it go. (Pause.) What are you getting <u>now</u>?
Jimmy:	I am okay. I really am okay.
Clinician:	When you focus on the original event (incident, experience), what do you get <u>now</u>?
Jimmy:	I see her face. I feel a little twinge in my chest.
Clinician:	Go with that (set of BLS). Good. Take a breath. (Pause.) Let it go. (Pause.) What are you noticing <u>now</u>?
Jimmy:	I see her walking away from me, except she is not moving. She is turning around and walking back toward me. She is hugging me. She says she loves me.
Clinician:	Go with that (set of BLS). Take a breath. (Pause.) Let it go. (Pause.) What is happening <u>now</u>?
Jimmy:	She's holding me.
Clinician:	When you focus on the original event (incident, experience), what do you get <u>now</u>?
Jimmy:	I can see her face. She's smiling … or kind of a half-smile.
Clinician:	Go with that (set of BLS). Take a breath. (Pause.) Let it go. (Pause.) What are you noticing <u>now</u>?
Jimmy:	We are both smiling. And we're holding each other … tightly.
Clinician:	When you bring up the original event (incident, experience), on a scale from 0 to 10, where 0 is no disturbance and 10 is the worst disturbance you can imagine, how disturbing does it <u>feel</u> to you <u>now</u>?
Jimmy:	It's a 0. She loves me and wants to grow old with me.

The clinician will be evaluating the degree of change from set to set by monitoring the client's responses between sets and client-reported changes in emotions and physical sensations. It is unnecessary to take a reading after each set. Remember that increases as well as decreases in a client's stress responses can indicate processing is occurring.

Clinician: Go with that (set of BLS). Take a breath. (Pause.) Let it go. (Pause.) What are you noticing <u>now</u>?
Jimmy: I feel good. I can see her grinning now and walking toward me. She loves me and is going to stay with me. I'm confident of that now.
Clinician: When you bring up the original event (incident, experience), on a scale from 0 to 10, where 0 is no disturbance and 10 is the worst disturbance you can imagine, how disturbing does it <u>feel</u> to you <u>now</u>?
Jimmy: It is still a 0.

INSTALLATION

Clinician: Focus on the original event (incident, experience). Do those words, "I do matter" *still fit*, or is there another positive statement you feel would be more suitable?

There are two reasons for asking this question: (a) the PC may have evolved to a more adaptive one since it was first asked during the Assessment Phase and (b) sometimes during the Assessment Phase the client is unable to come up with an adequate PC. Rather than causing them further discomfort by insisting the verbalize one, the clinician knows there is another opportunity for the client to voice what they would like to believe about themselves as they focus on the original event (incident, experience).

Jimmy: It feels totally appropriate.
Clinician: Focus on the <u>original</u> event (incident, experience) and those words, "I do matter." From 1, which is completely false, to 7, which is completely true, how <u>true</u> do they <u>feel now</u>?
Jimmy: 6.5.
Clinician: Focus on the event (incident, experience) and hold it together with the words "I do matter" (set of BLS; pause). On a scale of 1 to 7, how true do the words "I do matter" <u>feel</u> to you <u>now</u> when you focus on the original incident?
Jimmy: Now it's a 7.
Clinician: Go with that (set of BLS). Take a breath. (Pause.) Let it go. (Pause.) How <u>true</u> do they <u>feel now</u>?
Jimmy: 7!

BODY SCAN

Clinician: Close your eyes and focus on the original event (incident, experience) with those words, "I do matter," and scan your body from head to toe for physical discomfort. Any place you feel tension, tightness, or unfamiliar or unusual sensations, tell me.

The body scan is implemented at this stage of the process to ensure that there are no residual aspects of the target still in need of reprocessing.

Jimmy: There is nothing.
Clinician: What does "nothing" mean?
Jimmy: There is no discomfort. I feel calm and relaxed.
Clinician: Go with that (set of BLS). Take a breath. (Pause.) Let it go. (Pause.) What are you noticing <u>now</u>?

After a neutral body scan, the clinician implements an additional set of BLS to ensure a neutral or positive change. If body sensations change in either direction, the clinician will continue to do additional sets until the change is complete.

Jimmy: There is no change.
Clinician: Hold the event (incident, experience) in mind again and rescan your body. (Pause.) What do you get?
Jimmy: I still feel nothing.

CLOSURE

Clinician: The processing we have done today may continue after the session. You may or may not notice new insights, thoughts, memories, or dreams. If so, just notice what you are experiencing. Take a snapshot of what you are seeing, feeling, thinking, and any triggers and keep a log or TICES grid. Then do the Safe (Calm) Place exercise to rid yourself of the disturbance. We can work on this new material next time. If you feel it is necessary, you may call me.

In Chapter 4, the future template was illustrated using an example of skills building and imaginal rehearsal. After the session, the clinician helped target a positive template that incorporated appropriate future behaviors for Jimmy. A subsequent session followed that included appropriate education, modeling, and imagining, along with processed targeting to help Jimmy respond differently in the future.

Note: Anticipatory anxiety is usually processed in the same manner as a past event or present trigger using the standard EMDR protocol.

USE OF THE COGNITIVE INTERWEAVE DEMONSTRATED

Case Example: Kevin

Situation:	Kevin felt he had been teased at school as a child and snubbed by his coworkers in his present position.
Type of presentation:	One cluster of similar events.
Symptoms:	Uncomfortable in most situations involving other people; depression; recent difficulty going to and staying asleep; difficulty concentrating at work.
Issues:	His current position requires him to be a team player; he was having trouble trusting and working alongside his coworkers; he tended to isolate and distance himself from others.

Kevin had just turned 29 years old when he came to therapy. He is a competent worker but prefers to work alone. His recent promotion requires him to work with others more closely. This has become a stumbling block for him. As a child, Kevin felt ostracized by his peers. He did not relate well to others.

The following transcript was created to demonstrate how cognitive interweaves and unblocking and other strategies are introduced and used in a coherent manner. The chosen BLS is eye movement.

ASSESSMENT

Target: At age 7, Kevin was placed upside down into a donation bin at school by a group of his classmates.
Image: The look on the bystanders' faces as he lifted himself out of the donation bin.
NC: I'm worthless.
PC: I am worthwhile.
VoC: 2.
Emotion(s): Sadness, frustration, confusion.
SUD: 10.
Body: Stomach, throat.

DESENSITIZATION

Clinician: Kevin, bring up the image (or picture), those words, "I cannot take care of my-self," and where you feel it in your body. Just let whatever happens, happen (set of BLS). Take a breath. (Pause.) Let it go. (Pause.) What's coming up <u>now</u>?
Kevin: This same group of kids had been teasing me on and off since kindergarten. But it had been mostly verbal up to this time.
Clinician: Go with that (set of BLS). Good. Take a breath. (Pause.) Let it go. (Pause.) What comes up for you <u>now</u>?
Kevin: I can feel them crowding around me. I'm feeling faint. I can't breathe.
Clinician: Go with that (set of BLS). Good. Good. Take a breath. (Pause.) Let it go. (Pause.) What are you getting <u>now</u>?

The clinician may address the informational plateau of responsibility/defectiveness first in hope that the plateaus of safety/vulnerability and power/control (or choice) arise sponta-neously during the client's processing of the traumatic memory.

PLATEAU OF RESPONSIBILITY/DEFECTIVENESS

Kevin: I keep seeing the ringleader's face. There's a look in his eyes that scares me.
Clinician: Notice that (set of BLS). You're doing fine. Take a breath. (Pause.) Let it go. (Pause.) What are you getting now?
Kevin: I can't get rid of the image of his face. I ran into him every week up until I gradu-ated from high school, and he always had the same expression on his face when he chanced to look my way.
Clinician: Where is he now?

This cognitive interweave is an attempt to introduce current safety.

Kevin: He is off to the side of me and watching as the others began to pick on me.
Clinician: Where is he today?

The clinician makes a second attempt to orient to the safety of the present.

Kevin: I heard he went into the military after 9/11 and was deployed to Afghanistan. A couple of years ago, someone told me he was killed while on an enemy raid.

After two successive sets of negative responses with no change, the clinician infused a present referent by reminding the client where the bully is in the present.

Clinician: Go with that (set of BLS). Good. That's it. Take a breath. (Pause.) Let it go. (Pause.) What's coming up now?
Kevin: What did I do to deserve it? I always tried to get along with everyone.
Clinician: Go with that (set of BLS). Good. That's it. Take a breath. (Pause.) Let it go. (Pause.) What's coming up now?
Kevin: I know he can't hurt me now. But I always felt like I had done something to make him unhappy.
Clinician: Did you?
Kevin: No, of course not.
Clinician: Whose responsibility was it really?
Kevin: I don't know. I guess because I was unhappy back then. Like I had done something to deserve it.
Clinician: Did you?
Kevin: I was just a kid. I don't think so.

After two more successive sets of negative responses with no change, the clinician uses the Socratic method to help shape the client's thinking processes. Through these easily answered questions, the client was led to a logical conclusion. What the client discovered is that he had projected his anger and unhappiness on another person.

Clinician: Go with that (set of BLS). Good. You're doing fine. Take a breath. (Pause.) Let it go. (Pause.) What comes up for you now?
Kevin: I can still feel the intensity of his gaze as I focus on him.
Clinician: Where do you feel it in your body?
Kevin: In my stomach and throat.
Clinician: Is there anything you need to say to him?

The clinician provides the client opportunity to express unspoken words and to discharge his negative emotions.

Kevin: Go away. Leave me alone. I just want everyone to leave me alone.
Clinician: Go with that (set of BLS). You're doing fine. Take a breath. (Pause.) Let it go. (Pause.) What is coming up now?
Kevin: I am feeling much calmer.
Clinician: Go with that (set of BLS). That's it. That's it. Stay with it. You're doing fine. Take a breath. (Pause.) Let it go. (Pause.) What are you noticing now?

The clinician reinforced the client's positive processing.

Kevin: I am feeling much more relaxed.

PLATEAU OF SAFETY/VULNERABILITY

Clinician: When you focus on the <u>original</u> event (incident, experience), what do you get <u>now</u>?
Kevin: I can picture the other boys. They are all cheering as two of my classmates pick me up and dump me headfirst into the donation bin in the hall. Everyone is looking and cheering them on. I am so scared. I'm numb. I can't seem to move.
Clinician: Where do you feel it in your body?
Kevin: All over, but mostly in my stomach.
Clinician: Notice that (set of BLS). You're doing fine. Take a breath. (Pause.) Let it go. (Pause.) What are you getting now?
Kevin: I'm trying not to cry. I did that day, and they all laughed. I felt humiliated.
Clinician: Notice that (set of BLS; Kevin shakes and sobs uncontrollably). Let whatever needs to come up, come up. It's okay (eye movements are continued). That's good. Whatever it is, it's over. You're safe now (clinician changes speed of eye movements). Good. Good. You're doing fine. Just notice it. Take a breath. (Pause.) Let it go. (Pause.) What's happening <u>now</u>?

The client is obviously in distress, so the clinician encourages the continuation of the processing by maintaining verbal contact with him and establishing cadence between the eye movements and the words.

The clinician continues the eye movements if the client is abreacting and can tolerate the current affect.

Kevin: I'm overwhelmed with another image. This time of my father dunking my head in the toilet. I must have been 4 or 5. I think he was punishing me for wetting the bed. I thought I was going to drown. He's drunk. I'm afraid he won't let me up for air. He's so angry with me. I can't get the image out of my head. He's laughing. I am so afraid. I never saw my father that way before or ever again.

Another channel of association spontaneously emerges.

Clinician: Go with that (set of BLS). Good. Take a breath. (Pause.) Let it go. (Pause.) What are you noticing <u>now</u>?
Kevin: I can't get him out of my head. He was so big and scary that night.
Clinician: Go with that (set of BLS). Good. Take a breath. (Pause.) Let it go. (Pause.) What are you noticing <u>now</u>?
Kevin: No change.
Clinician: Change the image of your father in some way. Can you change his image to a still or black-and-white photo or something similar?

After two more successive sets of negative responses with no change, the clinician implements a distancing strategy to help the client manage his apparent high level of distress.

Kevin: I changed him into Sponge Bob.

Clinician: Notice that (set of BLS). You're doing fine. Take a breath. (Pause.) Let it go. (Pause.) What are you getting now?

Kevin: I am afraid my dad is going to do something like that again even though he is remorseful the next morning. He is so apologetic.

Clinician: Go with that (set of BLS). Good. That's it. Take a breath. (Pause.) Let it go. (Pause.) What's coming up now?

Kevin: My dad was a good guy. He scared me so badly that night that it was difficult for me to trust him again. From then on, I kept my distance. I never wanted him to hurt me again like that.

Clinician: Notice that (set of BLS). You're doing fine. Take a breath. (Pause.) Let it go. (Pause.) What are you getting now?

Kevin: He does not look so scary now.

Clinician: Are you still seeing your dad or Sponge Bob?

Kevin: My dad.

If the client were still seeing dad as Sponge Bob, the clinician will need to bring the client back to his dad for more processing. When using a distancing cognitive interweave, it is imperative that the clinician bring the client back to the original event to ensure that the client has completed reprocessing.

Clinician: Go with that (set of BLS). Good. Good. Just notice it. Take a breath. (Pause.) Let it go. (Pause.) What is coming up now?

Kevin: I am the one laughing at him. He keeps plunging and the more he does, the more the water gushes from the bowl. He can't hurt me.

Clinician: Go with that (set of BLS). Good. Good. Take a breath. (Pause.) Let it go. (Pause.) What are you getting now?

Kevin: I am back to feeling calm and relaxed. I felt the fear release and flow out the top of my head. He was a good father for the most part. Something just snapped in him that night. He did try to make up for it. It was just hard for me to shake.

Clinician: Go with that (set of BLS). Good. That's it. Take a breath. (Pause.) Let it go. (Pause.) What's coming up now?

Kevin: I am remembering some of the good times I had with my father when I let my guard down with him. He never did hurt me again.

PLATEAU OF POWER/CONTROL (OR CHOICE)

Clinician: When you focus on the original event (incident, experience), what do you get now?

Kevin: At the age of 5, I chose to distrust my father. And then I guess it just spread to everyone else.

Clinician: Go with that (set of BLS). You're doing fine. Take a breath. (Pause.) Let it go. (Pause.) What is coming up now?

Kevin: I felt so helpless and powerless. This is how I feel most of the time with my co-workers even though they have never really done anything to me.

Clinician: Go with that (set of BLS). That's right. That's right. Go with it. You're doing fine. Take a breath. (Pause.) Let it go. (Pause.) What are you noticing now?

Kevin: My biggest fear is that they are all laughing at me. I'm a joke. Just like that little boy whose head was upside down in the toilet bowl.

Clinician: Go with that (set of BLS). Good. Good. Just notice it. Take a breath. (Pause.) Let it go. (Pause.) What is coming up <u>now</u>?

Kevin: I feel my coworkers are laughing at me behind my back as well.

Clinician: I'm confused. Have you actually seen them laugh at you?

Kevin: Well, no. I just assumed they did. They never had much to do with me.

Clinician: I'm confused, was that about you or about them?

Kevin: Well, I guess that was about me. I keep my distance.

Clinician: Did you make a choice to distance yourself from your classmates as well?

Kevin: I guess I did.

The clinician used a cognitive interweave to help the client distinguish between fantasy and reality (i.e., internal vs. external locus of control).

Clinician: Go with that (set of BLS). Good. You're doing fine. Take a breath. (Pause.) Let it go. (Pause.) What comes up for you <u>now</u>?

Kevin: I guess I made an unconscious choice to distance myself from others, even my father after he did that to me. From then on, I felt powerless around people.

Clinician: Had your father ever treated you abusively *before* that night?

Kevin: I don't think so.

Clinician: Did your father ever treat you abusively *after* that night?

Kevin: No. He was extremely remorseful when my mother told him the next morning what he had done. He tried to make it up to me. He was always trying to make it up. I guess I chose not to let him.

Clinician: Go with that (set of BLS). You're doing fine. Take a breath. (Pause.) Let it go. (Pause.) What is coming up <u>now</u>?

Kevin: I didn't let anyone get close to me. I'm remembering that other kids did try to engage me. I discouraged them. Same thing happened at work. I discouraged my coworkers from trying to get to know me. I thought they would hurt me, too. I am beginning to understand that I hurt myself by keeping them at a distance. I set myself apart.

Clinician: Go with that (set of BLS). Good. Take a breath. (Pause.) Let it go. (Pause.) What are you noticing <u>now</u>?

Kevin: I am remembering it differently now. The kids were not maliciously teasing me that day. They were trying to engage me. The school had been sponsoring a charitable event. A tornado had touched down in the school district some months before. Local merchants had donated items to be raffled off to help those hardest hit. The donation bin was turned into a collection place for the raffle tickets. The day the winning tickets were to be selected, a couple of the older students picked me up and plunged me into the donation bin headfirst so I could pick the ticket for the grand prize. No one was laughing at me. They were laughing and cheering in the spirit of the moment. It took me by surprise. It happened so fast. I was so scared and embarrassed in that moment that I ran off and hid.

Clinician: Go with that (set of BLS). Good. That's it. Take a breath. (Pause.) Let it go. (Pause.) What's coming up now?

Kevin: I chose back then to interpret the events in the way I did, and now I can choose differently. It will be difficult, but I can do it.

Clinician: Go with that (set of BLS). Good. Take a breath. (Pause.) Let it go. (Pause.) What are you noticing <u>now</u>?

Kevin: I feel more empowered. I see now that my coworkers and team members try to draw me in all the time. It's not that they don't like or appreciate me. It's that I don't make the effort. I need to make the effort.

Clinician: Notice that (set of BLS). You're doing fine. Take a breath. (Pause.) Let it go. (Pause.) What are you getting <u>now</u>?

Kevin: I know it is going to be hard work and scary; and, with your help, I need to make the effort.

Clinician: When you focus on the original event (incident, experience) what do you get <u>now</u>?

Kevin: I continue to feel strong and empowered. I know what I need to do now to make my life better.

Clinician: Go with that (set of BLS). You're doing fine. Take a breath. (Pause.) Let it go. (Pause.) What is coming up <u>now</u>?

Kevin: I am strong and will do this. I can't live the same way I have all these years closing myself all these years. I made a choice years ago. I can make another choice now.

Clinician: When you focus on the original event (incident, experience), on a scale from 0 to 10, where 0 is neutral or no disturbance and 10 is the worst disturbance you can imagine, how disturbing is the event (incident, experience) to you <u>now</u>?

Kevin: 0. I feel so much stronger and safer.

Clinician: Notice that (set of BLS). You're doing fine. Take a breath. (Pause.) Let it go. (Pause.) What are you getting <u>now</u>?

Clinician: When you bring up the original event (incident, experience) on a scale from 0 to 10, where 0 is no disturbance and 10 is the worst disturbance you can imagine, how disturbing does it feel to you <u>now</u>?

Kevin: 0.

INSTALLATION

Clinician: Focus on the original event (incident, experience). Do those words, "I can protect myself," still *fit*, or is there another positive statement you feel would be more suitable?

Kevin: Yes. They fit. And I am going to do just that.

Clinician: Focus on the <u>original</u> event (incident, experience) and those words, "I can protect myself." From 1, which is *completely false*, to 7, which is *completely true*, how <u>true</u> do they <u>feel now</u>?

Kevin: 7.

Clinician: Notice that (set of BLS). Take a breath. (Pause.) Let it go. (Pause.) How <u>true</u> do they <u>feel now</u>?

Kevin: No change.

BODY SCAN

Clinician: Close your eyes and focus on the <u>original</u> event (incident, experience) and those words, "I can take care of myself." Now bring your attention to the different parts of your body, starting with your head and working downward. Any place you find tension, tightness, or unfamiliar or unusual sensations, let me know.

Kevin: I feel wonderful. I feel like I have a new beginning.

Clinician: Hold the event (incident, experience) in mind again and rescan your body. (Pause.) What do you get?

Kevin: I still feel wonderful.

The clinician may choose to use future resourcing to help Kevin strengthen this new learning by returning to the PC and asking if he anticipates a time soon when he will want to be able to remember this. If the response is affirmative, then ask Kevin to just notice that and add a short, slow set of BLS.

CLOSURE

Clinician: The processing we have done today may continue after the session. You may or may not notice new insights, thoughts, memories, or dreams. If so, just notice what you are experiencing. Take a snapshot of what you are seeing, feeling, thinking, and any triggers and keep a log or TICES grid. Then do the Safe (Calm) Place exercise to rid yourself of the disturbance. We can work on this new material next time. If you feel it is necessary, you may call me.

USE OF EYE MOVEMENT DESENSITIZATION (EMD)

Case Example: Harlan

Harlan had only been a deputy in a rural Kentucky county for less than a year. While riding shotgun along with his sergeant, the two were called to the home of an elderly man and his wife. The wife had become concerned over her husband's erratic behavior and called 911. By the time the two had arrived on the scene, the elderly man was seen running through the woods, yelling and screaming, all the while brandishing a shotgun. The man kept shouting "They're out to get me! They're out to get me!" He shot the gun several times up into the air and then turned the gun on himself. He fired. Harlan's heart sank to his stomach, and he began to retch violently. He could not force himself to look toward where the old man had been standing. It was several minutes before he learned that the old man had missed his mark and was sitting inside his house drinking coffee while waiting for an ambulance to take him to a local hospital.

It had only been a few days since the event, and Harlan was exhibiting extreme anxiety and other symptoms of an acute stress reaction. The clinician wanted to decrease the symptoms related to the specific event, but to contain the reprocessing and not allow the client to link to earlier memories that might be related. So, the clinician decided that EMD might be in order. Here is how the session was set up in terms of this procedure.

Clinician: Harlan, today we have decided to reprocess what happened to you at work. As you focus on it now, is there an <u>image</u> that represents the worst part of this memory?

The clinician orients the client to the event (incident, experience).

Harlan: Yes. I just heard the crack of the gunshot. I closed my eyes. I could not look up at the old man. I froze, and I felt like I went deaf. I could not hear anything except my own retching. I can still hear it.

The intrusive fragment identified earlier is the crack of the gunshot.

Clinician: What words go best with that image that express your negative belief about yourself now?
Harlan: I am powerless.
Clinician: When you bring up that image, what would you prefer to believe about yourself now?
Harlan: I have some power.
Clinician: When you bring up this image, how true do the words, "I have some power" feel to you now on a scale of 1 to 7, where 1 is completely false and 7 is completely true?
Harlan: 2.
Clinician: Okay. When you bring up the image and those words, "I am powerless," what emotions do you feel now?
Harlan: Horror! How could this happen?
Clinician: Harlan, on a scale from 0 to 10, where 0 is neutral or no disturbance and 10 is the highest disturbance you can imagine, how disturbing does the image feel to you now?
Harlan: 10+.
Clinician: Where do you feel it in your body?
Harlan: In my chest.
Clinician: Okay, now bring up the image and the negative belief, "I am powerless" (Initiate set of 12–15 BLS). Take a breath. (Pause.) Let it go. (Pause.) What are you noticing?
Harlan: I hear that crack of the shotgun and can't believe he's done it. I just can't believe it. I couldn't look. It made me so sick to my stomach that I started throwing up. I must have been there quite a while. I don't remember.
Clinician: When you bring up that image and those negative words, on a scale of 0 to 10 where 0 is no disturbance and 10 is the highest disturbance you can imagine, how disturbing does it feel to you now?
Harlan: It's still a 10.
Clinician: Just notice that (set of 12–15 BLS). Take a breath. (Pause.) Let it go. (Pause.) What are you noticing?
Harlan: He fired in the air a couple of times, and then he turned the gun on himself. I could see that, and I thought "No! No! Don't do it!" But, before I could do anything, I heard the shot. I had to look away. I didn't want to see it.
Clinician: Ok. When you bring up that image and those negative words, how disturbing does it feel to you now?
Harlan: It may be a 9.

Note that the clinician is asking for changes in SUD level after every set.

Clinician: Just notice that (set of 12–15 BLS). Take a breath. (Pause.) Let it go. (Pause.) What are you noticing now?

Harlan: Still no change.

Clinician: When you bring up that image and those negative words, how disturbing does it feel to you now?

Harlan: Still a 9.

If the client's SUD level does not decrease after two subsequent passes of BLS, ask: "Did any part of it change? Any change to the sound, your thoughts, or feelings?" "What do you get now?" or "Does anything else come up?"

If the SUD remains unchanged and the client can identify a body sensation in place of the emotion, have the client focus on it and resume processing.

Clinician: So, when you bring it up now, has anything changed?

Harlan: Yes. I hear the crack of the shotgun as clearly as I did when we started, but now I have this knot in my stomach.

Clinician: When you bring up that image and those negative words, how disturbing does it feel to you now?

Harlan: It's about an 8.

Clinician: Ok, just notice that (set of 12–15 BLS). Take a breath. (Pause.) Let it go. (Pause.) What are you noticing?

Harlan: It's getting better. My stomach is better. I guess it was quite a while before the Sarge found me. That's what he said. Sarge came to get me. Said the old man was inside. He missed and put the gun down and went inside. Go figure.

Clinician: When you bring up that image and those negative words, how disturbing does it feel to you now?

Harlan: It's a 6.

Clinician: Ok, just notice that (set of 12–15 BLS). Take a breath. (Pause.) Let it go. (Pause.) What are you noticing?

Harlan: I can still hear the shot, but my stomach isn't in knots. I'm thinking about that old man, running around out there in the woods with a gun. His wife must have been really scared too.

Clinician: When you bring up that image and those negative words, how disturbing does it feel to you now?

Harlan: Maybe a 5.

Clinician: Just notice that (set of 12–15 BLS). Take a breath. (Pause.) Let it go. (Pause.) What are you noticing?

Harlan: It's a lot better. I can hear the sergeant talking to me, telling me the old man is okay. Telling me he missed the shot and then went into the house. Backup was there with him waiting for the rest of the crisis team to come.

Clinician: When you bring up that image and those negative words, how disturbing does it feel to you now?

Harlan: It's only about a 3.

Clinician: Ok, just notice that (set of 12–15 BLS). Take a breath. (Pause.) Let it go. (Pause.) What are you noticing?

Harlan: I guess I learned a big lesson. I need to keep paying attention until everything is under control. I feel pretty silly about that.

Clinician:	When you bring up that image and those negative words, how disturbing does it feel to you now?
Harlan:	It's up a little. Maybe a 4.
Clinician:	Ok, just notice that (set of 12–15 BLS). Take a breath. (Pause.) Let it go. (Pause.) What are you noticing?
Harlan:	Everybody has to learn. I think I let it get to me. It was a tough call, but everybody has to learn. Guess it was my turn.
Clinician:	When you bring up that image and those negative words, how disturbing does it feel to you now?
Harlan:	It's down. 3.
Clinician:	Notice that (set of 12–15 BLS). Take a breath. (Pause.) Let it go. (Pause.) What are you noticing now?
Harlan:	I just kind of ran through the whole thing again. I can see why I got so upset. It makes sense—but I can't let it happen again. I'll need to remember this. I was powerless about what he was doing but not about my reaction.
Clinician:	When you bring up that image and those negative words, how disturbing does it feel to you now?
Harlan:	I would say a 1.
Clinician:	Notice that (set of 12–15 BLS). Take a breath. (Pause.) Let it go. (Pause.) What are you noticing now?
Harlan:	It was a tough call, but I had a good lesson to learn. I'm pretty new at this you know. Only been with the department for a year. Guess it happens to everyone sometime. I learned a lot.
Clinician:	When you bring up that image and those negative words, how disturbing does it feel to you now?
Harlan:	0.5.
Clinician:	Just notice that (set of 12–15 BLS). Take a breath. (Pause.) Let it go. (Pause.) What are you noticing now?
Harlan:	I'm feeling pretty good. I can see it all—the way it happened—and am okay.
Clinician:	When you bring up that image and those negative words, how disturbing does it feel to you now?
Harlan:	It's a 0.
Clinician:	Do the words, "I have some power" still fit, or is there another positive statement you feel would be more suitable?"
Harlan:	No, it still fits.
Clinician:	Good. So now when you think of the image, how true do the words, "I have some power" feel to you now from where 1 is completely false and 7 is completely true?
Harlan:	About a 5.
Clinician:	Focus on the original image along with those words, "I have some power" (set of eye movements). Take a breath. (Pause.) Let it go. (Pause.) How true does it feel to you now?
Harlan:	7. I really do have power over my reaction. That's the key.

The clinician should repeat the question above and take another VoC measure as long as it continues to increase.

Reprocessing is complete when the SUD = 0 and the VoC = 7. A body scan is not completed at the end of the installation of the PC. The clinician debriefs the client and closes down the session.

Special Note: Throughout this text, the clinician consistently says after each set, "Notice that. Take a breath. (Pause.) Let it go. (Pause.) What are you noticing?" and then, "Go with that" or something similar. In actual practice, these instructions often become intuitive for the client and do not require verbalization each set by the clinician. If the client veers off track and does not respond to the instructions as indicated above, the clinician may need to repeat the words again to bring the client back in line with the process.

DERAILMENT POSSIBILITIES

Derailment possibilities (see Tables 6.1–6.6) have been provided to further assist the clinician with keeping the "train on the track." The bolded text in these tables represents what a clinician could do to derail the process.

TABLE 6.1 Derailment Possibilities—General

Not adhering to the fidelity of the protocol
Failing to adhere to the EMDR Therapy protocol may result in stalled, derailed, or stopped processing.

Not identifying and processing etiological events that are the source of the maladaptive behaviors
With some exceptions, processing generally follows in this order: past event, present stimuli, and future desired outcome.

Not assessing the initial target based on the client's readiness and stability
Do not initiate target selection with the client who cannot tolerate high levels of emotion or does not have an appropriate therapeutic relationship with the clinician.

Beginning a new target session immediately after finishing another
Even when the client may have achieved a successful outcome on a targeted event, processing continues. Therefore, it is imperative that the client be provided enough opportunity to allow the processing to generalize to other parts of their life. One way to provide an opportunity for the material to generalize is to do a future template for each resolved present trigger.

Not allowing adequate time within a session to process the targeted material and conduct necessary closure
For there to be enough time to implement Phases 3 through 7, the recommended amount of time allowed for a reprocessing session is 50 or 90 minutes.

TABLE 6.2 Derailment Possibilities—Between Sets

AT THE BEGINNING OF A SET

"Go with that" or "Notice that"

Failure to say, "Notice that" or "Go with that"
If the clinician simply begins eye movements (or any other form of dual attention stimulus), the client may become confused and lose their concentration, or lose their previous train

---

(continued)

TABLE 6.2 Derailment Possibilities—Between Sets (continued)

of association. The client usually wants to know what they are to do every step of the way. Instruct and re-instruct at every turn. Be sure to continue to direct the client so they do not get disoriented and lose concentration (or train of thought) if they are unsure of what to do next.

Saying something other than, "Go with that" or "Notice that" (e.g., "Let's pick up where you left off")
The client is at a train stop, revved up and ready to go. The clinician wants to keep the train stoked and ready to go and keep the client on the train track. It is important to keep what is said between sets simple, consistent, and direct.

Asking the client to take a breath at the beginning of a set
The procedural steps clearly indicate the appropriateness of taking a breath—"Take a breath. Let it go."—at the end of a set of BLS. The breath should be taken after a set is completed, not before another set is initiated.

Directing the client to focus on something specific (e.g., "Let's go back to where you started")
Unless the client becomes distracted or confused or is experiencing some difficulty as to where to start, let the client start where they left off or are in the moment. Do not return to the original event until the client has come to the end of a channel of association. Simply say, "Go with that" or "Notice that."

Questioning the subjective nature of the client's reported change (e.g., "Is it different?")
The clinician should not question any reported change by the client because all changes, however slight, are indicative of information processing. Any efforts to obtain more information could possibly derail the client's processing.

Instructing the client to focus on what their body is processing by regularly and repeatedly asking about physical sensations or emotions
It is inappropriate to ask the client to focus on their body by saying, "Focus on the pain in your gut," "the tightness in your chest," "on your temple," or "on the spasms in your leg." This leads the client to consistently focus only on body sensations. If there is nothing extraneous going on (e.g., distraction, confusion, rambling) with the client, simply direct them to "Go with that" or "Notice that."

Describing the image, feelings, sensations reported by the client at the end of the set before saying, "Go with that" (e.g., "Focus on what you said about your brother running around the house in his underwear")
For the client's process to flow, it is imperative that the clinician simply say, "Go with that" or "Notice that" and nothing else.

AT THE END OF A SET

> *Take a breath (Pause). Let it go. What are you noticing now?*
> "What do you get now?"
> "What came up for you now?"
> "What's happening now?

(continued)

TABLE 6.2 Derailment Possibilities—Between Sets (continued)

Directing the client back to something other than the targeted event after a channel of association has been depleted
If the client's original event was when the German shepherd bit him, do not say, "Go back to the tightness in your chest" or "Go back to when your brother hit you in the elbow when you were 5." What the clinician should say is, "When you go back to the original incident/event, what are you noticing now?"

Failing to say, "Good" (or something similar) at the end of each set
Leaving this out would not derail the client's process, but it certainly tends to provide the client reinforcement, encouragement, and reassurance in terms of her process and progress.

Redirecting the client back to the original incident/event when associations continue to emerge
There are only a few reasons to have the client return to target: (a) the client is distracted and/or is initially experiencing difficulty getting started, (b) the client begins to ramble, (c) the clinician becomes distracted or confused, or (d) the client has come to the end of a channel of association. One of the primary reasons the client may initially have trouble starting the process is because they believe they are supposed to stay focused on the image/target. The image/target is meant to be the "starting," not "staying," point.

Saying, "Go with that" when the client responds to, "What are you noticing now?" by saying, "Nothing" or not responding at all
In this case it is okay to ask for details, such as changes in the initial image, thoughts, emotions or physical sensations. Respond by asking, "When you think of the incident, what do you get?"

Asking something other than, "What are you noticing now?" (e.g., "Any changes?" "Is your chest still tight?" "How are you feeling?")
"What are you noticing now?" or something similar is enough unless *client is unable or struggles to verbalize what has occurred during reprocessing.*

Filling in the blanks or probing for details when the client is unable or struggles to verbalize what has occurred during reprocessing
If the client cannot verbalize or experiences difficulty verbalizing what has occurred during a set, just allow her to "Go with that." It is important not to cause the client any undue distress during the process, and it is not always necessary for the clinician to know exactly where the client is in her process.

Encouraging dialogue
Unless processing is stuck, the clinician should not explore or probe for further information on an informational plateau. If shifts continue to occur, the client should be instructed to go with the cognition that was verbalized in the previous set. Simply allow the client to state what is happening at the time a set ends. Additional dialogue is not necessary or appropriate.

(continued)

TABLE 6.2 Derailment Possibilities—Between Sets (continued)

Saying, "What do you see?" or "What are you feeling?" at the end of a set
During reprocessing, shifts of any kind may occur—in the image, emotions or
body sensations, perspectives, or attitudes as well as the emergence of insight.
For that reason, the clinician should say, "What are you noticing now?" or something
similar. The clinician should be as non-demanding as possible. Allow the client to
determine what is most salient in the moment so that their processing may continue
unimpeded.

**Commenting, analyzing, interpreting, summarizing, restructuring, or reflecting in
terms of what the client says between sets**
Stay out of the client's way. This is the client's experience, and the clinician should
respect and allow their process to unfold by saying nothing or as little as possible
between sets. "What are you noticing now?" provides an opportunity for the clinician
to check in with the client to determine their overall condition, notice any new
information that may have surfaced, and assess any information that emerged to
determine if the client is appropriately processing the information so that a more
adaptive plateau may evolve.

Asking for specific information
To remain neutral and allow the client their process, the clinician should be deliberately
vague and open-ended in all inquiries. The clinician does not need to know the content.
What they need to know is that the client's process is shifting and changing as new
associations may emerge.

Making unnecessary cognitive interweaves
Cognitive interweaves should be a strategy of last resort. Use sparingly and rarely.

Intervening with unnecessary questions and goals
If the clinician has questions or goals to establish, it is advisable to wait until the end of the
EMDR session to do so.

Distracting the client by bringing up any issues unrelated to the image/target
The hallmark of reprocessing is to "Stay out of the way." Allow the client the power and
ability to follow their own flow of associations. Do not bring up any issues or information
that is unrelated to what is being reprocessed by the client in the moment.

Embarking on any discussions as to whether the client's memory is real or not
It is irrelevant whether the client's memory of events is real or not. It is how it is stored and
perceived that is important. Again, "stay out of the client's way."

**Distancing the client from the memory (e.g., train metaphor) when it is evident that
they can tolerate their emotions and remain in the present**
This statement is worth repeating: "Stay out of the way." If it is evident that the
client is effectively tolerating whatever emotions they are exhibiting at the time, it is
important to allow them to do so without interruption, distraction, or direction from
the clinician.

(continued)

TABLE 6.2 Derailment Possibilities—Between Sets (continued)

Taking too much time between sets for note-taking or taking notes during the eye movements
It is important not to slow down or stop the train (i.e., slow down or stop processing). If the client is on a 50-mile trip, it could take too long.

Abbreviation: BLS, bilateral stimulation.

TABLE 6.3 Derailment Possibilities—Intense Emotional Responses

Stopping the reprocessing when the client obviously continues to process negative associations
When the client is experiencing intense emotions, it is indicative that the processing continues. The distress and intense emotions that the client is experiencing will resolve more quickly if the clinician continues the BLS until it has subsided.

Talking while the client is experiencing an intense emotional response
Instead of trying to distract the client from this distress, it is suggested that the clinician offer support and encouragement to help the client tolerate their experience (e.g., "Good. You're doing fine," "It's over. You're safe now," or "It's in the past.").

Introducing a state-shift prematurely rather than continuing the reprocessing (e.g., breathing, safe place)
Again, it is important "to stay out of the way." If shifts and changes continue to occur with the client's processing, simply say, "Go with that" or "Notice that."

Failing to stop the reprocessing completely when the client requests
In this case, the clinician is encouraged to simply give the client a break and then return to reprocessing as soon as the client indicates they are able. If the client continues the request, stop immediately and do a container or other stabilization exercise. It is important not to push the client beyond their level of tolerance.

Not consulting the client's physician in the case where the client reports a serious medical problem (e.g., pregnancy, a cardiac or respiratory condition) as part of their clinical landscape
Because of the possibility of high levels of emotional response, the client's physician should be contacted before reprocessing is commenced under these and other medical circumstances.

Not assessing the client's current life situation before reprocessing is begun
High levels of emotional response are possible in any session. Therefore, the clinician must assess the client's current life responsibilities (e.g., work presentation scheduled immediately after a reprocessing session) prior to reprocessing. The clinician may also wish to assess the client's degree of psychological support before and after each session (e.g., If the client is scheduled to go on a long-term business trip, the clinician may want to schedule reprocessing upon the client's return).

(continued)

TABLE 6.3 Derailment Possibilities—Intense Emotional Responses (continued)

Allowing the client to leave the clinician's office during or immediately after an unresolved abreactive response
If a trauma is insufficiently processed, relatively high levels of disturbance may continue and increase even after the session ends. Adequate time needs to be taken to debrief and to allow the client to restore their sense of equilibrium before allowing them to leave the office. A closure procedure (e.g., Safe (Calm) Place, Lightstream Technique) should be agreed upon and in place before any processing has taken place. This procedure should be adequate to help the client contain affect and control and to help return them to a relative state of calm before leaving the clinician's office. Alternate arrangements may need to be made for transportation in the event the client is unable to drive safely. In some cases, it may be necessary to see the client later in the day or even later in the week to assure a continued sense of calm and mastery. The clinician may also call the client later in the week to check on their progress.

Abbreviation: BLS, bilateral stimulation.

TABLE 6.4 Derailment Possibilities—Emotions and Body Sensations

EMOTIONS

"When you bring up that picture and those words (NC), what emotion(s) do you feel now?"

Identifying the emotions without first pairing them with both the image and the NC
Follow the Assessment Phase in the order prescribed.

Discussing or naming the emotions for the client (e.g., "Are you feeling sadness or anger rather than regret?")
Stay out of the client's way. Allow them to identify and describe their own experience.

Not being attuned to the amount of emotional distress the client may be experiencing during reprocessing
The clinician should always be attending to the client during processing.

Allowing the client to provide an SUD score on positive emotions
In this case, the clinician will need to remind the client that they are only rating disturbing or negative emotions.

Targeting a new emotion in reference to a subsequent one
If a new emotion emerges, it should be targeted solely on its own. If the client reports anger, do not add a reference to previous emotions by asking, "Are you still feeling frustrated and confused?"

Failing to target smells or sounds in successive sets
If smells or sounds emerge, the clinician should target them in subsequent sets.

(continued)

TABLE 6.4 Derailment Possibilities—Emotions and Body Sensations (continued)

EMOTIONS

Accepting emotions that the client felt at the time of a disturbing event
The emotions solicited are those felt at the time of the assessment, not those the client experienced at the time of the event. Take care to discern when the client felt the emotions they are reporting—then or now.

Failing to utilize advanced strategies when the client begins looping
Looping is indicative that the client is experiencing high levels of disturbance and continues to report the same images, emotions, or body sensations. When looping occurs, the clinician may use a variety of strategies (e.g., strategies for blocked processing, cognitive interweaves) to mimic processing.

Failing to debrief the client on the possibility of intense emotions emerging
During the Preparation Phase, the clinician should briefly explain the possibility of intense emotions arising during processing. Explain that they are manifestations of old material. For example, the client may be experiencing fear during a session even though there is no immediate danger.

Asking for emotions in reference to the past
Elicit the emotions as the client is experiencing them "in the now."

Attempting to remove a negative emotion that may either be appropriate in a situation or an impetus to an appropriate reaction
The client with a snake phobia may exhibit irrational anxiety and fear at seeing a video of a recoiling snake on television. If, on the other hand, they were experiencing the same emotions while standing in front of a snake while out in the woods, this could be appropriate emotions under the circumstance, and EMDR processing could not remove them.

Redirecting the client back to an associated emotion when they report a physical sensation
If the client reports something other than an emotion(s), go where they go.

Stopping the client after they have identified only <u>one</u> emotion
There may be many emotions associated with the image/target.

Encouraging the client to judge or fear their emotions
The client should be encouraged to just *notice* their emotions.

Failing to address emotions as they emerge
A wide variety of emotions may sequentially emerge as the client is processing an event. When this happens, it is appropriate to ask, "Where do you feel it in your body?" Target the answer in the subsequent set.

BODY SENSATIONS

"Where do you feel it in your body?"

Asking, "What do you feel?"
The only relevant information is the location of the negative physical sensation in the client's body.

(continued)

TABLE 6.4 Derailment Possibilities—Emotions and Body Sensations (continued)

Treating a sensation that the client consistently reports in their head as an actual physical sensation
Treat it as a metaphoric construct instead.

Asking the client what the body sensation(s) is
It is not necessary for the clinician to ask for a description of a body sensation.

Dismissing the client's report of numbed, blocked, or separated body sensations
The clinician should pay attention to any response that denies body awareness or lack of feeling that simultaneously reveals a physical sensation. Redirect the client by saying, "Where do you feel blocked?" (i.e., in their body) and continue the BLS. Continue to reassure the client by explaining that this is part of the therapeutic process. The clinician may also ask the client, "What does numb mean?" (e.g., absence of feeling, insensitivity, paralysis, immobility, dead, unresponsive, unable to move). Numb sometimes may also mean the absence of negative body sensations.

Dismissing the client's inability to identify a body sensation
In this case, it is suggested that the clinician adjust subsequent instructions by directing the client to focus on other components of the target.

Failing to have the client verbalize unspoken words as a target to successive sets
Certain types of body sensations (e.g., tension or tightness in the throat or jaw) can indicate the presence of unspoken words (e.g., "Stop!"). It may represent something the client wished they could have said and could not say at the time of a traumatic event. When this occurs, encourage the client to say aloud whatever unspoken words arise during processing.

Continuing eye movements in the same direction when the client reports dizziness, pain, or nausea or if no movement at all
If the client reports any of these conditions after two sets, changing the direction of the eye movements may cause the physical sensations to shift.

Failing to educate the client on the skill of identifying body sensations
As a result of a continuing disturbance or a belief that needs cannot be fulfilled, the client may have learned to separate themself psychologically from their body. If the client encounters difficulties identifying a body sensation, the clinician may provide gentle instruction by saying, "You report a level of disturbance of _____ (fill in the blank). Where do you feel the _____ (fill in the blank) in your body?" If the client remains unable to respond, simply say, "Close your eyes and notice how your body feels. Now I will ask you to think of something; and, when I do, just notice what changes in your body. Okay, notice your body. Now, think of (or bring up the picture of) the memory. Tell me what changes. Now add the words [the clinician states the NC]. Tell me what changes."

Dismissing a small change in body sensations
All changes in body sensations are significant and should be targeted in subsequent sets. This will help the client become more aware of other sensations in their body.

(continued)

TABLE 6.4 Derailment Possibilities—Emotions and Body Sensations (continued)

Dismissing body sensations that represent an inhibited movement of any kind (e.g., a need to punch or kick)
When this occurs, the clinician may openly encourage the client's physical movement during progressive sets (e.g., kicking the air or punching a pillow).

Continuing eye movements when the client reports eye pain
If eye pain in reported by the client, stop the eye movement and continue with an alternate form of BLS. Unless the pain is simple fatigue, the client should be encouraged to have clearance by a physician before resuming eye movements.

Assuming all physical sensations are targets for subsequent sets
Physical sensations can also be products of the current moment (i.e., pain associated with a heart attack or stroke). Always be open to this possibility.

Attempting to remove a negative physical sensation that is caused by something other than a targeted event
During a body scan, the client may report physical symptoms that are unrelated to the targeted event and cannot be reprocessed (e.g., hunger pains).

Directing the client to focus on physical sensations reported in past sets
Direct the client to focus instead on wherever the sensation currently resides in the body.

Ascertaining what the client's body sensation feels like or ascribing a meaning to it
Shifts in body sensations (i.e., pain shifting upward from stomach to chest to throat) indicate that processing of information is taking place. As it shifts, direct the client to focus on the new location. There is no need to have the client describe it and tell you what it means to them.

Interpreting for the client what body sensations are connected to
Body sensations may be connected to an emotion(s) that arises during processing, may be the same sensations experienced at the time of the original trauma, or may be a nonspecific physical resonance of the NC. Refrain from interpreting for the client and simply say, "Go with that" or "Notice that."

Abbreviations: BLS, bilateral stimulation; NC, negative cognition; SUD, Subjective Units of Disturbance.

TABLE 6.5 Derailment Possibilities—Going Back to Target

"When you go back to the original memory, what are you noticing now?"

Saying, "When you go back to the original image/picture, what are you noticing?"
There is an important distinction between "original image/picture" and "original incident/issue." During the Assessment Phase, the questions are directed toward the original image/picture. During the reprocessing phases (i.e., desensitization, installation, and body scan), the client is directed to focus on the original memory/incident/issue. As reprocessing progresses, the original "image/picture" may have faded or resolved

(*continued*)

TABLE 6.5 Derailment Possibilities—Going Back to Target (continued)

and other associative memory networks may have surfaced. The goal here is to desensitize and bring adaptive resolution to all associated channels of information.

Saying, "What do you think?" or "What do you feel?" after instructing the client to go back to target
The only question the clinician should ask when instructing the client to go back to target is "When you go back to the original memory, what are you noticing now?" The primary reason for returning to target is to determine if there are additional channels of dysfunctional information linked to the original memory. In some cases, however, the client may appear to provide an "endless stream of associated distinct memories" (Shapiro, 2018). In this case and only after a series of 10 to 15 memories have been revealed sequentially should the client be returned to the target. This is a common occurrence with war veterans.

Bringing the client back to target when in the middle of processing an association
This is another "stay out of the way" situation. If there are shifts and changes in images, emotions, thoughts, and physical sensations, the primary instructions the clinician gives are "Go with that" or "Notice that." If the client appears distracted or seems to have gone off target, the clinician may want to bring the client back to target to get them back on the tracks.

Asking for an SUD level before cleaning out all channels of association (i.e., going back to target as needed)
All possible channels of association should be exhausted before asking for a SUD.

Describing the client's initial target/event anywhere during Phases 3–8
Once reprocessing commences, the original image (or picture) begins to fade as well as reprocessed channels of association.

Failing to return to target after two sets of neutral or positive sets, when the client's associations appear too diffuse, or when the client appears to be "lost" in terms of where they are during the processing
When any of the circumstances described above occur, it is necessary for the clinician to return the client back to target.

Going back to target immediately after a positive thought(s) or emotion(s) has emerged
It is important to strengthen any positive thought(s) or emotion(s) that emerge(s) which are adaptive for the client before returning to target. If negative and positive thoughts or emotions emerge simultaneously, focus on the negative.

Abbreviation: SUD, Subjective Units of Disturbance.

TABLE 6.6 Derailment Possibilities—SUD Measurement During Desensitization Phase

"When you bring up the original experience, on a scale of 0 to 10, where 0 is neutral or no disturbance and 10 is the highest disturbance you can imagine, how disturbing does it feel to you now?"

(continued)

TABLE 6.6 Derailment Possibilities—SUD Measurement During Desensitization Phase (continued)

Asking for the SUD on a scale of 1 to 10
Correct scale is 0 to 10

Eliciting an SUD without first going back to the original image/target
The clinician measures the client's current level of disturbance SUD *only* after redirecting the client back to the original incident/event and after all associated events appear to have been processed. This is to ensure that all levels of negative association related to the original incident/event have been integrated, resolved, and flushed out.

Asking for the SUD without going back to target after two consecutive sets of neutral passes
Only after the clinician has redirected the client back to target and initiates two more consecutive sets of BLS where the client reports "no change" or positive responses does the clinician take an SUD measurement.

Eliciting a rating on positive emotions
Be sure only disturbing emotions are being rated.

If the client's SUD level is 0 based on their responses
It is important to always ask the question, "How disturbing does it <u>feel now</u>?"

Asking for the VoC measurement before the Desensitization Phase has been completed
Follow the eight phases in order (i.e., history-taking and treatment planning, preparation, assessment, desensitization, installation, body scan, closure, and reevaluation). The Desensitization Phase, in all cases, precedes the Installation Phase (i.e., verification and installation of the PC).

Ending the Desensitization Phase before SUD = 0
Exceptions: (a) The session is incomplete; or (b) ecological validity has been established.

Asking, "What prevents it from being 0?" each time the client is brought back to target
This question should be asked when the client's SUD level does not get any lower than a 2 and only after the body sensations (i.e., "Where do you feel it in your body?") have been processed.

Or asking the client the same question above when the SUD remains relatively high (e.g., 5)
"What prevents it from being 0" should only be asked when the client is blocked at a SUD of 1 or 2, which indicates that there may be blocking beliefs or feeder memories impeding processing. A higher SUD level than this is indicative that there is more material that needs to be processed. If this is the case, the first question the clinician should ask is "Where do you feel it in your body?"

Continuing to the Installation Phase while the SUD equals 2 or higher
Unless the session is incomplete or there is ecological validity, the preferred SUD = 0.

Rating SUD on one emotion when several have been given
While the SUD is rated after obtaining the related emotion(s), the rating is on the entire target assessment, not just on the emotions. From 0, which is neutral or no disturbance, to 10, which is *the worst disturbance you can imagine,* how disturbing does it feel to you <u>now</u>?

(continued)

TABLE 6.6 Derailment Possibilities—SUD Measurement During
Desensitization Phase (continued)

Taking an SUD at the end of an incomplete session

It is not advisable to take an SUD at the very the end of an incomplete session unless there
is enough time to bring greater resolution to the targeted event. In doing so, the clinician
risks restimulating the memory and the memory network.

Abbreviations: BLS, bilateral stimulation; PC, positive cognition; SUD, Subjective Units of Disturbance; VoC, Validity
of Cognition.

Following is an explanation as to why a clinician should not have done what they did, or
what they should do instead.

SUMMARY STATEMENTS

Understanding and self-efficacy achieved at the end of a session by each of the clients
discussed in this chapter are *the hallmarks of a successful EMDR session* (Shapiro, 2018).
Remember that typically less than half of a clinician's reprocessing sessions occur without having to implement some type of clinical guidance or strategies to unblock stalled
processing. In either case, the result is the same—a client's previously reported negative
images, affect, cognitions, and physical sensations related to a stated trauma become
weaker or nonexistent, less colorful, less intense, or however the client happens to describe
them. The validity of the client's negative overall response to the trauma becomes absorbed
and replaced by the vividness of their positive images, affect, cognitions, and physical sensations of the same event. The client becomes more empowered, stable, secure, and has a
stronger sense of self.

Remember, EMDR therapy is not for everyone. Some problems presented by a client
may be remediated simply by using other means—education, stress management, or problem
solving. Others may require reprocessing of dysfunctionally stored material. If a client does
present with dysfunctional patterns of response, these should obviously be addressed first
and, in some cases, the success of the reprocessing may increase the assimilation of new skills
and eliminate the need for other means of treatment.

REFERENCES

Shapiro, F. (1995). *Eye movement desensitization and reprocessing: Basic principles, protocols and
procedures* (1st ed.). New York, NY: Guilford Press.

Shapiro, F. (2009–2017a). *The EMDR approach to psychotherapy—EMDR Institute basic training
Course: Weekend 1 of the two part basic training.* EMDR Institute.

Shapiro, F. (2009–2017b). *The EMDR approach to psychotherapy—EMDR Institute basic training
Course: Weekend 2 of the two part basic training.* EMDR Institute.

Shapiro, F. (2018). *Eye movement desensitization and reprocessing: Basic principles, protocols and procedures* (3rd ed.). Guilford Press.

7

Working With Special Populations

For the eye altering alters all.—William Blake (*Warner*, 1863)

INTRODUCTION

While not totally within the scope of this Primer, mention of three special client populations are included: military/veterans, children and adolescents, and culturally diverse populations. Below is a short review and a sample transcript for each population to help the reader understand some, but not all, of the issues and complications that can arise. For more information on these special populations, please visit the Francine Shapiro Library (emdria.omeka.net).

EMDR WITH MILITARY AND VETERAN POPULATIONS

Active military personnel and veterans using EMDR therapy treatment covers a wide range of potential issues. Besides the combat trauma experienced, the clinician may also need to address issues revolving around military sexual assault, addiction, anxiety, somatic disorders, natural and man-made disasters, grief, guilt, moral injury, couples and family, complex trauma with dissociative symptoms, and vicarious traumatization. Russell and Figley (2013) describe other types of stress with which military personnel contend beyond those inherent in combat—deployments, frequent geographical reassignments, disaster relief, peacekeeping missions, and training accidents.

Elements that clinicians working with military personnel need to be familiar with are the deployment cycle, military stressors and occupational hazards, military culture, and the spectrum of military stress injuries, including medically unexplained symptoms/conditions

(Russell & Figley, 2013), as well as a military client's past trauma history and how it might affect the client's current presentation.

There is a great need for more EMDR-trained clinicians who are willing and unafraid to serve this population. It is strongly suggested that any clinician who wants or attempts to treat active military personnel and veterans be highly familiar with both cultures before attempting to treat using EMDR therapy. There are a variety of resources and training opportunities available. Cultural competence in dealing with military personnel and/or veterans is paramount to successful treatment outcomes for these special populations. Anyone interested in serving this population could benefit by educating themselves in the military/veteran populations (see Department of Veterans Affairs and Military Onesource websites).

SAMPLE SESSION WITH VETERAN

A sample session with an Army veteran is described below to demonstrate possible themes that may arise during processing.

Example: While serving as a U.S. Army soldier on a mission in Afghanistan, Amalia and two others were patrolling and rooting out Sunni insurgents when the Humvee in which she was riding ran over an improvised explosive device (IED). It caused a blast so powerful that it knocked the vehicle on its side.

Amalia was severely injured and placed under "specialist care." The blast ripped the flesh off her left arm. She sustained a partial collapsed lung and lacerations to her face. A piece of shrapnel lodged in the right side of her body. As she was recovering consciousness from what she originally thought was from the force of the blast, a medic was getting ready to perform a field tracheotomy on her. It took Amalia 2 months to recover from her injuries before she was sent back to her unit. The two Army personnel who were injured along with her died two days after the explosion.

After another year in Afghanistan, Amalia's tour of duty ended. She was safely transported back to the United States, eventually mustered out of the Army, and returned to her family and civilian life. As the years passed, it became more and more difficult for her to shake the vivid images and negative emotions that continued to invade nearly every waking moment. She became more and more unable to tolerate the trauma due to the high levels of horror she experienced during this event and others, the helplessness and guilt she continued to feel about her inability to save injured colleagues, and the possibility that she shot and possibly killed a civilian as part of the outcome.

As she became more and more angry, Amalia began drinking and isolating from her husband, children, other family members, and friends. She survived the roadside blast, but years later her seemingly lifeless body was found next to an empty bottle of pills. Taken away by ambulance and revived, she was sent for psychological treatment. Amalia was eventually diagnosed with posttraumatic stress disorder (PTSD) and a traumatic brain injury (TBI), but only after many doctors' visits and a course of six different medications throughout the intervening months. It was from another veteran that she heard about EMDR therapy and decided to try it.

When Amalia presented to therapy, she reported intrusive memories in terms of images, thoughts,and smells; nightmares; flashbacks; inability to concentrate; avoidance of anything that reminded her of the event; and sleep difficulties. She often felt tearful, anxious, angry, and irritable. She reported a lot of shame and anxiety about letting her comrades down, and up to this point had been reluctant to openly discuss with others about the IED explosion and other traumatic events experienced while deployed in Afghanistan.

Even several years after her tour of duty, she was still living with debilitating symptoms from her brain injuries. She suffered from headaches, memory loss, and hearing and balance problems. She had difficulty getting and holding a job, found herself drinking too much, and dealt with high levels of anxiety on a daily basis. Finally, her clinician appropriately diagnosed her with PTSD.

Although Amalia grew up in a highly dysfunctional home where issues of verbal, physical, and sexual abuse were a daily occurrence, her prominent symptoms were obviously exacerbated by the combat trauma experienced in Afghanistan. A clinical decision was made to address first the trauma from her combat encounters. Here is an example of one of her most powerful sessions using the standard EMDR therapy protocol.

ASSESSMENT

Target:	IED explosion
Worst part:	When I woke up a medic was trying to perform a field tracheotomy on me.
Negative cognition (NC):	I'm powerless.
Positive cognition (PC):	I have some power.
Validity of Cognition (VoC):	2
Emotions:	Fear, anger, guilt
Subjective Units of Disturbance (SUD):	10
Body:	All over

DESENSITIZATION

Safety/Vulnerability Plateau

Clinician: Bring up the image (or picture), those words, "I'm powerless," and where you <u>feel</u> it in your body. Just let whatever happens, happen (set of bilateral stimulation [BLS]). Take a breath. (Pause.) Let it go. (Pause.) What's happening <u>now</u>?

Amalia: I had been unconscious. The first thing I remember is having a medic leaning over me with a knife. He was getting ready to make an incision in my neck so he could put in a tracheal tube. When I opened my eyes and gasped, he quit. Apparently my chest was pulsating, but I was not breathing. He couldn't hear any breath sounds. I was unconscious and, because my mouth was full of dirt and blood, I could not breathe. That's when I woke up. Even with a collapsed lung, I could breathe on my own.

Clinician: Go with that (set of BLS). Good. That's it. Take a breath. (Pause.) Let it go. (Pause.) What's coming up <u>now</u>?

Amalia: I saw a flash of light. And flames. I did not see it coming. The Humvee hit a big rock and went airborne. The rest is a blur.

Clinician: Go with that (set of BLS). Good. That's it. Take a breath. (Pause.) Let it go. (Pause.) What are you noticing <u>now</u>?

Amalia: I thought I was dying. When I woke up with the field medic over me, I could not believe it. Even with all the injuries I had sustained I was still able to stand up. My adrenaline was pumping. I was anticipating another IED hit, and I wanted to be ready. When I looked around, all I saw were Afghani civilians harvesting wheat in the fields. It was like nothing had happened.

Clinician: Go with that (set of BLS). Good. That's it. Take a breath. (Pause.) Let it go. (Pause.) What's happening <u>now</u>?

Amalia: I can feel the pain in my face and right side. I can't catch my breath.

Amalia is experiencing a body memory.

Clinician: Go with that (set of BLS). Good. That's it. Take a breath. (Pause.) Let it go. (Pause.) What's coming up <u>now</u>?

Amalia: Struggling to stand, the medic cut open my fatigue to get a look at what was lodged in my right side. It was a piece of shrapnel. My skin was stuck to my uniform. They cut the sleeve on my left arm and pulled the cloth away. It hurt like hell. The flesh had peeled away on my arm. I thought I was going to puke. I almost passed out.

Clinician: Go with that (set of BLS). Good. That's it. Take a breath. (Pause.) Let it go. (Pause.) What are you noticing <u>now</u>?

Amalia: I remember picking sand off my face and out of my ears. I had a massive headache. It was a couple of years before I was diagnosed with a TBI.

Clinician: Go with that (set of BLS). Good. That's it. Take a breath. (Pause.) Let it go. (Pause.) What's coming up <u>now</u>?

Amalia: I am starting to distance myself from the explosion. I feel better.

Clinician: Go with that (set of BLS). Good. That's it. Take a breath. (Pause.) Let it go. (Pause.) What's happening now?

Amalia: I just see an outline of the Humvee. Somehow it is no longer disturbing.

Clinician: Go with that (set of BLS). Good. That's it. Take a breath. (Pause.) Let it go. (Pause.) What are you noticing <u>now</u>?

Responsibility/Action ("I Did Something Wrong") Plateau

Amalia: I see my two companions lying next to the burned-out Humvee. They were not moving. Medics were trying to treat them. I could hear one of them moaning. Another informational plateau of the memory arises.

Clinician: Go with that (set of BLS). Good. That's it. Take a breath. (Pause.) Let it go. (Pause.) What's coming up <u>now</u>?

Amalia: I remember when I first saw them. They looked like they were not breathing. I was not sure. I felt dizzy and wanted to vomit. The medic told me that they were still alive. I got some comfort from that even though they were obviously severely injured.

Clinician: Go with that (set of BLS). Good. That's it. Take a breath. (Pause.) Let it go. (Pause.) What are you noticing <u>now</u>?

Amalia: When I finally got back to my unit, I heard that my two companions had died from their wounds. I felt so guilty. Why them and not me? It was my job to get them back to base unharmed.

Clinician: Go with that (set of BLS). Good. That's it. Take a breath. (Pause.) Let it go. (Pause.) What are you noticing now?

Amalia: It reminds me of another incident. I remember when we were just rolling down a hill. I was eating a mostly melted Hershey bar and minding my own business as we were riding along. I saw a flash to the front, and to the left of me was a passing fuel tanker in a convoy going the other way. The tanker was on fire and billowing orange smoke. My lieutenant pulled me down into the safety of the Humvee as the truck beside us exploded, and a torrential downfall of hot diesel fuel sprayed on and soaked me down to my underwear. Diesel was in my eyes, mouth, ears, and nose. I had to ride for hours with burning eyes and skin and a splitting headache. I could hear the soldiers in the other truck moaning and screaming. I should have done something then. I should have done something when the IED exploded. I should have reacted sooner. I let these soldiers down. It's my fault. I feel so weak.

Amalia tapped into an associative link. She feels intense guilt for not doing something more to save her comrades. She feels powerless because there was nothing she could do in either situation. These outcomes were beyond her control.

Clinician:	Go with that (set of BLS). Good. That's it. Take a breath. (Pause.) Let it go. (Pause.) What are you getting <u>now</u>?
Amalia:	I should have done something. I should have seen it coming. Two men are dead because of me.
Clinician:	Go with that (set of BLS). Good. That's it. Take a breath. (Pause.) Let it go. (Pause.) What is happening <u>now</u>?
Amalia:	I just feel so guilty and sad. You should have seen the look on their faces as they laid facing upward. I felt so bad.
Clinician:	Where do you feel it in your body?
Amalia:	In my back. It is a heavy burden to carry.
Clinician:	Notice that (set of BLS). Good. That's it. Take a breath. (Pause.) Let it go. (Pause.) What are you getting <u>now</u>?
Amalia:	It's my fault. I should have paid better attention.

Amalia is struggling with survivor's guilt. She is questioning the reasons she was spared and doubting her actions or lack of them before, during, and after the IED hit the Humvee. Survivor's guilt is a burden that many military personnel and veterans feel after surviving a battle or returning home when others did not. So many of their comrades never make it back home. This guilt often raises questions of responsibility and worthiness along with intense feelings, thoughts, and self-doubt coupled with the relief and gratitude that one might feel for surviving combat and the guilt and shame for the same when many comrades did not.

Clinician:	I'm confused. Did your friend Joe survive his deployment?

The clinician implements a cognitive interweave to dislodge Amalia's notion that it is not okay to survive the war when others did not.

Amalia:	Yes.
Clinician:	Did Joe deserve to die so others could live?
Amalia:	No. Of course not. No one deserves to die in combat. It's the roll of the dice. He died. I lived.
Clinician:	Notice that (set of BLS). Good. That's it. Take a breath. (Pause.) Let it go. (Pause.) What are you getting <u>now</u>?
Amalia:	I survived. It's okay.

Clinician: Notice that (set of BLS). Good. That's it. Take a breath. (Pause.) Let it go. (Pause.) What are you noticing <u>now</u>?

Amalia: It's okay. I'm okay. It's over.

Control/Power/Choice Plateau

Clinician: Amalia, go back to the original event and tell me what you are getting <u>now</u>.

Amalia: More memories of this event and others keep coming up. Some bad shit happened.

Clinician: Notice that (set of BLS). Good. That's it. Take a breath. (Pause.) Let it go. (Pause.) What's coming up <u>now</u>?

Amalia: It's becoming clearer. I was not knocked unconscious by the Humvee flipping over. Something else happened.

Clinician: Notice that (set of BLS). Good. That's it. Take a breath. (Pause.) Let it go. (Pause.) What's happening <u>now</u>?

Amalia: This is a part I have tried to forget. When the Humvee flipped over on its side, we all got out and tried to secure the area until we could evaluate all the wounded. We just shot hundreds of rounds down the road.

Clinician: Notice that (set of BLS). Good. That's it. Take a breath. (Pause.) Let it go. (Pause.) What are you noticing <u>now</u>?

Amalia: I caught sight of an Afghani darting in and out of cars as he was running down the road toward where other fighting was going on. I ran toward him. When he turned in a threatening way, I saw the threat, aimed, and fired. I hit him in his arm and side. The Afghani stumbled, darted into an alley, and disappeared inside a building. I never knew if I killed him or not. It all happened so fast. Seconds. Only seconds to potentially take a man's life for eternity. I don't even know if he was a soldier or not. He might have been a civilian. It was then that I collapsed and minutes later I woke up with the medic getting ready to put a field tracheotomy in my neck.

Amalia is beginning to question the decisiveness of her response that day. "Did I or did I not kill a civilian?" This is a question she has pondered long after her deployment in Afghanistan had ended.

Clinician: Notice that (set of BLS). Good. That's it. Take a breath. (Pause.) Let it go. (Pause.) What's happening <u>now</u>?

Amalia: We were in the middle of a firefight with wounded comrades to protect. I had to shoot. I couldn't risk it. I had to react so fast. I didn't have a choice.

Amalia knows even now why she made the decision to shoot the man, even though he might have been unarmed. The Afghani appeared to have acted in a strange and threatening way. The way he was moving made no sense. And, after just having extricated herself from a downed Humvee, shooting seemed the only viable option in that moment. This was war. She did not have the option of long deliberation before she acted. She only had seconds to decide.

Clinician: Notice that (set of BLS). Good. That's it. Take a breath. (Pause.) Let it go. (Pause.) What's coming up <u>now</u>?

Amalia: I began to second-guess myself. Insurgents are generally hardened, well-trained professionals and probably would not be dumb enough to act as erratically and threateningly in the way that he did. I worry that I shot a civilian and he was running for safety. He might not have posed any threat at all, and I shot and killed him.

Clinician: Notice that (set of BLS). Good. That's it. Take a breath. (Pause.) Let it go. (Pause.) What's happening <u>now</u>?

Amalia: I just felt like I had no choice. It was "us" or "them" in that moment. I chose "us."

Clinician: Notice that (set of BLS). Good. That's it. Take a breath. (Pause.) Let it go. (Pause.) What are you noticing <u>now</u>?

Amalia: I might have shot and killed an innocent man. This thought has caused me years of unbelievable emotional pain. There are days I cannot stop thinking about it.

Many soldiers return home to be continually haunted by what they did during wartime. This is called *moral injury,* and it can be more devastating than the physical wounds they bear that remind them every day where they have been and what they have done. It is a battlefield injury like no other.

Clinician: Notice that (set of BLS). Good. That's it. Take a breath. (Pause.) Let it go. (Pause.) What's coming up <u>now</u>?

Amalia: How does one justify killing someone unnecessarily? I don't know how to do that.

Amalia struggled to identify a different perspective to her experience in Afghanistan. Killing enemies may be justified during wartime, but the killing of a civilian is morally unacceptable at any time. At this point the clinician introduces an intervention to help her write a list and understand what her options were that day and an atonement metaphor as an alternative to punishment in the form of a cognitive interweave (Silver & Rogers, 2002).

Clinician: Let's explore other elements that influenced this method in an effort to help you gain a realistic self-appraisal of what really happened. I want you to draw a pie-shaped diagram on this sheet of paper and divide it into wedges to designate what portion of the responsibility belongs to each. Can you do that?

At this point, the clinician introduced a pie-shaped diagram which represented total responsibility for the killing. Each wedge of the pie was to designate different elements of responsibility.

Amalia: Yes.

Amalia quickly drew the diagram and filled out the wedges and then shared it with the clinician.

Clinician: What did you come up with?

Amalia: I had never thought about it in this way. What I came up with was my operating orders, the nature of the war in Afghanistan, my own psychological and physical fatigue at the time of the event, the necessity of my having to react quickly in a life-threatening situation, the fallen comrades who were my responsibility to protect from further harm, and the Afghani's decision to act strangely and erratically. I had no idea what he was up to or if he was a real threat to me. I just reacted. It was my finger on the trigger.

Clinician: Notice that (set of BLS). Good. That's it. Take a breath. (Pause.). Let it go. (Pause.) What's happening <u>now</u>?

Amalia: Wow. That was helpful. I still feel bad about the Afghani. I wish there was something I could do about it.

Note: At this point the clinician introduced the atonement metaphor. Using the knights of history and their moral codes (e.g., personal morality, church law, Code of Chivalry), the clinician explains how they rectified their guilt and remorse for the past acts of violence they had committed. Local priests realized early that acts of contrition or physical punishment did not work so well with the knights. The priests gave the knights a task to perform instead in the form of atonement (or payback). If the knight had become unwanted, unruly, and drunk and destroyed a tavern, he would be given the task of rebuilding it. But atonement in this form was not so easy to repair if one had killed or raped instead. In these cases, the scales of justice continued to remain out of balance. What the priests proposed was for the knights to rebalance the scale to place more weight on the positive side by performing a positive act of some kind (e.g., capturing outlaws and bandits, guarding the village so that the villagers felt safe; Silver & Rogers, 2002).

The primary tasks of atonement are offering something that makes an unusual demand on the client, should benefit others, and makes use of the client's abilities. With the clinician's help, the client is able to determine what would be appropriate for her (e.g., volunteer work of any kind with veterans, children, or animals). It must be appropriate for the client to succeed.

Clinician: The knights of yore had a similar issue after getting drunk and pillaging villages and raping their women. And, in doing so, they dishonored the moral code of knights. Upon waking up from a drunken rampage, they felt much guilt and sometimes found no relief wandering the country, feeling disconnected and alone, and often dying unnecessarily in battle to escape the pain. Acts of contrition and prayer or physical punishment did not work with them. Remember, pain was their profession. They were taught to endure pain and suffering for their people. So, the priests gave the knights tasks. They suggested that the knights perform some acts of atonement to help ease their pain. They rebuilt taverns they destroyed, replanted fields they burned, and mended fences they trampled. For those whose sins encompassed rape and murder, it was not so easy. So, the priests asked the knights to do something outside of their comfort zone that would benefit others and use what skills they possessed to do so. Is this something you would be interested in? Is there something you could do to atone for your action that would help you to feel better?

Amalia thought about it for a minute before she responded.

Amalia: I think that would make me feel better. I need to do something. I am willing to try. Maybe I could volunteer somewhere. I always wanted to work with children. Maybe I could do something with them.

Clinician: Notice that (set of BLS). Good. That's it. Take a breath. (Pause.) Let it go. (Pause.) What's coming up <u>now</u>?

Amalia: I am going to search my local community for a volunteer opportunity. I need to find a way to give back, to balance my own scales.

Clinician: Amalia, go back to the original event and tell me what you are getting <u>now</u>.

Amalia: It's hard to bring up. It's distant. I have so many other positive things to focus on now.

Clinician: Notice that (set of BLS). Good. That's it. Take a breath. (Pause.) Let it go. (Pause.) What are you noticing <u>now</u>?

Amalia: I am feeling pretty calm. It's difficult to focus on the event.

Clinician: Go back to the original event and tell me what you are getting <u>now</u>.

Amalia: It's all a blur. A good blur. I feel good for the first time in a long time.

Clinician: When you focus on the <u>original</u> event (incident, experience), on a scale from 0 to 10, where 0 is neutral or no disturbance and 10 is the worst disturbance you can imagine, how disturbing is the event (incident, experience) to you <u>now</u>?

Amalia: It's 0.5. I don't think it could ever be a 0. I might have killed an innocent person.

Because of the ecological validity inherent in this statement, the clinician readily accepts a SUD equal to 0.5, and the phase was completed as the clinician proceeded to the Installation and Body Scan phases. Nothing unordinary came up, and the client was sent home understanding what had happened and what she could do to continue to feel better.

Note: Humvee (HMMWV), high mobility multi-purpose wheeled vehicle; IED, improvised explosive device.

EMDR WITH CHILDREN

There are many problems potentially facing a child in today's world that cause ongoing stress (e.g., poverty, familial alcohol/drug problems, homelessness, food insecurity, school issues, peer difficulties, and family problems) that may have a detrimental impact on a child's development, learning, and behavior. In addition, a child may experience a traumatic event(s), such as sexual or physical abuse, vehicular or other accidents, community or school violence, losses, divorce, domestic violence, medical trauma, natural or man-made disasters, war or acts of terrorism, or medical care for unintentional injuries (e.g., dog bites, drownings, falls, fires) as well as circumstances of verbal or emotional abuse in the form of bullying, teasing, humiliation, embarrassment, and shame that may have become a frequent occurrence in a child's life.

Often when a child is traumatized by distressing or traumatic events, losses, or repeated failures, they may experience a loss of control/power over their life. This loss may result in symptoms of anxiety and depression; self-destructive behaviors (e.g., self-mutilation, over/undereating, pica, addiction); nightmares and other sleep disturbances; increased fear; decreased concentration; loss of interest in normal activities; poor self-esteem and self-confidence; irritability, anger, self-blame, guilt, and shame; somatic complaints (e.g., pain, digestive issues, constipation); feelings of helplessness and hopelessness; and negative behavioral issues at home and school. These distressing/traumatic events and subsequent symptoms may then affect the child's sense of self and identity in terms of ongoing development, self-esteem, and sense of security.

As children often respond very well to it, EMDR therapy becomes an effective approach for helping a child regain balance, restore trust, and move toward healthier thoughts, emotions, behaviors, and bodily states. EMDR therapy with children comes with its challenges and often with alternate pathways of organizing the eight phases of treatment to meet the developmental demands of each child. Other child-related psychotherapy interventions and strategies (e.g., play or art therapy) may be utilized in conjunction with EMDR therapy to make it more efficient and developmentally appropriate for children.

The modifications needed to successfully treat children occur in all eight phases and all prongs of EMDR therapy. Throughout the phases, the clinician needs to use developmentally appropriate language to ensure that the child understands the process at hand. Examples of the modifications often needed in using EMDR therapy with children are outlined below phase by phase.

PHASE 1—HISTORY-TAKING AND TREATMENT PLANNING

At the beginning of EMDR therapy, the clinician facilitates the completion of the child's trauma history with input from biological and foster parents, guardians (e.g., immediate family members, close family friends), counselors, case workers, and, obviously, with the child. Informed consent around the explanation of EMDR therapy is facilitated with the child and the parent(s), if available. Often in collaboration with the parent(s) and/or guardians, the development of a treatment plan can be implemented. Modified versions of direct questioning, floatback, and affect scan may be utilized to elicit a child's touchstone memory.

Target events could be preverbal or verbal. They may be identified using a memory wand (Gomez, 2013), mapping (Adler-Tapia & Settle, 2008), and other means. Targets are reported by parents/guardians and the child. It is in this stage that the clinician begins to actively assess for dissociation and will continue to do so through the rest of the phases as they occur.

PHASE 2—PREPARATION

There are a variety of stories, metaphors, and strategies (Adler-Tapia & Settle, 2008; Gomez, 2013; Greenwald, 1999) available to explain EMDR therapy to children. If the Safe (Calm) Place exercise is utilized, it may be real or imagined. The clinician will also work with the child and parents to ensure the child's capacity for self-regulation and interactive regulation as well as affect tolerance.

Because of the lack of conceptual understanding or ability to focus, some children, especially the young ones, respond better to something other than eye movements using the clinician's fingers to facilitate processing. If eye movements are implemented, they may be done with wands, puppets, or other forms of BLS, such as tactile (e.g., patty cake, butterfly hug, buzzies) and auditory (e.g., music, mechanical devices). In some cases, the systemic use of EMDR therapy may be necessary when adversity is currently occurring in the child's environment. It is especially true if the wounding is taking place in the parent-to-child relationship. During the Preparation Phase, significant work with caregivers may be indispensable if the child's symptoms reflect generational wounding. Restoring safety and connection in the parent-child relationship needs to be an important goal of the Preparation Phase with children. If dissociation is actively present, specific preparation strategies should be used to ensure that the child is able to maintain dual awareness.

PHASE 3—ASSESSMENT

Use of the standardized script for the assessment questions obviously does not work well with children, especially the young ones.

Image

Rather than asking a child what image/picture represents the worst part of a targeted memory, the clinician may elicit it by calling it something the child will understand, such as "yucky thing" (Gomez, 2013) or "owie" (Adler-Tapia & Settle, 2008), asking the child to draw a picture, using puppets or toys (or a therapy dog) to talk for them, or utilizing a sand tray to help distance the child from the event. In this case the question may be directed to a character of the story created by the child. The image may be elicited using drawing, collaging, or digital pictures (Adler-Tapia & Settle, 2008).

Cognitions

NC and PC need to be developmentally appropriate. When using with younger children, time is not necessarily taken to tease out the best phrased and compatible cognitions. With older children, pre-printed cards containing appropriate cognitions may be utilized if the child has difficulty coming up with one. Or a kid's list of cognitions (Adler-Tapia & Settle, 2008) may be utilized to help the child determine NC and PC that fit best with the image/event.

Validity of Cognition

In taking this measurement, developmentally appropriate language needs to be utilized for eliciting it. Trauma Recovery—Humanitarian Assistance Program (HAP) sells a placard with NC and PC on one side and numbered scales and faces which can help smaller children provide VoC and SUD measurements. A thought scale (Gomez, 2013), where the child points to a section of a large-scale number 1 to 7, or the VoC bridge (Adler-Tapia & Settle, 2008), where the child identifies the bad thought and the good thought on paper, may be utilized to identify the validity of the PC.

Emotions

If the child has a difficult time describing what is felt during this part of the assessment, the clinician could use a feelings poster where the child points to the face that corresponds to their feelings or use feeling cards, cubes, or a feeling finder/detector (Gomez, 2013) to identify the emotions associated with a specific traumatic or distressing image or event.

Subjective Units of Disturbance

See *VoC* above. The bother scale may also be utilized to determine the child's level of disturbance with the image/event (Gomez, 2013).

Body Sensations

The child may be able to point to the place on the body where there is discomfort. A feeling finder or detector (Gomez, 2013) could be a magnifying glass that the child uses to find where the emotions are being felt in the body.

PHASE 4—DESENSITIZATION

The sets of eye movements for reprocessing are generally shorter for younger children because of the inability to maintain focus for longer periods of time. Use of storytelling could facilitate smoother processing. Developmentally appropriate interweaves may be utilized that involve storytelling, metaphors, or the execution of responses the child could not complete during the traumatic event. In addition, the parent may be asked to accompany the child to provide interweaves which repair and meet the child's unmet attachment needs under the guidance of the clinician.

PHASE 5—INSTALLATION

Again, the HAP placard, VoC bridge (Adler-Tapia & Settle, 2008), or thought scale (Gomez, 2013) may be used to help the child determine the validity of the chosen PC in this phase. The PC may be embodied by asking the child to identify how the body would express the positive belief (Ogden & Gomez, 2013).

PHASE 6—BODY SCAN

Use of developmentally appropriate language is also needed here. A magnifying glass could be utilized in this phase to help a child determine the location on the child's body where the trauma is still felt. Playful ways of accessing the body, such as body outlines the child colors to denote the areas where sensations are experienced, may be used as well.

PHASE 7—CLOSURE

During this phase, the child may be directed back to use the container and the safe (calm) place developed during the Preparation Phase. However, it is important to select the closure activities and resources based on where the child is at the end of the session. For a child who is culminating the session in a state of hyperactivation, downregulating strategies that bring the child to a much calmer state are recommended. Conversely, for a child who ends the session in a state of hypoactivation or emotionally and physiologically shut down, upregulating strategies may be recommended. Running, jumping, singing, and using musical instruments as an alternative to the container exercise would be more effective in bringing the child into a state of balance.

PHASE 8—REEVALUATION

A discussion may be pursued with the child and the parent(s) or guardian as to the child's overall progress as a result of engaging in EMDR therapy. What changes have occurred? What had they noticed that is different? If the child is not showing progress, what are the barriers keeping the child from healing and moving forward?

OTHER PRONGS

As with adults, the clinician will process present and potential triggers with the child and install future templates to ensure adaptive responses.

SAMPLE SESSION WITH CHILD

A simple sample session using the standard EMDR therapy protocol with a male child is described below to demonstrate some of the possible themes that may arise during processing. The sample script was patterned after the script and props (i.e., thought and bothering scales, and thought cards, ball, or cubes, feeling finder or detector) utilized by Gomez (2013) to facilitate EMDR with children to demonstrate the different strategies and techniques that can be used with children during Phases 3 through 6.

When Andrés was 3 years old, he was diagnosed with hip dysplasia and subsequently had to endure an experimental surgery to realign his hip and lengthen one of his legs to match the other. He was placed in a body cast to prevent hip and leg movement after surgery and remained in the hospital for a period of 8 months as the doctors monitored the outcome and progress of the surgery. During the long months in the hospital, he experienced myriad negative emotions (e.g., fear, anger, loneliness, isolation, anxiety) and physical conditions associated with the discomfort of the after-surgery and the long, grueling months of being in a hospital room by himself.

Because it was an experimental surgery and he was only 3 years old, the physicians took great care to ensure he would not to be able to do anything which might hinder his progress. During the 8 months, Andrés suffered from a variety of physical conditions, such as cast burns from the heat by hardening; urinary tract infections and other complications caused by his pediatric catheter; severe pain, weakness, or numbness in his legs; pain and swelling in the hip area; skin and pressure sores; joint stiffness and muscle atrophy; numbness and tingling in his extremities; unusual odors, sensations, or wounds beneath the cast; extreme itching sensations under the cast; and circulation problems.

As he was unable to go to day care or hang out at home with his siblings, he suffered severe psychological symptoms caused by the isolation he felt. Although he saw them every day while in the hospital, he only saw his parents a couple of hours every day. His friends and classmates would come to visit once in a while to talk and play games with him. The people he interacted with most were his hospital caretakers. The loneliest time for him was at night when he was by himself, his room was dark, and he unable to fall asleep. The loneliness and social isolation took a bigger toll on him than his physical symptoms. He exhibited signs of depression and anxiety and began to have anxiety attacks while still in the hospital. He was tired and lost his motivation and experienced sleep issues and loss of appetite.

When he was 6 years old, his parents brought him to therapy because his anxiety had increased significantly and anxiety attacks, nightmares, and night terrors had become more frequent.

His parents provided a complete history during the initial intake. The clinician executed a thorough exploration of Andrés's life, including experiences with all his attachment figures. During the initial meetings with Andrés, the clinician worked on helping him build safety and trust as well as attunement in terms of pace and rhythm; the Safe (Calm) Place exercise was utilized in addition to other resources to increase his capacity to affect a state change; affect tolerance was increased by inviting him to "visit feelings" (Gomez, 2019); and the parents worked with the clinician to facilitate the likelihood of co-regulation with Andrés.

The following session targets his stay in the hospital immediately after his surgery. There were many other sessions after this to process things that occurred during his eight-month stay.

Assessment

Target
Clinician: How about we start with the *yucky thing* in the hospital we discussed today?
Andrés: Okay.

Andrés identified a target by creating a timeline with pictures and drawings of positive experiences and traumatic experiences that occurred throughout his life. The positive experiences Andrés identified were later installed using slow and short sets of BLS. The initial memory that Andrés and the clinician chose was the time he was taken to the hospital. Because Andrés was 6 years old at the time, the clinician referred to the hip surgery as a "yucky thing" (Gomez, 2013) throughout the session utilizing EMDR therapy.

Worst Part

Clinician: What is the worst part of the *yucky thing* in the hospital that happened to you? Can you draw a picture of it?

Andrés draws a picture of himself lying in a hospital bed with a full body cast.

Negative Cognition

Clinician: When you think of the *yucky thing*, what *mixed-up thought* do you have about yourself right now?

Andrés was given the choice of using the thought cards, ball, or cubes or the Thoughts Kit for Kids to find the *mixed-up thought* he had when he focused on the cast. As he had learned to read at an early age because of his condition, he elected to use the thought cubes.

Thought cubes (Gomez, 2013) are wooden cubes with negative beliefs suitable for children written on the sides. Andrés easily selected one he believed focused on his negative belief about himself as he focused on the picture he drew.

Andrés: I deserve bad things.

Positive Cognition

Clinician: When you focus on your drawing, what *good thought* would you like to have about yourself right now?

Andrés was again provided the option of the thought cards, ball, or cubes or the Thoughts Kit for Kids to find the *good thought*. He elected to use the thought cubes and chose a belief that was opposite to the one he selected above.

Andrés: I deserve good things.

Validity of Cognition

Clinician: We are going to use the thought scale in front on you. This scale will help you check how true the *good thought* that you chose feels to you now. This is how it works. The scale has numbers from 1 to 7. Number 1 means the thought does not feel very true and 7 means the thought really feels true. When you focus on your drawing, how true do the words, "I deserve good things," where 1 feels completely false and 7 feels completely true, feel to you now?

The thought scale is made up of foam squares with a number from 1 to 7. The squares are lined up in front of the child in a 1 to 7 sequence. With a helper or small doll chosen by the child before the beginning of the session, the child walks the doll down to the number that represents a measurement of how true a PC feels to him.

Andrés: It's not a 1. Maybe it's a 2. It's not a 3. It must be 2.

Emotions
Clinician: When you focus on your drawing and those words, "I deserve bad things," what feelings do you have now?

Feeling cards were given to Andrés for him to choose.

Andrés: I am mad. Sad. Scared.

Subjective Units of Disturbance
Clinician: We are going to use the bothering scale (Gomez, 2013) in front of you. This scale will help you check how much the *yucky thing* bothers you now. It has numbers from 0 to 10. The 0 means the *yucky thing* does not bother you at all and the 10 that it bothers you a lot. This is how it works. When you focus on your drawing and the *mixed-up thought*, how true do the words, "I deserve bad things," bother you now?

The bothering scale is made up of foam squares with a number from 0 to 10. The squares are lined up in front of the child in a sequence from 0 to 10. With a helper or small doll chosen by the child before the beginning of the session, the child walks the doll down to the number that best represents how disturbing the *yucky thing* is to him now.

Andrés: 10

Andrés slid the doll quickly down to the number 10.

Clinician: Now, use the feeling finder (or detector) to find where you feel it inside your body. (Pause.) Where do you feel it?
Andrés: All over.

Desensitization
Responsibility/Defectiveness Informational Plateau
Clinician: Andrés, focus on your drawing, the *mixed-up thought*, "I deserve bad things," and where you feel it in your body as I tap your knees.

Andrés selected tapping as his preferred mode of BLS.

Andrés: My legs hurt.
Clinician: Let's go with that (set of BLS). Good. That's it. Take a breath. (Pause.) What's coming up <u>now</u>?
Andrés: It is hot. Tight. (Andrés's breathing becomes shallower and restricted; his face reddens.)

Clinician: Let's go with that (set of BLS). Good. Good. Andrés, it's okay. It's in the past. (Andrés's breathing starts to even out, and his face begins to return to a pinkish hue.) Good (set of BLS continues). That's it. Let's take a breath. What is happening now?

Andrés: My mommy told me I was born with a bad hip. I thought it made me bad.

Clinician: Let's go with that (set of BLS). Good. That's it. Take a breath. (Pause.) Let it go. (Pause.) What's coming up now?

Andrés: Bad hip. Bad me.

Clinician: Let's go with that (set of BLS). Good. That's it. Take a breath. (Pause.) What's coming up now?

Andrés: I am good, not bad.

Clinician: Let's go with that (set of BLS). Good. That's it. Take a breath. (Pause.) What's coming up now?

Safety/Vulnerability Informational Plateau

Andrés: On the first week my daddy or mommy stayed with me all night. Then I had to stay by myself. It was so scary. I kept hearing scary noises. Loud footsteps outside my door. (Andrés covers his ears with his hands.)

What Andrés is describing are the noises from the machines he was hooked up to that measured his vital signs.

Clinician: Let's go with that (set of BLS). Good. That's it. Take a breath. (Pause.) What's coming up now?

Andrés: Nightmares of spiders. I would wake up and see huge spider webs coming out of me. I could not move. I wanted my mommy.

Andrés was hooked up to an IV, a blood pressure monitor, and a variety of other machines to monitor how he was doing. When he would wake up in the middle of the night from a deep sleep, what he saw were something that resembled spider webs.

Clinician: Let's go with that (set of BLS). Good. That's it. Take a breath. (Pause.) What's coming up now?

Andrés: I see my bed at home. And my Spiderman blankie. It's so soft.

Clinician: Let's go with that (set of BLS). Good. That's it. Take a breath. (Pause.) What's coming up now?

Andrés: The Spiderman blankie. It was there with me. My mommy brought it from home, and it was on the bed in the hospital.

Clinician: Let's go with that (set of BLS). Good. That's it. Take a breath. (Pause.) What's coming up now?

Control/Power/Choice Informational Plateau

Andrés: I couldn't get out of bed by myself. I was stuck.

Clinician: Let's go with that (set of BLS). Good. That's it. Take a breath. (Pause.) What's coming up now?

Andrés: I couldn't get up to go to the bathroom by myself.

Clinician: Let's go with that (set of BLS). Good. That's it. Take a breath. (Pause.) What's coming up now?

Andrés: It was so hard to roll over. I am on my back. I had something stuck up my pee-pee. It hurt.

Because he needed to stay immobile as much as possible, he had to have a pediatric catheter inserted.

Clinician: Let's go with that (set of BLS). Good. That's it. Take a breath. (Pause.) What's coming up <u>now</u>?

Andrés: I hurt all over. Itchy. Smelly. (Andrés pinched his nostrils together with his index finger and thumb.) Phewie!

Clinician: Let's go with that (set of BLS). Good. That's it. Take a breath. (Pause.) What's coming up <u>now</u>?

Andrés: I had peed on myself so much that my mommy had to throw away my Spiderman jammies and blankie. It made me cry.

Clinician: Let's go with that (set of BLS). Good. That's it. Take a breath. (Pause.) What's coming up <u>now</u>?

Andrés: The next Christmas Santa gave me new Spiderman jammies. And a Spiderman blankie.

The level of disturbance for this memory, VoC, and body scan all cleared with this memory. Because Andrés suffered from a variety of traumas over a period of 9 months, several other targets needed to be processed before his symptoms resolved and he returned to normal functioning. Andrés's mother accompanied him during some of the processing sessions. When information processing was stuck, the clinician at times would invite a parent to participate. In one of the sessions, Andrés reported repeatedly feeling fearful and not safe. The clinician then used interweaves that could repair and meet the needs that were not met during the traumatic event. Here is an example of what could occur:

Clinician: Andrés, as you see your scary feelings while you are in the hospital, can you ask "little Andrés" what he wanted to have and what he needed right there?

Andrés: I needed my mommy and felt lonely and scared.

Clinician: Let's go with that (set of BLS). Good. That's it. Take a breath. (Pause.) What's coming up <u>now</u>?

Andrés: I needed my mommy, I feel scared.

Clinician: Can we invite mom to be right there with you and "little Andrés?"

Andrés: Okay.

Clinician: Mom, may I invite you to sit by Andrés? Andrés, can you tell mom what you wanted her to do and say?

Andrés: I want mommy to hold me and tell me I am okay.

Clinician: Mom, can you hold Andrés and tell him that he and "little Andrés" are now okay?

Mother: *(holding Andrés):* Andrés and "little Andrés, I am right here with you, and, guess what? You are safe and okay now. It is over … it is over and we are safe now.

The clinician initiates BLS while the mother is providing a reparative interweave that restores safety and helps Andrés locate the memory in time and space (i.e., "It's over. You are okay and safe now") and meets the need of companionship.

Clinician: Let's go with that (set of BLS). Good. That's it. Take a breath. (Pause.) What's coming up <u>now</u>?
Andrés: I feel good.
Clinician: Let's go with that.

Unfortunately, it is beyond the scope of the Primer to highlight specifically all the wonderful strategies, techniques, metaphors, and other resources created throughout the past 30 years to deal with the child population.

EMDR WITH CULTURALLY DIVERSE POPULATIONS

Treating mental health issues presented by clients with an awareness of cultural context is a growing trend for a widening diversity of social identities and cultural populations. The stories abound in our multicultural society of the discrimination and mistreatment of individuals as a result of, but not limited to, gender, ethnicity and race, socio-economic status, sexual orientation, geographic origin, gender identification, age, and religious affiliation. Detailed considerations for specific cultural populations are beyond the scope of this Primer; however, cultural competency is not. As there is not the time or space to cover the differing and specific nuances and needs of each of the special groups mentioned above, the discussion below will evolve around the members of the transgender community as a specific example of the types of issues that may arise when working with different populations of clients.

Just like the military/veteran population described earlier, it is important for a clinician to develop cultural competency around dealing with transgender and gender non-conforming self-identities. For all special populations, cultural competency (aka multicultural competence; Pederson, 1988) is imperative when dealing with clients with transidentities (i.e., transgender identities, LGBTQ) and acts as an important and effective means of creating safe conditions for healing in contrast to the commonly experienced bias and phobias that constantly assail them. As a clinician, it is important to hone sensitivity to the challenges this cultural group routinely faces and to learn the terminology and language specific to their experience and culture. In doing so, the clinician is more likely to create and continue to provide a safer, more welcoming, well-informed, nondiscriminatory environment for transgender and other non-gender conforming clients to share their deepest fears and struggles.

As the transcript below demonstrates, transgender people traditionally have routinely been met with violence, harassment, and discrimination (Grant et al., 2011). Cultural competency ensures a clinician greater ability to communicate, understand, and interact with transgender clients (Office of Minority Health, 2013). Some of the other issues common to this cultural population relate to gender dysphoria and issues with same in early childhood (i.e., social discomfort), puberty (i.e., dealing with unwanted body changes), and early adulthood (i.e., addressing transgender issues, transitioning); post-transition issues; workplace discrimination; difficulties with stigma of being different and lack of acceptance; social discrimination; isolation; anxiety, depression and suicidal thoughts; and other mental health issues that arise outside of the transgender experience (Kaplan, 2019).

As Nickerson (2017a, 2017b) has stated, EMDR therapy is a culturally competent intervention that has become "a model of cultural competence" over the past 30 years. Covering a broad range of cultural contexts, it has proven efficacious; its clinicians have taken humanitarian efforts to aid culturally diverse peoples all over the world; it invites attunement and cultural awareness for both client and clinician; and it has the ability to resolve and heal the effects of oppression and social discrimination (Nickerson, 2017a, 2017b). Toward these culturally succinct goals, EMDR therapy clinicians worldwide have devised alternate treatment and protocols to specially deal with oppression, discrimination, and social prejudice. As these protocols are beyond the scope of the Primer, the standard EMDR therapy protocol will be utilized to highlight some of the possible issues that may surface when dealing with a female transgender client.

The following session with a transgender female demonstrates the relevance of cultural competence when treating a client who belongs to a culturally diverse population.

SAMPLE SESSION WITH A TRANSGENDER FEMALE

A sample session using the standard EMDR therapy protocol with a transgender female is described below to demonstrate some of the possible themes that may arise during processing.

Renee, meaning "born again" (formerly Liam) is a transgender female who grew up in a small town. Her family belonged to a church where women were still regarded as little better than cattle. It was in this same church where she dared to dream and pray to magically be transformed into a girl. But, believing men were supreme beings and God was a bully who hated women, Renee kept her secret tightly packed away until she was much older and living away from her family. When she was 18, she moved to a larger city north of where she lived so that she could be around others who struggled with the same issues of gender dysphoria.

It was not until she moved away that Renee decided to become "the woman" she so longed to be. She was at a place where to her there was no other alternative but to finally begin her transition to womanhood. Unfortunately, Renee was not able to begin her transition for another six years, at which point she started taking hormones and began the inquiry about getting an orchiectomy to finally remove her testicles. She came from a financially successful family, and she had a trust that became accessible to her when she turned 25 years old.

Once the trust had been granted, Renee began the long process of gender reassignment surgery (or sexual reassignment surgery) from male to female, which from start to finish would end by reshaping her penis and testicles into a vagina and clitoris so she could function emotionally, physically, and sexually as a female. Before this feminization process could even be accomplished, she had to spend a grueling year on hormone replacement therapy. She also opted for facial hair removal. At each stage, she planned the next stage based on the progress and outcome of the last. She eventually also elected to have a vaginoplasty and facial feminization surgery. These were all long, drawn out, and wearying processes for which she had to endure both physical and emotional suffering. Seeking out a qualified surgeon to perform the surgery also proved to be a difficult endeavor in the area in which she lived. There were still few choices at the time as to who could perform this type of gender-affirming surgery because of knowledge, skill, or bias. She only found one surgeon who was qualified to perform the surgery, but he worked for a hospital that did not agree with these types of surgeries and was not allowed to perform them on Renee. She finally did find one, but she had to move even further away from her hometown to obtain these much-desired procedures.

After a year or more of taking estrogen and anti-androgens, Renee's body started to change. Feminization was occurring. Her body hair started to slowly diminish on her torso and extremities and the fat on her body started redistributing to her thighs and buttocks. Her breasts began to develop slightly; her skin became softer. Her muscle mass changed significantly, and her testes and penis lessened in size. It was becoming more and more obvious to her and the local community that something was different with Renee. Except for the people closest to her in the LGBT community, most people still only knew her as Liam. She had not officially changed her name or affirmed her physical sex.

Because the hormones she recently began to take were at work rapidly changing the nature of her body, she began to fear going out in public—afraid that people in her neighborhood would notice, judge, and react negatively. Rapid changes were being made to her body that she would be hard pressed to explain to those around her. She became despondent and depressed. She was confused by the hospital's decision to prevent her from living a more normal life where she could live to be who she was and feel safe and happy. She wanted so much to feel relief from her gender dysphoria.

At the same time, as a result of the physical changes that her body was experiencing, Renee became more about living her life as a transgender woman and began to go shopping at the local shops for feminine clothes and to the local hair salons. However, the town in which she had chosen to live was not very accepting. One day while she was shopping for dresses, a representative of the store approached her and told her, "This is not a place for a person like you. Please leave immediately." Something similar happened to her at a salon the day she visited for a new hairdo. When the hair stylist saw that she was transgender, she made offensive, transphobic remarks to Renee. The hairdresser adamantly refused to cut Renee's hair. Renee left the dress shop and salon embarrassed, afraid, and ashamed. Her sense of self-worth was deeply affected by these and other similar experiences.

One night while in a local bar celebrating someone's birthday with other trans friends, a straight couple began to harass them by calling them "men" and other transphobic names. One man and his female companion attacked her, and another man knocked her off her chair and tried to physically shove her out the door. Not long after, the bouncer threw her and all her trans friends out into the street. These kinds of occurrences were common and left many in the transgender community on edge.

Renee eventually was able to find a doctor in a larger city to perform the sexual reassignment surgeries she continued to desperately want. Sex reassignment surgery (SRS) or gender-affirming surgery had always been her goal, but it was not the end of her journey from once being a man to becoming forever a woman. Post-surgery, she initially felt that the surgery was a terrible mistake, and she silently harbored much regret as she became excessively fatigued and disappointed. The lack of physical energy caused by the sex hormone depletion was overwhelming. She suffered from increased anxiety, panic attacks, depression and suicidal ideation, and mood swings mainly due to hormonal deficiency and metered hormonal care. Friends reported a marked change in her personality. She struggled with cognitive deficiencies, such as memory loss and concentration difficulties, frequent headaches, and other generalized aches and pains.

Assessment

Target:	Being verbally and physically attacked with friends in a bar
Worst part:	Being called names, such as tranny, he-she, and freak
NC:	I am in danger.
PC:	It's over. I am safe now.
VoC:	2
Emotions:	Fear, sadness, disgust
SUD:	10
Body:	Heart, stomach

Desensitization

Safety/Vulnerability Plateau

Clinician: Bring up the image (or picture), those words, "I am in danger," and where you <u>feel</u> it in your body. Just let whatever happens, happen (set of BLS). Take a breath. (Pause.) Let it go. (Pause.) What's happening <u>now</u>?

Renee: I am shaking … it's difficult to breathe. I continue to see the hatred in their eyes and hear the disgust in the tone of their voices.

Clinician: Go with that (set of BLS). Good. That's it. Take a breath. (Pause.) Let it go. (Pause.) What's coming up <u>now</u>?

Renee: When we walked in and sat down, I saw this couple looking at us strangely. I don't think it took them very long to realize that we were trans. The man and then the woman started calling us "tranny" and "men" and "he-she" and "it," or, worse yet, "freak." As their anger and hatred toward us escalated and they continued to call us other names, other men and women at the bar started chanting some hate words as well. It was chilling. It was then that the man who called us "men" started to approach me. Then he and the woman who was with him attacked me and pulled me by my belt and tried to shove me out the door.

Clinician: Go with that (set of BLS). Good. That's it. Take a breath. (Pause.) Let it go. (Pause.) What are you noticing <u>now</u>?

Renee: I can still feel myself pushing against this couple who were trying to shove me out the door. Then I saw this big man barreling toward me with a baseball bat in his hand, yelling at me to "get out." He told us all to leave or he would start swinging.

Clinician: Go with that (set of BLS). Good. That's it. Take a breath. (Pause.) Let it go. (Pause.) What's happening <u>now</u>?

Renee: Someone called the police; but by the time they arrived the man and the woman were gone as well as the big guy with the bat. They just disappeared into nowhere. The police interviewed us all and said they were going to file the attack as a possible bias crime. We never heard from them again, and we were just too afraid to pursue it.

Clinician: Go with that (set of BLS). Good. That's it. Take a breath. (Pause.) Let it go. (Pause.) What's coming up <u>now</u>?

Renee: The next day my whole body hurt. I felt like I had been hit by a truck. My arms and legs were bruised, and my knees ached. My friend's nose was broken.

Clinician: Go with that (set of BLS). Good. That's it. Take a breath. (Pause.) Let it go. (Pause.) What's coming up <u>now</u>?

Responsibility/Defectiveness ("I Am Something Wrong") Plateau

Renee: All that hate I saw in their eyes. I remember it from when I was a kid. I thought I had left that behind.

Clinician: Go with that (set of BLS). Good. That's it. Take a breath. (Pause.) Let it go. (Pause.) What's happening <u>now</u>?

Renee: In the church where I grew up, anything that did not look white and male was an abomination. I could never reveal my true female identity in that environment. I feared that I might be castrated or killed. To them, gender was determined by biological sex, not by self-perception. I was an abomination.

Clinician: Go with that (set of BLS). Good. That's it. Take a breath. (Pause.) Let it go. (Pause.) What are you noticing <u>now</u>?

Renee: The people in my hometown, in my church, abhorred and feared anything that deviated from their perception of what they thought things should be—even me if they knew my truth. I could never let that happen. I sensed their hatred and fear of anything that was different, but I never saw it like I did that night in the bar. It was terrifying.

Clinician: Go with that (set of BLS). Good. That's it. Take a breath. (Pause.) Let it go. (Pause.) What's happening <u>now</u>?

Renee: That's why I left that town as soon as I was 18. I knew I could not survive. I did what I needed to do to be who I really am.

Clinician: Go with that (set of BLS). Good. That's it. Take a breath. (Pause.) Let it go. (Pause.) What's coming up <u>now</u>?

Renee: I am not broken. They are.

Clinician: Go with that (set of BLS). Good. That's it. Take a breath. (Pause.) Let it go. (Pause.) What are you noticing <u>now</u>?

Control/Power/Choice Plateau

Renee: I thought when I made the decision to transition, I thought it was the right one. It was something I had always wanted. The post-surgery aftermath was just horrible. I thought I was going to feel the joy of finally being in my own female skin and loving it. Instead, I was miserable. Before the surgery I felt like a girl, but I had a boy's body. I had no control over what I looked like, and I had no control over what I felt like. It was agony. I felt no better right after the first surgery.

Clinician: Go with that (set of BLS). Good. That's it. Take a breath. (Pause.) Let it go. (Pause.) What's happening <u>now</u>?

Renee: I wanted so badly to be a female after the sex reassignment operation. I just wanted to finally feel like a total woman. I was despondent and disappointed and mostly full of regret and did not understand why.

Clinician: Go with that (set of BLS). Good. That's it. Take a breath. (Pause.) Let it go. (Pause.) What's coming up <u>now</u>?

Renee: There were so many complications in the beginning from the orchiectomy and after. I had usually been upbeat and positive, and I did not feel like myself. I thought, "Oh, what have I done?"

Clinician: Go with that (set of BLS). Good. That's it. Take a breath. (Pause.) Let it go. (Pause.) What are you noticing <u>now</u>?

Renee: Once I got my hormones regulated, I started to feel better and felt more like myself. I finally felt like I found my true power and it was feminine power. I could finally be who I always felt I was.

Clinician: Go with that (set of BLS). Good. That's it. Take a breath. (Pause.) Let it go. (Pause.) What's happening <u>now</u>?

Connectiveness/Belongingness Plateau

Renee: I remember when I first moved out of my parents' house and started to transition. People were not very accepting of what they saw. I could not go buy a dress or get my hair cut and styled without ugly stares and even uglier comments. I didn't fit. I didn't seem to belong anywhere.

Clinician:	Go with that (set of BLS). Good. That's it. Take a breath. (Pause.) Let it go. (Pause.) What's coming up <u>now</u>?
Renee:	It took a while for the sting of these past experiences to recede. People fear what they don't understand. I had to forgive them to move on. I had to be bigger and more understanding than them.
Clinician:	Go with that (set of BLS). Good. That's it. Take a breath. (Pause.) Let it go. (Pause.) What's happening <u>now</u>?
Renee:	It's different now. I live in a very accepting community and have friends who just love me for me. And I look and feel the way I have always wanted to look and feel. The awkwardness I used to feel is gone, and it is evident to everyone. People still question and judge me. After all I have undergone to get to be who I am today, I don't care what people think. Let me be me, and I will accept them for who they are as well.
Clinician:	Renee, go back to the original event and tell me what you are getting <u>now</u>.
Renee:	This all seems so long ago. I look in the mirror each morning, and I like what I see. Life still has its struggles and people can be asses, but I still like what I see and feel. There are still challenges and struggles that I encounter every day because of who I have chosen to be.
Clinician:	Go with that (set of BLS). Good. That's it. Take a breath. (Pause.) Let it go. (Pause.) What's coming up <u>now</u>?
Renee:	I am sure I will experience prejudice and bias in the future because of who I decided to be, but it's okay. I would not change a thing.
Clinician:	Go back again to the original event and tell me what you are getting <u>now</u>.
Renee:	It's different now for me and it's okay.
Clinician:	When you focus on the <u>original</u> event (incident, experience), on a scale from 0 to 10, where 0 is neutral or no disturbance and 10 is the worst disturbance you can imagine, how disturbing is the event (incident, experience) to you <u>now</u>?
Renee:	0. It just does not matter much anymore. I succeeded in getting what I wanted and what I needed the most.

Renee proceeded quickly through the Installation and Body Scan phases. Nothing extraordinary came up.

There are several EMDR therapy strategies and protocols that have been developed to increase clinician cultural attunement, to build upon cultural resources, and to assist individuals to reprocess and recover from the internalized impact of culturally related trauma and adversity (Nickerson, 2017a).

It is strongly suggested that the clinician become knowledgeable and adept at working with EMDR therapy (i.e., eight phases, three prongs) before deviating from the EMDR standard protocol in any way. It is then, and only then, that if they do so that they know they have a good reason to do so.

SUMMARY STATEMENTS

Since its introduction in 1989, the positive treatment effects of EMDR therapy are experienced worldwide by clients who have suffered from anxiety, depression, obsessions, phobias and panic, stress, relationship conflicts, addictions, chronic and phantom limb pain, and grief, among others. Thousands of clinicians have been trained worldwide in this efficacious method since its inception, but some of them have chosen not to practice EMDR therapy. They chose to continue using their previously learned treatment methods. Some may have deemed EMDR therapy not a good fit with their current therapeutic model, work setting, or clinical population. Or, perhaps, managed care or limited sessions appeared to render EMDR therapy impractical or impossible. Whatever the reason, the desire in writing this Primer is to help newly trained EMDR therapy practitioners keep on track and to offer a refresher for those who have not consistently used EMDR therapy in their practices.

The intent of the Primer is to provide a learning tool to assist newly trained and previously EMDR-trained clinicians to better understand the basic principles, protocols, and procedures of EMDR therapy. This Primer is a substitute neither for formal EMDR training nor for Dr. Shapiro's basic text, *Eye Movement Desensitization and Reprocessing: Basic Principles, Protocols and Procedures*, 3rd edition (2018).

Now that you have reached the end of the Primer, you are encouraged to go back and reread Dr. Shapiro's basic text. Read other texts and manuals written and/or edited by Dr. Shapiro (Shapiro, 2002, 2009–2017a, 2009–2017b; Shapiro & Forrest, 2016; Shapiro, Kaslow, & Maxfield, 2007) as you continue to enrich your understanding of EMDR therapy. Over the past 26 years, numerous skilled clinicians, researchers, and students have also written books, articles, and dissertations and have presented papers on EMDR therapy at major trauma conferences worldwide.

Hopefully, your understanding of EMDR therapy has been enriched and deepened and your excitement and commitment to use it with your clients have increased. If it has been many years since you were trained in EMDR therapy and you are reading this Primer because EMDR therapy is something you are considering to initiate with your clients in the future, it would be advisable to seek the training again and obtain consultation from an EMDRIA-Approved Consultant. Whatever the case, it is hoped that your interest in and enthusiasm for EMDR therapy have been rekindled and that you have learned something along the way and had fun while doing it.

REFERENCES

Adler-Tapia, R., & Settle, C. (2008). *EMDR and the art of psychotherapy with children.* Springer Publishing Company.

Gomez, A. M. (2013). *EMDR therapy and adjunct approaches with children: Complex trauma, attachment, and dissociation.* Springer Publishing Company.

Gomez, A. M. (2019). *Let's have a visit with our feelings: A book for children to increase emotional tolerance and acceptance.* AGATE Books.

Grant, J. M., Mottet, L. A., Tanis, J., Harrison, J., Herman, J. L., & Keisling, M. (2011). *Injustice at every turn: A report of the national transgender discrimination survey.* http://issuu.com/lgbtagingcenter/docs/ntds_report

Greenwald, R. (1999). *Eye movement desensitization and reprocessing (EMDR) in child and adolescent psychotherapy.* Jason Aronson.

Kaplan, A. (2019). *Discussions of mental health issues for gender-variant and transgender individuals, friends, and family.* Retrieved October 24, 2019 from https://tgmentalhealth.com/basic-issues-in-transgender-mental-health/.

Nickerson, M. (2017a). Cultural competence and EMDR therapy. In Nickerson, M. (Ed.), *Cultural competence and healing culturally-based trauma with EMDR therapy: Innovative strategies and protocols* (pp. 3–14). Springer Publishing Company.

Nickerson, M. (2017b). *Ten keys to culturally attuned and effective EMDR therapy* [Paper presentation]. Presentation at the 22nd EMDR International Association Conference, Bellevue, WA.

Office of Minority Health. (2013). *National standards for culturally and linguistically appropriate services in health and health care: A blueprint for advancing and sustaining CLAS policies and practice*. U.S. Department of Health and Human Services. Retrieved October 21, 2013, from https://www.minorityhealth.hhs.gov/.

Ogden, P., & Gomez, A. M. (2013). EMDR therapy and sensorimotor psychotherapy with children. In Gomez, A. (Ed.), *EMDR therapy and adjunct approaches with children* (pp. 247–271). Springer Publishing Company.

Pederson, P. (1988). *A handbook for developing multicultural awareness*. American Association for Counseling and Development.

Russell, M. C., & Figley, C. R. (2013). *Treating traumatic stress injuries in military personnel: An EMDR practitioner's guide*. Routledge Publishing.

Shapiro, F. (2002). *EMDR as an integrative psychotherapy approach: Experts of diverse orientations explore the paradigm prism*. American Psychological Association Press.

Shapiro, F. (2009–2017a). *The EMDR approach to psychotherapy—EMDR Institute basic training Course: Weekend 1 of the two part basic training*. EMDR Institute.

Shapiro, F. (2009–2017b). *The EMDR approach to psychotherapy—EMDR Institute basic training Course: Weekend 2 of the two part basic training*. EMDR Institute.

Shapiro, F. (2012). *Getting past your past: Take control of your life with self-help techniques from EMDR therapy*. Rodale Books.

Shapiro, F., & Forrest, M. S. (2016). *EMDR: The breakthrough therapy for overcoming anxiety, stress, and trauma* (2nd ed.). New York, NY: Basic Books.

Shapiro, F., Kaslow, F. W., & Maxfield, M. (2007). *Handbook of EMDR and family therapy processes*. Hoboken, NJ: John Wiley.

Silver, S. M., & Rogers, S. (2002). *Light in the heart of darkness: EMDR and the treatment of war and terrorism survivors* (1st ed.). New York, NY: W. W. Norton & Co.

8

Resources, Scripts, and Exercises

A: EMDR PHASE 2 EXERCISES

GROUNDING

When an individual is grounded, it says three things. An individual who is grounded is in their body, is present, and is available to experience anything that happens.

Being grounded means "being in your feet." It means being rooted to the ground. It means being solid, stable, and empowered. An individual can ground themself anywhere. They can ground themself in nature by gardening, for instance, or with anything that anchors or connects them to the earth. Being with animals is grounding. Walking, hiking, running, or just stomping or wiggling your feet on the floor is grounding. Simply moving your feet may compress the energy in your feet and serve to ground you. Being grounded gives one an energetic connection to the earth. Anything that gives you a sense of the earth beneath your feet is grounding.

During the Preparation Phase, along with a brief introduction to EMDR therapy, try teaching the client to ground and breathe correctly before leading them into the Safe (Calm) Place or sacred space exercises. The exercise that follows is one of the easiest and quickest ways to teach clients how to ground.

Grounding Exercise

Close your eyes. Try to relax and imagine thick tree roots growing out of the soles of your feet and shooting down into the ground as deeply as you can possibly imagine. Take them to the earth's core. Find something to wrap the roots around (e.g., a tree root, a rock) so that you feel drawn tight and taut against the earth. The earth has an energy field just like you and me. As you inhale into your diaphragm (see sections Diaphragmatic Breathing and Chin Mudrā), draw the earth's energy up through these roots, up through the soles of your feet, and up into the rest of your body. You may feel it. It may feel cool, warm, pulsating, tingly, and/or your feet may start to feel heavier. Continue to do this until you can feel the earth's energy pulsating throughout your body.

When the client is ready, ask, "How does it feel? What is the difference between now and before you began this exercise?" Ask the client to practice this grounding exercise daily or until it becomes first nature.

This exercise is taught so that clients can remain grounded all the time. For clients who may present as unstable, dissociative, disoriented, or dysregulated, it may be necessary to have a repertoire of grounding exercises. These techniques may be successfully employed in sessions when the client is dysregulated or unable to maintain dual awareness (i.e., past vs. present). Clients may be panicky, disoriented, demonstrate signs of overwhelm, or just freeze. In these cases, techniques are employed that bring the client back to the present situation in the clinician's office. The clinician may play ball with the client using a wadded-up piece of paper, a tissue, or a pillow. The clinician's voice will also be an invaluable tool in bringing the client back into the present moment, as will reminding the client to breathe or to feel the room with all their five senses. Ask the client to smell the air (or provide an essence for them to smell, such as peppermint or lavender), have them touch the fabric of the chair, or listen to the noise of the traffic outside. Ask the client to count, add, subtract, multiply numbers, or count backward. Any of these tasks will require the client to shift their focus of attention from affective to a cognitive focus of attention.

Outside the session, the client may ground themself by taking a bath or shower, eating or drinking something, calling someone, chewing gum, stomping their feet on the ground, or any number of other activities that involve all five senses.

DIAPHRAGMATIC BREATHING

Diaphragmatic breathing is the way that we breathe when we are born. It is the way we need to breathe in order to maintain a balance of oxygen and carbon dioxide. This assists the body in maintaining a relaxed state and staving off perpetual anxiety. Diaphragmatic breathing is effective with clients in reducing stress-related symptoms, anxiety, depression, and fatigue. Along with the grounding exercise, breathing from the diaphragm can give the client a big boost in terms of overall health, elevated self-esteem, and a sense of well-being.

Not surprisingly, many clients are shallow or chest breathers. They breathe into and through their chests rather than into their diaphragms. Many may present stressed out and anxious or report mind chatter. To help alleviate these symptoms, retraining clients to breathe diaphragmatically can be effective.

When we are in danger, our autonomic, automatic response is to inhale quickly into our chest as a signal to all our senses to go on hyperalert. This is a startle response. We become more alert, tense, and hypervigilant until the danger is over. The body's natural response is to then return to breathing from the diaphragm and into a state of relaxation.

Clients who present as chest breathers are often in a hypervigilant state and will need to retrain themselves to breathe into their diaphragm as a way of lessening the stress, anxiety, tightness, and tenseness with which they present.

Breathing Exercise

The client should be sitting comfortably in a chair. Their knees should be bent, and their feet flat on the floor.

> *Try to relax your shoulders, head, and neck as much as possible. Now place your right hand on your diaphragm and your left hand on your upper chest. This will allow you to better feel your diaphragm move as you breathe. Your diaphragm is just below your rib cage and above the stomach. It will rise as you inhale and fall as you exhale. Breathe in through your nose and out through your mouth. Inhale and hold your breath for a slow count of five, and exhale on another slow count of five. Repeat two or more times. There is to be no movement in your chest or lower abdomen. The key is motionlessness in these two areas. Breathe in your nose and out your mouth. Breathe smoothly, slowly, and evenly.*

Note: When clients are first introduced to this exercise, they may tend to breathe too deeply and get lightheaded. At first, the diaphragmatic breathing may not feel comfortable. Clients may also experience tiredness after only a few minutes of breathing in this way. Although the benefits of this type of breathing are immediate, it needs to be practiced. It is suggested that clients practice this exercise 3 to 4 times daily for 5 to 10 minutes.

CHIN MUDRĀ AS AN ALTERNATIVE TO TEACHING CLIENT DIAPHRAGMATIC BREATHING

The mudrā (i.e., yoga of the fingers; a hand posture) exists in many traditions, including Indian, Buddhist, and Japanese. The chin mudrā is one of the most commonly used and recognized of the mudrās (literally meaning, "Gesture of Wisdom") and it is used here as an alternative to teaching diaphragmatic breathing. It is created by lightly touching the thumb and index finger of each hand to form a zero (Figure A.1) and extending the other three fingers outward, but not so rigid (Carroll, 2013). The hands are placed palms down on the thighs or knees. When used, this mudrā activates and redirects the client's breathing back to the diaphragm.

As this mudrā activates the diaphragm, this becomes a quick test to see if the client is a chest or a diaphragm breather and it allows the client to instantly notice the emotional and physical differences between the two types of breathing. Instruct the client to breathe deeply through their nose as they notice the air enter the back of their throat and to feel their belly as their diaphragm expands, pushing the abdominal wall. Encourage the client to practice it until diaphragmatic breathing becomes the more natural way.

FIGURE A.1 Chin mudrā.

ANCHORING IN THE PRESENT

The present moment is the only moment that counts. If you are truly in the moment, you are not being pulled back into the past or drawn into the future. It is the space between the past and the future where time can stand still. This is an important concept for the client to experience, enjoy, and understand. The following exercise is designed to engage the client in the moment and serves as a precursor to better understanding mindfulness. In this space, the client may experience calm, clarity, safety, security, strength, and hope that their life can be different.

This exercise can be conducted routinely with clients. Make sure the client is sitting comfortably and erect in a chair with their feet firmly planted on the ground and then instruct them to do the following:

Close your eyes and become aware of what is going on around you. Feel your feet. Move them. The best way to ground yourself quickly is to feel your feet. Can you feel your socks? (Pause.) Can you feel the inner soles of your shoes? (Pause.) Can you feel the rug under your feet? (Pause.) Can you feel the concrete under the rug? (Pause.) Can you feel the hardness under your feet? (Pause.) How about what is under the concrete? (Pause.) Can you feel the coldness of the damp earth beneath the concrete? (Pause.) Now feel the texture of the upholstery of the chair on which you are sitting. (Pause.) Feel it. Take it in. (Pause.) Can you feel the foam under the fabric? (Pause.) Can you feel the wood structure that supports the chair? (Pause.)

Listen to the sound of my voice as I talk. Listen to what other sounds you can hear. Can you hear the overhead fan? (Pause.) Can you hear the traffic outside? (Pause.) Can you hear voices in the hall outside? (Pause.) What else can you hear? (Pause.) Listen to all the sounds that you were consciously unaware of 30 seconds ago.

Take a breath. What do you smell? Feel the cool air in your nostrils. How does it feel? What do you smell? Taste the saliva in your mouth. Feel what your skin feels.

Please open your eyes now and look around. What shapes do you see? (Pause.) Look at the colors, shapes, patterns, designs, and textures of everything in the room. (Pause.) Count 10 things in the room that are blue. (Pause.) Now count 10 things that are red. (Pause.)

How are you feeling? Are you feeling differently than before we started this exercise?

Seeing, or, in this case, feeling, is believing. An important offshoot of this exercise is that the client has an opportunity to feel the difference between living in the present versus living in the past or future. Once the client appears to be fully present, ask them to notice how it feels and report their experience of being here. Then ask them to focus on a disturbing event in their past. "How does that feel?" Have them come back to the present. Then ask them to focus on something disturbing that may be happening in the future. "How does that feel?" Often the client can experience what it is truly like to be "in the present."

SAFE (CALM) PLACE (SHAPIRO, 2006, P. 45, 2009–2017a, P. 43, 2018, PP. 117–119)

Dr. Shapiro (2018) recommends the use of the Safe (Calm) Place exercise throughout the EMDR process. It assists in preparing the client to process traumatic events, to close an incomplete session, and to help equalize or stabilize the client's distress in session if the information that emerges is too emotionally disruptive. It is called a safe (calm) place because some clients have been traumatized to such a high degree that it is not ecologically possible for them to even imagine that a "safe" place could exist. Any positive state that is accessible to the client can be substituted for the words "calm" or "safe." This process, if successful and strengthened by bilateral stimulation (BLS), also serves to introduce the client to BLS in a comfortable way before the BLS is used on disturbing material.

It is important to instruct clients extensively on the correct use of the safe (calm) place and its potential effects. For instance, if disturbing events arise during the Safe (Calm) Place exercise, they may halt processing and cause the client to shift cognitively, emotionally, or physiologically. Or, they may increase the current distress level in some clients. And, when a disturbing event is paired with BLS, there is the potential for intensifying negative affect with which the client presents or activate the processing of the client's presenting issue (Shapiro, 2018). As with any technique utilized with the client, use caution. A scripted version of the Safe (Calm) Place exercise follows:

Identify the Image

Clinician: Bring up a place, some place real or imagined, that feels safe (calm). Can you think of such a place? A mountaintop or beside a babbling stream, perhaps? Or on a beach? Where would it be?

Client: Oh, that's easy. When I was looking over the Urubamba Valley in Peru from Machu Picchu.

The client is asked to visualize or create a place where they can find calm and safety.

Identify the Associated Emotions and Sensations

Clinician: Good. Focus on this safe (calm) place—everything in it. What sights, sounds, and smells, if any, come up for you? What are you noticing?

Client: It is so calm and peaceful up there. I could stay there forever.

The client focuses on the image, the feelings evoked by the image, and where they feel it in their body.

Enhancing the Sensations

Clinician: Good. Concentrate on this image and where you feel the pleasant sensations in your body. Allow yourself to connect to and enjoy them. As you are concentrating on these images, follow my fingers. (Pause.) How do you feel now?

Client: I am feeling calm and peaceful and safe as well.

The clinician uses guided imagery to enhance the safe (calm) place by stressing the positive feelings and sensations being experienced by the client. The BLS utilized with the safe (calm) place is slow and consists of 4 to 6 passes.

Clinician: Good. Focus on that and follow my fingers once more. (Pause.) What do you notice now?

Client: The sensations have strengthened and deepened.

If positive feelings come up, continue with soothing guided imagery and the positive feelings and sensations expressed by the client, along with additional sets of BLS (4–6 passes). Keep repeating as long as the client's sensations continue to be enhanced (i.e., "Bring up your safe (calm) place and those pleasant sensations.").

Establishing a Cue Word

Clinician: Good. Is there a word or phrase that might represent your safe (calm) place?

The client is asked to identify a single word or phrase that best represents their safe (calm) place.

Client: "Sacred."

Clinician: Focus on the word "sacred" and notice positive feelings that arise when you do. Focus on those sensations and the word "sacred" and follow my fingers. (Pause.) What do you notice now?

The clinician verbally enhances the positive feelings and sensations identified by the client with slow short sets of BLS (4–6 passes).

Client: I feel like I am in a sacred cocoon.

Repeat the instruction, along with short sets of BLS (4–6 passes) in an attempt to further enhance the positive feelings experienced by the client. Continue if the positive feelings keep being enhanced.

Because the clinician does not want to expose the client to premature linkages to trauma material, the clinician does not implement BLS after this point.

Self-Cuing Instruction

Clinician: Now do the same thing on your own. Say the word "sacred" and notice what you feel and follow my fingers.

Cuing With Disturbance

Clinician: Think of a *minor* annoyance (This disturbance is about a 1 or 2 on a 10-point scale where 10 = the worst and 0 = calm or neutral. Higher levels of disturbance may cause the client to be unable to successfully use the safe (calm) place. Perhaps something that happened this week. Now go to your safe (calm) place and notice how it feels. Bring up the word "sacred" and notice if there are shifts in your body sensations. What did you notice?

If a negative shift occurs, the clinician will attempt to guide the client through the process until a shift to positive emotions and sensation occurs.

Client: I felt my whole body sink when I focused on the conflict I had with my boss earlier in the week. When I repeated the word "sacred" to myself, I felt uplifted and strong.

Self-Cuing With Disturbance

Clinician: Good. Now bring up another mildly annoying event (i.e., SUD 1–2). Bring up the word "sacred" on your own and notice changes in your body as you do.

Client: Same thing happened as before. I just feel so strong and impenetrable.

At the end of the exercise, instruct the client to use their cue word and safe (calm) place every time they feel even a little annoyed between sessions. The client can keep track of this by keeping what is called a trigger, image, cognition, emotion, and sensation (TICES) log (Shapiro, 2018, 2009–2017a, 2009–2017b). Clients are also alerted that attempts to use their safe (calm) place when they are experiencing high levels of disturbance may not work, especially when they are learning this process. The process will work better as they gain more skill with practice. See Chapter 8, C: Informed Consent and EMDR Therapy for an explanation of the TICES log.

There are some cautionary elements for the clinician:

1. The initial development of a safe (calm) place may be disturbing to the client and increase their levels of distress. If this does occur, reassure the client that it is not unusual for this to happen. Then immediately assist the client in developing another safe (calm) place or initiate another self-regulating exercise.

2. Pairing the BLS with the development of the safe (calm) place may bring some clients to high levels of negative affect very quickly. For example, the client may be in the process of developing a safe (calm) place in a meadow, and suddenly the image of the rapist appears as a dark figure overshadowing it. In cases like this, try to develop a place that continues to be safe and/or calm to them, probably a different place, as the current place has been "intruded" upon by distressing material. It is sometimes useful to tell the client that this is their own space, real or imaginary, where no one else or no other thing may intrude. It is just for them.

3. Negative associations may also emerge when the safe (calm) place is developed and the BLS is introduced. For example, the client who happens to be a police officer is preparing to reprocess a memory of seeing their partner shot in a shootout with a gang member. Upon introducing BLS to their newly developed safe (calm) place, a memory of exchanging gunfire with a group of marauding student protesters emerges. When this happens, the clinician can assist the client in developing another safe (calm) place.

SACRED SPACE

This sacred space exercise was developed by the author as an alternative to safe (calm) place. Clients who have been severely abused or have experienced horrifying life events sometimes have a difficult time finding an external safe (calm) place. This exercise provides them with an opportunity to create such a place internally where no one else has tread and no one else knows where it is or what it is.

Grounding the Client in the Moment

Place your feet flat on the floor and, if possible, keep your eyes closed throughout the duration of this exercise. Become aware of your surroundings and your sense of self in them. Pay attention to your breathing. Imagine that you have big, thick tree roots growing out of the soles of your feet. Shoot them down as deep into the earth as you can possibly imagine. Wrap these roots around anything you can imagine (e.g., a root, rock) so that you are drawn taut and tight against the floor beneath your feet. Let them anchor you to the earth. Like ourselves, the earth possesses an energy field and, as you inhale, draw the earth's energy up the roots, up through the soles of your feet, and up into the rest of your body. With each breath, this energy can travel further and further up your body until you can feel it at the top of your head. You may feel the energy. It may feel cool, warm, tingling, or you may not feel it at all. It does not matter. Breathe like this until you can feel your breath tingle in your torso and upper extremities. Breathe evenly and consistently.

Finding Sacred Space

Take the essence of who you are at this moment in time and go inside your body, starting at the top of your head, and go to the tips of your toes in search of what is called a sacred space. This is a space that you will create where you can go when you need solace or solitude, comfort or calm, safety or support. It can be anywhere in your body. I do not want or need to know where it is as I want this to remain your own very special place. [Option: If you cannot find a sacred space, just pick a space that you feel might be appropriate.] Take your time, and when you are finished just say, "okay."

Preparing the Sacred Space

Wait patiently and silently until the client indicates by saying, "okay" or in some way that they have located an appropriate spot in their body for a sacred space. When they have done so, instruct the client as follows:

Now prepare your sacred space. Bring into this space anything and everything that you might need to help resolve the issues you bring here today. If you need courage, faith, strength, or peace, bring these into your sacred space. Anything and everything. The sky is your limit. Paint it, texture it, design it, and furnish it. Make this sacred space as comfortable as you can possibly make it. Take your time. When you are finished, just say, "okay."

Getting Comfortable in Sacred Space

Once the client has indicated that they have finished preparing their sacred space, invite them to go there.

Now go to your sacred space. Nestle down among the things you have placed there. This is your sacred space, and you should be comfortable in it. When you are comfortable, just say, "okay."

Preparing the Way for Wisdom's (or Guidance's) Message

Imagine a bright light coming through your forehead, creating a channel to your sacred space. Through this channel, graciously and respectfully invite wisdom (or guidance) into your sacred space. Wisdom (or guidance) may come in any form. It may come in the form of a book, a picture, an object, a symbol, a person, or a group of persons. When wisdom (or guidance) is there, just say, "okay."

Listening for Wisdom's (or Guidance's) Message

Wisdom (or guidance) has brought you a very special message today. Graciously and respectfully ask wisdom (or guidance) for that message. When you have it, just say, "okay." (Pause.)

Note: If the client does not answer, prompt her by saying, "Just say the first thing that comes to your mind."

When the client indicates that she has the message, say, "What is the message?"

Make sure you write it down and say, "Now graciously and respectfully thank wisdom (or guidance) for the message and remember that wisdom (or guidance) may come any time it is called into your sacred space."

Remarkably, most clients do hear messages, such as "I can make it," "I can do this," "I know what I have to do now," or "I am in the right place."

Closing the Sacred Space

And, realize as you leave here today, you take this space with you. It is your very own special space. No one knows where it is but you. This is your special place. You can go there often. Go there when you need comfort or calm, solace or solitude, safety or support. When you are ready, you may open your eyes.

This sacred space exercise can be a very empowering experience. The sacred place becomes the client's safe place, a place for silence, a retreat. It is a place where the client can go to resettle their mind, gather their strength, and regain their footing.

Note: Use BLS throughout the entire exercise. The BLS is slow and consistent. During the actual EMDR therapy session, the client can be instructed to go to their sacred space in the same way that others use the safe (calm) place.

REFERENCES

Carroll, C. (2013). *Mudras of yoga: 72 hand gestures for healing and spiritual growth*. Singing Dragon.

Shapiro, F. (2006). *EMDR: New notes on adaptive information processing with case formulations principles, forms, scripts and worksheets, version 1.1*. EMDR Institute.

Shapiro, F. (2018). *Eye movement desensitization and reprocessing: Basic principles, protocols and procedures* (3rd ed.). Guilford Press.

Shapiro, F. (2009–2017a). *The EMDR approach to psychotherapy—EMDR Institute basic training Course: Weekend 1 of the two part basic training*. EMDR Institute.

Shapiro, F. (2009–2017b). *The EMDR approach to psychotherapy—EMDR Institute basic training Course: Weekend 2 of the two part basic training*. Watsonville, CA: EMDR Institute.

B: EMDR THERAPY SCRIPTS

RESOURCE DEVELOPMENT STEPS—AFFECT MANAGEMENT AND BEHAVIOR CHANGE (SHAPIRO, 2009–2017a, PP. 70–71)

1. **Resource:** Client identifies the needed resource or affect management skill. Examples: calm place, container, breathing technique, courage, focus, and so on.
2. **Image:** Client images a time, activity, or place (real or imagined) when that resource had been successfully used.
3. **Emotions and sensations:** Client focuses on image and feelings and identifies location of positive sensations associated with the resource.
4. **Enhancement:** Clinician verbally enhances the resource with guided imagery stressing its positive behavior, feelings, and sensations.
5. **BLS:** Once enhanced, add several brief sets of BLS (6–8 slow passes). "Bring up your resource and those pleasant feelings" (BLS 6–8 slow passes). Repeat several times if process has enhanced client's positive feelings and sensations. If not positive, consider returning to step 1 and identify another resource.
6. **Cue word:** Have client identify a word or phrase that represents the resource. Use that word/phrase to verbally enhance the pleasant feelings and sensations. Once fully accessed, further enhance by using a short set (BLS 6–8 slow passes). If positive, repeat several times. If negative, return to step 1 and consider an alternative coping skill.
7. **In order to avoid premature linkage with trauma material, no BLS is used from this point on.**
8. **Self-cuing:** Instruct client to repeat procedure on their own, bringing up the image of the resource and its positive emotions and sensations.
9. **Cuing with disturbance:** Have the client think of a recent, mild disturbance, then instruct them to imagine how using their resource would have helped in managing the situation. Guide client through the process until they are able to experience positive emotions and sensations.
10. **Self-cuing with disturbance:** Without any help from the clinician, have the client think of another mild, recent disturbing event, imagining using the resource and experiencing positive emotions and sensations.
11. **Keep a TICES log:** A TICES log is used to evaluate the effectiveness of the safe (calm) place or any other stress management strategy being used by the client.

CONTAINER EXERCISE

At the end of an incomplete session, the client is encouraged to "contain" whatever aspects of their trauma that still linger. This entails the client placing their residual trauma in a container of their choice.

Containers may be as simple as a box, a jar, or vase, or as complex as a safe that is thrown into the bottom of the ocean, a key box buried in their backyard, or being bound by bubble wrap and duct tape and placed in a closet.

Some clients may wish to place a sign on the container stating, "Do not open until next session," to lessen their contact with the thoughts of the trauma between sessions. Others, who are unable to visualize with any success, may wish to write whatever they are upset about on a piece of paper and place it in a box or put it into a drawer. And still others may wish to leave residue of the nearly reprocessed trauma in the clinician's office. The container visualization may be reinforced and strengthened with slow, short sets of BLS. For a more comprehensive example of this container exercise, see Murray (2011).

Dr. Shapiro (2018) suggests using vertical eye movements when closing an incomplete session because of the calming effect they appear to produce.

BREATHING SHIFT (SHAPIRO, 2017, P. 91)

Here is a scripted version of the breathing shift:

Clinician: Bring up a good or positive memory … a memory that is a good or happy memory.

Use whatever affect is the most useful.

Client: Okay.
Clinician: Just notice where your breath starts and then place your hands over it.
Client: Okay.
Clinician: (Pause.) Just notice how it feels. Good. (Pause.) Bring up a memory with a low level of disturbance (Pause.) Notice how your breath changes (Pause.) Place your hand over the location where you feel the change (Pause.) Now place your hand where you had it before and deliberately change your breathing pattern accordingly.

If this technique does not cause the disturbance to dissipate, try something else (e.g., spiral technique).

DIAPHRAGMATIC BREATHING (SHAPIRO, 2017, P. 92)

A scripted version of diaphragmatic breathing follows:

Clinician: Take a deep breath and fill your lungs completely so you can get the most out of your breathing. Please scoot forward in your chair and place one hand over your abdomen and the other over your chest.

Demonstrate for the client.

Client: Okay.
Clinician: Start by exhaling in all the way with your *abdomen* for a count of 2. Then breathe in again all the way with your *chest* for a count of 2.
Client: Okay.
Clinician: Hold that breath for a count of 7 and then breathe out all the way with your abdomen for a count of 4 and breathe in with your *chest* for a count of 4.
Client: Okay.

Demonstrate for the client and/or do it together. Repeat this sequence 4 times.

SPIRAL TECHNIQUE (SHAPIRO, 2006, P. 46, 2017, P. 90)

A scripted version of the spiral technique follows:

Clinician: Bring up a disturbing memory and concentrate on body sensations that emerge. This is an imaginal exercise, so there are no right or wrong responses.

Client: Okay.

Clinician: When you think of the *original* event (or incident), on a scale from 0 to 10, where 0 is neutral or no disturbance and 10 is the worst disturbance you can imagine, how disturbing is the event (or incident) to you *now?*

Client: 9.

Clinician: Where do you feel it in your body?

Client: In my stomach.

Clinician: Concentrate on what you are feeling in your body. Imagine that the feelings are energy. If the energy is going in a spiral, what direction is it going? Clockwise? Or counterclockwise?

Client: Clockwise.

Clinician: Good. Focus on the feelings and change the direction of the spiral to counter-clockwise. Just notice what happens as you do.

Client: Okay.

Clinician: What happens?

Client: The sensations seem to be lessening.

If this technique is working, the client's sensations may dissipate and the Subjective Units of Disturbance (SUD) level may drop. If it does not work, try something else (e.g., breathing shift).

LIGHTSTREAM TECHNIQUE (SHAPIRO, 2020, P. 155)

A stress management strategy the clinician can use with the client is the Lightstream Technique. Utilizing this technique, the clinician asks the client to concentrate on an upsetting body sensation and helps the client identify the shape, size, color, temperature, texture, and sound, by asking, "If it had _____ (fill in the blank), what would it be?

Example: Sam is talking about his mother and is getting more and more upset. He keeps getting cramps in his chest as he continues to talk. The clinician instructs Sam to focus on the cramps in his stomach. The clinician says, "If it had a shape, what would it be? (Pause.) If it had a size, what would it be? (Pause.) If it had a color, what would it be? (Pause.) If it had a temperature, what would it be? (Pause.) If it had a texture, what would it be? (Pause.) If it had a sound, what would it be? (Pause.) What is your favorite color you associate with healing?" (Shapiro & Laliotis, 2020).

The clinician then says, "Imagine that this favorite colored light is coming in through the top of your head and directing itself at the shape identified above in your body. Let's pretend that the source of this light is the cosmos, so the more you use, the more you have available. The light directs itself at the shape and resonates, vibrates in and around it. And, as it does, what happens to the shape, size, or color?"

If the client reports that the shape is changing in any way, the clinician will repeat a version of the underlined portion below of this technique and say, "*Today, I'd like to suggest that we work on how you will respond in the future to similar situations.*"

Lightstream Transcript

Ask client to concentrate on upsetting body sensations.

Identify the following by asking, "If it had a _____(fill in the blank), what would it be?"

a. shape   d. size
b. color   e. temperature
c. texture   f. sound (high-pitched or low)

- Ask, "What favorite color do you associate with healing?"
- Say, "Imagine that this favorite colored light is coming in through the top of your head and directing itself at the shape in your body. Let's pretend that the source of this light is the cosmos, so the more you use, the more you have available. The light directs itself at the shape and resonates, vibrates in and around it. And as it does, what happened to the shape, size, or color?" If the client gives feedback that it is changing in any way, continue repeating a version of the underlined portion and ask for feedback until the shape is completely gone. This usually correlates with the disappearance of the upsetting feeling. After it feels better, bring the light into every portion of the client's body and give them a positive statement for peace and calm until the next session. Ask the client to become externally aware at the count of five.

The Lightstream Technique is a combination of ancient meditation and recent Neurolinguistic Programming strategies that help ease stress for most clients.

FUTURE TEMPLATE

Future Template Script

(Shapiro, 2020, pp. 94–96)

Introduction
We have worked on past experiences relating to your presenting problem, as well as the present situations that have triggered your distress.

Today, I'd like to suggest that we work on how you will respond in the future to similar situations.

Desired Outcomes Steps
1. **Identifying the future situation** (i.e., previously identified recent experience or present trigger): *Identify a future situation and a positive belief you would like to have about yourself in that situation.*
2. **Run the movie:** *While holding the positive belief about yourself in mind, run the movie of the situation as you would like to be able to respond, from beginning to end. Let me know if there are any parts of the movie that are uncomfortable or challenging.*
3. **What are you noticing now?**
   a. If the client's response is POSITIVE, run movie of adaptive responses(s), adding BLS sets as long as positive response is strengthening.
   b. If the client's response is NEUTRAL, ask for clarification (lacks familiarity, need for a plan). Generate with client desired response; run movie of desired response with sets of BLS until client has a positive response.

    c.   If client's response is NEGATIVE, focus on body sensations; add sets of BLS until client response is neutral. Elicit from client desired response and run movie with sets of BLS until client has achieved a positive response.

        If negative associations arise, the clinician may need to return the client to reprocessing.

4.   **Install positive cognition (PC) to Validity of Cognition (VoC) = 7:** *Hold your positive belief with that situation. On a scale of 1–7, how true does it feel? Install to VoC of 7 with BLS.*

Problem-Solving Situation Steps

1.   **Create a problem-solving situation:** *I'd like you to think of some challenge you may experience in that situation.*

2.   **What are you noticing now?**

    Positive: Add BLS sets as long as additional positives are reported.
    Negative: Focus on body sensation and add BLS until sensations dissipate.

3.   **Install PC to VoC = 7 with each situation:** *Hold your PC with that situation. On a scale of 1–7, how true does it feel now? Install VoC = 7 with BLS.*

See Figure B.1 for the steps to these two important processes.

STEPS FOR RECENT TRAUMATIC EVENTS PROTOCOL (SHAPIRO, 2020, PP. 121–122)

The Recent Traumatic Events Protocol was designed for use with single traumatic events that have occurred within two to three months (maybe longer) and in situations characterized by a lack of safety.

The standard EMDR protocol referred to throughout this entire Primer: (a) focuses on an entire traumatic memory; (b) focuses on an image (or picture) that is representative of the entire memory; and (c) results in the entire memory being reprocessed as it generalizes to other associative channels of information which arise throughout the processing. What Dr. Shapiro discovered when working with clients from the 1989 San Francisco Bay Area earthquake is that processing the most traumatic part of a memory did not necessarily generalize to other parts of the same memory. As the clients were able to provide a serial description of the event, it was clear to Dr. Shapiro that the memory had consolidated at some level. But, because the treatment effect did not generalize to other associative parts of the memory, they were not "integrally linked" (Shapiro, 2018).

With this in mind, Dr. Shapiro developed the Recent Traumatic Events Protocol to account for the differences in processing of a more distant memory versus a more recent one. After providing a narrative account of the event, the client will target each disturbing aspect separately using the standard protocol in the Assessment Phase (i.e., image, negative cognition [NC], PC, VoC, emotions, and SUD) and through to the Installation Phase. In a recent event, it is not unusual for the image to present as a sound or a smell.

All aspects of client selection and preparation are the same as in the standard protocol. It may be necessary to provide some preparation or stabilization skills before completing the history-taking. It is also important to determine if the client has had any earlier trauma that may get reactivated by reprocessing with the standard protocol.

1. **Obtain a narrative history:** The clinician asks the client to relate the details of the event in narrative form.
2. **Target the most disturbing aspect of the memory:** As the client is providing a narrative, the clinician records each separate event identified by the client.
3. **Target the remainder of the narrative in chronological order:** At this point, the clinician needs to target each of the chronological events in the client's narrative. If they were to have identified one of the events to be more disturbing than the rest, the clinician would target this one first and then the remainder as they occurred during the telling of their story. Each target is treated separately in terms of the standard EMDR procedure up to the Installation Phase, being mindful to exclude the body scan for each. The body scan is initiated only after the last target of this traumatic event has been identified and addressed so that all the associated negative physical sensations can be eliminated.
4. **Visualize entire sequence of the event with eyes closed:** Once all the separate events in the narrative have been identified and reprocessed, the client is asked to visualize the entire sequence of the event from start to finish.

   If something disturbing arises and it is still disturbing, the clinician may implement the EMDR procedure through to the Installation Phase again with this most recent disturbance. Once this has been processed, the clinician would then ask the client to visualize the entire sequence of the event once again to see if further disturbances arise. If so, the client would reprocess each disturbance that surfaces using the standard EMDR procedure.
5. **Visualize entire sequence of events with eyes open:** When the client has run the experience through and no distressing material comes up, have them run the experience coupling it with the PC visualizing the entire sequence of the event one more time with their eyes open. Then initiate a long set of BLS. The client is asked to scan the experience mentally and to give the "stop" signal when their processing has been completed.
6. **Conclude with body scan:** Once this open-eyed visualization has been completed, the body scan is done.
7. **Process present triggers:** Process all present triggers (e.g., causes of startle responses, avoidance of locations similar to where the event occurred, nightmares, or any negative reminders of the experience).
8. **Create future template:** Before treatment is complete, create a future template for each present trigger. Create a future template of desired responses for coping in the future. Include accessing the PC, additional resources or skills, or new information.

TICES LOG (SHAPIRO, 2018, PP. 441-442)

The TICES log (i.e., trigger = image, cognitions, emotions, and sensations) is a log the client is asked to keep between sessions to record disturbing experiences. The log provides a means of informing the clinician what occurred with the client after the reprocessing session. What got activated? What, if anything, was disturbing? What did the client notice when they got triggered? What changed? What is unresolved? The client is instructed at the end of each session to record their experiences in this log. Once this is done, the client is instructed to use one of the self-control techniques learned in their therapy to dissipate the remaining disturbance.

At the end of each session, the clinician may remind and instruct the client to utilize the TICES log in the following manner: "The processing we have done today may

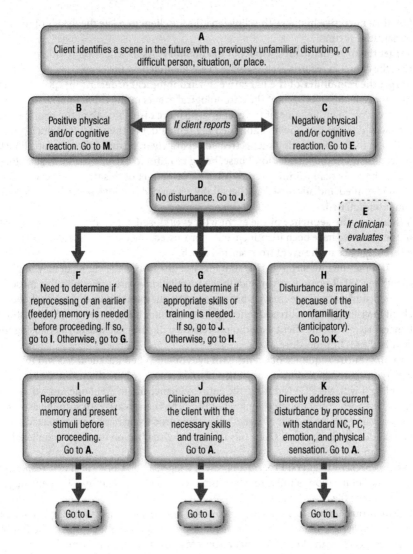

FIGURE B.1 Future template flow chart: Skills building and imaginal rehearsal.

continue after the session. You may or may not notice new insights, thoughts, memories, or dreams. If so, notice what you are experiencing and record it in your TICES log. Use the Safe (Calm) Place exercise to rid yourself of disturbance. Remember to use a relaxation technique daily. We can work on this new material next time. If you feel it is necessary, call me" (Shapiro, 2018).

The recommended format for the client's weekly log report is demonstrated in Table B.1, TICES Log (Shapiro, 2018).

As the titles of the columns indicate, the client is asked for only brief descriptions of any disturbing experiences encountered between sessions. Note that the order of the titles in the columns mirrors the information needed to target an event in a subsequent session in the

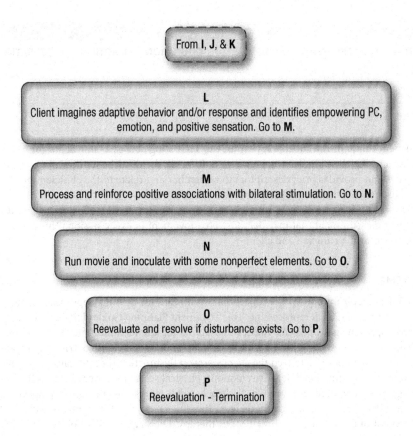

FIGURE B.1 (continued).

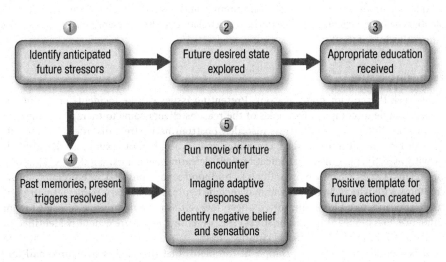

FIGURE B.2 Future template: Skills building and imaginal rehearsal.

TABLE B.1 TICES Log					
DATE	TRIGGER =	IMAGE	COGNITION	EMOTION	SENSATION AND SUD

Abbreviation: SUD, Subjective Units of Disturbance.

Assessment Phase of EMDR therapy. Thus, the TICES log acts as a clinical aid for both the clinician and the client. It also trains the client to break the disturbance down into its attendant parts and provides brief descriptors to remember and relate to the clinician the details of the experience in the event future processing is needed.

The TICES log provides an outcome measure for every session of reprocessing. It is a self-report measurement that may demonstrate movement in every session. This is valuable information for the clinician and client.

TREATMENT PLANNING GUIDE

In 2006, Dr. Shapiro proposed the conceptual framework for defining appropriate targets for treatment utilizing EMDR reprocessing. This Treatment Planning Guide (TPG) follows a three-pronged approach (past, present, future) that allows for the identification of the presenting problem (i.e., the presenting issue), critical incident, and any previous contributing incidents or memories that continue to feed the client's *present* dysfunction (i.e., the cause), the *present* symptoms (i.e., dysfunctional negative emotions, physical sensations, behavior, or belief), *present* triggers, current manifestations (i.e., flashbacks, nightmares), and the future template.

The TPG is one of many methods (e.g., timeline, genogram) designed to assist in the development of a treatment plan for EMDR therapy. Dr. Shapiro (2006) originally conceptualized the TPG to assist clinicians in identifying targets: past events (first, worst, and other contributing experiences) that continue to fuel the client's current pathology, current triggers that remain due to second-order conditioning, and desired outcomes or preparation for potential challenges clients may face in the future relating to their presenting issues. Table B.2 outlines the flow of the TPG.

Presenting Issues

Clients seek therapy for many reasons. Presenting issues can be incident- or symptom-focused, simple or complex. Examples of the reasons clients come to therapy are myriad: relationship difficulties, acute stress disorder, posttraumatic stress disorder (PTSD), eating disorders, recent trauma (such as a motor vehicle accident or sexual assault), difficulties with assertiveness or communication, self-defeating behaviors, psychosexual issues, work-related issues, chronic pain or illness, childhood sexual, physical, or emotional abuse. Symptoms with which clients present may include depression, anxiety, panic, fears or phobias, bereavement and loss, unresolved anger, low self-esteem, negative self-image, loss of confidence, loss of meaning, and/or stress. The presenting issues are generally identified in the History-Taking and Treatment Planning Phase.

It is around the presenting complaint (problem) that the TPG is structured and formulated. In some cases, there may be more than one presenting issue, and a TPG should be completed for each issue. Consider the case of Clara:

Six months ago, Clara met Harry; and they fell deeply in love. Harry has been pressing Clara more and more insistently to marry him. Clara is having difficulty resisting the urge to flee. She loves Harry and does not want to lose him.

Clara is commitment phobic. She has had one long-term relationship since she graduated from college 15 years ago. After 5 years of dating Roger and nearing a marriage proposal, she abruptly terminated their relationship without any reasonable explanation. That was 5 years ago. In the meantime, Clara has settled for or pursued inappropriate or unattainable partners. She frequently entered into instant relationships or fled any relationship that felt like a stable, enduring union. Clara's biggest fear is fear of betrayal from a loved one.

When Clara was a child, she was close to her father. She remembers standing patiently and watchfully by the living room window in the early evenings waiting to see his car round the bend on his way from work. She would wait for him to open the door to the garage and fling herself joyfully into his arms. They would play and sing and read books together every night before she had to go to bed.

Clara's mother died while giving birth to her. From the moment of her birth, her aunt became her surrogate mother. Unfortunately, the aunt was mean and sultry and resentful that she had to take care of Clara rather than have children of her own.

One day, Clara waited and waited for her father's car to round the bend. It kept getting darker and darker and still no father. Her father never came that day. He had a head-on collision with a semi-tractor trailer and was seriously injured. As his recovery was long and burdened with numerous setbacks, her aunt assumed full responsibility for Clara's care. Throughout long months of worry, Clara watched helplessly and hopelessly as her father quickly deteriorated and sunk into a deep depression from which he never fully recovered. He remained sullen and unavailable. As a result, Clara became distant and disconnected from her father and aunt and immersed herself in her school activities. She felt alone and betrayed by her father's condition and their loss of relationship.

Clara's relationship with her aunt was no better. Her aunt's anger and resentment worsened with the increased responsibility for Clara's care. She would often say to Clara, "I don't know what I did to deserve this. I have no life because of you." When Clara was fourteen or fifteen, her aunt went into a fit of rage when Clara spilled soda on the living room carpet. Her aunt screamed at her, "I wish you were dead."

The talk of a long-term relationship or marriage terrifies her. The mere mention of the word "marriage" causes her to flinch uncontrollably. Whenever a man talks of having a future with her, Clara initially freezes up, removes herself from his company, and flees as fast as she can. She becomes anxious as well at the idea of any long-term contract—leases, mortgages, and so on.

Treatment Planning Guide Script

Presenting Issue (Complaint)

Clinician: Clara we had determined last week that we would directly take a look at your fear of commitment today. Is this still agreeable?

Clara: Yes.

Incident

Clinician: Tell me a specific recent situation where you had experienced anything related to your fear of commitment.

Clara: On our six-month anniversary, Harry began talking about our future together.

TABLE B.2 Treatment Planning Guide—Three-Pronged Approach: Adaptive Information Processing-Informed Treatment Planning Flowchart

PRESENTING ISSUE

Identify specific event where client experienced presenting complaints	Elicit recent examples of presenting complaint	Elicit current NC and PC

PAST EVENTS

Presenting problems are often informed by maladaptively stored past experiences.

Identify touchstone event (if one) and other contributing memories utilizing:	Cluster groups of memories together.	Determine if remaining memories exist and are still disturbing. If so, reprocess each using Phases 3–8.
	Identify first and worst events and other contributing past experiences.	
Direct Questioning		
Floatback		
Affect Scan	Reprocess touchstone event using Phases 3–8	

PRESENT TRIGGERS

Additional maladaptive information may still be contained in present triggers that continue to be disturbing even after past experiences have been reprocessed. These will need to be targeted separately.

Identify and reprocess remaining triggers, situations, and people and address any residual physical sensations or urges (usually identified during history-taking, reprocessing, and re-evaluation) using Phases 3–8.	Reprocess current triggers that remain active as a result of second-order conditioning.	Identify and reprocess traumatic events (e.g., accidents, injuries) that have no obvious historical component but where the symptoms are the same. Target separately.

(*continued*)

TABLE B.2 Treatment Planning Guide—Three-Pronged Approach: Adaptive Information Processing-Informed Treatment Planning Flowchart (continued)

FUTURE TEMPLATE

In order to meet current life demands, the client develops and encodes in memory adaptive responses to future scenarios. Every present trigger reprocessed should be followed by the installation of a future template.

Once past and present experiences have been identified and successfully reprocessed, develop multiple adaptive responses to similar situations.	Identify and reprocess desired outcome and potential future challenges for each trigger identified earlier.	Once a desired response has been successfully developed in the future, multiple challenge situations are developed to strengthen positive connections.
	If client needs assistance due to lack of familiarity and requires needed skills, clinician teaches what is needed.	

REEVALUATION

If symptom resolution, then determine if the client's symptoms have been eliminated or decreased.	If comprehensive treatment, determine if main themes have been successfully integrated into client's current life.

SUCCESSFUL EMDR REPROCESSING SESSION

Abbreviations: NC, negative cognition; PC, positive cognition.

Clinician: What picture represents the worst part of that incident?

Clara: I literally froze and did not say anything. I was quiet all the way home. I could not *speak*.

Negative Belief

Clinician: What words go best with the picture that express your negative belief about yourself now?

Clara: I don't deserve love.

Positive Belief

Clinician: When you bring up that picture, what would you like to believe about yourself now?

Clara: I deserve love.

Clinician may also elicit the emotions(s) and physical sensation(s) associated with the image (or picture) in the event the floatback technique is needed to identify the touchstone event.

First Incident (Touchstone Memory)

Clinician: What is the first incident in your life when you thought you did not deserve love?

Clara: I was 12 when my father was involved in an automobile accident. My father was never the same. I lost my best friend. I lost my first love.

Use direct questioning initially to find the earliest event accessible that laid the groundwork for the client's present pathology.

If the client is unable to identify a touchstone event but has identified a NC which appears to be a significant element of the presenting issue (or the present event is not fully accessed), the clinician may use the floatback technique (Browning, 1999; Zangwill, 1997) to help identify it. And remember, there is not always a touchstone event.

The NC is not necessarily needed in order to identify a touchstone event. An adaptation of the Watkins and Watkins (1997) affect scan has been developed to utilize when the NC is unclear. The affect scan is utilized when the NC is sketchy; the current memory is already accessible at a high level of disturbance; and when time is an issue.

Worst Incident

Clinician: If not the time with your father, what is the worst incident when you thought you did not deserve love?

Clara: My mother died while giving birth to me. I was denied and didn't deserve her love either. I got her sister instead.

Other Incidents

Clinician: Were there other incidents in your life when you believed you did not deserve love?

Clara: When I was 13 my aunt became upset and frustrated with me, more than usual this time. I don't remember exactly what had happened, but the words she screamed at me still burn in my ears. She said, "I don't know what I did to deserve this. I have no life because of you."

Clinician: Can you think of any other incidents where you believed you did not deserve love?

Clara: Again, when I was around 14 or 15, I had spilled a can of soda on the carpet. My aunt became irate with me and yelled, "I wish you were dead."

Clinician: Are there any other events in your life when you believe you did not deserve love?

Clara: The only other one I can think of that still causes emotional upset is the breakup with Roger.

Future Desired Outcomes

Clinician: How would you like to see yourself successfully handling relationships in the future?

Clara: I would like to be comfortable and agreeable when Harry talks about our long-term future together. I would like to be able to picture a long life with him.

Treatment Plan

Clinician: Well it seems like we have identified several incidents in your past that would be appropriate to address using EMDR therapy. Generally, I suggest starting with the earliest incident. However, since both occurred when you were very young, we have some choices. When you think of each incident, what incident gives a feeling most similar to the situation with Harry?

Clara: The one with my father. I love Harry and my father so much.

Clinician: Okay, we will start addressing that disturbing memory involving the loss of your father at our next session. Once this has been resolved, we will check back and see if the memory of your mother dying still has a negative emotional charge. If it does, we will work with this memory as well.

Table B.3 provides the clinician with a summary of the steps to an Adaptive Information Processing (AIP)-Informed Treatment Plan for Clara.

TABLE B.3 AIP-Informed Treatment Planning

Presenting issue: Fear of commitment

Specific event where client experienced her fear of commitment: When boyfriend Harry talked about marrying after celebrating 6 months of dating each other.

NC: I don't deserve love.

PC: I deserve love.

Touchstone event: Father was severely injured in a car accident when she was 12 years old.

Other contributing events: (a) Mother died in childhood. (b) Aunt told her, "I don't know what I did to deserve this. I have no life because of you." (c) Aunt also stated, "I wish you were dead." (d) Abrupt breakup with Roger.

Present triggers: (a) Talking of a long-term relationship, (b) anyone talking about her future in any way, and (c) legal commitments of any sort.

Future template: Clara clearly states that she would like to be able say "yes" to Harry's proposal and live out the rest of her life with him.

Abbreviations: NC, negative cognition; PC, positive cognition.

The TPG is a good conceptual tool for teaching the newly trained EMDR therapy clinician to think strategically in terms of past, present, and future when developing a treatment plan.

Cautionary Note

As mentioned earlier, the TPG is one of many ways to conceptualize and develop an EMDR treatment plan. In developing the TPG, it is not an unusual occurrence for the client's distress to be activated during this process. If activation occurs, additional self-soothing measures may need to be taught and used, or another means of gathering the data may need to be considered.

Symptom Reduction Versus Comprehensive Treatment

When developing an initial treatment plan, the clinician may use different criteria and/or history-taking strategies for symptom reduction than they may when developing a plan for more comprehensive treatment. Symptom reduction focuses on a specific symptom(s) or a specific disorder(s) while a comprehensive treatment plan addresses the client's entire clinical picture. Clients may present themselves for therapy requesting only symptom reduction. Occasionally, once the symptoms are reduced, they may elect to switch to request comprehensive therapy. Table B.4 focuses on the similarities and differences in these treatment plans, and Table B.5 illustrates the differences between the clinical presentations of simple and complex PTSD.

PHOBIA (AND ANXIETY) PROTOCOL

A phobia is an irrational fear response to a situation which often poses little or no danger. If the client cannot avoid the feared object or situation, they may experience panic and fear, rapid heartbeat, shortness of breath, tunnel vision, trembling, a strong desire to flee, or worse. Phobias generally form after some type of traumatic event. For instance, Tanisha was in an earthquake when she was 8 when she was trapped under debris before rescuers could dig her out. As a result, she developed a phobia of enclosed spaces (i.e., claustrophobia). She is unable to tolerate elevators, closets, and windowless rooms. Even tight clothing causes her to go into a panic. In the case of phobia, it is important to identify and reprocess the ancillary and antecedent events.

EMDR has been found to be highly effective in dealing with phobias. An adaptation of the EMDR trauma protocol is outlined below for use with phobias. Figure B.3 provides a visual representation to the steps involved in the Phobia Protocol.

Steps for Processing Phobias

Prior to reprocessing, the clinician needs to educate their client about their symptoms and to address any secondary-gain issues that may be present.

1. Teach client self-control techniques to deal with client's "fear of fear."
2. Identify and reprocess targets (in this order):
   a. Ancillary or antecedent events that contribute to the phobia (e.g., precipitating event may be separate from the actual phobic response).
   What events were occurring at the time of the first phobic response that may have contributed to the development of the phobia? Do any childhood experiences

TABLE B.4 Symptom Reduction Versus Comprehensive Treatment		
Directed at the reduction/ elimination of specific symptom(s), for example, emotions, physical sensations, patterns of behavior.	Take a thorough history.	Addresses entire clinical picture.
Usually large "T" (e.g., single incident, single phobia).		Large "T" or disturbing life event. Childhood or adult onset.
External to identity.		Internal to identity; pervasive self-belief.
PAST		
Identify and process first or worst traumatic event.		Identify single or multiple issues, complex presentation; identify touchstone event(s) or larger-T traumas or disturbing life events if any; establish treatment plan.
PRESENT		
	Target and process present triggers and/or other stimuli; use TICES log.	
FUTURE		
Anticipated fears.	Future projection.	Anticipated fears/developmental fears.

Abbreviation: TICES, trigger, image, cognition, emotion, and sensation.

exist which might have contributed to the fear being experienced by the client? Ask, "What happened or was happening just prior to experiencing this fear for the first time?" "Did you experience these same feelings or physical sensations before the onset of your phobia?"

b. Memories related to the phobia should be reprocessed in the following order: first, worst, and most recent.

c. Any associated present stimuli (e.g., any people, places, situations, or events that trigger the fear response) and physical sensations or other manifestations of fear

TABLE B.5 Treatment Planning Guide

SIMPLE-SYMPTOM PRESENTATIONS	COMPREHENSIVE CLINICAL PRESENTATIONS
Acute stress response (i.e., fight or flight) Recent-event trauma. Single incident. Specific presenting problem (e.g., negative irrational belief, pattern of behavior, affects, physical sensations, or people, situations, or specific time periods). Circumscribed set of experiences (or problem, acute or longstanding) in a time-limited context. Diagnoses (e.g., adjustment disorder, ASD, PTSD).	Multiple problems/issues. Pervasive experiences of severe childhood abuse/neglect. Adult-onset traumatic experiences. Comorbidity of disorders. Pervasive history of early trauma. Vague or diffuse presentations. Diagnoses: Complex PTSD, addictions, compulsive disorders, personality disorders, mood disorders, phobias, dissociative disorders. In taking pervasive history of early trauma or symptoms clusters across various contexts: 1. Investigate client's history of early abuse/neglect and its impact on the client's psychosocial development, family relationships, school performance, social development, etc. 2. Explore history of disrupted attachments. 3. Assess negative impact on self-esteem. 4. Examine secondary/tertiary loss/gain issues.
TARGETS	**TARGETS**
Single PTSD *(i.e., symptoms stem from a critical incident.)* *Present manifestation of the problem* (e.g., flashbacks, nightmares). *Primary* event (e.g., raped late at night within the last 6 months), including *aftermath of identified trauma* (e.g., invasive medical procedures after a rape) and *feeder memories* (e.g., previous assaults or rapes). Use direct questioning, floatback, and affect scan to identify touchstone memories that may be feeding the feelings (e.g., helplessness, powerlessness), if any.	**Complex PTSD** *(i.e., presents with more complex diagnoses or issues.)* *Present manifestation of the problem* (e.g., isolates; feels too clingy; unable to trust people, especially men). *Touchstone memories*, if any (e.g., raped by maternal uncle at age 5). Use direct questioning, floatback, and affect scan using a current situation as focal point.

(continued)

TABLE B.5 Treatment Planning Guide (continued)

Clinician will determine what is targeted first.
Present triggers (e.g., walking to car after work late at night, seeing someone out of the corner of their eye).
Future template
Incorporate for each trigger (e.g., imagining themself walking to car late at night comfortably, but cautiously).

Other past events (e.g., previous assaults or rapes).

Present triggers (e.g., sleeping with the bedroom door closed, hearing strange noises in the middle of the night).
Future template
Incorporate for each trigger (e.g., imagining what they might do is they hear a strange noise at night).

Abbreviation: PTSD, posttraumatic stress disorder.

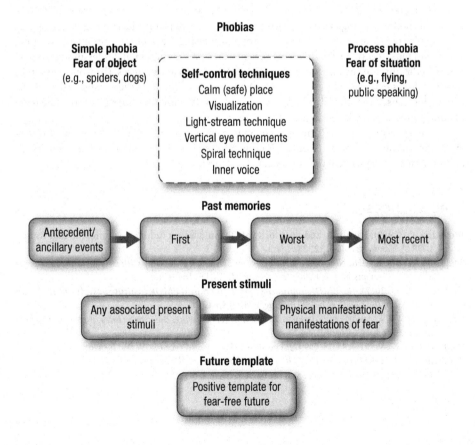

FIGURE B.3 EMDR protocol for simple and process phobias—Processing order.

(e.g., fear symptoms, such as hyperventilation) should be reprocessed. Ask, "What triggers your fear response?" "What are your fear symptoms in terms of this phobia?" or "What are the internal triggers?"

3. Incorporate a positive template for a fear-free future action.
4. Create a contract for action.
5. **Run a mental videotape of the full sequence:**
   a. Instruct the client to close their eyes and run a mental videotape of participating with every aspect of the feared situation. If any anxiety or physical discomfort arises, instruct the client to open their eyes and reprocess that aspect. Restart the video from the beginning. Continue to do this until every aspect of the situation that causes anxiety or physical discomfort has been reprocessed and the client can view the entire experience without any disturbance. If no disturbance, go to Step 6.
6. Complete processing of targets revealed between sessions—Reevaluation. Instruct the client to maintain a TICES log between sessions. Often additional targets can be identified from the log.

In all cases, be sure to conclude with a rehearsal of the feared situation with stimuli in the real world. Prepare the client to expect some anxiety during this transitory period of real-life exposure and to use a log and self-control technique: There is no failure; it is only feedback.

Shapiro (2018) stresses the importance of reprocessing the phobic events in terms of first, worst, and most recent for the following reasons: (a) first—assumes it includes all stimuli pertinent to the onset of the fear and its associated physiological responses, (b) worst—assumes that it includes exacerbating stimuli, and (c) most recent—assumes the second-order conditioning has caused the stimuli to become more potent. It is also necessary to address the issue of anticipatory anxiety if it exists.

Note: In terms of EMDR therapy, Dr. Shapiro no longer distinguishes treatment differences for specific or process phobias. Each is processed using the steps outlined earlier. In addition, this same protocol may be used to treat anxiety.

REFERENCES

Browning, C. (1999). Floatback and float forward: Techniques for linking past, present, and future. *EMDRIA Newsletter, 4*(3), 12, 34.

Shapiro, F. (2006). *EMDR: New notes on adaptive information processing with case formulations principles, forms, scripts and worksheets, version 1.1.* EMDR Institute.

Shapiro, F. (2009–2017). *The EMDR approach to psychotherapy—EMDR Institute basic training course: Weekend 1 of the two part basic training.* EMDR Institute.

Shapiro, F. (2018). *Eye movement desensitization and reprocessing: Basic principles, protocols and procedures* (3rd ed.). Guilford Press.

Watkins, J. G., & Watkins, H. H. (1997). *Ego states: Theory and therapy.* W. W. Norton.

Zangwill, W. M. (1997). *The dance of the cognitive interweave* [Paper presentation]. EMDR International Association Conference, San Francisco, CA.

C: INFORMED CONSENT AND EMDR THERAPY

Informed consent, like EMDR therapy, is a process, not an event. It is a two-way communication process whereby the clinician provides information and encourages the client to ask questions or make comments. It is important that the clinician create an environment in which the client can make informed choices as to the types of treatments—medical, psychological, or otherwise—in which they choose to engage.

The criteria for informed consent have been defined over the years by such organizations as the American Medical Association and the American Psychological Association. It is a process of communication that serves as an ethical obligation and a legal requirement. An informed choice is a voluntary decision based on information provided by the clinician, understanding by the client, and a discussion of available options. Informed consent is introduced in the Preparation Phase of EMDR therapy. In terms of EMDR therapy and informed consent, Shapiro (2018) strongly recommends that the following criteria be explained thoroughly and in a way that the client can understand: (a) EMDR therapy and how it works; (b) the nature and purpose of EMDR therapy and its procedural steps; (c) treatment effects; (d) the possibility of emotional disturbance before, during, and after reprocessing; (e) the risks and benefits; and (f) alternative treatments and their risks and benefits.

Prior to implementing reprocessing, the client agrees to the treatment as explained by the clinician. In cases where legal proceedings are imminent, further caution needs to be taken. If legal proceedings may be an option, Shapiro (2018) further suggests:

1. It is important for the EMDR therapy clinician to be familiar with the nature of memory and be aware that memory records not what the client remembers but what the client perceives.
2. The client may not be able to access a vivid picture of the event after reprocessing. Memories tend to fade or even disappear as they become less intense after reprocessing. For example, the client may have forgotten the color of a perpetrator's clothing and other finer details of the traumatic event. If court proceedings are a possibility, the client's legal counsel is contacted prior to reprocessing because the quality of the client's memories can be further degraded by the reprocessing of the traumatic event.
3. The client may not be able to access the event again with extreme emotion (i.e., EMDR processing can take away the intense negative emotional charge associated with the event).
4. The client may also be able to access more information than they had previous to processing. The images that were originally remembered may be more vivid and contain more detail. In addition, a heightened level of emotion may occur when the client is reprocessing highly charged information associated with the event. What is remembered is not necessarily factual as the legal system would define it. It is valid to the client and reflects what was stored in the client's memory at the time of the event. However, it may be what was perceived, not necessarily what is factual.
5. The process may tend to be compared to hypnosis by the court.
6. In the case of the client in recovery from substance abuse, relapse may be a possibility when they access information from highly charged memories or other reprocessing information that arises from the targeted traumatic events.

The client has the right and the clinician has an ethical obligation to ensure that they are fully informed regarding EMDR therapy. This includes information on what the client may or may not expect if it is used as part of their treatment (e.g., possibility of high levels of distressing emotions during processing, memory may fade or disappear, affect around memory may change, shift in recall of details, information that emerges may not be accurate, mechanisms or behaviors used to cope with the distress at the time of the original memory may be reactivated), possible responses, and additional information that paints a picture of why EMDR therapy is used, how it works, and what the treatment effects may be.

Informed consent allows the client to make an informed decision based on the facts that are presented to them before agreeing to EMDR therapy. This also includes relating the legal ramifications if there is a pending lawsuit. In this instance, it is important to discuss court involvement in terms of how memory works with EMDR therapy and other forensic issues (i.e., fading or disappearing memories, lack of intense emotional affect when discussing the events, and the emergence of more information surrounding the event and the accuracy of it) that can emerge as a result of EMDR processing. In all cases, the clinician or the client needs to consult with the client's legal counsel to ensure that all the necessary details of the event have been fully investigated and all notes and depositions have been completed pre-Phases 3–6. It is unwise to initiate reprocessing prior to consultation with the client's attorney.

The client is also informed of the high levels of emotion that may occur during this process, as well as the possible emergence of new or unexpected memories. In addition, the client will need to be aware of the potential processing difficulties or benefits encountered if they also present with a history of substance abuse. In some cases, an addiction can be reactivated by processing. In others, it may decrease, especially if the trauma identified and processed is a contributing factor to the client's past substance abuse or relapses.

REFERENCE

Shapiro, F. (2018). *Eye movement desensitization and reprocessing: Basic principles, protocols and procedures* (3rd ed.). Guilford Press.

D: EMDR THERAPY–RELATED RESOURCES

EMDR INTERNATIONAL ASSOCIATION, EMDR RESEARCH FOUNDATION, TRAUMA RECOVERY/EMDR-HUMANITARIAN ASSISTANCE PROGRAMS, AND THE EMDR INSTITUTE: WHAT ARE THE DIFFERENCES?

Understanding the ownership and relationship between the original organizations that arose in the 1990s and 2000s to oversee EMDR therapy's functioning across all boundaries is of importance to all EMDR therapy clinicians. Figure D.1 graphically defines the important differences among the EMDR International Association (EMDRIA), the EMDR Institute, and Trauma Recovery/EMDR-Humanitarian Assistance Programs (HAP).

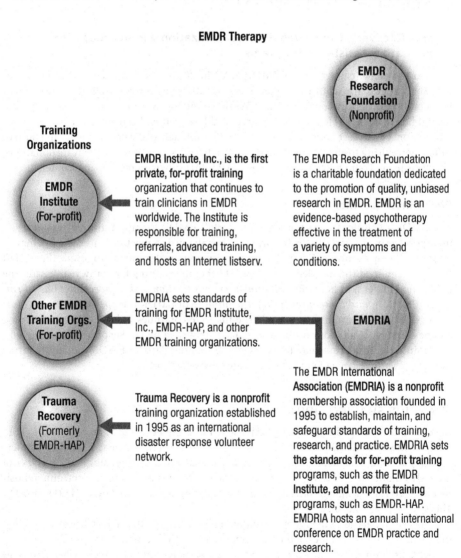

FIGURE D.1 EMDR Therapy and Associated Organizations in the United States.

EMDR International Association

EMDRIA is a 501(c)6 nonprofit membership association founded in 1995 to establish, maintain, and safeguard standards of training, research, and practice for EMDR therapy. EMDRIA is comparable to the American Psychiatric Association, American Psychological Association, or American Counseling Association. This association's mission is to be "a membership organization of mental health professionals dedicated to the highest standards of excellence and integrity in EMDR." EMDRIA's website can be found at www.emdria.org. EMDRIA was the first of the regional EMDR associations. As of this writing, the additional regional associations include EMDR Europe, EMDR IberoAmerica (Central and South America), EMDR Canada, and EMDR Asia.

Trauma Recovery/Eye Movement Desensitization and Reprocessing- Humanitarian Assistance Programs

Trauma Recovery (changed from EMDR-HAP in 2013) was the brainchild of Dr. Francine Shapiro. It is also a 501(c)3 nonprofit organization that offers EMDR therapy training to mental health professionals in Third World countries, as well as domestic community mental health agencies, for free or for a reduced fee. Trauma Recovery/EMDR-HAP is an international volunteer network of mental health providers dedicated to alleviating human suffering resulting from man-made and natural disasters. It is funded by private donations. The website for Trauma Recovery/EMDR-HAP is https://www.emdrhap.org/content/.

EMDR Institute, Inc.

The EMDR Institute, Inc. is the first "for profit" EMDR therapy training organization, incorporated in the early 1990s by Dr. Francine Shapiro to meet the increasing demands of EMDR therapy training. Other than university-approved training programs, the EMDR Institute remained the sole deliverer of EMDR therapy training for many years. After the publication of her first book, *Eye Movement Desensitization and Reprocessing: Basic Principles, Protocols, and Procedures* (1995), the number of EMDR therapy training programs proliferated rapidly around the world. The institute continues to be the longest running and best known of all the training programs. Established by Dr. Shapiro in the early 90s, this training institute continues to represent the gold standard for EMDR therapy. Institute training schedules can be found at its website (www.emdr.org).

FRANCINE SHAPIRO LIBRARY

Created and developed by Barbara J. Hensley, EdD, the Francine Shapiro Library (FSL) was presented to the EMDR therapy community at the 12th Annual EMDRIA Conference in Phoenix, Arizona, in September 2008. Named after the originator and developer of the (AIP) model and EMDR therapy, the library is the world's premier electronic repository and largest assemblage of EMDR citations. The library is hosted by EMDRIA (EMDR Therapy Database, 2020).

Special thanks go to the following individuals for helping this library become a reality: Irene Giessl, EdD, co-founder of the Cincinnati Trauma Connection; Marilyn Schleyer, PhD, former assistant professor, and other faculty members at Northern Kentucky University; and Scott Blech, former executive director, EMDRIA. As of the fall of 2014, EMDRIA became the new host of the library. The link for the FSL is as follows: https://emdria.omeka.net/. Thanks to Michael Wells, Northern Kentucky University Systems librarian, and Joshua Kramer, IT consultant, for helping in this transition.

COUNCIL OF SCHOLARS

In the fall of 2018, EMDRIA formed a steering committee under the auspices of Louise Maxfield, PhD, editor of (JEMDR), to form the Future of EMDR Therapy Project. The initial steering committee was primarily responsible for the selection of EMDR scholars, design of the initial symposium, and the structure of the working groups which led to an inaugural symposium in September 2019 after the EMDRIA Conference in Anaheim, California (Michael Bowers, personal communication, December 19, 2019).

The original group of esteemed scholars included Benedikt Amann, Tamaki Amano, Joyce Baptist, Ian Barron, Ad de Jongh, Carlijn de Roos, Tonya Edmond, Elise Faretta, Derek Farrell, Ana Gomez, Ricky Greenwald, E. C. Hurley, Masaya Ichii, Ignacio Jarero, Emre Konuk, Deborah Korn, Deany Laliotis, Chris Lee, Andrew Leeds, Marilyn Luber, Suzy Matthijssen, Louise Maxfield, Paul Miller, Sushma Mehrotra, Ana Moreno-Alcazar, Udi Oren, Luca Ostacoli, Elan Shapiro, Nancy Smyth, Jonas Tesarz, and Juliane Tortes Saint Jammes. The Council also included representatives from the EMDR Research Foundation, EMDR Europe, and EMDRIA, as well as Mark Nickerson, who was later added as a member working on clinical practice issues.

As an intellectual community, these international EMDR thought leaders were brought together to work toward the goal of advancing the field of EMDR therapy, establishing parameters of EMDR efficacy, and identifying areas of future research.

RESOURCE DEVELOPMENT AND INSTALLATION

Although not covered at length in this Primer, stabilization and ego strengthening are not to be overlooked. They are an inherent and important part of the Preparation Phase of EMDR therapy, especially for difficult and challenging clients, those who are unstable or inadequately resourced, dissociative clients, and clients with low affect tolerance. These topics deserve separate focus and intense study by the clinician.

Resource Development and Installation (RDI) is an effective intervention in the initial stabilization phase of treatment with Complex PTSD/Disorders of Extreme Stress Not Otherwise Specified. RDI is similar to hypnotherapeutic ego-strengthening methods and is compatible with Dialectical Behavior Therapy and other relationally and skill-focused methods of resource development. RDI is an EMDR-related protocol focused on strengthening the connections to resources in the client's positive (i.e., functional) memory network while not intentionally stimulating the client's negative (i.e., dysfunctional or traumatic) memory networks. "Again, the inclusion of bilateral stimulation in the protocol appears to lead to spontaneous, rapid increases in affective intensity within an initially selected memory network and to rich, emotionally vivid associations to other functional (positive) memory networks. These increases in intensity of positive emotion and new functional associations bring additional ego-strengthening material into consciousness" (Korn & Leeds, 2002). Unlike the EMDR protocol, RDI uses fewer (6–12) and slower sets of BLS to facilitate the aforementioned.

There are no published controlled studies of RDI currently available, but there are articles on RDI that discuss it as an effective intervention for stabilization. Clinicians trained in EMDR therapy are encouraged to reference the following resources for RDI:

Korn, D., & Leeds, A. (2002). Preliminary evidence of efficacy for EMDR resource development and installation in the stabilization phase of treatment of complex posttraumatic stress disorder. *Journal of Clinical Psychology, 58*(12), 1465–1487. https://doi.org/10.1002/jclp.10099

Leeds, A. M. (1998). Lifting the burden of shame: Using EMDR resource installation to resolve a therapeutic impasse. In P. Manfield (Ed.), *Extending EMDR: A casebook of innovative applications* (1st ed., pp. 256–281). W. W. Norton.

Leeds, A. M. (2001). Principals and procedures for enhancing current functioning in complex posttraumatic stress disorder with EMDR resource development and installation. *EMDRIA Newsletter,* Special Edition, 4–11.

Leeds, A. M., & Shapiro, F. (2000). EMDR and resource installation: Principles and procedures for enhancing current functioning and resolving traumatic experiences. In J. Carlson & L. Sperry (Eds.), *Brief therapy with individuals and couples* (pp. 469–534). Zeig, Tucker & Theisen.

As a precursor to RDI, see:

Lendl, J., & Foster, S. (1997). Brief intervention focusing protocol for performance enhancement. In J. Lendl & S. Foster (Eds.), *EMDR and performance enhancement for the workplace: A practitioners' manual.* Author.

This publication is currently self-published and available through Mentor Books.

DISSOCIATIVE DISORDERS

Clinical Signs and Symptoms of Dissociative Disorders

Dissociation is something we all experience at some level. We may "lose ourselves in a book" or not be able to recall the details of our car ride to work or school (i.e., highway hypnosis) or find ourselves daydreaming while watching television or mowing the lawn (i.e., zoning out, autopilot mode). In these instances, we tend to lose touch with our present surroundings. Everyone experiences these forms of dissociation at one time or another.

More severe forms of dissociation develop as an effective coping/defense mechanism for some individuals with repeated exposure to overwhelming and life-threatening events (i.e., abuse, violence, war) with extreme physical, emotional, and/or sexual abuse in childhood being the most common cause. Derealization, depersonalization, and dissociative identity disorder constitute the most severe form of dissociation.

A full explanation of dissociation is beyond the scope of this Primer.

Refer to the following references for clinical signs and symptoms of dissociative disorders:

Carlson, E. B., & Putnam, F. W. (1993). An update on the dissociative experiences scale. *Dissociation, 6,* 16–27.

Dell, P. F., & O'Neil, J. A. (2009). *Dissociation and the dissociative disorders.* Routledge.

EMDR Therapy Database (2020). *Francine Shapiro Library (by Barbara J. Hensley).* http://emdria.omeka.net

Kluft, R. P. (1985). The natural history of multiple personality disorder. In R. P. Kluft (Ed.), *The childhood antecedents of multiple personality.* American Psychiatric Press.

Kluft, R. P. (1987). First-rank symptoms as a diagnostic clue to multiple personality disorder. *American Journal of Psychiatry, 144,* 293–298. https://doi.org/10.1176/ajp.144.3.293

Loewenstein, R. J. (1991). An office mental status examination for complex, chronic dissociative symptoms and multiple personality disorder. *Psychiatric Clinics of North America, 14,* 567–604.

Putnam, F. W. (1989). *Diagnosis and treatment of multiple personality disorder.* Guilford Press.

Putnam, F. W., Guroff, J. J., Silberman, E. K., Barban, L., & Post, R. M. (1986). The clinical phenomenology of multiple personality disorder. *Journal of Clinical Psychiatry, 47,* 285–293.

Ross, C. A., Miller, S. D., Reagor, P., Bjornson, L., Fraser, G. A., & Anderson, G. (1990). Schneiderian symptoms in multiple personality disorder and schizophrenia. *Comprehensive Psychiatry, 31,* 111–118.

Spiegel, D. (1993). Multiple posttraumatic personality disorder. In R. P. Kluft & C. G. Fine (Eds.), *Clinical perspectives on multiple personality disorder.* American Psychiatric Press.

In addition, there are resources available that deal with dissociation and EMDR by Catherine Fine, PhD; Carol Forgash, LCSW; Gerald Puk, PhD; Sandra Paulsen, PhD; and others. Search the FSL for these valuable resources.

Dissociative Experiences Scale

Both authorized versions of the Dissociative Experiences Scale (DES) are self-report measures that assess the degree and types of dissociative experiences. The DES is used primarily as a *screening* device for identifying major dissociative pathology and secondarily as a research tool. It is not meant to be utilized as a *diagnostic* tool. Depending on when and by whom the clinician was trained, some EMDR therapy training manuals contain copies of the DES. If not, the clinician may refer to the following resources for an explanation and/or copies of the DES for use with their clients.

The Colin A. Ross Institute for Psychological Trauma provides an excellent description of the DES at www.rossinst.com/dissociative_experiences_scale.html.

For further reading, refer to the following citations:

Dissociative Experiences Scale-I

Bernstein, C., & Putnam, F. (1986). Development, reliability, and validity of a dissociation scale. *Journal of Nervous and Mental Diseases, 174,* 727–735. https://doi.org/10.1097/00005053-198612000-00004

Dissociative Experiences Scale-II

Carlson, E. B., & Putnam, F. W. (1993). An update on the dissociative experiences scale. *Dissociation, 6,* 16–27.

There is a reproducible copy of the Dissociative Experiences Scale-II (DES-II) in this article. Serving as a manual for the DES-II, this article summarizes data on psychiatrically healthy and clinical samples.

Copies of both versions of the DES can be purchased online from the Sidran Foundation at www.sidran.org/product-category/assessment-tools or by contacting the Foundation at the following address:

Sidran Institute
7220 Muncaster Mills Road,
Suite 376
Derwood, MD 20855

Scoring the Dissociative Experiences Scale

The original DES used a visual analog scale that required the client to mark their responses along a numerically anchored 100-mL line. The item responses range from 0% (i.e., "This never happens to you") to 100% (i.e., "This always happens to you"). The newer form of the DES is easier to score in that the responses are made by circling a percentage ranging from 0% to 100% at 10% intervals. The DES-II uses an 11-point Likert scale.

Total scores for both scales can be obtained by averaging the scores of the 28 items. It yields a score in the range of 0 to 100.

Interpreting the Dissociative Experiences Scale

Generally, the higher the score, the more likely the diagnosis of a dissociative disorder. More specifically, the better the likelihood that dissociation exists.

The DES is available in several different languages.

EGO STATE THERAPY

For more information on Ego State Therapy, you are encouraged to access the following resources:

Forgash, C. A., & Copeley, M. (2008). *Healing the heart of trauma and dissociation with EMDR and ego state therapy.* Springer Publishing.
Watkins, H. H., & Watkins, J. G. (1997). *Ego states, theory and therapy.* W. W. Norton.
For formal training in trauma and dissociation, contact the International Society for the Study of Trauma and Dissociation (www.isst-d.org).

SCHEMA THERAPY

Jeffery Young developed Schema therapy for use in the treatment of personality disorders, most especially borderline personality disorder (Young et al., 1994). For more information, refer to the following resources:

Rafaeli, E., Berstein, D. P., & Young, J. E. (2010). *Schema therapy distinctive features.* Routledge.
Young, J. E., Klosko, J. S., & Beck, A. T. (1994). *Reinventing your life: The breakthrough program to end negative behavior ... and feel great again.* Plume.
Young, J. E., Klosko, J. S., & Weisharr, M. E. (2006). *Schema therapy: A practitioner's guide.* Guilford.
Young, J. E., Zangwill, W. M., & Behary, W. E. (2002). Combining EMDR and schema-focused therapy: The whole may be greater than the sum of the parts. In F. Shapiro (Ed.), *EMDR as an integrative psychotherapy approach: Experts of diverse orientations explore the paradigm prism* (1st ed., pp. 181–208). American Psychological Association.

REFERENCES

Bernstein, C., & Putnam, F. (1986). Development, reliability, and validity of a dissociation scale. *Journal of Nervous and Mental Diseases, 174,* 727–735. https://doi.org/10.1097/00005053-198612000-00004
Carlson, E. B., & Putnam, F. W. (1993). An update on the dissociative experiences scale. *Dissociation, 6,* 16–27.

Dell, P. F., & O'Neil, J. A. (2009). *Dissociation and the dissociative disorders*. Routledge.

Forgash, C. A., & Copeley, M. (2008). *Healing the heart of trauma and dissociation with EMDR and ego state therapy*. Springer Publishing Company.

Kluft, R. P. (1985). The natural history of multiple personality disorder. In R. P. Kluft (Ed.), *The childhood antecedents of multiple personality*. American Psychiatric Press.

Kluft, R. P. (1987). First-rank symptoms as a diagnostic clue to multiple personality disorder. *American Journal of Psychiatry, 144*, 293–298. https://doi.org/10.1176/ajp.144.3.293

Korn, D., & Leeds, A. (2002). Preliminary evidence of efficacy for EMDR resource development and installation in the stabilization phase of treatment of complex posttraumatic stress disorder. *Journal of Clinical Psychology, 58*(12), 1465–1487. https://doi.org/10.1002/jclp.10099.

Leeds, A. M. (1998). Lifting the burden of shame: Using EMDR resource installation to resolve a therapeutic impasse. In P. Manfield (Ed.), *Extending EMDR: A casebook of innovative applications* (1st ed., pp. 256–281). W. W. Norton.

Leeds, A. M. (2001). Principals and procedures for enhancing current functioning in complex posttraumatic stress disorder with EMDR resource development and installation. *EMDRIA Newsletter*, Special Edition, 4–11.

Leeds, A. M., & Shapiro, F. (2000). EMDR and resource installation: Principles and procedures for enhancing current functioning and resolving traumatic experiences. In J. Carlson & L. Sperry (Eds.), *Brief therapy with individuals and couples* (pp. 469–534). Zeig, Tucker & Theisen.

Lendl, J., & Foster, S. (1997). Brief intervention focusing protocol for performance enhancement. In J. Lendl & S. Foster (Eds.), *EMDR and performance enhancement for the workplace: A practitioners' manual*. Author.

Loewenstein, R. J. (1991). An office mental status examination for complex, chronic dissociative symptoms and multiple personality disorder. *Psychiatric Clinics of North America, 14*, 567–604.

Putnam, F. W. (1989). *Diagnosis and treatment of multiple personality disorder*. Guilford Press.

Putnam, F. W., Guroff, J. J., Silberman, E. K., Barban, L., & Post, R. M. (1986). The clinical phenomenology of multiple personality disorder. *Journal of Clinical Psychiatry, 47*, 285–293.

Rafaeli, E., Berstein, D. P, & Young, J. E. (2010). *Schema therapy distinctive features*. Routledge.

Ross, C. A., Miller, S. D., Reagor, P., Bjornson, L., Fraser, G. A., & Anderson, G. (1990). Schneiderian symptoms in multiple personality disorder and schizophrenia. *Comprehensive Psychiatry, 31*, 111–118.

Shapiro, F. (2018). *Eye movement desensitization and reprocessing: Basic principles, protocols and procedures* (3rd ed.). Guilford Press.

Spiegel, D. (1993). Multiple posttraumatic personality disorder. In R. P. Kluft & C. G. Fine (Eds.), *Clinical perspectives on multiple personality disorder*. American Psychiatric Press.

Watkins, H. H., & Watkins, J. G. (1997). *Ego states, theory and therapy*. W. W. Norton.

Young, J. E., Klosko, J. S., & Beck, A. T. (1994). *Reinventing your life: The breakthrough program to end negative behavior … and feel great again*. Plume.

Young, J. E., Klosko, J. S., & Weisharr, M. E. (2006). *Schema therapy: A practitioner's guide*. Guilford.

Young, J. E., Zangwill, W. M., & Behary, W. E. (2002). Combining EMDR and schema-focused therapy: The whole may be greater than the sum of the parts. In F. Shapiro (Ed.), *EMDR as an integrative psychotherapy approach: Experts of diverse orientations explore the paradigm prism* (1st ed., pp. 181–208). American Psychological Association.

E: EFFICACY OF EMDR THERAPY

The research so heavily emphasized and encouraged by Dr. Shapiro since her famous walk in the park in the late 1980s has repeatedly proven the efficacy of EMDR therapy. It has become the treatment of choice for various trauma centers and mental health groups around the world. It may be helpful for clinicians to have familiarity with the growing number of endorsements given to EMDR therapy by the leading international health associations. Table E.1 describes the organizations to date that have included EMDR therapy in their International Treatment Guidelines for Trauma, particularly PTSD.

A wide variety of research studies have been implemented using various treatment aspects and protocols as their focus since its initial development. Many of these studies support EMDR therapy as an empirically validated treatment of trauma. Several types of research models are utilized. Among these are meta-analyses (Table E.2), randomized clinical trials (Table E.3), and nonrandomized studies (Table E.4).

TABLE E.1 EMDR International Guidelines

American Psychiatric Association. (2004). *Practice guidelines for the treatment of patients with acute stress disorder and posttraumatic stress disorder.* American Psychiatric Association Practice Guidelines. http://www.psych.org/psych_pract/treatg/pg/prac_guide.cfm

American Psychological Association. (2017). *Clinical practice guideline for the treatment of posttraumatic stress disorder (PTSD) in adults.* https://www.apa.org/ptsd-guideline/ptsd.pdf

Bleich, A., Kotler, M., Kutz, E., & Shaley, A. (2002*). A position paper of the (Israeli) National Council for Mental Health Guidelines for the assessment and professional intervention with terror victims in the hospital and in the community.* https://emdria.omeka.net/items/show/16077

California Evidence-Based Clearinghouse for Child Welfare. (2010). *Trauma treatment for children.* http://cebc4cw.org

Clinical Resource Efficiency Support Team. (2003). *The management of post traumatic stress disorder in adults.* Clinical Resource Efficiency Support Team of the Northern Ireland, Department of Health, Social Services and Public Safety. http://www.gain-ni.org/Guidelines/post_traumatic_stress_disorder.pdf

Department of Veterans Affairs & U.S. Department of Defense. (2017). *VA/DoD clinical practice guideline for the management of post-traumatic stress disorder and acute stress disorder.* The Management of Posttraumatic Stress Disorder Work Group, Office of Quality and Performance Publication. https://www.healthquality.va.gov/guidelines/MH/ptsd/VADoDPTSDCPGFinal012418.pdf

Dutch National Steering Committee Guidelines Mental Health Care. (2003). *Multidisciplinary guidelines anxiety disorders.* Quality Institute Heath Care CBO/Trimbos Institute.

Institut national de la santé et de la recherche médicale. (2004). *Psychothérapie, trois approches évaluées [Psychotherapy: An evaluation of three approaches].* https://www.inserm.fr/en/Publicationsandstatistics/Publications/PublicationsPolicyAndGuidance/DH_4007323.

(continued)

TABLE E.1 EMDR International Guidelines (continued)

International Society for Traumatic Stress Studies. (2018). *PTSD prevention and treatment guidelines methodology and recommendations.* ISTSS. http://www.istss.org/treating-trauma/new-istss-prevention-and-treatment-guidelines.aspx

Substance Abuse and Mental Health Services America. (2012). *Comparative effectiveness research series. Eye movement desensitization and reprocessing: An information resource.* SAMHSA's National Registry of Evidence-based Programs and Practices. https://cdn.ymaws.com/www.emdria.org/resource/resmgr/research/treatment_guidelines/samhsa.2012.nrepp-comparativ.pdf

Sjöblom, P. O., Andréewitch, S., Bejerot, S., Mörtberg, E., Brinck, U., Ruck, C., & Körlin, D. (2003). *Regional treatment recommendation for anxiety disorders.* Medical Program Committee/Stockholm City Council.

The Cochrane Database of Systematic Reviews. (2013). *Psychological therapies for chronic post-traumatic stress disorder (PTSD) in adults.* https://www.cochrane.org/CD003388/DEPRESSN_psychological-therapies-chronic-post-traumatic-stress-disorder-ptsd-adults

Therapy Advisor. (2004–2007). Retrieved October 19, 2011 from http://www.therapyadvisor.com

United Kingdom Department of Health. (2001). *Treatment choice in psychological therapies and counseling evidence based clinical practice guidelines.* London: Department of Health.

World Health Organization (2013). *Guidelines for the management of conditions specifically related to stress.* Author.

TABLE E.2 Meta-Analyses of EMDR

Bisson, J., & Andrew, M. (2007). Psychological treatment of post-traumatic stress disorder (PTSD). *Cochrane database of systematic reviews, 3,* Article CD003388. doi:10.1002/14651858.CD003388.pub3

Bradley, R., Greene, J., Russ, E., Dutra, L., & Westen, D. (2005). A multidimensional meta-analysis of psychotherapy for PTSD. *American Journal of Psychiatry, 162*(2), 214–227. https://doi.org/10.1176/appi.ajp.162.2.214

Chen, Y. R., Hung, K. W., Tsai, J. C., Chu, H., Chung, M. H., Chen, S. R., Liao, Y. M., Ou, K. L., Chang, Y. C., Chou, K. R. (2014). Efficacy of eye-movement desensitization and reprocessing for patients with posttraumatic-stress disorder: A meta-analysis of randomized controlled trials. *PloS One, 9*(8), e103676. https://doi.org/10.1371/journal.pone.0103676

Davidson, P. R., & Parker, K. C. H. (2001). Eye movement desensitization and reprocessing (EMDR): A meta-analysis. *Journal of Consulting and Clinical Psychology, 69,* 305–316. https://doi.org/101037//0022-006x.69.2.305

Ho, M. S. K., & Lee, C. W. (2012). Cognitive behaviour therapy versus eye movement desensitization and reprocessing for post-traumatic disorder—Is it all in the homework then? *European Review of Applied Psychology/Revue Européenne de Psychologie Appliquée, 62*(4), 253–260. https://doi.org/10.1016/j.erap.2012.08.001

(continued)

TABLE E.2 Meta-Analyses of EMDR (continued)

Lee, C. W., & Cuijpers, P. (2012). A meta-analysis of the contribution of eye movements in processing emotional memories. *Journal of Behavior Therapy and Experimental Psychology, 44*(2), 231–239. https://doi.org/10.1016/j. jbtep.2012.11.001

Maxfield, L., & Hyer, L. A. (2002). The relationship between efficacy and methodology in studies investigating EMDR treatment of PTSD. *Journal of Clinical Psychology, 58*, 23–41. https://doi.org/10.1002/jclp.1127

Rodenburg, R., Benjamin, A., de Roos, C., Meijer, A. M., & Stams, G. J. (2009). Efficacy of EMDR in children: A meta-analysis. *Clinical Psychology Review, 29*(70), 599–606. https://doi.org/10.1016/j.cpr.2009.06.008

Seidler, G. H., & Wagner, F. E. (2006). Comparing the efficacy of EMDR and trauma-focused cognitive-behavioral therapy in the treatment of PTSD: A meta-analytic study. *Psychological Medicine, 36*(11), 1515–1522. https://doi.org/10.1017/S0033291706007963

Watts, B. V., Schnurr, P. P., Mayo, L., Yinong, Y., Weeks, W. B., & Friedman, M. J. (2013). Meta-analysis of the efficacy of treatments for posttraumatic stress disorder. *Journal of Clinical Psychiatry, 74*(6), e541–e550. https://doi.org/10.4088/JCP.12r08225

TABLE E.3 Randomized Clinical Trials

Abbasnejad, M., Mahani, K. N., & Zamyad, A. (2007). Efficacy of "eye movement desensitization and reprocessing" in reducing anxiety and unpleasant feelings due to earthquake experience. *Psychological Research, 9*(3–4), 104–117.

Acarturk, C., Konuk, E., Cetinkaya, M., Senay, I., Sijbrandij, M., Gulen, B., & Cuijpers, P. (2016). The efficacy of eye movement desensitization and reprocessing for post-traumatic stress disorder and depression among Syrian refugees: Results of a randomized controlled trial. *Psychological Medicine, 46*(12), 2583–2593. https://doi.org/10.1017/S0033291716001070

Ahmad, A., Larsson, B., & Sundelin-Wahlsten, V. (2007). EMDR treatment for children with PTSD: Results of a randomized controlled trial. *Nordic Journal of Psychiatry, 61*(5), 349–354. https://doi.org/10.1080/08039480701643464

Ahmadi, K., Hazrati, M., Ahmadizadeh, M., & Noohi, S. (2015). REM desensitization as a new therapeutic method for post- traumatic stress disorder: A randomized controlled trial. *Acta Medica Indonesiana, 47*(2), 111–119.

Arabia, E., Manca, M. L., & Solomon, R. M. (2011). EMDR for survivors of life-threatening cardiac events: Results of a pilot study. *Journal of EMDR Practice and Research, 5*(1), 2–13. https://doi.org/10.1891/1933-3196.5.1.2

Capezzani, L., Ostacoli, L., Cavallo, M., Carletto, S., Fernandez, I., Solomon, R., Pagani, M., Cantelmi, T. (2013). EMDR and CBT for cancer patients: Comparative study of effects on PTSD, anxiety, and depression. *Journal of EMDR Practice and Research, 7*(3), 134–143. https://doi.org/10.1891/1933-3196.7.3.134

Carletto, S., Borghi, M., Bertino, G., Oliva, F., Cavallo, M., Hofmann, A., & Ostacoli, L. (2016). Treating post-traumatic stress disorder in patients with multiple sclerosis: A randomized controlled trial comparing the efficacy of eye movement desensitization and reprocessing and relaxation therapy. *Frontiers in Psychology, 7*, 526. https://doi.org/10.3389/fpsyg.2016.00526

(continued)

TABLE E.3 Randomized Clinical Trials (continued)

Carlson, J., Chemtob, C. M., Rusnak, K., Hedlund, N. L., & Muraoka, M. Y. (1998). Eye movement desensitization and reprocessing (EMDR): Treatment for combat-related posttraumatic stress disorder. *Journal of Traumatic Stress, 11*, 3–24. https://doi.org/10.1023/A:1024448814268

Chemtob, C. M., Nakashima, J., & Carlson, J. G. (2002). Brief-treatment for elementary school children with disaster-related PTSD: A field study. *Journal of Clinical Psychology, 58*, 99–112. https://doi.org/10.1002/jclp.1131

Cvetek, R. (2008). EMDR treatment of distressful experiences that fail to meet the criteria for PTSD. *Journal of EMDR Practice and Research, 2*(1), 2–14. https://doi.org/10.1891/1933-3196.2.1.2de Bont, P. A., van den Berg, D. P., van der Vleugel, B. M., de Roos, C., de Jongh, A., van der Gaag, M., & van Minnen, A. M. (2016). Prolonged exposure and EMDR for PTSD v. a PTSD waiting-list condition: Effects on symptoms of psychosis, depression and social functioning in patients with chronic psychotic disorders. *Psychological Medicine, 46*(11), 2411–2421. https://doi.org/10.1017/S0033291716001094

de Bont, P. A., van Minnen, A., & de Jongh, A. (2013). Treating PTSD in patients with psychosis: A within-group controlled feasibility study examining the efficacy and safety of evidence-based PE and EMDR protocols. *Behavior Therapy, 44*(4), 717–730. https://doi.org/10.1016/j.beth.2013.07.002

de Roos, C., Greenwald, R., den Hollander-Gijsm, M., Noorthoorn, E., van Buuren, S., & de Jongh, A. (2011). A randomised comparison of cognitive behavioural therapy (CBT) and eye movement desensitisation and reprocessing (EMDR) in disaster-exposed children. *European Journal of Psychotraumatology, 2*, 5694. https://doi.org/10.3402/ejpt.v2i0.5694

de Roos, C., van der Oord, S., Zijlstra, B., Lucassen, S., Perrin, S., Emmelkamp, P., & de Jongh, A. (in press). Comparison of EMDR therapy, cognitive behavioral writing therapy, and waitlist in pediatric PTSD following single-incident trauma: A multi-center randomized clinical trial. *Journal of Child Psychology and Psychiatry, 58*(11), 1219–1228. https://doi.org/10.1111/jcpp.12768

Devilly, G. J., & Spence, S. H. (1999). The relative efficacy and treatment distress of EMDR and a cognitive behavioral trauma treatment protocol in the amelioration of posttraumatic stress disorder. *Journal of Anxiety Disorders, 13*(1–2), 131–157. https://doi.org/10.1016/S0887-6185(98)00044-9

Diehle, J., Opmeer, B. C., Boer, F., Mannarino, A. P., & Lindauer, R. J. (2015). Trauma-focused cognitive behavioral therapy or eye movement desensitization and reprocessing: What works in children with posttraumatic stress symptoms? A randomized controlled trial. *European Child & Adolescent Psychiatry, 24*(2), 1–10. https://doi.org/10.1007/s00787-014-0572-5

Edmond, T., Rubin, A., & Wambach, K. (1999). The effectiveness of EMDR with adult female survivors of childhood sexual abuse. *Social Work Research, 23*, 103–116. https://doi.org/10.1093/swr/23.2.103

Edmond, T., Sloan, L., & McCarty, D. (2004). Sexual abuse survivors' perceptions of the effectiveness of EMDR and eclectic therapy: A mixed-methods study. *Research on Social Work Practice, 14*, 259–272. https://doi.org/10.1177/1049731504265830

(continued)

TABLE E.3 Randomized Clinical Trials (continued)

Gil-Jardiné, C. Evrard, G., Al Joboory, S., Saint Jammes, J. T., Masson, F., Ribéreau-Gayon, R., Galinski, M., Salmi, L. R., Revel, P., Régis, C. A., Valdenaire, G., & Lagarde, E. (2018). Emergency room intervention to prevent post concussion-like symptoms and post-traumatic stress disorder: A pilot randomized controlled study of a brief eye movement desensitization and reprocessing intervention versus reassurance or usual care. *Journal of Psychiatric Research, 103*, 229–236. https://doi.org/10.1016/j.jpsychires.2018.05

Högberg, G., Pagani, M., Sundin, Ö., Soares, J., Aberg-Wistedt, A., Tarnell, B., & Hallstrom, T. (2007). On treatment with eye movement desensitization and reprocessing of chronic post-traumatic stress disorder in public transportation workers—A randomized controlled trial. *Nordic Journal of Psychiatry, 61*, 54–61. https://doi.org/10.1080/08039480601129408

Follow-up: Högberg, G., Pagani, M., Sundin, Ö., Soares, J., Aberg-Wistedt, A., Tarnell, B., & Hallström, T. (2008). Treatment of post-traumatic stress disorder with eye movement desensitization and reprocessing: Outcome is stable in 35-month follow-up. *Psychiatry Research, 159*(1–2), 101–108. https://doi.org/10.1016/j.psychres.2007.10.019

Ironson, G. I., Freund, B., Strauss, J. L., & Williams, J. (2002). Comparison of two treatments for traumatic stress: A community-based study of EMDR and prolonged exposure. *Journal of Clinical Psychology, 58*, 113–128. https://doi.org/10.1002/jclp.1132

Jaberghaderi, N., Greenwald, R., Rubin, A., Zand, S. O., & Dolatabadim, S. (2004). A comparison of CBT and EMDR for sexually abused Iranian girls. *Clinical Psychology and Psychotherapy, 11*, 358–368. https://doi.org/10.1002/cpp.395

Jarero, I., Artigas, L., & Luber, M. (2011). The EMDR protocol for recent critical incidents: Application in a disaster mental health continuum of care context. *Journal of EMDR Practice and Research, 5*, 82–94. https://doi.org/10.1891/1933-3196.5.3.82

Jarero, I., Givaudan, M., & Osorio, A. (2018). Randomized controlled trial on the provision of the EMDR integrative group treatment protocol adapted for ongoing traumatic stress to female patients with cancer-related posttraumatic stress disorder symptoms. *Journal of EMDR Practice and Research, 12*(3), 94–104. https://doi.org/10.1891/1933-3196.12.3.94

Jarero, I., Uribe, S., Artigas, L., & Givaudan, M. (2015). EMDR protocol for recent critical incidents: A randomized controlled trial in a technological disaster context. *Journal of EMDR Practice and Research, 9*, 166–173. https://doi.org/10.1891/1933-3196.9.4.166

Johnson, D. R., & Lubin, H. (2006). The counting method: Applying the rule of parsimony to the treatment of posttraumatic stress disorder. *Traumatology, 12*(1), 83. https://doi.org/10.1177/153476560601200106

Karatzias, T., Power, K., Brown, K., McGoldrick, T., Begum, M., Young, J., Loughran, P., Chouliara, Z., & Adams, S. (2011). A controlled comparison of the effectiveness and efficiency of two psychological therapies for posttraumatic stress disorder: Eye movement desensitization and reprocessing vs. emotional freedom techniques. *Journal of Nervous Mental Disease, 199*(6), 372–378. https://doi.org/10.1097/NMD.0b013e31821cd262

Kemp, M., Drummond, P., & McDermott, B. (2010). A wait-list controlled pilot study of eye movement desensitization and reprocessing (EMDR) for children with post-traumatic stress disorder (PTSD) symptoms from motor vehicle accidents. *Clinical Child Psychology and Psychiatry, 15*(1), 5–25. https://doi.org/10.1177/1359104509339086

Laugharne, J., Kullack, C., Lee, C. W., McGuire, T., Brockman, S., Drummond, P. D., & Starkstein, S. (2016). Amygdala volumetric change following psychotherapy for posttraumatic stress disorder. *The Journal of Neuropsychiatry and Clinical Neurosciences.* https://doi.org/10.1176/appi.neuropsych.16010006

(continued)

TABLE E.3 Randomized Clinical Trials (continued)

Lee, C., Gavriel, H., Drummond, P., Richards, J., & Greenwald, R. (2002). Treatment of posttraumatic stress disorder: A comparison of stress inoculation training with prolonged exposure and eye movement desensitization and reprocessing. *Journal of Clinical Psychology, 58,* 1071–1089. https://doi.org/10.1002/jclp.10039

Marcus, S., Marquis, P., & Sakai, C. (1997). Controlled study of treatment of PTSD using EMDR in an HMO setting. *Psychotherapy, 34,* 307–315. https://doi.org/10.1037/h0087791

Marcus, S., Marquis, P., & Sakai, C. (2004). Three- and six-month follow-up of EMDR treatment of PTSD in an HMO setting. *International Journal of Stress Management, 11,* 195–208. https://doi.org/10.1037/1072–5245.11.3.195

Nijdam, M. J., Gersons, B. P. R., Reitsma, J. B., de Jongh, A., & Olff, M. (2012). Brief eclectic psychotherapy v. eye movement desensitisation and reprocessing therapy in the treatment of post-traumatic stress disorder: Randomised controlled trial. *British Journal of Psychiatry, 200,* 224–231. https://doi.org/10.1192/bjp.bp.111.099234

Novo, P., Landin-Romero, R., Radua, J., Vicens, V., Fernandez, I., Garcia, F., Pomarol-Clotet, E., McKenna, P. J., Shapiro, F., & Amann, B. L. (2014). Eye movement desensitization and reprocessing therapy in subsyndromal bipolar patients with a history of traumatic events: A randomized, controlled pilot-study. *Psychiatry Research, 219*(1), 122–128. https://doi.org/10.1016/j.psychres.2014.05.012

Osorio, A., Pérez, M. C., Tirado, S. G., Jarero, I., & Givaudan, M. (2018). Randomized controlled trial on the EMDR integrative group treatment protocol for ongoing traumatic stress with adolescents and young adults patients with cancer. *American Journal of Applied Psychology, 7*(4), 50–56. https://doi.org/10.11648/j.ajap.20180704.11

Power, K., McGoldrick, T., Brown, K., Buchanan, R., Sharp, D., Swanson, V., & Karatzias, A. (2002). A controlled comparison of eye movement desensitization and reprocessing versus exposure plus cognitive restructuring, versus waiting list in the treatment of post-traumatic stress disorder. *Journal of Clinical Psychology and Psychotherapy, 9,* 299–318. https://doi.org/10.1002/cpp.341

Rothbaum, B. O. (1997). A controlled study of eye movement desensitization and reprocessing in the treatment of post-traumatic stress disordered sexual assault victims. *Bulletin of the Menninger Clinic, 61,* 317–334.

Rothbaum, B. O., Astin, M. C., & Marsteller, F. (2005). Prolonged exposure versus eye movement desensitization and reprocessing (EMDR) for PTSD rape victims. *Journal of Traumatic Stress, 18,* 607–616. https://doi.org/10.1002/ jts.20069

Scheck, M., Schaeffer, J. A., & Gillette, C. (1998). Brief psychological intervention with traumatized young women: The efficacy of eye movement desensitization and reprocessing. *Journal of Traumatic Stress, 11,* 25–44. https://doi.org/10.1023/A:1024400931106

Shapiro, E., & Laub, B. (2015). Early EMDR intervention following a community critical incident: A randomized clinical trial. *Journal of EMDR Practice and Research, 9*(1), 17–27. https://doi.org/10.1891/1933-3196.9.1.17

Shapiro, F. (1989a). Efficacy of the eye movement desensitization procedure in the treatment of traumatic memories. *Journal of Traumatic Stress Studies, 2,* 199–223. https://doi.org/10.1007/BF00974159

Soberman, G. B., Greenwald, R., & Rule, D. L. (2002). A controlled study of eye movement desensitization and reprocessing (EMDR) for boys with conduct problems. *Journal of Aggression, Maltreatment, and Trauma, 6,* 217–236. https://doi.org/10.1300/J146v06n01_11

(continued)

TABLE E.3 Randomized Clinical Trials (continued)

Tarquinio, C., Rotonda, C., Houllé, W. A., Montel, S., Rydberg, J. A., Minary, L., Dellucci, H., Tarquinio, P., Fayard, A., & Alla, F. (2016). Early psychological preventive intervention for workplace violence: A randomized controlled explorative and comparative study between EMDR-recent event and critical incident stress debriefing. *Issues in Mental Health Nursing, 37*(11), 787–799. https://doi.org/10.1080/01612840.201 6.1224282

Taylor, S., Thordarson, D., Maxfield, L., Fedoroff, I., Lovell, K., & Ogrodniczuk, J. (2003). Comparative efficacy, speed, and adverse effects of three PTSD treatments: Exposure therapy, EMDR, and relaxation training. *Journal of Consulting and Clinical Psychology, 71*, 330–338. https://doi.org/10.1037/0022-006X.71.2.330

ter Heide, F. J. J., Mooren, T. M., van de Schoot, R., de Jongh, A., & Kleber, R. J. (2016). Eye movement desensitisation and reprocessing therapy v. stabilisation as usual for refugees: Randomised controlled trial. *The British Journal of Psychiatry, 209*(4), 311–318. https://doi.org/10.1192/bjp.bp.115.167775

van den Berg, D. P. G., de Bont, P. A. J. M., van der Vleugel, B. M., de Roos, C., de Jongh, A., van Minnen, A., & van der Gaag, M. (2015). Prolonged exposure vs eye movement desensitization and reprocessing vs waiting list for posttraumatic stress disorder in patients with a psychotic disorder: A randomized clinical trial. *Journal of the American Medical Association Psychiatry, 72*(3), 259–267. https://doi.org/10.1001/jamapsychiatry.2014.2637

van der Kolk, B. A., Spinazzola, J., Blaustein, M. E., Hopper, J. W., Hopper, E. K., Korn, D. L., & Simpson, W. B. (2007). A randomized clinical trial of eye movement desensitization and reprocessing (EMDR), fluoxetine, and pill placebo in the treatment of posttraumatic stress disorder: Treatment effects and long-term maintenance. *Journal of Clinical Psychiatry, 68*(1), 37–46. https://doi.org/10.4088/JCP.v68n0105

Vaughan, K., Armstrong, M. F., Gold, R., O'Connor, N., Jenneke, W., & Tarrier, N. (1994). A trial of eye movement desensitization compared to image habituation training and applied muscle relaxation in post- traumatic stress disorder. *Journal of Behavior Therapy & Experimental Psychiatry, 25*, 283–291. https://doi.org/10.1016/0005-7916(94)90036-1

Wanders, F., Serra, M., & de Jongh, A. (2008). EMDR versus CBT for children with self-esteem and behavioral problems: A randomized controlled trial. *Journal of EMDR Practice and Research, 2*(3), 180–189. https://doi.org/10.1891/1933-3196.2.3.180

Wilson, S., Becker, L. A., & Tinker, R. H. (1995). Eye movement desensitization and reprocessing (EMDR): Treatment for psychologically traumatized individuals. *Journal of Consulting and Clinical Psychology, 63*, 928–937. https://doi.org/10.1037/0022-006X.63.6.928

Wilson, S., Becker, L. A., & Tinker, R. H. (1997). Fifteen-month follow-up of eye movement desensitization and reprocessing (EMDR) treatment of post-traumatic stress disorder and psychological trauma. *Journal of Consulting and Clinical Psychology, 65*, 1047–1056. https://doi.org/10.1037/0022-006X.65.6.1047

Yurtsever, A., Konuk, E., Akyüz, T., Zat, Z., Tükel, F., Çetinkaya, M., Savran, C., & Shapiro, E. (2018). An eye movement desensitization and reprocessing (EMDR) group intervention for Syrian refugees with posttraumatic stress symptoms: Results of a randomized controlled trial. *Frontiers in Psychology, 9*, 493. https://doi.org/10.3389/fpsyg.2018.00493

TABLE E.4 Nonrandomized Studies

Adúriz, M. E., Bluthgen, C., & Knopfler, C. (2009, May). Helping child flood victims using group EMDR intervention in Argentina: Treatment outcome and gender differences. *International Journal of Stress Management, 16*(2), 138–153. https://doi.org/10.1037/a0014719

Devilly, G. J., & Spence, S. H. (1999). The relative efficacy and treatment distress of EMDR and a cognitive behavioral trauma treatment protocol in the amelioration of post-traumatic stress disorder. *Journal of Anxiety Disorders, 13*, 131–157. https://doi.org/10.1016/S0887-6185(98)00044-9

Fernandez, I. (2007). EMDR as a treatment of post-traumatic reactions: A field study on child victims of an earthquake. *Educational and Child Psychology, Special Issue: Therapy, 24*(1), 65–72.

Fernandez, I., Gallinari, E., & Lorenzetti, A. (2004). A school-based EMDR intervention for children who witnessed the Pirelli Building airplane crash in Milan, Italy. *Journal of Brief Therapy, 2*, 129–136.

Grainger, R. D., Levin, C., Allen-Byrd, L., Doctor, R. M., & Lee, H. (1997). An empirical evaluation of eye movement desensitization and reprocessing (EMDR) with survivors of a natural catastrophe. *Journal of Traumatic Stress, 10*(4), 665–671. https://doi.org/10.1023/A:1024806105473

Hensel, T. (2009). EMDR with children and adolescents after single-incident trauma: An intervention study. *Journal of EMDR Practice and Research, 3*(1), 2–9. https://doi.org/10.1891/1933–3196.3.1.2

Hurley, E. C. (2018). Effective treatment of veterans with PTSD: Comparison between intensive daily and weekly EMDR approaches. *Frontiers in Psychology, 9*(1458), 1–10. https://doi.org/10.3389/fpsyg.2018.01458

Jarero, I., & Artigas, L. (2010). The EMDR integrative group treatment protocol: Application with adults during ongoing geopolitical crisis. *Journal of EMDR Practice and Research, 4*(4), 148–155. https://doi.org/10.1891/1933– 3196.4.4.148

Jarero, I., Artigas, L., & Hartung, J. (2006). EMDR integrative group treatment protocol: A postdisaster trauma intervention for children and adults. *Traumatology, 12*(2), 121–129. https://doi.org/10.1177/1534765606294561

Jarero, I., Artigas, L., Montero, M., & Lopez-Lena, L. (2008). The EMDR integrative group treatment protocol: Application with child victims of a mass disaster. *Journal of EMDR Practice and Research, 2*(2), 97–105. https://doi.org/10.1891/1933-3196.2.2.97

Jarero, I., Artigas, L., Uribe, S., García, L. E., Cavazos, M. A., & Givaudan, M. (2015). Pilot research study on the provision of the eye movement desensitization and reprocessing integrative group treatment protocol with female cancer patients. *Journal of EMDR Practice and Research, 9*(2), 98–105. https://doi.org/10.1891/1933-3196.9.2.98

Jarero, I., Roque-López, S., & Gomez, J. (2013). The provision of an EMDR-based multicomponent trauma treatment with child victims of severe interpersonal trauma. *Journal of EMDR Practice and Research, 7*(1), 17–28. https://doi.org/10.1891/1933-3196.7.1.17

Jarero, I., & Uribe, S. (2011). The EMDR protocol for recent critical incidents: Brief report of an application in a human massacre situation. *Journal of EMDR Practice and Research, 5*, 156–165. https://doi.org/10.1891/1933-3196.5.4.156

Jarero, I., & Uribe, S. (2012). The EMDR protocol for recent critical incidents: Follow-up report of an application in a human massacre situation. *Journal of EMDR Practice and Research, 6*, 50–61. https://doi.org/10.1891/1933-3196.6.2.50

(continued)

TABLE E.4 Nonrandomized Studies (continued)

Konuk, E., Knipe, J., Eke, I., Yuksek, H., Yurtsever, A., & Ostep, S. (2006). The effects of eye movement desensitization and reprocessing (EMDR) therapy on post-traumatic stress disorder in survivors of the 1999 Marmara, Turkey, earthquake. *International Journal of Stress Management, 13*(3), 291–308. https://doi.org/10.1037/1072-5245.13.3.291

McLay, R. N., Webb-Murphy, J. A., Fesperman, S. F., Delaney, E. M., Gerard, S. K., Roesch, S. C., Nebeker, B. J., Pandzic, I., Vishnyak, E. A., & Johnston, S. L. (2016). Outcomes from eye movement desensitization and reprocessing in active-duty service members with posttraumatic stress disorder. *Psychological Trauma: Theory, Research, Practice, and Policy.* http://dx.doi.org/10.1037/tra0000120

Puffer, M., Greenwald, R., & Elrod, D. (1998). A single session EMDR study with twenty traumatized children and adolescents. *Traumatology, 3*(2), Article 6. https://doi.org/10.1037/h0101053

Ribchester, T., Yule, W., & Duncan, A. (2010). EMDR for childhood PTSD after road traffic accidents: Attentional, memory, and attributional processes. *Journal of EMDR Practice and Research, 4*(4), 138–147. https://doi.org/10.1891/1933-3196.4.4.138

Russell, M. C., Silver, S. M., Rogers, S., & Darnell, J. (2007). Responding to an identified need: A joint Department of Defense-Department of Veterans Affairs training program in eye movement desensitization and reprocessing (EMDR) for clinicians providing trauma services. *International Journal of Stress Management, 14*, 61–71. https://doi.org/10.1037/1072-5245.14.1.61

Schubert, S. J., Lee, C. W., de Araujo, G., Butler, S. R., Taylor, G., & Drummond, P. (2016). The effectiveness of eye movement desensitization and reprocessing (EMDR) therapy to treat symptoms following trauma in Timor Leste. *Journal of Traumatic Stress, 1–8.* https://doi.org/10.1002/jts.22084

Silver, S. M., Brooks, A., & Obenchain, J. (1995). Eye movement desensitization and reprocessing treatment of Vietnam war veterans. *Journal of Traumatic Stress, 8,* 337–342.

Silver, S. M., Rogers, S., Knipe, J., & Colelli, G. (2005). EMDR therapy following the 9/11 terrorist attacks: A community-based intervention project in New York City. *International Journal of Stress Management, 12*(1), 29–42. https://doi.org/10.1037/1072-5245.12.1.29

Solomon, R. M., & Kaufman, T. E. (2002). A peer support workshop for the treatment of traumatic stress of railroad personnel: Contributions of eye movement desensitization and reprocessing (EMDR). *Journal of Brief Therapy, 2,* 27–33.

Sprang, G. (2001). The use of eye movement desensitization and reprocessing (EMDR) in the treatment of traumatic stress and complicated mourning: Psychological and behavioral outcomes. *Research on Social Work Practice, 11,* 300–320. https://doi.org/10.1177/104973150101100302.

Wadaa, N. N., Zaharim, N. M., & Alqashan, H. F. (2010). The use of EMDR in treatment of traumatized Iraqi children. *Digest of Middle East Studies, 19*(1), 26–36. https://doi.org/10.1111/j.1949-3606.2010.00003.x

Zaghrout-Hodali, M., Alissa, F., & Dodgson, P. (2008). Building resilience and dismantling fear: EMDR group protocol with children in an area of ongoing trauma. *Journal of EMDR Practice and Research, 2*(2), 106–113. https://doi.org/10.1891/1933-3196.2.2.106

REFERENCES

Abbasnejad, M., Mahani, K. N., & Zamyad, A. (2007). Efficacy of "eye movement desensitization and reprocessing" in reducing anxiety and unpleasant feelings due to earthquake experience. *Psychological Research, 9*(3–4), 104–117. https://doi.org/10.1017/S0033291716001070

Acarturk, C., Konuk, E., Cetinkaya, M., Senay, I., Sijbrandij, M., Gulen, B., & Cuijpers, P. (2016). The efficacy of eye movement desensitization and reprocessing for post-traumatic stress disorder and depression among Syrian refugees: Results of a randomized controlled trial. *Psychological medicine, 46*(12), 2583–2593. https://doi.org/10.1017/S0033291716001070

Adúriz, M. E., Bluthgen, C., & Knopfler, C. (2009). Helping child flood victims using group EMDR intervention in Argentina: Treatment outcome and gender differences. *International Journal of Stress Management, 16*(2), 138–153. https://doi.org/10.1037/a0014719

Ahmad, A., Larsson, B., & Sundelin-Wahlsten, V. (2007). EMDR treatment for children with PTSD: Results of a randomized controlled trial. *Nordic Journal of Psychiatry, 61*(5), 349–354. https://doi.org/10.1080/08039480701643464

Ahmadi, K., Hazrati, M., Ahmadizadeh, M., & Noohi, S. (2015). REM desensitization as a new therapeutic method for post- traumatic stress disorder: A randomized controlled trial. *Acta Medica Indonesiana, 47*(2), 111–119.

American Psychiatric Association. (2000). *Diagnostic and statistical manual of mental disorders* (4th ed., text rev.). Author.

American Psychiatric Association. (2004). *Practice guidelines for the treatment of patients with acute stress disorder and posttraumatic stress disorder.* American Psychiatric Association Practice Guidelines. http://www.psych.org/psych_pract/treatg/pg/prac_guide.cfm

American Psychological Association. (2017). *Clinical practice guideline for the treatment of posttraumatic stress disorder (PTSD) in adults.* https://www.apa.org/ptsd-guideline/ptsd.pdf

Arabia, E., Manca, M. L., & Solomon, R. M. (2011). EMDR for survivors of life-threatening cardiac events: Results of a pilot study. *Journal of EMDR Practice and Research, 5*(1), 2–13. https://doi.org/10.1891/1933-3196.5.1.2

Bisson, J., & Andrew, M. (2007). Psychological treatment of post-traumatic stress disorder (PTSD). *Cochrane Database of Systematic Reviews, 3*, Article CD003388. https://doi.org/10.1002/14651858.CD003388.pub3

Bleich, A., Kotler, M., Kutz, E., & Shaley, A. (2002). *A position paper of the (Israeli) National Council for Mental Health Guidelines for the assessment and professional intervention with terror victims in the hospital and in the community.* https://emdria.omeka.net/items/show/16077

Bradley, R., Greene, J., Russ, E., Dutra, L., & Westen, D. (2005). A multidimensional meta-analysis of psychotherapy for PTSD. *American Journal of Psychiatry, 162*(2), 214–227. https://doi.org/10.1176/appi.ajp.162.2.214

California Evidence-Based Clearinghouse for Child Welfare. (2010). *Trauma treatment for children.* http://cebc4cw.org.

Capezzani, L., Ostacoli, L., Cavallo, M., Carletto, S., Fernandez, I., Solomon, R., Pagani, M., Cantelmi, T. (2013). EMDR and CBT for cancer patients: Comparative study of effects on PTSD, anxiety, and depression. *Journal of EMDR Practice and Research, 7*(3), 134–143. https://doi.org/10.1891/1933-3196.7.3.134

Carletto, S., Borghi, M., Bertino, G., Oliva, F., Cavallo, M., Hofmann, A., & Ostacoli, L. (2016). Treating post-traumatic stress disorder in patients with multiple sclerosis: A randomized controlled trial comparing the efficacy of eye movement desensitization and reprocessing and relaxation therapy. *Frontiers in Psychology, 7*, 526. https://doi.org/10.3389/fpsyg.2016.00526

Carlson, J., Chemtob, C. M., Rusnak, K., Hedlund, N. L., & Muraoka, M. Y. (1998). Eye movement desensitization and reprocessing (EMDR): Treatment for combat-related posttraumatic stress disorder. *Journal of Traumatic Stress, 11*, 3–24. https://doi.org/10.1023/A:1024448814268.

Chemtob, C. M., Nakashima, J., & Carlson, J. G. (2002). Brief-treatment for elementary school children with disaster-related PTSD: A field study. *Journal of Clinical Psychology, 58*, 99–112. https://doi.org/10.1002/jclp.1131

Chen, Y. R., Hung, K. W., Tsai, J. C., Chu, H., Chung, M. H., Chen, S. R., Liao, Y. M., Ou, K. L., Chang, Y. C., Chou, K. R. (2014). Efficacy of eye-movement desensitization and reprocessing for patients with posttraumatic-stress disorder: A meta-analysis of randomized controlled trials. *PloS One*, *9*(8), e103676. https://doi.org/10.1371/journal.pone.0103676

Clinical Resource Efficiency Support Team. (2003). *The management of post traumatic stress disorder in adults*. Clinical Resource Efficiency Support Team of the Northern Ireland, Department of Health, Social Services and Public Safety. http://www.gain-ni.org/Guidelines/post_traumatic_stress_disorder.pdf

Cvetek, R. (2008). EMDR treatment of distressful experiences that fail to meet the criteria for PTSD. *Journal of EMDR Practice and Research*, *2*(1), 2–14. https://doi.org/10.1891/1933-3196.2.1.2

Davidson, P. R., & Parker, K. C. H. (2001). Eye movement desensitization and reprocessing (EMDR): A meta-analysis. *Journal of Consulting and Clinical Psychology*, *69*, 305–316. https://doi.org/101037//0022–006x.69.2.305

de Bont, P. A., van den Berg, D. P., van der Vleugel, B. M., de Roos, C., de Jongh, A., van der Gaag, M., & van Minnen, A. M. (2016). Prolonged exposure and EMDR for PTSD v. a PTSD waiting-list condition: Effects on symptoms of psychosis, depression and social functioning in patients with chronic psychotic disorders. *Psychological Medicine*, *46*(11), 2411–2421. https://doi.org/10.1017/S0033291716001094

de Bont, P. A., van Minnen, A., & de Jongh, A. (2013). Treating PTSD in patients with psychosis: A within-group controlled feasibility study examining the efficacy and safety of evidence-based PE and EMDR protocols. *Behavior Therapy*, *44*(4), 717–730. https://doi.org/10.1016/j.beth.2013.07.002

de Roos, C., Greenwald, R., den Hollander-Gijsm, M., Noorthoorn, E., van Buuren, S., & de Jongh, A. (2011). A randomised comparison of cognitive behavioural therapy (CBT) and eye movement desensitisation and reprocessing (EMDR) in disaster-exposed children. *European Journal of Psychotraumatology*, *2*, 5694. https://doi.org/10.3402/ejpt.v2i0.5694

de Roos, C., van der Oord, S., Zijlstra, B., Lucassen, S., Perrin, S., Emmelkamp, P., & de Jongh, A. (in press). Comparison of EMDR therapy, cognitive behavioral writing therapy, and waitlist in pediatric PTSD following single-incident trauma: A multi-center randomized clinical trial. *Journal of Child Psychology and Psychiatry*, *58*(11), 1219–1228. https://doi.org/10.1111/jcpp.12768

Department of Veterans Affairs & Department of Defense. (2004). *VA/DoD clinical practice guideline for the management of posttraumatic stress*. Veterans Health Administration, Department of Veterans Affairs and Health Affairs, Department of Defense. Office of Quality and Performance Publication 10Q-CPG/PTSD-04.

Department of Veterans Affairs & U.S. Department of Defense. (2017). *VA/DoD clinical practice guideline for the management of post-traumatic stress disorder and acute stress disorder*. The Management of Posttraumatic Stress Disorder Work Group, Office of Quality and Performance Publication. https://www.healthquality.va.gov/guidelines/MH/ptsd/VADoDPTSDCPGFinal012418.pdf

Devilly, G. J., & Spence, S. H. (1999). The relative efficacy and treatment distress of EMDR and a cognitive behavioral trauma treatment protocol in the amelioration of posttraumatic stress disorder. *Journal of Anxiety Disorders*, *13*(1–2), 131–157. https://doi.org/10.1016/S0887-6185(98)00044-9

Diehle, J., Opmeer, B. C., Boer, F., Mannarino, A. P., & Lindauer, R. J. (2015). Trauma-focused cognitive behavioral therapy or eye movement desensitization and reprocessing: What works in children with posttraumatic stress symptoms? A randomized controlled trial. *European Child & Adolescent Psychiatry*, *24*(2), 1–10. https://doi.org/10.1007/s00787-014-0572-5

Dutch National Steering Committee Guidelines Mental Health Care. (2003). *Multidisciplinary guidelines anxiety disorders*. Quality Institute Heath Care CBO/Trimbos Institute.

Edmond, T., Rubin, A., & Wambach, K. (1999). The effectiveness of EMDR with adult female survivors of childhood sexual abuse. *Social Work Research*, *23*, 103–116. https://doi.org/10.1093/swr/23.2.103

Edmond, T., Sloan, L., & McCarty, D. (2004). Sexual abuse survivors' perceptions of the effectiveness of EMDR and eclectic therapy: A mixed-methods study. *Research on Social Work Practice*, *14*, 259–272. https://doi.org/10.1177/1049731504265830

Fernandez, I. (2007). EMDR as a treatment of post-traumatic reactions: A field study on child victims of an earthquake. *Educational and Child Psychology, Special Issue: Therapy, 24*(1), 65–72.

Fernandez, I., Gallinari, E., & Lorenzetti, A. (2004). A school-based EMDR intervention for children who witnessed the Pirelli Building airplane crash in Milan, Italy. *Journal of Brief Therapy, 2*, 129–136.

Foa, E. B., Keane, T. M., & Friedman, M. J. (2000). *Effective treatments for PTSD: Practice guidelines of the International Society for Traumatic Stress Studies.* Guilford Press.

Follow-up: Högberg, G., Pagani, M., Sundin, Ö., Soares, J., Aberg-Wistedt, A., Tarnell, B., & Hallström, T. (2008). Treatment of post-traumatic stress disorder with eye movement desensitization and reprocessing: Outcome is stable in 35-month follow-up. *Psychiatry Research, 159*(1–2), 101–108. https://doi.org/10.1016/j.psychres.2007.10.019

Gil-Jardiné, C. Evrard, G., Al Joboory, S., Saint Jammes, J. T., Masson, F., Ribéreau-Gayon, R., Galinski, M., Salmi, L. R., Revel, P., Régis, C. A., Valdenaire, G., & Lagarde, E. (2018). Emergency room intervention to prevent post concussion-like symptoms and post-traumatic stress disorder. A pilot randomized controlled study of a brief eye movement desensitization and reprocessing intervention versus reassurance or usual care. *Journal of Psychiatric Research, 103*, 229–236. https://doi.org/10.1016/j.jpsychires.2018.05

Grainger, R. D., Levin, C., Allen-Byrd, L., Doctor, R. M., & Lee, H. (1997). An empirical evaluation of eye movement desensitization and reprocessing (EMDR) with survivors of a natural catastrophe. *Journal of Traumatic Stress, 10*(4), 665–671. https://doi.org/10.1023/A:1024806105473

Hensel, T. (2009). EMDR with children and adolescents after single-incident trauma: An intervention study. *Journal of EMDR Practice and Research, 3*(1), 2–9. https://doi.org/10.1891/1933-3196.3.1.2

Ho, M. S. K., & Lee, C. W. (2012). Cognitive behaviour therapy versus eye movement desensitization and reprocessing for post-traumatic disorder—is it all in the homework then? *European Review of Applied Psychology/Revue Européenne de Psychologie Appliquée, 62*(4), 253–260. https://doi.org/10.1016/j.erap.2012.08.001

Högberg, G., Pagani, M., Sundin, Ö., Soares, J., Aberg-Wistedt, A., Tarnell, B., & Hallstrom, T. (2007). On treatment with eye movement desensitization and reprocessing of chronic post-traumatic stress disorder in public transportation workers—A randomized controlled trial. *Nordic Journal of Psychiatry, 61*, 54–61. https://doi.org/10.1080/08039480601129408

Hurley, E. C. (2018). Effective treatment of veterans with PTSD: Comparison between intensive daily and weekly EMDR approaches. *Frontiers in Psychology, 9*(1458), 1–10. https://doi.org/10.3389/fpsyg.2018.01458

Institut national de la santé et de la recherche médicale. (2004). *Psychothérapie, trois approches évaluées [Psychotherapy : An evaluation of three approaches].* http://www.dh.gov.uk/en/Publicationsandstatistics/Publications/PublicationsPolicyAndGuidance/DH_4007323.

International Society for Traumatic Stress Studies. (2018). *PTSD prevention and treatment guidelines methodology and recommendations.* ISTSS. http://www.istss.org/treating-trauma/new-istss-prevention-and-treatment-guidelines.aspx

Ironson, G. I., Freund, B., Strauss, J. L., & Williams, J. (2002). Comparison of two treatments for traumatic stress: A community-based study of EMDR and prolonged exposure. *Journal of Clinical Psychology, 58*, 113–128. https://doi.org/10.1002/jclp.1132

Jaberghaderi, N., Greenwald, R., Rubin, A., Zand, S. O., & Dolatabadim, S. (2004). A comparison of CBT and EMDR for sexually abused Iranian girls. *Clinical Psychology and Psychotherapy, 11*, 358–368. https://doi.org/10.1002/cpp.395

Jarero, I., & Artigas, L. (2010). The EMDR integrative group treatment protocol: Application with adults during ongoing geopolitical crisis. *Journal of EMDR Practice and Research, 4*(4), 148–155. https://doi.org/10.1891/1933-3196.4.4.148

Jarero, I., Artigas, L., & Hartung, J. (2006). EMDR integrative group treatment protocol: A postdisaster trauma intervention for children and adults. *Traumatology, 12*(2), 121–129. https://doi.org/10.1177/1534765606294561

Jarero, I., Artigas, L., & Luber, M. (2011). The EMDR protocol for recent critical incidents: Application in a disaster mental health continuum of care context. *Journal of EMDR Practice and Research*, 5, 82–94. https://doi.org/10.1891/1933-3196.5.3.82

Jarero, I., Artigas, L., Montero, M., & Lopez-Lena, L. (2008). The EMDR integrative group treatment protocol: Application with child victims of a mass disaster. *Journal of EMDR Practice and Research*, 2(2), 97–105. https://doi.org/10.1891/1933-3196.2.2.97

Jarero, I., Artigas, L., Uribe, S., García, L. E., Cavazos, M. A., & Givaudan, M. (2015). Pilot research study on the provision of the eye movement desensitization and reprocessing integrative group treatment protocol with female cancer patients. *Journal of EMDR Practice and Research*, 9(2), 98–105. https://doi.org/10.1891/1933-3196.9.2.98

Jarero, I., Givaudan, M., & Osorio, A. (2018). Randomized controlled trial on the provision of the EMDR integrative group treatment protocol adapted for ongoing traumatic stress to female patients with cancer-related posttraumatic stress disorder symptoms. *Journal of EMDR Practice and Research*, 12(3), 94–104. https://doi.org/10.1891/1933-3196.12.3.94

Jarero, I., Roque-López, S., & Gomez, J. (2013). The provision of an EMDR-based multicomponent trauma treatment with child victims of severe interpersonal trauma. *Journal of EMDR Practice and Research*, 7(1), 17–28. https://doi.org/10.1891/1933-3196.7.1.17

Jarero, I., & Uribe, S. (2011). The EMDR protocol for recent critical incidents: Brief report of an application in a human massacre situation. *Journal of EMDR Practice and Research*, 5, 156–165. https://doi.org/10.1891/1933-3196.5.4.156

Jarero, I., & Uribe, S. (2012). The EMDR protocol for recent critical incidents: Follow-up report of an application in a human massacre situation. *Journal of EMDR Practice and Research*, 6, 50–61. https://doi.org/10.1891/1933-3196.6.2.50

Jarero, I., Uribe, S., Artigas, L., & Givaudan, M. (2015). EMDR protocol for recent critical incidents: A randomized controlled trial in a technological disaster context. *Journal of EMDR Practice and Research*, 9, 166–173.https://doi.org/10.1891/1933-3196.9.4.166

Johnson, D. R., & Lubin, H. (2006). The counting method: Applying the rule of parsimony to the treatment of posttraumatic stress disorder. *Traumatology*, 12(1), 83. https://doi.org/10.1177/153476560601200106

Karatzias, T., Power, K., Brown, K., McGoldrick, T., Begum, M., Young, J., Loughran, P., Chouliara, Z., & Adams, S. (2011). A controlled comparison of the effectiveness and efficiency of two psychological therapies for posttraumatic stress disorder: Eye movement desensitization and reprocessing vs. emotional freedom techniques. *Journal of Nervous Mental Disease*, 199(6), 372–378. https://doi.org/10.1097/NMD.0b013e31821cd262

Kemp, M., Drummond, P., & McDermott, B. (2010). A wait-list controlled pilot study of eye movement desensitization and reprocessing (EMDR) for children with post-traumatic stress disorder (PTSD) symptoms from motor vehicle accidents. *Clinical Child Psychology and Psychiatry*, 15(1), 5–25. https://doi.org/10.1177/1359104509339086

Konuk, E., Knipe, J., Eke, I., Yuksek, H., Yurtsever, A., & Ostep, S. (2006). The effects of eye movement desensitization and reprocessing (EMDR) therapy on post-traumatic stress disorder in survivors of the 1999 Marmara, Turkey, earthquake. *International Journal of Stress Management*, 13(3), 291–308. https://doi.org/10.1037/1072-5245.13.3.291

Laugharne, J., Kullack, C., Lee, C. W., McGuire, T., Brockman, S., Drummond, P. D., & Starkstein, S. (2016). Amygdala volumetric change following psychotherapy for posttraumatic stress disorder. *The Journal of Neuropsychiatry and Clinical Neurosciences*. https://doi.org/10.1176/appi.neuropsych.16010006

Lee, C., Gavriel, H., Drummond, P., Richards, J., & Greenwald, R. (2002). Treatment of posttraumatic stress disorder: A comparison of stress inoculation training with prolonged exposure and eye movement desensitization and reprocessing. *Journal of Clinical Psychology*, 58, 1071–1089. https://doi.org/10.1002/jclp.10039

Lee, C. W., & Cuijpers, P. (2012). A meta-analysis of the contribution of eye movements in processing emotional memories. *Journal of Behavior Therapy and Experimental Psychiatry*, 44(2), 231–239. https://doi.org/10.1016/j.jbtep.2012.11.001

Marcus, S., Marquis, P., & Sakai, C. (1997). Controlled study of treatment of PTSD using EMDR in an HMO setting. *Psychotherapy, 34*, 307–315. https://doi.org/10.1037/h0087791

Marcus, S., Marquis, P., & Sakai, C. (2004). Three- and six-month follow-up of EMDR treatment of PTSD in an HMO setting. *International Journal of Stress Management, 11*, 195–208. https://doi.org/10.1037/1072-5245.11.3.195

Maxfield, L., & Hyer, L. A. (2002). The relationship between efficacy and methodology in studies investigating EMDR treatment of PTSD. *Journal of Clinical Psychology, 58*, 23–41. https://doi.org/10.1002/jclp.1127

McLay, R. N., Webb-Murphy, J. A., Fesperman, S. F., Delaney, E. M., Gerard, S. K., Roesch, S. C., Nebeker, B. J., Pandzic, I., Vishnyak, E. A., & Johnston, S. L. (2016). Outcomes from eye movement desensitization and reprocessing in active-duty service members with posttraumatic stress disorder. *Psychological Trauma: Theory, Research, Practice, and Policy, 8*(6), 702–708. http://dx.doi.org/10.1037/tra0000120

Nijdam, M. J., Gersons, B. P. R., Reitsma, J. B., de Jongh, A., & Olff, M. (2012). Brief eclectic psychotherapy v. eye movement desensitisation and reprocessing therapy in the treatment of post-traumatic stress disorder: Randomised controlled trial. *British Journal of Psychiatry, 200*, 224–231. https://doi.org/10.1192/bjp.bp.111.099234

Novo, P., Landin-Romero, R., Radua, J., Vicens, V., Fernandez, I., Garcia, F., Pomarol-Clotet, E., McKenna, P. J., Shapiro, F., & Amann, B. L. (2014). Eye movement desensitization and reprocessing therapy in subsyndromal bipolar patients with a history of traumatic events: A randomized, controlled pilot-study. *Psychiatry Research, 219*(1), 122–128. https://doi.org/10.1016/j.psychres.2014.05.012

Osorio, A., Pérez, M. C., Tirado, S. G., Jarero, I., & Givaudan, M. (2018). Randomized controlled trial on the EMDR integrative group treatment protocol for ongoing traumatic stress with adolescents and young adults patients with cancer. *American Journal of Applied Psychology, 7*(4), 50–56. https://doi.org/10.11648/j.ajap.20180704.11

Power, K., McGoldrick, T., Brown, K., Buchanan, R., Sharp, D., Swanson, V., & Karatzias, A. (2002). A controlled comparison of eye movement desensitization and reprocessing versus exposure plus cognitive restructuring, versus waiting list in the treatment of post-traumatic stress disorder. *Journal of Clinical Psychology and Psychotherapy, 9*, 299–318. https://doi.org/10.1002/cpp.341

Puffer, M., Greenwald, R., & Elrod, D. (1998). A single session EMDR study with twenty traumatized children and adolescents. *Traumatology, 3*(2), Article 6. https://doi.org/10.1037/h0101053

Ribchester, T., Yule, W., & Duncan, A. (2010). EMDR for childhood PTSD after road traffic accidents: Attentional, memory, and attributional processes. *Journal of EMDR Practice and Research, 4*(4), 138–147. https://doi.org/10.1891/1933-3196.4.4.138

Rodenburg, R., Benjamin, A., de Roos, C., Meijer, A. M., & Stams, G. J. (2009). Efficacy of EMDR in children: A meta-analysis. *Clinical Psychology Review, 29*(70), 599–606. https://doi.org/10.1016/j.cpr.2009.06.008

Rothbaum, B. O. (1997). A controlled study of eye movement desensitization and reprocessing in the treatment of post-traumatic stress disordered sexual assault victims. *Bulletin of the Menninger Clinic, 61*, 317–334.

Rothbaum, B. O., Astin, M. C., & Marsteller, F. (2005). Prolonged exposure versus eye movement desensitization and reprocessing (EMDR) for PTSD rape victims. *Journal of Traumatic Stress, 18*, 607–616. https://doi.org/10.1002/jts.20069

Russell, M.C., Silver, S.M., Rogers, S., & Darnell, J. (2007). Responding to an identified need: A joint Department of Defense-Department of Veterans Affairs training program in eye movement desensitization and reprocessing (EMDR) for clinicians providing trauma services. *International Journal of Stress Management, 14*, 61–71. https://doi.org/10.1037/1072-5245.14.1.61

Scheck, M., Schaeffer, J. A., & Gillette, C. (1998). Brief psychological intervention with traumatized young women: The efficacy of eye movement desensitization and reprocessing. *Journal of Traumatic Stress, 11*, 25–44. https://doi.org/10.1023/A:1024400931106

Schubert, S.J., Lee, C.W., de Araujo, G., Butler, S.R., Taylor, G., & Drummond, P. (2016). The effectiveness of eye movement desensitization and reprocessing (EMDR) therapy to treat symptoms following trauma in Timor Leste. *Journal of Traumatic Stress, 29*(2), 141–148. https://doi.org/10.1002/jts.22084

Seidler, G. H., & Wagner, F. E. (2006). Comparing the efficacy of EMDR and trauma-focused cognitive-behavioral therapy in the treatment of PTSD: A meta-analytic study. *Psychological Medicine, 36*(11), 1515–1522. https://doi.org/10.1017/S0033291706007963.

Shapiro, E., & Laub, B. (2015). Early EMDR intervention following a community critical incident: A randomized clinical trial. *Journal of EMDR Practice and Research, 9*(1), 17–27. https://doi.org/10.1891/1933-3196.9.1.17

Shapiro, F. (1989a). Efficacy of the eye movement desensitization procedure in the treatment of traumatic memories. *Journal of Traumatic Stress Studies, 2*, 199–223. https://doi.org/10.1007/BF00974159

Silver, S. M., Brooks, A., & Obenchain, J. (1995). Treatment of Vietnam War veterans with PTSD: A comparison of eye movement desensitization and reprocessing, biofeedback, and relaxation training. *Journal of Traumatic Stress, 8*, 337–342. https://doi.org/10.1007/BF02109568

Silver, S. M., Rogers, S., Knipe, J., & Colelli, G. (2005). EMDR therapy following the 9/11 terrorist attacks: A community-based intervention project in New York City. *International Journal of Stress Management, 12*(1), 29–42. https://doi.org/10.1037/1072-5245.12.1.29

Sjöblom, P. O., Andréewitch, S., Bejerot, S., Mörtberg, E., Brinck, U., Ruck, C., & Körlin, D. (2003). *Regional treatment recommendation for anxiety disorders*. Medical Program Committee/Stockholm City Council.

Soberman, G. B., Greenwald, R., & Rule, D. L. (2002). A controlled study of eye movement desensitization and reprocessing (EMDR) for boys with conduct problems. *Journal of Aggression, Maltreatment, and Trauma, 6*, 217–236. https://doi.org/10.1300/J146v06n01_11

Solomon, R. M., & Kaufman, T. E. (2002). A peer support workshop for the treatment of traumatic stress of railroad personnel: Contributions of eye movement desensitization and reprocessing (EMDR). *Journal of Brief Therapy, 2*, 27–33.

Sprang, G. (2001). The use of eye movement desensitization and reprocessing (EMDR) in the treatment of traumatic stress and complicated mourning: Psychological and behavioral outcomes. *Research on Social Work Practice, 11*, 300–320. https://doi.org/10.1177/104973150101100302

Substance Abuse and Mental Health Services America. (2012). *Comparative effectiveness research series. Eye movement desensitization and reprocessing: An information resource.* SAMHSA's National Registry of Evidence-based Programs and Practices. https://cdn.ymaws.com/www.emdria.org/resource/resmgr/research/treatment_guidelines/samhsa.2012.nrepp-comparativ.pdf

Tarquinio, C., Rotonda, C., Houllé, W. A., Montel, S., Rydberg, J. A., Minary, L., Dellucci, H., Tarquinio, P., Fayard, A., & Alla, F. (2016). Early psychological preventive intervention for workplace violence: A randomized controlled explorative and comparative study between EMDR-recent event and critical incident stress debriefing. *Issues in Mental Health Nursing, 37*(11), 787–799. https://doi.org/10.1080/01612840.2016.1224282

Taylor, S., Thordarson, D., Maxfield, L., Fedoroff, I., Lovell, K., & Ogrodniczuk, J. (2003). Comparative efficacy, speed, and adverse effects of three PTSD treatments: Exposure therapy, EMDR, and relaxation training. *Journal of Consulting and Clinical Psychology, 71*, 330–338. https://doi.org/10.1037/0022-006X.71.2.330

ter Heide, F. J. J., Mooren, T. M., van de Schoot, R., de Jongh, A., & Kleber, R. J. (2016). Eye movement desensitisation and reprocessing therapy v. stabilisation as usual for refugees: Randomised controlled trial. *The British Journal of Psychiatry*, 1–8. https://doi.org/10.1192/bjp.bp.115.167775

The Cochrane Database of Systematic Reviews. (2013). *Psychological therapies for chronic posttraumatic stress disorder (PTSD) in adults.* https://www.cochrane.org/CD003388/DEPRESSN_psychological-therapies-chronic-post-traumatic-stress-disorder-ptsd-adults

Therapy Advisor. (2004–2007). Retrieved October 19, 2011 from http://www.therapyadvisor.com

United Kingdom Department of Health. (2001). *Treatment choice in psychological therapies and counseling evidence based clinical practice guidelines.* http://www.doh.gov.uk/mentalhealth/treatmentguideline/

van den Berg, D. P. G., de Bont, P. A. J. M., van der Vleugel, B. M., de Roos, C., de Jongh, A., van Minnen, A., & van der Gaag, M. (2015). Prolonged exposure vs eye movement desensitization and reprocessing vs waiting list for posttraumatic stress disorder in patients with a psychotic disorder: A randomized clinical trial. *Journal of the American Medical Association Psychiatry, 72*(3), 259–267. https://doi.org/10.1001/jamapsychiatry.2014.2637

van der Kolk, B. A., Spinazzola, J., Blaustein, M. E., Hopper, J. W., Hopper, E. K., Korn, D. L., & Simpson, W. B. (2007). A randomized clinical trial of eye movement desensitization and reprocessing (EMDR), fluoxetine, and pill placebo in the treatment of posttraumatic stress disorder: Treatment effects and long-term maintenance. *Journal of Clinical Psychiatry, 68*(1), 37–46. https://doi.org/10.4088/JCP.v68n0105

Vaughan, K., Armstrong, M. F., Gold, R., O'Connor, N., Jenneke, W., & Tarrier, N. (1994). A trial of eye movement desensitization compared to image habituation training and applied muscle relaxation in post- traumatic stress disorder. *Journal of Behavior Therapy & Experimental Psychiatry, 25*, 283–291. https://doi.org/10.1016/0005-7916(94)90036-1

Wadaa, N. N., Zaharim, N. M., & Alqashan, H. F. (2010). The use of EMDR in treatment of traumatized Iraqi children. *Digest of Middle East Studies, 19*(1), 26–36. https://doi.org/10.1111/j.1949-3606.2010.00003.x

Wanders, F., Serra, M., & de Jongh, A. (2008). EMDR versus CBT for children with self-esteem and behavioral problems: A randomized controlled trial. *Journal of EMDR Practice and Research, 2*(3), 180–189. https://doi.org/10.1891/1933-3196.2.3.180

Watts, B. V., Schnurr, P. P., Mayo, L., Yinong, Y., Weeks, W. B., & Friedman, M. J. (2013). Meta-analysis of the efficacy of treatments for posttraumatic stress disorder. *Journal of Clinical Psychiatry, 74*(6), e541–e550. https://doi.org/10.4088/JCP.12r08225

Wilson, S., Becker, L. A., & Tinker, R. H. (1995). Eye movement desensitization and reprocessing (EMDR): Treatment for psychologically traumatized individuals. *Journal of Consulting and Clinical Psychology, 63*, 928–937. https://doi.org/10.1037/0022-006X.63.6.928

Wilson, S., Becker, L. A., & Tinker, R. H. (1997). Fifteen-month follow-up of eye movement desensitization and reprocessing (EMDR) treatment of post-traumatic stress disorder and psychological trauma. *Journal of Consulting and Clinical Psychology, 65*, 1047–1056. https://doi.org/10.1037/0022-006X.65.6.1047

World Health Organization (2013). *Guidelines for the management of conditions specifically related to stress.* Author.

Yurtsever, A., Konuk, E., Akyüz, T., Zat, Z., Tükel, F., Çetinkaya, M., Savran, C., & Shapiro, E. (2018). An eye movement desensitization and reprocessing (EMDR) group intervention for Syrian refugees with posttraumatic stress symptoms: Results of a randomized controlled trial. *Frontiers in Psychology, 9*, 493. https://doi.org/10.3389/fpsyg.2018.00493

Zaghrout-Hodali, M., Alissa, F., & Dodgson, P. (2008). Building resilience and dismantling fear: EMDR group protocol with children in an area of ongoing trauma. *Journal of EMDR Practice and Research, 2*(2), 106–113. https://doi.org/10.1891/1933-3196.2.2.106

F: HISTORY OF EMDR THERAPY AND THE EMDR RESEARCH FOUNDATION

See Table F.1 for truncated history of EMDR Therapy.

TABLE F.1 History of EMDR Therapy
1987
Dr. Francine Shapiro took her historic "walk in the park" in Los Gatos, California. As a result: She discovered the effects of spontaneous eye movements on memory quality
Along with the eye movements, she added other elements, including a cognitive component, and developed procedures around the effects and called it EMD
1988
Shapiro began conducting research and introducing EMD to the world
She conducted her first presentations on EMD to professional organizations in the United States
She traveled to Israel to introduce EMD to various researchers
1989
Shapiro published her first controlled treatment outcome studies for PTSD:
Shapiro, F. (1989a). Efficacy of the eye movement desensitization procedure in the treatment of traumatic memories. *Journal of Traumatic Stress, 2*(2), 199–223. https://doi.org/10.1007/BF00974159
Shapiro, F. (1989b). Eye movement desensitization: A new treatment for post-traumatic stress disorder. *Journal of Behavior Therapy and Experimental Psychiatry, 20*(3), 211–217. https://doi.org/10.1016/0005-7916(89)90025-6
Shapiro opened an office and began working at the MRI in Palo Alto, California
1990
EMD becomes EMDR
EMDR Institute was established. It was originally operated out of the Mental Research Institute and later relocated to Pacific Grove, California. The EMDR Institute is now located in Watsonville, California
Shapiro presented her first workshops on EMD to licensed mental health professionals in San Jose and Palo Alto, California
Shapiro trained the first EMD research teams at the University of Pennsylvania and Veteran's Affairs Medical Center in Philadelphia
Shapiro was invited to present at EMD training at the ISSTS Annual Conference in New Orleans, Louisiana
Concerned that clinicians would attempt to learn EMDR through journal articles, Shapiro incorporated training restrictions with institute facilitators asking them not to train other clinicians in EMDR until her text was published (Shapiro, 2001)
At the annual conference of Association for Advancement of Behavior Therapy, Dr. Shapiro presented her EMD research

(continued)

TABLE F.1 History of EMDR Therapy (continued)

Joseph Wolpe declared EMD to be a "breakthrough" in the treatment of PTSD

Other forms of BLS (i.e., tones, taps) were discovered and utilized

The first Part 2 weekend training (then called Intermediate Training) was instituted and held in San Jose

1991

EMD becomes EMDR to recognize the shift from desensitization to information processing

Shapiro, F. (1991). Eye movement desensitization and reprocessing procedure: From EMD to EMD/R—A new treatment model for anxiety and related traumata. *The Behavior Therapist, 14*(5), 133–135.

Recognizing that the effects of EMD extended beyond those accounted for by desensitization, Shapiro focused on information processing theories based on AIP as a better explanation

The first trainings in Paris, Amsterdam, and El Salvador were also held

EMDR Network Association was formed

The EMDR Networker, the first EMDR-specific publication, was published and distributed to all members of the network. There was a membership fee at the time that included the earlier publication and an annual directory

Composed of clinicians from the MRI and others, an EMDR ethics and professional issues committee was created to fortify and regulate training requirements and restrictions

EMDR-trained clinicians created specialized protocols for dissociative disorders and critical incidents

The first humanitarian trainings were provided by Institute trainers to local clinicians in Nicaragua

Wolpe published an independent study on EMD:

Wolpe, J., & Abrams, J. (1991). Post-traumatic stress disorder overcome by eye movement desensitization: A case report. *Journal of Behavior Therapy and Experimental Psychiatry, 22*(1), 39–43. https://doi.org/10.1016/0005-7916(91)90032-Z

1992

The first EMDR conference was sponsored by EMDR Network Association in San Jose, California. Clinicians came together to teach applications of EMDR therapy for various populations and presenting problems beyond the standard protocol

EMDR training was brought to Australia

1993

The EMDR Institute was incorporated. Robbie Dunton is its first administrative coordinator

The first randomized clinical trial was published using a veteran sample with PTSD:

Boudewyns, P. A., Stwertka, S. A., Hyer, L. A., Albrecht, S. A., & Sperr, E. V. (1993). Eye movement desensitization for PTSD of combat: A treatment outcome pilot study. *The Behavior Therapist, 16*(2), 30–33.

The distinguished *Scientific Achievement in Psychology Award* was presented to Shapiro by the California Psychological Association

EMDR training was brought to Canada

(continued)

TABLE F.1 History of EMDR Therapy (continued)

1994

Humanitarian trainings were provided by institute trainers (Steve Silver, PhD, Gerald Puk, PhD, and Susan Roger, PhD) to local clinicians in Croatia (Zagreb) and Sarajevo (Bosnia and Herzegovina) during the war

A position paper was published by the EMDR Dissociative Disorder Task Force (Catherine Fine, PhD, Marilyn Luber, PhD, Sandra Paulsen, PhD, Gerald Puk, PhD, Curt Rouanzion, PhD, and Walter Young, MD)

EMDR training was brought to England

1995

Shapiro's published her first EMDR textbook. This book introduced a detailed explanation of her theory of the AIP model:

Eye movement desensitization and reprocessing: Basic principles, protocols, and procedures (1st ed.). Guilford Press.

Because of the independent research support and the clinical standards articulated and published in this text, the previous imposed restrictions placed on EMDR-trained clinicians were lifted. EMDR-trained clinicians could now train other clinicians who were not previously trained in the model

The first randomized clinical trial on EMDR treatment of civilian PTSD is published. This paper provided evidence of EMDR's efficacy in the treatment of PTSD:

Wilson, S., Becker, L., & Tinker, R. (1995). Eye movement desensitization and reprocessing (EMDR) treatment for psychologically traumatized individuals. *Journal of Consulting & Clinical Psychology, 63*(6), 928–937. https://doi.org/10.1037/0022-006X.63.6.928

Born out of the EMDR community's response to the Oklahoma City bombings, the EMDR HAP (Sandra Wilson, PhD) was created

The EMDRIA was formed. EMDRIA is a membership organization that replaced the EMDR Network. Carol York was the first director and Steve Lazrove the first president. It had 473 charter members at the time of its creation

Protestants and Catholics were brought together in Belfast, Northern Ireland, with its first EMDR-HAP training

EMDR training was brought to Germany

EMDR Institute, Inc., became a Continuing Education Unit (CEU) provider

EMDR was used in Japan by Masaya Ichii after an earthquake. At this time, the EMDR training manual was translated into Japanese

1996

EMDR trainings were conducted in Argentina, Colombia, and South Africa

The EMDRIA Newsletter is first published

EMDRIA held its first conference in Denver, Colorado

Francine Shapiro received a Humanitarian Assistance Award from the EMDRIA

1997

EMDR trainings were conducted in Mexico, Guatemala, Brazil, Chile, and Japan

After Hurricane Pauline ravaged the western coast of Mexico, the EMDR Integrative Group Treatment Protocol (i.e., butterfly hug) was developed by members of EMDR-HAP and the Asociacion para Ayuda Mental en Crisis

(continued)

TABLE F.1 History of EMDR Therapy (continued)

Shapiro and Forrest wrote the first book on EMDR that was written specifically for the lay person:

Shapiro, F., & Forrest, M. S. (1997a). *EMDR: The breakthrough therapy for overcoming anxiety, stress, and trauma* (1st ed.). Basic Books.

Barbara Korzun, PhD, becomes the HAP's first response coordinator

EMDR-HAP conducts trainings in Bogota, Colombia

The first study in an HMO setting was conducted:

Marcus, S. V., Marquis, P., & Sakai, C. (1997). Controlled study of treatment of PTSD using EMDR in an HMO setting. *Psychotherapy, 34*(3), 307–315. https://doi.org/10.1037/h0087791

1998

EMDR Association of Australia and EMDR Association of Canada were formed

The Clinical Division of the American Psychological Association recognized EMDR as "probably efficacious for civilian PTSD":

Chambless, D. L., Baker, M. J., Baucom, D. H., Beutler, L. E., Calhoun, K. S., Crits-Christoph, P., (1998). *Update of empirically validated therapies, II. The Clinical Psychologist, 51*, 3–16.

A randomized clinical trial on the treatment of military veterans was published. This study demonstrated that 12 sessions of EMDR resulted in 77% remission of PTSD diagnosis:

Carlson, J. G., Chemtob, C. M., Rusnak, K., Hedlund, N. L., & Muraoka, M. Y. (1998). Eye movement desensitization and reprocessing (EMDR) treatment for combat-related posttraumatic stress disorder. *Journal of Traumatic Stress, 11*(1), 3–24. https://doi.org/10.1023/A:1024448814268

The first meta-analysis comparing EMDR and other cognitive behavioral therapies was published. This study reported equivalent effects and less treatment for EMDR therapy:

van Etten, M. L., & Taylor, S. (1998). *Comparative efficacy of treatments for posttraumatic stress disorder: A meta-analysis.* Clinical Psychology and Psychotherapy, 5(3), 126–144. https://doi.org/10.1002/(SICI)1099-0879(199809)

EMDR-HAP trained local clinicians in Bangladesh and India

Barbara Korzun, PhD, becomes HAP's first executive director

1999

EMDR Europe was formed

EMDR training was brought to India after the Gujarat earthquake and Turkey after the earthquake in Marmara

The first training in Turkey occurred after an earthquake

The first randomized clinical trial involving adult survivors of sexual abuse was published. This study demonstrated that EMDR was superior to routine treatment:

Edmond, T. E., Rubin, A., & Wambach, K. G. (1999). The effectiveness of EMDR with adult female survivors of childhood sexual abuse. *Social Work Research, 23*(2), 103–116. https://doi.org/10.1093/swr/23.2.103

Professional development programs were created by EMDRIA, including programs for EMDRIA Credit, EMDRIA Certification Program, and EMDRIA-Approved Consultant programs

EMDRIA LatinoAmerica is formed

(continued)

TABLE F.1 History of EMDR Therapy (continued)

2000

The International Society for Traumatic Stress Studies found EMDR efficacious for PTSD:
Foa, E.B., Keane, T.M., & Friedman, M.J. (2000). *Effective treatments for PTSD: Practice guidelines of the International Society for Traumatic Stress Studies.* Guilford Press.

Led by Israeli EMDR-HAP volunteers, the first training of Palestinian clinicians from the Gaza Strip was held

EMDR Europe held its first conference in Utrecht, the Netherlands

HAP responds to the Columbine High School shootings in Littleton, Colorado

---

2001

Shapiro published the second edition of her first book which explained the change from Accelerated Information Processing model to the Adaptive Information Processing model:
Eye movement desensitization and reprocessing: Basic principles, protocols, and procedures (2nd ed.). Guilford Press.

After the terrorist attacks of September 11, 2001, EMDR-HAP launched a major initiative in its service to victims of families, survivors, and first responders. It was during the aftermath of 9/11 that EMDR-HAP attempted the first model of a trauma recovery network

Also, in response to 9/11, EMDR-HAP conducted refresher courses for clinicians in New York, New Jersey, and Washington, DC

EMDR-HAP TPO (Transcultural Psychological Organization) Project in France trained French-speaking clinicians in Algeria and other African countries

The United Kingdom proclaimed that the best evidence of efficacy was reported for EMDR, exposure, and stress inoculation:
United Kingdom Department of Health. (2001). *Treatment choice in psychological therapies and counseling evidence based clinical practice guidelines.* London, Department of Health.

EMDR-HAP trainings were conducted in Palestine

2002

Shapiro was presented the International Sigmund Freud Award for Psychotherapy by the city of Vienna in conjunction with the World Council of Psychotherapy

As one of the first of many recommendations by various national health councils for EMDR treatment of PTSD, the Israeli National Council for Mental Health recommended EMDR as one of three therapies recommended for treatment of terror victims:
Bleich, A., Kotler, M., Kutz, E., & Shaley, A. (2002). *A position paper of the (Israeli) National Council for Mental Health: Guidelines for the assessment and professional intervention with terror victims in the hospital and in the community.* Israeli National Council for Mental Health.

Reporting positive treatment effects with elementary school children who were victims of Hurricane Iniki, the first randomized study of EMDR with children who had been diagnosed with PTSD was published:
Chemtob, C., Nakashima, J., & Carlson, J. (2002). Brief treatment for elementary school children with disaster-related posttraumatic stress disorder: A field study. *Journal of Clinical Psychology, 58*(1), 99–112. https://doi.org/10.1002/jclp.1131

(continued)

TABLE F.1 History of EMDR Therapy (continued)

A study was published that demonstrated that EMDR may reduce behavioral problems in conduct-disordered boys:

Soberman, G. B., Greenwald, R., & Rule, D. L. (2002). A controlled study of eye movement desensitization and reprocessing (EMDR) for boys with conduct problems. *Journal of Aggression, Maltreatment and Trauma, 6*(1), 217–236. https://doi.org/10.1300/J146v06n01_11

Resource Installation and Development demonstrated preliminary evidence for effectiveness in the stabilization phase in the treatment of complex PTSD:

Korn, D., & Leeds, A. (2002). Preliminary evidence of efficacy for EMDR resource development and installation in the stabilization phase of treatment of complex posttraumatic stress disorder. *Journal of Clinical Psychology, 58*(12), 1465–1487. https://doi.org/10.1002/jclp.10099

Another study was published that demonstrated that more rigorous studies utilizing EMDR produced larger effects and that treatment fidelity correlated with effect size:

Maxfield, L., & Hyer, L. (2002). The relationship between efficacy and methodology in studies investigating EMDR treatment of PTSD. *Journal of Clinical Psychology, 58*(1), 23–41. https://doi.org/10.1002/jclp.1127

Two randomized clinical trials were published that showed relatively comparative effects between CBT and EMDR for adult PTSD. EMDR demonstrated some superiority and had no homework. One study reported that participants used fewer treatment sessions with EMDR (Power et al., 2002):

Ironson, G., Freund, B., Strauss, J., & Williams, J. (2002). Comparison of two treatments for traumatic stress: A community-based study of EMDR and prolonged exposure. *Journal of Clinical Psychology, 58*(1), 113–128. https://doi.org/10.1002/jclp.1132

Power, K., McGoldrick, T., Brown, K., Buchanan, R., Sharp, D., Swanson, V., & Karatzias, A. (2002). A controlled comparison of eye movement desensitization and reprocessing versus exposure plus cognitive restructuring, versus waiting list in the treatment of post traumatic stress disorder. *Journal of Clinical Psychology and Psychotherapy, 9*(5), 299–318. https://doi.org/10.1002/cpp.341

Shapiro's third book was published:

Shapiro, F. (2002). *EMDR as an integrative psychotherapy approach: Experts of diverse orientations explore the paradigm prism.* American Psychological Association Books.

2003

Robert Gelbach became EMDR-HAP's second executive director

CREST listed EMDR as one of the treatments of choice for EMDR in Northern Ireland:

Clinical Resource Efficiency Support Team. (2003). *The management of posttraumatic stress disorder in adults.* Clinical Resource Efficiency Support Team of the Northern Ireland Department of Health, Social Services and Public Safety

EMDR-HAP expanded trainings to mental health nonprofit agencies

EMDR and CBT were both designated as treatments of choice for PTSD by the Dutch National Steering Committee in their guidelines for mental health care:

Dutch National Steering Committee Guidelines Mental Health Care. (2003). *Multidisciplinary guidelines anxiety disorders.* Quality Institute Heath Care CBO/Trimbos Institute.

Sweden recommended CBT and EMDR as the treatments of choice for PTSD

(continued)

TABLE F.1 History of EMDR Therapy (continued)

2004

The American Psychiatric Association recommended EMDR as an effective treatment for trauma:

> Practice guideline for the treatment of patients with acute stress disorder and posttraumatic stress disorder. American Psychiatric Association Practice Guidelines.

U.S. Department of Veterans Affairs and Department of Defense recommended EMDR placed in the "A" category as "strongly recommended" for the treatment of trauma:

> Department of Veterans Affairs & Department of Defense. (2004). VA/DoD clinical practice guideline for the management of posttraumatic stress.

EMDR-HAP expanded humanitarian assistance trainings to clinicians at the U.S. Veterans Administration and Defense Department

Reporting positive treatment effects with 236 children involved in a plane crash in Italy, a study utilizing the EMDR group protocol was published:

> Fernandez, I., Gallinari, E., & Lorenzetti, A. (2004). A school-based EMDR intervention for children who witnessed the Pirelli Building airplane crash in Milan, Italy. Journal of Brief Therapy, 2(2), 129–136.

In a randomized clinical trial involving sexually abused Iranian girls, EMDR and CBT were found effective, although the preliminary findings did suggest that EMDR may be more efficient:

> Jaberghaderi, N., Greenwald, R., Rubin, A., Zand, S. O., & Dolatabadim, S. (2004). A comparison of CBT and EMDR for sexually abused Iranian girls. Clinical Psychology and Psychotherapy, 11, 358–368. https://doi.org/10.1002/cpp.395

The National Institute of Mental Health (NIMH)-sponsored website, Therapy Advisor, listed EMDR as an empirically validated treatment for PTSD

EMDR was considered the treatment of choice by French National Institute of Health and Medical Research, Paris, France:

> Institut national de la santé et de la recherche médicale. (2004). [Psychotherapy: An evaluation of three approaches]. French

2005

NICE stated that EMDR is one of the empirically supported treatments of choice:

> National Institute for Clinical Excellence. (2005). Trastorno de estrés postraumatico (TEPT): Gestión del TEPT en niños y adultos en atención primaria y secundaria [posttraumatic stress disorder (PTSD): Management of PTSD in children and adults in primary and secondary care]. NICE.

EMDR-HAP instituted training projects in Sri Lanka, Thailand, and India following a tsunami in Southeast Asia

EMDR-HAP trained 240 clinicians and serves 600 first responders in response to the aftermath of hurricanes Katrina and Rita

The first study of victims of a terrorist attack with EMDR was published. This study reported successful outcomes in the immediate aftermath of 9/11:

> Silver, S. M., Rogers, S., Knipe, J., & Colelli, G. (2005). EMDR therapy following the 9/11 terrorist attacks: A community-based intervention project in New York City. International Journal of Stress Management, 12(1), 29–42. https://doi.org/10.1037/1072-5245.12.1.29

The EMDRIA Foundation was incorporated as a Texas corporation. The original board members were Wendy Freitag, president; Jim Gach; and Rosalie Thomas

(continued)

TABLE F.1 History of EMDR Therapy (continued)

2006

According to a single case study published, preliminary evidence was provided that EMDR may prove effective in the treatment of borderline personality disorder:

Brown, S., & Shapiro, F. (2006). EMDR in the treatment of borderline personality disorder. *Clinical Case Studies, 5*(5), 403–420. https://doi.org/10.1177/1534650104271773

Positive effects of EMDR were reported with studies evaluating large-scale treatment after natural disasters:

Jarero, I., Artigas, L., & Hartung, J. (2006). EMDR integrative group treatment protocol: A postdisaster trauma intervention for children and adults. *Traumatology, 12*(2), 121–129. https://doi.org/10.1177/1534765606294561

Konuk, E., Knipe, J., Eke, I., Yuksek, H., Yurtsever, A., & Ostep, S. (2006). The effects of eye movement desensitization and reprocessing (EMDR) therapy on post-traumatic stress disorder in survivors of the 1999 Maramara, Turkey, earthquake. *International Journal of Stress Management, 13*(3), 291–308. https://doi.org/10.1037/1072-5245.13.3.291

At the annual EMDR International Conference in Philadelphia, Shapiro introduced *New Notes on Adaptive Information Processing:*

Shapiro, F. (2006). *New notes on adaptive information processing: Case formulation principles, scripts, and worksheets.* EMDR Humanitarian Assistance Programs.

EMDR-HAP conducted Gulf Coast trainings in response to hurricanes Katrina and Rita

EMDR-HAP commenced the TRN Project

2007

EMDR Iberoamerica Association was formed; it is currently composed of 17 members: Argentina, Brazil, Chile, Colombia, Costa Rica, Ecuador, El Salvador, the Iberian Peninsula, Guatemala, Mexico, Nicaragua, Panama, Portugal, Puerto Rico, the Spanish Caribbean, Uruguay, and Venezuela

A Cochrane Review recognized EMDR as an efficacious treatment for PTSD:

Bisson, J., & Andrew, M. (2007). Psychological treatment of post-traumatic stress disorder (PTSD). *Cochrane Database of Systematic Reviews, 3*, Article CD003388. https://doi.org/10.1002/14651858.CD003388.pub3

Springer published the first issue of the *Journal of EMDR Practice and Research*

EMDR is shown to be more successful in achieving sustained reductions in PTSD. First study comparing EMDR to pharmacological treatment for PTSD showed EMDR to be more successful in achieving sustained symptom reductions in PTSD in the first study comparing pharmacological treatment to EMDR:

van der Kolk, B. A., Spinazzola, J., Blaustein, M. E., Hopper, J. W., Hopper, E. K., Korn, D. L., & Simpson, W. B. (2007). Randomized clinical trial of eye movement desensitization and reprocessing (EMDR), fluoxetine, and pill placebo in the treatment of posttraumatic stress disorder: Treatment effects and long-term maintenance. *Journal of Clinical Psychiatry, 68*(1), 37–46. https://doi.org/10.4088/JCP.v68n0105

EMDR-HAP conducted trainings in Indonesia, Lebanon, Kenya, and Philippines

Handbook of Family Therapy Processes was published:

Shapiro, F., Kaslow, F. W., & Maxfield, L. (2007). *Handbook of EMDR and family therapy processes.* John Wiley & Sons, Inc.

Curriculum requirements for Basic EMDR Training were established by EMDRIA

The second study of EMDR was funded by NIMH

(continued)

TABLE F.1 History of EMDR Therapy (continued)

2008

The FSL was introduced at the annual EMDRIA Conference in Phoenix, Arizona, by the library's creator and curator, Dr. Barbara Hensley. Originally hosted by Northern Kentucky University, the FSL is a comprehensive electronic resource for journal articles and other references related to EMDR

In recognition of the development and the contributions of EMDR therapy, Shapiro received State of Connecticut General Assembly and City of New Haven Board of Alderman official citations

EMDR Institute contracted with AMEDD to conduct military trainings

2009

Presented by the American Psychological Association Division 56, Shapiro received the *Award for Outstanding Contributions to Practice in Trauma Psychology*

The first issue of the *Japanese Journal of EMDR Practice and Research* was published

During the EMDR-Europe Association annual meeting, plans were made for the establishment of an EMDR-Asia Association in 2010

Initiatives in Africa and the Middle East were launched by EMDR-HAP

The ISSTS Practice Guidelines endorsed EMDR:

Foa, E. B., Keane, T. M., Friedman, M. J., & Cohen, J. A. (2009). *Effective treatments for PTSD: Practice guidelines from the International Society for Traumatic Stress Studies*. Guilford Press.

EMDR-HAP conducted trainings in Rwanda to work with survivors of the 1994 genocide

EMDR celebrated its 20-year anniversary at the annual EMDRIA Conference in Atlanta, Georgia

2010

The first Asian EMDR Conference, titled "Building Bridges Between East & West Through EMDR," was held in Bali, Indonesia

EMDR Asia was established at its first Asian conference

EMDR-HAP conducted trainings in China in response to the earthquake in Chengdu and in collaboration with clinicians in Ethiopia with HELP for Children Orphanage. It also trained Iraqi clinicians in Jordan and Kenya. EMDR-HAP played a role in coordinating French and Belgian clinicians to train Haitians in response to a major earthquake

The California Evidence-Based Clearinghouse for Child Welfare Trauma Treatments for Children supported trauma-focused CBT and EMDR as "well-supported by research evidence"

EMDR-HAP trained Iraqi clinicians in Jordan, clinicians in collaboration with Help for Children Orphanage in Ethiopia, and clinicians in Kenya

2011

Carol Martin became EMDR-HAP's third executive director

The EMDRIA Foundation was renamed the EMDR Research Foundation

Sarah Haley Memorial Award for Clinical Excellence at the IST SS 27th Annual Meeting: Social Bonds and Trauma Through the Life Span was awarded to the EMDR Humanitarian Assistance Programs

(continued)

TABLE F.1 History of EMDR Therapy (continued)

EMDR-HAP conducted trainings in Tuscaloosa, Alabama, and Joplin, Missouri, in
response to tornadoes
SAMHSA's NREPP recognized EMDR as an evidence-based practice in the treatment
of PTSD and its symptoms (anxiety and depression) and stated that EMDR aids in the
improvement of overall mental health functioning:
Substance Abuse and Mental Health Services Administration. (2010). *Eye movement
desensitization and reprocessing.* National Registry of Evidence-Based Programs and
Practices, U.S. Department of Health and Human Services (HHS). Retrieved March 25,
2011, from http://nrepp.samhsa.gov/ViewIntervention.aspx?id=199

2012
Dr. Shapiro wrote and published Getting Past Your Past:
Shapiro, F. (2012). *Getting past your past.* Rodale Books.
TRN/EMDR-HAP chapters responded to Hurricane Sandy in New York, Connecticut,
and New Jersey

2013
World Health Organization (WHO) recognizes EMDR as a psychotherapy recommended
for children, adolescents and adults with PTSD.
World Health Organization. (2013). *Guidelines for the Management of Conditions That are
Specifically Related to Stress.* Geneva, WHO.
EMDR-HAP changed its formal name to TRN/EMDR-HAP
The first MSc in EMDR was validated at the University of Worcester (UK) with the help of
Derek Farrell (PhD)
TRN/EMDR-HAP chapters responded to a shooting in Newtown, Connecticut; fires in
Arizona and California; a tornado in Oklahoma; and a typhoon in the Philippines

2014
EMDR celebrated its 25-year anniversary at the annual EMDRIA Conference in Denver
The Francine Shapiro Library came home to EMDRIA
The United Nations Committee on Non-Governmental Organizations recommended that the
United Nations Economic and Social Council grant EMDR-HAP Special Consultative Status
Dr. Francine Shapiro renamed from EMDR to EMDR therapy to recognize it officially as a
distinct integrative psychotherapeutic approach
TRN/EMDR-HAP chapters responded to the Boston Marathon bombing and to the Oso
mudslide in Washington state

2016
Shapiro and Forrest wrote the first book on EMDR specifically for the lay person
Shapiro and Forrest published the second edition of their book on EMDR for the client:
Shapiro, F., & Forrest, M. S. (1997b). *EMDR: The breakthrough therapy for overcoming
anxiety, stress, and trauma* (2nd ed.). Basic Books

2018
Shapiro published the third edition of her EMDR textbook:
Eye movement desensitization and reprocessing: Basic principles, protocols, and procedures
(3rd ed.). Guilford Press

(continued)

TABLE F.1 History of EMDR Therapy (continued)

2019

Francine Shapiro died in Sea Ranch, California, on June 16

Council of Scholars was formed by EMDRIA (see above)

2020

Ireland separates from the United Kingdom to establish their own EMDR Association.

As the COVID-19 pandemic invades the United States, many EMDR-trained therapists find themselves implementing EMDR therapy through telehealth for the first time.

The first online EMDRIA conference is conducted due to the pandemic.

Note: Special thanks to Roberta "Robbie" Dunton for providing and/or verifying the accuracy of the above history of EMDR therapy.

Abbreviations: AIP, Adaptive Information Processing; CBT, cognitive behavioral therapy; CREST, Clinical Resource Efficiency Support Team; EMD, eye movement desensitization; EMDRIA, EMDR International Association; FSL, Francine Shapiro Library; HAP, Humanitarian Assistance Program; ISSTS, International Society for Traumatic Stress Studies; MRI, Mental Research Institute; NICE, National Institute for Clinical Excellence; NREPP, National Registry of Evidence-Based Programs and Practices; PTSD, posttraumatic stress disorder; SAMHSA, Substance Abuse and Mental Health Services Administration; TRN, Trauma Recovery Network.

See Table F.2 for truncated history of the EMDR Research Foundation.

TABLE F.2 History of EMDR Research Foundation

The EMDR Research Foundation envisions a world where people are transformed to wellness and vibrancy by effective, compassionate mental health treatment that is driven by quality research (EMDR Research Foundation, 2020)

2005

Incorporated originally in Texas, the original board members were Wendy Freitag, president, and board directors Rosalie Thomas and Jim Gach

2009

The original board was expanded to include additional directors: Barbara Hensley, Zona Scheiner, Tonya Edmond, and Dennis Hall

The board's first $100,000 fundraising goal was announced and exceeded in 2010

2010

The Dissertation Research Award in the amount of $5,000 was inaugurated and the first recipient was announced at the EMDRIA Annual Conference in Minneapolis, Minnesota

2011

Katy Murray joined the board as a director

Four research awards in the amount of $10,000 were granted

The Visionary Alliance was formed to encourage recurring donations

The EMDR Research Board developed and adopted a 5-year strategic plan with the end in mind of increasing EMDR research by 10%, contacting a minimum 10,000 clinicians, publishing guidelines for quality EMDR research, and providing non-monetary support for the same

(continued)

TABLE F.2 History of EMDR Research Foundation (continued)

Chris Lee was awarded a plaque for his successful efforts toward ensuring EMDR therapy was recognized by SAMHSA as an evidence-based treatment

2012
Scott Blech, former EMDRIA executive director, was added as a director
Three grant awards totaling $25,000 were awarded
The first article of TRIP was published in the Journal of EMDR Practice and Research: Murray, K. (2012). EMDR with grief: Reflections on Ginny Sprang's 2001 study. *Journal of EMDR Practice and Research, 6*(4), 187–191. https://doi.org/10.1891/1933-3196.6.4.187
The board's research priorities were expanded to include suicide and somatic and medical conditions

2013
Two $10,000 grants were awarded
The first $1000 Consultation Award was given
A Research Resource Directory was launched on the board's website
The board created and disseminated the Military in Action and Clinical Information newsletters
Karen Forte joined the board as a director
The second article of TRIP was published in the Journal of EMDR Practice and Research: Bellecci-St. Romain, L. (2013). EMDR with recurrent "flash-forwards": Reflections on Engelhard et al.'s 2011 study. *Journal of EMDR Practice and Research, 7*(2), 106–111. https://doi.org/10.1891/1933-3196.7.2.106

2014
A $1,000 Research Dissemination Travel Award was launched
The board redefined its research priorities to include advancing evidence-based practice, addressing the global burden of trauma, and building clinical evidence
A grant of $25,000 was offered for 25 years of EMDR research
The Early EMDR Interventions Researchers' Toolkit was created and published on the board's website
Susan Rogers and Susan Brown joined the board as directors

2015
The amount of the Research Grant Award was increased from $10,000 to $25,000
The third article of TRIP was published in the *Journal of EMDR Practice and Research:* Myers, K. (2015). EMDR with choking phobia: Reflections on the 2008 study by de Roos and de Jongh. *Journal of EMDR Practice and Research, 9*(1), 64–70. https://doi.org/10.1891/1933-3196.9.1.64
Three research grants in the amount of $25,000 were awarded
David Sherwood joined the board as a director

2016
The $5,000 Sandra Wilson Memorial Dissertation Grant Award was announced

2017
Research grants totaling $32,850 were awarded

(continued)

TABLE F.2 History of EMDR Research Foundation (continued)

Dedicated to research into suicide prevention and survivor support, the Marcia Murray Memorial Fund was created and announced

---

2018

Three research grants totaling $75,000 were awarded to expand the EMDR therapy evidence base to include addiction-focused EMDR therapy, PTSD following acute coronary syndromes, and treatment of suicidal drivers

The EMDR EEI Fund was created to explore long-term effectiveness of EEI and evaluate whether it can prevent the eventual development of PTSD

A study partially funded by the EMDR Research Foundation on how eye movements may reduce fear-related trauma was published:

de Voogd, L. D., Kanen, J. W., Neville, D. A., Roelofs, K., Fernández, G., & Hermans, E. J. (2018). Eye-movement intervention enhances extinction via amygdala deactivation. *Journal of Neuroscience, 38*(40), 8694–8707. https://doi.org/10.1523/JNEUROSCI.0703-18.2018

Another partially funded study was published on how effective and safe EMDR therapy is in the psychological treatment of an oncology population:

Roberts, A. K. P. (2018). The effects of the EMDR group traumatic episode protocol with cancer survivors. *Journal of EMDR Practice and Research, 12*(3), 105–177. https://doi.org/10.1891/1933-3196.12.3.105

2019

Two research grants totaling $50,000 were awarded to encourage expansion of the evidence base for EMDR therapy across a range of populations and disorders (e.g., anorexia nervosa, PTSD in forensic mental health services)

Another study partially funded by the EMDR Research Foundation was published that focused on the efficacy of EMDR therapy to reduce the severity of posttraumatic stress symptoms in recent rape victims:

Covers, M. L. V., de Jongh, A., Huntjens, R. J. C., de Roos, C., van den Hout, M., & Bicanic, I. A. E. (2019). Early intervention with eye movement desensitisation and reprocessing (EMDR) therapy to reduce the severity of posttraumatic stress symptoms in recent rape victims: Study protocol for a randomised controlled trial. *European Journal of Psychotraumatology, 10*(1), 1632021. https://doi.org/10.1080/20008198.2019.1632021

A partially funded study evaluating the efficacy of EMDR therapy compared to TAU in breast cancer survivors who also suffer from PTSD was published:

Careletto, S., Porcaro, C., Settanta, C., Vizzari, V., Stanizzo, M. R., Oliva, F., Torta, R., Fernandez, I., Coletti Moja, M., Pagani, M., & Ostacoli, L. (2019). Neurobiological features and response to eye movement desensitization and reprocessing treatment of posttraumatic stress disorder in patients with breast cancer. *European Journal of Psychotraumatology, 10*(1), 1600832. https://doi.org/10.1080/20008198.2019.1600832

Another partially funded study was published in the Journal of Psychotraumatology that investigated how oculomotion (i.e., eye movements) influence the retrieval of autobiographical traumatic memories:

(continued)

TABLE F.2 History of EMDR Research Foundation (continued)
Harricharan, S., McKinnon, M. C., Tursich, M., Densmore, M., Frewen, M., Théberge, J., van der Kolk, B., & Lanius, R. A. (2019). Overlapping frontoparietal networks in response to oculomotion and traumatic autobiographical memory retrieval: implications for eye movement desensitization and reprocessing. *European Journal of Psychotraumatology, 10*(1), 1586265. https://doi.org/10.1080/20008198.2019.1586265
In honor of Dr. Francine Shapiro, who died on June 16, 2019, the EMDR Research Foundation established the Francine Shapiro Memorial Fund

Abbreviations: EEI, EMDR Early Intervention; PTSD, posttraumatic stress disorder; SAMHSA, Substance Abuse and Mental Health Services Administration; TRIP, Translating Research into Practice; TAU, treatment as usual.

REFERENCES

Bellecci-St. Romain, L. (2013). EMDR with recurrent "flash-forwards": Reflections on Engelhard et al.'s 2011 study. *Journal of EMDR Practice and Research, 7*(2), 106–111. https://doi.org/10.1891/1933-3196.7.2.106

Bisson, J., & Andrew, M. (2007). Psychological treatment of post-traumatic stress disorder (PTSD). *Cochrane Database of Systematic Reviews, 3*, Article CD003388. https://doi.org/10.1002/14651858.CD003388.pub3

Bleich, A., Kotler, M., Kutz, E., & Shaley, A. (2002). *A position paper of the (Israeli) National Council for Mental Health: Guidelines for the assessment and professional intervention with terror victims in the hospital and in the community*. Israeli National Council for Mental Health.

Boudewyns, P. A., Stwertka, S. A., Hyer, L. A., Albrecht, S. A., & Sperr, E. V. (1993). Eye movement desensitization for PTSD of combat: A treatment outcome pilot study. *The Behavior Therapist, 16*(2), 30–33.

Brown, S., & Shapiro, F. (2006). EMDR in the treatment of borderline personality disorder. *Clinical Case Studies, 5*(5), 403–420. https://doi.org/10.1177/1534650104271773

Careletto, S., Porcaro, C., Settanta, C., Vizzari, V., Stanizzo, M. R., Oliva, F., Torta, R., Fernandez, I., Coletti Moja, M., Pagani, M., & Ostacoli, L. (2019). Neurobiological features and response to eye movement desensitization and reprocessing treatment of posttraumatic stress disorder in patients with breast cancer. *European Journal of Psychotraumatology, 10*(1), 1600832. https://doi.org/10.1080./20008198.2019.1600832

Carlson, J. G., Chemtob, C. M., Rusnak, K., Hedlund, N.L., & Muraoka, M. Y. (1998). Eye movement desensitization and reprocessing (EMDR) treatment for combat-related posttraumatic stress disorder. *Journal of Traumatic Stress, 11*(1), 3–24. https://doi.org/10.1023/A:1024448814268

Chambless, D. L., Baker, M. J., Baucom, D. H., Beutler, L. E., Calhoun, K. S., Crits–Christoph, P. (1998). Update of empirically validated therapies, II. *The Clinical Psychologist, 51*, 3–16.

Chemtob, C., Nakashima, J., & Carlson, J. (2002). Brief treatment for elementary school children with disaster-related posttraumatic stress disorder: A field study. *Journal of Clinical Psychology, 58*(1), 99–112. https://doi.org/10.1002/jclp.1131

Covers, M. L. V., de Jongh, A., Huntjens, R. J. C., de Roos, C., van den Hout, M., & Bicanic, I. A. E. (2019). Early intervention with eye movement desensitisation and reprocessing (EMDR) therapy to reduce the severity of posttraumatic stress symptoms in recent rape victims: Study protocol for a randomised controlled trial. *European Journal of Psychotraumatology, 10*(1), 1632021. https://doi.org/10.1080/20008198.2019.1632021

Clinical Resource Efficiency Support Team. (2003). *The management of posttraumatic stress disorder in adults*. Clinical Resource Efficiency Support Team of the Northern Ireland Department of Health, Social Services and Public Safety.

de Voogd, L. D., Kanen, J. W., Neville, D. A., Roelofs, K., Fernández, G., & Hermans, E. J. (2018). Eye-movement intervention enhances extinction via amygdala deactivation. *Journal of Neuroscience, 38*(40), 8694–8707. https://doi.org/10.1523/JNEUROSCI.0703-18.2018

Department of Veterans Affairs & Department of Defense. (2004). *VA/DoD clinical practice guideline for the management of posttraumatic stress.* Washington, DC: U.S. Department of Veteran Affairs.

Dutch National Steering Committee Guidelines Mental Health Care. (2003). *Multidisciplinary guidelines anxiety disorders.* Quality Institute Heath Care CBO/Trimbos Institute.

Edmond, T. E., Rubin, A., & Wambach, K. G. (1999). The effectiveness of EMDR with adult female survivors of childhood sexual abuse. *Social Work Research, 23*(2), 103–116. https://doi.org/10.1093/swr/23.2.103

Fernandez, I., Gallinari, E., & Lorenzetti, A. (2004). A school-based EMDR intervention for children who witnessed the Pirelli Building airplane crash in Milan, Italy. *Journal of Brief Therapy, 2*(2), 129–136.

Foa, E. B., Keane, T. M., & Friedman, M. J. (2000). *Effective treatments for PTSD: Practice Guidelines of the International Society for Traumatic Stress Studies.* Guilford Press.

Foa, E. B., Keane, T. M., Friedman, M. J., & Cohen, J. A. (2009). *Effective treatments for PTSD: Practice guidelines from the International Society for Traumatic Stress Studies.* Guilford Press.

Harricharan, S., McKinnon, M. C., Tursich, M., Densmore, M., Frewen, M., Théberge, J., van der Kolk, B., & Lanius, R. A. (2019). Overlapping frontoparietal networks in response to oculomotion and traumatic autobiographical memory retrieval: implications for eye movement desensitization and reprocessing. *European Journal of Psychotraumatology, 10*(1), 1586265. https://doi.org/10.1080/20008198.2019.1586265

Ironson, G., Freund, B., Strauss, J., & Williams, J. (2002). Comparison of two treatments for traumatic stress: A community-based study of EMDR and prolonged exposure. *Journal of Clinical Psychology, 58*(1), 113–128. https://doi.org/10.1002/jclp.1132

Jaberghaderi, N., Greenwald, R., Rubin, A., Zand, S. O., & Dolatabadim, S. (2004). A comparison of CBT and EMDR for sexually abused Iranian girls. *Clinical Psychology and Psychotherapy, 11*, 358–368. https://doi.org/10.1002/cpp.395

Jarero, I., Artigas, L., & Hartung, J. (2006). EMDR integrative group treatment protocol: A postdisaster trauma intervention for children and adults. *Traumatology, 12*(2), 121–129. https://doi.org/10.1177/1534765606294561

Konuk, E., Knipe, J., Eke, I., Yuksek, H., Yurtsever, A., & Ostep, S. (2006). The effects of eye movement desensitization and reprocessing (EMDR) therapy on post-traumatic stress disorder in survivors of the 1999 Maramara, Turkey, earthquake. *International Journal of Stress Management, 13*(3), 291–308. https://doi.org/10.1037/1072-5245.13.3.291

Korn, D., & Leeds, A. (2002). Preliminary evidence of efficacy for EMDR resource development and installation in the stabilization phase of treatment of complex posttraumatic stress disorder. *Journal of Clinical Psychology, 58*(12), 1465–1487. https://doi.org/10.1002/jclp.10099

Marcus, S. V., Marquis, P., & Sakai, C. (1997). Controlled study of treatment of PTSD using EMDR in an HMO setting. *Psychotherapy, 34*(3), 307–315. https://doi.org/10.1037/h0087791

Maxfield, L., & Hyer, L. (2002). The relationship between efficacy and methodology in studies investigating EMDR treatment of PTSD. *Journal of Clinical Psychology, 58*(1), 23–41. https://doi.org/10.1002/jclp.1127

Murray, K. (2012). EMDR with grief: Reflections on Ginny Sprang's 2001 study. *Journal of EMDR Practice and Research, 6*(4), 187–191. https://doi.org/10.1891/1933-3196.6.4.187

Myers, K. (2015). EMDR with choking phobia: Reflections on the 2008 Study by de Roos and de Jongh. *Journal of EMDR Practice and Research, 9*(1), 64–70. https://doi.org/10.1891/1933-3196.9.1.64

National Institute for Clinical Excellence (2005). *Trastorno de estrés postraumatico (TEPT): Gestión del TEPT en niños y adultos en atención primaria y secundaria* [Posttraumatic stress disorder (PTSD): Management of PTSD in children and adults in primary and secondary care]. Author.

Power, K., McGoldrick, T., Brown, K., Buchanan, R., Sharp, D., Swanson, V., & Karatzias, A. (2002). A controlled comparison of eye movement desensitization and reprocessing versus exposure plus cognitive restructuring, versus waiting list in the treatment of post traumatic stress disorder. *Journal of Clinical Psychology and Psychotherapy, 9*(5), 299–318. https://doi.org/10.1002/cpp.341

Practice guideline for the treatment of patients with acute stress disorder and posttraumatic stress disorder. Falls Church, VA: American Psychiatric Association.

Roberts, A. K. P. (2018). The effects of the EMDR group traumatic episode protocol with cancer survivors. *Journal of EMDR Practice and Research, 12*(3), 105–177. https://doi.org/10.1891/1933-3196.12.3.105

Shapiro, F. (1989a). Efficacy of the eye movement desensitization procedure in the treatment of traumatic memories. *Journal of Traumatic Stress, 2*(2), 199–223. https://doi.org/10.1007/BF00974159

Shapiro, F. (1989b). Eye movement desensitization: A new treatment for post-traumatic stress disorder. *Journal of Behavior Therapy and Experimental Psychiatry, 20*(3), 211–217. https://doi.org/10.1016/0005-7916(89)90025-6

Shapiro, F. (1991). Eye movement desensitization and reprocessing procedure: From EMD to EMD/R— A new treatment model for anxiety and related traumata. *The Behavior Therapist, 14*(5), 133–135.

Shapiro, F. (1995). *Eye movement desensitization and reprocessing: Basic principles, protocols, and procedures* (1st ed.). Guilford Press.

Shapiro, F. (2001). *Eye movement desensitization and reprocessing: Basic principles, protocols, and procedures* (2nd ed.). Guilford Press.

Shapiro, F. (2002). *EMDR as an integrative psychotherapy approach: Experts of diverse orientations explore the paradigm prism.* American Psychological Association Books.

Shapiro, F. (2006). *New notes on adaptive information processing: Case formulation principles, scripts, and worksheets.* EMDR Humanitarian Assistance Programs.

Shapiro, F. (2012). *Getting past your past.* Rodale Books.

Shapiro, F. (2018). *Eye movement desensitization and reprocessing: Basic principles, protocols, and procedures* (3rd ed.). Guilford Press.

Shapiro, F., & Forrest, M. S. (1997a). *EMDR: The breakthrough therapy for overcoming anxiety, stress, and trauma* (1st ed.). Basic Books.

Shapiro, F., & Forrest, M. S. (1997b). *EMDR: The breakthrough therapy for overcoming anxiety, stress, and trauma* (2nd ed.). Basic Books.

Shapiro, F., Kaslow, F. W., & Maxfield, L. (2007). *Handbook of EMDR and family therapy processes.* John Wiley & Sons, Inc.

Silver, S. M., Rogers, S., Knipe, J., & Colelli, G. (2005). EMDR therapy following the 9/11 terrorist attacks: A community-based intervention project in New York City. *International Journal of Stress Management, 12*(1), 29–42. https://doi.org/10.1037/1072-5245.12.1.29

Soberman, G. B., Greenwald, R., & Rule, D. L. (2002). A controlled study of eye movement desensitization and reprocessing (EMDR) for boys with conduct problems. *Journal of Aggression, Maltreatment and Trauma, 6*(1), 217–236. https://doi.org/10.1300/J146v06n01_11

Substance Abuse and Mental Health Services Administration. (2010). *Eye movement desensitization and reprocessing.* National Registry of Evidence-Based Programs and Practices, U.S. Department of Health and Human Services (HHS). Retrieved March 25, 2011 from http://nrepp.samhsa.gov/ViewIntervention.aspx?id=199

van der Kolk, B. A., Spinazzola, J., Blaustein, M. E., Hopper, J. W., Hopper, E. K., Korn, D. L., & Simpson, W. B. (2007). A randomized clinical trial of eye movement desensitization and reprocessing (EMDR), fluoxetine, and pill placebo in the treatment of posttraumatic stress disorder: Treatment effects and long-term maintenance. *Journal of Clinical Psychiatry, 68*(1), 37–46. https://doi.org/10.4088/JCP.v68n0105

van Etten, M. L., & Taylor, S. (1998). Comparative efficacy of treatments for posttraumatic stress disorder: A meta-analysis. *Clinical Psychology and Psychotherapy, 5*(3), 126–144. https://doi.org/10.1002/(SICI)1099-0879(199809)

Wilson, S., Becker, L., & Tinker, R. (1995). Eye movement desensitization and reprocessing (EMDR) treatment for psychologically traumatized individuals. *Journal of Consulting & Clinical Psychology, 63*(6), 928–937. https://doi.org/10.1037/0022-006X.63.6.928

Wolpe, J., & Abrams, J. (1991). Post-traumatic stress disorder overcome by eye movement desensitization: A case report. *Journal of Behavior Therapy and Experimental Psychiatry, 22*(1), 39–43. https://doi.org/10.1016/0005-7916(91)90032-Z

Glossary

Adverse life experiences. These types of traumatic events may be more subtle and tend to impact one's beliefs about self, others, and the world. Adverse life experiences are those that can affect our sense of self, self-esteem, self-definition, self-confidence, and optimal behavior. They influence how we see ourselves as a part of the bigger whole. They are often ubiquitous (i.e., constantly encountered) in nature and are stored in state-dependent mode in our memory network. Formerly referred to as small "t" traumas.

Affect scan. The client is asked to focus on the most recent memory of an event as a starting point for floating back into time through similar memories to find the original memory or cause of the client's presenting problem/issue. The affect scan (Shapiro, 1995: independently developed and without the hypnotic/reliving component contained in Watkins & Watkins, 1971) is probably the easiest and quickest way to get to the touchstone event and can be the most powerful.

Ancillary targets. These types of targets are contributory factors that may lead to blocked processing. Blocking beliefs and feeder memories are ancillary targets.

Back to target. Instructing the client to return to the original incident/event currently being processed.

Bilateral stimulation (BLS). BLS is any stimulation—visual, auditory, or kinesthetic—that addresses both the left and right sides of the brain in sequence. EMDR processing neutralizes negative events by means of BLS.

Blocking belief. A blocking belief is a belief that stops the processing of an initial target. This type of belief may resolve spontaneously during reprocessing or may require being targeted separately.

Channels of association. Within the targeted memory, events, thoughts, and physical and emotional sensations may spontaneously arise or arise when the client is instructed to go back to target (i.e., return to the original event, incident, image, incident, etc.). These are called channels of association and may arise any time during the reprocessing phases (i.e., 3–6).

Circumstances. Situations that stimulate a disturbance.

Cluster memories. These memories form a series of related or similar events and have shared cues, such as an action, person, or location. Each event is representational or generalizable to the other. These nodes are not targeted in the sessions in which they have been identified. The clinician usually keeps an active list of any nodes that arise during reprocessing and reevaluates them at a later date to see if further treatment is necessary.

Developmental trauma. Events that occur over time and gradually affect and alter the client's neurological system to the point that it remains in a traumatic state. This type of trauma may cause interruptions in a child's natural psychological growth.

Dual awareness. This is what Dr. Shapiro calls "dual focus of attention" (2018). It allows the client to maintain a sense of present awareness and for the client's internal processes to function without interference during reprocessing.

Ecological validity. Appropriate to the client given their present circumstances.

Eye Movement Desensitization (EMD). EMD is a simple desensitization technique whose primary focus is on reducing the anxiety, and the primary modality is behavioral. Dr. Shapiro changed the name of EMD to EMDR in 1990 to reflect the information processing mechanism involved as well as the cognitive and emotional restructuring nature of the method.

Fears. Fear in the processing of targeted information can become a blocking mechanism. It stalls the process. Dr. Shapiro identified fears to include fear of the clinical outcome of EMDR therapy or the process itself, fear of going crazy, fear of losing good memories, and fear of change. Fear of the process can be readily recognized whenever a client begins to identify elements of EMDR therapy that appear to be problematic for them (2018). Also check to ensure that any expressed fears of the process are not related to secondary gain.

Feeder memory. This type of memory has been described by Shapiro (2018) as an inaccessible or untapped, earlier memory that contributes to the client's current dysfunction and that subsequently blocks the reprocessing of it.

Flashforward. A technique used to address the client's irrational fears.

Floatforward. A technique used to help clients to identify and cope with unspecified future fears.

Floatback technique. If the client is unable to identify the touchstone through direct questioning, the clinician's next option is to use the floatback technique developed by William Zangwill (Browning, 1999; Young et al., 2002) to elicit the past event that is responsible for the client's current dysfunction. The floatback is an imagery exercise that acts as a bridge to earlier dysfunctional memories.

Future desired state. The third prong of EMDR focuses on targeting a positive template that will assist in incorporating anticipatory events. This stage may involve teaching the client assertiveness skills, modeling good decision-making, or having the client imagining future situations, such as coaching people to help them respond more appropriately.

Future rehearsal. Unlike a future template, which is utilized after resolution of each trigger to solidify a desired outcome or direction, future rehearsal is used to help a client to deal with a demand situation prior to the complete resolution of a trauma.

Internal or external triggers. Internal and external cues that are capable of stimulating dysfunctionally stored information and eliciting emotional or behavioral disturbances.

Inverted (Hofmann, 2009) *or Reverse* (Adler-Tapia, 2012) *Protocol.* Simply reversing the order of processing from past, present, future to future, past, present to help the more unstable client to reduce their symptoms so that they are able to work on past events. These protocols work well with more fragile clients.

Negative cognition (NC). This is the negative self-belief associated with the unprocessed and dysfunctional negatively stored incident/event.

Node. In terms of the AIP model, a node is an associated system of information (i.e., associatively stored material). It is a pivotal place among physiologically associated material.

Associated channels may consist of specific events or dreams; a person; an actual, fantasied or projected event, whether actual, fantasized, or projected; or some aspect of experience, including a body sensation or a specific thought. Example: If the client's presenting issue is their response to a coworker's unpredictable outbursts, there may be a constellation of associated experiences linked to it. If they react with fear or anger, there may be a constellation of associated experiences that are linked to it. These events may be linked to previous experiences with the coworkers or with a sibling or a friend. In order for the client to react and respond to these outbursts appropriately, it is necessary to clean out all the associated channels connected to the node. A node is also a touchstone or a primary, self-defining life event.

Original target. Selected node out of which all negative associated channels of information emerge.

Peelback memory. A peelback memory usually occurs when a touchstone has not been identified and, during reprocessing, other associations begin to "peel back" to expose prior disturbing memories. There is often confusion between a progression and a peelback memory. A peelback memory is an earlier unsuspected memory, while a progression is any new associated memory.

Positive cognition (PC). The positive belief which reflects the client's desired direction of change.

Positive template (imaginal future template development). A process where the client uses the adaptive information learned in the previous two prongs to ensure future behavioral success by incorporating patterns of alternative behavioral responses. These patterns require the client to imagine responding differently and positively to real or perceived negative circumstances or situations or significant people.

Polar shift. A polar shift occurs when a negative emotion is replaced by a positive one in the early part of the processing (e.g., client is crying and then laughs).

Primary events. These are standalone events that may emerge during the History-Taking and Treatment Planning, Reprocessing, and Reevaluation phases as well as over the course of treatment itself. Dr. Shapiro (2018) defines these as events that have the greatest significance or that have been identified by the clinician as representing critical areas of dysfunction to the client.

Progression. While processing an identified target, another target may emerge that may be salient to the client's clinical picture. If this memory does not resolve during the current processing, the clinician should take note of this for possible processing at a later date.

Primary events. These are stand-alone events that may emerge during the History-Taking and Treatment Planning, Reprocessing, and Reevaluation phases as well as over the course of treatment itself. Dr. Shapiro (2018) defines these as events that have the greatest significance or that have been identified by the clinician as representing critical areas of dysfunction to the client.

Secondary gain. A secondary-gain issue has the potential of keeping a presenting issue from being resolved.

Second-order conditioning. A classical conditioning or Pavlovian (1927) term that refers to a situation in which a previously neutral stimulus (e.g., associating a bell with light, "second" order) is paired with a conditioned stimulus (e.g., associating a bell with food, "first" order) to produce the same conditioned response as the conditioned stimulus. In other words, he is using a previously successful conditioned stimulus (i.e., the bell) as the unconditioned stimulus (i.e., the light) to provide further conditioning to produce the same conditioned response.

Set. Round-trip passes of eye movements.

Shock trauma. Involves a sudden threat that is perceived by the central nervous system as overwhelming and/or life threatening. It is a single-episode traumatic event.

Starburst effect. This occurs when multiple events come out during processing.

State change. A state change is momentary or transitory. A state change is a change of mind. It instills a sense of hope in the client. A state change also requires the use of coping mechanisms to continue the change.

Subjective Units of Disturbance (SUD). Measures the level of distress associated with an incident/event.

Target. Incident/event selected for reprocessing in the Assessment Phase.

Three-pronged protocol. Past events, present triggers, future template selected for processing.

Touchstone memory. A memory that lays the foundation for the client's current presenting issue or problem. This is the memory that formed the core of the maladaptive network or dysfunction. It is the first time the client may have believed, "I am not good enough" or that this conclusion was formed. The touchstone event often, but not necessarily, occurs in childhood or adolescence. Reprocessing will be more spontaneous for the client if the touchstone events can be identified and reprocessed earlier in the treatment.

Trait change. A trait change reflects a permanent change and, as such, requires no coping mechanisms. With a trait change, the client changes how they see or view the event and, as a result, can experience it differently.

Trauma. Trauma can be defined as any event that causes an unusually high level of emotional stress and has a long-lasting negative effect on a person. However, it is the client's subjective emotional experience of an event that determines whether it was traumatic, not the objective facts of the event itself. In short, any situation or event that leaves the client feeling overwhelmed and unable to cope in the present may be defined as traumatizing, regardless of whether physical harm was involved. So, it is important to ask the client, "Is the trauma still disturbing?" when developing an AIP-informed treatment plan.

Validity of Cognition (VoC). Measurement of how true the selected PC feels when paired with the target incident/event.

Wellsprings of disturbance. This phenomenon is indicative of "the presence of a large number of blocked emotions that can be resistant to full EMDR processing" (Shapiro, 2018) and is often caused by the existence of an extensive negative belief system. A wellspring is similar to a feeder memory in that both are feeding the emerging emotions. Clients who are resistant to therapy or who seek therapy involuntarily at the urging of someone else (e.g., therapy is court-ordered or requested by a persistent and threatening spouse) are most susceptible to this phenomenon. They are in therapy because of someone else and possess no desire to report or deal with any feelings (Shapiro, 2018).

Abbreviations

AIP	Adaptive Information Processing
BLS	bilateral stimulation
C-PTSD	complex posttraumatic stress disorder
CAT	computed axial tomography
CBT	Cognitive Behavioral Therapy
CEU	Continuing Education Units
CPA	Certified Public Accountant
CREST	Clinical Resource Efficiency Support Team
DES	Dissociative Experiences Scale
DES-II	Dissociative Experiences Scale-II
EEI	EMDR Early Intervention
EFRS	EMDR Fidelity Rating Scale
EMD	Eye Movement Desensitization
EMDDRRIIA	experiential, modulation, defense, developmental repair, relational, informational, integration, and action interweaves
EMDRIA	EMDR International Association
FSL	Francine Shapiro Library
HAP	Humanitarian Assistance Program
HMMWV	high mobility multi-purpose wheeled vehicle
IED	improvised explosive device
ISST-D	International Society for the Study of Trauma and Dissociation
ISTSS	International Society for Traumatic Stress Studies
MID	Multidimensional Inventory of Dissociation
MRI	Mental Research Institute
NC	negative cognition
NICE	National Institute for Clinical Excellence
NIMH	National Institute of Mental Health
NREPP	National Registry of Evidence-Based Programs and Practices
PC	positive cognition
PTSD	posttraumatic stress disorder
RDI	Resource Development and Installation
REM	rapid eye movement
SAMHSA	Substance Abuse and Mental Health Services Administration
SCID-D	Structured Clinical Interview of Dissociative Disorders
SRS	sex reassignment surgery

SUD	Subjective Units of Disturbance
TAU	treatment as usual
TBI	traumatic brain injury
TICES	trigger, image, cognition, emotion, and sensation
TPG	Treatment Planning Guide
TR	trauma recovery
TRIP	Translating Research into Practice
TRN	Trauma Recovery Networks
VoC	Validity of Cognition

Index